CRIMES OF HATE

For Mom and Dad
—P. B. G.

For people everywhere who are dedicated to social justice
—D. R. G.

CRIMES OF **HATE**
SELECTED READINGS

EDITED BY

Phyllis B. Gerstenfeld
California State University, Stanislaus

Diana R. Grant
Sonoma State University

SAGE Publications
International Educational and Professional Publisher
Thousand Oaks ▪ London ▪ New Delhi

For information:

Sage Publications, Inc.
2455 Teller Road
Thousand Oaks, California 91320
E-mail: order@sagepub.com

Sage Publications Ltd.
6 Bonhill Street
London EC2A 4PU
United Kingdom

Sage Publications India Pvt. Ltd.
B-42, Panchsheel Enclave
Post Box 4109
New Delhi 110 017 India

Printed in the United States of America

Library of Congress Cataloging-in-Publication Data

Crimes of hate: Selected readings / Phyllis B. Gerstenfeld and Diana R. Grant, editors.
    p. cm.
Includes bibliographical references and index.
ISBN 0-7619-2942-8 (cloth: alk. paper)
ISBN 0-7619-2943-6 (pbk.: alk. paper)
    1. Hate crimes-United States. 2. Hate groups-Government policy-United States. 3. Hate crimes-United States-Prevention. I. Gerstenfeld, Phyllis B. II. Grant, Diana Ruth.
HV6773.52.C75 2004
364.15-dc21

                                              2003013098

03   04   05   06   10   9   8   7   6   5   4   3   2   1

Acquisitions Editor:	Jerry Westby
Editorial Assistant:	Vonessa Vondera
Production Editor:	Denise Santoyo
Typesetter:	C&M Digitals (P) Ltd.
Indexer:	Kathy Paparchontis
Cover Designer:	Michelle Lee Kenny

Contents

PREFACE

Hate crimes have occurred since time immemorial, but only quite recently has the law recognized such actions as crimes. We created this anthology to help readers learn more about the social and legal aspects of hate crime as an emerging domain of law. Our goal is to contribute to the growing societal debate about hate crimes and the law by creating this anthology to serve as a resource to provoke thought and discussion on the policy implications of the emerging hate crime paradigm. The articles and cases presented in this anthology were drawn from a variety of fields and perspectives. Each of the eight sections focuses on a particular aspect of the central legal and societal issues raised by hate crimes and hate crime legislation. Each article is preceded by a brief introduction and followed by questions for discussion. The anthology was designed so that it could be used in tandem with *Hate Crimes: Causes, Controls, and Controversies* (Gerstenfeld, 2004) or used independently or as an accompaniment to other primary texts in a variety of disciplines. As is always the case when creating an anthology, editors face hard choices about which articles to include. Our choices here reflect considerations such as whether the selection was current, empirical, accessible to a wide audience, not widely available elsewhere, and, of course, fit page/space constraints. Thus, there were many articles that we would have liked to include but were not able to, unfortunately.

Ultimately, we believe that a better understanding of the human costs of hate violence for both individuals and societies will lead to better prevention strategies. We hope that this text is a valuable resource for you. We welcome your comments and suggestions.

—Phyllis B. Gerstenfeld, J.D., Ph.D.

—Diana R. Grant, Ph.D.

ACKNOWLEDGMENTS

We would like to thank all of the authors and journals who kindly gave us permission to include their articles in this book. We would also like to thank the reviewers for their helpful comments:

Kristen Kuehnle, Salem State University

Sarah Soule, University of Arizona

Valerie Jenness, University of California, Irvine

Karen Franklin, California School of Professional Psychology

Katherine Culotta, Indiana State University

Sue Cote, California State University, Sacramento

We would also like to give special thanks to Humayun Deura and Dennis Behrens for their support and encouragement.

Part I

INTRODUCTION

In the article that follows, Petrosino sets the stage for our understanding of hate crimes by tracing the historical roots of modern hate crimes against minorities. A comparison of historic and modern-era hate crimes reveals similarities in the antecedent conditions leading to such crimes, yet it also reveals some distinct differences between earlier and current eras in the nature and scope of hate crimes. For example, the relationship between the law and hate crimes in the two eras is distinctly different in many, although not all, respects; where previously the law and law-makers were either silent or sometimes actually condoned hate crimes, the law is now an important policy forum for attempts to prevent and sanction hate crimes.

1

CONNECTING THE PAST TO THE FUTURE

Hate Crime in America

CAROLYN PETROSINO

On June 7, 1998, James Byrd, Jr., a Black man, was hitchhiking home following a relative's bridal shower when a truck pulled up. However, instead of receiving a lift home, Byrd was kidnapped, taken to a wooded area, beaten to unconsciousness, chained to the back of the truck, and then dragged for several miles. His head and right arm were torn from his body during the dragging and were later found in a ditch along the road. His assailants were three White men with links to racist groups (Hohler, 1998). It is believed that the genesis for this gruesome murder was racial hatred.

Hate crimes are despicable acts. Their toll only begins with the victim. Harm expands to the victim's family, group, and society itself. Its greatest cost is not only measured in property damages, medical expenses, or the loss of wages, but also in the depreciation of the human spirit in dignity, liberty, and security. Furthermore, lethal hate crimes like the Byrd murder take on a quality of frenzied killing; they attest to a revelry in the destruction of a human being. Hamm (1998a) refers to this as "the carnival of violence" (p. 250). The costs of such acts upon society are immeasurable.

The savagery that ended Byrd's life is not an isolated incident; it has occurred over and over in U.S. history (Bureau of Justice Assistance, 1997; J. Levin & McDevitt, 1993). This examination reviews a sample of historical events in light of recent hate crime legislation. The primary objective here is to answer the question that some scholars have posed: Is American hate crime a distinctively modern phenomenon? (Czajkoski, 1992). As this article will show, substantial evidence exists to suggest that hate crime as a behavior has existed in America for more than 300 years; however, only recently—relatively speaking—has it become recognized as a violation of law.

EDITORS' NOTE: From Petrosino, C. (1999, February). Connecting the Past to the Future: Hate Crime in America. *Journal of Contemporary Criminal Justice, 15*(1), 22-47. © 1999 Sage Publications, used with permission.

Searching for examples of historical hate crimes means moving away from legal definitions. Instead, a definition based on intrinsic justice is needed because many hate crimes discussed here were not considered illegal at the time (Jordan, 1968; Miller, 1979; Stampp, 1956; Steinfield, 1973; Takaki, 1994a, 1994b; Wells-Barnett, 1969). Intrinsic justice is an inherent balance scale of justice. Natural law is written upon the conscious of mankind by his Creator allowing him to discern good versus evil (Devlin, 1986). It is an internal compass causing consciousness of moral and immoral behavior (for more information on this topic refer to St. Thomas Aquinas [Feinberg & Gross, 1986], or the Holy Bible, Book of Romans 2:14–15). Intrinsic justice has great value because it overrides self-serving special interests that sometimes lead to codified law. It possesses a universal quality causing most community members to collectively consider a behavior right or wrong (e.g., incest [Pallone, 1990]). Harms perpetrated on individuals because of their race, gender, culture, or social status may meet this universal standard. Such behaviors are *malum in se* or wrong in themselves; they are naturally evil.

In addition to responding to the initial question posed, this article accomplishes four objectives: to (a) redefine hate crime, permitting a definition that covers legal but immoral acts in history; (b) identify historical events that meet the new definition; (c) provide a comparative analysis of past and present hate crimes; and (d) predict the scope of future hate crimes and system response.

DEFINING HATE CRIME ACTS

Contemporary hate crime legal concepts are often varied and complex. What identifies a hate crime in one jurisdiction, may not be useful in another (Burk, 1994; Martin, 1996). Similar to this, statutory definitions of hate crimes vary across jurisdictions (Hamm, 1994). For instance, some statutes will list race, color, religion, or national origin as specific categories protected by hate crime legislation. Other states may also include gender, sexual orientation, and the physically disabled in their laws. Hate crime scholarship argues that victim categories extend from the traditional—race, ethnicity, religion, and sexual orientation—to gender, disabilities,

age, class, and even political persuasion (Bureau of Justice Assistance, 1997; Gerstenfeld, 1992). Historically, such perspectives of crime victims were nonexistent.

To begin constructing a more adequate definition, characteristics of modern American hate crime victims were identified. These include (a) most victims are members of distinct racial or ethnic (cultural) minority groups (Bureau of Justice Assistance, 1997; Hamm, 1994); (b) most victim groups are decidedly less powerful politically and economically than the majority group (Hamm, 1993); and last, (c) victims represent to the perpetrator a threat to their quality of life (i.e., economic stability and/or physical safety) (J. Levin & McDevitt, 1993). These common factors suggest the following base definition of hate crime: the victimization of minorities due to their racial or ethnic identity by members of the majority. This definition focuses on the imbalance of power between the perpetrator (majority) and the victim (minority)—emphasizing harm potential in hate crimes. Although hate crimes certainly occur across racial and socioeconomic categories, (i.e., perpetrators can be minorities and victims from the majority group) the most typical incidents are covered by the base definition (Bureau of Justice Assistance, 1997).

Although hate crimes are more easily identified today, this is not true historically. Among the reasons for this include the lack of criminalization; the absence of constitutional, statutory, or other legal rights of victims; the normative values of past eras that denied personhood to victims; and the complicitous or direct role of governments and other authorities in hate acts.

Recorded history reveals that although acts such as assault, theft, murder, and rape were considered crimes under the common law, the same acts when motivated by racism or ethnocentrism were not (Hoffer, 1992; Jordan, 1968). The reasons lie in the foundation of law itself. Laws and the criminal justice system often express the intent of powerful interest groups (Mann, 1993; Walker, Spohn, & DeLone, 1996). Few would argue that the protective authority of the law in America did not routinely extend to the poor or non-Whites. In fact, many states disallowed non-Whites full legal redress particularly in matters that accused Whites (Perlmutter, 1992; Steinfield, 1973; Takaki, 1994a, 1994b).

The Value of Intrinsic
Justice and Moral Theory

Although the law emphasizes some aspects of morality, it does not pronounce all moral behavior. It has biased qualities that at times reflect the interests of only some segments of society while ignoring others (Messner & Rosenfeld, 1997) and is inherently flawed (Hoffer, 1992; Mackie, 1977; Pollock-Byrne, 1989). Moreover, some laws could be viewed as immoral (e.g., Three Strikes Law, the death penalty, abortion, the federal sentencing guidelines for powder cocaine vs. crack cocaine offenders, etc.). To some, such laws legitimize immoral acts. Although laws fall short of embodying morality, intrinsic justice transcends the moral shortcomings of codified law (Haskins, 1969; Pound, 1938).

In some ways, intrinsic justice is reflected in morality. The dominant moral theories in American—as well as in most Western cultures—are teleological and deontological in nature. To define briefly, teleological moral theory states that the rightness or wrongness of an action depends on its consequences. Whereas, deontological moral theory states that the rightness or wrongness of an action is intrinsic to the act itself. More familiar than the term *teleological* is *utilitarianism* that defines moral behavior as that which brings the greatest good to the greatest number. Kantian ethics[1] best illustrates deontological theory, and it advocates that one has a duty to act according to universal principles of morality. These theories appeal to a rational logic that determines moral behavior. However, deontological theory more closely resembles intrinsic justice because of its appeal to universal standards. Under the lens of deontological theory, hate crimes are clearly immoral due to their inherent nature.

A Definition of Hate Crime and
Selection Criteria for Historical Events

In this article, the following definition of hate crime is used: The victimization of minorities due to their racial or ethnic identity by members of the majority. However, an additional measure was applied to further underscore the imbalance of power between the victim and perpetrator. The consideration of whether the legal authorities of that time would have responded to the acts in a similar fashion if victims were White Anglo-Saxon[2] Protestants.

Selection of historical events was based on the following criteria: (a) moral offensiveness; (b) the presence, at least in part, of a racial or ethnic bias motive; (c) intentional harming; (d) existence of the likelihood that the justice system would have responded differently if the victim(s) had been White; and (e) occurred before the first wave of hate crime legislation in the 1980s.[3]

Most events selected occurred during the 17th, 18th, and 19th centuries. In addition, the incidents were drawn from the historical experiences of racial minority populations in America. Although historical hate crimes were not an experience solely of racial or ethnic minorities, longevity of victimization uniquely applied to them (Perlmutter, 1992). This pattern is also reflected in contemporary hate crime statistics (Bureau of Justice Assistance, 1997). It is recognized that other ethnic and racial groups have sustained prolonged periods of persecution (i.e., Jewish and Mexican Americans). However, the documented evidence of harms in the form of murder and other destructive acts perpetrated against Native Americans, Blacks, and Asians are very compelling. It is further noted that although there are countless historical events that could have been selected, it is not the purpose of this article to document each episode; but rather, the purpose is to highlight those events that demonstrate the nature of historical hate crime. Historical records as reported in secondary and tertiary sources are relied on in the examination of selected events due to their high recognition and frequent representation in archival and other sources.

MANIFEST DESTINY: THE
AMERICAN CULTURE OF HATE

Before reviewing specific historical incidents, it is important to describe an essential feature in American culture that helped to foster racial hatred. Several scholars have noted that hate crime acts are rationalized through an established ideology (Arendt, 1963; Gibbs, 1989; Hamm, 1994; J. Levin & McDevitt, 1993). The hate crime perpetrator is often ethnocentric and devalues his victims. Such beliefs are not created in a vacuum. American culture, both past and present, includes similar beliefs and values. Systematic bigotry and discrimination, or the "culture of hate" (J. Levin & McDevitt, 1993), continuously reaffirms the identity of unworthy members of society, thus instigating and ensuring their victimization. In this article, *Manifest Destiny* is examined as a contributor to ethnocentrism, intolerance, and hate crime in America.

Manifest Destiny was the belief that America was to be governed by White Anglo-Saxon Protestants, as ordained by "God Almighty." Although not a formal policy until 1845, its tenets were evident from the earliest moments of White colonization (Horsman, 1981; Perlmutter, 1992). The idea of a divine mission was present in the 17th century (Horsman, 1981; Perlmutter, 1992). Colonial America linked Christianity to racial purity or Whiteness and heathenism with racial impurity or non-Whiteness. Therefore, destiny, Christianity, and racial identity were culturally conjoined early in American history (Jordan, 1968). In fact, racial superiority permeated American culture to the point where being American was synonymous with being White. Other races were viewed as foreigners. Prophylactic measures were applied to maintain the distinctions. Thus, practices such as systematic exclusion and discrimination further legitimized bigotry and hatred. Manifest Destiny, in the minds of many, justified American expansionism by any means necessary (Merk, 1963). Therefore, if discrimination, racism, fraud, theft, rape, kidnapping, and even murder achieved destiny objectives, such acts were considered to be acceptable consequences.

The following sections examine a selected sample of historical events. After a brief description of the racial attitudes comprising the social climate of that era, a review of the incident and a discussion of its legitimacy as a hate crime are presented.

NATIVE AMERICANS AS VICTIMS OF HATE CRIME

The Social Climate

Many historians have described early contacts between Europeans and Native Americans as nonviolent. However, the nature of their relationship changed with the self-serving acts of the Europeans[4] (Sanders, 1978; Spindler, 1972; Steinfield, 1973; Tebbel and Jennison, 1960). The term *noble savage* came to represent the European image of the Native American (Farb, 1968; Harjo, 1998), a phrase that indicated both disdain and regard. Eventually, this image became more malevolent. As Native Americans increasingly resisted European encroachment and deceptive practices, they were depicted as barbaric (Harjo, 1998; Riding In, 1998). Frequently infantilized stereotyped groups are perceived as dangerous when docile behavior is replaced with assertiveness (J. Levin & Levin, 1982; J. Levin & McDevitt, 1993). Records maintained by the Department of Indian Affairs illustrate attitudes once held toward the Native American.[5]

Historical Events: The Near Genocide of the Yuki and Cheyenne Indians

The Yuki of northern California numbered approximately 5,000[6] when first encountered by White settlers in 1848. By this time, many atrocities had been routinely committed against Native Americans in the form of kidnapping, theft, fraud, forced indentured servitude, sexual assault, intentional spread of disease, depletion of food supplies, starvation,[7] and murder (Riding In, 1998). Targeting the Yuki for similar treatment, therefore, was not an aberrant act. Military records indicated interest in exterminating them for the sake of White settlements (Cook, 1943; Miller, 1979). Private efforts were substituted by state sponsored kill parties to affect the goal (Chalk & Jonassohn, 1990; Perlmutter, 1992). The following is an excerpt of the 1851 annual state message given by California Governor Burnett (Perlmutter, 1992, p. 136):

> A war of extermination will continue to be waged between the two races until the Indian race becomes extinct . . . while we cannot anticipate this result with but painful regret, the inevitable destiny of the race is beyond the power and wisdom of man to avert.

As a result of Burnett's pogroms, the Yukis lost 90% of their population in a 32-year period (Chalk & Jonassohn, 1990).

The Cheyenne were victims of similar acts as described in the 39th U.S. Congressional record, 2nd session, Senate Report 156. The following is an account of a mass murder on November 28, 1864, as told by eyewitness Robert Bent (Brown, 1970, p. 73):

> When the troops fired, the Indians ran. . . . I think there were six-hundred Indians in all . . . about sixty [men] in all. . . . I saw five squaws under a bank for shelter . . . but the soldiers shot them all. . . . There seemed to be indiscriminate slaughter of men, women, and children. There were some thirty or forty squaws collected in a hole for protection; they sent out a little girl about six years old with a white flag on a stick; she had not proceeded but a few steps when she was shot and killed. Every one I saw dead was scalped. I saw one squaw cut open with an unborn child. . . . I saw the body of a leader, with the privates cut off, and I heard a soldier say he was going to make a tobacco pouch out of them. I saw quite a number of infants in arms killed with their mothers.[8]

Argument for the Classification of These Events as Hate Crime

Few would disagree that these acts were anything less than barbaric, but are they hate crimes? The acts committed against the Yuki and Cheyenne clearly intended to cause significant harm. The nature of the acts also indicates a potent disregard of the victims' humanity. Evidence of racial animus toward Native Americans, which permeated White American culture then, is prolific (Berthrong, 1963). For instance, it was not until 1891[9] that a U.S. Supreme Court decision declared that Indians were human beings. Note the writing of an Oregon settler (Kennedy, 1959, p. 10):

> It was customary [for the Whites] to speak of the Indian man as a buck; of the woman as a squaw; until at length in the general acceptance of the terms, they ceased to recognize the rights of humanity in those to whom they were applied. By a very natural and easy transition, from being spoken of as brutes they came to be thought of as game to be shot, or as vermin to be destroyed.[10]

It could be concluded that racial bias was a primary motive in the events described. The case for moral offensiveness is apparent. Kant's morality test includes whether it would be desirable and appropriate if such acts were universalized, thus permitting any person to commit them. The genocidal actions described would not have been embraced by 19th-century America if the aggressor and victim groups were reversed. It is unlikely that the government would have financed genocidal acts of Native Americans against Whites, nor would the justice system have remained passive to such acts (Riding In, 1998).

AFRICANS AND AFRICAN DESCENDANTS AS VICTIMS OF HATE CRIME

The Social Climate

It is well documented that perceptions of Africa and African people have been articulated through a Eurocentric perspective (Fredrickson, 1991; Jordan, 1968; Pieterse, 1992). Although the early images of Africans were dynamic,[11] once Europe focused economic interest on the New World, the utility of a particular image was needed. Some have argued that early African enslavement by Europeans was based on culture rather than race, yet some evidence suggests otherwise. The racial characterizations attributed to African people by Europeans were inextricably linked to the devaluation of African cultures. For example, Jordan (1968) and others contend that the British associated blackness with negativity, evil,[12] and foulness. The Africans' skin color and non-Christian religious practices made it less complicated for the British to view them as uncivilized heathens. Subsequently, it became rational for them to associate heathenism—with its inferences to inferiority—with blackness.

By 1625, Africans were enslaved internationally (Jordan, 1968). In fact, being African became synonymous with being enslavable (Morris, 1996; Rome, 1998). The perception of the African as inferior did not change in the colonies. From their earliest experiences in colonial America, Africans were treated in a debased manner. This discriminatory treatment[13] predated the institution of slavery (Horsman, 1981; Morris, 1996). When the legalization of African slavery occurred in the colonies, the scientific community offered evidence of the African's racial inferiority. Moreover, the Black or Slave Codes beginning in 1640 further distinguished Blacks from all other groups in America. These initiatives reinforced the racial animus and prejudice Whites held toward them.

Historical Event: Black Slavery

Before the actual tenure of slavery began, the transoceanic voyage from the west coast of Africa to the Caribbean and then to the colonies proved to be an extraordinarily brutal event. The following account is an observer's description of the nature of the Middle Passage voyage (Perlmutter, 1992, p. 18):

> The sense of misery and suffocation was so terrible that in the 'tweendecks—where the height was sometimes only eighteen inches, so that the unfortunate slaves could not turn around, were wedged immovably in fact, and chained to the deck by the neck and legs—that the slaves not infrequently would go mad before dying or suffocating. In their frenzy some killed others in the hope of procuring more room to breathe. Men strangled those next to them and women drove nails into each other's brains.

Conservative estimates place the death toll during the voyages at approximately 100,000 (Higginbotham, 1978). Shortly after slavery was established, it received the legal status of *perpetual* (Jordan, 1968), making the loss of freedom lifelong and complete. The status of children born to slaves was clarified when slavery was defined by law as an inherited condition. Servitude dismissed the humanity of Blacks in White society. As chattel, a Black's value was simply contingent on age, health, strength, and other factors related to work ability. The value of African women was determined by their ability to bear future slaves and work the fields; they were viewed as beasts of burden. As a result, they were often made to give birth in plantation fields (Jordan, 1968).

Despite an enormous effort from religious, political, and scientific quarters to justify slavery, there existed a flaw in the proslavery thesis.

Blacks were forced to accept their natural status. Slaveholders often employed various techniques to coerce Blacks to accept their conditions (Stampp, 1956). Military protocols for breaking the will of Africans and creating manageable slaves were implemented (Jordan, 1968; Stampp, 1956). The system of slavery necessitated crimes of fraud, kidnapping, assault, torture, inhumane treatment,[14] forced labor, rape, and psychological abuse propelled by economic interests, and racial bias.

Historical Event: Lynching

The history of American lynching has not been widely studied, despite the significance of its occurrence. Named for Charles Lynch who popularized the act during the 18th century, lynching or lynch law involved the execution of an accused individual without due process of law. Although Whites were also lynched, Blacks were disproportionately victimized (Cutler, 1969). For example, the victimization rate of Blacks in southern states was 350% greater than that of Whites (Cutler, 1969; Dennis, 1984; Wells-Barnett, 1969).

Black lynching in southern states escalated following emancipation. It was a response to the federal government's effort to remove legal constraints on Black participation in America's political, social, and economic systems. Little provocation was required for Blacks to be victimized. Social activist Ida B. Wells provided commentary on two 1892 lynchings, epitomizing the vulnerability of Blacks at that time (Wells-Barnett, 1969, p. 17): "John Hughes of Moberly (Missouri) and Isaac Lincoln of Fort Madison (S. Carolina) and Will Lewis in Tullahoma, Tenn. suffered death for no more serious charge than that they were 'saucy' to white people."

According to some records, "lynching was so common it was impossible to keep accurate accounts" (Perlmutter, 1992, p. 151).[15] The *Chicago Tribune* reported that between 1882 and 1903, a total of 3,337 Blacks were known to have been lynched by White mobs (Cutler, 1969). The following is an account of a July 15, 1921, lynching in Moultrie, Georgia. An eyewitness described the incident for a local newspaper (Steinfield, 1973, pp. 40–42):

Williams was brought from Moultrie on Friday night by sheriffs. . . . Saturday court was called. . . . The trial took half an hour. Then Williams, surrounded by fifty sheriffs armed with machine guns, started out of the courthouse door toward the jail . . . 500 poor pecks rushed the sheriffs, who made no resistance. . . . They tore the negro's [sic] clothing off. . . . The negro [sic] was unsexed, as usual, and made to eat a portion of his anatomy. . . . The negro [sic] was chained to [a] stump. . . . The pyre was lit and a hundred men . . . women, old and young, grandmothers among them, joined hands and danced around the negro [sic] while he burned.

Argument for the Classification of These Events as Hate Crime

Both slavery and lynching were uniquely applied to Blacks,[16] indicating a bias motive. Particularly in the case of slavery, only Africans were selected for perpetual bondage (Higginbotham, 1978; Stampp, 1956). The intentional harm incorporated in both acts are obvious—including the theft of another's liberty for economic gain and the theft of another's life without due process. Moreover, slavery and lynching are morally reprehensible,[17] inasmuch as neither fit Kant's criteria for moral behavior. It is unlikely that either would have been embraced as appropriate universal behavior. If Whites had been routinely the victims of activities necessary to enslave or lynch, governmental and law enforcement bodies would have responded differently (Morris, 1996).

ASIAN IMMIGRANTS AS VICTIMS OF HATE CRIME

The Social Climate

Asian laborers were invited to the United States to assist the transcontinental railroad construction and to work Hawaiian sugar plantations (Healey, 1995). Although initially viewed as industrious, images of Asians were influenced by several factors. During the latter 19th century, the scientific community focused on racial classifications. Not unlike Africans and Native Americans, Asians did not fair well in these schemes. For instance, some contended

that the adult Mongoloid was equivalent to an adolescent Caucasian (Gould, 1981). Many stereotypes used to depict Native Americans and Africans were used against Asians as well (Takaki, 1994a, p. 66).

> White workers called the Chinese "nagurs," [sic] and a magazine cartoon depicted a Chinese man as a bloodsucking vampire with slanted eyes, a pigtail, dark skin, and thick lips. Like blacks, the Chinese were described as heathen, morally inferior, savage, childlike, and lustful. Chinese women were condemned as a "depraved class" and said to resemble Africans.

Several states enacted laws during the 1800s to constrain Asian liberties. These statutes segregated them and culminated in an effort to banish them from the United States. The pervasiveness of anti-Asian sentiments from that era is illustrated by a statement attributed to Theodore Roosevelt. He never approved of Japanese immigration, and regarding the Hawaiian islands, he said that they should have "a white population representing American civilization" (Takaki, 1994a, p. 76). Roosevelt also believed America should be preserved as a heritage for Whites, and that because Asians were entirely different, they should not live in the country (Takaki, 1994a)."

Other political organizations echoed similar sentiments. The Native Sons of the Golden West is credited with the following statement (Chronister, 1992, pp. 40–41): "that the state of California should remain what it had always been and God himself intended it shall always be—the White Man's Paradise . . . the 31st star shall never become dim or yellow."

Historical Event: Kearneyism

Asian unemployment surged at the completion of the railway, but it was short-lived. Most took jobs that Whites declined, or they started their own businesses. Asians found steady work in menial labor, and White unemployment became an increasing problem.[18] Labor leader Denis Kearney and others inflamed anti-Asian sentiments (Steinfield, 1973). He sent a very clear message that the presence of Chinese people was among the chief causes of economic woes for the region. Moreover, with their removal, the economic problems of Whites would eventually dissipate. This message, along with preexisting norms of prejudice and racism, created an atmosphere that prompted spontaneous acts of violence against Asians. During this period of Kearneyism, Asian-owned businesses were frequently vandalized and burned down. Asians were also robbed, assaulted, and murdered. However, because they lacked basic civil liberties, little was done by the legal system in response to their victimization. The murder of Asians became so casual that the print media frequently chose not to report its occurrence (Steinfield, 1973; Takaki, 1994a).

Historical Event: The Japanese Internment

Following Pearl Harbor, Roosevelt issued Executive Order 9066 (Steinfield, 1973). Pursuant to the order, the land borders of the United States were closed to all enemy aliens and all persons of Japanese ancestry, even American citizens. This caused the mass arrest and incarceration of more than 100,000 persons of Japanese ancestry—of which two thirds were American citizens. Based on race, this action occurred as a result of long-standing suspicions and prejudice. Evidence of this attitude is demonstrated in a statement attributed to Commanding General John DeWitt (Chronister, 1992, p. 43):

> In the war in which we are now engaged racial affinities are not severed by migration. The Japanese race is an enemy race and while many second and third generation Japanese born on US [sic] soil, possessed of US [sic] citizenship have become "Americanized," the racial strains are undiluted.

Those destined for the internment camps required only one eighth of Japanese blood to lose their liberty (Chronister, 1992). This determination of guilt was based on racial heritage—an abnormal evidentiary standard. Besides mass incarceration, the urgency of the evacuation and relocation caused many Japanese to lose accumulated wealth and possessions (Daniels, 1993; Takaki, 1994b).

Argument for the Classification of These Events as Hate Crime

Both Kearneyism and the internment camp experience caused significant psychological, physical, and economic harm. Total disruption of family and community life, compounded with the sudden loss of financial security, brought irreparable damages. Also, these incidents were morally offensive. Based on Kantian principles, the victims were treated merely as ends rather than as means (i.e., ridding White males of job competitors and the incapacitation of an imagined threat to national security that was easy to identify). Evidence of racial bias is easily perceived.

Once again, such attitudes were prevalent in American culture. For example, during the early 1900s, the *San Francisco Chronicle* printed a series of articles that depicted Asians in a contemptuous manner: "Brown Men Are Made Citizens Illegally"; "Japanese a Menace to American Women"; "Brown Men an Evil in the Public Schools"; and "The Yellow Peril—How Japanese Crowd Out the White Race" (Steinfield, 1973; Takaki, 1994b). In addition, in 1981 the Commission of Wartime Relocation formally acknowledged that the internment of Japanese Americans was based on racism (Daniels, 1993; Davis & Graham, 1995). The United States was also at war with Germany and Italy, yet German and Italian Americans were not subjected to the same collective suspicion and persecution at the hands of the federal government. The government's position reflected the mindset that White Americans would not be scrutinized due to their ethnicity or race as were Asian Americans. Likewise, the consequences of Kearneyism would have been brought under control quickly had the attackers been Asian and the victims White Americans.

DISCUSSION

Similarities Between the Past and Present

America's current hate crime problem is not a distinctly modern phenomenon; rather, it has deep historical roots. Harmful acts motivated by racist attitudes and ethnocentrism have

Table 1.1   Comparisons Between Historical and Modern Hate Crime Factors

Common Items From Historical Events	Historical Events[a]	Modern Events
Factor A: Perpetrator group reflected ideals similar to the mainstream	x	x
Factor B: Perpetrator group believed the target group to be inadequate, inferior, and undeserving (culture of hate in place)	x	x
Factor C: Diversity not well tolerated	x	x
Factor D: Targets were identified as anti-American, blamed for the ills of the country, inflation, unemployment, crime, loss of morality	x	x
Factor E: Perpetrator rarely punished	x	_[b]
Factor F: Perpetrators were primarily White males	x	x
Factor G: Targets were primarily people of color	x	x
Factor H: Hate crime was characteristically violent	x	_[c]
Factor I: Targeted groups have constitutional protections by federal and state law	–	x
Factor J: Hate groups were affiliated with legitimate political parties (or sought affiliation)	x	x[d]

a. An event is considered historical if it is pre-hate crime legislation.
b. Punishment is relatively lenient.
c. Much of it is crime against properties, yet incidents of violence are increasing.
d. For example, extremists infiltrated the Buchanan and Dole organizations and the David Duke and Tom Metzger early runs on Democratic and Republican tickets.

frequently occurred throughout American history.

There are many parallels between historical and present-day hate crimes. The most apparent similarity is the presence of White racism in American culture. Racially motivated acts are born out of racist attitudes, making those attitudes powerful predictors of subsequent hate crime (Hamm, 1993). Racism was as prevalent in the past as it is today. Evidence of it was found in institutional and cultural practices. Governmental policies encouraged institutional racism with Indian Relocation programs, Black Codes, and anti-Asian legislation. Social sentiment supported and was reinvigorated by such policies. Evidence of modern racist attitudes, unfortunately, are also well documented (Barkan & Cohn, 1994; Brown, 1995; Hacker, 1995; Mann, 1993).

Other similarities between past and present hate crimes include characteristics of the crimes, perpetrators, and victims. Table 1.1 summarizes these factors.

Historical and modern hate crime acts are compared in Table 1.1. Historical events are those that occurred before the first wave of hate crime legislation beginning in the 1980s. The two categories are compared using common characteristics gleaned from a review of the historical events.

Factors A to D are concerned with the prevailing attitudes of the times and indicate a social and political environment that facilitated division and acts of intolerance. Modern and historical social climates are viewed similarly across these elements. Factors F and G describe the identities of the typical perpetrator and victim of hate crime. Similarities are found once again. With regard to Factor H, historical hate crimes frequently involved significant bodily harm and death, whereas most modern hate crimes do not. Some research indicates that a higher percentage of bias crimes result in physical harm than nonbias offenses; however, the clear majority of hate crimes are property related (B. Levin, 1992–1993).

Factor J denotes the presence of affiliation of organized hate groups like the Ku Klux Klan with legitimate political parties. In historical events, government officials were often active participants in the crimes, implying representation in mainstream political organizations (Jordan, 1968; Steinfield, 1973). Likewise, modern events indicate infiltration of extremists in traditional political parties (Hamm, 1993).

Factor E compares the level of punishment received by hate crime perpetrators. Analysis of historical events suggests that perpetrators acted with impunity—punishment was a rare occurrence. Modern hate crime perpetrators often receive lenient punishment due to their age and absence of prior record (J. Levin & McDevitt, 1993). However, these offenders are recognized across all jurisdictions as criminals. Factor I compares the level of constitutional or other statutory protections afforded hate crime victim groups. Historical evidence indicates the general absence of such protections, whereas modern victims have received the benefit of various legal mechanisms for protection.

The Future of American Hate Crime

Recent changes in hate crime suggest their prevention and control will become more difficult. They include the following: (a) a greater ability to cause mass destruction, (b) a growing acceptance of extremist ideology in the marketplace of political ideas, (c) the legal protection of extremists in the court system, (d) an increase in religious zealotry among hate crime perpetrators, and (e) an increased adoption of extremist agenda into the concerns of middle America.

Mass Destruction

Whereas the examined historical events caused the victimization of countless persons, they also required the participation of many. Conversely, modern hate crime perpetrators have the capacity to cause large-scale destruction single-handedly. In 1989, Patrick Purdy, described as a dysfunctional transient with a criminal record, acquired a semiautomatic assault rifle and shot Asian children during recess in their Stockton, California elementary school. Purdy wounded 30 children

and killed 5 (J. Levin & McDevitt, 1993). Likewise, Colin Ferguson, the Long Island shooter, wounded 19 and killed 6 (Van Biema, 1995); and Terry Nichols and Tim McVeigh wounded more than 400 people, and caused the death of 168 persons (Federal Emergency Management Agency, 1995).

In addition, hate crime perpetrators have learned the value of forming alliances and coalitions (Christensen, 1994; Hamm, 1994; J. Levin & McDevitt, 1993). Information is shared regarding bomb manufacturing, as well as other techniques to disrupt vital infrastructure such as energy sources, water systems, telecommunications and transportation systems (Southern Poverty Law Center Report, 1997a). With computer technology, such coalitions transverse states as well as continents. The Federal Bureau of Investigation has long reported links between American hate groups and middle-eastern state-sponsored terrorist organizations (J. Levin & McDevitt, 1993; Sloan, 1997). These developments have enabled modern perpetrators to compile arsenals that give pause to many law enforcement agents. Raids have uncovered a panoply of sophisticated weaponry (Valentine, 1995), in addition to plans to secure missiles, biochemical agents, and nuclear weaponry (Southern Poverty Law Center Report, 1997b). Thus, modern advancements allow hate crime perpetrators to become major threats to society. As we approach the new millennium, several watch groups report that extremists are planning acts with the potential for massive loss of life (Hamm, 1998b).

Growing Acceptance of Extremist Ideology

Even more disturbing is the quiet acquiescence and adoption of extremist views in mainstream political platforms and ideologies (Hagan, 1997; Horowitz, 1996; J. Levin & McDevitt, 1993; McLemee, 1997). Although Tom Metzger is considered by some to be the leading force behind the revitalization of the racist skinhead movement in the United States (Hamm, 1994), he consistently sought to enter into the foray of mainstream politics early in his career. He supported Republican Presidential Candidate Barry Goldwater in 1964, George

Wallace in 1968, and he found agreement in much of the Reagan platform. Metzger ran for a congressional seat in 1980. His extreme views were present in his political vision; he may have been one of the original critics of affirmative action policies (Hamm, 1993). Today, affirmative action is moot in California, and it is currently under challenge in several other states. Also, Metzger advocated legislation to end immigration with particular emphasis on sealing U.S. borders from Mexican illegals. Similar to this, Patrick Buchanan, in his Republican primary bid, announced a platform that harmonized strongly with many of Metzger's views (Project Vote Smart, 1992–1998).

Gain of Legal Protection

The courts may be ineffectual in stemming actions that facilitate intolerance. Court decisions reveal increasing hesitancy to interfere with hate speech. First Amendment purists argue for the constitutional right of extremists to espouse their vitriol in public (Heumann & Church, 1997)—even cross burning has been construed as protected speech (see Lawrence [1996] discussion of *R.A.V. v. City of St. Paul, Minnesota*). Using the same First Amendment argument, extremist organizations are using the Internet to provide provocative information. They are able to proselytize, to announce rallies and White Power rock concerts, and to provide additional disturbing information (Hamm, 1993; Southern Poverty Law Center Report, 1997a). Hate advocates have discovered a market in how-to books, such as *Bacteriological Warfare: A Major Threat to North America—A Guide for the Development, Preservation and Deployment of Biological Agents,* authored by Larry Wayne Harris; and William Powell's *Anarchist Cookbook.* Chapters include the following: "How to Make Tear Gas in Your Basement," "How to Build a Silencer for a Submachine Gun," or "How to Make Nitroglycerin." These works have been protected by the U.S. Constitution and the courts.

Increase in Religious Zealotry

Although America has denounced religion-based terrorism in Ireland, Bosnia, India, Pakistan, and the Middle East, some contend that the United States is witnessing the start of the same turmoil on its own soil (Southern Poverty Law Center Report, 1997b). American hate crime perpetrators, organized groups, and other extremist affiliations are often connected by a mutual belief in Christian Identity theology. A pseudo-religion, Christian Identity promotes a doctrine that the White race will be involved in a cataclysmic war against other races and political enemies (Barkun, 1994). This religion has been repeatedly claimed by many organized extremists such as the Aryan Nation and the White Aryan Resistance (Barkun, 1994; Christensen, 1994). Timothy McVeigh reportedly was influenced by the Identity movement. These individuals are devoted to their theology.

Middle America is Becoming More Sympathetic

Since the popularity of political conservatism in the 1980s, Americans have continued to embrace conservative beliefs and values. Although the Clinton administration and many economists describe America's economic health as robust, some Americans are skeptical. As corporations, businesses, and banking institutions merge and local economic conditions are affected, Americans become increasingly concerned and increasingly conservative (Bryjak and Soroka, 1997). In fact, working class Americans are a growing populace of alienated, hostile, frustrated individuals who are expressing views not unlike some extremists (Horatio Alger Association, 1996; "Pool points," 1996). Scapegoating is at an all-time high. Not unlike the viewpoints of the patriot, separatist, survivalist, supremacist, militia, or other anarchist movements, anxiety-filled working class Americans have pointed the finger of blame at everything from working women, the nation of Israel, and non-English-speaking Hispanics to liberalism, the New World Order, and the Bureau of Alcohol Tobacco and Firearms. Add to this mix Americans who are seduced by extremist rhetoric, and the potential is there for an escalation of hate crimes or domestic terrorism in this country that is fueled by racial hatred (Goldhagen, 1996).

CONCLUSION

Historical hate crimes were shaped by the forces of their day. Prevailing societal attitudes that legitimized ethnocentrism provided conditions that facilitated attacks on the devalued, disfranchised, and isolated subpopulations in America. With the involvement of the government in several instances, historical hate crime had a subsuming and fatalistic quality. Historical victims had little to no legal rights, let alone the capability of mounting adequate defense strategies. In addition, because they were frequently isolated and/or segregated physically and psychologically from the dominant populace, their victimization was largely unnoticed.

Although modern hate crime perpetrators are far more dangerous (i.e., greater access to weapons of mass destruction [Wooden, 1994]), today's hate crime targets do not have the disadvantages of historical victims. Minority populations are generally more integrated and far less isolated, making targeting more difficult. They also have a greater ability to engage political and economic platforms that would prevent or frustrate attacks. Nevertheless, it is clear that the potential of modern hate crime exponentially surpasses harms that were committed in the past.

Scholars such as Sloan (1997) recognize a blurring of the line between foreign and domestic terrorism. Likewise, in several ways hate crime and domestic terrorism have converged (Gibbs, 1989; Hamm, 1994). Due to the growing political sophistication of hate organizations (J. Levin & McDevitt, 1993), American hate crime has clearly evolved into domestic terrorism. The National Advisory Committee's Task Force on Disorders and Terrorism's Report included the definitions of various forms of terrorism. The objective of political terrorism corresponds with the goal of most hate organizations (Hagan, 1997, p. 134): "violent criminal behavior [is] designed primarily to generate fear in the community for political purposes."

Some would say that much of hate crime targets property and, therefore, does not approach any degree of terrorism. This author disagrees. Even the anonymous spray painting of a swastika on a tombstone evokes fear, intimidation, and sends a political message even if that was not the intention. Hate crime perpetrators range from naive impulsive teenagers to trained members of well-structured and financed organizations bent on procuring destruction. Both terrorists and hate crime perpetrators use fear to achieve purposes that often extend beyond immediate objectives.

Lessons from the past, the present, and the evolving nature of hate crimes suggest further examination of the problem as a form of domestic terrorism. This would be an important change in law enforcement and prosecutorial attitude toward hate crimes. Hate crime viewed as a form of domestic terrorism increases its priority. Law enforcement training, resource allocation, and intelligence gathering would likely receive greater emphasis and fiscal support. However, law enforcement and prosecutors may be hesitant to embrace this new perspective due to the general undercurrent of systemic devaluation of minority, poor, homosexual, and female crime victims (Hernandez, 1990). To legislatively upgrade the classification of hate crime as a form of domestic terrorism is to impute additional importance on the hate crime victim. Perhaps only then will society have sent a cogent message—not sent historically, nor well sent today—that the victimization of the James Byrd, Jrs of the world will receive a higher standard of justice than what has occurred through the last 300 years.

NOTES

1. See J. M. Pollock (1994, p. 18) for a substantive discussion of Kantian ethics. The following are some principles of Kant's ethical formalism:

1. Act only on that maxim which you can at the same time will that it should become a universal law. In other words, for any decision of behavior to be made, examine whether that behavior would be acceptable if it were a universal law to be followed by everyone.

2. Act in such a way that you always treat humanity, whether in your own person or that of any other, never simply as a means but always at the same time as an end. *In other words, one should not use people for one's own purposes.*

3. Act as if you were, through your maxims, a lawmaking member of a kingdom of ends. This principle directs that the individual's actions should contribute

to and be consistent with universal law. Also, because we freely choose to abide by moral law and these laws are self-imposed rather than imposed from the outside, they are a selection of the higher nature of humans.

2. See Horsman (1981, p. 4) for more information on Anglo-Saxon. The term *Anglo-Saxon* race is truly a misnomer. In reality, the term represents a combination of different European ethnicities, including Germanic and Celtic tribes, and Nordics and Normans who conquered and eventually settled among the indigenous people of England. However, the term began to represent the distinction between English-speaking Caucasians in general and Native Americans, Africans, descendants of Africans, Mexicans, and Asians.

3. One could argue that the antecedents for modern hate crime legislation lie in the Thirteenth and Fourteenth Amendments or in the seminal U.S. Supreme Court decision of *Brown v. Board of Education* (1954). However, in 1981 the Anti-Defamation League drafted the model legislation for hate crimes that stood to facilitate state legislatures (for additional information see Freeman [1992–1993] or Jost [1993]). Based on Freeman (1992–1993) and Jost (1993), the writer uses 1980 as indicative of the hate crime legislation era.

4. See Steinfield (1973, p. 56), regarding the early treatment of Indians.

5. The following is a statement made by Commissioner W. A. Jones in the Annual Report of the Commissioner of Indian Affairs in 1903 (Steinfield, 1973, p. 52):

> It is probably true that the majority of our wild Indians have no inherited tendencies whatever toward morality or chastity, according to an enlightened standard. Chastity and morality among them must come from education and contact with the better elements of the whites.

6. Some have set their approximate numbers closer to 20,000.

7. "They were practically starving on government rations, and the government had told them that they could no longer supplement their diets by hunting game" (Carnes, 1995, p. 62; cited in Spindler, 1972).

8. See Brown (1970, p. 90). "Robert Bent's description of the atrocities was corroborated by Lieutenant James Connor":

> In going over the battleground the next day I did not see a body of man, woman, or child but was scalped. . . . Bodies were mutilated in the most horrible manner; I heard another say he had cut the fingers off an

Indian to get the rings. . . . I also heard of numerous instances in which men had cut out the private parts of females and stretched them over the saddle-bows and wore them over their hats while riding in the ranks.

9. Native Americans did not legally receive some form of citizenship until 1924, as a result of their significant participation in World War I.

10. Regarding the manifestation of the dehumanization of the American Indian, as noted in Kennedy (1959, p. 10): "In the opening up of Oregon to white settlement, even Methodist clergymen expressed no regret at seeing Indian women being clubbed to death and Indian babies dashed against trees by white settlers."

Found in Brown (1970, p. 90), and in Berthrong (1963, p. 1850), in a public speech made in Denver, Colonel Chivington advocated the killing and scalping of all Indians, even infants: "Nits make lice!" he declared.

11. See Pieterse (1992) for further clarification on the change in Africa's image. A summarizing paragraph is found on page 29:

> From antiquity to the early Middle Ages the dominant image changed from positive to negative, while the early to late Middle Ages saw the transformation of the black from an infernal demon to the highly honoured representative of a remote Christendom—Europe's redeemer and help in distress.

The developments described are significant against the background of later developments, when gradually a negative image of Africans comes again to predominate.

12. See Jordan (1968, p. 24), on the symbolism of color and spiritual values:

> In the Christian period a significant break occurred with the views of antiquity. In the writings of several of the church fathers of western Christendom . . . the color black began to acquire negative connotations, as the color of sin and darkness. Origen, head of the catechetical school in Alexandria in the third century, introduced the allegorical theme of Egyptian darkness as against spiritual light. The symbolism of light and darkness was probably derived from astrology, alchemy . . . in itself it had nothing to do with skin color, but in the course of time it did acquire that connotation.

13. See Horsman (1981, p. 100):

> The process of debasing blacks had been carried out in the daily life of America, and whatever the theory, blacks in practice were not regarded merely as men and women of a different complexion. Blacks were not simply regarded as debased because they were slaves: they were also enslaved because of what was regarded as their different and debased nature. Whites, by the

very laws they passed and the attitudes they assumed, placed blacks on a different human level.

Also, in Pieterse (1992, p. 41):

In his study of British attitudes vis-à-vis blacks at the time of the slave trade, Anthony Barker argues that before 1770 blacks were regarded as inferior more on grounds of cultural traits, and the traditional association in Christian culture of blackness with evil, than on those of any theory of in-bred racial inferiority.

See Horsman (1981, p. 123). Thomas R. Dew's review of the debate (regarding Virginia debates on emancipation and equality):

Dew's main contention was that to end slavery would be a disaster. . . . Dew thought that the presence of large numbers of free blacks would be disastrous to both races. Slaves, were "utterly unfit for a state of freedom among the whites." Blackness, not slavery, was the essential cause of the Negro condition, for "the emancipated black carries a mark that no time can erase; he forever wears the indelible symbol of his inferior condition."

14. See Stampp (1956), regarding the systematic effects of slavery on Black mortality rates.

15. Wells-Barnett (1969, p. 54) on the casualness of lynch incidents:

Perhaps the most characteristic feature of this record of lynch law for the year 1893, is the remarkable fact that five human beings were lynched and that the matter was considered of so little importance that the powerful press bureaus of the country did not consider the matter of enough importance to ascertain the causes for which they were hanged. . . . Lynch Law had become so common in the United States that the finding of the dead body of a Negro, suspended between heaven and earth to the limb of a tree, is of so slight importance that neither the civil authorities nor press agencies consider the matter worth investigating.

16. See Jordan (1968) regarding the significance of color and the political status of slavery.

17. See Perlmutter (1992, p. 144) regarding the Dred Scott decision. "Unlike European immigrants who could become citizens after 5 years, Blacks born abroad or in America could not. They were simply property. This was the ruling in the 1857 Supreme Court case of Dred Scott v. Sanford."

18. Cited in Steinfield (1973, p. 132) from Elmer Clarence Sandmeyer in *The Anti-Chinese Movement in California* (1939). Sandmeyer quoted Senator Morton:

There would have been a depression in 1870s if the entire population had been made up of lineal descendants of George Washington. . . . If the Chinese in California were white people, being in all other respects what they are, I do not believe that the complaints and warfare against them would have existed to any considerable extent.

REFERENCES

Arendt, H. (1963). *Eichmann in Jerusalem: A report on the banality of evil.* New York: Viking Press.

Barkan, S. E., & Cohn, S. F. (1994). Racial prejudice and support for the death penalty by Whites. *Journal of Research in Crime and Delinquency, 31,* 202–209.

Barkun, M. (1994). *Religion and the racist right: The origins of the Christian Identity movement.* Chapel Hill: University of North Carolina Press.

Berthrong, D. J. (1963). *The southern Cheyennes.* Norman: University of Oklahoma Press.

Brown, D. (1970). *Bury my heart at Wounded Knee. An Indian history of the American west.* New York: Holt, Rinehart & Winston.

Brown, T. (1995). *Black lies, white lies.* New York: William Morrow.

Brown v. Board of Education, 347 U.S. 483 (1954).

Bryjak, G. J., & Soroka, M. P. (1997). *Sociology: Cultural diversity in a changing world* (3rd ed.). Boston: Allyn & Bacon.

Bureau of Justice Assistance. (1997). *A policymaker's guide to hate crimes* (BJA Monograph #NCJ 162304). U.S. Department of Justice: Office of Justice Programs.

Burk, R. A. (1994). Foreword. In M. S. Hamm (Ed.), *Hate crime: International perspectives on causes and control* (pp. v-x). Cincinnati, OH: Anderson Publishing and Academy of Criminal Justice Sciences.

Chalk, F., & Jonassohn, K. (1990). *The history and sociology of genocide: Analyses and case studies.* New Haven: Yale University Press.

Christensen, L. (1994). *Skinhead street gangs.* Boulder, CO: Paladin Press.

Chronister, A. (1992). *Japan-bashing: How propaganda shapes Americans' perception of the Japanese.* Unpublished master's thesis, Lehigh University, Bethlehem, PA.

Cutler, J. E. (1969). *Lynch-law. An investigation into the history of lynching in the United States.* Chicago: Negro Universities Press.

Czajkoski, E. H. (1992). Criminalizing hate: An empirical assessment. *Federal Probation, 56(8),* 36–40.

Daniels, R. (1993). *Prisoners without trial. Japanese Americans in World War II.* New York: Hill & Wang.

Dennis, D. (1984). *Black history.* New York: Writers and Readers Publishing.

Devlin, P. (1986). Morals and criminal law. In J. Feinberg & H. Gross (Eds.), *Philosophy of law* (3rd ed.). Belmont, CA: Wadsworth.

Farb, P. (1968). *Man's rise to civilization as shown by the Indians of North: America from primeval times to the coming of the industrial state.* Chicago: E. P. Dutton.

Federal Emergency Management Agency. (1998, January 19). *Oklahoma City bombing disaster* [On-line]. Available: Internet http://www.fema. gov/okc95/okcudt8.htm

Feinberg, J., & Gross, H. (1986). *Philosophy of law* (3rd ed., pp. 11–23). Belmont, CA: Wadsworth.

Fredrickson, G. M. (1991). *White supremacy. A comparative study in American and South African history.* New York: Oxford University Press.

Freeman, S. M. (1992–1993). Hate crime laws: Punishment which fits the crime. *Annual Survey of American Law, 4.*

Gerstenfeld, P. B. (1992). Smile when you call me that! The problems with punishing hate motivated behavior. *Behavioral Sciences and the Law, 10,* 259–285.

Gibbs, J. P. (1989). Conceptualization of terrorism. *American Sociological Review, 54,* 329–340.

Goldhagen, D. J. (1996). *Hitler's willing executioners: Ordinary Germans and the Holocaust.* New York: Vintage.

Gould, S. J. (1981). *The mismeasurement of man.* New York: Norton.

Hacker, A. (1995). *Two nations black and white, separate, hostile, and unequal.* New York: Ballantine.

Hagan, F. E. (1997). *Political crime: Ideology and criminality.* Needham Heights, MA: Allyn & Bacon.

Hamm, M. S. (1993). *American skinheads: The criminology and control of hate crime.* Westport, CT: Praeger.

Hamm, M. S. (1994). Conceptualizing hate crime in a global context. In M. S. Hamm (Ed.), *Hate crime: International perspectives on causes and control* (pp. 173–189). Cincinnati, OH: Anderson Publishing and Academy of Criminal Justice Sciences.

Hamm, M. S. (1998a). The laundering of white crime. In C. R. Mann and M. S. Zatz (Eds.), *Images of color images of crime* (pp. 244–256). Los Angeles, CA: Roxbury.

Hamm, M. S. (1998b). Terrorism, hate crime, and antigovernment violence: A review of the research. In H. W. Kushner (Ed.), *The future of terrorism: Violence in the new millennium.* Thousand Oaks, CA: Sage.

Harjo, S. S. (1998). Redskins, savages, and other Indian enemies: An historical overview of American media coverage of Native peoples. In C. R. Mann and M. S. Zatz (Eds.), *Images of color images of crime* (pp. 30–46). Los Angeles, CA: Roxbury.

Haskins, G. L. (1969). The beginnings of partible inheritance in the American colonies. In D. H. Flaherty (Ed.), *Essays in the history of early American law* (pp. 204–244). Chapel Hill: University of North Carolina Press.

Healey, J. F. (1995). *Race, ethnicity, gender and class: The sociology of group conflict and change.* Thousand Oaks, CA: Sage.

Hernandez, T. K. (1990). Bias crimes: Unconscious racism in the prosecution of "racially motivated violence." *Yale Law Journal, 99,* 845–864.

Heumann, M., & Church, T. W. (1997). General introduction. In M. Heumann & T. W. Church (Eds.), *Hate speech on campus. Cases, case studies and commentary* (pp. 3–13). Boston: Northeastern University Press.

Higginbotham, A. L., Jr. (1978). *In the matter of color. Race and the American legal process: The colonial period.* New York: Oxford University Press.

Hoffer, P. C. (1992). *Law and people in colonial America.* Baltimore: Johns Hopkins University.

Hohler, B. (1998, June 28). Klan rally bares hatred, but Jasper thwarts violence. *Boston Globe,* pp. A1, A16.

Horatio Alger Association. (1996). *Immigration polls: Why doesn't Congress listen to the American people?* [On-line]. Available: Internet http:// www/horatioalger.com/pubmat/pubmat.htm

Horowitz, C. (1996). Anti-semitic violence is increasing. In P. A. Winters (Ed.), *Current controversies series: Hate crimes* (pp. 18–24). San Diego, CA: Greenhaven.

Horsman, R. (1981). *Race and manifest destiny. The origins of American racial Anglo-Saxonism.* Cambridge, MA: Harvard University Press.

Jordan, W. D. (1968). *White over black. American attitudes toward the Negro, 1550–1812.* Chapel Hill: University of North Carolina Press.

Jost, K. (1993). Hate crimes. *CQ Researcher,* January, 3–19.

Kennedy, S. (1959). *Jim Crow guide to the U.S.A. The laws, customs and etiquette governing the conduct of nonwhites and other minorities as second-class citizens.* Westport, CT: Greenwood.

Lawrence, C. R., III. (1996). Hate crimes violate the free speech rights of victims. In P. A. Winters (Ed.), *Current controversies: Hate crimes* (pp. 60–67). San Diego, CA: Greenhaven.

Levin, B. (1992–1993). Bias crimes: A theoretical and practical overview. *Stanford Law and Policy Review,* Winter, 165–180.

Levin, J., & Levin, W. C. (1982). *The functions of discrimination and prejudice.* New York: Harper & Row.

Levin, J., & McDevitt, J. (1993). *Hate crimes. The rising tide of bigotry and bloodshed.* New York: Plenum Press.

Mackie, J. L. (1977). *Ethics: Inventing right and wrong.* New York: Penguin.

McLemee, S. (1997). The militia movement is dangerous. In C. P. Cozic (Ed.), *The militia movement. At issue. An opposing viewpoints series* (pp. 50–58). San Diego, CA: Greenhaven Press.

Mann, C. R. (1993). *Unequal justice: A question of color.* Bloomington: University of Indiana Press.

Martin, S. (1996). Investigating hate crimes: Case characteristics and law enforcement responses. *Justice Quarterly, 13*(3), 455–480.

Merk, F. (1963). *Manifest Destiny and mission in American history. A reinterpretation.* New York: Knopf.

Messner, S. F., & Rosenfeld, R. (1997). *Crime and the American dream* (2nd ed.). New York: Wadsworth.

Miller, V. P. (1979). *Ukomno'm: The Yuki Indians of Northern California.* Socorro, NM: Ballena Press.

Morris, T. D. (1996). *Southern slavery and the law, 1619–1860.* Chapel Hill: University of North Carolina Press.

Pallone, N. J. (1990). *Rehabilitating criminal sexual psychopaths.* New Brunswick, NJ: Transaction.

Perlmutter, P. (1992). *Divided we fall. A history of ethnic, religious, and racial prejudice in America.* Ames: Iowa State University Press.

Pieterse, J. N. (1992). *White on black. Images of Africa and Blacks in western popular culture.* New Haven, CT: Yale University Press.

Pollock-Byrne, J. M. (1989). *Ethics in crime and justice. Dilemmas and decisions.* Pacific Grove, CA: Brooks/Cole.

Pool points to conservative electorate. (1996). *USA Today* [On-line].

Pound, R. (1938). *The formative era of American law.* Gloucester, MA: Little, Brown.

Project Vote Smart. (1992–1998). *Candidate for President of the United States. Patrick Joseph Buchanan* [On-line].

Riding In, J. (1998). American Indians in popular culture: A pawnee's experiences and views. In C. R. Mann & M. S. Zatz (Eds.), *Images of color*

images of crime (pp. 15–29). Los Angeles, CA: Roxbury.

Rome, D. M. (1998). Murderers, rapists, and drug addicts. In C. R. Mann & M. S. Zatz (Eds.), *Images of color images of crime* (pp. 85–95). Los Angeles, CA: Roxbury.

Sanders, R. (1978). *Lost tribes and promised lands. The origins of American racism.* Boston: Little, Brown.

Sloan, S. (1997). An Unholy Alliance. The Internationalization of Domestic Terrorism. *Intelligence Report. Winter 1997.* (Vol. 85, pp. 10–11). Atlanta, GA: Klanwatch.

Southern Poverty Law Center Report. (1997a). *New Klanwatch project monitors internet hate* (Vol. 27, p. 3). Atlanta, GA: Southern Poverty Law Center.

Southern Poverty Law Center Report. (1997b). Intelligence Briefs. *Intelligence Report. Winter 1997* (Vol. 85, p. 2). Montgomery, AL: Klanwatch Publishers. A Project of the Southern Poverty Law Center.

Spindler, W. H. (1972). *Tragedy strikes at Wounded Knee and other essays on Indian life in South Dakota and Nebraska.* Vermillion: University of South Dakota Press.

Stampp, K. M. (1956). *The peculiar institution: Slavery in the ante-bellum south.* New York: Vintage.

Steinfield, M. (1973). *Cracks in the melting pot. Racism and discrimination in American history* (2nd ed.). New York: Glencoe.

Takaki, R. (1994a). *Journey to gold mountain. The Chinese in 19th-century America.* New York: Chelsea House.

Takaki, R. (1994b). *Issei and Nisei. The settling of Japanese America.* New York: Chelsea House.

Tebbel, J., & Jennison, K. (1960). *The American Indian wars.* New York: Harper & Row.

U.S. Congress. 39th. 2nd session. Senate Report 156.

Valentine, B. (1995). *Gang intelligence manual. Identifying and understanding modern-day violent gangs in the United States.* Boulder, CO: Paladin.

Van Biema, D. (1995). Justice. A fool for a client. *Time Domestic, 145*(6).

Walker, S., Spohn, C., & DeLone, M. (1996). *The color of justice.* New York: Wadsworth.

Wells-Barnett, I. B. (1969). *Wells-Barnett: On lynchings southern horrors a red record mob rule in New Orleans.* New York: Arno Press.

Wooden, W. S. (1994). *Renegade kids, suburban outlaws.* New York: Wadsworth.

QUESTIONS

1. How does the history of our legal system's approach to crimes against individuals from powerless groups illustrate the political nature of lawmaking in terms of what is—and what isn't—defined as a crime?

2. Consider the distinction between "utilitarian" and "universal principles of morality" moral theories. The utilitarian approach looks at the consequences of an action to determine whether it is right or wrong. In contrast, the universal principles approach defines the morality of an action in terms of the inherent character of the action (i.e., whether it violates universal principles of morality). What are the implications of these contrasting approaches for hate crime laws?

3. What criteria does Petrosino use to evaluate whether or not a historical episode of violence can be defined as a hate crime? According to these criteria, were members of minority groups subject to hate crimes during historic times?

4. Describe and discuss how violence against Native Americans, African Americans, and Asian immigrants reflected the social and legal climate of the times. In what ways was the law used to justify this violence?

5. Why does Petrosino propose that the prevention and control of hate crimes will become increasingly difficult? Discuss the reasons she provides.

6. In what ways do modern hate crime perpetrators have greater power to create destruction than historic hate crime perpetrators had?

7. How has the advent of technology and the media increased the ability of modern hate crime perpetrators to cause harm?

8. What are some examples of the "growing acceptance of extremist ideology" that Petrosino discusses? Why do you think this is happening?

9. How do recent societal debates on civil liberties and immigration illustrate the growing acceptance of extremist views by many Americans?

10. In what ways do court decisions (e.g., on hate speech) influence the ability of extremists to spread their message?

11. In what ways do hate crimes resemble domestic terrorism in terms of their consequences on affected individuals and communities?

12. What are the similarities between hate crimes in the historic and the modern era? What are the differences?

Part II

HATE CRIME LAWS

In this section, the authors detail legal developments related to hate crime. The articles in this section collectively describe some of the complexities associated with legislation and judicial interpretations of hate crime laws, including how to define a hate crime and a hate crime victim, and the challenge of distinguishing between expressive behavior that is and is not protected by the First Amendment. The articles in this section raise important questions that become recurring themes throughout this reader: How do law and policy making on hate crimes illustrate the dynamic relationship between societal and legal change? To what degree do emerging law and policy responses to the historic problem of hate crime reflect growing social awareness of the problem, media attention to the problem, political activism by individuals and groups, and to what degree is it a reflection of top-down policy-making efforts?

2

The Birth and Maturation of Hate Crime Policy in the United States

Ryken Grattet

Valerie Jenness

In this article, the authors trace the emergence of hate crime as a legally recognized type of crime. How has hate-based offending changed from being an unacknowledged part of the American historical landscape to being an evolving new "policy domain," where such behavior is explicitly recognized and defined as a societal and legal problem? The authors discuss how societal interpretations of discriminatory violence have changed over the years, culminating in legal recognition of the harms of hate crimes for those officially defined as hate crime victims.

It is beyond question that the recent eruptions of racist, anti-Semitic, and antigay violence have focused unprecedented attention on the topic of hate crime. Indeed, the media chronicles of hate crimes are given fresh installments at alarmingly regular intervals. It seems we are in the midst of a hate "crime wave" (Fishman, 1978). It is fitting, then, that a national law journal has dubbed the 1990s the "decade of hate—or at least of hate crime" (Rovella, 1994).

Hate-motivated violence, however, is perhaps more accurately characterized as an age-old problem approached with a new sense of urgency. This urgency stems from a social process that was set in motion several decades ago. During the 1980s and 1990s, multiple social movements began to devote considerable material and symbolic resources to the problem. Government agencies analyzed the issue. Legislative campaigns sprang forth from every level of government. New sentencing rules and categories of criminal behavior were established in law. Prosecutors and law enforcement developed training policies and specialized enforcement units. The U.S. Supreme Court weighed in

EDITORS' NOTE: From Grattet, R., & Jenness, V. (2001). The Birth and Maturation of Hate Crime Policy in the United States. *American Behavioral Scientist, 45,* 668-696. © 2001 Sage Publications. Reprinted with permission.

with its rejection of one statutory formula and its acceptance of another. Scholarly commentary and social science research on the topic have exploded. These extraordinary developments attest to the growing concern with and public visibility of violence motivated by bigotry, hatred, or bias. In the process, criminal conduct that was once undistinguished from ordinary crime has been parsed out, redefined, and condemned more harshly than before (Jenness & Grattet, 2001), reflecting the increasing acceptance of the idea that criminal conduct is different when it involves an act of discrimination. In short, hate crime has clearly secured a place in the American public sphere.

In this article, we argue that hate crime cannot be understood solely in terms of its behavioral manifestations, its statistical frequency, and/or its causal precursors. Instead, as the developments catalogued above indicate, hate crime involves a significant mobilization of people, bureaucracies, and institutions. What we are witnessing is a common, but undertheorized, phenomena: the birth and structuring of a domain of public policy. Accordingly, the way this policy domain has emerged, its key players, organizational practices, and substantive foci, form the backdrop against which the behavior and consequences of hate crime can best be understood.

CONCEPTUALIZING HATE CRIME AS A POLICY DOMAIN

Throughout this article, we frequently refer to hate crime as a policy domain. As Burstein (1991) noted in his review of the literature on the formation and evolution of policy domains, "Sociologists interested in politics have increasingly turned in recent years to the study of policy domains" (p. 328). He used the term to denote "components of the political system organized around substantive issues" (p. 327).[1]

Policy domains are fundamentally rooted in definitional and classification schemes that are properly characterized as social constructions. This means that the substantive focus and boundaries of policy domains are not based on inherent qualities of "problems." Instead, the distinctions reflect dominant modes of conceptualizing

issues. Such distinctions are routinely revealed as "constructed" by social analysts who point out the social conditions are assigned meanings that define their parameters and content (for a review, see Mauss & Jenness, 2001). Therefore, how issues are constructed has clear implications for how policy domains are structured and the kinds of policies that are brought to bear on any particular social problem.[2]

Our use of the term *policy domain* implies that the causes and consequences of a problem cannot be fully comprehended apart from an understanding of the larger processes that identified, defined, and ultimately propelled it. More specifically, we use the term *policy domain* to refer to two things. First, it refers to the range of collective actors—for example, politicians, experts, officials, enforcers, and interest groups—who have gained sufficient legitimacy to speak about or act on a particular issue. Second, it refers to the cultural logics, theories, frameworks, and ideologies those actors bring to bear in constructing the problem and the appropriate policy responses.

These dimensions of a policy domain orient us to several considerations with respect to hate crime. Most generally, they suggest that the organization and culture of the hate crime policy domain have shaped the way the problem of hate crime has been defined and the kinds of policies that have been formulated and adopted. Moreover, focusing on policy domains requires recognizing that "policy change takes place through the conjunction of three streams of activity moving fairly independently: problem recognition and agenda setting; the specification of policy options; and the politics of selecting among proposals and enacting legislation" (Burstein, 1991, p. 346). To these three streams we add one more: Policy change continues throughout the lifecourse of policy as the procedures of application in judicial and law enforcement settings are elaborated and refined (Jenness & Grattet, 2001). Finally, the above conceptualization of policy domains implies a focus on the relationship between social organization and meanings; therefore, it suggests that the problem of hate crime is likely to be understood differently over time, across space, and between institutional locations within the domain.

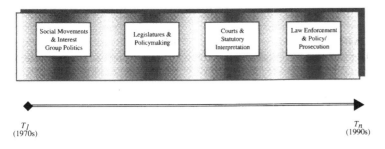

T_1
(1970s)

T_n
(1990s)

Figure 2.1   Summary of Select Institutional Spheres Composing the Policy Domain of Hate Crime

Temporal, spatial, and institutional variation in the meaning of hate crime occurs because the formation of a policy domain is rooted in the social processes of innovation, diffusion, and institutionalization. That is, the social construction of hate crime and its official responses diffuse not only across jurisdictional and geographical space, but also across the four streams of policy-making process identified above. This phenomenon is contingent on institutionalization, the process by which the meanings and practices that constitute hate crime stabilize, become cognitively taken for granted by actors, and/or attain a high level of normative consensus (DiMaggio & Powell, 1983; Meyer & Rowan, 1977; Powell & DiMaggio, 1991; R. Scott, 1987; Zucker, 1991).

It seems clear, then, that studying hate crime requires exploring the birth and evolution of a policy domain. Accordingly, the analysis presented below is motivated by a series of questions about how social problems, law, and policy domains come into being, are transformed, and are institutionalized over time. For example, with regard to social problems, why is the concept of hate crime only now being applied to age-old conduct? As for law, how have legal and extralegal subjects and conduct related to hate-motivated crime been constructed by key players, most notably, activists, lawmakers, judges, and law enforcement agents?

To address these and related questions, our approach involves an examination of how the concept of hate crime emerged, how its meaning has been transformed across multiple segments of the policy domain, and how it has become institutionalized as a social fact and set of policies. Specifically, we focus on how social

movements have constructed the problem of hate-motivated violence, how politicians at both the federal and state level have made legislation that defines the parameters of hate crime, how judges have interpreted those laws, and how law enforcement officials classify and manage that which is defined as criminal by statutes. Summarized in Figure 2.1, we examine the work of these collective actors to reveal the social processes that have resulted in the production of hate crime and hate crime policy, both inside and outside of the justice system.

THE ROLE OF SOCIAL MOVEMENTS IN THE CONSTRUCTION OF HATE CRIME

The idea of hate crime emerged through the confluence of several social movement discourses, most notably the Black civil rights movement, the women's movement, the gay and lesbian movement, the disabilities rights movement, and the crime victims' rights movement (Jenness & Broad, 1997). These movements converged to compose the modern anti–hate crime movement (Jenness, 1999; Jenness & Grattet, 2001; Maroney, 1998), which in turn proved crucial to the development of hate crime in the United States.

The Black civil rights movement of the 1960s was predominantly concerned with the broad issue of discrimination and was therefore geared largely toward establishing and enhancing opportunities within specific sectors of social life, such as employment, education, voting and governmental practice, and public accommodations. There was an understanding within the movement that discrimination was the overarching problem and intergroup violence could be mitigated, at least in part, by using government policy to increase economic opportunities and guarantee civil rights. In other words, the systems that maintained Black marginality were seen as the cause, and occasional episodes of violent repression were a symptom (West, 1993). Thus, efforts to curb the violence were central to the broader goal of inclusion. In addition, the "axes" of discrimination focused on by 1960s civil rights campaigns were restricted to race, religion, national origin, and ancestry (Bensinger, 1992; Morsch, 1991).

The 1970s civil rights movements, specifically the women's movement and the gay and lesbian movement, borrowed heavily from the language and strategies of the earlier movement (Goldberg, 1991; McAdam, 1982; Morris, 1984). They did so to expand the scope of activism in important ways (Jenness, 1995; Jenness & Broad, 1997; Minkoff, 1995; Vaid, 1995). Most notably, the women's movement and the gay and lesbian movement enlarged the legal conception of what constitutes standard and legitimate subjects of discrimination. Specifically, the axes of discrimination that the law recognized and sought to ameliorate were broadened to include women, as well as gays and lesbians. Although each of these "second wave civil rights movements" (Goldberg, 1991), like the earlier movement, are strongly geared toward expanding opportunities for its constituencies, each movement also sponsors antiviolence projects to combat discriminatory violence directed at its constituency (Jenness, 1995; Jenness & Broad, 1997). The emergence and institutionalization of the antiviolence projects reflect a growing understanding that violence is not merely epiphenomenal to the various systems of discrimination; rather, it is central to their maintenance.

The final movement that significantly contributed to the development of the anti–hate crime movement was the crime victims' movement (Maroney, 1998). The crime victims' movement is composed of a fairly diverse range of groups, including some of the groups discussed above. The basic grievance put forth by the crime victim movement is simple: Victims of crime, especially violent crime, not only need but are entitled to special assistance, support, and rights as crime victims. From the point of view of those involved in the crime victim movement, "the criminal justice system was not perceived as providing certainty of justice for the criminal or the victim" (Weed, 1995, p. 21). As a result, advocates for victims' rights argue that legal and extralegal mechanisms are needed to recognize and serve those injured by crime, especially violent crime. Such mechanisms include counseling services and an array of statutes and state constitutional amendments that allow for increased participation of victims in the criminal justice process, protection from retaliation and harassment, and civil actions for compensation (Weed, 1995).

The anti–hate crime movement emerged through a fusion of the strategies and goals of several identifiable precursor movements that laid the foundation for a new movement to question, and make publicly debatable, issues of rights and harm as they relate to a variety of constituencies. One of the major achievements of the anti–hate crime movement is that it unites disparate social movements, what some would refer to as strange bedfellows (Jenness & Grattet, 2001). As liberal, progressive movements, the civil rights, women's, and gay and lesbian movements "called attention to the personal costs of minority groups' political victimization," whereas the more conservative victims' rights movement "called attention to the political context of personal victimization" (Maroney, 1998, p. 579). As portrayed in Figure 2.2, these liberal and conservative movements combined to instigate public discussions about violence born of bigotry and to demand legal changes, especially in criminal law, to remedy the problem.[3]

The history of the formation of the anti–hate crime movement directly affected the changing character of the hate crime policy domain. Like the broader history of the modern rights movements, participation in the anti–hate crime movement was staggered. Racially and religiously oriented organizations such as the Anti-Defamation League (ADL) and the Southern Poverty Law Center (SPLC) led the way, whereas lesbian and gay and women's groups as well as disability activists joined later. For example, early on, the ADL and the SPLC activity concentrated on compiling statistical

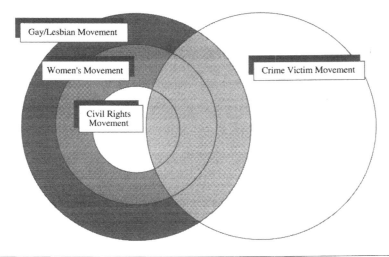

Figure 2.2   The Convergence of Civil Rights Movements and the Emergence of an Anti-Hate Crime Movement in the Latter Part of the 20th Century

reports to establish the empirical credibility of hate crimes directed at the groups they represented, primarily racial, religious, and ethnic minorities. Gender, sexual orientation, and disability were not incorporated into their statistics-gathering efforts and, in the case of the ADL, were not included in the early model hate crime statutes promoted in the early 1980s. Thus, early on the empirical credibility of gender-based and antigay offenses as a type of hate crime was not established by the work of these organizations.[4] As a result, such acts remained outside the operative construction of hate crime until considerably later in the history of the concept, as we describe below.

SOCIAL MOVEMENT MOBILIZATION TRANSLATED INTO FEDERAL AND STATE LEGISLATION

Once the anti–hate crime movement was able to bring the issue of discriminatory violence into the public consciousness, the struggle turned to creating some sort of legal and policy response. This activity targeted state and federal legislators to enact statutes embodying social movement goals. In 1981, the ADL created and

began to promote a model hate crime law. Five kinds of statutes were included: institutional vandalism (vandalism directed at religious institutions), intimidation (including assault, trespass, vandalism, or harassment), a civil action for both kinds of crime, data collection, and police training law (for a review, see Grattet, Jenness, & Curry, 1998; Jenness & Grattet, 1996). These elements continue to form the core policy agenda for the hate crime policy domain.

Proposed early on, however, the ADL model did not initially include sexual orientation, disability, and gender as provisions in hate crime law. Other early advocates, such as the National Institute Against Prejudice and Violence and the Coalition on Hate Crimes[5] also operated with an emphasis on hate crime as offenses involving violence stemming from racial, religious, and ethnic prejudice. Later, as the gay and lesbian and women's activists gained a higher profile on the issue, the ADL modified its model statute to include gender and sexual orientation. This, once again, underscores the staggered way that the different movements and hence different categories or persons were incorporated into the concept of hate crime.

By the mid-1980s, the issue of hate crime reached the U.S. Congress. As of 2000, nine U.S. Congresses had devoted attention to the task of responding to hate-motivated violence, resulting in hundreds of hours of congressional hearings and debates, as well as three new federal laws: ❘Hate Crimes Statistics Act (HCSA), the Violence Against Women Act, and the Hate Crimes Sentencing Enhancement Act (HCSEA). The legislative histories of these laws reveal how the inclusion of status provisions in hate crime law (i.e., "race, religion, and ethnicity," "sexual orientation," and "gender") ensured that the concept of hate crime expanded to recognize women, gays and lesbians, and people with disabilities as constituencies implicated in the hate crime problem (Jenness, 1999).

Consistent with the recommendation of the Coalition on Hate Crimes, early claims from local-, regional-, and state-level organizations—especially the ADL—focused on the scope and consequences of race-, religion-, and ethnicity-based violence, thus expressing the parameters of the problem in comparatively narrow terms. A growing awareness of this type of violence became grounds for promoting federal hate crime legislation by a limited number of social movement organizations and their representatives. This activity cemented a trio of statuses—race, religion, and ethnicity—as the anchoring provisions of all hate crime law. This occurred without controversy over the legitimacy of these status provisions and in light of the fact that race, religion, and ethnicity were already institutionalized as a legitimate subject for federal discrimination law.

Later, the character of hate crime law was reshaped when the domain of federal law expanded to include additional provisions. Shortly after federal hate crime law was envisioned, proposals were made by representatives from the gay and lesbian movement to further differentiate hate crime victims by adding sexual orientation to the list of provisions in federal hate crime law. Through direct and sustained testimony in federal hearings, social movement organization representatives were able to bestow empirical credibility on the violence connected with this provision (i.e., antigay violence), just as the ADL and other social movement organizations previously bestowed empirical credibility on violence organized around race, religion, and ethnicity. After much heated debate, advocates for the inclusion

of sexual orientation in hate crime law convinced legislators that the meaning of sexual orientation was more similar to than dissimilar from the meanings already attached to race, religion, and ethnicity insofar as all are core axes of systematic discrimination. By successfully engaging in these linking strategies, gay and lesbian movement activists and their allies proved crucial to the expansion of hate crime law to cover sexual orientation, despite the fact that sexual orientation has not been recognized as a legitimate provision in previous federal discrimination law.

Other provisions initially recommended for inclusion in the law, but not added to the bill prior to its passage, did not attract significant and sustained social movement mobilization in congressional hearings. Prior to the passage of the HCSA, for example, during hearings legislators made passing references to the possibility of including "octogenarians," "union members," "children," "the elderly," and "police officers" in hate crime law. In the absence of formal hearings on violence against these groups, however, there was never an opportunity for representatives from these groups to establish the empirical credibility of the problem as it pertains to their constituencies. Similarly, there was no opportunity for representatives of these groups to engage in the necessary claims making required to legitimate these provisions. As a result, provisions for these constituencies have not been written into federal hate crime law. U.S. Representative John Conyers Jr. acknowledged this facet of lawmaking in hearings on hate crime when he said,

> The reason we did not include octogenarians who are assaulted is because there was no testimony that suggested that they ought to be, as awful as the crimes visited upon them are, and the reason we did not account for policemen killed in the line of duty, is that there was no request that they be separated out from the uniform crime statistics. (Cong. Rec. 11395 [1988])

For comparative purposes, an examination of the legislative history of gender as a provision in federal hate crime law reveals that later in the history of federal lawmaking around hate crime, the importance of collective action, as measured through the presence of social movement organizations at congressional hearings and in

Table 2.1   Social Movement Organization (SMO) Mobilization and the Adoption of Select Status
                  Provisions in Federal Hate Crime Law, 1985-1998

| SMO Mobilization | Status Provision | | | |
| | Proposed | | Adopted | |
	Early (pre-1990)	*Late (post-1990)*	*Early (pre-1990)*	*Late (post-1990)*
Yes	Race/religion/ ethnicity, sexual orientation		Race/religion/ ethnicity, sexual orientation	
No	Octogenarians, union members, children, elderly, police officers	Gender, disabilities		Gender, disabilities

congressional debates, declined. Once a corpus of hate crime law was established and select provisions were cemented in law (i.e., race, religion, ethnicity, and sexual orientation), new provisions—in this case gender—were adopted without direct pressure applied by sustained mobilization from relevant social movement organizations and their representatives, and despite the fact that it was purposely excluded from law in the incipient stages of the lawmaking process. `•

Although there have been many federal hearings on hate crime that address violence against women, none of these hearings have been initiated or sustained by feminist social movement organizations. Instead, lawmakers simply incorporated gender into the existing framework of hate crime laws established in previous hearings, whereas feminist advocates—most notably representatives from the National Organization for Women and the Feminist Majority—gave testimony only after the imminent passage of the bill was predicted (Jenness & Broad, 1997). This occurred without much fanfare and without relevant social movement organizations engaging in direct and sustained lobbying work. It was only possible because gender, like race, religion, and ethnicity, was already a standard subject of federal discrimination law.

Declining involvement of social movement organizations is also evident in the history of the disability provision. Disability was added to both the reauthorization of the HCSA, the

original and final version of the HCSEA, and the current bill pending in Congress: the Hate Crimes Prevention Act (§ 1529). The changing character of the law along these lines occurred despite the fact that federal lawmakers have never held a hearing on violence directed at those with disabilities and no contestation occurred over this provision. Moreover, the official records of federal-level hate crime lawmaking reveal that representatives from the disabilities movement have yet to make an appearance and offer testimony related to federal hate crime legislation. Regardless, disabilities, and thus persons with disabilities, have found a home in hate crime legislation, albeit rather late in the history of lawmaking on hate crime. Here, too, this occurred in light of the fact that disability, like race, religion, and gender, was already a standard subject of federal discrimination law, in large part because of the earlier passage of the Americans With Disabilities Act in 1990 (Shapiro, 1993).

This history of status provisions included and excluded from federal legislation is instructive. Theoretically speaking, the pattern described above and summarized in Table 2.1 suggests that the effects of social movements on hate crime lawmaking are twofold. On one hand, those movements give rise to activist organizations that in turn generate the individuals who promote and publicize a particular reform and then testify before Congress and other legislative bodies. This activity affects which groups are visibly associated with an issue and, ultimately, which groups are included in the law. On the other hand, in many cases it is really not the mobilization around the specific issue that is crucial, especially once a policy approach is available and established. Later in the formation of a policy domain, the approach and the category of persons must merely be seen as compatible by policy makers (e.g., Does disability "fit" under the hate crimes rubric?). Yet, in order for this to happen, a movement must have been successful over the long term in laying claim to inclusion within these types of issues (e.g., equal rights and violence issues).

As social movement goals were translated into a legal and policy issue, the term *hate crime* was refocused and specified, resulting in changes in its fundamental nature. In addition to the expansion of the hate crime concept described above, it was necessarily reconstituted in universal terms as concrete groups such as Blacks, immigrants, and Jews were folded into more abstract categories such as race, national origin, and religion. In other words, as the concept was translated into legal discourse, hate crime became something that members of minority and majority groups— Blacks and Whites, homosexuals and heterosexuals, immigrants and natives, women and men—could potentially be victims of and were thus given equal protection under the law. Thus, the domain of the concept was expanded beyond the mere addition of new provisions.

The Diffusion of Hate Crime Statutes

As direct and sustained activism declined in importance with regard to shaping the concept, legislative institutions began to determine the precise rules and policies that would constitute the official definition of and response to the problem. The legislative arena subjected the concept to a new set of pressures that reshaped it once again. Here, we focus on the making and remaking of hate crime as a state-level statutory construct and, in so doing, ask a broader question about the formation of the policy domain: Once developed, how do legal concepts circulate, take shape, and become institutionalized across distinct, but interrelated, polities (i.e., states)?

As of 1999, criminal hate crime laws had passed in 41 states (Jenness & Grattet, 2001; Soule & Earl, 1999). These laws differ in important ways, however. They share the same core elements. In particular, they all create or enhance penalties for criminal behavior motivated by some combination of status categories, such as race, religion, national origin, sexual orientation, gender, and disability. As we describe below, variation in the distribution of status provisions is extensive, but patterned. In particular, the approach an individual state took was largely shaped by when it adopted a law. In other words, the timing of adoption strongly influenced the specific wording used and the content included. For example, hate crime laws have employed four different ways of characterizing the motivational requirement for conviction under the statute. Some states, such as New Hampshire and Rhode Island, use phrasing that requires prosecutors to show that an act was precipitated by "animus, hostility, maliciousness, or hatred." Such wording implies that a high degree of emotional intensity be behind the offense; thus, a prosecutor must demonstrate the particular subjective state(s) that motivated the crime to obtain a conviction. In contrast, other states, such as California and New York, employ more restrained language that only requires that the perpetrator have an "intent to harass and intimidate the victim." This too requires the prosecutor to demonstrate that the perpetrator intended (a mental state) to cultivate a sense of fear and intimidation (another mental state) in the victim. And, this too is a difficult requirement to meet. A third type of motivational phrasing contains the least stringent requirement for the prosecutor. Louisiana and Ohio, for example, simply require that the offense be committed "because of" race, religion, ancestry, and so forth.[6]

As Figure 2.3 shows, the employment of these phrasings is time dependent. Each of these phrasings was employed prior to 1983, reflecting little consensus in the initial wave of adoptions between 1977 and 1987. However, by 1990, two forms—the "because of" wording and "intent to harass or intimidate" wording—began to

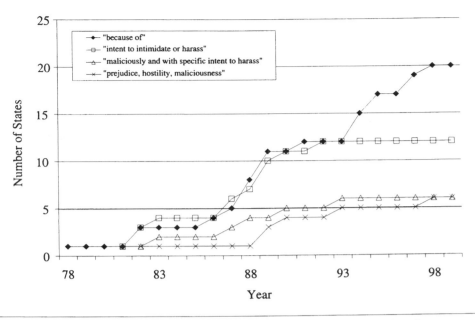

Figure 2.3   Cumulative Frequency of Alternative Motivational Phrasings in Hate Crime Statutes, 1978-1999

emerge as the most popular. Finally, after 1993, the because of phrasing became the dominant form, with roughly half of the adopting states using such language. The event responsible for this development was the U.S. Supreme Court decision in *Wisconsin v. Mitchell* (1993), in which the Court upheld a statute that employed the because of formulation. This ensured that the least stringent form of motivational phrasing was increasingly deemed legitimate.

The process of convergence around a specific motivational phrasing reflects legislative dynamics that are well known to students of state policy making and the diffusion of innovations (Gray, 1973; Strang & Meyer, 1993; J. L. Walker, 1969). Within the system of state governments, innovative policies evolve through a series of characteristic phases. The initial phase is characterized by a diversity of approaches because there are no clear models or guides on which to act. As time passes, other states begin to respond; however, they no longer operate in the absence of precedent and are instead confronted with various options and the experience of their predecessors about what

works and what is a legitimate approach (e.g., constitutional or politically). Subsequent policy making results from informed mimicry of early innovators, which tends to lead to one or two approaches becoming understood as the best approach. In the aggregate, this means that a period of experimentation and diversity of approaches tends to be followed by a convergence, or homogenization, of approaches. As we have demonstrated above, hate crime law certainly follows this pattern of homogenization over its life course insofar as approaches to the law were once diverse but are increasingly convergent.

Despite the convergence in method of phrasing, however, hate crime statutes have become more expansive in terms of the categories of persons they cover. Figure 2.4 displays the status provisions included in the laws as of 1988 and then 10 years later in 1998. In both periods, nearly every state law in existence covered acts motivated by race, religion, color, and national ancestry. In 1988, only 11%, 21%, and 26% of the statutes in existence included sexual orientation, gender, and disability, respectively. By 1998, however, half of the statutes had sexual

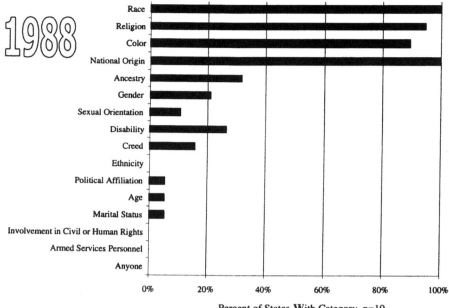

Percent of States With Category, n=19.

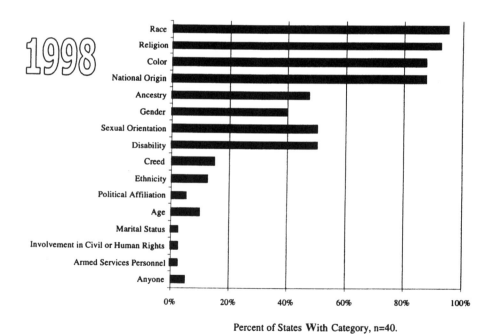

Percent of States With Category, n=40.

Figure 2.4   Status Provisions in State Hate Crime Laws, 1988 and 1998

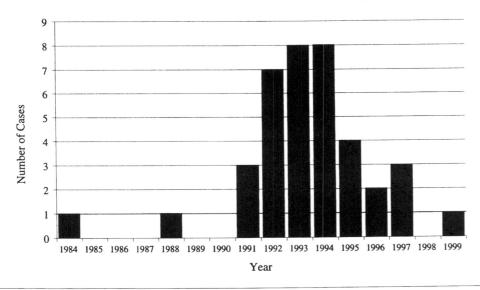

Figure 2.5   Number of Appellate Cases Challenging Hate Crime by Year, 1984-1999

orientation and disability and 40% had gender included. Figure 2.4 also makes apparent that many statutes now contain some miscellaneous categories that have not been replicated in any substantial way. Thus, three tiers emerge: categories that are always included, categories that are included with increasing regularity, and anomalous categories that are included but not with any regularity.

The interpretation of the pattern of status provisions over time is clear. The most pervasive categories reflect the oldest, most established, and most recognized axes of oppression. The salience of these categories reflects the success of the 1960s-era civil rights movement in galvanizing particular categories in the public consciousness and in legal discourse (Grattet et al., 1998). Legislators, by and large, do not contest the prevalence and seriousness of hate crime motivated by these categories (Jenness, 1999). Sexual orientation, gender, and disability reflect more recent, and therefore less embedded, rights movements that still face considerable opposition when claiming membership in issues such as hate crime (Jenness, 1999). Finally, the miscellaneous categories have little or no history to sustain claims for inclusion in

the laws and therefore have made much less systematic inroads into the issue.[7]

Thus far, we have seen that the hate crime concept undergoes a common process within each new institutional arena into which it is placed. That is, its institutionalization is accompanied by a refocusing of the concept relative to constraints of each new arena into which it moves. Its meaning is sharpened and, as we have seen, expanded and elaborated in novel ways. Indeed, the twin processes that characterize the evolution of hate crime within the legislative arena, homogenization and expansion, are reiterated as the concept moves into the judicial realm.

THE RESTRICTION AND EXPANSION OF HATE CRIME IN APPELLATE CASES

If legislatures provide the general templates for law, the job of courts, particularly appellate courts, is to flesh out the specific meanings of a statute. Between 1984 and 1998, U.S. appellate courts considered the constitutionality of hate crime statutes 38 times.[8] As Figure 2.5 shows, the bulk of these cases occurred over a 3-year period stretching from 1992 to 1995. During this period, hate crime statutes were embroiled in a highly visible constitutional crisis (Bader, 1994; Brooks, 1994; Gaumer, 1994; Grannis, 1993; Kagan, 1992; Morsch, 1991; Strossen, 1993; Tribe, 1993; Winer, 1994). By 1997, however, that crisis was largely resolved, and the frequency of hate crime cases and attendant legal commentary subsided dramatically. This signals that the rules governing hate crime are becoming more "settled" in judicial discourse (Phillips & Grattet, 2000).

Before being resolved, however, the constitutional crisis had important effects on the legal conception of hate crime. Namely, appellate judges rejected certain approaches and endorsed others, thus creating a jurisprudential foundation for the statutes. Although the statutes are themselves quite broad and potentially cover all sorts of things, courts have restricted their meaning in ways that result in the concept of hate crime becoming increasingly delineated and demarcated. A review of constitutional challenges reveals how this has occurred and with what consequence.

The central concern expressed by challengers of the statutes is whether laws punish speech. Indeed, First Amendment violations have been the most successful strategy in challenging specific statutory forms (*R.A.V. v. Saint Paul,* 1992; *State v. Kearns,* 1994; *State v. Talley,* 1993). This is not surprising given that almost all of the statutes cover activity that clearly borders on speech, such as intimidation and harassment. In response to these concerns, courts have consistently restricted the coverage of hate crime law to the "conduct" side of the speech-conduct continuum (Phillips & Grattet, 2000). This has meant that intimidation and harassment can only refer to speech that involves direct threats. That is, a speech act must qualify as a "true threat," an established standard that requires demonstration that a speaker has both the intent and the capacity to carry out the threat. It is, in practical terms, a speech act verging on conduct. Racial epithets and taunts that do not meet the legal standard of true threats do not qualify as hate crime under this interpretation. Thus, the possible meanings of hate crime as covering, say, the conscious creation of an intimidating environment or general expressions of a desire to do violence to members of a particular group

would be extremely difficult, if not impossible, to prosecute under the prevailing judicial interpretation of the laws.

In contrast to the restrictions implied by considerations of First Amendment violations, there are some identifiable ways in which the settling of the hate crime concept in the hands of judges has led to an expansion of the domain of coverage. This is most evident through an examination of the way the motivational standard has been interpreted. As we detailed in the previous section, there is considerable diversity in terms of the ways statutes define the specific motivational requirements. The because of construction is relevant to the issue of whether hate crime laws punish speech, underlying motives, and political viewpoints. By endorsing the because of phrasing, courts maintain that it does not matter what political views or ideologies motivated the act. Rather, all that matters is that a victim was selected because of his or her race, religion, ancestry, and so forth, quite apart from the degree of malice involved on the part of the perpetrator (Phillips & Grattet, 2000).

By endorsing the because of form of the law, courts drew a parallel with established antidiscrimination principles within which

> it does not matter why a woman is treated differently than a man, a black differently than a white, a Catholic differently than a Jew; it matters only that they are. So also with section 775.085 [Florida's hate crime statute]. It doesn't matter that Dobbins hated Jewish people or why he hated them; it only mattered that he discriminated against Daly by beating him because he was Jewish. (*Dobbins v. State,* 1992)

This interpretation situates hate crime jurisprudence within the broader and more established body of antidiscrimination law; in so doing, it broadens its applicability by defining biased selection of the victim, rather than hate, as the requisite motivational precursor. The consequence is that acts by virulent racists or offenders with "only" a mild disrespect for the victim's group are punished equally, with an offender's underlying philosophy and degree of bigotry being irrelevant. In short, this expands the domain of the law because, properly speaking, "hate" is not a necessary element, only bias.[9]

In sum, as hate crime statutes came under the scrutiny of the courts, yet another round of reworking of the concept was set in motion. As with the social movement and legislative arenas described earlier, a refocusing and sharpening of the concept resulted from the circulation of hate crime within courts. And once again, the institutionalization of hate crime is reflected in its refinement and the emergent consensus about what the laws cover and do not cover. The courts have had a unique influence insofar as judicial discourse regarding hate crime has framed the topic as discriminatory violence, in large part by subsuming it under antidiscrimination laws. In the process, its meaning was further delimited, and a range of circumstances was ruled outside of the domain of the concept. Most notably, the judicial translation of hate crime into bias crime has meant that hate crime law might be enforced in circumstances where hate is absent. The remaining question, then, is what happens to the concept once the law is legitimated by the courts and it is placed in the hands of law enforcers?

ENFORCING HATE CRIME LAWS

If the efforts of legislators in responding to hate crimes peaked in the late 1980s and the court challenges played out mostly prior to 1995, then the late 1990s witnessed enormous attention to law enforcement—especially policing and prosecution—as the principal problem areas with respect to hate crime. At this point in the history of the concept, the legislative issues regarding who and what should be covered by the laws, as well as the judicial issues regarding the legitimacy and constitutionality of the laws, have given way to pragmatic issues about the organizational changes required to enforce the laws. Efforts along these lines are currently ongoing in federal, state, and local policing institutions. Indeed, law enforcement officials at federal (Reno, 1999), state (Lockyer, 1999), and local (Garcetti, cited in Boxall, 1998) levels have recently announced plans to redouble efforts at policy training and the enforcement of hate crime statutes.

Much of the social science research on hate crimes focuses on the multitude of ways police departments are responding to the legal mandate to pursue bias-motivated crime (Boyd, Berk, & Hamner, 1996; Martin, 1996; S. Walker & Katz, 1995; Wexler & Marx, 1986). Conducted in the early 1990s when the precise definition of hate crime was still being negotiated in legislatures and courts, these early studies reveal that hate crime policing is quite variable across jurisdictions and across divisions within the same jurisdiction. In large part, this variation is attributable to differences in the philosophies, organizational structures, and routine practices in different departments, as well as the newness of the criminal category itself. Given that the latter is only a temporary condition, there is reason to believe that variation in the policing of hate crime is decreasing and will continue to do so as the concept becomes settled. Just as social movement activism, lawmaking, and judicial decision making around hate crime have done over the past two decades, newfound police practices related to hate crime are likely to become established and taken for granted. Indeed, preliminary evidence suggests this is the case.[10]

In recent years, efforts to formulate uniform police training guidelines have revolved around the Federal Bureau of Investigation's (FBI's) promotion of its own program (Reno, 1997, 1999). Large states such as California, for example, have revised and updated their police training guidelines to reflect changing definitions and judicial interpretations of the law and to bring their guidelines into alignment with the FBI's. In particular, our research on California shows that the FBI and the California guidelines are both aware of the judicial rulings relevant to the question of how to classify cases where bias is only one of several motivations. Reflecting recent court decisions in California, both sets of guidelines—California's and the FBI's—stipulate that an incident should be classified as a hate crime when it appears to have been caused "in whole, or in part" by race, religion, and so forth (Jenness & Grattet, 2001). In other words, at both the state and federal levels, training is being altered to reflect the more recent conceptualization of hate crime law, with homogenization in policing policy and practice following suit.

Many California police departments have recently adopted general orders relative to hate crime. These orders articulate local department policies about hate crime, thus embodying law enforcement's response to the issue. They typically include a working definition of the concept, as well as a list of indicators reflecting the kinds of evidence that suggest a hate crime has occurred and a set of procedures for processing cases that might be classifiable as hate crimes. Since hate crime constitutes a relatively new criminal category for law enforcement, it is not surprising that the production and dissemination of these orders are a recent development.

In light of being handed this new crime to enforce, some police officers express complaints about the law, and others comply—to greater or lesser degrees—with the mandate to enforce it. With regard to the former, some officers register complaints that resemble those made in relation to domestic violence laws in the 1970s and 1980s and stalking laws in the 1990s. Namely, opponents argue that hate crime laws are hopelessly vague and too ambiguous to enforce; moreover, law enforcement personnel have more serious problems to contend with (S. Walker & Katz, 1995). In contrast, Boyd et al. (1996) found out that many officers express the opposite view. They do not view the complexities of the categorization processes that surround the enforcement of hate crime as fundamentally different from other kinds of crimes and attendant required police work. In part, these contrasting views reflect the newness of the concept and the diversity of police practices and personnel in the United States.

The newness of the concept is further reflected in the variation in departmental general orders. For example, as Figure 2.6 shows, few of the general orders cite anything other than race, religion, and ancestry as relevant status provisions in their definitions of hate crime. These departments are operating with definitions of hate crime that date back to the early 1980s. This is even more surprising when we consider that California has one of the most expansive definitions of hate crime, including coverage of transsexuals and that all the authors of the order needed to do is read the statute to realize the categories of persons covered under the law. With such variations existing at the local level, it is not surprising that there is considerable diversity of interpretations.

From a social science point of view, classic and contemporary studies of policing demonstrate that variation in interpretative practices across departments and officers is not uncommon in law enforcement (Kitsuse & Cicourel, 1963; Saunders, 1977). Officers frequently deal with circumstances that are difficult to classify and require them to understand complex motivations and the interpersonal dynamics of the persons involved. Thus, the question that must be asked about hate crime is, Does the variation we currently see correspond to other innovations in crime policy at this stage of their development? In other words, the appropriate comparison for hate crime policing is not crimes such as theft, which is a deeply settled concept in American law and police practice and thus raises comparatively little disagreement about its behavioral attributes, but stalking, domestic violence, and sexual harassment, all of which are recent innovations, like hate crime, that have become increasingly settled in law enforcement practice.

The other side of law enforcement, the prosecution of hate crime, is in roughly the same shape. Prosecutors express mixed opinions about the viability and value of enforcing hate crime law. Some prosecutors have gone on record rejecting hate crime laws as useless and unenforceable (Jacobs & Potter, 1998), whereas others have strongly embraced them as a meaningful response to community strife (Boxall, 1998). With regard to the former, at least in the abstract, hate crime implies greater evidentiary burdens, more effort to spell out the intricacies of the law to juries, and more time and energy to prepare cases. For prosecutors who are understaffed and subjected to heavy caseloads, such laws may represent an extra set of burdens they prefer to avoid in an occupation where one's work is usually evaluated in terms of conviction rates. Other prosecutors, however, view hate crime laws as an extra tool to contribute to the management of crime and intergroup conflict in their community.

Although there is currently little published social science research on hate crime prosecution to draw conclusions about which of these predominates among American prosecutors, the publication of initial statistics on hate crime prosecutions, convictions, and plea bargains is revealing. In particular, four recent years of data

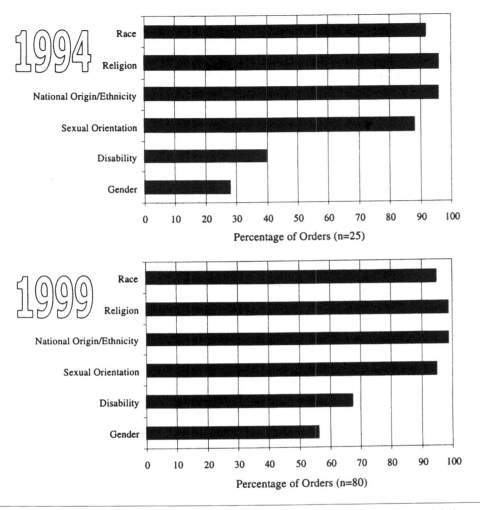

Figure 2.6 Inclusion of Particular Status Provisions in California Police Department General Orders Regarding Hate Crimes, 1994 and 1999

on prosecution in California begin to tell the story (see Figure 2.7). From 1995 to 1998, all of the major indicators of the hate crime processing have varied. Only about 6% of hate crime incidents in 1995 and 1996 led to successful convictions. In 1997, that figure rose to more than 17%, but in 1998 it fell back to 10%. On the surface, these percentages may seem dismal. However, to put these percentages in perspective, consider that the more recently reported percentages fall between the percentages for aggravated assault (a crime known for

being comparatively easy to police and prosecute) and vandalism (a crime known for being fairly difficult to police and prosecute). Of course, hate crime runs the gamut from assault to vandalism, so it is not surprising that it is somewhere between the two in terms of the ratio of incidents to convictions. However, these data only tell us about the slippage between the police's classification of incidents and the ability of prosecutors to obtain convictions.

A more useful way of evaluating prosecution is to determine the proportion of cases that, once

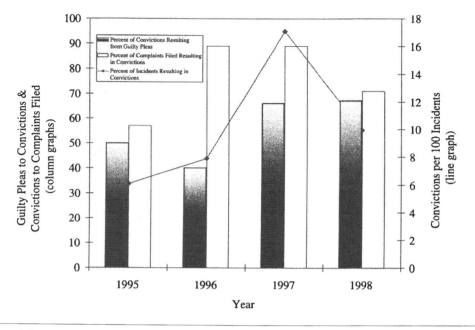

Figure 2.7   California Prosecution Data on Hate Crime, 1995-1998

filed by the prosecutors, leads to convictions. Although there is again a lot of variability, in general, the ratio has improved and falls within the range of other crimes. This suggests that once prosecutors decide to proceed to prosecute a crime as a hate crime, they do not seem to be struggling greatly with obtaining convictions, at least not any more so than with other crimes. This evidence contradicts arguments about the unenforceability of hate crime law. A final piece of evidence worth contemplating is guilty pleas. If, as some have contended (Jacobs & Potter, 1998), hate crimes are considerably more ambiguous and contestable than "parallel crimes" (Lawrence, 1999) and thus a misuse of justice system resources, then we would expect that plea bargains rarely happen. Defendants would be encouraged to challenge the charge on constitutional or evidentiary grounds. However, as is the case with most crimes, the majority of hate crime cases result in guilty pleas rather than trials, and that number has increased in recent years.

Thus, the pessimistic view of hate crime prosecutions as causing enormous problems for prosecutors is simply not borne out by initial available

evidence. Although only a small portion of incidents produces convictions, when prosecutors do decide to file cases as hate crimes they are successful in obtaining convictions, usually by guilty plea. This suggests that the prosecution of hate crime is proceeding in a conservative rather than liberal or indiscriminate fashion, something we would expect from a newly initiated policy. Moreover, hate crime prosecutions are beginning to resemble patterns for other crimes, something we would expect to be increasingly the case as the concept becomes more and more settled in the law enforcement arena.

In theoretical terms, law enforcement represents the end point of the movement of the hate crime concept across the various policy arenas we have discussed. It should not be surprising that it is less institutionalized than the other arenas. Nonetheless, although evidence is only recently beginning to be compiled, it appears that—as in the legislative and judicial realms—the process of settling of the concept hate crime is occurring within law enforcement. Thus, across the different arenas in which hate crime policies have been defined, we observe a striking similarity in core social processes. Taking these processes seriously has implications for how hate crime statistics are understood, where future social science research might focus next, and what the future might hold for hate crime policy making.

DISCUSSION AND CONCLUSION

Over the past three decades, hate crime has been defined, promoted, and addressed as a contemporary social problem. As Senator Edward Kennedy proclaimed,

> Civil rights are still the unfinished business of America. Hate crimes are uniquely destructive and divisive, because their impact extends far beyond the victim. They poison entire communities and undermine the ideals for which America stands. They deserve to be punished with the full force of law. (cited in Lawrence, 1999, jacket note)

Interestingly, it was not until the end of the 20th century that comments like this were expressed by senior elected officials and that policy reform designed to combat discriminatory violence was forthcoming and institutionalized. This marks an important moment in the history of crime control efforts, the development of criminal and civil law, the allocation of civil rights, and the symbolic status of select minorities in the United States. So, it is fair to ask, How have the many changes that accompany this moment come about such that an entirely new policy domain has emerged to redefine age-old conduct—discriminatory violence—as a crime problem? From our point of view, an answer to this question necessarily forms the backdrop against which the behavior and consequences of hate crime can best be understood by social scientists and addressed by activists, policy makers, and citizens.

As the above discussion illustrates, the birth and structuring of the hate crime policy domain have occurred as a sequence of stages. In its journey from social movement frame to legislative concept to judicial theory to law enforcement practice, the meaning and policy significance of hate crime have undergone a series of transformations. As we have seen, each change reflects the unique demands placed on the concept in the different institutional arenas that compose the American policy process. Its meaning has been pushed and pulled in new directions both within and across each new context, mutating in ways that ensure constancy as well as innovation.

As the policy concept circulates within and across institutional spheres, common social processes operate. Specifically, within each arena hate crime begins as an imprecise multivalent concept whose definition and attendant policy implications become more refined and settled over time. This settling takes two seemingly contradictory paths, each of which reflects countervailing forces evident within select institutional spheres as well as between these spheres. On one hand, the concept becomes more specified and restricted in terms of the circumstances under which it is applicable. That is, it becomes possible to rule out certain behaviors and circumstances from the domain of the concept. On the other hand, the concept becomes more embedded and more established. As it is increasingly applied in novel circumstances, its definition expands as new phenomena are assembled under its rubric. Even the process by which a broader foundation or framework is sought can result in enlarging the meaning and implication of the concept. Finally, it is important to understand that the core features of this process—the sequential formation of a policy domain, the solidification of the definition of the policy concept, and its institutionalization occurring both through expansion and restriction of its scope—are not unique to hate crime. Indeed, these are characteristics of policy domain formation processes more generally.

With these understandings in mind, it is possible to confront some of the major criticisms of hate crime policy. A central concern has been that hate crime is by definition a highly subjective and vague concept and therefore will lead to resource waste as officials strain to determine how best to implement the laws. This research suggests that the ambiguity of the concept is decreasing over time in all of the spheres we have examined. Specifically, social movement players have generally reached agreement on how to operationalize the concept. A dominant model of hate crime has emerged in the legislative arena. Judicial interpretations of the law have largely converged. And, the law enforcement practices appear to be solidifying. Within this context, to critique a concept because it appears ambiguous to some officials amounts to a critique of the concept's newness, which, in our view, is not a particularly compelling basis for critique.

The questions raised by this phenomenon are not whether a concept is hopelessly ambiguous, but rather, what features of the social organization of various sectors of the legal system influence variation in understandings and uses. Thus, the vagueness of the concept of hate crime must be analyzed longitudinally rather than concluded from a static impression gathered early in the career of a concept. Likewise, comparison cases are extremely important to evaluating hate crime laws. There is heterogeneity in the interpretation of many kinds of laws. The question should not be "Do understandings of hate crime vary across jurisdictions?" but "How does the variability in hate crime compare with other crimes?" To address this question, the comparison case should not be crimes such as assault or burglary, whose meaning and associated policing practices have been institutionalized for centuries. Instead, hate crime should be compared with categories of law, such as sexual harassment, stalking, and domestic abuse, which are comparatively new categories that have traveled the same path from social movement construct to law enforcement tool.

A similar response is appropriate to the critique of hate crime statistics. Because the statistics are so contingent on the part of the hate crime policy domain that is the least institutionalized (i.e., policing), data collection remains problematic in the pursuit of evaluating the extent and character of hate crime in the United States. But, this should not be the final judgment. In fact, given the efforts to improve the knowledge of law enforcement and to homogenize the data collection techniques currently under way by federal and some state law enforcement agencies, we expect data collection to become more systematic and reliable and, incidentally, more useful for traditional criminological analyses as well. Certainly, this has been the case with other recently invented, diffused, and institutionalized categories of crime, such as stalking.

Finally, the policy implications that derive from this analysis are simple. Programs that are designed to facilitate the transfer of knowledge and techniques to prosecutors and police officers are precisely what will hasten the institutionalization process we have discussed. Cautious prosecution is also advisable, not only because case-building strategies and expertise are at an early stage of development but also because the symbolic value of prosecuting cases as hate crimes diminishes with volume and with particular controversial applications. Ironically, hate crimes may be a kind of law that we would not want to see implemented with great regularity. The more it is applied, the more "normalized" hate crimes become, and what was once front-page news slips to the third page of the metro section. The symbolic force of law diminishes as a result.

NOTES

1. Other terms have been used to describe much the same combination of cultural and organizational elements of political processes (e.g., "policy areas" [Amenta & Carruthers, 1988, p. 666], "sectors" [Freeman, 1985; W. R. Scott & Meyer, 1983, p. 137], "subsystems" [Freeman, 1985], "issue domains" [McDonagh, 1989, p. 121], "fields" [Grattet, 1994, p. 15], and "programs" [Rose, 1985, p. 9]).

2. Recognizing that policy domains are rooted in social constructions does not, however, mean that the social conditions they address are not real or, by extension, that the social facts and attendant suffering underlying a problem are only illusory. Rather, it merely acknowledges that how problems are defined and responded to are contingent on available frameworks of meaning that are appropriated and deployed in key institutional settings.

3. In the context of waning legislative support for progressive civil rights–based movements in the early 1980s, enhancing punishments for hate crimes could be justified as part of the larger "get tough on crime" campaign. Under this rubric, it was difficult for conservative policy makers to oppose it. Wittingly or not, hate crime law advocates capitalized on an era in American policy making in which it would be difficult for members of either party to vote against crime legislation promoted by various sectors of the anti–hate crime movement.

4. Establishing empirical credibility for a social problem is crucial to the development of a policy domain. Claims are empirically credible "to the extent that there are events and occurrences that can be pointed to as documentary evidence" (Snow & Benford, 1992, p. 140).

5. The Coalition on Hate Crimes was composed of civil rights, religious, ethnic, and law enforcement groups, as well as a diverse array of professional organizations, including the Anti-Defamation League, the American Bar Association, 30 attorneys general, the National Institute Against Prejudice and Violence, the National Gay and Lesbian Task Force, the American Psychological Association, the American Psychiatric Association, the Center for Democratic Renewal, the American Civil Liberties Union, the American Jewish Congress, People for the American Way, the National Organization of Black Law Enforcement Executives, the U.S. Civil Rights Commission, the Police Executives Research Forum, the Criminal Justice Statistics Administration, the International Association of Chief of Police, the National Council of Churches, the National Coalition of American Nuns, and the American Arab Anti-Discrimination Committee.

6. Although technically speaking these phrasings suggest different requirements for prosecutors, appellate courts have tended to view them as meaning the same thing (Phillips & Grattet, 2000).

7. Paralleling the pattern of growth in status provisions, there is a similar pattern of growth in the kinds of activities referenced in hate crime statutes (Grattet, Jenness, & Curry, 1998). As the laws diffused, states began to expand the range of covered crimes from assault, vandalism, and intimidation to blocks of crimes (e.g., felonies), and more recently, some states have even passed laws that permit any crime to be converted into a hate crime (e.g., Vermont).

8. This refers only to cases considering the "facial validity" of hate crime laws. Cases involving constitutionality challenges based on how the laws were applied (i.e., "as applied" challenges) are not included here because the latter deal with case-specific circumstances of enforcement and application rather than the more general jurisprudential questions that constitute our focus.

9. Incidentally, this is also why many scholars suggest a terminology shift such that the subject and the laws should be referred to as "bias crime" rather than "hate crime."

10. As envisioned in Figure 2.1, law enforcement falls in the last phase of the formation of the hate crime policy domain; thus, it is the institutional sphere on which we have the least amount of valid and reliable data. Accordingly, in this section, we are left to hypothesize to a greater extent than in previous sections.

REFERENCES

Amenta, E., & Carruthers, B. (1988). The formative years of U.S. social spending polices. *American Sociological Review, 53,* 661–678.

Bader, H. F. (1994). Penalty enhancement for bias-based crimes. *Harvard Journal of Law and Public Policy, 17,* 253–262.

Bensinger, G. (1992). Hate crimes: A new/old problem. *International Journal of Comparative and Applied Criminal Justice, 16,* 115–123.

Boxall, B. (1998, February 13). D.A. seeks to expand hate crimes unit. *Los Angeles Times,* B3.

Boyd, E., Berk, R., & Hamner, K. (1996). Motivated by hatred or prejudice: Categorization of hate-motivated crimes in two police divisions. *Law & Society Review, 30,* 819–850.

Brooks, T. D. (1994). First Amendment-penalty enhancement for hate crimes: Content regulation, questionable state interests and non-traditional sentencing. *Journal of Criminal Law and Criminology, 84,* 703–742.

Burstein, P. (1991). Policy domains: Organization, culture, and policy outcomes. *Annual Review of Sociology, 17,* 327–350.

134 Cong. Rec. H 3373, No. 70 (May 18, 1988). Hate Crime Statistics Act. 100th Congress, 2nd session.

DiMaggio, P., & Powell, W. W. (1983). The iron cage revisited: Institutional isomorphism and collective rationality in organizational fields. *American Sociological Review, 48,* 147–160.

Dobbins v. State, 605 So. 2d 922 (Fla. App. 1992), LEXIS 10062, 17 Fla. Law W. D 2222 (1992).

Fishman, M. (1978). Crime waves as ideology. *Social Problems, 25,* 531–543.

Freeman, G. P. (1985). National styles and policy sectors: Explaining structured variation. *Journal of Public Policy, 5,* 467–496.

Gaumer, C. P. (1994). Punishment for prejudice: A commentary on the constitutionality and utility of state statutory responses to the problem of hate crimes. *South Dakota Law Review, 39,* 1–48.

Goldberg, R. A. (1991). *Grassroots resistance: Social movements in the twentieth century.* Belmont, CA: Wadsworth.

Grannis, E. J. (1993). Fighting words and fighting freestyle: The constitutionality of penalty enhancement for bias crimes. *Columbia Law Review, 93,* 178–230.

Grattet, R. (1994). *At play in the field of the law: Professionals and the transformation of industrial accident law.* Unpublished dissertation manuscript.

Grattet, R., Jenness, V., & Curry, T. (1998). The homogenization and differentiation of hate crime law in the United States, 1978–1995: Innovation and diffusion in the criminalization of bigotry. *American Sociological Review, 63,* 286–307.

Gray, V. (1973). Innovation in the states: A diffusion study. *American Political Science Review, 67,* 1174–1185.

Jacobs, J., & Potter, K. (1998). *Hate crimes: Criminal law & identity politics.* New York: Oxford University Press.

Jenness, V. (1995). Social movement growth, domain expansion, and framing processes: The gay/lesbian movement and violence against gays and lesbians as a social problem. *Social Problems, 42,* 145–170.

Jenness, V. (1999). Managing difference and doing legislation: Social movement mobilization, categorization processes, and identity politics in the making of hate crime law in the U.S., 1985–1997. *Social Problems, 46,* 548–571.

Jenness, V., & Broad, K. (1997). *Hate crimes: New social movements and the politics of violence.* Hawthorne, NY: Aldine de Gruyter.

Jenness, V., & Grattet, R. (1996). The criminalization of hate: A comparison of structural and polity influences on the passage of "bias-crime" legislation in the United States. *Sociological Perspectives, 39,* 129–154.

Jenness, V., & Grattet, R. (2001). *Making hate a crime: From social movement to law enforcement.* New York: Russell Sage.

Kagan, E. (1992). The changing faces of first amendment neutrality: R.A.V. v. St. Paul, Rust v. Sullivan, and the problem of content-based underinclusion. *Supreme Court Review, 2,* 29–77.

Kitsuse, J., & Cicourel, A. (1963). A note on the uses of official statistics. *Social Problems, 11,* 131.

Lawrence, F. M. (1999). *Punishing hate: Bias crimes under American law.* Cambridge, MA: Harvard University Press.

Lockyer, B. (1999, August 16). *Announcement of Civil Rights Commission and rapid response protocol for combating hate crimes* [Press release]. Sacramento: State of California, Attorney General's Office.

Maroney, T. A. (1998). The struggle against hate crime: Movement at a crossroads. *New York University Law Review, 73,* 564–620.

Martin, S. (1996). Investigating hate crimes: Case characteristics and law enforcement responses. *Justice Quarterly, 13*(3), 455–480.

Mauss, A., & Jenness, V. (2001). Social problems. In E. Borgatta & M. Borgatta (Eds.), *The encyclopedia of sociology* (pp. 2759–2766). New York: Macmillan.

McAdam, D. (1982). *Political process and the development of Black insurgency.* Chicago: University of Chicago Press.

McDonagh, E. L. (1989). Issues and constituencies in the progressive era: House roll call voting on the Nineteenth Amendment, 1913–1919. *Journal of Politics, 51,* 119–136.

Meyer, J. W., & Rowan, B. (1977). Institutional organizations: Formal structure as myth and ceremony. *American Journal of Sociology, 83,* 340–363.

Minkoff, D. C. (1995). *Organizing for equality: The evolution of women's and racial-ethnic organizations in America, 1955–1985.* New Brunswick, NJ: Rutgers University Press.

Morris, A. D. (1984). *The origins of the civil rights movement: Black communities organizing for change.* New York: Free Press.

Morsch, J. (1991). The problem of motive in hate crimes: The argument against presumptions of racial motivations. *Journal of Criminal Law and Criminology, 82,* 659–689.

Phillips, S., & Grattet, R. (2000). Judicial rhetoric, meaning making, and the institutionalization of hate crime. *Law and Society Review, 34*(3), 567–606.

Powell, W. W., & DiMaggio, P. J. (Eds.). (1991). *The new institutionalism in organizational analysis.* Chicago: University of Chicago Press.

R.A.V. v. Saint Paul, 505 U.S. 377; 112 S. Ct. 2538; 1992 U.S. LEXIS 3863; 120 L. Ed. 2d 305; 60 U.S.L.W. 4667; 92 Cal. Daily Op. Service 5299; 92 Daily Journal DAR 8395; 6 Fla. Law W. Fed. S 479 (1992).

Reno, J. (1997). *Memo: Implementation of hate crime initiative* [U.S. Department of Justice, Attorney General memo] [Online]. Available from: http://www.usdoj.gov/ag/readingroom/ag_foia1.htm

Reno, J. (1999, March). *FY 2000 summary performance plan Section 3.1.1. Hate crimes* [U.S. Department of Justice, Office of Attorney General] [Online]. Available from: http://www.usdoj.gov/ag/summary/part1.htm

Rose, R. (1985). The programme approach to the growth of government. *British Journal of Political Science, 15,* 1–28.

Rovella, D. E. (1994, August). Attack on hate crime is enhanced. *National Law Journal, 29,* A1.

Saunders, W. (1977). *Detective work: A study of criminal investigations.* New York: Free Press.

Scott, R. (1987). The adolescence of institutional theory. *Administrative Science Quarterly, 32,* 493–511.

Scott, W. R., & Meyer, J. W. (1983). The organization of societal sectors. In J. W. Meyer & W. R. Scott (with B. Rowan & T. E. Deal)

(Eds.), *Organizational environments.* Beverly Hills: Sage.

Shapiro, J. P. (1993). *No pity: People with disabilities forging a new civil rights movement.* New York: Random House.

Snow, D. A., & Benford, R. D. (1992). Master frames and cycles of protest. In A. C. Morris & C. McClurg Mueller (Eds.), *Frontiers in social movement theory* (pp. 133–155). New Haven, CT: Yale University Press.

Soule, S., & Earl, J. (1999, August). *All men are created equal: The differential protection of minority groups in hate crime legislation.* Paper presented at the annual meeting of the American Sociological Association, Chicago.

State v. Kearns, 136 N.J. 56; 642 A.2d 349; 1994 N.J. LEXIS 430; 63 U.S.L.W. 2015 (1994).

State v. Talley, 122 Wash. 2d 192; 858 P.2d 217; 1993 Wash. LEXIS 227 (1993).

Strang, D., & Meyer, J. W. (1993). Institutional conditions for diffusion. *Theory and Society, 22,* 487–512.

Strossen, N. (1993). Yes: Discriminatory crimes. *ABA Journal, 79,* 44.

Tribe, L. (1993). The mystery of motive, private and public: Some notes inspired by the problems of hate crime and animal sacrifice. *Supreme Court Review, 1,* 1–36.

Vaid, U. (1995). *Virtual equality: The mainstreaming of gay & lesbian liberation.* New York: Anchor Books.

Walker, J. L. (1969). The diffusion of innovations among the American states. *American Political Science Review, 63,* 880–897.

Walker, S., & Katz, C. M. (1995). Less then meets the eye: Police department bias-crime units. *American Journal of Police, 14,* 29–48.

Weed, F. (1995). *Certainty of justice: Reform in the crime victim movement.* New York: Aldine.

West, C. (1993). *Race matters.* Boston: Beacon.

Wexler, C., & Marx, G. T. (1986). When law and order works: Boston's innovative approach to the problem of racial violence. *Crime & Delinquency, 32,* 205–223.

Winer, A. S. (1994). Hate crimes, homosexuals, and the Constitution. *Harvard Civil Rights-Civil Liberties Law Review, 29,* 387–438.

Wisconsin v. Mitchell, 113 S. Ct. 2194; 1993 U.S. LEXIS 4024; 124 L. Ed. 2d 436; 61 U.S.L.W. 4575; 21 Media L. Rep. 1520; 93 Cal. Daily Op. Service 4314; 93 Daily Journal DAR 7353 (1993).

Zucker, L. G. (1991). The role of institutionalization in cultural persistence. In W. W. Powell & P. J. DiMaggio (Eds.), *New institutionalism in organizational analysis* (pp. 83–107). Chicago: University of Chicago Press.

QUESTIONS

1. Do you think that the growing societal and legal concern with hate crimes described in this article could counteract the prediction made by Petrosino in Part I that hate crimes may become worse due to a variety of factors?

2. Do motives matter? Should the central criterion for defining a hate crime be the motive of the perpetrator? Why or why not? What other criterion might be preferable as a way to define hate crime, and why?

3. In what way do policy domains represent "social constructions," according to the authors? How does the hate crimes policy domain illustrate this?

4. The authors note that " . . . violence is not merely epiphenomenal to the various systems of discrimination; rather, it is central to their maintenance." How and why is this the case? Discuss using examples.

5. What social movements have contributed to the recognition of hate crime and its emergence as a policy domain?

6. Compare the definitions of hate crime victims that emerged during the first and second phases of hate crime policy making. Who was included in each phase, and who was not? What are some reasons that some categories of people now defined as hate crime victims were not included earlier?

7. How did existing federal laws regarding gender discrimination and discrimination against people with disabilities serve as the foundation for the inclusion of these groups in hate crime legislation?

8. The authors discuss how the concept of hate crimes was "reconstituted in universal terms" such that it refers to *categories* such as race, sexual orientation, and religion rather than "concrete groups" such as Blacks, gays, and Jews. What are the implications of this shift in terms of equal protection for potential victims of hate crimes?

9. The authors discuss some of the most commonly used ways that hate crime statutes

define the motive component that must be proven by the government. What are the differences between the most frequently used "motivational phrasings"?

10. What roles have legislatures and courts played in defining and interpreting hate crime laws? Are these roles distinct or overlapping?

11. The authors note that some prosecutors view hate crime laws as an extra burden, whereas other prosecutors see such laws as a useful legal tool. What are some of the reasons that might help explain such differing prosecutorial views of hate crime statutes?

12. The authors suggest that the more hate crimes are prosecuted, the more "normalized" such crimes may become, thereby diminishing the "symbolic value" of hate crime laws. Do you agree or not? Why?

3

CONSEQUENCES FOR VICTIMS

A Comparison of Bias- and Non-Bias-Motivated Assaults

JACK MCDEVITT

JENNIFER BALBONI

LUIS GARCIA

JOANN GU

This article builds on earlier empirical research to investigate the question of whether the experiences of bias-crime (i.e., hate-crime) victims are different from those of non-bias-crime victims. For example, discussions of whether hate crimes should be punishable by enhanced penalties is often centered on the question of whether hate crimes have an especially harmful impact on victims and the community. Research comparing the reactions of hate crime victims with other kinds of victims is also relevant to the question of what should be considered a hate crime. Should hate crimes be legally defined as a category consisting of only certain specific crimes, or should any crime be prosecutable as a hate crime depending upon the particular circumstances of the crime?

In the impassioned debate about hate crime legislation, assertions are made on both sides about the consequences of bias-motivated crimes on their victims. In one camp, several scholars claim that bias crimes are a political construct, devised to promote identity politics. Critics argue that distinguishing hate crime from other comparable crimes is superfluous because the bias motivation of the offender does not cause additional injurious impact on the primary victim. Implicit in this assumption is that bias crimes are not intrinsically different

EDITORS' NOTE: From McDevitt, J., Balboni, J., Garcia, L., & Gu, J. (2001). Consequences for Victims: A Comparison of Bias- and Non-Bias-Motivated Assaults. *American Behavioral Scientist, 45,* 697-713. © 2001 Sage Publications. Reprinted with permission.

from similar nonbias offenses. Legal scholars Jacobs and Potter (1998) cogently summed this argument: "We do not believe that crimes motivated by hate invariably are morally worse or lead to more severe consequences for the victims than the same criminal act prompted by other motivations" (p. 147). Critics cite the example that a bias murder victim is just as dead as a nonbias murder victim as a reason for treating these crimes similarly.

Although the no additional injury argument is based on apparently rational arguments, no empirical evidence is available to support it. Furthermore, this assumption about the differences between murder victims is misleading because, among other things, it does not address the fact that the overwhelming majority of bias crimes in this country involve intimidation, vandalism, or assault, not murder (Uniform Crime Reports, Hate Crime Reports, 1998). Most people readily would agree that a cross burning is different from a typical trespassing/vandalism offense. In this article, we focus on differences between bias and nonbias crimes in terms of their impact on assault victims, differences that have not been fully explored in prior research. This article reports the findings of our analysis of survey data from bias and nonbias assault victims regarding the psychological consequences of their victimization experiences.

DIFFERENCES BETWEEN BIAS AND NONBIAS OFFENSES

We posit that hate crimes are inherently more harmful to the social fabric of society than comparable crimes without bias motive. Several authors have suggested dimensions of bias crimes that may increase the impact these crimes would have on their victims. The first unique dimension of bias crimes is the aspect of victim interchangeability inherent in many of these crimes (Levin & McDevitt, 1993). Interchangeability means that any individual who possesses, or is perceived to possess, a specific trait could be selected as a target. Bias crime victims are selected for victimization because of some actual or perceived status that they are powerless to change. For instance, an African American person can not change his or

her race after an attack to prevent future victimization; he or she will continue to be African American.

The second unique dimension of bias crime is the capacity for secondary victimization. Bias crime offenders generally intend for their acts to reach far beyond the primary victim, to affect all members of a particular minority group. For example, a cross burning not only affects the immediate family, but any African American who becomes aware of the incident. Consider the differences in the following scenarios:

1. A teenage couple demonstrates their undying love by spray painting "Joe loves Mary" across the back wall of their community high school.

2. A hate monger professes his views of Nazism by spraying "Hitler was right" on a local synagogue.

Technically, both incidents are vandalism. The first scenario presents somewhat of a petty nuisance, whereas the second incident attacks a distinct segment of the population—attempting to intimidate a segment of the community by indicating approval of the annihilation of that group and signaling to all people of Jewish descent that the offender believes they are inferior. It would be difficult to argue that the racial slur does not victimize more people, in a more serious fashion, than the teenagers' prank in the first scenario.

Moreover, the effects of victim interchangeability and secondary victimization can interact to disrupt the community in serious and often violent ways. The U.S. Supreme Court referred to this dimension of bias crime as "the distinct emotional harm" that such crimes inflict, noting the potential to "incit[e] community unrest" (*Wisconsin v. Mitchell,* 1993). Civil disturbances following the incidents in Bensonhurst and Howard Beach, New York, as well as the violence and destruction that followed court decisions in the Rodney King case illustrate the courts' fear that bias crimes could exacerbate existing racial tensions to the point of community violence. The Oregon Court of Appeals refers to this elusive attribute of bias crime as the power to "escalate from individual conflicts to mass disturbances" (Harvard Law Review, 1996). Although the Supreme Court and other courts across the country have noted the difference between the two types of crime, research is scant as to precisely how this type of crime affects the victims.

Prior Literature on Hate Crime Victimizations

Research regarding the impact of bias crimes is limited. Although there has been significant research about the general victimization process, very little examines the complex relationship between bias motivation, incidence of crime, and victimization consequences. Moreover, of the few that do examine the extent of psychological and emotional injury suffered by bias crime victims, most fail to provide comparative data for victims of similar non-bias-motivated offenses.

Whereas numerous studies have been conducted to describe the psychosocial consequences of particular types of victimization (e.g., Freedy, Resnick, Kilpatrick, Dansky, & Tidwell, 1994; Frieze, Greenberg, & Hymer, 1987; Kilpatrick, Saunders, Veronen, Best, & Von, 1987; Sales, Baum, & Shore, 1984), only a handful compare symptoms across crime types (Davis & Brickman, 1996; Lurigio, 1987; Resick, 1987; Riggs & Foa, 1995; Wirtz & Harrell, 1987), and even fewer are specific to bias crime victimization (Barnes & Ephross, 1994; Ehrlich, Larcom, & Purvis, 1994; Ephross, Barnes, Ehrlich, Sandnes, & Weiss, 1986; Herek, Cogan, & Gillis, 1999; Herek, Gillis, Cogan, & Glunt, 1997). In part due to methodological issues, the results of these studies on bias crime victimization are somewhat inconsistent in their conclusions.

According to Barnes and Ephross (1994), the most prevalent emotional reaction of the 59 bias victim respondents was anger toward the offender, followed by fear. When comparing the victims of bias and nonbias assault, their data indicated that

> a major difference in the emotional response of hate violence victims appears to be the absence of lowered self-esteem. The ability of some hate violence victims to maintain their self-esteem may be associated with their attribution of responsibility

for the attacks to the prejudice and racism of the perpetrators. (p. 250)

Although these data are notable, the purposive sampling technique and small sample of respondents raise questions about the generalizability of the findings.

Conversely, Ehrlich et al. (1994) in their national telephone victimization survey (2,078 respondents) revealed marked differences in the traumatic effects of hate violence. They indicated that among four subgroups (i.e., nonvictims, group defamation victims, personal crime victims, and bias crime victims), bias crime victims demonstrated the greatest average number of symptoms and behavior variations on a scale of 19 psychophysiological symptoms of posttraumatic stress and 12 social and behavioral changes. The authors reported a clear overall pattern of pervasive consequences in the lives of victims of bias crime and concluded that "ethnoviolence [bias crime] victims suffer greater trauma than do victims of . . . violence which is committed for other reasons" (p. 27). Specifically, ethnoviolence victims reported experiencing 5.98 negative psychophysiological aftereffects, whereas personal victims had 4.77, and group defamation victims reported 4.02. According to this study, victims of ethnoviolence were also significantly more nervous, lost more friends, had more trouble sleeping or concentrating, had more interpersonal difficulties, and felt angrier than those victims of personal crimes.

In a related study to Ehrlich et al. (1994) on the effects of ethnoviolence in the workplace, once again the victims of ethnoviolence reported the greatest number (5.6) of psychophysiological symptoms on the same 19-point list. Whereas personal victims reported only 3.5, victims of prejudicial insults or jokes reported 5.0 (Barnes & Ephross, 1994). The limitation to this study, however, is the broad definition of bias incidents asked of workers during the interview. Participants were asked, "In the past 3 years, have you ever been mistreated at this company?" They were then asked to determine whether they felt this was due to some prejudice.

More recently, Herek et al. (1999) explored the psychological sequelae of gay, lesbian, and bisexual bias crime victims. Recruiting from gay/lesbian community events (i.e., Gay Pride celebration, etc.), gay bars, or community organizations, the research team recruited more than 2,000 participants to fill out a self-administered questionnaire. This study marks the most expansive empirical effort to include bias crime victims, and although the sample is somewhat skewed toward gay/lesbians who are public about their sexuality (i.e., are able to attend gay/lesbian/bisexual functions, community organizations, etc.), this research is notable for its sample size.

The data indicate that those respondents who reported experiencing a bias crime (compared with victims of nonbias crimes) within the past 5 years consistently had more intense feelings of adverse psychological sequelae. Statistically significant relationships were found for depressive symptoms, traumatic stress, and anger. One of the methodological limitations in this study, however, is how the research team coded bias and nonbias events; events were classified as bias or nonbias by asking respondents whether they felt they were victimized because of their sexual orientation. It is possible that this subjective interpretation might be related to other characteristics of the victim, such as the victim's political orientation toward gay, lesbian, and bisexual issues, and thus may also influence the impact of the crime. Despite this limitation, these data indicate additional support for the belief that bias crime victims endure more intense effects of victimization on several dimensions.

With the exception of these few studies, little is known about the differences between bias and nonbias victimization. These studies represent the first attempt by researchers to quantify the psychological and behavioral impact of bias crime victimization. The current study attempts to provide further information on some of these issues.

RESEARCH DESIGN/METHOD

The present study takes a comparative look into the experience of bias and nonbias victims. One of the primary goals of the design is to be able to make comparisons between similar bias and nonbias crime victims in an effort to understand if bias crime victims experience differential impacts. To achieve this goal, this study surveys a comparable group of violent bias and nonbias assault victims identified from law enforcement and advocacy agency legal records.

When designing this study, we estimated that the most powerful data about the victimization experience would be from the victims themselves. To this end, we created a mail survey instrument to be sent to all victims of bias-motivated aggravated assault in the city of Boston[1] within the years of 1992 to 1997 and a random sample of nonbias assault victims. The notable exceptions to this list were domestic assaults and child abuse. Because both of these categories touch on specific phenomena, the team felt that their inclusion would be inappropriate. Therefore, all incidents coded as a domestic assault or child abuse (by the responding officers at the Boston Police Department) have been excluded from both the experimental and control groups in this study.

Because there were considerably more nonbias assaults during the same time frame, the research team used a 10% random sample of this group. Once the lists were constructed, each name was given a numeric identifier, allowing the research team to track which victims had or had not responded.

In addition to the databases accessed through the Boston Police, the research project staff reviewed records from a prominent Boston gay/lesbian community advocacy center. From these records, researchers contacted by mail victims of violent bias crime assaults from the years 1992 to 1997 who had not been previously identified through law enforcement records.

Several points of contact were made with victims to maximize response rates. First, the research team and advisory board all agreed that victims should be given advanced notification of the study so as not to shock a victim with a highly sensitive survey about his or her victimization. Therefore, victims were sent a preliminary letter, notifying them that they were selected to participate in a study on the effects of victimization. To be sensitive to all victims, victims were given the option to elect not to participate in the study by contacting a representative to remove their name from the list for future mailings. Several victims called to request information, but very few people called to say they did not wish to participate.

Next, the self-administered questionnaire was compiled with advice from an advisory board with several distinguished bias crime scholars.[2] The final survey instrument employed the Horowitz Impact of Events Scale (Horowitz, Walker, & Alvarez, 1979) to gain insight into the psychological sequelae involved in the victimization process. In addition to being used in several settings to enhance reliability of the instrument, this instrument has also been employed in prior research with bias crime victims (Ehrlich et al., 1994). Also included in the survey packet was a copy of the police incident report[3] so that victims could correctly remember the particular incident that we were requesting information about; victims were also encouraged to include any additional information and/or correct anything on the original police report. For those victims who had experienced more than one victimization, it clarified which incident that our survey was targeting. In addition, to reduce the trauma associated with reliving the incident, a list of social service and advocacy agencies was provided with the questionnaire so that those victims who felt they needed additional help could access support services. Finally, respondents who had difficulty writing were given the option for a member of the research team to assist them either by phone or in person.

Unfortunately, nearly 50% of the initial mailings were returned with address unknown; "moved, left no forwarding address"; and so forth. In an attempt to find these victims, the research team used the computer-tracking program Autotrack and was able to locate a little more than half of the unknown addresses. Still, even after locating many of the victims' addresses, the response rate remained low. In an effort to increase the response rate, the research team decided to offer victims compensation ($15) for their time to complete the survey, a method that has been employed in several previous victim studies (Davis & Brickman, 1996; Herek et al., 1997; Rothbaum, Foa, Riggs, Murdock, & Walsh, 1992). Despite the monetary incentive, the personalization of the second survey mailing, and the repetition of sending another reminder/mailing, the overall response rate did not significantly improve. Unfortunately, the response still remained quite low at approximately 23% for the bias assault victims and 11% for the nonbias victims. It must be noted that with such a low response rate, it is likely that our sample is nonrepresentative in many ways. We do expect, however, that similar response problems will affect both our bias and nonbias assault victim samples.

The final draft of the victim survey contained sections about the incident, the psychological and behavioral aftermath, family and community responses to the event, perceptions of police and prosecutors' roles and efficacy, and demographic information. The survey also attempted to address the impact of the victimization by relating the incident to other major life events (i.e., major illness, divorce, death of family member, etc.). Several scales of coping strategies were devised, drawing from a comprehensive review of previous crime victim research literature. This article will focus on the psychological and behavioral impact of violent bias crime victimization.

SAMPLE CHARACTERISTICS

A review of the characteristics of the two samples reveals surprising similarities considering the difficulties encountered in obtaining survey responses (see Table 1). About 40% of each sample of victims are female (37.8% vs. 40%), and the racial and ethnic makeups are similar for the two respondent samples. When we consider the age breakdown of the samples, the bias crime sample is slightly younger, with nonbias victims about twice as likely to be older than 45 years. In addition, the samples are very similar in terms of income and education. Finally, as expected, the bias crime sample is more likely to include victims who identify themselves as gay, lesbian, and bisexual.

Characteristics of Incident

In general, there were few differences between the location of the incident and whether the incident was or was not bias related. It does appear, however, that slightly more of the bias sample were victimized in the area of their home (37% vs. 30%), and nonbias assaults were more likely to occur at work (14% vs. 7%).

Our data are consistent with 1997 UCR Hate Crime Reporting data regarding location of the incident. Approximately one third of both samples were victimized in the area of their home. The UCR location category "street/transportation" is similar to our category of "enroute to/from somewhere" from our survey. Both measures are imprecise in illuminating whether the particular spot was just outside a victim's residence or many miles away. For this reason, we speculate that some percentage of those who are victimized "on the street" or traveling are within a very short distance from their homes due to the fact that an individual's home is usually the pivotal point (going to and coming from) for most travel. Such distance is relevant in interpreting subsequent psychological sequelae for victims.

Prior research has looked at the impact of location on victimization and subsequent post-traumatic stress disorder. Schepple and Bart (1983) found in their study of sexual assault victims that women who believed they were in a safe place during the attack were more likely to experience more severe trauma. The authors speculated that victims who are attacked in a perceived safe place are not able to employ "victim blaming" techniques and thus have no buffer from the severe psychological impact of victimization. Victim blaming allows the victim to feel that if he or she had augmented his or her behavior, he or she could have prevented the incident. The important corollary to this is that victims can use this strategy to reduce their fears about future victimization, asserting that if they change their behavior, they can be safe. However, because it is difficult to determine whether our measure of "passing through the area" indicates near the victim's home or not, we are unable to understand the context of location for a substantial percentage of victims. Although the differences between the bias and nonbias group are not significant, it is notable that a larger percentage of bias victims are victimized near their homes, thus making the victims more vulnerable to the postincident effects mentioned above.

The one measure that more closely approximates the context of whether the place of victimization is considered safe by the victim is the question about frequency. We asked victims whether they had been to this location (before the incident occurred) "never," "a few times," "quite often," or "almost every day." When we collapse these categories into never/a few times and quite often/almost every day, we find that bias victims are more likely to be victimized in locations that are familiar to them. More than three quarters of the bias group tended to frequent the location where the incident occurred often, compared to only two thirds of the nonbias group. After the incident, only 28% of the bias victims and 34% of the nonbias victims returned almost every day. Although these differences are not statistically significant, they are instructive in understanding the context of the crime.

Next, bias crime victims were also more likely to be attacked by a group of attackers than our comparison sample of nonbias victims (49% vs. 35%). The bias victims had a mean of 2.04 attackers, compared to the nonbias group, who had a mean of 1.84 attackers. It is interesting to note that in this sample, about one quarter of each group were attacked by a group of four or more offenders (23% vs. 25%).

Relationship to Offender

Several studies have explored the relationship between victim and offender in cases of sexual assault (Katz, 1991; Koss & Cox, 1984; Ullman & Seigel, 1993). Although these studies focus on different aspects of the healing process, Ullman and Seigel (1993) found that fear and anxiety were more common for women sexually assaulted by strangers. Katz (1991), however, found that women victimized by strangers are more likely to retain a positive self-image than women who are raped by nonstrangers.

In our sample, bias crime victims were significantly less likely to have a prior relationship with the offender than were nonbias victims (83.5% to 68.2%). One quarter of the nonbias group reported that they knew their attacker for at least 1 year, compared to less than 7% of the bias crime victims.

The survey also asked victims to relay how they describe the nature of the incident. They

Table 3.1 Comparative Statistics Between the Samples of Bias and Nonbias Assault Victim Respondents

Demographic Variables Subcategory	Bias Victim Respondents (n = 91)	Nonbias Victim Respondents (n = 45)
Gender		
Male	62.2	60.0
Female	37.8	40.0
Age (years)		
Younger than 18	12.5	11.1
18-24	11.4	13.3
25-44	62.5	48.9
45 and older	13.6	26.7
Race and Latino ethnicity		
White	62.2	52.4
Black	23.3	33.3
Asian	6.7	7.1
Other	2.2	2.4
Latino ethnicity	5.6	4.8
Household income ($)		
< 20,000	42.7	38.9
20,000-39,999	28.0	22.2
40,000-59,999	8.5	13.9
60,000-79,999	12.2	11.1
80,000-99,999	3.7	8.3
100,000 or more	4.9	5.6
Education		
< high school/NA	26.1	17.8
High school/some college	35.2	46.7
College graduate	22.7	20.0
Postgraduate	15.9	15.6
Sexual orientation		
Heterosexual	68.8	94.4
Bisexual	2.5	0.0
Lesbian	6.3	2.8
Gay male	22.5	2.8
Transgender	0.0	0.0

were asked if the assault was "an unprovoked attack against me," "an ongoing dispute," "a minor disagreement that got out of hand," a case of "mistaken identity," or "a poor response to a situation by the offender." This is important because several critics of bias crime legislation have suggested that many bias crimes are simply the result of disputes between individuals of different groups. The data here contradict this assertion; nearly all the bias crime assaults were committed by strangers (84%), and most victims reported that the assault was the result

of an unprovoked attack (76%). Only 8% of the bias crime victims reported that the attack was a result of an ongoing dispute. When comparing the two samples, bias crime victims were more likely to have been attacked by strangers and more likely to see the attack as unprovoked (76% vs. 53%). This supports the prior contention in the literature that bias crime victims are chosen because of their membership in a group and not because of any prior actions they may have taken. As opposed to many other assault victims, bias crime victims are interchangeable; as far as the offender is concerned, any member of the group could be selected as a target.

Whereas these questions are helpful in understanding the qualitative context of the precipitants of the assault, the next set of questions asks the victims to directly attribute levels of responsibility to the victim, offender, or other individual. Specifically, we asked victims to assess responsibility for the incident on a scale of 0 to 10, with 0 indicating that the victim had no responsibility for the attack and 10 indicating that the victim assumed full responsibility. Once again, the responses are consistent with the earlier conclusions. Bias crime victims are more likely to report that they had no responsibility for the incident than nonbias crime victims (76% vs. 58%). This again fits with the prior descriptions of bias crimes that most bias crime victims feel that they did nothing to provoke or initiate the attack.

Many nonbias victims reinforced the lack of responsibility for the assault in their qualitative remarks when asked how to reduce/prevent these types of crimes in the future. Whereas bias crime victims often pointed to a community responsibility, nonbias victims were more likely to respond that the reduction/prevention of assault was within their own control, inferring they may have precipitated the crime by their own overt actions. Many responses from nonbias victims involved changing their own behaviors. The following responses were typical for the nonbias group when asked what they might do to prevent such crimes in the future.

- "Walk away from the incident."
- "Be polite."
- "Look away, but it is hard not to . . ."
- "Not to settle quarrels physically."

On the contrary, bias crime victims expressed feelings of frustration when asked how to prevent or reduce such crimes in the future. They generally did not indicate that their actions had done anything to provoke or exacerbate a situation, confirming the responses from earlier questions about the nature of the assault. Because most bias crime victims did not believe they could do anything to prevent future victimization, they felt frustrated. The following

response captures many of the bias crime respondents' feelings about preventing victimization: "Not to be in the wrong place at the wrong time. In other words, it's impossible." Such remarks indicate that bias crime victims feel largely powerless to protect themselves in the future.

Collectively, the responses to questions about the level of responsibility, precipitating incident events, and prior relationship paint a picture of bias crime assaults that is different in many ways from that of nonbias assaults. These events are less likely to involve victims and offenders who are friends or acquaintances and to be precipitated by any overt actions by the victim, and the onus of responsibility appears to lie much more fully with the offender.

Medical Treatment

We asked victims whether they sought medical assistance as a result of the incident. Because our sample included only aggravated assault victims, we expected that some physical harm would be involved in most of these incidents. There was little difference in the number of victims from each sample who required overnight hospital treatment (15% vs. 16%), but bias crime victims reported that they went to the hospital emergency room for treatment less often (29% vs. 43%). However, less than 60% of the sample answered this question. In retrospect, our measure may have been imprecise, and the low response rate is a reaction to ill-fitting response categories. This conclusion may indicate that nonbias victims in our sample were more likely to suffer serious injury, or it may indicate that bias crime victims are reluctant to go to the emergency room after being attacked. Whatever the reason, definitive conclusions regarding the extent of medical treatment for comparable victims are not supported from these data. Further analysis is necessary to determine if bias crime victims are more likely to receive more serious physical injury in their attacks.

Reporting Practice

When victims were asked if they had spoken to anyone prior to reporting the crime to the police, bias crime victims were more likely to report that they had sought out someone to discuss the incident with prior to reporting the assault to the police (40% vs. 29%). In most cases, the victim went to a family member or a friend before he or she reported the crime to the police. The fact that nearly half of the bias-motivated victims report discussing the attack with someone before formally reporting to the police may have important implications for improving the reporting of bias crimes nationally. It may be necessary to broaden the previctimization outreach efforts to include families of victims as well as the victims themselves. In addition, it may be necessary to increase the availability of victim support programs, where victims can go to obtain support and assistance before they become formally involved in the criminal justice system.

VICTIM REACTIONS

Behavioral Reactions

Twelve separate indicators measured postvictimization behavioral changes, each with a dichotomous variable (yes or no). Surprisingly, there were no significant differences between the bias and nonbias groups. Both groups of assault victims appear to take the same steps postvictimization: The overwhelming majority of victims in both groups (77.4% for bias, 77.8% for nonbias victims) stated that they pay more attention to where they walk now. More than a third of both samples stated that they try to be less visible since the incident (37.8% for bias, 38.6% for nonbias victims). Twenty-two percent of both samples responded that they had become more active in the community because of the victimization. Overall, however, the similarities in behavior modifications between the groups are striking. The same can not be said, however, for the psychological sequelae of the bias and nonbias victims. We will return to the findings of the behavioral responses during the discussion section of this report.

Psychological Reactions

Using Horowitz's Impact of Event Scale (Horowitz et al., 1979) to understand some of the psychological sequelae, we asked victims from both groups the same questions about postevent distress. Horowitz has suggested that the psychological themes in his scale can be grouped into two major components: intrusiveness and avoidance. Our scale incorporated one major change from the original scale; although we used basically the same symptoms, we measured the response differently. Originally, Horowitz employed a "not at all, rarely, sometimes, often" response framework for each of the scale items, within a time frame of "within the last seven days." On the suggestion of our advisory group, we decided to account for differences between the groups while incorporating a time dimension, thus further refining the sometimes category of the original scale. In addition, because our sample included victims who had been victimized spanning 1 month to 6 years prior to the administration of the survey, asking whether the respondent encountered the adverse stimuli or reaction always, sometimes, rarely, or not at all as was done in the original Horowitz instrument would conceal the time-sensitive nature of the impact. Respondents were asked whether they experienced the particular emotion or coping technique "not at all," "for a few days," "for a few weeks," "for a few months," or "for a few years." In short, our measures represent an attempt to incorporate both a measure of intensity and duration.

Although there were only six items from Horowitz's Psychological Scale where significant differences exist between the bias and nonbias victim groups, every psychological impact measure from this scale had a higher mean value from the bias group than from the nonbias group. This means bias crime victims experienced the adverse psychological sequelae more often than the nonbias control group on every item we measured. Although the levels of significance vary, the relationship does not vary; bias crime victims clearly experienced more negative impacts and experienced these impacts for longer periods of time than the nonbias victim group.

The psychological impact of crime on the victim is measured in our study by 19 separate scale items. A *t* test was performed between the bias-motivated and non-bias-motivated assault victim groups on each reaction category. A (moderate) statistically significant difference was detected between the two groups within 5 of the 19 categories ($p < .05$). The largest categorical difference was in "feeling angry" with a t score of 2.625 and a mean difference of .54 on a 5-point scale (i.e., not at all, days, weeks, months, and years).

All of the five variables that are statistically significant at the .05 level are related to Horowitz's intrusiveness theme. Bias crime victims cite that they are more nervous, more depressed, have more trouble concentrating, think about the incident when they do not mean to, and feel like not wanting to live any longer more often than nonbias victims. Collectively, we see that the bias group has more difficulty coping with the victimization and that they appear to have additional problems with their recovery process due to increased fear and more frequent intrusive thoughts.

One could, however, persuasively argue that due to imprecisely characterizing the mean as an instrument of comparison in the t test, we may have somehow blurred the test of significance. To address this, the research team split these variables in several different ways. First, we collapsed the psychological variables into two categories: either the presence of the symptom (coded as 1) or the absence of it (coded as 0). Collapsing these categories yields very similar results. Once again, feelings of depression, nervousness, difficulty concentrating at work, and feeling ashamed/losing confidence are significant below the .05 level. These results indicate that there is a relationship between the element of bias in assault that is strongly related to whether the victim experiences these adverse psychological sequelae at all.

At this point in the analysis, the research team wished to test the bivariate relationships further within the psychological sequelae. Specifically, one could argue that the difference between having symptoms for a few days and not having them at all is not very remarkable. For this reason, we created a separate dichotomous variable that collapsed categories into not at all/for a few days (coded as 0) and a few weeks, months, years. This division makes the implicit objective assumption that most victims of violence will sustain some impact; however, when the impact duration creeps into

weeks or months, there is something notable about it.

The results from this analysis are congruent with earlier tests of significance. Four variables— more nervous than usual, thought about when I didn't mean to, didn't feel like living any longer, and had trouble concentrating at work— all indicated a Pearson value below the .05 level of significance. Again, we see that the level of intrusiveness for the bias crime victim is greater than for the nonbias victims. In this version of the analysis, only more depressed falls from being significantly different between the two groups.

The research team also designed the 19-item Impact of Event Scale into a collective score. We did this by taking the mean of each respondent's 19 answers, excluding surveys where more than 5 answers on the scale were missing. We ran these collective scale scores and found that once again, the differences between the two groups are significant (Pearson's value .041), with the bias group more likely to have a mean above 1.5 (67% to 48.9%). There is also a significant correlation between the mean score for the Psychological Scale and whether the victim is from the bias or nonbias group (.03). Once again, this indicates the strength of the relationship between psychological sequelae and the presence of bias in the incident. By nearly every bivariate measure, the bias victims are affected more intensely, with more intrusive psychological sequelae.

Feelings of Safety

When asked how safe the victims feel after the crime, bias crime victims are significantly less likely to feel safe. Almost one half of the nonbias victims reported feeling less safe after the incident (46%), but a significantly higher number of bias crime victims reported feeling unsafe after their attack (59%). This increased fear is interesting because the nonbias attacks were more likely to have involved reported injury. One possible reason for this increased fear may be that bias crime victims are more likely to be concerned that a similar crime may happen in the future, especially because they have experienced previous attacks more frequently. Fully 52% of the bias crime sample reported that they were very concerned about becoming a victim of a similar crime in the future; this compares to 37% of the nonbias crime sample who reported that they were very concerned about future victimization. In addition, after the incident, bias crime victims were more likely to report that they felt unsafe alone in their neighborhood at night (42% vs. 32%) and that they felt unsafe returning to the area of the incident (52% vs. 44%). Taken together, these findings indicate that bias crime assault victims are more likely to experience increased fear and reduced feelings of safety after the crime than nonbias crime assault victims.

Other Victimization Consequences

We asked both samples if they had experienced other negative life events since the assault. In most areas, the bias crime sample reported that they had endured more negative experiences since the assault. For example, bias crime victims were more likely to report that they had lost employment (50% vs. 34%) since the assault. In addition, bias crime victims reported that they had had significant health problems after the assault (48% vs. 32%). Conversely, the nonbias group was more likely to experience a divorce or separation (15% vs. 7%). Although it is impossible to determine if these changes are related to the assault that preceded them, it is true that many of the bias crime victims in this sample experienced more traumatic events in their lives following the original assault.

In addition, we asked each sample a summary question: "Overall, how difficult was it for you to overcome the effects of this incident?" Here again, the bias crime sample was almost three times more likely to report that overcoming this incident had been very difficult (36% vs. 13%).

CONCLUSION

Our data have several limitations. First, the limited sample size reinforces the need for replication. Second, the nonrepresentative sample raises questions about generalizability. However,

the difficulties we encountered in getting victims to respond, and our efforts to improve responses, can inform future research projects. Both bias and nonbias victim groups were hard to locate, and when correct addresses were found, they were hesitant to respond through the mail. This population may need more intensive efforts, such as interviews instead of self-administered questionnaires, as a methodology to encourage participation in sharing their victimization experiences.

Despite our methodological difficulties, our data confirm several previously posited hypotheses. First, compared to non-bias-motivated assaults, the incidence of bias crime tends to be perpetrated by multiple offenders upon strangers, and the victims of bias crimes are more likely to be victims selected only because they belong to a particular group. Bias crimes are more likely to occur in locations familiar to the victim, and bias crime victims are much more likely to experience increased fear after the incident. In addition, victims of bias assault are more likely to feel the effects of victimization more intensely and for a longer period of time. Whether this is a result of the inability to employ traditional coping mechanisms or due to some other phenomena, bias crime victims suffer more intense intrusive psychological sequelae than do nonbias assault victims.

Although the behavioral responses may initially seem surprising, we believe these also confirm earlier hypotheses. First, the element of victim interchangeability injects a unique dynamic into the victimization process. Victims are aware that their overt actions did nothing to precipitate their victimization; being the "wrong person," at the wrong time and place, qualifies the bias victim. Therefore, if the impetus for victimization is something that is outside of the bias victim's control before the incident, it is reasonable that there would be little that the victim would do differently subsequent to the incident. Qualitative responses from open-ended questions on the survey confirmed that victims were aware of their distinct vulnerability, whereas nonbias victims indicated that their behavior may have encouraged the offender or exacerbated a tense situation among acquaintances. Psychological sequelae, however, are less easily controlled by the victim. The level of intrusive thoughts created by the incident and the feelings of helplessness associated with bias-motivated victimization all point to a unique victimization process for bias victims.

This research supports the conclusion that bias crimes affect their victims differently from nonbias crimes. Victims of bias crimes are more fearful after the incident and are more likely to experience a series of intrusive thoughts. This is true even if we control on the type of crime, in this case, assaults. Although it is beyond the scope of our study to definitively conclude whether various hate crime legislation is justified, it is clear that bias victims have distinct needs. These conclusions support the claim that bias crimes do in fact affect their victims differently and that consequently law enforcement and social service agencies should be cognizant of these differences in assisting bias crime victims.

Lastly, this project does not begin to address the impact that bias crimes have on the secondary victims, the community. Because bias crimes have the unique impact of reaching far beyond the primary victim, due to the dimension of victim interchangeability, every member of the minority group who is aware of the crime is affected by a solitary crime against one individual minority member. Unfortunately, this is well beyond the scope of the current study. With these considerations in mind, we hope that the research community will both attempt to replicate this research with additional bias victim samples, as well as tap into the important dimension of secondary victimization.

NOTES

1. The city of Boston was selected due to its comprehensive strategies for investigating bias crimes through the Community Disorders Unit, formed in 1979 in response to heightened racial tensions within the city. Because of this, the research team had access to an extensive database of bias crime offenses.

2. The advisory board was composed of representatives from the U.S. Attorneys Office, the Anti-Defamation League, the district attorney's office, the victim/witness office, the NAACP, gay/lesbian community centers, the Boston Police Community Disorders Unit, the Massachusetts Office of Corrections, and members of the academic community who specialize in both international and domestic bias crime studies.

3. All offender information was redacted according to the Boston Police Department's legal guidelines.

REFERENCES

Barnes, A., & Ephross, P. H. (1994, May). The impact of hate violence on victims: Emotional and behavioral responses to attacks. *Social Work, 39*(3), 247–251.

Davis, R., & Brickman, E. (1996). Supportive and unsupportive aspects of the behavior of others toward victims of sexual and non-sexual assault. *Journal of Interpersonal Violence, 11*(2), 250–262.

Ehrlich, H. J., Larcom, B.E.K., & Purvis, R. D. (1994, May). *The traumatic effects of ethnoviolence*. Towson, MD: Prejudice Institute, Center for the Applied Study of Ethnoviolence.

Ephross, P. H., Barnes, A., Ehrlich, H. J., Sandnes, K. R., & Weiss, J. C. (1986, October). *The ethnoviolence project: Pilot study*. Baltimore: National Institute Against Prejudice and Violence.

Freedy, J., Resnick, H., Kilpatrick, D., Dansky, B., & Tidwell, R. (1994). The psychological adjustment of recent crime victims in the criminal justice system. *Journal of Interpersonal Violence, 9*(4), 450–468.

Frieze, I. H., Greenberg, M. S., & Hymer, S. (1987). Describing the crime victim: Psychological reactions to victimization. *Professional Psychology: Research and Practice, 18*(4), 299–315.

Harvard Law Review. (1996). Penalty enhancement does not punish free speech or thoughts. In B. Leone & P. A. Winters (Eds.), *Hate crimes* (pp. 121–129). San Diego, CA: Greenhaven Press.

Herek, G., Gillis, J. R., Cogan, J. C., & Glunt, E. K. (1997, April). Hate crime victimization among lesbian, gay, and bisexual adults: Prevalence, psychological correlates, and methodological issues. *Journal of Interpersonal Violence, 12*(2), 195–215.

Herek, G. M., Cogan, J. C., & Gillis, J. R. (1999). Psychological sequelae of hate crime victimization among lesbian, gay and bisexual adults.

Journal of Consulting and Clinical Psychology, 67(6), 945–951.

Horowitz, M., Walker, N., & Alvarez, W. (1979, May). Impact of Events Scale: A measure of subjective stress. *Psychosomatic Medicine, 41*(3), 209–218.

Jacobs, J., & Potter, K. (1998). *Hate crime: Criminal law and identity politics.* New York: Oxford Press.

Katz, B. (1991). The psychological impact of stranger versus nonstranger rape on victims' recovery. In A. Parrot & L. Bechhofer (Eds.), *Acquaintance rape: The hidden crime* (pp. 251–269). New York: John Wiley.

Kilpatrick, D. G., Saunders, B. E., Veronen, L. J., Best, C., & Von, J. M. (1987). Criminal victimization: Lifetime prevalence, reporting to police, and psychological impact. *Crime & Delinquency, 33*(4), 479–489.

Koss, D., & Cox, S. (1984). Stranger and acquaintance rape: Are there differences in the victim's experience? *Psychology of Women Quarterly, 12,* 1–24.

Levin, J., & McDevitt, J. (1993). *Hate crimes: The rising tide of bigotry and bloodshed.* New York: Plenum.

Lurigio, A. J. (1987). Are all victims alike? The adverse, generalized, and differential impact of crime. *Crime and Delinquency, 33*(4), 452–467.

Resick, P. (1987). Psychological effects of victimization: Implications for the criminal justice system. *Crime and Delinquency, 33*(4), 468–478.

Riggs, R., & Foa, E. (1995). A prospective examination of symptoms of post-traumatic stress disorder in victims of nonsexual assault. *Journal of Interpersonal Violence, 10*(2), 201.

Rothbaum, B., Foa, E., Riggs, D., Murdock, T., & Walsh, W. (1992). A prospective examination of post-traumatic stress disorder in rape victims. *Journal of Traumatic Stress, 5*(3), 455–475.

Sales, E., Baum, M., & Shore, B. (1984). Victim readjustment following assault. *Journal of Social Issues, 40*(1), 117–136.

Schepple, K. L., & Bart, P. B. (1983). Through women's eyes: Defining danger in the wake of sexual assault. *Journal of Social Issues, 39*(2), 63–81.

Ullman, S. E., & Seigel, J. M. (1993). Victim-offender relationship and sexual assault. *Violence and Victims, 8*(2), 121–133.

Wirtz, P., & Harrell, A. (1987). Victim and crime characteristics, coping responses, and short and long-term recovery from victimization. *Journal of Consulting and Clinical Psychology, 55*(6), 866–871.

Wisconsin v. Mitchell, 508 U.S. 476 (1993).

QUESTIONS

1. Do you think that bias crimes have a significantly different impact on victims and/or the community than non-bias crimes do? Discuss your reasons as part of your answer.

2. When bias-crime victims perceive that they had no responsibility for their victimization, how might this influence the victims' psychological reactions to the crime, especially their perception of how to prevent such crimes in the future?

3. Describe the concept of "victim interchangeability." How can this concept help explain the nature and scope of the impact of bias crimes?

4. According to the victims, did the characteristics of the crime incident vary significantly depending upon whether it was a bias-related or non-bias-related crime?

5. Did most victims report knowing or not knowing their attacker(s)? Were there differences between bias-crime and non-bias-crime victims in the proportion who reported knowing the offender(s)?

6. Did most victims report talking to someone before reporting the crime to the police, or not? Were there differences between bias-crime and non-bias-crime victims in this respect?

7. What kinds of behavioral reactions did bias-crime and non-bias-crime victims report having after their victimization? Were there differences between the two kinds of victims in the nature or frequency of behavioral reactions that they reported?

8. What kinds of psychological reactions did bias-crime and non-bias-crime victims report experiencing after their victimization? In what ways did the psychological reactions of bias-crime victims differ from those of other victims?

9. According to the research presented in this article, how did the responses of non-bias-crime victims and bias-crime victims to their victimization compare? In what ways were their responses similar? In what ways did their responses differ?

10. According to the authors, what are the methodological limitations of this research?

4

RETALIATION, FEAR, OR RAGE

An Investigation of African American and White Reactions to Racist Hate Crimes

KELLINA M. CRAIG

This article describes research exploring the question of whether hate crimes may be more likely to provoke retaliation than other crimes. If hate crimes are more likely than others to lead to retaliatory violence, it would support the argument that hate crimes can have uniquely destructive effects on the social fabric—for example, harming community relations by fostering mistrust. The question of whether hate crimes are more likely than other crimes to provoke retaliation is another key element in the debate about how to define and punish hate crimes.

Almost every U.S. advocacy group reports that hate crimes are on the rise (e.g., Anti-Defamation League [ADL] of B'nai B'rith, 1994; National Gay and Lesbian Task Force, 1994; Southern Poverty Law Center, 1994), and represent both a national and global problem. A host of researchers are also in agreement (Brown, 1997; Herek & Berrill, 1992; Levin & McDevitt, 1993; Pinkney, 1994). Results of a survey by the Center for the Study of Ethnic and Racial Violence (1993) suggest that hate crimes occurred at the alarming rate of one every 14 minutes during the period studied.

To the extent that hate crimes provoke retaliatory hate crimes, this rate is likely to continue to increase. The present study examines one aspect of hate crime victimization: responses of members of victims' groups.

Definition and Conceptualization of a Hate Crime

A hate crime is an illegal act involving intentional selection of a victim based on a perpetrator's bias or prejudice that relates to either the actual or perceived status of the

EDITORS' NOTE: From Craig, K. M. (1999). Retaliation, Fear, or Rage: An Investigation of African American and White Reactions to Race Hate Crimes. *Journal of Interpersonal Violence, 14,* 138-151. © 1999 Sage Publications Inc. Used with permission.

victim. Hate crimes may include harassment, intimidation, verbal and physical assaults, property damage, and, in extreme cases, murder. Attributions concerning the causes of these events range from deep-seated historical resentment, actual or imagined economic competition, racial integration of neighborhoods, and insensitive media coverage of minority groups (e.g., Herek & Berrill, 1992; Langer, 1993; Levin & McDevitt, 1993), and are located within the context of the state of current race relations.

In 1990, Congress enacted the Hate Crime Statistics Act that required law enforcement personnel to systematically record hate crime incidents. This law has subsequently been amended (1993) to ensure continuous mandatory reporting. Because victims of hate crimes can belong to a variety of social categories simultaneously (e.g., an African American lesbian or a physically challenged Jew), an accurate assessment of the basis for the bias is often difficult. For this reason, legal scholars who study hate crimes have suggested a variety of ways to improve current statutes and sentencing proscriptions for hate crimes (e.g., Gellman, 1991; Gerstenfeld, 1992; Weisburd & Levin, 1994). Interestingly, however, none have questioned the veracity of the claim that hate crimes engender greater emotional distress and expressions of revenge than similar crimes not motivated by hate for members of the victim's group. The present project addresses this issue.

Victims of hate crimes include members of racial, ethnic, and religious minority groups, gays, lesbians, and bisexuals as well as the physically challenged. Although most researchers and law enforcement personnel agree that perpetrators of hate crimes are primarily male (e.g., Berk, 1990; Herek, Gillis, Cogan, & Glunt, 1997; Massachusetts Executive Office of Public Safety, 1990), there is little consensus regarding the characteristics of the most frequent victims of hate crimes. For example, Sanchez and Castenda (1994) contend that African Americans are most likely to be victims. Indeed, they report that since 1990, hate crimes against African Americans have increased dramatically. In contrast, a National Institute of Justice report concluded that "homosexuals are probably the most frequent victims" (Finn & McNeil, 1987, p. 2). Thus, there is some ambiguity concerning

which type of minority group experiences the most frequent rates of hate crime victimization. However, to the extent that hate crimes are on the rise for members of *all* stigmatized groups, it would seem fruitful to consider all groups to be potentially at risk and to begin empirical investigations by focusing on at least one type of hate crime. The present study examined responses to racist hate crimes.

Postvictimization Experiences

Generally, victims of crimes may experience a wide range of aversive psychological states, including but not limited to depression, anxiety, hostility, fear, and post-traumatic stress (Norris, Kaniasty, & Scheer, 1990; Thompson & Norris, 1992). Researchers have begun to focus on the postvictimization experiences of hate crime, victims in particular. Indeed, results of one study investigating the experiences of victims of heterosexist hate crimes reveal that increased perceptions of vulnerability and fear of crime, as well as a decreased perception of benevolence in the world and lower self-esteem, were common for victims following a hate crime (Herek et al., 1997). Moreover, the responses of the more than 140 lesbians and gay men who reported heterosexist victimization revealed that the psychological distress experienced by hate crime survivors continued for almost 3 years longer than that of victims of nonbias crimes.

In addition to the increased magnitude and duration of the psychological distress experienced by hate crime survivors, there may also be an increased likelihood for retaliation. Here, retaliation refers to an aversive action that is directed at the initial perpetrators or those believed to be in some way related to the perpetrators. The State of Wisconsin and amici (e.g., Brief for the United States as Amicus Curiae 1–15; Brief for the American Civil Liberties Union as Amicus Curiae 9–10) suggest that hate crimes inflict both greater individual and societal harm because "they are likely to provoke retaliatory crimes . . . and incite community unrest" (*Wisconsin v. Mitchell,* 1993, p. 13). Similarly, Weinstein (1992) has written that hate crimes (unlike nonbias crimes) "can have a powerful *in terrorem* effect, particularly for members of minority groups who historically have been, or currently are, victims of racist violence" (p. 10). Thus, the impact of hate crimes is believed to extend well beyond the initial victim to members of the victim's category and may be manifested in retaliatory activities.[1]

The present experimental study was exploratory and sought to examine the potential consequences of hate crimes for members of victims' groups. As noted above, both researchers and legislators have suggested that, among other things, revenge carried out by members of the hate crime victim's group may be especially likely to occur (Weisburd & Levin, 1994). Indeed, the near twofold increase in hate crimes in New York City following the infamous Howard Beach incident in 1986, in which an African American man was killed after being chased by a mob of White youths, is often cited as evidence of this.[2] Thus, it may well be that hate crimes are more likely than nonbias crimes to elicit retaliatory crimes or revenge fantasies.

Conceptual Framework

Early work in sociology on the norm of reciprocity provides a framework for the present investigation (Gouldner, 1960). According to this approach, much of human behavior is governed in a quid pro quo manner: People respond to others in ways and to the degree that resembles that of the other person's initial response. More recent research has suggested that the recipient of a harmful act tends to respond to its provider with a harm that is comparable in both quantity and quality (Youngs, 1986). Thus, recipients of harm should feel a normative obligation to respond to harm similarly. In a study investigating the nature of conflict spirals, Youngs (1986) found that retaliatory exchanges did occur such that both perceived threats and punishments were reciprocated (although no measure of revenge fantasies were obtained). The present study examines the likelihood that members of a hate crime victim's category will engage in one form of negative reciprocity: expressed desire for revenge.

This study is based in part on the notion that the likelihood of retaliation by members of the hate crime victim's category is enhanced as a result of two distinguishing characteristics of hate crimes. First, members of the victim's category typically perceive the interchangeability dynamic of such crimes and, unlike the members of the nonbias crime victim's social group, are extremely likely to believe that "they could be next." Second, anger experienced by members of the victim's category is especially likely to be extreme because of the inherent unjustifiability of the instigating act. That is, the victims of the crime were victimized as a result of factors over which they had no control, but because of which they were singled out.

In the present study, I sought to determine whether observation of a racist hate crime encouraged greater expressed desire for retaliation than did observation of a nonbias crime for an observer who was a member of the victim's racial group. According to some (e.g., Brown, 1997), racist hate crimes are especially problematic because they create an atmosphere of suspicion, anger, and anomie. Indeed, in one study examining people's perceptions of hate crimes, perpetrators, and victims, participants regarded racist hate crimes as more extreme and problematic than nonbias crimes and nonracist hate crimes (Craig & Waldo, 1996).[3]

In the current study, African American and White males observed videotaped assaults in which the race of the perpetrators was systematically varied to reflect same-race assaults or assaults in which the perpetrators were of a different race than the victim.[4] Assaults in which the perpetrators were of a different race than the victim represented the hate crimes. The assault in which perpetrator and victim were of the same racial group was not a hate crime. Whether the hate-motivated assault was more likely than the other assault to elicit expressed desires for revenge by members of the victim's category was investigated. Furthermore, whether members of the hate crime victim's social group would express greater emotional distress following observation than did those who observed a general assault was also of interest and was investigated.

METHOD

Design and Overview

African American and White male participants each viewed, alone, two videotaped scenes in which the order of the scenes was systematically varied. In each of the two experimental scenes, participants observed two males assaulting a lone male who was always of the same race as the participant. In one of the experimental scenes, the perpetrators were the same race as the victim (and the participant), and in the other experimental scene, the perpetrators were a different race than the victim (and the participant). After observation of each of the videotaped scenes, participants' reactions were obtained.

Participants

Twenty-four African American and 49 White males from an introductory psychology course at a large Midwestern university participated in partial fulfillment of a course requirement. Participants were between the ages of 18 and 24 and were conducted through the procedure one at a time.

Materials

The videotaped scenes observed by participants were performed and recorded for the purpose of the present study and each lasted 3 minutes. Participants observed five scenes, of which the third and last constituted the experimental manipulation, and the order of their presentation was counterbalanced. The two experimental scenes were embedded in three control scenes in an effort to reduce the demand characteristics of the experiment. In Scene 1, all participants viewed a street in town that was presumably shot from the window of a moving automobile. There was an accompanying audio track in which the sounds of traffic as well as some dialogue were detectable although unremarkable. In Scene 2, all participants observed passers-by walking to and from a large open area on campus. Again, the accompanying audio track revealed small exchanges of unremarkable conversation. In Scene 4, participants viewed two kittens playing with toys. In Scenes 3 and 5, all participants observed a physical assault by two males on one male, who was chased and later escaped. The settings in the two scenes were outdoors but different. The actors in the scene could be heard taunting the victim, who screamed at times during the attack. Although the race of the perpetrators was varied in the two experimental scenes,

the victim was always of the same race as the participant. For the scene in which the perpetrators were of a different race than the victim, they were overheard making racially provocative remarks (i.e., they did not use racist epithets but when the victim was an African American, referred to him as "boy" and when White referred to him as "punk White boy"). When the victim was of the same race as the perpetrators he was called "stupid." Before the experiment was conducted, the videotaped scenes were shown to three "blind" research assistants who identified the scene in which the perpetrators were a different race than the victim as a hate crime and did not do so for the scene in which they were of the same racial status as the victim.

Procedure

On arrival at the experimental suite, participants were greeted by a female experimenter who was of Asian descent. Thus, any potential experimenter effects resulting from shared racial status with the participant or actors was eliminated. Consent to participate was then obtained from each of the participants and they were led into the viewing room. Participants were led to believe that the purpose of the study was to investigate differences in recall for a variety of different types of visual stimuli. It was explained that because participants would be asked to view a total of five different stimulus events recorded on videotape, it would be necessary to obtain their responses to a questionnaire at five different times during the procedure. After answering any questions, the experimenter seated the participant directly in front of a 19-inch color monitor and turned on the VCR. She instructed the participant to watch carefully, turned on the recorder, and stepped out of the participant's line of sight. When each scene ended, the experimenter immediately shut off the video recorder and provided the participant with a one-page questionnaire containing 13 to 15 items.

Following each scene, in an open-ended response format, participants indicated the content of the scene they had just observed. The next item required participants to rate on a 7-point scale, where 1 = *not likely* and 7 = *very likely,* the likelihood that they would find themselves in such a situation. Additional items assessed participants' recall for details in the scenes as well as their perceptions of the likelihood that such events could occur. For the experimental scenes, the questionnaire also included items that assessed the likelihood that participants in a similar situation would have fought back, would want revenge, would have called for help, and would have returned to the scene with friends at a later date, each on the 7-point scale. Each of these options represents a possible response to hate crime victimization that is consistent with the testimonies of real-life victims (see Herek & Berrill, 1992, for survivors' stories). This was followed by two items that required participants to circle the response that applied regarding what the victim should have done during the attack and following the attack. Response options to the first item were: fight back, run for help, contact the police, lie down and pretend to be unconscious, and holler loudly for help. Options to the second included: report incident to the police station, avoid coming down that street again, report incident to the local newspaper, contact a social service agency, and return to the scene later with friends to look for assailants. Respondents selected one response to each item. These judgments about the videotaped events made up the primary dependent variable.

Finally, all questionnaires also contained seven mood adjectives on a 7-point scale that assessed the extent to which the participant found the scene to be boring, interesting, and pleasant, and whether they felt excited, pleased, anxious, or irritated following observation. These items were included to determine the extent to which the hate-motivated, non-hate-motivated, and control scenes would be perceived as such among participants, and whether participants would express increased distress following observation of a hate-motivated attack on a member of their racial group.

Following completion of the one-page questionnaire after the final scene, the experimenter told the participant that the primary experiment was complete. All participants were extensively debriefed, thanked for their participation, and dismissed.

RESULTS

Before examining whether the experimental videotaped scenes elicited different emotional

responses from participants, content analysis of responses to the open-ended item that assessed participants' identification and recall of what occurred in each of the scenes was first conducted. In the case of the two experimental scenes, all participants indicated that they had observed a fight or an assault. Furthermore, all participants correctly identified the content of the three nonexperimental scenes.

Emotional Responses

Whether the three different types of videotaped scenes (hate-motivated assault, assault not motivated by hate, and control) elicited different emotional responses from participants was first examined. Analysis of the seven items that assessed reactions to and feelings about each of the scenes was carried out in three separate repeated-measures MANOVAs where responses to the video containing the hate-motivated assault were compared with the control videos, responses to the video containing the nonbias assault were compared with the control videos, and responses to the hate crime assault were compared with the nonbias assault. Separate MANOVAs were conducted as a result of sample size limitations. Results for each are reported below.

The repeated measures MANOVA comparing the scene containing the assault motivated by hate to the average of the responses to the control scenes was significant, $F(7, 65) = 41.5$, $p < .0001$. Significant univariate effects (all $ps < .0001$) were observed for each of the items, such that participants indicated that the control scenes were more boring ($M = 5.41$), less interesting ($M = 2.67$), and more pleasant ($M = 3.89$) than the hate-motivated assault scene ($M = 2.51$, $M = 5.06$, $M = 2.42$, respectively). Participants also reported feeling more excited ($M = 4.22$ vs. $M = 2.13$), less pleased ($M = 2.36$ vs. $M = 3.11$), more anxious ($M = 3.54$ vs. $M = 2.09$), and more irritated ($M = 4.36$ vs. $M = 2.77$) following observation of the hate-motivated assault than they did after viewing the control scenes.

The repeated measures MANOVA that compared the assault that was not motivated by hate to the average of the responses to the control scenes was also significant, $F(7, 63) = 36.5$, $p < .0001$. Significant univariate effects (all $ps < .001$) were observed for each of the items such that participants indicated that the control scenes were more boring ($M = 5.44$), less interesting ($M = 2.64$), and more pleasant ($M = 3.90$) than the nonbias assault scene ($M = 2.67$, $M = 4.94$, $M = 2.51$, respectively). Participants also reported feeling more excited ($M = 4.03$ vs. $M = 2.09$), less pleased ($M = 2.52$ vs. $M = 3.11$), more anxious ($M = 3.37$ vs. $M = 2.09$), and more irritated ($M = 3.95$ vs. $M = 2.77$) following observation of the nonbias assault than they did after viewing the control scenes. The repeated measures MANOVA that compared responses on these items for the hate-motivated assault and the nonbias assault was not significant. Furthermore, neither the multivariate effects of participant race or any of the interaction effects were significant. Thus, although reactions to the experimental scenes were significantly different than reactions to the control scenes, participants did not report different emotional responses to the two types of assaults, and reported emotions were similar for African American and White participants.

Judgments of Stimulus Events

Although the initial repeated measures MANOVA that compared participants' judgments of the nonbias assault with judgments about the hate-motivated assault did not reveal systematic differences in judgments about the assaults, subsequent analyses that took account of participant race revealed significant findings. When separate MANOVAs were conducted for the nonbias assault and hate-motivated assaults, including participant race as a factor, only the analysis of the hate-motivated assault resulted in significant differences between African American and White participants. The multivariate effect of race was significant, $F(6, 67) = 3.00$, $p < .05$, and significant univariate effects were observed for three of the event judgments. African American participants ($M = 2.68$) indicated that the observed hate-motivated assault was more likely to occur than did White participants ($M = 2.06$), $F(1, 72) = 3.99$, $p < .05$. African Americans also indicated that the observed assault was more typical ($M = 3.80$ vs. $M = 2.67$), $F(1, 72) = 9.77$, $p < .01$, and that they would be more likely to return to the scene later with friends ($M = 5.04$ vs. $M = 4.02$), $F(1, 72) =$

4.00, $p < .05$. There were no differences associated with racial status in participants' judgments about the nonbias assaults.

Responses to the two event judgments—What should the victim have done during the attack? and What should the victim do after the attack?—were obtained in a closed format such that participants were instructed to circle the response option that applied. Responses were treated as 0, 1 data and were coded such that *1* indicated the participant's judgment that the victim should engage in that behavior and *0* indicated that he shouldn't.

Neither of the chi-square tests of association that examined whether the type of assault viewed (hate crime versus not hate-motivated) was associated with participants' judgments about what the victim should have done during and following the attack was significant. However, when participants' responses to these items were analyzed as a function of their racial status, significant differences emerged, $\chi^2(5, N = 49) = 20.00$, $p < .001$. These differences occurred only for responses of White participants to the item, What should the victim have done during the attack? Although 20% of White participants indicated that the victim should have fought back following observation of a nonbias (i.e., same race) attack, only 2% selected this option when the perpetrators were African Americans. Furthermore, greater proportions of White participants indicated that the victim should have fled (27% vs. 6%), called the police (4% vs. 2%), and pretended to be unconscious (6% vs. 0%) when the assault was perceived to be a hate crime (i.e., the perpetrators were African Americans) than when it was not. Interestingly, although 12% of participants who viewed a nonbias attack indicated that the victim should have screamed, only 8% did so in response to the hate crime.

DISCUSSION

What is perhaps especially noteworthy about the results of this study concerns participants' almost identical reactions to both the hate-motivated assault and the assault that was not motivated by hate, that is, the general assault. Participants expressed similar emotional reactions to the two assaults and their responses indicated that they found both assaults to be arousing and unpleasant. Participants' responses also indicated an overall negative affective state (e.g., they were less pleased, more irritated, and more anxious) following both assault scenes that was greater than their average reaction to the control scenes.

Results of the analysis comparing participants' judgments of the two assault scenes also failed to reveal differences in response patterns. Participants judged the likelihood and typicality of the two types of assaults similarly, and selected similar proscriptions and recommendations for the victims in both cases. Only when the race of the participant was taken into account did differences in event judgments appear, and those differences were limited to the hate-motivated assault.

African American participants regarded the racially motivated assault as more likely to occur and more typical than did White participants. They were also more likely to express desire for revenge, given that they more frequently indicated that were they in a similar situation, they would return to the scene later with friends.[5] That African Americans regarded a racist hate crime in which an African American was the victim as likely and typical may reflect the extent to which members of this racial group are statistically more likely to be victims of a racist hate crime than are Whites, as well as historical circumstances.

There were also differences among participants in their proscriptions for victim responses during the attack. When White participants viewed the hate crime, they more frequently suggested that the victim respond passively either by running away or pretending to be hurt and not fighting back. In contrast, when the perpetrators were the same race as the victim and as themselves, they were no more likely to suggest one type of response over another. What accounts for these differences in White participants' proscriptions for victim responses?

Although it is difficult to do more than speculate because participants were not asked to provide reasons for their responses, these differences may reflect Whites' inherent beliefs about the relative danger associated with interracial and intrarracial violent interactions. These beliefs are associated with contemporary patterns of interaction between African Americans

and Whites, as well as cultural stereotypes about African Americans. With respect to the former, some researchers have noted an increased militancy in African Americans' responses to Whites in simulated interracial interactions (Wilson & Rogers, 1975). Furthermore, results of the General Social Survey (GSS) reveal that many White Americans believe that African Americans are more violent than are Whites (Smith, 1990). To the extent that this is true, White proscriptions for victim reactions such as the ones obtained in the present study are not surprising.

As with any laboratory study that has potential applications to real-world circumstances, the ecological validity of the present study may have been compromised. Whether observation of a videotaped assault observed in a psychology experiment has the same impact on viewers as does a real-world event is questionable. However, it should be noted that most individuals become aware of such events today as a result of viewing a 2- to 3-minute videotaped excerpt from the news. For example, the Rodney King beating, which probably represents the most notorious racist hate crime in recent years, was initially filmed by an amateur film maker on a home video (Jacobs, 1996). African American viewers' reactions surveyed following this event were consistent with the results obtained in the present study—although angered, few expressed surprise.

Implications for Hate Crime Sentencing

When participants in the present study observed the hate crime, they did not report more negative emotional reactions than when viewing the assault that was not motivated by racial hatred. However, differences did occur in the judgments about the events that were associated with differences in the cognitive appraisals of the events. Cognitive appraisals represent the complex evaluations individuals arrive at following an event. Given this, policy makers may wish to focus discussions on the cognitive appraisals surrounding these types of events rather than on emotional reactions. In this study, participants' cognitive appraisals of the assaults differed according to whether it was perceived as a hate crime or not. These appraisals affected the likelihood that they regarded the event as likely, expressed a desire for revenge, and chose to fight back, among other things.

At least part of the rationale for sentencing in hate crime cases is based on legislative intuition about the likelihood that members of hate crime victims' groups will want and seek revenge. The present findings reveal that, among African Americans (who some contend are the most frequent victims of racist hate crimes) (Sanchez & Castenda, 1994), retaliation may appear to be an especially practical option. Therefore, policy makers are accurate in their conceptualization of hate crimes as especially heinous and egregious because, for at least some populations, they are likely to provoke retaliation. Future research is necessary to examine the generalizability of the current laboratory findings to real-world settings.

NOTES

1. A related issue here is the extent to which victims and members of victims' groups are in agreement with perpetrators' perceptions of their group membership. Although the present discussion focuses on the affective experiences of hate crime victims, it is recognized that victim's group identification is an important factor in predicting victim responses.

2. Interestingly, in the case of racist hate crimes, Garofalo (1991) presents evidence of reciprocity between African American and White perpetrators and victims. That is, there may be a greater willingness for revenge between these two groups than among other groups.

3. According to some law enforcement personnel, although racist hate crimes are disproportionately directed at members of racial minority groups, in some instances, minority group members are perpetrators of hate crimes (Levin & McDevitt, 1993; Massachusetts Executive Office of Public Safety, 1990). Indeed, African Americans have the dubious distinction of being the only group of people who are categorized in significant numbers as both victims and perpetrators of hate crimes (as cited in Brown, 1997).

4. It is acknowledged that there are problems with using racial classification systems. These problems concern the fact there are more within-group differences than between-group differences in the characteristics used to define racial groups (Zuckerman, 1990). Thus, I am in agreement with many social scientists who contend that race is not a scientific category. As such, race represents a social construct that continues to demarcate patterns of social interaction.

5. At the end of the procedure, participants completed a number of personality inventories for use in an unrelated study and among them was the Vengeance Scale (Stuckless & Goranson, 1992). Analysis of participant responses revealed no significant differences between African Americans ($M = 69.92$, $SD = 26.59$) and Whites ($M = 73.84$, $SD = 23.21$), and Whites generally scored higher.

REFERENCES

Anti-Defamation League. (1994). *Hate crime laws: A comprehensive guide.* New York: Author.

Anti-Defamation League of B'nai B'rith. (1994). *Audit of anti-Semitic incidents.* New York: Author.

Berk, R. (1990). Thinking about hate-motivated crimes. *Journal of Interpersonal Violence, 5,* 334–349.

Brown, T. (1997). Hate crimes, stress, and bigotry in the late twentieth century: Where are we headed? *African American Research Perspectives, 3*(1), 21–29.

Center for the Study of Ethnic and Racial Violence. (1993). Unpublished manuscript. Edgewater, CA: Author.

Craig, K. M., & Waldo, C. (1996). "So, what's a hate crime anyway?" Young adults' perceptions of hate crimes, victims, and perpetrators. *Law and Human Behavior, 20,* 113–129.

Finn, P., & McNeil, T. (1987). *The response of the criminal justice system to bias crime: An exploratory review* (Contract Report submitted to the National Institute of Justice, U.S. Department of Justice). Available from ABT Associates, Inc., 55 Wheeler St., Cambridge, MA 02138-1168.

Garofalo, J. (1991). Racially motivated crimes in New York City. In M. J. Lynch & E. B. Patterson (Eds.), *Race and criminal justice* (pp. 161–173). Albany, NY: Harrow & Heston.

Gellman, S. (1991). Sticks and stones can put you in jail, but can words increase your sentence? Constitutional and policy dilemmas of ethnic intimidation laws. *UCLA Law Review, 39,* 333–396.

Gerstenfeld, P. B. (1992). Smile when you call me that: The problems with punishing hate-motivated behavior. *Behavioral Sciences and the Law, 10,* 259–285.

Gouldner, A. W. (1960). The norm of reciprocity: A preliminary statement. *American Sociological Review, 25,* 161–178.

Hate Crime Statistics Act. (1990). Pub. L. No. 101–275, 104 Stat. 140 (codified as amended 28 U.S.C.A. § 534 [West, 1993]).

Herek, G. M., & Berrill, K. T. (1992). *Hate crimes: Confronting violence against lesbians and gay men.* Newbury Park, CA: Sage.

Herek, G. M., Gillis, J. R., Cogan, J. C., & Glunt, E. K. (1997). Hate crime victimization among lesbian, gay, and bisexual adults: Prevalence, psychological correlates, and methodological issues. *Journal of Interpersonal Violence, 12,* 195–215.

Jacobs, R. N. (1996). Civil society and crisis: Culture, discourse, and the Rodney King beating. *The American Journal of Sociology, 101,* 1238.

Langer, E. (1993). The American neo-Nazi movement. In D. Gioseffi (Ed.), *On prejudice. A global perspective.* New York: Doubleday.

Levin, J., & McDevitt, J. (1993). *Hate crimes. The rising tide of bigotry and bloodshed.* New York: Plenum.

Massachusetts Executive Office of Public Safety. (1990). *Hate crime in Massachusetts preliminary annual report: January-December 1990.* Boston: Executive Office of Public Safety and Criminal History Board, Crime Reporting Unit.

National Gay and Lesbian Task Force. (1994). *Anti-gay/lesbian violence, victimization and defamation in 1993.* Washington, DC: National Gay and Lesbian Task Force Policy Institute.

Norris, F., Kaniasty, K., & Scheer, D. (1990). Use of mental health services among victims of crime: Frequency, correlates, and subsequent recovery. *Journal of Consulting and Clinical Psychology, 58,* 538–547.

Pinkney, A. (1994). *Lest we forget. . . . White hate crimes.* Chicago, IL: Third World Press.

Sanchez, S., & Castenda, C. J. (1994). Hate-crime report: Blacks targeted most. *USA Today* (Nationline).

Smith, T. W. (1990). *Ethnic images* (Topical Report No. 19). Chicago: National Opinion Research Center.

Southern Poverty Law Center. (1994). *Klanwatch intelligence report.* Montgomery, AL: Author.

Stuckless, N., & Goranson, R. (1992). The vengeance scale: Development of a measure of attitudes towards revenge. *Journal of Social Behavior and Personality, 7,* 25–42.

Thompson, M. P., & Norris, F. H. (1992). Crime, social status, and alienation. *American Journal of Community Psychology, 20,* 97–119.

Weinstein, J. (1992). First amendment challenges to hate crime legislation: Where's the speech? *Criminal Justice Ethics, 11*(6), 10.

Weisburd, S., & Levin, B. (1994, Spring). On the basis of sex. *Stanford Law and Policy Review,* pp. 21–47.

Wilson, L., & Rogers, R. W. (1975). The fire this time: Effects of race of target, insult, and potential retaliation on black aggression. *Journal of Personality and Social Psychology, 32,* 857–864.

Wisconsin v. Mitchell, 113 S. Ct. 2194 (1993).

Youngs, G. A. (1986). Patterns of threat and punishment reciprocity in a conflict setting. *Journal of Personality and Social Psychology, 51,* 541–546.

Zuckerman, M. (1990). Some dubious premises in research and theory on racial differences: Scientific, social, and ethical issues. *American Psychologist, 45,* 1297–1303.

QUESTIONS

1. Can you think of circumstances which may *decrease* the likelihood of retaliation in response to hate crimes? What factors might conceivably *increase* the likelihood of retaliation?

2. Why do the "victim interchangeability" and inherent unjustifiability of hate crimes suggest that these crimes may be especially likely to provoke retaliation?

3. Can you think of circumstances under which hate crimes could potentially result in increased cohesion among community members? For example, in one instance, scores of town residents of varying religions responded to an anti-Semitic hate crime by placing menorahs (Jewish religious symbols) prominently in their windows to demonstrate their rejection of such crimes.

4. When interracial assaults occur, should they always be considered hate crimes? Why or why not? If not, how would one distinguish between assaults that were hate crimes and those that were not?

5. Should society, through legislation on hate crimes, convey strong symbolic condemnation of particular crimes as a way to strengthen the social fabric?

6. How persuasive are the conclusions this article presents regarding the likelihood of retaliation in response to hate crimes?

7. What are the methodological limitations of this study?

8. If hate crimes are especially likely to provoke retaliation, is this a factor that would support enhanced penalties for hate crimes?

5

R. A. V. v. City
of St. Paul, Minnesota

United States Supreme Court
505 U.S. 377 (1992)

This case illustrates the importance of the wording used in statutes defining and penalizing hate crimes. At issue in R. A. V. was the distinction between expressive behavior protected by the First Amendment and actions outside the scope of such protection that can be regulated via statutory prohibitions and penalties.

Justice Scalia Delivered
the Opinion of the Court

In the predawn hours of June 21, 1990, petitioner and several other teenagers allegedly assembled a crudely made cross by taping together broken chair legs. They then allegedly burned the cross inside the fenced yard of a black family that lived across the street from the house where petitioner was staying. Although this conduct could have been punished under any of a number of laws, one of the two provisions under which respondent city of St. Paul chose to charge petitioner (then a juvenile) was the St. Paul Bias-Motivated Crime Ordinance, St. Paul, Minn., Legis. Code § 292.02 (1990), which provides: "Whoever places on public or private property a symbol, object, appellation, characterization or graffiti, including, but not limited to, a burning cross or Nazi swastika, which one knows or has reasonable grounds to know arouses anger, alarm or resentment in others on the basis of race, color,

creed, religion or gender commits disorderly conduct and shall be guilty of a misdemeanor."

Petitioner moved to dismiss this count on the ground that the St. Paul ordinance was substantially overbroad and impermissibly content based and therefore facially invalid under the First Amendment. The trial court granted this motion, but the Minnesota Supreme Court reversed. That court rejected petitioner's overbreadth claim because, as construed in prior Minnesota, the modifying phrase "arouses anger, alarm or resentment in others" limited the reach of the ordinance to conduct that amounts to "fighting words," i.e., "conduct that itself inflicts injury or tends to incite immediate violence . . . ," and therefore the ordinance reached only expression "that the first amendment does not protect." The court also concluded that the ordinance was not impermissibly content based because, in its view, "the ordinance is a narrowly tailored means toward accomplishing the compelling governmental interest in protecting the community against bias-motivated threats to public safety and order."

In construing the St. Paul ordinance, we are bound by the construction given to it by the Minnesota court. Accordingly, we accept the Minnesota Supreme Court's authoritative statement that the ordinance reaches only those expressions that constitute "fighting words" within the meaning of *Chaplinsky*. Petitioner and his amici urge us to modify the scope of the Chaplinsky formulation, thereby invalidating the ordinance as "substantially overbroad." We find it unnecessary to consider this issue. Assuming, arguendo, that all of the expression reached by the ordinance is proscribable under the "fighting words" doctrine, we nonetheless conclude that the ordinance is facially unconstitutional in that it prohibits otherwise permitted speech solely on the basis of the subjects the speech addresses.

The First Amendment generally prevents government from proscribing speech, or even expressive conduct because of disapproval of the ideas expressed. Content-based regulations are presumptively invalid. From 1791 to the present, however, our society, like other free but civilized societies, has permitted restrictions upon the content of speech in a few limited areas, which are "of such slight social value as a step to truth that any benefit that may be derived from them is clearly outweighed by the social interest in order and morality." We have recognized that "the freedom of speech" referred to by the First Amendment does not include a freedom to disregard these traditional limitations. Our decisions since the 1960's have narrowed the scope of the traditional categorical exceptions for defamation, but a limited categorical approach has remained an important part of our First Amendment jurisprudence.

We have sometimes said that these categories of expression are "not within the area of constitutionally protected speech," or that the "protection of the First Amendment does not extend" to them. Such statements must be taken in context, however, and are no more literally true than is the occasionally repeated shorthand characterizing obscenity "as not being speech at all." What they mean is that these areas of speech can, consistently with the First Amendment, be regulated because of their constitutionally proscribable content (obscenity, defamation, etc.)—not that they are categories of speech entirely invisible to the Constitution, so that they may be made the

vehicles for content discrimination unrelated to their distinctively proscribable content. Thus, the government may proscribe libel; but it may not make the further content discrimination of proscribing only libel critical of the government. We recently acknowledged this distinction in *Ferber*, where, in upholding New York's child pornography law, we expressly recognized that there was no "question here of censoring a particular literary theme. . . ."

Our cases surely do not establish the proposition that the First Amendment imposes no obstacle whatsoever to regulation of particular instances of such proscribable expression, so that the government "may regulate [them] freely." That would mean that a city council could enact an ordinance prohibiting only those legally obscene works that contain criticism of the city government or, indeed, that do not include endorsement of the city government. Such a simplistic, all-or-nothing-at-all approach to First Amendment protection is at odds with common sense and with our jurisprudence as well. It is not true that "fighting words" have at most a "de minimis" expressive content, or that their content is in all respects "worthless and undeserving of constitutional protection;" sometimes they are quite expressive indeed. We have not said that they constitute "no part of the expression of ideas," but only that they constitute "no essential part of any exposition of ideas."

The proposition that a particular instance of speech can be proscribable on the basis of one feature (e.g., obscenity) but not on the basis of another (e.g., opposition to the city government) is commonplace and has found application in many contexts. We have long held, for example, that nonverbal expressive activity can be banned because of the action it entails, but not because of the ideas it expresses—so that burning a flag in violation of an ordinance against outdoor fires could be punishable, whereas burning a flag in violation of an ordinance against dishonoring the flag is not. Similarly, we have upheld reasonable "time, place, or manner" restrictions, but only if they are "justified without reference to the content of the regulated speech." And just as the power to proscribe particular speech on the basis of a noncontent element (e.g., noise) does not entail the power to proscribe the same speech on the basis of a content element; so also, the power to proscribe it on the basis of one content element (e.g., obscenity) does not entail the power to proscribe it on the basis of other content elements.

In other words, the exclusion of "fighting words" from the scope of the First Amendment simply means that, for purposes of that Amendment, the unprotected features of the words are, despite their verbal character, essentially a "nonspeech" element of communication. Fighting words are thus analogous to a noisy sound truck: Each is, as Justice Frankfurter recognized, a "mode of speech;" both can be used to convey an idea; but neither has, in and of itself, a claim upon the First Amendment. As with the sound truck, however, so also with fighting words: The government may not regulate use based on hostility—or favoritism—towards the underlying message expressed.

The concurrences describe us as setting forth a new First Amendment principle that prohibition of constitutionally proscribable speech cannot be "underinclusive"—a First Amendment "absolutism" whereby "within a particular 'proscribable' category of expression, . . . a government must either proscribe all speech or no speech at all. That easy target is of the concurrences' own invention. In our view, the First Amendment imposes not an "underinclusiveness" limitation but a "content discrimination" limitation upon a State's prohibition of proscribable speech. There is no problem whatever, for example, with a State's prohibiting obscenity (and other forms of proscribable expression) only in certain media or markets, for although that prohibition would be "underinclusive," it would not discriminate on the basis of content.

Even the prohibition against content discrimination that we assert the First Amendment requires is not absolute. It applies differently in the context of proscribable speech than in the area of fully protected speech. The rationale of the general prohibition, after all, is that content discrimination "raises the specter that the Government may effectively drive certain ideas or viewpoints from the marketplace." But content discrimination among various instances of a class of proscribable speech often does not pose this threat.

When the basis for the content discrimination consists entirely of the very reason the entire class of speech at issue is proscribable, no significant danger of idea or viewpoint discrimination exists. Such a reason, having been adjudged neutral enough to support exclusion of the entire class of speech from First Amendment protection, is also neutral enough to form the basis of distinction within the class. To illustrate:

A State might choose to prohibit only that obscenity which is the most patently offensive in its prurience—i.e., that which involves the most lascivious displays of sexual activity. But it may not prohibit, for example, only that obscenity which includes offensive political messages. And the Federal Government can criminalize only those threats of violence that are directed against the President—since the reasons why threats of violence are outside the First Amendment (protecting individuals from the fear of violence, from the disruption that fear engenders, and from the possibility that the threatened violence will occur) have special force when applied to the person of the President. But the Federal Government may not criminalize only those threats against the President that mention his policy on aid to inner cities. And to take a final example, a State may choose to regulate price advertising in one industry but not in others, because the risk of fraud (one of the characteristics of commercial speech that justifies depriving it of full First Amendment protection) is in its view greater there. But a State may not prohibit only that commercial advertising that depicts men in a demeaning fashion.

Another valid basis for according differential treatment to even a content-defined subclass of proscribable speech is that the subclass happens to be associated with particular "secondary effects" of the speech, so that the regulation is "justified without reference to the content of the . . . Speech." A State could, for example, permit all obscene live performances except those involving minors. Moreover, since words can in some circumstances violate laws directed not against speech but against conduct (a law against treason, for example, is violated by telling the enemy the Nation's defense secrets), a particular content-based subcategory of a proscribable class of speech can be swept up incidentally within the reach of a statute directed at conduct rather than speech. Thus, for example, sexually derogatory "fighting words," among other words, may produce a violation of Title VII's general prohibition against sexual discrimination in employment practices. Where the government does not target conduct on the basis of its expressive content, acts are not shielded from regulation merely because they express a discriminatory idea or philosophy.

These bases for distinction refute the proposition that the selectivity of the restriction is "even arguably 'conditioned upon the sovereign's agreement with what a speaker may intend to say.'" There may be other such bases as well. Indeed, to validate such selectivity (where totally proscribable speech is at issue) it may not even be necessary to identify any particular "neutral" basis, so long as the nature of the content discrimination is such that there is no realistic possibility that official suppression of ideas is afoot. (We cannot think of any First Amendment interest that would stand in the way of a State's prohibiting only those obscene motion pictures with blue-eyed actresses.) Save for that limitation, the regulation of "fighting words," like the regulation of noisy speech, may address some offensive instances and leave other, equally offensive, instances alone.

Applying these principles to the St. Paul ordinance, we conclude that, even as narrowly construed by the Minnesota Supreme Court, the ordinance is facially unconstitutional. Although the phrase in the ordinance, "arouses anger, alarm or resentment in others," has been limited by the Minnesota Supreme Court's construction to reach only those symbols or displays that amount to "fighting words," the remaining, unmodified terms make clear that the ordinance applies only to "fighting words" that insult, or provoke violence, "on the basis of race, color, creed, religion or gender." Displays containing abusive invective, no matter how vicious or severe, are permissible unless they are addressed to one of the specified disfavored topics. Those who wish to use "fighting words" in connection with other ideas—to express hostility, for example, on the basis of political affiliation, union membership, or homosexuality—are not covered. The First Amendment does not permit St. Paul to impose special prohibitions on those speakers who express views on disfavored subjects.

In its practical operation, moreover, the ordinance goes even beyond mere content discrimination, to actual viewpoint discrimination. Displays containing some words—odious racial epithets, for example—would be prohibited to proponents of all views. But "fighting words" that do not themselves invoke race, color, creed, religion, or gender aspersions upon a person's mother, for example—would seemingly be usable ad libitum in the placards of those arguing in favor of racial, color, etc., tolerance and equality, but could not be used by those speakers' opponents. One could hold up a sign saying, for example, that all "anti-Catholic bigots" are misbegotten; but not

that all "papists" are, for that would insult and provoke violence "on the basis of religion." St. Paul has no such authority to license one side of a debate to fight freestyle, while requiring the other to follow Marquis of Queensberry rules.

What we have here, it must be emphasized, is not a prohibition of fighting words that are directed at certain persons or groups (which would be facially valid if it met the requirements of the Equal Protection Clause); but rather, a prohibition of fighting words that contain (as the Minnesota Supreme Court repeatedly emphasized) messages of "bias motivated" hatred and in particular, as applied to this case, messages "based on virulent notions of racial supremacy." One must wholeheartedly agree with the Minnesota Supreme Court that "it is the responsibility, even the obligation, of diverse communities to confront such notions in whatever form they appear," but the manner of that confrontation cannot consist of selective limitations upon speech. St. Paul's brief asserts that a general "fighting words" law would not meet the city's needs because only a content-specific measure can communicate to minority groups that the "group hatred" aspect of such speech "is not condoned by the majority." The point of the First Amendment is that majority preferences must be expressed in some fashion other than silencing speech on the basis of its content.

Despite the fact that the Minnesota Supreme Court and St. Paul acknowledge that the ordinance is directed at expression of group hatred, Justice Stevens suggests that this "fundamentally misreads" the ordinance. It is directed, he claims, not to speech of a particular content, but to particular "injuries" that are "qualitatively different" from other injuries. This is wordplay. What makes the anger, fear, sense of dishonor, etc., produced by violation of this ordinance distinct from the anger, fear, sense of dishonor, etc., produced by other fighting words is nothing other than the fact that it is caused by a distinctive idea, conveyed by a distinctive message. The First Amendment cannot be evaded that easily. It is obvious that the symbols which will arouse "anger, alarm or resentment in others on the basis of race, color, creed, religion or gender" are those symbols that communicate a message of hostility based on one of these characteristics. St. Paul concedes in its brief that the ordinance applies only to "racial, religious, or gender-specific symbols" such as "a burning cross, Nazi swastika or other instrumentality of like import." Indeed, St. Paul argued in the Juvenile Court that "the burning of a cross does express a message and it is, in fact, the content of that message which the St. Paul Ordinance attempts to legislate."

The content-based discrimination reflected in the St. Paul ordinance comes within neither any of the specific exceptions to the First Amendment prohibition we discussed earlier nor a more general exception for content discrimination that does not threaten censorship of ideas. It assuredly does not fall within the exception for content discrimination based on the very reasons why the particular class of speech at issue (here, fighting words) is proscribable. As explained earlier, the reason why fighting words are categorically excluded from the protection of the First Amendment is not that their content communicates any particular idea, but that their content embodies a particularly intolerable (and socially unnecessary) mode of expressing whatever idea the speaker wishes to convey. St. Paul has not singled out an especially offensive mode of expression—it has not, for example, selected for prohibition only those fighting words that communicate ideas in a threatening (as opposed to a merely obnoxious) manner. Rather, it has proscribed fighting words of whatever manner that communicate messages of racial, gender, or religious intolerance. Selectivity of this sort creates the possibility that the city is seeking to handicap the expression of particular ideas. That possibility would alone be enough to render the ordinance presumptively invalid, but St. Paul's comments and concessions in this case elevate the possibility to a certainty.

St. Paul argues that the ordinance comes within another of the specific exceptions we mentioned, the one that allows content discrimination aimed only at the "secondary effects" of the speech. According to St. Paul, the ordinance is intended, "not to impact on [sic] the right of free expression of the accused," but rather to "protect against the victimization of a person or persons who are particularly vulnerable because of their membership in a group that historically has been discriminated against." Even assuming that an ordinance that completely proscribes, rather than merely regulates, a specified category of speech can ever be considered to be directed only to the secondary effects of such speech, it is clear that the St. Paul ordinance is not directed to secondary effects within the meaning of *Renton*. As we said in *Boos v. Barry*, "Listeners' reactions to speech

are not the type of 'secondary effects' we referred to in *Renton*." "The emotive impact of speech on its audience is not a 'secondary effect.'"

It hardly needs discussion that the ordinance does not fall within some more general exception permitting all selectivity that for any reason is beyond the suspicion of official suppression of ideas. The statements of St. Paul in this very case afford ample basis for, if not full confirmation of, that suspicion.

Finally, St. Paul and its amici defend the conclusion of the Minnesota Supreme Court that, even if the ordinance regulates expression based on hostility towards its protected ideological content, this discrimination is nonetheless justified because it is narrowly tailored to serve compelling state interests. Specifically, they assert that the ordinance helps to ensure the basic human rights of members of groups that have historically been subjected to discrimination, including the right of such group members to live in peace where they wish. We do not doubt that these interests are compelling, and that the ordinance can be said to promote them. But the "danger of censorship" presented by a facially content-based statute, requires that that weapon be employed only where it is "necessary to serve the asserted [compelling] interest." The existence of adequate content-neutral alternatives thus "undercuts significantly" any defense of such a statute, casting considerable doubt on the government's protestations that "the asserted justification is in fact an accurate description of the purpose and effect of the law." The dispositive question in this case, therefore, is whether content discrimination is reasonably necessary to achieve St. Paul's compelling interests; it plainly is not. An ordinance not limited to the favored topics, for example, would have precisely the same beneficial effect. In fact the only interest distinctively served by the content limitation is that of displaying the city council's special hostility towards the particular biases thus singled out. That is precisely what the First Amendment forbids. The politicians of St. Paul are entitled to express that hostility—but not through the means of imposing unique limitations upon speakers who (however benightedly) disagree.

Let there be no mistake about our belief that burning a cross in someone's front yard is reprehensible. But St. Paul has sufficient means at its disposal to prevent such behavior without adding the First Amendment to the fire.

The judgment of the Minnesota Supreme Court is reversed, and the case is remanded for proceedings not inconsistent with this opinion.

It is so ordered.

JUSTICE WHITE, CONCURRING (JOINED BY JUSTICES BLACKMUN, O'CONNOR, AND STEVENS)

I agree with the majority that the judgment of the Minnesota Supreme Court should be reversed. However, our agreement ends there.

This case could easily be decided within the contours of established First Amendment law by holding, as petitioner argues, that the St. Paul ordinance is fatally overbroad because it criminalizes not only unprotected expression but expression protected by the First Amendment. Instead, "finding it unnecessary" to consider the questions upon which we granted review, the Court holds the ordinance facially unconstitutional on a ground that was never presented to the Minnesota Supreme Court, a ground that has not been briefed by the parties before this Court, a ground that requires serious departures from the teaching of prior cases and is inconsistent with the plurality opinion in *Burson v. Freeman,* which was joined by two of the five Justices in the majority in the present case.

This Court ordinarily is not so eager to abandon its precedents. . . . But in the present case, the majority casts aside long-established First Amendment doctrine without the benefit of briefing and adopts an untried theory. This is hardly a judicious way of proceeding, and the Court's reasoning in reaching its result is transparently wrong. . . .

Today, the Court has disregarded two established principles of First Amendment law without providing a coherent replacement theory. Its decision is an arid, doctrinaire interpretation, driven by the frequently irresistible impulse of judges to tinker with the First Amendment. The decision is mischievous at best and will surely confuse the lower courts. I join the judgment, but not the folly of the opinion.

JUSTICE BLACKMUN, CONCURRING

I regret what the Court has done in this case. The majority opinion signals one of two possibilities: It will serve as precedent for future cases, or it will not. Either result is disheartening. . . .

I concur in the judgment, however, because I agree with Justice White that this particular ordinance reaches beyond fighting words to speech protected by the First Amendment.

[Justice Stevens also wrote a concurring opinion.]

QUESTIONS

1. The court's opinion in *R. A. V.* notes that "We have long held . . . that nonverbal expressive activity can be banned because of the action it entails, but not because of the ideas it expresses—so that burning a flag in violation of an ordinance against outdoor fires could be punishable, whereas burning a flag in violation of an ordinance against dishonoring the flag is not" (p. 68, this volume). How does this example help illustrate the court's distinction between actions and ideas? What are the implications of this distinction for hate crime legislation?

2. This case illustrates the idea that from a First Amendment perspective, "all content is not equal." Why is the nature of the content of a communication a key legal issue in this case?

3. What are some examples of "fighting words"? Are "fighting words" protected or not protected as free speech under the First Amendment? Why or why not?

4. If you were one of the Supreme Court justices, would you have upheld the St. Paul ordinance or not? Explain your reasoning.

5. How does this case illustrate the need to carefully define the legal basis for proposed hate crime statutes?

6. Why was the *mode* of expression of ideas a key to the decision in this case?

7. Do you agree with the court that the "emotive impact" of speech on the audience should not be a basis for prohibiting speech?

8. *R. A. V. v. City of St. Paul* illustrates some of the complexity of First Amendment jurisprudence. For example, clearly the First Amendment does not protect all expressive communications. What kinds of expression do not fall within the scope of First Amendment protection?

Part III

POLICY PROBLEMS

How do we create laws that define what constitutes a hate crime? The definition of *hate crime* involves complex legal and ethical questions about what circumstances should be taken into account in defining whether something is a hate crime and which categories of people should be included in the legal designation of hate crime victim. Similarly, how can we design policies to facilitate law enforcement recognition and reporting of hate crimes? This section discusses the complex public policy issues raised by such questions and demonstrates that the creation and implementation of public policies on hate crimes reflect the influence of political and practical considerations as much as strictly legal considerations.

6

WISCONSIN v. MITCHELL

United States Supreme Court
508 U.S. 476 (1993)

This case illustrates some of the key First Amendment issues raised by statutes providing enhanced penalties for hate crimes. As you read this case, consider how it compares to *R. A. V. v. St. Paul*. The free speech question raised in *Wisconsin v. Mitchell* is whether enhancing penalties for defendants convicted of hate crimes amounts to punishing defendants for their beliefs rather than for their actions. As you read, think about the reasoning the justices used in deciding that the defendant's First Amendment rights were not violated by Wisconsin's penalty enhancement law.

JUSTICE REHNQUIST,
WRITING FOR A UNANIMOUS COURT

Respondent Todd Mitchell's sentence for aggravated battery was enhanced because he intentionally selected his victim on account of the victim's race. The question presented in this case is whether this penalty enhancement is prohibited by the First and Fourteenth Amendments. We hold that it is not.

On the evening of October 7, 1989, a group of young black men and boys, including Mitchell, gathered at an apartment complex in Kenosha, Wisconsin. Several members of the group discussed a scene from the motion picture "Mississippi Burning," in which a white man beat a young black boy who was praying. The group moved outside and Mitchell asked them: "'Do you all feel hyped up to move on some white people?'" Shortly thereafter, a young white boy approached the group on the opposite side of the street where they were standing. As the boy walked by, Mitchell said: "'You all want to fuck somebody up? There goes a white boy; go get him.'" Mitchell counted to three and pointed in the boy's direction. The group ran toward the boy, beat him severely, and stole his tennis shoes. The boy was rendered unconscious and remained in a coma for four days.

After a jury trial in the Circuit Court for Kenosha County, Mitchell was convicted of aggravated battery. That offense ordinarily carries a maximum sentence of two years' imprisonment. But because the jury found that Mitchell had intentionally selected his victim because of the boy's race, the maximum sentence for Mitchell's offense was increased to seven years under § 939.645. That provision enhances the maximum penalty for an offense whenever the defendant "intentionally selects the person against whom the crime . . . is committed . . . because of the race, religion, color, disability, sexual orientation, national origin or ancestry of that person. . . ." The Circuit Court sentenced Mitchell to four years' imprisonment for the aggravated battery.

Mitchell unsuccessfully sought postconviction relief in the Circuit Court. Then he appealed his conviction and sentence, challenging the constitutionality of Wisconsin's penalty-enhancement provision on First Amendment grounds. The Wisconsin Court of Appeals rejected Mitchell's challenge, but the Wisconsin Supreme Court reversed. The Supreme Court held that the statute "violates the First Amendment directly by punishing what the legislature has deemed to be offensive thought." It rejected the State's contention "that the statute punishes only the 'conduct' of intentional selection of a victim." According to the court, "the statute punishes the 'because of' aspect of the defendant's selection, the *reason* the defendant selected the victim, the *motive* behind the selection." And under *R. A. V.* v. *St. Paul,* "the Wisconsin legislature cannot criminalize bigoted thought with which it disagrees."

The Supreme Court also held that the penalty-enhancement statute was unconstitutionally overbroad. It reasoned that, in order to prove that a defendant intentionally selected his victim because of the victim's protected status, the State would often have to introduce evidence of the defendant's prior speech, such as racial epithets he may have uttered before the commission of the offense. This evidentiary use of protected speech, the court thought, would have a "chilling effect" on those who feared the possibility of prosecution for offenses subject to penalty enhancement. Finally, the court distinguished antidiscrimination laws, which have long been held constitutional, on the ground that the Wisconsin statute punishes the "subjective mental process" of selecting a victim because of his protected status, whereas antidiscrimination laws prohibit "objective acts of discrimination."

We granted certiorari because of the importance of the question presented and the existence of a conflict of authority among state high courts on the constitutionality of statutes similar to Wisconsin's penalty-enhancement provision. We reverse.

Mitchell argues that we are bound by the Wisconsin Supreme Court's conclusion that the statute punishes bigoted thought and not conduct. There is no doubt that we are bound by a state court's construction of a state statute. In *Terminiello,* for example, the Illinois courts had defined the term "'breach of the peace,'" in a city ordinance prohibiting disorderly conduct, to include "'stirs the public to anger . . . or creates a disturbance.'" We held this construction to be binding on us. But here the Wisconsin Supreme Court did not, strictly speaking, construe the Wisconsin statute in the sense of defining the meaning of a particular statutory word or phrase. Rather, it merely characterized the "practical effect" of the statute for First Amendment purposes ("Merely because the statute refers in a literal sense to the intentional 'conduct' of selecting, does not mean the court must turn a blind eye to the intent and practical effect of the law—punishment of motive or thought"). This assessment does not bind us. Once any ambiguities as to the meaning of the statute are resolved, we may form our own judgment as to its operative effect.

The State argues that the statute does not punish bigoted thought, as the Supreme Court of Wisconsin said, but instead punishes only conduct. While this argument is literally correct, it does not dispose of Mitchell's First Amendment challenge. To be sure, our cases reject the "view that an apparently limitless variety of conduct can be labeled 'speech' whenever the person engaging in the conduct intends thereby to express an idea." Thus, a physical assault is not by any stretch of the imagination expressive conduct protected by the First Amendment.

But the fact remains that under the Wisconsin statute the same criminal conduct may be more heavily punished if the victim is selected because of his race or other protected status than if no such motive obtained. Thus, although the statute punishes criminal conduct, it enhances the maximum penalty for conduct motivated by a discriminatory point of view more severely than the same conduct engaged in for some other reason or for no reason at all. Because the only reason for the enhancement is the defendant's discriminatory motive for selecting his victim, Mitchell argues (and the Wisconsin Supreme Court held) that the statute violates the First Amendment by punishing offenders' bigoted beliefs.

Traditionally, sentencing judges have considered a wide variety of factors in addition to evidence bearing on guilt in determining what sentence to impose on a convicted defendant. The defendant's motive for committing the offense is one important factor. Thus, in many States the commission of a murder, or other capital offense, for pecuniary gain is a separate aggravating circumstance under the capital sentencing statute.

But it is equally true that a defendant's abstract beliefs, however obnoxious to most people, may not be taken into consideration by a sentencing judge. In *Dawson,* the State introduced evidence at a capital sentencing hearing that the defendant was a member of a white supremacist prison gang. Because "the evidence proved nothing more than [the defendant's] abstract beliefs," we held that its admission violated the defendant's First Amendment rights. In so holding, however, we emphasized that "the Constitution does not erect a *per se* barrier to the admission of evidence concerning one's beliefs and associations at sentencing simply because those beliefs and associations are protected by the First Amendment." Thus, in *Barclay* v. *Florida,* we allowed the sentencing judge to take into account the defendant's racial animus towards his victim. The evidence in that case showed that the defendant's membership in the Black Liberation Army and desire to provoke a "race war" were related to the murder of a white man for which he was convicted. Because "the elements of racial hatred in [the] murder" were relevant to several aggravating factors, we held that the trial judge permissibly took this evidence into account in sentencing the defendant to death.

Mitchell suggests that *Dawson* and *Barclay* are inapposite because they did not involve application of a penalty-enhancement provision. But in *Barclay* we held that it was permissible for the sentencing court to consider the defendant's racial animus in determining whether he should be sentenced to death, surely the most severe "enhancement" of all. And the fact that the Wisconsin Legislature has decided, as a general matter, that bias-motivated offenses warrant greater maximum penalties across the board does not alter the result here. For the primary responsibility for fixing criminal penalties lies with the legislature.

Mitchell argues that the Wisconsin penalty-enhancement statute is invalid because it punishes the defendant's discriminatory motive, or

reason, for acting. But motive plays the same role under the Wisconsin statute as it does under federal and state antidiscrimination laws, which we have previously upheld against constitutional challenge. Title VII of the Civil Rights Act of 1964, for example, makes it unlawful for an employer to discriminate against an employee "*because of* such individual's race, color, religion, sex, or national origin." In *Hishon,* we rejected the argument that Title VII infringed employers' First Amendment rights. And more recently, in *R. A. V.* v. *St. Paul,* we cited Title VII (as well as 18 U.S.C. § 242 and 42 U.S.C. §§ 1981 and 1982) as an example of a permissible content-neutral regulation of conduct.

Nothing in our decision last Term in *R. A. V.* compels a different result here. That case involved a First Amendment challenge to a municipal ordinance prohibiting the use of "'fighting words' that insult, or provoke violence, 'on the basis of race, color, creed, religion or gender.'" Because the ordinance only proscribed a class of "fighting words" deemed particularly offensive by the city—*i.e.,* those "that contain . . . messages of 'bias-motivated' hatred," we held that it violated the rule against content-based discrimination. But whereas the ordinance struck down in *R. A. V.* was explicitly directed at expression (*i.e.,* "speech" or "messages"), the statute in this case is aimed at conduct unprotected by the First Amendment.

Moreover, the Wisconsin statute singles out for enhancement bias-inspired conduct because this conduct is thought to inflict greater individual and societal harm. For example, according to the State and its *amici,* bias-motivated crimes are more likely to provoke retaliatory crimes, inflict distinct emotional harms on their victims, and incite community unrest. The State's desire to redress these perceived harms provides an adequate explanation for its penalty-enhancement provision over and above mere disagreement with offenders' beliefs or biases. As Blackstone said long ago, "it is but reasonable that among crimes of different natures those should be most severely punished, which are the most destructive of the public safety and happiness.

Finally, there remains to be considered Mitchell's argument that the Wisconsin statute is unconstitutionally overbroad because of its "chilling effect" on free speech. Mitchell argues (and the Wisconsin Supreme Court agreed) that the statute is "overbroad" because evidence of the defendant's prior speech or associations may be used to prove that the defendant intentionally selected his victim on account of the victim's protected status. Consequently, the argument goes, the statute impermissibly chills free expression with respect to such matters by those concerned about the possibility of enhanced sentences if they should in the future commit a criminal offense covered by the statute. We find no merit in this contention.

The sort of chill envisioned here is far more attenuated and unlikely than that contemplated in traditional "over-breadth" cases. We must conjure up a vision of a Wisconsin citizen suppressing his unpopular bigoted opinions for fear that if he later commits an offense covered by the statute, these opinions will be offered at trial to establish that he selected his victim on account of the victim's protected status, thus qualifying him for penalty enhancement. To stay within the realm of rationality, we must surely put to one side minor misdemeanor offenses covered by the statute, such as negligent operation of a motor vehicle; for it is difficult, if not impossible, to conceive of a situation where such offenses would be racially motivated. We are left, then, with the prospect of a citizen suppressing his bigoted beliefs for fear that evidence of such beliefs will be introduced against him at trial if he commits a more serious offense against person or property. This is simply too speculative a hypothesis to support Mitchell's overbreadth claim.

The First Amendment, moreover, does not prohibit the evidentiary use of speech to establish the elements of a crime or to prove motive or intent. Evidence of a defendant's previous declarations or statements is commonly admitted in criminal trials subject to evidentiary rules dealing with relevancy, reliability, and the like. Nearly half a century ago, in *Haupt* v. *United States,* we rejected a contention similar to that advanced by Mitchell here. Haupt was tried for the offense of treason, which, as defined by the Constitution, may depend very much on proof of motive. To prove that the acts in question were committed out of "adherence to the enemy" rather than "parental solicitude," the Government introduced evidence of conversations

that had taken place long prior to the indictment, some of which consisted of statements showing Haupt's sympathy with Germany and Hitler and hostility towards the United States. We rejected Haupt's argument that this evidence was improperly admitted. While "such testimony is to be scrutinized with care to be certain the statements are not expressions of mere lawful and permissible difference of opinion with our own government or quite proper appreciation of the land of birth," we held that "these statements . . . clearly were admissible on the question of intent and adherence to the enemy."

For the foregoing reasons, we hold that Mitchell's First Amendment rights were not violated by the application of the Wisconsin penalty-enhancement provision in sentencing him. The judgment of the Supreme Court of Wisconsin is therefore reversed, and the case is remanded for further proceedings not inconsistent with this opinion.

It is so ordered.

Questions

1. Do you agree with the court's reasoning supporting its decision in this case? Why or why not?

2. Why was the wording of the Wisconsin statute about "selection" of a victim a critical aspect of this case?

3. How does this case illustrate the Supreme Court's focus on prohibited conduct (actions) versus speech?

4. Should evidence of a defendant's previous biased statements be admissible as part of the sentencing hearing? Why or why not?

5. Do you see any inconsistencies between the *Mitchell* decision and the decision in *R. A. V. v. St. Paul*?

6. What factors explain the St. Paul hate crime ordinance being struck down, whereas the Wisconsin ordinance was supported?

7. The appellant in this case, Mitchell, argued that Wisconsin's penalty enhancement statute for hate crimes essentially amounted to punishing offenders for their bigoted beliefs, in violation of their First Amendment rights. What is your opinion of this argument? Is it persuasive? Discuss your reasons.

7

GOOD INTENTIONS

The Enforcement of Hate
Crime Penalty-Enhancement Statutes

KAREN FRANKLIN

This article demonstrates that there is far more than meets the eye when it comes to penalty enhancement statutes. As the author demonstrates, such statutes may even backfire, illustrating that public policies intended to achieve social and legal goals with respect to crime must be carefully planned to minimize possible unintended consequences.

In the past two decades, a curious marriage of civil rights groups and the crime victims' rights movement has given birth to a national movement against hate crime in the United States (Jenness & Ryken, 2001; Maroney, 1998). With this reframing of the age-old problem of intergroup conflict and violence, hate crimes have come to the forefront of political discourse as a significant social problem. In response, the federal government and the majority of U.S. states have enacted legislation to combat hate crime.

Hate crime statutes are typically enacted due to a confluence of political lobbying by interest groups, specific triggering events, and consequent media attention (e.g., Becker, 1999; Jenness, 1999; Jenness & Broad, 1997).

They are intended by their drafters to remedy— at both the symbolic and practical levels—the special harms of crimes motivated by bias or prejudice by increasing public awareness of the serious consequences of intergroup violence and providing protection for victims. Other goals include lengthening the sentences of apprehended offenders, deterring prospective offenders, identifying patterns in intergroup violence, and—ultimately—reducing violence against traditionally victimized groups.

Hate crime laws vary widely. Some states provide civil remedies for victims of hate crimes, whereas others require data collection or law enforcement training. The most widespread, and most controversial, laws are so-called

EDITORS' NOTE: From Franklin, K. (2002). Good Intentions: The Enforcement of Hate Crime Penalty-Enhancement Statutes. *American Behavioral Scientist, 46,* 154-172. © 2002 Sage Publications, Inc. Used with permission.

penalty-enhancement statutes, which increase the standard criminal penalties when crimes target members of specified groups. Penalties are enhanced either through assigning a higher sentencing range for bias-motivated crimes or "upgrading" a bias-driven offense to a more serious category of crime (Grattet, Jenness, & Curry, 1998). Either way, the penalty is increased if a defendant intentionally selects victims "because of" or "due to" their membership in certain categories. Currently, all but seven states have penalty-enhancement statutes, most based on a model by the Anti-Defamation League of the B'nai B'rith (2001; White, 1996). All statutes list race, religion, and ethnicity as protected categories; some also include sexual orientation, gender, and disability status.

Penalty-enhancement statutes raise an interesting issue in that they are enacted due to lobbying by civil rights groups, yet enforced by the criminal justice system—police, prosecutors, and judges whose social values and practical priorities are frequently at odds with those of the civil rights movement. Thus, the practical enforcement of hate crime statutes may be quite different from that envisioned by the laws' drafters.

This article explores what is known about the enforcement of penalty-enhancement statutes, as well as their practical impact within the legal system and in U.S. society more broadly. For example, once they are passed, how evenly and widely are the laws enforced? How successfully are they prosecuted? Do they benefit traditionally victimized minority individuals and/or groups? Do they increase social tolerance? Do they function as deterrents? Based on this exploration, suggestions for future research are provided.

Police Enforcement: Trouble in the Trenches

Although penalty-enhancement statutes for hate crimes are on the books in 43 U.S. states (Anti-Defamation League of the B'nai B'rith, 2001), accounts by legal scholars (e.g., Maldonado, 1992/1993) suggest that prosecutions are rare and, when attempted, they often fail due to practical and legal difficulties. Complications arise at every stage of the process, from the initial decision by a victim

about whether to report a crime as bias-related to the ultimate decision by a judge or jury about what penalty to impose.[1]

In terms of effective enforcement, probably the most important decisions are those made at the outset by investigating officers, who decide whether to categorize a crime as bias driven. Explorations of this process (Boyd, Hamner, & Berk, 1996; Martin, 1995) suggest that hate crime rates and patterns in a given jurisdiction are heavily influenced by the idiosyncratic practices of local police, which, in turn, are influenced by local politics, rank-and-file attitudes, and other subjective factors.

In a study conducted in Baltimore, one of the earliest cities to establish a special hate crimes unit, Martin (1995) found that police classifications of suspected hate crimes were guided by a subjective weighing of conflicting accounts, motivations, and provocation. Martin found that police in Baltimore took all suspected hate crimes seriously and tried to proactively reduce racial conflicts before they erupted into violence. Thus, she stated that the very existence of a hate crimes policy may sensitize police and serve as "a symbol of the department's affirmative commitment to correct prior biases" (p. 323). At the same time, she concluded that hate crimes "ultimately emerge through police definitions of situations and interpretations of laws and policies" (p. 323).

In contrast to the Baltimore police, detectives in two separate divisions in a large, unidentified city studied by Boyd et al. (1996) believed that true hate crimes were exceedingly rare. Despite this shared belief, the two divisions produced widely divergent hate crime rates due to their different categorization methods. One division focused on inferring motivations, with the explicit goal of unfounding as many potential hate crimes as possible. The other division focused on facts and categorized a case as a hate crime if it contained any element even remotely suggestive of prejudice: "Any incident during which racial, ethnic, or religious epithets were hurled, regardless of how peripheral to the crime, would be counted by the division as a hate crime" (p. 842).

As examples of how the divisions' philosophies produced different results (Boyd et al., 1996), in the first division, juveniles "were treated categorically as immune from hate motives; rather, their actions were most often dismissed as acts of irresponsibility" (p. 837). When a group of teenagers shouted "Sieg Heil" outside a synagogue, they were scolded by police and dismissed as "just screwing around" (p. 837). By contrast, in the other division, when an unknown suspect drove a golf cart across a fairway and crashed it into a hedge, the case was tallied as a hate crime based solely on the complainant's statement that the incident was similar to one 2 years earlier that had likewise occurred on the eve of Rosh Hashanah.

Three other studies support the notion that local implementation of hate crime laws is highly variable and contingent on numerous subjective factors, including the attitudes, beliefs, and practices of individual officers, the perceived tractability of the problem, police funding and training, and public opposition to hate crime policies (Haider-Markel, 2000; Nolan & Akiyama, 1999; Walker & Katz, 1995). Surveying 16 police departments that claimed to have special bias crime units, Walker and Katz (1995) found that the agencies varied greatly in their procedures and in their commitment to enforcing hate crime laws, with only half providing officers with any specialized training. Furthermore, only one fourth of the agencies that claimed to have a special bias-crime unit actually had such a unit. Nolan and Akiyama (1999) also reported disparate practices among police agencies depending partly on geographic locale, with Northeastern and Western police tending to be more committed to hate crime data collection than were Central or Southern police. Similarly, examining local implementation of hate crime laws in 250 large U.S. cities, Haider-Markel (2000) reported that the traditional discretion afforded individual officers in enforcing the law is even greater when it comes to enforcing hate crime laws. Variables influencing effective enforcement included the attitudes of rank-and-file officers, the support of police leaders, the levels of funding and training for hate crime procedures, and public attitudes toward hate crime policies.

Taken together, these studies suggest that despite recent efforts by the Federal Bureau of Investigation to provide training at the local level, variable practices among individual police agencies exert tremendous influence on the rates and patterns of reported hate crimes and thus on the public's understanding of the nature and size of the hate crime problem.

The Next Hurdle: Proving Motivation

When police do record an arrest as a hate crime, prosecutors must then decide whether to attach a penalty enhancement (in the states in which this applies), whether to take a case to trial, and how to present evidence if a trial ensues. For a criminal penalty to be enhanced, statutes typically require that a defendant committed the act "by reason of" or "because of" the victim's membership (or, in some cases, perceived membership) in a protected group. One of the major constraints faced by district attorneys—and one that it is sometimes hard for the lay public to understand—is the inherent difficulty in proving hatred or bias as a primary motivation.

An example of the potential difficulties, as well as the potential intrusion into free speech and privacy rights, is *State v. Wyant,* a landmark 1992 Ohio case involving an interracial dispute at a campground. When the defendant, a White man, testified that he was not a racist and that he had many Black friends, the prosecutor challenged: "All these Black people that you have described that are your friends, I want you to give me one person, just one, who was really a good friend of yours." The prosecutor then cross-examined the defendant about his relationship with an elderly Black neighbor, asking whether the two had ever dined, drank beer, or gone to a movie together (cited in Jacobs & Potter, 1998, pp. 106–107). Thus, the quality of a defendant's interracial friendships can be explored for evidence of bias, which in turn is assumed to underlie hate crimes.

As this case suggests, it is frequently difficult to prove a biased motive. Indeed, based on her in-depth study in Baltimore (described earlier), Martin (1995) concluded that bias was only a secondary motivation in "a sizable proportion" of reported hate crimes. For example, people may hurl racist, sexist, or antigay epithets in the heat of a confrontation that is rooted in more tangible concerns. Or, the symbolic status of a victim may engender crimes based on actuarial goals, such as when women, gay men, or disabled people are robbed because they are perceived as easy targets (e.g., Steadman, 1999).

A vivid example of the complexities in assessing the role of bias was a highly publicized 1991 case in Atlantic Beach, New York. Initial media accounts described the incident as follows: A White high school student, Shannon Siegel, became angry when he saw a Black man flirting with a White woman at a party. Shouting racial epithets, he started a fight, and was ejected from the gathering. Later that evening, he and four friends returned, stalking and brutally attacking the Black man with a bat. Siegel was taken to trial under an aggravated harassment statute requiring that the victim was harassed "because of" his race (Fleisher, 1994).

At Siegel's trial, the motivations became more murky. The White woman in question turned out to be the defendant's former girlfriend. The Black victim had been the defendant's friend. The defendant's father testified that three fourths of Siegel's friends were Black, and that he "idolized" one Black friend in particular. Other friends testified that Siegel hung out with a mainly Black crowd that routinely used racial epithets with each other. Not only that, Siegel walked and talked as if he himself were Black and, according to one Black friend's testimony, seemed to feel that he was "really Black on the inside" (Fleisher, 1994, p. 35). Jurors rejected the bias motivation, deciding the crime would have occurred anyway, due to a combination of jealousy and Siegel's bruised ego about being ejected from the party. As this case illustrates, the truth, invariably, is more complex and elusive than the initial media sound bites suggest.[2]

In another detailed case analysis, Hutchinson (1999) illustrated how even when a crime was clearly motivated by bias, the reductionistic nature of hate crime politics may cause different interest groups to vie for claim to the victim. Thus, after the highly publicized beating of Loc Minh Truong, a Vietnamese American, on a gay section of Laguna Beach, California, in 1993 by a large group of White teenagers, Vietnamese and gay activists argued over which victim label should apply, with prosecutors ultimately choosing to prosecute for antigay animus. Through such essentialism, individuals who may belong to more than one oppressed group

are made invisible, as are questions of wealth, poverty, and power, Hutchinson (1997, 1999) argued.

With motivations so difficult to pin down, it falls on police, prosecutors, judges, and jurors to sort out whether the victim's group status was a contributing factor, an irrelevant factor, or even "a nonexistent but objectively possible reason" (Gellman, 1992/1993, p. 514). The inherent subjectivity of this process invites arbitrary and uneven application of penalty enhancements. As Gellman (1992/1993, p. 514) pointed out, "some prosecutors, courts, and juries might apply the statute to some mixed motive situations and others would not, inviting arbitrary and even discriminatory application and inconsistent results."

Confronted by the vicissitudes of penalty-enhancement statutes, anecdotal evidence suggests that jurors and judges may be reticent to convict and sentence under them. Migdalia Maldonado, a former prosecutor in the Brooklyn, New York, civil rights bureau, reports that many jurors view hate crime laws as "an example of how public officials cave in to special interest groups" (Maldonado, 1992/1993, p. 561); jurors also believe that some groups are more likely than others to report *regular* crimes as hate crimes to promote a political agenda. Maldonado further reports that many judges are disinclined to mete out harsh sentences based on penalty enhancements. Although the judges may thus be perceived as insensitive to hate crime victims, they may be reluctant because they do not believe that incarceration will engender greater tolerance, particularly in youthful offenders "perceived to be exercising a rite of passage" by participating in a group assault (p. 561).

Other than recent mock jury studies examining factors that might influence decision-making (Marcus-Newhall, Blake, & Baumann, 2002), there has been little systematic study of prosecutions or dispositions in hate crime cases.[3] For example, there have been few attempts to empirically determine specific characteristics of either the crime, the offender, or the victim that might influence decisions to prosecute and/or to convict. However, Hernández (1995) argued that unconscious racism leads prosecutors to trivialize or ignore bias crimes, engendering a systematic bias toward nonenforcement. This bias remains largely undetected, she argued, because prosecutorial discretion is traditionally not reviewed by outside authorities.

Punishing Minorities?

The suggestion of racial bias in prosecutorial decision making is troubling in light of evidence that members of traditionally oppressed groups, which hate crime laws were ostensibly enacted to protect, appear to be disproportionately arrested under penalty-enhancement statutes. This can occur because the laws are operationalized without regard to societal power dynamics. In other words, bias crimes that target Whites, heterosexuals, or Protestants are regarded as seriously under these statutes as those targeting traditionally victimized social groups. Commenting on FBI arrest data for antiheterosexual bias crimes, Bufkin (1999, p. 170) conjured up the ludicrous image of "a lone heterosexual attacked, perhaps almost beaten to death, by a group of young, inebriated gay men who are bragging about their homoerotic prowess."

Bufkin uses this facetious portrayal to argue that hate crime control may end up creating as much oppression as it controls. Indeed, in a foreshadowing of things to come, one of the first applications of an enhancement statute was against an African American man in Florida who called a police officer who was arresting him a "cracker" (Gey, 1997). Similarly, the controlling Supreme Court case in this area, *Wisconsin v. Mitchell* (508 U.S. 476, 1993), involved a Black-on-White crime. In that case, a penalty enhancement was imposed against Todd Mitchell for inciting his friends to attack a White boy after the group watched a scene from the movie *Mississippi Burning,* in which a White man attacks a Black child.

Both national and local data indicate that these two cases are not anomalies, as African Americans are disproportionately represented among identified assailants. For example, in 1993, the Southern Pacific Leadership Conference, which maintains a national hate crimes database, announced that 46% of racially motivated killings were committed by Blacks and concluded that "hate violence committed by Blacks in the United States is escalating at an alarming rate" (Appleborne, 1993, p. A12). Statistics from the Federal Bureau of Investigation

also document that African Americans are accused of hate crimes in numbers exceeding their proportion of the population. For example, in 1999, about 19% of known-race hate crime offenders were African American; anti-White hate crimes accounted for about 18% of racially motivated hate crimes (Federal Bureau of Investigation, Criminal Justice Information Services, 2000).

Echoing FBI data, disproportionate arrest rates of African Americans have been documented at the state and local levels as well. For example, in the first year of data collection under a Florida hate-crime-reporting act, Whites were the largest category of reported victims, 50%, with Blacks representing 38% of victims. Of known offenders, 27% were Black, compared with 33% White and 40% unknown (Czajkoski, 1992). In Kings County, New York, of the 238 bias-related complaints referred to the district attorney's office in one 18-month period, anti-White crimes were the second-largest category (after anti-Semitic), with 46 cases (compared with 44 anti-Black and 14 anti-homosexual incidents) (Maldonado, 1992/1993).

The statistics are less extreme in California, which was the first state to pass a penalty-enhancement statute and which has the most extensive data-collection system, reporting about a quarter of the nation's hate crimes. Of 1,321 known suspects in racially based incidents in 1999, 15% had committed anti-White crimes (California Attorney General, 2000). However, even in California, two researchers identified non-White youths as major perpetrators of racist hate crimes in Los Angeles, based on analyses of geographic locales with high rates of reported hate crimes (Umemoto & Mikami, 2000).

The irony of using the term *hate crime* to describe crimes by members of traditionally oppressed groups against members of the dominant culture is apparently lost on these researchers, as it is on White activists who have protested that anti-White hate crimes are not sufficiently publicized or prosecuted. "Newspapers just don't report on hate crimes by non-European Americans," wrote a San Jose, California, organization dedicated to combating slurs against European Americans. "In 1991 . . . 71% of 85 local hate crimes were perpetrated by non-European Americans, who provide about 55% of the population. . . . There were no local news stories at all about such hate crimes" (Resisting Defamation, 1996, p. 33).

The disproportionate representation of African Americans among reported offenders may reflect several factors. It is possible that African Americans commit higher rates of intergroup crime (or use more racial epithets) than do other groups. If so, the question is whether these crimes merit greater punishment than do Black-on-Black crimes (based on a theory of greater harm to victims as a class). Another factor is that some groups—including African Americans, immigrants, and gays and lesbians of color—are less likely to report crime victimization (Czajkoski, 1992; Hutchinson, 1999; Umemoto & Mikami, 2000). Last, the legal system's traditional, well-documented bias against certain classes of offenders and toward certain classes of victims (e.g., Davis, Estes, & Schiraldi, 1996; Males & Macallair, 2000) undoubtedly manifests itself in hate crimes just as it does in other types of crimes (Bufkin, 1999). For example, both police and crime victims may be more likely to label an event as a hate crime if the offender is African American than if he or she is White (Gerstenfeld, 1998; also see Green, McFalls, & Smith, 2001). This consequence of hate crime laws, similar to the disproportionate use of the death penalty against Blacks who kill Whites (Fleisher, 1994), will undoubtedly reinforce African Americans' long-standing perception that the legal system responds more harshly to crimes by Blacks against Whites than to either Black-on-Black or White-on-Black crimes.

Who Offends, and Why?

The open question of why African Americans are disproportionately represented among reported assailants raises the issue of what is known about hate crime offenders. Is there a distinguishable type of individual who is driven by bias or prejudice to commit crimes against members of specific, legally defined minority groups, as implied in hate crime legislation? If so, what are this individual's characteristics? What motivates him or her to commit hate crimes? Information on who commits hate crimes and why is essential to the design of effective rehabilitative interventions, as well as educational and policy interventions to deter potential offenders (see Cogan, 2002).

Our current knowledge of offenders comes primarily from the following three sources: arrest data, information provided by crime victims and witnesses, and hate crime databases,[4] which typically include information from both police sources and victim reports. Analyses of these databases have not revealed any demographic patterns that distinguish hate crime offenders from violent offenders overall, other than possible younger age. Rather, typical offenders appear to be fairly average young men acting as part of an informal group. However, the available data are limited by several factors.

First, arrest data are limited because only a small percentage of crimes categorized as bias related are resolved through arrests. For example, a 1995 national study found that only 16% of antigay violence reported to police resulted in arrests, compared with 45% of violent crime overall (National Coalition of Anti-Violence Programs, 1996). Furthermore, suspects are more likely to be identified and arrested for offenses at the two extremes of severity, that is, those involving extreme violence or those involving nuisance behaviors such as repeat telephone or mail harassment. The individuals who commit the broad majority of hate crimes—such as threatening behaviors, property damage, shouted epithets, and graffiti spraying—are much less likely to be apprehended. Thus, arrested assailants cannot be generalized as representative of hate crimes offenders overall.[5]

Information from eyewitnesses and victims is also limited. Witnesses and victims can provide rudimentary demographic data (e.g., approximate age, race, and sex) in incidents that were observed. But despite being the primary data source, victim accounts are not always reliable when it comes to inferring an offender's motivation. For example, if an assailant shouts a presumably hateful epithet such as "nigger," "faggot," or "bitch," it is not always obvious whether this is due to hatred per se or, rather, is because name-calling is "the parlance of violent struggle" (Green et al., 2001). This was illustrated in Franklin's (1996, 1998) in-depth interviews with offenders. For example, one young man insisted that he assaulted a group of male strangers because of anger over a traffic dispute (Franklin, 1998), and that he only used the term "fag" to provoke a fight:

> It's a way to talk to put them down, to make them lower, to make them mad. Usually a confrontation comes up after that. They're supposed to throw something at that point. . . . I don't know if they were gay. You can't tell by looking at someone, you have to get to know them a bit. (p. 162)

To overcome the limitations of arrest data and victim accounts, Franklin (2000) conducted a survey of potential perpetrators, asking 484 young adults to explain the reasons for any acts committed against homosexuals. The results suggested multiple motivations underlying acts that could be labeled as hate crimes. These motivations include not only intergroup prejudice but also peer group dynamics, thrill seeking, and perceived self-defense.

Qualitative interviews with 11 assailants, several convicted under penalty-enhancement statutes, suggested two additional, often overlooked factors relevant to understanding hate crimes (Franklin, 1996, 1998; see Dong, 1997, for similar interviews). The first is that the more violent hate crimes are typically committed by individuals who were raised in violent milieus and who practice violence frequently and indiscriminately in their lives. Although these individuals typically cite larger cultural norms to justify their actions, they are living on the social fringe and are riding express trains toward the nearest penitentiary. Thus, because extreme crimes tend to garner media attention, the popular image of the hate crime problem is based on the actions of a small minority of pervasively violent individuals at the bottom of the social order.

A second, related dynamic that is typically neglected but is necessary to a full understanding of hate crimes is the role of social class divisions. Connell (1995) has described how economically and socially disempowered men may pursue violence as a means of distracting themselves from their relative powerlessness. Several assailants in Franklin's (2000) study expressed class resentment toward gay men in particular, describing them not only as sexual deviants but also as affluent, powerful, and blessed with undeserved special rights. This conflation of sexuality and economic class (which has historical roots beyond the scope of this discussion) (see Healy, 1996) helps to explain why gay men serve as an ideal target for socially powerless men to vent their rage. As a young Texan who terrorized and murdered a gay man so cogently expressed it (Bissinger, 1995),

> I work all my life tryin' to have something nice and make something of myself. About the best job I can get is working in a restaurant makin' minimum wage. . . . From the time I was a kid it seemed like there was a lot against me, and yet here they [homosexuals] are, they're doing something that God totally condemns in the Bible. But look at everything they've got. . . . They've got all these good jobs, sit back at a desk or sit back in an air-conditioned building not having to sweat, not having to bust their ass, and they've got money. They've got the cars, they've got the apartments. They've got all the nice stuff in 'em. So, yeah, I resented that. (p. 88)

Thus, homosexuals in particular may be targeted not only as sexual deviants but also as archetypal symbols of ruling-class oppression. This motivation was evidenced, for example, in the Matthew Shepard case. Speaking of the economic divide in Laramie, Wyoming, the Rev. Stephen Johnson, leader of a Unitarian Universalist congregation there, told a news reporter, "This is going to happen again and again and again unless the have-nots of this town become part of the community again" (Lewan & Paulson, 1998). In exploring this motivation, Green et al. (2001) pointed out that hate crime does not mechanistically derive from group power differentials or macroeconomic changes but, rather, from a group's collective beliefs that its status or way of life is threatened by outsiders.

Ethnographic studies suggest that similar, misplaced resentments may contribute to the victimization of racial and religious minorities as well (e.g., Ezekiel, 1995; Pinderhughes, 1993).

Indeed, there likely are both similarities and differences in the motivations underlying assaults on different minority groups. For example, minority group members are fairly interchangeable for thrill-seeking assailants (Franklin, 2000; Levin & McDevitt, 1993). However, assailants motivated by perceived self-defense might view themselves as protecting their bodies from sexually predatory homosexuals, their neighborhoods from intruding African Americans or Asians (Green, Strolovitch, & Wong, 1998), and their traditionally male workplaces from women. This has implications for hate crime prevention because a one-size-fits-all campaign against hatred is likely to be ineffective if different motivations underlie hate crimes targeting different minority groups.

Given the variety of motivations underlying bias crimes, it is not surprising that the stereotype of offenders as members or affiliates of extremist organizations has not been borne out by research. Comparing apprehended offenders in North Carolina with known White supremacists, Green, Abelson, and Garnett (1999) found significant differences between the racial beliefs of offenders and White supremacists, despite both groups' greater racism and social conservatism than a matched sample from the general population. Furthermore, a full 16% of the White general population fit the profile of either hate crime offenders or organized extremists. In other words, both extremists and offenders "may be drawn from a much larger pool of like-minded individuals" (p. 17) who refrain from illegal displays of their biased beliefs. This supports the commonsense notion that extremist rhetoric sways vulnerable individuals, perhaps explaining the finding of sharp increases in cross-burnings following public demonstrations by White extremist groups (Green & Rich, 1998).

These findings suggest the importance of focusing not only on individual factors but also on environmental factors that may contribute to intergroup violence. In this regard, Green et al. (1998) found evidence of increased crime against racial minorities in "defended" White urban neighborhoods that had recently experienced in-migrations of minorities. Similarly, Medoff (1999), using economics methodology, found a correlation between hate crime rates and a state's unemployment and education levels, among other factors. Although Medoff's methodology was flawed (and hate crime data are not sufficiently accurate to permit such studies), such a meta-approach does suggest the utility of examining larger structural variables, including the role of economic disenfranchisement suggested earlier in this discussion as well as the related roles of political discourse and the media, factors that have received more attention from European scholars (for a discussion see Green et al., 2001).

Deterrent Effects

The obvious impact of the environment on individual behavior suggests that hate crime laws might be beneficial in establishing a tone of decreased social tolerance for bigotry and intergroup violence. Unfortunately, due to the vagaries of hate crime reporting, as well as the difficulties inherent in measuring deterrence, an accurate estimate of the deterrent value of hate crime laws is unlikely to be achieved. In addition, penalty enhancements do not impose punishment where none previously existed; they merely increase the severity of punishment. In general, this has not been found to be an effective deterrence strategy.

On an individual level, it is unlikely that penalty enhancements alone will deter apprehended offenders from committing future hate crimes. Among offenders interviewed by Franklin (1996, 1998), prosecution increased their belief that they were the victims of oppression by a more socially privileged and powerful elite. Thus, penalty enhancements paradoxically increased, rather than decreased, their resentment of minorities. The likelihood that enhancements will strengthen offenders' bias is even greater if they are sent to prison, where virulent racism and homophobia are the norm. However, it is possible that bias might be reduced in offenders who receive some type of educational intervention or treatment; this would be a fruitful area for further study.[6]

In terms of more generalized deterrent effects, there is some indication that a widely publicized hate crime may paradoxically cause a spike in reported hate crimes (Richardson, 1992) similar to regional spikes in murder rates following a highly publicized execution. For example, New York City experienced a near-twofold increase in reported hate crimes following the infamous Howard Beach incident in 1986, in which three African Americans were attacked by a group of White teenagers. Finding that a single hate offense is often followed by a large number of follow-up attacks, Levin and McDevitt recently expanded their original typology of hate crimes (Levin & McDevitt, 1993) to include a category of "retaliatory hate crimes" (McDevitt, Levin, & Bennett, in press). Copycat crimes have also been implicated (along with economic incentives to collect on insurance claims) in the 1995 to 1996 rash of Black church burnings in the Southern United States (Greenberg, 1997).

Several factors may account for this observed pattern. These include (a) copycat crimes by other bias offenders; (b) victims' greater willingness to report incidents (due to increased awareness of the laws and/or increased belief that they will be taken seriously); (c) false reports by individuals seeking personal or group attention or other forms of gain; and/or (d) retaliatory strikes by members of a victim's social group.

Only the last of these factors has been addressed by research, in a laboratory study by Craig (1999). The research goal was to ascertain whether hate crimes were more likely than intragroup assaults to provoke a desire for retaliation by members of the victim's racial group. Craig found that desire for retaliation differed by race, with African American men more likely than White men to endorse returning to the scene of victimization with friends, to look for the offender.

A rash of false hate crime reports on college campuses around the United States in the wake of the Matthew Shepard murder (Gose, 1999) suggests that false reporting may be a significant barrier to accurate assessment of the hate crime problem. Some false reports are motivated by the desire for personal attention, whereas for others, the goal is furthering a political cause. For example, among Black students, "The hate crime hoax is usually conceived as an effort to energize Black student activism or to press the administration to move more quickly on Black students' concerns" ("When a Hate Crime," 1998/1999, p. 52). Other motivations for the filing of false hate crime reports include financial gain in insurance cases (Journal of Blacks in Higher Education, 1998/1999) and obtaining investigative priority (e.g., Boyd et al., 1996)[7] or harsher treatment of an offender in routine assault or vandalism cases. Based on her experiences as a hate crime prosecutor in New York City, Maldonado (1992/1993) reported that complainants frequently embellish accounts to obtain a hate crime designation and thereby be taken more seriously. Interestingly, Maldonado reported that many false reports come from heterosexual White men rather than members of traditionally victimized groups.

In summary, penalty-enhancement statutes, on their face, do convey the message that intergroup violence is unacceptable. However, there is currently little evidence that, in and of themselves, they will lead to a reduction in intergroup conflict. Furthermore, publicity surrounding their enforcement may frequently lead to increases in both true and false reporting of hate crimes.

Social and Political Impact

Hate crime laws are aimed not only at decreasing the actual incidence of hate crimes but also at creating a more tolerant social climate by framing intergroup violence as a social problem. The passage of these statutes signals society's moral condemnation of heinous conduct based on prejudice. Hate crime advocates share a commitment to using the laws as a tool to fight racism, heterosexism, anti-Semitism, and other prejudices.

The use of penalty enhancements to achieve these social goals has proved quite controversial. Penalty enhancements have been widely criticized by legal scholars, often out of concern about potentially negative social ramifications such as infringement on free speech (e.g., Gellman, 1992/1993; Gerstenfeld, 1992; Jacobs & Potter, 1998; Morsch, 1991). Indeed, legal scholars have argued that for such laws to pass constitutional muster on First Amendment grounds, bias-motivated crimes must be shown to cause "a more particularized and specific harm" than nonbias crimes (Gey, 1997, p. 1044).

This idea of special harm, dovetailing with the social movements for victims' rights over the past two decades, gets at another fundamental purpose of hate crime laws. That is, they are designed in part to provide redress for groups that have historically been the victims of societal prejudice: "Crimes of hate can happen to anyone, but hate crimes justifying penalty enhancement happen to traditional victims of bias" (Hughes, 1998, p. 621).

Thus, one research goal has been to establish that crimes based on a victim's symbolic status are indeed more psychologically damaging than random crimes. In a large-scale study of the effects of hate crimes on victims, Herek, Gillis, and Cogan (1999) found significantly greater psychological sequelae among gay male and lesbian hate crime victims than among a matched sample of homosexuals who were the victims of similar nonbias crimes. Activists have also noted the terrorizing impact of hate crimes on entire communities.

The establishment of greater harm to victims and victim groups does not in and of itself establish, however, that victims are necessarily benefited by enhanced penalties for offenders. As described earlier, African Americans do not uniformly benefit from the laws because they compose a disproportionate percentage of those arrested. Furthermore, it remains an open question as to whether penalty enhancements will lead to increased tolerance of minorities among the general public. Some critics argue that the laws, although well intentioned, may actually increase the social divisions they are designed to ameliorate (e.g., Crocker, 1992/1993; Gey, 1997). They cite the popular belief that hate crime laws are an example of certain groups receiving special rights not accorded to other citizens.

CONCLUSION

Hate crime penalty-enhancement statutes have been promulgated by socially concerned people with justifiable intentions. And it is precisely because these statutes are intended to address not just the victimization of individuals but broader social injustices that they must be evaluated to determine how well their actual effects match the intentions of their promulgators.

Without question, the laws are meeting some of their intended goals. They are identifying patterns in the commission of intergroup crimes. They are drawing public attention to an important social problem. To the extent that they are prosecuted, they will probably result in longer incarceration of apprehended offenders. They have also been highly successful in some jurisdictions in sensitizing police, prosecutors, and judges to the problems faced by minority crime victims (e.g., Paynter, 2000).

These effects must be weighed against the statutes' unintended negative consequences. One particularly pernicious consequence is that the laws appear to be contributing to increased criminal penalties against African Americans, one of the groups they were designed to protect.[8] This has occurred because hate crime laws have been operationalized with little or no attention to societal power dynamics and social inequalities (Miller & Myers, 2000). Indeed, Umemoto and Mikami (2000) argued that many gang-related assaults by one minority group of another should be prosecuted as race-based hate crimes, thereby further expanding the domain of hate crime statutes and meting out additional punishment to the already dispossessed. Given the well-documented race and class biases within the legal system (e.g., Baldus, Woodworth, & Pulaski, 1990; Davis et al., 1996; Harris, 1997; Males & Macallair, 2000), it is not surprising that without explicit attention to issues of social power, hate crime laws will end up replicating the very power imbalances and inequalities they were designed to ameliorate.

Another highly significant and paradoxical problem is that hate crime laws may increase divisions between social groups at a time when boundaries in U.S. society are becoming more fluid. As Crocker (1992/1993) pointed out, increased racial categorization will not lead to less racial discrimination: "Racism will decline as [racial] classifications become more difficult [and] of less significance. . . . [It will] turn out to be a losing antiracist strategy to give operational significance to—and to emphasize—racial divisions" (pp. 506–507).

Penalty-enhancement statutes are "part of a larger American syndrome of adopting harsh punishment as an expedient response that deals only with the most superficial manifestations of complex, deep-seated problems" (Weinstein, 1992, p. 16). They provide politicians with an easy way to demonstrate that they are doing something about a perceived social problem, while sidestepping the complex causes of prejudice and violence in American society.

These criminal justice sanctions did not materialize in a political vacuum. They were drafted during a conservative period in U.S. history, the Reagan Era, due to an alliance between some civil rights groups and the conservative victims' rights movement (Jenness & Ryken, 2001). Ironically, by focusing on the narrow concept of hate, these laws have helped to restrict the enforcement of civil rights laws dating back to Reconstruction (White, 1996). They are part of a broader judicial trend over the past two decades to ignore societal patterns of discrimination in favor of individual explanations (Harris, 1997). That is, rather than focusing on group and institutional sources of animus as did the earlier laws, hate crime statutes shine the spotlight on a small minority of violent individuals who are merely reflecting—rather than creating—larger social norms that allow if not encourage intergroup violence. In the long run, this may not do much to ameliorate prejudice, discrimination, or the harmful consequences of intergroup violence.

NOTES

1. The significant problems in data collection go beyond the scope of this article and have been the topic of recent attention (e.g., Grattet, 2000; Nolan & Akiyama, 1999; Steadman, 1999). Although proponents of hate crime legislation frequently claim a growing "epidemic" of hate crimes or, more dramatically, a "rising tide of bigotry and bloodshed" (Levin & McDevitt, 1993), these claims are premature due to the recency of efforts to collect data and the vagaries in the ensuing data. Indeed, some Southern and Midwestern states that never passed hate crime statutes report little or no hate crimes to the FBI, leaving the impression that hate crimes are highest where enforcement is strictest; California, for example, accounts for nearly a quarter of all reported incidents (Grattet, 2000). Studies of individual police departments also suggest that their data are highly

unreliable; for example, only one fourth of the agencies who reported to the federal government that they had bias-crime units actually did have such units (Walker & Katz, 1995).

2. The Atlantic Beach case was far from an aberration. Typically, hate crimes are initially presented simplistically and, as the public and the media obtain more information, complexities gradually emerge that shed doubt on hatred as a pure motivation. For an excellent example of the subtleties of another well-known case, the 1986 killing of Yusuf Hawkins by a group of White teens in Bensonhurst, New York, see Fleisher (1994).

3. One exception is the state of California Department of Justice, which publishes comprehensive data on prosecution rates. For 1999, of 1,962 total hate crimes reported, 1,039 were referred by police for prosecution, and 372 (19%) resulted in the filing of criminal complaints. Of these, 46.8% resulted in hate crime convictions, including 109 through pleas of guilty or no contest, and 65 through convictions at trial (California Attorney General, 2000).

4. Databases in the United States include those of the Federal Bureau of Investigation and several national organizations, including the Anti-Defamation League of the B'nai B'rith, the National Gay and Lesbian Task Force, and the Southern Poverty Law Center. Local organizations also collect data in many large U.S. cities. Because of their partisan nature, these watchdog groups may provide unreliable data (Green, McFalls, & Smith, 2001).

5. A related problem is the conceptualization of hate crimes as primarily stranger-on-stranger assaults. Harassment in schools, workplaces, and institutional settings such as the military, prisons, and law enforcement is grossly underreported. Victimization data may also overrepresent those with more social status. For example, in the case of homosexuals, White gay men are more likely than lesbians or non-White gay men to report victimization (Berrill, 1992). There is also some evidence that non-minorities are proportionately more likely to report hate crime victimization than are members of traditionally victimized groups (see discussion and citations in text).

6. Outcome research has yet to be conducted on diversion programs, which include Juvenile Offenders Learning Tolerance (JOLT) in Los Angeles (Wessler, 2000), Stamp Out Hate Crimes in New Jersey (Greenberg, 1997), and the Anti-Defamation League of the B'nai B'rith's programs for anti-Semitic offenders in New York City and Boston.

7. Boyd, Hamner, and Berk (1996) explained how, in the city they studied, suspected hate crimes

are automatically assigned to a special hate crimes detective and receive a level-1 priority, requiring the investigation to be completed within 10 days. In contrast, level-2 cases must be investigated within 30 days, and level-3 cases may not require any follow-up investigation at all.

8. A controlling Supreme Court case, *Wisconsin v. Mitchell,* has been used in a similarly paradoxical manner to rebut First Amendment challenges to the Don't Ask, Don't Tell policy excluding gays from the military, and to punish environmental dissidents protesting old-growth logging in Oregon (Gey, 1997). As Gey pointed out, this use of the Mitchell case is "an example of a common phenomenon: A politically progressive speech-regulation theory that ends up providing the government with an excellent justification for suppressing politically progressive speech" (p. 1015).

REFERENCES

Anti-Defamation League of the B'nai B'rith. (2001). *Hate crime laws.* Retrieved from www.adl.org/99hatecrime/provisions.html

Appleborne, P. (1993, December 13). Rise is found in hate crimes committed by blacks. *The New York Times,* p. A12.

Baldus, D. C., Woodworth, G., & Pulaski, C. (1990). *Equal justice and the death penalty.* Boston: Northeastern University Press.

Becker, P. J. (1999). The creation of Ohio's ethnic intimidation law: Triggering events, media campaigns, and interest group activity. *American Journal of Criminal Justice, 23*(2), 247–265.

Berrill, K. T. (1992). Anti-gay violence and victimization in the United States: An overview. In G. M. Herek & K. T. Berrill (Eds.), *Hate crimes: Confronting violence against lesbians and gay men* (pp. 19–45). Newbury Park, CA: Sage.

Bissinger, H. G. (1995, February). The killing trail. *Vanity Fair,* pp. 80–88, 142–145.

Boyd, E., Hamner, K., & Berk, R. (1996). "Motivated by hatred or prejudice": Categorization of hate-motivated crimes in two police divisions. *Law & Society Review, 30*(4), 819–850.

Bufkin, J. L. (1999). Bias crime as gendered behavior. *Social Justice, 26*(1), 155–176.

California Attorney General. (2000). *Hate crime in California, 1999.* Retrieved from http://caag.state.ca.us/cjsc/hc99/netone.pdf

Cogan, J. C. (2002). Hate crimes as a crime category worthy of policy attention. *American Behavioral Scientist, 46*(1), 173–185.

Connell, R. W. (1995). *Masculinities.* Berkeley: University of California Press.

Craig, K. M. (1999). Retaliation, fear, or rage: An investigation of African American and white reactions to racist hate crimes. *Journal of Interpersonal Violence, 14*(2), 138–151.

Crocker, L. (1992/1993). Hate crime statutes: Just? Constitutional? Wise? *Annual Survey of American Law,* 485–508.

Czajkoski, E. H. (1992). Criminalizing hate: An empirical assessment. *Federal Probation, 56*(3), 36–40.

Davis, C., Estes, R., & Schiraldi, V. (1996). *"Three Strikes": The new apartheid.* Washington, DC: Justice Policy Institute.

Dong, A. (Director, Writer, Editor). (1997). *Licensed to kill* [Motion picture]. San Francisco: Deep Focus Productions.

Ezekiel, R. S. (1995). *The racist mind: Portraits of American neo-Nazis and Klansmen.* New York: Penguin.

Federal Bureau of Investigation, Criminal Justice Information Services. (2000). *Uniform Crime Report: Crime in the United States—1999.* Retrieved from www.fbi.gov/ucr/Cius_99/ 99crime/

Fleisher, M. (1994). Down the passage which we should not take: The folly of hate crime legislation. *Journal of Law & Policy, 2,* 1–53.

Franklin, K. (1996). *Hate crime or rite of passage? Assailant motivations in antigay violence.* Unpublished doctoral dissertation, California School of Professional Psychology, Alameda.

Franklin, K. (1998). Unassuming motivations: Contextualizing the narratives of antigay assailants. In G. Herek (Ed.), *Stigma and sexual orientation: Understanding prejudice against lesbians, gay men, and bisexuals* (pp. 1–23). Thousand Oaks, CA: Sage.

Franklin, K. (2000). Antigay behaviors among young adults: Prevalence, patterns, and motivators in a noncriminal population. *Journal of Interpersonal Violence, 15*(4), 339–362.

Gellman, S. (1992/1993). Hate crime laws are thought crime laws. *Annual Survey of American Law,* 509–532.

Gerstenfeld, P. (1992). "Smile when you call me that!" The problem with punishing hate motivated behavior. *Behavioral Sciences & the Law, 10,* 259–285.

Gerstenfeld, P. (1998). Reported hate crimes in America. *Journal of Research, 2,* 35–43.

Gey, S. (1997). What if *Wisconsin v. Mitchell* had involved Martin Luther King, Jr.? The Constitutional flaws of hate crime enhancement statutes. *George Washington Law Review, 65*(6), 1014–1070.

Gose, B. (1999, January 8). Hate-crime hoaxes unsettle campuses. *Chronicle of Higher Education,* p. A55.

Grattet, R. (2000). Hate crimes: Better data or increasing frequency? *Population Today, 28*(5), 1, 4.

Grattet, R., Jenness, V., & Curry, T. (1998). The homogenization and differentiation of hate crime law in the United States, 1978 to 1995: Innovation and diffusion in the criminalization of bigotry. *American Sociological Review, 63*(2), 286–307.

Green, D. P., Abelson, R. P., & Garnett, M. (1999). The distinctive political views of hate crimes perpetrators and white supremacists. In D. Prentice & D. T. Miller (Eds.), *Cultural divides: Understanding and overcoming group conflict* (pp. 429–464). New York: Russell Sage.

Green, D. P., McFalls, L. H., & Smith, J. K. (2001). Hate crime: An emergent research agenda. *Annual Review of Sociology, 27,* 479–504.

Green, D. P., & Rich, A. (1998). White supremacist activity and cross-burnings in North Carolina. *Journal of Quantitative Criminology, 14*(3), 263–282.

Green, D. P., Strolovitch, D. Z., & Wong, J. S. (1998). Defended neighborhoods, integration, and racially motivated crime. *American Journal of Sociology, 104*(2), 372–403.

Greenberg, S. (1997). The Massachusetts Hate Crime Reporting Act of 1990: Great expectations yet unfulfilled? *New England Law Review, 31*(2), 103–158.

Haider-Markel, D. P. (2000, August). *Enforcers and activists: The politics of hate crime policy implementation.* Paper presented at American Psychological Association conference, Washington, DC.

Harris, P. (1997). *Black rage confronts the law.* New York: New York University Press.

Healy, M. (1996). *Gay skins: Class, masculinity and queer appropriation.* London: Cassell.

Herek, G. M., Gillis, J. R., & Cogan, J. C. (1999). Psychological sequelae of hate-crime victimization among lesbian, gay, and bisexual adults. *Journal of Consulting & Clinical Psychology, 67*(6), 945–951.

Hernández, T. K. (1995). Bias crimes: Unconscious racism in the prosecution of "racially motivated violence." In A. S. Lopez (Ed.), *Criminal justice and Latino communities* (pp. 139–158). New York: Garland.

Hughes, J. (1998). Can anyone be the victim of a hate crime? *University of Dayton Law Review, 23*(3), 591–622.

Hutchinson, D. L. (1997). Out yet unseen: A racial critique of gay and lesbian theory and political discourse. *Connecticut Law Review, 29*(2), 561–645.

Hutchinson, D. L. (1999). Ignoring the sexualization of race: Heteronormativity, critical race theory and anti-racist politics. *Buffalo Law Review, 47*(1), 1–116.

Jacobs, J., & Potter, K. (1998). *Hate crimes: Criminal law and identity politics.* New York: Oxford University Press.

Jenness, V. (1999). Managing difference and making legislation: Social movements and the racialization, sexualization, and gendering of federal hate crime law in the U.S., 1985–1998. *Social Problems, 46*(4), 548–571.

Jenness, V., & Broad, K. (1997). *Hate crimes: New social movements and the politics of violence.* New York: Aldine.

Jenness, V., & Ryken, G. (2001). *Making hate a crime: From social movement to law enforcement.* New York: Russell Sage Foundation.

Levin, J., & McDevitt, J. (1993). *Hate crimes: The rising tide of bigotry and bloodshed.* New York: Plenum.

Lewan, T., & Paulson, S. (1998, October 16). *A crime borne of poverty, not hate? Murder of gay man highlights class divide in Wyoming town.* Retrieved from the Associated Press Web site, http://wire.ap.org

Maldonado, M. (1992/1993). Practical problems with enforcing hate crimes legislation in New York. *Annual Survey of American Law, 555,* 557–558.

Males, M., & Macallair, D. (2000). *The color of justice: An analysis of juvenile adult court transfers in California.* Washington, DC: Justice Policy Institute. Retrieved from www.cjcj.org/jpi/publications.html

Marcus-Newhall, A., Blake, L. P., & Baumann, J. (2002). Perceptions of hate crime perpetrators and victims as influenced by race, political orientation, and peer group. *American Behavioral Scientist, 46*(1), 108–135.

Maroney, T. (1998). The struggle against hate crime: Movement at a crossroad. *New York University Law Review, 73,* 564–620.

Martin, S. (1995). A cross-burning is not just an arson: Police social construction of hate crimes in Baltimore County. *Criminology, 33,* 303–326.

McDevitt, J., Levin, J., & Bennett, S. (in press). Hate crime offenders: An expanded typology. *Journal of Social Issues.*

Medoff, M. H. (1999). Allocation of time and hateful behavior: A theoretical and positive analysis of hate and hate crimes. *American Journal of Economics and Sociology, 58*(4), 959–973.

Miller, J. K., & Myers, K. A. (2000, April). *Are all hate crimes created equal?* Paper presented at the annual meeting of the Southern Sociological Society, New Orleans, LA.

Morsch, J. (1991). The problem of motive in hate crimes: The argument against presumption of racial motivation. *Journal of Criminal Law & Criminology, 82,* 659–689.

National Coalition of Anti-Violence Programs. (1996). *Anti-lesbian/gay violence in 1995.* San Francisco: Community United Against Violence.

Nolan, J., & Akiyama, Y. (1999). An analysis of factors that affect law enforcement participation in hate crime reporting. *Journal of Contemporary Criminal Justice, 15*(1), 111–127.

Paynter, R. L. (2000). Protecting all the people. *Law Enforcement Technology, 27*(4), 62–66.

Pinderhughes, H. L. (1993). The anatomy of racially motivated violence in New York City: A case study of youth in Southern Brooklyn. *Social Problems, 40,* 478–492.

Resisting Defamation. (1996). Hate crimes against whites are a serious problem. In P. Winters (Ed.), *Hate crimes.* San Diego, CA: Greenhaven.

Richardson, L. (1992, January 28). 61 acts of bias: One fuse lights many different explosions. *The New York Times,* p. B1.

Steadman, G. (1999, April). *Review of 12 cities' survey data: A test of hate crime data collection.* Paper presented at Hate Crimes: Their Definition and Measurement conference, School of Criminal Justice, State University of New York at Albany.

Umemoto, K., & Mikami, C. K. (2000). Profile of race-bias hate crime in Los Angeles County. *Western Criminology Review, 2*(2), 1–34.

Walker, S., & Katz, C. M. (1995). Less than meets the eye: Police department bias-crime units. *American Journal of Police, 14*(1), 29–48.

Weinstein, J. (1992). First Amendment challenges to hate crime legislation: Where's the speech? *Criminal Justice Ethics, 11*(2), 6–19.

Wessler, S. (2000). *Promising practices against hate crimes: Five state and local demonstration projects.* Unpublished monograph, U.S. Department of Justice, Bureau of Justice Assistance. Retrieved from www.ncjrs.org/pdffiles1/bja/181425/pdf

When a hate crime isn't a hate crime: Racial hoaxes on college campuses. (1998/1999). *Journal of Blacks in Higher Education, 22,* 52.

White, J. V. (1996). Vindicating rights in a federal system: Rediscovering 42 U.S.C. § 1985(3)'s equality right. *Temple Law Review, 69*(1), 145–243.

QUESTIONS

1. What are the difficulties prosecutors face in proving motivation in hate crimes cases?

2. What is an example of an actuarial hate crime? Would you consider this a hate crime in the same sense as other crimes committed because of the offender's bias or hatred of the victim's group? Why or why not?

3. According to the research discussed in this article, why does police enforcement of hate crime laws vary between jurisdictions?

4. Consider the argument that implementing hate crime laws without considering the underlying societal dynamics of oppression can actually result in harming members of the groups that such laws are intended to protect. Why is this the case? Discuss using examples.

5. Why are members of some minority groups disproportionately represented among defendants charged with hate crimes? What are some possible explanations for this?

6. Is it possible that members of different ethnic groups vary in their likelihood of reporting their victimization as hate crime targets? If so, what are the implications of this for statistics on hate crimes?

7. According to research, what kinds of motivations have driven offenders to commit hate crimes? Are there any motivations you would add to the list?

8. Compare the popular perception of hate crimes with the reality of hate crimes shown by research. How do the two compare?

9. How might perpetrators' feelings of relative economic and social powerlessness be related to their commission of hate crimes?

10. Are most hate crime offenders members of extremist groups? Based on the research, how would you describe the typical hate crime offender?

11. Why are hate crime laws unlikely to be effective as a deterrent to hate crimes?

12. Discuss the arguments for and against the proposition that hate crime penalty enhancements will ultimately help (a) reduce hate crimes and/or (b) help victims of hate crimes.

8

AN ANALYSIS OF FACTORS THAT AFFECT LAW ENFORCEMENT PARTICIPATION IN HATE CRIME REPORTING

JAMES J. NOLAN

YOSHIO AKIYAMA

These authors highlight the fact that police, as the gatekeepers of the criminal justice system, play a critical role in efforts to identify, report, and prosecute hate crimes. The authors identify a wide range of factors that influence police recognition and reporting of hate crimes, and they suggest strategies for improving police reporting of hate crimes.

In May 1994, at a beach resort in Delaware, five men wielding baseball bats and empty champagne bottles attacked and brutally beat three homosexual men as they sat talking together just past midnight on the resort's boardwalk. One of the victims suffered a fractured skull, causing paralysis and speech problems. The other victims also sustained severe head lacerations. The suspects are alleged to have attacked the men solely because they were homosexuals (Harvey, 1994).

In December 1995, three White soldiers from the prestigious 82nd Airborne Division stationed at Fort Bragg, North Carolina, decided to harass Blacks. After a night of drinking, the men (alleged to be White supremacists) drove to a predominately Black section of Fayetteville where they selected an African American couple standing on the street and killed them with a 9mm pistol. It appears that the single motivation for this murder was that the victims were Black (*Time*, December 18, 1995).

EDITORS' NOTE: Nolan, J. J., & Akiyama, Y. (1999). An Analysis of Factors That Affect Law Enforcement Participation in Hate Crime Reporting. *Journal of Contemporary Criminal Justice, 15,* 111-127. © 1999 Sage Publications, Inc. Reprinted with permission.

Table 8.1 Law Enforcement Participation in Reporting Hate Crimes to the Federal Bureau of Investigation

Year	States	Agencies	Agencies Reporting at Least One Hate Crime (N)	Agencies Reporting at Least One Hate Crime (%)	U.S Population Covered by Participating Agencies (%)
1991	33	2,215	739	33.4	29
1992	42	6,181	1,099	18	51
1993	47	6,865	1,326	19.3	58
1994	44	7,298	1,150	16	58

NOTE: Many police agencies that participate in the hate crime program report that no hate crimes have occurred in their jurisdictions.

Senseless, brutal crimes, like the ones described above, that are motivated by bias or hatred for a person or group are referred to as *hate crimes*. The Federal Bureau of Investigation (FBI) defines a hate crime as "a criminal offense committed against a person or property, which is motivated, in whole or in part, by the offender's bias against a race, religion, disability, ethnic/national origin, or sexual orientation" (U.S. Department of Justice, Federal Bureau of Investigation, 1992, p. 14; Eisler, 1993). The motivation for the criminal offense is what makes the offense a hate crime. A hate crime is not a separate type of crime. Instead it is a traditional crime, like murder, rape, burglary, robbery, and intimidation. The distinction is that these crimes are motivated by hatred that is deeply grounded in bigotry (J. Levin & McDevitt, 1994).

Hate crimes often have profound effects not only on the individual victims, but also on an entire group that shares the same characteristic for which the victim was targeted (Barnes & Ephross, 1994). Hate crimes also can tear at the very fabric of the community, regardless of the seriousness of the offense (Martin, 1995). In an attempt to gain a better understanding of the nature and scope of hate crimes occurring in the United States, political leaders, policy makers, victim advocacy groups, and others have expressed the need for national data. In response, on April 13, 1990, President George Bush signed into law the Hate Crime Statistics Act (the Act), requiring the attorney general to collect and report data on hate crime in the United States (U.S. Congress, 1990).

The task of collecting the data was given to the FBI and was incorporated into the existing Uniform Crime Reporting (UCR) Program. The FBI's Programs Support Section of the Criminal Justice Information Services Division has been responsible for collecting hate crime data from state and local law enforcement agencies since passage of the Act. The FBI compiles this information and publishes an annual hate crime report titled *Hate Crime Statistics* (U.S. Department of Justice, Federal Bureau of Investigation, 1996). Supporters of the legislation believe that collecting hate crime data is extremely important for several reasons: (a) it raises the public's awareness of the existence of these crimes; (b) it provides baseline information for research and program development in this area; (c) it helps support the development of local, state, and federal anti-hate crime legislation; (d) it provides law enforcement professionals with both the information to prevent hate crimes from occurring in the first place, and the tools needed to work with communities in dealing with these crimes when they do occur; and (e) it encourages victims to come forward and ultimately get the support and assistance they may need.

Law enforcement participation in this initiative increased quickly during the first 4 years of the program but, by 1994, it seemed to have reached a plateau. Table 8.1 describes the law enforcement participation rates in hate crime reporting to the FBI from the passage of the Act through 1994.

In 1994, 7,298 law enforcement agencies participated in the hate crime program. At the time of this study, this was the highest number of participating agencies since the program's inception. However, this number was still less than half of the more than 16,000 law enforcement agencies that report Index crimes[1] to the FBI's Uniform Crime Reporting program. Also of interest is the large number of agencies that participate in the program but report that no hate crimes have occurred. Of the 7,298 participating agencies, only 1,150 (or 16%) reported hate crimes as having actually occurred in their jurisdictions. The remaining 84% of participating agencies reported that no hate crimes had occurred.

The Problem

Law enforcement agencies that do participate in hate crime reporting programs are often accused by private advocacy groups of underreporting these crimes. The New York City Gay and Lesbian (NYCGL) Anti-Violence Project's *Report on Anti-Gay/Lesbian Violence in the United States* (1995) cited wide disparities between hate crime figures provided by local organizations versus those that were provided by law enforcement agencies. Comparing 1994 hate crime numbers, the group found that for every single antigay or antilesbian incident that police agencies reported, community agencies identified 4.67 such incidents.

Many victims do not report hate crimes to the police for one reason or another. The most frequently cited reason among victims of antigay or antilesbian violence for failure to report bias incidents to police was fear of secondary victimization (i.e., insensitivity and abuse by police [NYCGL Anti-Violence Project, 1995]). However, according to the same source, victims of antigay or antilesbian violence did report crimes to the police 37% of the time. However, only 68% of these reports were officially labeled as bias crimes by police. This failure on the part of the police to correctly identify bias crimes as such was explored by Jack McDevitt (1987), a Northeastern University criminology professor, in research he conducted at the Boston Police Department. In his 1987 study, McDevitt examined 452 bias incidents handled by the Boston Police Department, and found that only 19 (4.2%) had been appropriately identified as bias incidents by reporting officers (B. Levin, 1992). It seems that the failure of

crime victims to report bias incidents to police, combined with police misidentification or failure to identify these crimes, add to the already burdensome and complex task of collecting meaningful data on hate crimes.

Law enforcement officers have reported informally several reasons why they misidentify or choose not to identify hate crimes. Some police officers, for example, have attributed their lack of participation to burdensome, albeit well-intentioned, departmental policies which sensationalize hate crimes.[2] The officers explain that when relatively minor crimes like simple assault or intimidation get labeled as hate crimes, the incidents can become so high-profile that they would have preferred not to have made such a distinction. Other officers have indicated that they personally do not believe that it is appropriate to treat hate crimes as something special. Instead, they believe that all crimes of similar magnitude should be treated the same.[3] B. Levin (1992) writes that critics of police cite "personal prejudice as the main cause of misidentification." Levin also cites organizational conditioning as a problem. He writes, "Police officers are conditioned to identify crimes based on the severity of injury or the magnitude of property damage . . . not on the basis of motive" (p. 173). Levin contends that this organizational conditioning inhibits officers from understanding the subtleties and importance of bias crimes in the context of a larger, community-wide perspective.

Anecdotal accounts from law enforcement officers have also identified some of the factors that prevent or inhibit law enforcement agency participation in national hate crime data collection efforts. For example, some law enforcement agencies have attributed their lack of participation to insufficient resources. Higher public demand for service combined with shrinking budgets and manpower have prohibited some agencies from developing a mechanism to collect and report hate crime data. In some situations, law enforcement administrators have decided not to participate because they believe that the identification of traditional crimes as hate crimes could divide their jurisdictions along racial lines.

On the other end of the spectrum, information regarding factors that encourage participation

Table 8.2   Hate Crime Data Collection: The Sequence of Events

Step 1	Victim's report
Step 2	Police officer's record
Step 3	Police determine and verify hate bias
Step 4	Police agencies participate in hate crime program

have included increased public support, passage of the Hate Crime Statistics Act, and the support of well-established advocacy groups like the Anti-Defamation League of B'nai B'rith (ADL), the National Association for the Advancement of Colored People (NAACP), the International Association of Chiefs of Police (IACP), the National Sheriff's Association (NSA), and the National Organization of Black Law Enforcement Executives (NOBLE), to name just a few.

From these explanations one can see that there are a number of social forces that might prevent individuals and agencies from fully participating in a program to identify and report hate crimes. Some forces are based within the organization (e.g., resources, policies, and organizational culture). Others are based outside the organization (e.g., the political climate, local laws, or social norms). Still others are based on individual convictions (e.g., religious beliefs and personal commitment). Social forces that encourage participation also seem to lie both inside and outside the law enforcement organization. Although statistical data are available regarding the number of law enforcement agencies that collect hate crime data, no empirical data currently exists regarding the forces that either encourage or discourage either individual officers' participation or law enforcement agency participation in hate crime data collection. The study presented here attempts to fill this empirical void by examining the forces that affect hate crime reporting as they coexist in the social field of the law enforcement agency.[4]

The Scope of This Research

Once a hate crime occurs, several things must happen before the crime is counted as part of the national data. First, the victim must report the

crime to the police. Next, the police officer must record the crime by filing an incident report. Then, the police department must have a mechanism in place to review the incident to determine and verify a bias motivation. Finally, the police agency must participate in the national data collection program (see Table 8.2).

The primary foci of this study are the police officer recording of hate crime and police agency participation in hate crime data collection programs (Steps 2 and 4). The fact that a police officer might misidentify (e.g., fail to recognize a hate bias [Step 3]) is also considered. It is important to note that this research is based on hate crime as defined by the Hate Crime Statistics Act of 1990, and as set forth by the Federal Bureau of Investigation. This means that *hate crimes*, as it applies herein, refers only to criminal acts: street crimes such as murder, rape, robbery, assault, intimidation, and the like.

METHOD

Focus group interviews and survey research were the two methods used in this study. The focus groups involved interviews with police officers and civilian specialists from six jurisdictions in two east coast states. The jurisdictions included two city police departments, two suburban county police departments, one state police agency, and one university police department. The 47 participants in the five focus groups were police administrators, midlevel managers, supervisors, detectives, patrol officers, and civilian specialists. The results of these interviews were used by the researchers to construct a survey instrument, the Hate Crime Reporting Climate Survey (HCRCS), for distribution to a larger sample of law enforcement professionals. The collection and analysis of HCRCS data comprised the second stage in this study. The 147 respondents to the HCRCS were selected from four jurisdictions, one in each region of the United States: Northeast, West, Central, and South. Two of the participating agencies were city police departments and two were suburban police departments. Two of the participating agencies reported hate crimes to the FBI in 1994, and two did not. The survey

Table 8.3   Comparison of Law Enforcement Agencies Participating in Study

Region/Type Agency	Population	Crime Rate	Violent Crime Rate	Property Crime Rate	Hate Crimes Reported	Total Police Officers
Northeast (suburban county)	717,879	6,241.4	1,001.3	5,240.2	93	1,487
West (city)	389,458	10,323.7	1,206.3	9,120.4	40[a]	569
South (city)	38,624	11,894.2	1,421.4	10,472.8	0	80
Central (suburban county)	121,799	2,572.3	201.15	2,371.1	0	169

NOTE: All crime figures were obtained from the Federal Bureau of Investigation's (FBI) Uniform Crime Reporting Program.
a. This agency collected hate crime statistics in 1994, but did not report them to the FBI. This figure was obtained directly from this city police department.

participants were also police administrators, midlevel managers, supervisors, detectives, patrol officers, and civilian specialists. Table 8.3 compares the police departments that participated in the survey across a number of variables, including population of jurisdiction, crime rate, hate crimes reported, and number of police officers. The agencies from the Northeast and West reported hate crimes in 1994. The police agencies in the South and Central regions did not.

RESULTS

Focus Group Findings

The focus group participants identified a number of significant variables that affect whether police officers properly identify and record hate crimes when they are reported by the victim. They also provided an enormous amount of insight regarding the variables that affect whether police agencies participate in hate crime reporting initiatives. The focus groups were organized to elicit information about forces that affect hate crime reporting. Information was collected and organized into four categories: agency encouragers, agency discouragers, individual encouragers, and individual discouragers. Agency encouragers and agency discouragers are the forces that affect (i.e., encourage or discourage) whether the police department participates in hate crime data collection. Individual

encouragers and individual discouragers are the forces that either encourage or discourage the individual police officer's active participation. Collectively, the focus group participants identified 30 variables that they believed could affect a police department's participation in hate crime data collection; 15 variables were identified as encouraging forces, and 15 were identified as discouraging forces. Likewise, there were 30 variables that the respondents identified that could affect the individual police officer's participation in the identification and reporting of hate crime. Fifteen of these variables were identified as encouraging forces, and 15 were identified as forces that discouraged participation. Table 8.4 provides a summary list of the encouraging and discouraging variables at the agency level, and Table 8.5 summarizes the variables at the individual officer level.

The researchers used the findings from the focus groups to develop the HCRCS. The purpose of the HCRCS was to assess the degree to which each of the 60 variables existed respectively within the participating police departments. The survey provided several important insights, including the recognition that each department had its own unique field of forces (i.e., the degree to which each variable from the focus groups existed in the department, and in what combination was different for each department). However, most useful was the ability to statistically reduce the 60 variables into 10 common factors. The findings from the factor analysis of the HCRCS data are presented in the section that follows.[5]

Table 8.4   Variables That Affect Whether Agencies Report Hate Crimes

Agency Encouragers	*Agency Discouragers*
Ability to assess intergroup tensions in community	Not deemed important by department
Desire to give support to communities	Perception on part of police that no problem exists
Belief that hate crime reporting will improve police/community relations	Insufficient support staff to process, record, and submit hate crime data.
Belief that police help set level of acceptable behavior in the community	Perceived as not being real police work
Understanding that community wants police to report hate violence	A belief that reporting hate crimes will make things worse for victim
Need to know extent of problem as first step to developing solutions	A belief that reporting hate crimes will make things worse for communities
Lets community know that department takes hate crimes seriously	Perception that some minority groups complain unnecessarily
A belief that victims will get help	Not a priority of local government
Will help diffuse racial tensions within the police department	A belief that identifying a crime as a hate crime will have no effect on the outcome
The right thing to do politically	A belief that it is wrong to make these types of crimes special
The right thing to do morally	A belief that hate crime reporting will result in negative publicity for the community
Will help maintain department's good relationship with diverse groups	A belief that hate crime reporting supports the political agendas of gay and minority groups (which is seen as a negative thing)
Consistent with values of department	It creates too much additional work
A belief that identifying problem will keep others safe	Hate crimes are not as serious as other crimes (i.e., a lower priority)
Citizens appreciate the hate crime reporting efforts of the police	Agency does not have the adequate technological resources

Survey Findings

In the present study a relatively large number of variables (total of 60) were used to describe agency and individual encouragers and discouragers. Factor analysis was used to identify overarching factors (constructs) that connect and represent these variables. The researcher found that the 30 police agency variables loaded high on five common factors. These five factors are described as (a) shared attitudes and beliefs about hate crime reporting, (b) utility in community relations, (c) organizational self-preservation, (d) efficacy of police involvement, and (e) resource allocation. The 30 individual officer variables also loaded high on five common factors. These factors are described as (a)

supportive organizational policies and practices, (b) individual attitudes/beliefs about hate crime reporting, (c) professional self-preservation, (d) work-related difficulties, and (e) organization's commitment. Singularly and in combination, these 10 factors affect the levels at which law enforcement participates in hate crime reporting. The 10 factors are described below.

Agency-Level Factors

Shared attitudes/beliefs about hate crime reporting. Shared attitudes/beliefs about hate crime reporting refers to the attitudes and beliefs about hate crime reporting that are held within the agency. These are attitudes and beliefs that

Table 8.5   Variables That Affect Whether Police Officers Record Crime

Individual Encouragers	Individual Discouragers
Departmental policy mandates hate crime reporting	Belief that it is not viewed as important by department officials
Belief that early identification of problem is key to effective solution	Too much additional work
Belief that it is an important part of the job	Sometimes runs counter to officer's personal beliefs
Belief that it will help prevent problems	Belief that hate crimes are not serious
Belief that reporting hate crimes will prevent personal (officer) liability	Belief that hate crimes should not be treated as special
Belief that hate crimes are morally wrong	Little concern for some minority groups (e.g., homosexuals and others)
Encouraged to report by department officials	Not the job of the police (more like social work)
Encouraged and supported by supervisors and colleagues	Not recognized or rewarded for reporting hate crimes
A clear, understood, and accepted departmental policy	Informally encouraged to adjust complaints (no reports) because of the large number of calls for service.
It benefits victims and communities	Lack of common definition of hate crime
Internal checks to make sure officers do not misidentify hate crime	Incident will be blown out of proportion—unnecessarily become high profile
Recognized as good for investigating and recording hate crime	Officers already too busy; not enough police officers to investigate properly
Desire to be considered a good police officer	Personally opposed to supporting gay and minority political agendas
It is encouraged and rewarded by the department	Lack of training: How to identify and respond to hate crimes
Personal desire to comply with departmental policy	Victims do not want to assist in prosecution

are shared by most of the members of the agency. These attitudes/beliefs relate to whether the department membership perceives that citizens want them to report hate crimes, whether the community will appreciate the police department's efforts in this area, whether it is morally the right thing to do, and whether hate crimes should be treated as special—to name just a few.

Perceived utility in community relations. This refers to the perception on the part of the police agency that hate crime reporting will be useful in the area of community relations—specifically if it will improve the police/community relationship. It also refers to the agency's belief regarding the utility of hate crime reporting for assessing intergroup tensions in the community.

Organizational self-preservation. This refers to the department's desire to survive in its environment. This includes its desire to improve relations with diverse community groups and to remain consistent with the values that are held (and shaped) by the larger society in which the agency exists.

Efficacy of police involvement. Efficacy of police involvement refers to the belief on the part of the organization that police involvement in hate crime data collection can have a positive effect. This includes beliefs regarding whether identifying hate crimes will make things better or worse for victims and communities, whether hate crime reporting is real police work, and whether hate crime reporting is helping victims or merely serving to advance political agendas.

Resource allocation. This refers to the department's desire to distribute resources toward priority areas. With limited resources, police departments must prioritize. If there is a perception that hate crime reporting is not a priority, then few resources (i.e., training and support staff) will be directed to it.

Individual-Level Factors

Supportive organizational policies and practices. This refers to the degree to which the organization's policies and practices support hate crime reporting. If the police agency does not have a hate crime reporting policy or has a policy that is not followed in practice, officers are not likely to recognize and record these crimes. However, if the police agency has a strong policy that is reinforced by an internal system of training, quality control checks, and recognition for reporting, then police officers are more likely to recognize and record these crimes at higher levels.

Individual attitudes and beliefs about hate crime reporting. This refers to the officers' personal beliefs about hate crime and hate crime reporting. These personal beliefs include whether hate crime reporting is effective, whether it is the job of the police to do it, or whether the officers believe hate crime is really a problem that needs to be addressed—to name just a few.

Professional self-preservation. Professional self-preservation refers to the officer's personal desire to survive and to be successful in the police environment. This includes the officer's desire to comply with departmental policies and to be considered a good police officer.

Work-related difficulties. This refers to the real-life difficulties experienced by the officers when trying to investigate hate crimes. These difficulties include additional effort that may or may not get recognized, pressure from supervisors and colleagues to quickly adjust citizens' complaints (with no report) because of a large number of pending calls for police service, and the reluctance of victims to assist in the prosecution of hate crime.

Organization's commitment. This refers to the officers' beliefs about their organization's commitment to hate crime reporting. One measure of this commitment is the amount of training resources directed to hate crime investigation and reporting.

DISCUSSION AND CONCLUSION

The problem presented at the outset of this study was that the law enforcement community, although fully committed to the collection and reporting of crime data to the UCR Program, does not fully participate in the collection and reporting of hate crime data. This problem exists at two levels, (a) the police officer level, and (b) the police agency level.

For a hate crime to be counted in the national data, it must first be recorded by the police officer. In other words, the officer must write a police report that correctly identifies the crime as a hate crime. Once the crime is recorded by the police officer it must be sent by the police agency to either the state UCR Program or to the FBI in order to be counted. In some cases police officers correctly identify and record a hate crime, but the agency does not submit this information to the national program. In other cases, police agencies might participate in the national data collection program, but report that no hate crimes had occurred in their jurisdiction because officers did not record or properly identify the crime. So, factors at both the police officer and the police agency levels were considered in this study.

The reluctance on the part of some police agencies and officers to fully participate in reporting hate crimes creates problems for those who count on reliable data to create policies, draft legislation, conduct research, direct police resources, and more. Without the full participation of the law enforcement community, it is difficult to use the existing national hate crime data in any meaningful way.

Questions are often asked: "Why do some police departments participate in hate crime reporting and others don't?" "How can we get the police to fully participate in this effort?" Prior to this research the only information available regarding police participation in hate crime data collection was anecdotal accounts offered by individual officers. Experts in the field also have their best guesses as to why this phenomenon is occurring.

The research presented here explores this issue in some detail. The foundations of this research, including the interpretations of the results, are in force-field analysis (an application of Lewin's field theory) that holds the following assumptions:

1. Social phenomena, like hate crime reporting, can only be fully understood by examining them together in the social field and not as isolated parts.

2. Within a social field there are counteracting forces at work, both internal and external, that affect behavior.

3. A state of quasi-stationary equilibrium will occur within a social field that will stabilize behavior at a certain level.

Field theory provides not only the framework for assessing counteracting forces, but also a mechanism for identifying effective change strategies (Lewin, 1948; Cartwright, 1951).

To explore the field of forces that affect police officer participation in hate crime reporting, the researchers conducted a series of focus group interviews with a diverse group of police officers and civilian specialists from two states. Although it is possible that there could be an infinite number of variables that affect law enforcement participation, the focus groups identified 60 variables. These 60 variables were identified as either encouragers (driving forces for police participation) or discouragers (restraining forces inhibiting police participation). These 60 variables provided the substance of the HCRCS that was developed to learn more about the presence of these factors in law enforcement agencies. The HCRCS was distributed in four police agencies, one in each region of the country. The analysis of the results revealed two important findings that are outlined below.

Each police agency has its own unique field of forces affecting behavior. Each police agency in this study was found to have its own unique combination of variables (or forces) that affect hate crime reporting behavior. By quantifying and analyzing these variables as a field of forces, one could easily identify strategies to change behavior in the desired direction. For example, if increased hate crime reporting is the goal, then specific encouragers (e.g., supportive departmental policies and systems for recognition and rewards) can be increased, and specific discouragers (e.g., lack of training and support staff) are decreased. These actions, then, are likely to result in an increased level of hate crime reporting. Similarities and differences in the presence of these hate-crime-reporting variables across police agencies could provide clues regarding the changes that might work to improve reporting behavior.

There are a small number of common factors that combine to affect law enforcement participation in hate crime reporting. There appear to be 10 factors that both alone and in combination significantly affect law enforcement participation in hate crime reporting. These factors are summarized in Tables 8.6 and 8.7.

The research findings have provided a thorough look at the forces present in police agencies that affect individual and organizational behavior and its relation to hate crime reporting. These findings point directly to forces both within police agencies and within individual police officers that either encourage or discourage hate crime reporting. This analysis suggests change strategies that could improve the level at which the law enforcement community participates in hate crime reporting.

The findings from this research have implications in two areas: (a) the formation of departmental policies and procedures, and (b) the development of hate crime training curricula.

Recommendations for Departmental Hate Crime Policies and Procedures

Based on the results of this study, the researchers make the following recommendations regarding departmental hate crime policies and procedures:

1. An organizational policy should be implemented requiring police officers to investigate

Table 8.6   Factors That Affect Law Enforcement Participation in Hate Crime Reporting

Agency Factors	Description
Shared attitudes/beliefs about hate crime reporting	Refers to organizational attitudes and beliefs, both negative and positive, about hate crime reporting. These beliefs include whether citizens want the police to report, whether the community will appreciate the police department's efforts, whether it is morally the right thing to do, or whether hate crimes should be treated as special.
Utility in community relations	Refers to the police organization's perception that hate crime reporting will be useful in the area of community relations.
Organizational self-preservation	Refers to the department's desire to survive in its social environment. It also refers to the organization's desire to improve relations with diverse community groups, and to remain consistent with organizational values (that are shaped by the culture of the society in which the agency exists).
Efficacy of police involvement	Refers to the organization's belief that police involvement can have a positive effect.
Resource allocation	Refers to the department's desire to distribute resources toward priority areas.

and take official police reports in all cases where a bias motivation is suspected.

2. Policies should set forth formal, step-by-step procedures for the investigation and recording of reported hate crimes, the verification of the bias motivations, effective strategies for dealing with victims and affected communities, and the reporting of verified hate crimes to the UCR program.

3. Policy statements should include explicit statements of values, specifically those relating to the recognition and appreciation of diversity within the jurisdiction and within the police department. These value statements should be consistent with organizational practices.

4. Police officers who aggressively and effectively investigate hate crimes should be recognized and rewarded for their efforts.

5. Data regarding the occurrence of hate crimes within the jurisdiction should be shared with community groups at face-to-face meetings between the police and community. This will let the community know that the police are aware that these crimes are occurring, and that they take them seriously.

6. Training and personnel resources for hate crime investigations should remain a priority.

Inadequate training and resources in the area of hate crimes sends the message to employees that the program is not a priority.

Recommendations for Hate Crime Training

A hate crime training curriculum should include the following components:

1. the mechanics of investigating and recording the hate crime, verifying the bias motivation, and reporting the offense to the UCR program;

2. effective methods for working with victims and communities in the prevention and response to hate crimes—this includes the initial response by the investigating officers when an incident first occurs as well as the follow-up response from the top police administration;

3. local, state, and federal hate crime and civil rights laws—this should include methods and procedures for successful prosecutions;

4. the opportunity for officers to meet and dialogue with members of affected community groups;

5. an exploration of the positive and negative effects of reporting hate crimes from the victim's,

Table 8.7   Factors That Affect Police Officers' Participation in Hate Crime Reporting

Individual Factors	Description
Supportive organizational policies and practices	Refers to the degree to which the organization's policies and practices support hate crime reporting. This includes formal and informal systems for recognition and rewards.
Individual attitudes/beliefs about hate crime reporting	Refers to the police officer's individual beliefs about hate crime and hate crime reporting.
Professional self-preservation	Refers to the police officer's desire to survive and to be successful in the police organization. This includes the desire to be considered a good police officer.
Work-related difficulties	Refers to the difficulties experienced on the job by the police officers as they try to investigate hate crimes. This might include busy case loads and a reluctance on the part of the victim to assist in the prosecution of hate crimes.
Organization's commitment	Refers to the officer's beliefs about their organization's commitment to hate crime reporting. One measure of this commitment is the amount of training resources directed to hate crime investigation and reporting.

community's, and officer's perspective—real-life experiences should be the focus of these discussions whenever and wherever possible;

6. the effect of organizational culture on employee attitudes and behaviors, especially as it applies to law enforcement hate crime initiatives—this includes organizational change strategies where appropriate; and

7. a social psychology segment that includes topics such as prejudice, discrimination, stereotyping, ethnocentrism, nationalism, interpersonal relations, and group dynamics.

These recommendations are based on the findings of this study and are presented to assist law enforcement in developing effective hate crime reporting strategies. For it is only with the full support of the law enforcement community that the nation will ever have comprehensive and valid hate crime statistics.

NOTES

1. Index crimes are those crimes that, because of their frequency, severity, and likelihood of coming to the attention of police, are collected and reported to the FBI. Index crimes combine to form the annual crime index. These crimes include murder and nonnegligent manslaughter, forcible rape, aggravated assault, robbery, burglary, larceny theft, motor vehicle theft, and arson.

2. This refers to a telephone interview with a city police officer in an east coast state (1995).

3. This refers to an interview with a state police trooper in an east coast state (1995).

4. This study was conducted in 1996 in response to concerns about the relatively low level of law enforcement participation in the FBI's Hate Crime Data Collection Program (1996) (a part of the Uniform Crime Reporting Program). Since 1996, law enforcement participation in hate crime reporting has continued to increase at a moderate pace. However, efforts are still under way at the federal, state, and local levels to increase law enforcement participation in the national hate crime program.

5. The results of the Hate Crime Reporting Climate Survey were examined several different ways using a number of robust statistical techniques (Akiyama, 1996). For example, survey responses were examined and compared between the four agencies—two of the agencies were actually participating in the hate crime program, and two were not. A between-item examination of survey responses was also conducted. Both studies resulted in a number of interesting findings. However, the purpose of this chapter is to release the most general findings that

were the results of the focus groups and the factor analysis of the survey data.

REFERENCES

Akiyama, Y. (1996). *The u statistic.* Unpublished internal research document. Washington, DC: Federal Bureau of Investigation.

Barnes, A., & Ephross, P. H. (1994). The impact of hate violence on victims: Emotional and behavioral responses to attacks. *Social Work, 39*(3), 247–251.

Cartwright, D. (Ed.). (1951). *Field theory in social science: Selected theoretical papers by Kurt Lewin.* New York: Harper & Brothers.

Chua-eoan, H. (18 December, 1995). Enlisted killers. *Time.*

Eisler, B. (1993). The Hate Crime Statistics Act of 1990. *Criminal Law Bulletin, 29*(2), 99–123.

Harvey, C. (1994). Attack prompts debate. *The Washington Times.*

Hate Crime Statistics Act of 1990. Pub. L. 101–275.

Levin, B. (1992). Bias crimes: A theoretical & practical overview. *Stanford Law & Policy Review, Winter,* 165–181.

Levin, J., & McDevitt, J. (1994). *Hate crimes: The rising tide of bigotry and bloodshed.* New York: Plenum.

Lewin, G. (Ed.). (1948). *Resolving social conflicts.* New York: Harper & Brothers.

Martin, S. E. (1995). A cross-burning is not just an arson: Police social construction of hate crimes in Baltimore County. *Criminology, 33*(3), 303–326.

New York City Gay and Lesbian (NYCGL) Anti-Violence Project. (1995). *Report on anti-gay/lesbian violence in the United States.* New York: Author.

U.S. Congress (101st Congress). (1990). Hate Crimes Statistics Act. PL 101–275. Washington, DC.

U.S. Department of Justice, Federal Bureau of Investigation. (1992). *Training guide for hate. Crime data collection.* Washington, DC: Government Printing Office.

U.S. Department of Justice, Federal Bureau of Investigation. (1996). *Hate crime statistics.* Washington, DC: Government Printing Office.

QUESTIONS

1. In your opinion, is it the perpetrator's motivation or the discriminatory selection of a victim that defines an action as a hate crime?

2. If an offender deeply hates a person and attacks the person due to this personal animus, could the offense be considered a hate crime regardless of the demographic characteristics of the victim?

3. What is the Hate Crime Statistics Act? What requirements does it impose on the attorney general?

4. What factors might explain why many law enforcement agencies that participate in the collection of hate crime statistics report that no hate crimes occurred in their jurisdictions?

5. Why might police underreport or misidentify hate crimes? Discuss economic, social, political, organizational, and attitudinal reasons that can help explain underreporting.

6. What factors encourage police reporting of hate crimes, and what could be done to increase police reporting?

7. Could perceptions of lack of community support for hate crime reporting explain comparatively low rates of reporting in southern and central states?

8. What individual factors are significant in police officers' decisions to report hate crimes?

9. Why is accurate, reliable, and complete data on hate crimes important?

10. What recommendations do the authors make to improve police department policies and procedures for reporting hate crimes?

11. The authors recommend that police training include information on topics such as prejudice, discrimination, and similar issues. If you were designing a segment of the police curriculum so it reflected social psychological principles, what would it look like?

Part IV

HATE CRIME OFFENDERS

W ho are the perpetrators of hate crimes? Why are hate crimes committed? The articles in this section approach these questions using diverse theoretical perspectives and a wide range of methods. Taken together, the results illustrate how developing an adequate understanding of hate crimes requires us to look past the characteristics of the perpetrators to the social context surrounding hate crimes. When we do this, we discover that hate violence often reflects extant societal and legal norms that legitimize violence against particular groups.

9

HATE CRIME OFFENDERS

An Expanded Typology

JACK McDEVITT

JACK LEVIN

SUSAN BENNETT

All hate crime offenders are not the same, the authors of this article argue. Their research examines how hate crimes can reflect a variety of motivations and how these crimes and the offenders who commit them can be distinguished from one another along a variety of dimensions.

In recent years, much controversy has surrounded the passage of hate crime legislation both nationally and at the local level. The debate has challenged a variety of issues involving hate crimes, from questions regarding whether hate-motivated offenses differ from other similar crimes to concerns about the ability of criminal justice personnel to distinguish an offender's motivation (Iganski, 1999; Petrosino, 1999). Building on the earlier work of J. Levin and McDevitt (1993), this article seeks to inform the hate crime debate by constructing an offender typology in which the major motivations are represented.

BACKGROUND

Definition of Hate Crimes

Hate or bias crimes, as defined by the Federal Bureau of Investigation (FBI), are crimes that manifest evidence of prejudice based on race, religion, sexual orientation, or ethnicity (FBI, 1999). This definition has been expanded to include both physical and mental disabilities and gender. The Hate Crimes Statistics Act of 1990 requires that the attorney general develop procedures to collect information regarding hate offenses. The act does not single out hate

EDITORS' NOTE: From McDevitt, J., Levin, J., & Benett, S. (2001). Hate Crime Offenders: An Expanded Typology. *Journal of Social Issues, 58,* 303-317. Reprinted with permission from Blackwell Publishing, Ltd.

crimes as a new, distinct crime but assigns the determination of bias motivation in conjunction with traditional offenses (FBI, 1999).

Distinguishing Elements of Hate Crimes

Research concerning hate crime victims, offenders, society, and government has been undertaken to better understand and address the issue. Factors assessed in understanding hate crimes and measuring their impact have been generated from the victim's psychological and behavioral responses (Garcia & McDevitt, 1999), attitudes and perceptions of hate crimes among various groups within society (Craig, 1999), police records, and official data. Given the relative infrequency with which hate crimes are reported, and to a lesser degree, an offender is identified, research on offender motivation remains sparse.

Some researchers have looked at specific areas of hate crime motivation. For example, Van de Ven's (1995) study of violence against gay males and lesbians found that most of the offenders in his sample had engaged in antigay violence and that most of this violence was associated with the offender's antigay stereotypes. In a more recent study, Byers and his colleagues (Byers, Crider, & Biggers, 1999) identified various neutralization techniques used by hate crime offenders to justify their attacks on Amish victims. Recent research suggests also that the issue of heightened potential for retaliation is a valid concern among victims' groups and should continue to be addressed (B. Levin, 1999). It appears that victims in hate crime incidents are frequently threatened with revenge if they report the harassment to the police or if they do not act as the offender demands (e.g., move out of the neighborhood).

Identifying Hate Crimes

In the most horrendous of cases, bias intent may be obvious; in less severe incidents, however, detecting and identifying bias motivation becomes more complex and often goes undocumented. For example, if a victim reports to the police that he was attacked because he is Hispanic, but upon investigation the police discover that the offender had himself been an assault victim recently and was trying to retaliate for that attack, many police officers are less likely to categorize such an assault as a hate crime. One indicator police officers use to determine bias intent is lack of other motivation. In instances of hate crimes, there appear to be no gains for the assailant: There is no attempt to take money or other personal items, and there is no prior relationship between the victim and offender. Often only unprovoked attacks are designated as hate crimes, and those in which the offender perceives himself as retaliating for some perceived slight or bias are considered too complicated to allow for prosecution as a bias crime.

Two of the most recent and horrific hate crime incidents left little doubt as to the mindset and motivation of the murderers. In 1998 in Jasper, Texas, a Black man was dragged to his death behind a pickup truck, and that same year in Laramie, Wyoming, a young gay man was beaten, tied to a fence, and left to die. These homicides further served to demonstrate to Americans that bias could lead to some of the most violent actions that one person can perpetrate against another. But what of the numerous incidents in which indicators of bias intent are hazy, absent, or unknown to the victim or police officer investigating? Additionally, in a number of violent bias crimes, the offender has previously engaged in less severe acts of intimidation. All too often these actions go unrecognized by the police, and thus the offender is empowered and the victims further traumatized. When hate crimes go unaddressed, we as a society send a message to offenders that this behavior is acceptable and possibly even appreciated. This reinforces the behavior and empowers the perpetrators to continue and in many cases to escalate their attack (McDevitt, 1989). In addition, by ignoring hate crimes we are revealing a general lack of concern for the victim and reinforcing the notion that many people in the community may in fact agree with the offender. In August 2001, for example, Donald Butler, a 29-year-old Black resident of Pemberton Township, Pennsylvania, was targeted by two White supremacists who shouted racial slurs at him as he stood on the front lawn of his home. Perhaps seeing the verbal abuse against their neighbor as an isolated and trivial event, Butler's White neighbors did absolutely nothing to assure him of their support or indignation. Three weeks later, the same two hatemongers returned with baseball bats, this time invading Butler's home in the dead of night, where they brutally beat him and his wife. The Butlers escaped with stitches and broken bones, but they also felt hurt and alone, as if no one really cared. They have since relocated to another community.

Offender Typology

In 1993 J. Levin and McDevitt suggested that hate crime offenders could be grouped into three major categories according to the motivation of the offenders involved. Based on interviews with police officials, victims, and several hate crime offenders, J. Levin and McDevitt developed a typology that identified three primary motivations: offenders who committed their crimes for the excitement or the thrill, offenders who saw themselves as defending their turf, and finally a small group of offenders whose life's mission had become to rid the world of groups they considered evil or inferior.

The primary position of the present chapter is that the current typology used to assist law enforcement in investigating and identifying hate crimes is incomplete. Based on discussions with hate crime investigators after the release of the original typology, it occurred to us that there are sometimes additional factors and indicators present that seem to relate to bias motivation but are not currently specified in the literature. Offenses that involve these factors and indicators are bias motivated but include distinct characteristics that indicate a retaliatory theme. Therefore, we propose that the category "retaliatory" be included within the hate crime offender typology. Although the categories "defensive" and "retaliatory" share some features, we maintain that they are separate because of the different precipitants that spark violence in each.

The basic underlying factor found throughout all of the hate offender groups is bigotry (J. Levin & McDevitt, 1993). This is considered a primary motivation for the hate offense to occur. However, each offender category differs with respect to the conditions, both psychologically and environmentally, that ultimately lead to a violent attack. In thrill crimes, for example, the offender is set off by a desire for excitement and power; defensive hate crime offenders are provoked by feeling a need to protect their resources under conditions they consider to be threatening; retaliatory offenders are inspired by a desire to avenge a perceived degradation or assault on their group; and mission offenders perceive themselves as crusaders who hope to cleanse the earth of evil.

METHODS

To provide empirical grounding for the expanded typology, case files used to develop the original typology were reanalyzed. The Community Disorders Unit (CDU) of the Boston Police Department provided these case files to the research team. The final sample of 169 cases constituted the total number of cases in which the offender was known and represented: 47% of the 358 hate crimes reported and investigated by the Boston police during the 18-month period from July 1991 through December 1992. The review was limited to cases involving either a known suspect or an offender who was arrested.

One concern about using official reports to identify offender motivation is important to note. Although any study of motivation that is inferred from indirect data (as opposed to direct interviews conducted by the researcher) introduces potential bias, the investigators from the CDU are a rather unique source of information. These investigators are experienced police investigators who have been trained and had experience investigating hate crimes in Boston. All investigators have been instructed in the elements necessary to prove bias motivation in court. They have, for example, been trained that the use of language alone cannot be an indicator of motivation.

For each case in the sample, research assistants from Northeastern University reviewed the entire case file to discover potential sources of information regarding offender motivation. These sources included the original incident report filed by the responding officer, statements made by the offender to the victim, case notes from the CDU officer investigating the case, and any statements made by the offender prior to his/her arrest.

The research assistants were graduate students from the master's program in criminal justice at Northeastern University. All students participated in a 2-day training program to familiarize them with the goals of the study, the previous work on the typology, and most importantly the forms and language used by the investigators from the CDU serving as a source of the data set. Three different students assessing interrater reliability coded the first 25 cases independently. After some sources of confusion were identified and resolved, all cases were coded, including the original 25. The intercoder reliability check resulted in more than 90% total agreement (three out of three coders agreed) as to the placement of incidents.

A code sheet was then completed for each case in the sample. Relevant data coded from the CDU files consisted of location of incident, offense type, bias indication, type of injury, offender's motivation, relationship of parties involved, involvement of organized groups, and victim and offender characteristics. Data were also coded that described the outcome of the offender's case at each step in the criminal justice system (e.g., dismissed because of insufficient evidence during grand jury). These data were coded onto the hate crime typology code sheet.

RESULTS AND DISCUSSION

The analysis of the hate crime case files indicated that the most common type of hate crime was an attack committed for the thrill or excitement of the act. As shown in Table 9.1, fully 66% of the cases under review in this study were motivated by a desire for excitement or thrills. In this category of crimes, youths often told police they were just bored and looking for some fun. In 91% of these thrill-motivated cases, the perpetrators reported having left their own neighborhood to search for a victim in a gay bar, a temple in another part of town, or a minority neighborhood. It is important to stress that their target was not selected randomly but was chosen because the offender perceived that the victim was somehow different. This was indicated by the CDU following its investigation, which determined that the crime was motivated by bias. Following nationally accepted standards, investigators from the CDU

Table 9.1   Frequency of Offender Motivation in Boston Police Department Cases, 1991–1992

Offender motivation	Number of cases	Percentage of cases
Thrill	111	66%
Defensive	43	25%
Retaliatory	14	8%
Mission	1	<1%
Total	169	100%

employed the following bias indicators: the offenders' use of slurs or epithets, the offenders' history of bias and violence, the coincidence of a triggering event, the presence of bias graffiti, and the location of the attack. Although the underlying factor was bigotry, according to interviews with CDU investigators, the attack in these thrill-motivated cases was triggered by an immature desire to display power and to experience a rush at the expense of someone else. In discussions with the police, several of these young offenders revealed that their only benefit from the attack was some vague sense of their own importance: a sadistic high as well as bragging rights with their friends who believed that hatred was cool. In a recent study, Byers et al. (1999) similarly reported that for most hate crime offenders, thrill seeking seemed to be a key motivation. Moreover, in a study focusing on antigay behavior among young adults, Franklin (2000) separates the two aspects of what we refer to as thrill motivation into two themes, peer dynamics and thrill seeking. As we discuss later, this distinction may be important for assigning degree of culpability to thrill-seeking offenders.

As indicated in Table 9.1, some 25% of the hate crimes reported to the Boston Police were categorized as defensive. Unlike thrill-motivated offenses, defensive bias attacks were committed, from the offender's prejudiced point of view, in order to protect his neighborhood from those he considered to be outsiders or intruders. In interviews with police investigators and in several police reports, offenders expressed their belief that members of another group, whether Black, Latino, or Asian, had undeservedly moved into a home on their previously all-White block. According to these reports, the objective of these crimes was to convince the outsider to relocate elsewhere and also to send a message to other members of the victim's group that they too were not welcome in the neighborhood. Previous research has suggested that hate crimes are associated with demographic shifts at the neighborhood level. More specifically, Greene (Greene, Glaser, & Rich, 1998) has indicated that hate crimes tend to increase in what he refers to as "defended neighborhoods," those previously all-White areas that have begun to transition, with a growing population of Black residents. Similarly, research conducted by the *Chicago Reporter* (Gordon, 1997) has similarly found that Chicago-area suburbs with growing minority population have recently experienced increasing numbers of hate offenses directed against Blacks and Latinos.

Reviewing the occurrences of hate crimes in America, it has been noted that a single hate offense is often followed by a large number of follow-up attacks. For example, the month with the most hate crimes in New York City's history was the period following the deadly attack on a young Black man, Yusuf Hawkins, in the White working-class community known as Bensonhurst (Levin, 1999). Many of the attacks in the subsequent month were retaliatory in nature. Many offenders felt that someone should pay for the death of Hawkins. Once this cycle of action and reaction takes hold, it is difficult to end, especially when the media get involved and young offenders see themselves as avenging their honor.

In retaliatory hate crimes, whether the original incident actually occurred is often irrelevant. Sometimes a rumor of an incident may cause a group of offenders to take vengeance, only to learn later that their original information was merely unfounded hearsay. According to interviews with investigators from the CDU, some retaliatory hate crimes are committed after rumors circulate about a crime and before anyone has had a chance to verify the accuracy of the original rumor.

In discussing retaliatory offenses, we refer specifically to incidents in which offenders act in response to a hate crime, whether real or perceived. We do not include those actions in which offenders see themselves as reacting against the presence of a group or individual. Attacks based on revenge tend to have the greatest potential for fueling and refueling additional hate offenses. For example, a recent hate-related killing spree committed by a Black resident of suburban Pittsburgh most likely triggered a retaliatory rampage perpetrated by a White resident of the same area just weeks later. In March 1999, shortly after Ronald Taylor attacked several Whites in what can be described as a classic mission-killing spree, Richard Baumhammers decided to get even with immigrants and minorities by targeting them in a retaliatory mass murder. Although it is only speculated that Baumhammers sought revenge for the actions of Taylor, the likelihood of such extreme and similar events occurring in such proximity in time and space seem to be more than coincidental. In the present study, approximately 8% of all hate crimes were concluded to be retaliatory in their motivation.

In an earlier study, J. Levin and McDevitt (1993) suggested a forth category of hate offenses in which a perpetrator becomes totally committed to bigotry, making it the primary focus of his life. In so-called mission hate crimes, the perpetrator seeks to rid the world of evil rather than to respond to any specific event that threatens him. He may join an organized hate group, such as the Ku Klux Klan or the National Alliance, or he may operate alone, as did Timothy McVeigh, the convicted murderer of 168 Americans in the bombing of the Murrah Federal Building in Oklahoma City. He makes hate a career rather than a hobby. In the present study, we determined that only 1 out of 169 hate offenses could be categorized as a mission hate crime.

Implications for Policy

One reason why the original typology has been so widely adopted by law enforcement is that, early on, it offered a way to categorize hate crime offenders and suggested some clues as to methods of investigating hate offenses. If a department determines that a hate crime is defensive (this can sometimes be determined by certain elements, such as a series of prior threats and/or a victim who recently moved into a neighborhood), then the investigation can focus on those who would be considered at risk. If, for example, a Black family that moves into an all-White neighborhood receives a couple of threats on the answering machine and then finds that its windows are broken, it is highly unlikely that some person from another city or state is responsible. More likely, it is a neighbor whose house is in proximity to that of the victim.

It is sometimes difficult to determine which crimes are bias motivated. For this reason, the FBI has developed a set of indicators that it encourages officers to employ when they identify bias-motivated offenses. The *Uniform Crime Reports* present 13 indicators, some of which should be evident in a particular crime in order for a determination of bias to be made (U.S. Department of Justice, 1990). These include information such as similar previous incidents committed by the offender, previous hate crimes that have occurred in the same neighborhood as the incident in question, and the relevance of the date of the incident (e.g., Martin Luther King Day). Additionally, the *Uniform Crime Reports* guidelines caution investigators to weigh facts on a case-by-case basis, to attend to misleading and feigned facts, to be aware that offenders may have been mistaken in their perception of the victim's characteristics, and to change bias designations when bias intent is established after the fact or withdrawn after original reporting. With growing understanding of what indicators to look for, the investigation process can be greatly enhanced.

The most crucial piece of information currently collected to establish bias motive is the offender's use of language. Hate crime data collected by the Los Angeles Human Rights Commission (1997) indicates that 90% of the incidents documented were determined to be bias related because of hate speech or symbols used in the commission of the crime. Although some critics claim that punishing this behavior is a legal infringement of a person's freedom of speech (Jacobs & Potter, 1998), it must be kept in mind that hate speech alone does not qualify as a crime. The criminal act that accompanies hate speech is the deplorable action, and hate speech is merely one piece of information that is used to assess bias motivation. The *Uniform*

Crime Reports' data collection guidelines warn that, before an incident can be reported as a hate crime, sufficient objective facts must be present to lead a reasonable and prudent person to conclude that the offender's actions were motivated, in whole or in part, by bias.

Based on previous work by Nolan and Akiyama (1999), McDevitt, Balboni, and Bennett (2000) recently conducted a national survey of police officials to examine perceptions of hate crimes held by law enforcement agencies across the country. The study found that the majority of police chiefs and hate crime investigators believe that hate-motivated offenses are more serious than those not motivated by hatred and that victims often fail to report hate crime incidents because they either fear the police or believe the police will not take the incident seriously. This mindset of the victim also reveals the lack of confidence officers apparently harbor and display when dealing with hate crime incidents.

Yet hate crime training for the majority of police officers is minimal (U.S. Department of Justice, 2000). This is an area in which training and clear guidelines could greatly increase positive interactions and encourage reporting by hate crime victims. Currently, officers lack appropriate knowledge regarding the most effective and appropriate ways to inquire about potential bias intent. It is believed that typical hate crime victims are also among the groups that have traditionally had strained relations with law enforcement (McDevitt et al., 2000). A clumsy approach by the police toward inquiring about possible bias motivation may further damage relations between victims' groups and law enforcement.

In addition to clear guidelines necessary for hate crime investigators, and for that matter, all law enforcement officers who may be the first on the scene of a potential hate attack, appropriate standards should be established for other criminal justice actors who must deal with more complex issues of establishing and prosecuting hate motivation in the commission of an offense.

Table 9.2 provides a descriptive summary of the various types of hate crime offenders and specific characteristics often associated with a particular type of attack. If the full range of

Table 9.2   Characteristics of Hate Crimes by Motivation of the Offender

Attack Characteristics	Thrill	Defensive	Retaliatory	Mission
Number of offenders	Group	Group	Single offender	Group
Age of offender(s)	Teens–young adults	Teens–young adults	Teens–young adults	Young adults–adults
Location	Victim's turf	Offender's turf	Victim's turf	Victim's or offender's turf
Weapon	Hands, feet, rocks	Hands, feet, rocks	Hands, feet, rocks, sticks, guns	Bats, guns
Victim offender history	None	Previous acts of intimidation	Often no history	None
Commitment to bias	Little	Moderate	Moderate	Full
Deterrence	Likely	Unlikely	Unlikely	Most unlikely

motivations and related outcomes are understood, more confident and accurate bias determinations can hopefully be made by all criminal justice actors.

The model can be useful in identifying different types of bias motivation. For instance, in distinguishing retaliatory from defensive attacks, the presence and/or absence of certain factors should be apparent. In the case of defensive bias crimes, there is not a particular hate incident that has spurred the attack. The attack stems from an overall defensive posture maintained by an individual against a particular group (or groups) of people who are considered a growing threat to resources and a cause of problems occurring in the life of the offender. The precipitant for a defensive attack consists of an intrusion of outgroup members into the offender's neighborhood, workplace, or campus. Consequently, these crimes often occur in or near the offender's turf (i.e., home, work, school) and involve groups of young offenders who have a history of previous acts of intimidation. By contrast, in retaliatory hate crimes, in which the offender is getting even for a specific (real or perceived) hate attack, we would observe that the offender is more likely to act alone, to perpetrate the attack outside of his own turf, and possibly to use more extreme violence.

Retaliation crimes also differ from defensive crimes in that in retaliation crimes, the threat of

an attack is not constant. Offenders will attack a victim only after they perceive that an incident has occurred in which the members of a particular group have somehow attacked someone from their own group. The location of an attack, in the case of retaliatory incidents, is comparable to that of thrill episodes, in that the attack is less likely (albeit not unheard of) to occur in the neighborhood of the offender. The offender actively seeks a target from the group considered responsible for the wrongdoing, and this is generally in the neighborhood of the victim or in an opportune area some distance from the residence of the offender. In avoiding targets close to their own turf, perpetrators make themselves less vulnerable to a counterattack.

In addition to offering a new dimension to the hate crime offender typology, the revised model suggests a continuum of culpability that will hopefully assist criminal justice decision makers in assessing the role of each individual hate crime offender in an incident (see Table 9.2). A common complaint from those who are empowered to arrest, charge, prosecute, and sentence hate crime offenders is that there are often multiple offenders, each with a different level of involvement in the crime. These levels of culpability affect many decisions made within the criminal justice system. For example, was one of the offenders not involved in the beating? Or did that offender attempt to stop the

Table 9.3   Culupability of Individuals Involved in Hate Crimes by Motivation of the Offender

Level of Culpability	Thrill	Defensive	Retaliatory	Mission
Leader	Encourages others			
Fellow traveler	Actively or hesitantly participates in crime	Actively participates in planning or crime	Actively or hesitantly participates in crime	Actively participates in hate group and crime
Unwilling participant	Does not actively participate in crime but does not attempt to stop crime or help victim	Does not actively participate in crime but does not attempt to stop crime or warn victim	Does not actively participate in crime but does not attempt to stop crime or warn victim	Does not actively participate in crime but cannot withdraw from the group
Hero	Attempts to stop crime	Warns victim	Attempts to stop crime and warns victim	Reports group behavior to police

Color Key

	= Highly Amenable to Change
	= Moderately Amenable to Change
	= Change Highly Unlikely

attack but get rebuffed by his friends? We are suggesting that in hate crimes, offenders often play different roles in a single incident and that these roles reflect differing levels of culpability. We base these dimensions on the review of hate crime case files from the Boston Police Department cited above and a set of interviews from police officers who have investigated hate crime incidents.

Levels of Culpability

The additional dimension that we suggest as necessary to appropriately address, prosecute, and sentence hate crimes is the degree of culpability of the offenders. This element is particularly useful in discussing levels of responsibility associated with group attacks. Such discussion does not address the issue of hate crimes as generally more harmful than identical crimes not motivated by hate. It is used only to discuss the usefulness of identifying levels of culpability for increased understanding of multiple-offender involvement in a hate-motivated attack.

Based on the cases we reviewed and the interviews with police investigators we conducted, those cases in which the offender was not a full participant in the crime offer particular challenges for law enforcement. In the cases we reviewed, if a young person was with a group that committed a hate crime but did not fully participate in it, that individual was not usually charged in the incident. In some cases the young person actually disagreed with the sentiment of the group but did not know how to get out of the situation and save face with his/her peers. It is important to note that most hate crime offenders are young males for whom respect from their peers is incredibly important. Sometimes, simply to prevent being rejected, these young people will go along with their friends, even if they disagree.

It is also important to acknowledge that in some cases young people have made heroic efforts at great personal cost to prevent hate crimes from occurring. The dimensions of culpability we suggest here are intended to acknowledge and assist in the identification of the full range of culpability in most hate crimes. We suggest that there are three levels of culpability, as depicted in Table 9.3: the leader in an incident, the fellow traveler, and the unwilling participant. Also to distinguish those who are culpable from those who are not, we offer the category of hero to acknowledge those individuals who actively try to intervene to protect the victim of bias-motivated violence.

Most hate crimes could not occur at all if someone didn't suggest that the group engage in this kind of violence. The leader performs this role; he (in the vast majority of cases in our data, the leader was a male) might suggest that the group go out and look for someone to terrorize or beat; he might be the one who, for the sake of a thrill, begins an altercation with someone who is crossing his turf.

Fellow travelers (a concept originally developed by political scientist Meredith Watts) may not have initiated the crime but—once a leader makes a suggestion to the group—are happy to go along (Watts & Zinnecker, 1998). These individuals are almost as culpable as the leaders, since they are willing to act on their hatred, so long as someone else initiates the crime.

By contrast, unwilling participants find themselves in a situation of which they do not approve, yet they also do not actively attempt to stop the attack. Such an unwilling participant may be the young man who is with a group of friends when an attack begins (e.g., when a Black man is seen walking through their neighborhood). Although he may not agree with the notion of attacking an innocent victim, he also does not know how to get out of the situation while saving face with his friends. For young teenage males, this is particularly difficult.

A number of police officers have told us about situations involving unwilling participants, because they are among the most difficult to decide to prosecute. Unwilling participants are clearly less at fault, since in many cases they do not join in the beating, but they also lacked the courage to resist and seldom report an attack to the police after the fact. Our typology suggests that these individuals have less culpability for the crime but are still culpable to some extent.

We have included a final category, heroes, to distinguish those individuals who actively attempt to stop the attack from the unwilling participants who acquiesce. Heroes may intervene to stop the beating and/or report the attack to the police. Their actions require a certain immunity to social influence and a strong sense of conscience. In most cases, heroes are asked to turn in their close friends in an effort to protect someone they have never met. We include this category as an example of behavior we should strive for and reward because it is an example of doing the right thing at a very difficult time.

Sentencing Options Based on Culpability

Determining culpability is also useful in assessing the kind of sanction to be imposed on the offender. Once the level of culpability is determined, the offender can be more effectively matched with a sentencing option that would be of optimal benefit to the offender and the victim. For instance, individuals determined to be unwilling participants may benefit most by community sanctions designed to promote understanding of the victim's group. Fellow travelers might also gain from such an option but would be considered a more reluctant group and might therefore require more intensive programming. It is particularly unlikely that leaders representing defensive, retaliatory, or mission groups would be amenable to alternative sanctions involving integration of or education about the victim's group. On the other hand, leaders associated with thrill hate crimes may benefit from such an option. It is believed that thrill leaders may not possess the level of distrust or perceive the victim's group to be as threatening or despicable as leaders of defensive, retaliatory, or mission groups.

CONCLUSION

The description provided to us by some retaliatory hate crime offenders was that the perpetrators needed to realize that they couldn't get away with attacking someone like them. Although the motivation was somewhat defensive in nature, the attack was based on more than the need to protect a neighborhood, a workplace, or a school.

As with any single study, the present work is limited in a number of ways. The typology we propose is based on research in a single urban jurisdiction and represents investigations conducted by only one police agency. Future research should attempt to replicate these findings in other settings, for example, in suburban and rural jurisdictions and in other parts of the country. In addition, it would be interesting to see if similar results were obtained from non-criminal-justice samples—for example, in school settings. Similarly, research should be done to assess the predictive capability of the revised typology.

Understanding different types of hate motivation and specific indicators associated with these have been shown to be useful in identifying and prosecuting hate crimes and providing appropriate services to hate crime victims. If police departments are not encouraged and trained to properly investigate bias intent, to record hate incidents, and to respond appropriately to the victims of such incidents, then we, as a society, are essentially making a statement that hate crimes are not important enough to receive our serious attention. This mindset only serves to isolate hate crime victims and their communities from the rest of humanity.

Historically, the criminal justice system has been charged with relieving the burden of retribution from crime victims. In the case of hate crimes, this service is especially important, because the magnitude of the victimization often extends throughout a community. By ignoring hate crimes, the system is refusing to acknowledge the suffering of these victims, making the burden for closure rest entirely on the victim or the victim's group. Tools that assist government agencies in understanding and effectively dealing with hate crime incidents may be our best effort toward curtailing this brand of violence. In J. Levin and McDevitt's original typology, this category was referred to as "reactive"; however, after careful consideration the category has been renamed "defensive." We feel that this term more accurately depicts the set of behavioral and

psychological influences that affect this type of hate crime offender. Renaming the category serves to reduce any confusion in understanding new elements of the typology.

REFERENCES

Byers, B., Crider, B., & Biggers, G. (1999). Bias crime motivation. *Journal of Contemporary Criminal Justice, 15*(1), 78–96.

Craig, K. M. (1999). Retaliation, fear, or rage: An investigation of African American and White reactions to racist hate crimes. *Journal of Interpersonal Violence, 14,* 138–151.

Franklin, K. (1999). Antigay behaviors among young adults: Prevalence, patterns, and motivators in a noncriminal population. *Journal of interpersonal Violence, 15*(4), 339–362.

Federal Bureau of Investigation (FBI). (1999). *(Annual) Uniform crime reports: Hate crime reporting statistics.* Washington, DC: Author.

Garcia, L., & McDevitt, J. (1999). *The psychological and behavioral effects of bias and nonbias motivated assault.* Washington, DC: U.S. Department of Justice, National Institute of Justice.

Gordon, D. (1997, September). Hate crimes strike changing suburbs. *Chicago Reporter,* p. 1.

Greene, D. P., Glaser, J., & Rich, A. (1998). From lynching to gay bashing: The elusive connection between economic conditions and hate crime. *Journal of Personality and Social Psychology, 75,* 82–92.

Iganski, P. (1999). Why make "hate" a crime? *Critical Social Policy, 19,* 386–395.

Jacobs, J. B., & Potter, K. A. (1997). Hate crimes: A political perspective. *Crime and Justice, 22,* 1–50.

Jacobs, J. B., & Potter, K. A. (1998). *Hate crime: Criminal law and identity politics.* New York: Oxford University Press.

Jenness, V., & Grattet, R. (1996). The criminalization of hate: A comparison of structural and policy influences on the passage of "bias-crime" legislation in the United States. *Sociological Perspectives, 39,* 129–154.

Levin, B. (1999). Hate crimes: Worse by definition. *Journal of Contemporary Criminal Justice, 15*(1), 6–21.

Levin, J., & McDevitt, J. (1993). *Hate crimes: The rising tide of bigotry and bloodshed.* New York: Plenum.

Los Angeles Human Rights Commission. (1997). Data provided to the Center for Criminal Justice

Policy Research by the L.A. Human Rights Commission, Los Angeles, CA.

McDevitt, J. (1989). *The study of the character of civil rights violations in Massachusetts (1983–1987).* Paper presented at the American Society of Criminology.

McDevitt, J., Balboni, J., & Bennett, S. (2000). *Improving the quality and accuracy of bias crime statistics nationally: An assessment of the first ten years of bias crime data collection.* Report to the Department of Justice's Bureau of Justice Statistics. Washington, DC: Department of Justice.

Nolan, J., & Akiyama, Y. (1999). An analysis of factors that affect law enforcement participation in hate crime reporting. *Journal of Contemporary Criminal Justice, 15*(1), 111–127.

Petrosino, C. (1999). Connecting the past to the future: Hate crime in America. *Journal of Contemporary Criminal Justice, 15*(1), 22–47.

U.S. Department of Justice. (1990). *Hate crime statistics 1990: A resource book.* Washington, DC: Bureau of Justice Statistics.

Van de Ven, P. (1995). Talking with juvenile offenders about gay males and lesbians: Implications for combating homophobia. *Adolescence, 30*(117).

Watts, M. W., & Zinnecker, J. (1998). Varieties of violence-proneness among male youth. In M. W. Watts (Ed.), *Cross-cultural perspectives on youth and violence* (pp. 117–145). New York: JAI Press.

QUESTIONS

1. Why is societal failure to recognize and condemn hate crimes potentially a source of encouragement to hate crime perpetrators or potential perpetrators?

2. What is the basic factor underlying all types of hate crime offenders, according to the authors?

3. Describe the five types of hate crime offenders. How do they differ from one another?

4. What is the most common type of hate crime motivation? What is the least common type?

5. How is defensive hate crime associated with social change (e.g., neighborhood changes)?

6. Why do retaliatory hate crimes carry especially high potential for creating community unrest?

7. What does the FBI list as possible indicators of hate crime? How could these indicators be used by police investigators to help recognize hate crimes?

8. Should hate speech be used as an indicator of a hate crime? Why or why not?

9. The authors assert that hate crime offenders can be ranked along a "continuum of culpability." Do you agree that hate crime perpetrators may be differentially culpable? For example, should offenders who participate in a hate crime only marginally be considered equally responsible along with more active perpetrators of the crime, or not? Discuss your reasons.

10. In what ways are conformity and social influence key factors in the commission of hate crimes?

11. What could we do to encourage more people to be heroes who intervene in hate crimes?

12. What do you think would be appropriate sentencing strategies in cases of thrill hate crimes? What type(s) of sentence might be most effective at preventing reoffending and addressing the needs of hate crime victims?

10

BIAS CRIME MOTIVATION

*A Study of Hate Crime
and Offender Neutralization
Techniques Used Against the Amish*

BRYAN BYERS

BENJAMIN W. CRIDER

GREGORY K. BIGGERS

How can hate crime perpetrators commit their crimes and live with their consciences? This article takes a close look at how a small group of offenders explained their hate crimes against the Amish to others—and to themselves. The offenders used classic psychological techniques to rationalize their actions after the fact by dehumanizing and even blaming their victims. Examining the strategies that these offenders used sheds light on how hate crime offenders may fail to see their crimes as harmful or unjust.

A Stoning in Fulham County (1988) is a movie based on an actual manslaughter case of an Amish baby in Fulham County (a pseudonym for an Indiana county) that occurred on August 31, 1979. The film begins with an Amish family, including small children and an infant, traveling home by buggy from a gathering at a fellow Amish family's farm. Four young men in a truck begin harassing the family on a country road. One of the young men throws a clay tile at the buggy. The tile strikes and kills the infant in the mother's arms (Byers & Crider, 1997b). The stoning depicted in the film is an example of claping (pronounced *clay-ping*). *Claping* is a local term that may be used to describe harassment, intimidation, and vandalism

EDITORS' NOTE: From Byers, B., Crider, B. W., & Biggers, G. K. (1999). Bias Crime Motivation: A Study of Hate Crime and Offender Neutralization Techniques Used Against the Amish. *Journal of Contemporary Criminal Justice, 15*(1), 78-96. © 1999 Sage Publications. Used with permission.

against Amish. However, similar acts of harassment and other crimes have occurred in Amish communities found in Pennsylvania, Wisconsin, and other parts of Indiana.

Some examples of claping include, but may not be limited to, throwing firecrackers or other objects at buggies, forcing buggies off roads with cars, yelling obscenities at the Amish, or smashing Amish mailboxes. The derogatory term *clape* or *clapes* (along with the term *crows* due to the traditional Amish male black attire) is still in use in Fulham County. This study examines the experiences of former and present Fulham County English (non-Amish) residents who have engaged in claping. This is accomplished through interviews designed to study offender claping accounts. Throughout this article, we use the pseudonym *Fulham County* to describe the site of this study, to preserve the anonymity of the Amish community under study, and to protect the community at large (Byers & Crider, 1997a).

As a cultural and social group, the Amish have been well researched (Good, 1985; Good & Good, 1979; Hostetler, 1983, 1993; Kraybill, 1989; Kraybill & Olshan, 1994), but this body of research has not involved a particular focus on those who have committed hate crimes against the Amish. To satisfy this need, this study uses personal accounts (Scott & Lyman, 1968) of bias crime events reported and recanted by offenders who have engaged in claping, and it builds on the need for additional qualitative research on hate crimes in society (Hamm, 1994a, 1994b).

❧ Neutralizations as Accounts

Techniques of neutralization are linguistic accounts that are used after an offense has been committed. First noted by Sykes and Matza (1957), several authors have since examined neutralizations within a variety of contexts (Agnew, 1994; Agnew & Peters, 1986; Baumeister, Stillwell, & Wotman, 1990; Gonzales, Pederson, Manning, & Wetter, 1990; Hazani, 1991; Mitchell, Dodder, & Norris, 1990). Each of these works is based, at least in part, on the classic work of Sykes and Matza (1957). Sykes and Matza (1957) believed that one of the nine components to Edwin

Sutherland's theory of differential association deserved additional attention. That dimension, as Sutherland put it, was the potential use of "rationalization" to justify and excuse delinquent behavior based on favorable associations with delinquent peers (Sutherland, 1947/1994). The basic component to the neutralization, as Sykes and Matza (1957) state, is that the strategies attempt to separate the act from personal responsibility for the act. In other words, the techniques of neutralization are used after the act has been committed to either justify or rationalize the act.

Research Questions

Four research questions (RQ 1–4) are examined. First (RQ 1), why did the subjects engage in claping? This question is based on the absence of any literature-based, systematic examination of the motivations for claping behavior. Second (RQ 2), do individuals who engage in acts of claping use neutralization techniques? Third (RQ 3), what techniques, if any, might such individuals use after the event or events have taken place? Fourth (RQ 4), what are the most frequently used techniques? The latter three questions are examined because previous researchers have used neutralization techniques when examining various forms of deviant and criminal behavior. However, there has been no previous application of these techniques to the field of hate crimes research, nor to research on deviance and criminal behavior committed against the Amish.

Methods and Procedures

This study used confidential, face-to-face, in-depth interviews. Interviews were audio taped with the subject's permission, and they were based on established qualitative interview procedures (Holstein, 1995; McCracken, 1988). This study used a snowball sampling technique with confidential informants, and the sampling procedure consisted of two segments.

First, the authors used personal knowledge of an informant who served as the study's gatekeeper. This person had personal knowledge of other individuals who could speak about their claping experiences and activities. Second, from these personal and confidential contacts, subjects were asked by the gatekeeper if they would be willing to assist the investigators in obtaining additional subjects for interviews in order to build a sample. The rationale for the second sampling procedure was the gatekeeper's assumption that those who have claped did so in friendship groups during adolescence. Therefore, subjects, with the trust of the investigators established, served as valuable resources in participant recruitment. The gatekeeper, a person trusted by each subject, assisted during the interviews with clarifying questions. The gatekeeper also helped to build rapport between each subject and the interviewer. The sample was exhausted when interviewees repeated the same names of potential subjects to the researchers, and the original confidential informant (gatekeeper) indicated that the sample was as complete as possible.

The sampling procedure resulted in 8 subjects who agreed to in-depth confidential interviews. The interviewees were from middle-class to upper- middle-class families. Subjects were very articulate and several had gone on to college. Overall, one might say the subjects were mainstream kids, and they were quite popular with their peers during high school. It is noteworthy that none of the subjects were viewed by the community as bad boys. Rather, the interviewees were perceived as good kids when they were younger. Five of the subjects went to college, and the others have been successful in their life and occupational endeavors. All subjects were male due to the fact that claping among adolescent females was unheard of among the subjects. The subjects belonged to three different friendship groups, and they ranged from 18 to 26 years of age at the time of the interview. Seven of the 8 subjects were raised in Mennonite (a form of Anabaptists) homes, and 1 subject actually had Amish relatives. All subjects had some form of regular contact with the Amish. Some had contact through family businesses in the exchange of goods and services.

A semistructured interview schedule was used whereby questions were allowed to emerge from the interview. Although questions were used that were designed to determine if neutralizations were used, open rapport and dialogue were also used to build on the questions. This provided the authors with an opportunity to capitalize on themes that emerged during conversation with each subject. As a result, this study used a recursive interview methodology, whereby the interviewer used responses from subjects to spontaneously develop questions during an interview, as well as wording of questions for subsequent subjects (Schwartz & Jacobs, 1979, p. 45). Although the phrasing of questions may have changed slightly as a result of the interviews (e.g., to establish better flow, to enhance clarity, to speak at the level of the subject, etc.), the basic content remained the same and focused on the reasons for claping and how such behavior was neutralized.

Each interview lasted between 1 hour and 2½ hours. The length of each interview was the result of our ability to establish rapport with the subject, and to discuss their lives and behavior. As a result, the entire data set consisted of approximately 16 hours of recorded conversations with individuals who had claped.

ANALYSIS

As practiced by Berg (1995), the present analysis treated each transcribed interview as a written document source for purposes of content analysis. From each interview that was transcribed verbatim from audiotape, two units of analysis were examined: the theme and the concept (Berg, 1995). Efforts were made to uncover participant quotations addressing the themes and concepts represented in each of the research questions. Also, coding was intended to reveal emergent themes and concepts. Therefore, the coding procedure used here represented a hybrid approach. As Berg (1995) notes, "Because of the creative component [of qualitative research], it is impossible to establish a complete step-by-step operational procedure that will consistently result in qualitative analysis" (p. 59). However, one can draw from a variety of qualitative data analytical procedures and strategies (Berg, 1995; Marshall & Rossman, 1989; Strauss & Corbin, 1990) in an effort to establish an analytical approach tailored to the data. As a result, the following multistage analysis process was used.

Transcribed interviews were analyzed by three individuals. The first individual to examine the transcripts was not involved in the interview process at all but did have knowledge of claping and the use of neutralizations. This coder read the transcripts and attempted to draw themes and concepts from the data that might suggest the use of neutralizations and reasons for the behavior. Next, a second individual (our gatekeeper) who was at each interview read the transcripts. Our gatekeeper searched the transcripts for the reasons for claping and neutralizations themes/concepts, in addition to checking for transcription accuracy. Once each person was satisfied with the independent analyses, the two individuals met with their coded transcripts on at least five occasions to make comparisons. Together, deliberations took place on how various statements were coded in an effort to reach consensus on whether certain statements constituted neutralizations, how the statements could be classified by the five techniques, and what other motivations might account for claping. Once this consensus was reached, the findings were presented to the interviewer for final analysis. The interviewer agreed with all of the classifications and results. The final analysis resulted in 38 neutralizations used by the 8 subjects as well as examples of reasons why the subjects claped.

FINDINGS

Why They Claped

Pertaining to the first research question (RQ 1), it seemed clear from our interviews that subjects had certain beliefs about the Amish that motivated them to engage in this type of activity. The beliefs seemed to have three sources: (a) relatives, (b) peers, and (c) personal experiences or contacts with the Amish. Some respondents reported that their parents and/or relatives held similar beliefs and, in some cases, actually claped when they (the relatives) were teens. Parents and relatives were also a source of stereotypes and negative opinions toward the Amish. Peers also played a role by

reinforcing—within friendship groups—negative perceptions of the Amish. Although contact is often a way to reduce ill feelings toward another group, the type of contact is relevant. Typical contact occurred on the streets and in schools. Within both contexts, the Amish were viewed as different and subordinate. On the streets, there was a tendency to view the Amish negatively based on the inconveniences they produced (namely, buggies and horse manure on roadways). In school, the Amish kids were different and not considered equal. Given the size of the Amish community studied, with a total of roughly 600 Amish households, the Amish sent their children to public schools through the eighth grade (the minimum required by state law), rather than having separate Amish schools. Amish schools are more common in larger Amish settlements.

Many subjects thought the Amish were subordinate to the English community. For example, respondents commented on how the Amish were stupid, dirty, stunk, backward, and hypocritical. Such characterizations have been common in describing other minority groups by those in the majority. This seems to be the case here as well. Given the Amish practice of only attending school through the eighth grade, the source of the belief that the Amish are stupid seems obvious. However, although not highly educated, the Amish are far from this characterization. They tend to be avid readers and information gatherers within their communities. The belief that the Amish are dirty and unclean is generated from the Amish practice of living a 19th century lifestyle. Old Order Amish, the most traditional and the type victimized by the subjects, use outhouses and do not have running water in their homes for easy bathing. Beliefs in Amish backwardness and hypocrisy are somewhat interrelated. All Old Order Amish, to a certain extent, reject technology which makes them appear backward and unsophisticated. The Amish were viewed by the subjects as hypocrites because they (the Amish they saw) would use technology even though the Anabaptist faith would generally reject it. For example, the Amish—even many Old Order Amish—will ride in cars and use telephones, but will own neither. For the subjects this was difficult to understand, and it contributed to their loathing of the Amish culture, and it fed the belief of hypocrisy. Such descriptions and related beliefs among the subjects seemed to elevate the subjects to a level of social superiority that justified claping.

Subjects also seemed to view the Amish as an easy mark. The Amish presence in the community, due to their dress and customs, was obvious to anyone. The Amish appearance made them easily identifiable to the youth. In addition to their easy identification, there are two additional elements that make the Amish easy targets. These are their theologically based beliefs in pacifism, and an unwillingness, for the most part, of participating in the American criminal justice system (however, please note that the Amish are, overall, extremely law abiding and respectful of the law). Therefore, when harassed or attacked, the Amish are unlikely to retaliate or report the incident to criminal justice authorities. Moreover, the Amish place a high value on forgiveness toward those who trespass against them.

Finally, the subjects reported that claping was fun. That is, for them it was an enjoyable activity that was thrilling. Levin and McDevitt (1994) refer to this type of hate crime offender as the thrill seeker. The thrill seeker tends to commit hate crimes with peer group members, but he or she is not typically associated with an organized hate group. This was clearly the case in our subject pool. In fact, when asked if a person were to clape alone, subjects responded that the person would have to be "sick" to do such a thing. Claping was clearly a peer-group-based activity. Such offenders commit their hate crimes against vulnerable and targeted group members outside their (the offender's) normal turf, and they purposely travel to areas frequented by those in such groups. Our subjects traveled the county back roads looking for victims—often while out drinking—cruising for Amish. Once found, the Amish were often targets. These attacks tend to be random and anonymous (or at least difficult to identify the offender). Our offenders almost always victimized the Amish at night when it was hard for them (the subjects) to be identified. Harassment and vandalism are the hallmark offenses, and this was the case among our subjects. An

ideology of hate is typically absent among thrill seekers. Rather than an ideology of hate, offending rests largely with the thrill or excitement experienced. This was certainly the case with our subjects.

Findings

Neutralization Techniques

Through an examination of interview data, it became clear that subjects did not always attempt to neutralize their behaviors (RQ 2). When subjects did not attempt to neutralize, there was lack of remorse or shame for the behavior. One would expect this given that Sykes and Matza (1957) suggest that not all individuals will use neutralization techniques. Our subjects selectively used the techniques to rationalize certain conduct, but not all conduct.

After completing the coding and analysis phases, themes pertaining to specific neutralization techniques emerged. All five techniques are present in the data (RQ 3). However, the preponderance of statements made by the 8 interviewees fell into the categories of the denial of injury and the denial of the victim (RQ 4). Although some statements were made that were coded as denial of responsibility, condemnation of the condemners, and appeal to higher loyalties, these were fewer in frequency.

For purposes of summary, subjects tended to neutralize injury (31.5%), the victim (23.7%), loyalty (18.4%), condemnation (15.8%), and responsibility (10.5%), in that order. In a word, the interviewees tended to spend more time neutralizing their actions based on two techniques—the denial of the victim and the denial of injury. Thirty-eight neutralizations were used with 4.75 neutralizations used per subject.

To present examples of statements that pertain to neutralization techniques made by respondents about their hate crime activity against the Amish, the following is provided. The data presented is consistent with an established format in reporting neutralizations (LaBeff, Clark, Haines, & Diekhoff, 1990) and accounts (Stamp & Sabourin, 1995). Data are organized by technique and interviewee number. Although many subject statements could be offered that would demonstrate the various techniques, attempts are made below to include quotes from a few subjects representative of each technique.

Denial of Injury

Attempts are made to neutralize behavior by suggesting that no real harm was done to the victim. Perpetrators, when using this account, do not typically deny that they (the perpetrators) engaged in the act. Rather, the tendency is to view the behavior as not causing great harm, and that the acts were merely mischief. For example, the following statement made by a current college student reflects this notion:

> No, no one really ever got hurt, and it wasn't really all that much property damage. It was pretty much just a mess to clean up. The outhouse was the most damaged though. I guess I was just thinking that it is just an outhouse, [and the Amish could] throw up [easily build] another one. (Interviewee 2)

This subject went on to say:

> I don't really regret any of it. . . . It was all, I always thought clean fun . . . Yes, all of it wasn't but. . . . We always looked at it as there are a lot worse things that we could be doing. (Interviewee 2)

Another subject, still living and working in the community, made the following claim:

> For me, it was mostly mischief. Why? Just because it was what our friends were doing at that time to pass the summer months away or whatever. That was what we were doing on Friday nights. (Interviewee 3)

His justifications continued when he said,

> I didn't hurt anybody for the plain and simple fact that that is really not me. I mean, [the name of another subject] can testify that I'm not exactly the most violent person, and I mean that out of the group, I would be the one leaning more towards the "let's not" [do it]. I would be more of the conscience. You know, we had better not do this. But then, you know, several times I got a little worked up. (Interviewee 3)

The following subject, a bright young man with a skilled labor job, denied injury in a rather unique fashion: "I really didn't hurt anybody, because I didn't try to. I always thought that if I tried to hurt somebody then I am going to hurt them. I never tried to do bodily harm, physical harm" (Interviewee 5). He went on to reflect on his main motivations and the probability of getting caught claping:

> It was just going out and having fun. It was just mischief. You want to cause trouble but the odds are that you probably aren't going to get caught, and that is the kind of mischief that there is. Not getting caught is how I saw it. (Interviewee 5)

Another subject, a college student, denied the victim's injury based on his belief that the Amish should be accustomed to the abuse, and the Amish have their own way of retaliating against the English:

> I don't think any harm was inflicted on them [the Amish]. Stuff like that happens to them. It happens to them all the time. They are used to it I think. . . . They [the Amish] get everyone back when their horses shit on the road, and they do stuff that we don't like. The White people or whatever they want to call us. . . . I didn't see them crying when I did it. I mean I didn't get real close to them or anything . . . because I really didn't want to hurt anybody. It was just fun and games. (Interviewee 7)

Yet another subject attempted to neutralize his individual behavior, and simultaneously project blame on the belief that Amish are ill-treated by others as well. For example,

> As far as from anything that I did, really not any [injury]. Not much from me, maybe as a whole from everybody harassing them, I mean the whole community where all the kids were out harassing them maybe a little bit of harm. I think that they are used to that, and I think that they catch a lot of shit from a lot of different people so any one thing that I might have personally said to them or stuff that I have done to them I don't think that too much harm came just from what I have done. . . . I don't think that I really hurt them mentally or psychologically, I don't think that I did any harm to them. (Interviewee 8)

Based on the aforementioned examples, a few summary remarks might be made concerning the use of this neutralization technique. First, subjects readily used "denial of injury," and tended to elaborate on their responses. Second, the acts of claping were rationalized based on the perpetrator's perception that little harm, if any, was done to the Amish, and the acts were simply mischief perpetrated during adolescence. Finally, there is some evidence to suggest that the subjects denied injury based on the perception that the Amish should be accustomed to such treatment.

Denial of the Victim

This technique suggests that the victim either had it coming (i.e., the act was justifiably correct), or the victim is of such low status that any injury has no real social or legal impact. In a word, the denial of injury involves, at least to a certain extent, some aspect of dehumanization of the victim or the group to which the victim belongs.

For example, the following subject, one of the college students and a major in the behavioral sciences, stated,

> You know, I guess I just had the mentality that they are just Amish. . . . I guess I looked at them as not really being a part of society in a way. It is like, we can pick on them because they are so different. (Interviewee 2)

He continued with his own form of analysis:

> I always thought they were lesser intelligent. I mean in school they just didn't compare. I mean they only went to the eighth grade, and after that you know they quit, and I guess that I looked down on them. Not being, they were just a lower status than we were. You don't want to pick on anyone with the same status as you or above you. It is easier to pick on someone with lower status and weaker and vulnerable. And then we had a thing of not really having any way of getting back at you. There really wasn't any way of getting back at you. You know. . . . To dehumanize the Amish makes them not as people. That is how I look at it. Didn't think about what we were doing. When we were doing things, we didn't think of them as people. . . . Their social status was so far

below ours, because they weren't even actual acting humans. They were dehumanized. They are below us. I guess relative below us is that they live so simple that they were like almost not even anything to me. I guess we just picked on them. (Interviewee 2)

Although not a college student, but instead a worker still living in the community, the following subject reflected a very similar sentiment: "It is because I still have some feeling that they almost 'deserved it' for some unknown reason just because they are different" (Interviewee 3).

He continued with some additional reasons why the Amish should be denied victim status when he stated,

> The dusting [driving by an Amish buggy on a dirt road creating a cloud of dust], or trying to spook the horse, or whatever, in some cases I would almost justify that because of the fact that they were in the middle of the road. I mean, that would be just like you being behind a car doing two miles an hour and all you see is blue hair [old people]. . . . The dusting, they had it coming because . . . they blocked the road, and we probably thought part of the time they deserved it. With the chicken shit [spraying Amish with a mixture made of chicken feces and water], the reason you could say they deserved it would be because they were just Amish. (Interviewee 3)

The following subject suggested that perhaps the Amish may have been unfortunate victims of circumstance:

> I don't consider them [the Amish] as a victim. . . . I just never really thought about it that much. It was just something that we went out and did. I never considered them a victim. Unlucky maybe . . . [they were in the] wrong place [at the] wrong time. (Interviewee 5)

Surprisingly, the same subject justified claping based on the belief that the victim should expect such treatment:

> They [the Amish] expect you to antagonize them. I think they almost expect you to. It is not like they go out in there buggies and they think, they know. They know that there is the possibility that they are going to get antagonized. (Interviewee 5)

For the next subject, the belief in Amish hypocrisy played an important role in his neutralization strategies. Incidentally, his contact with the Amish may have been more common and frequent than most other subjects because he remained in the community. He seems to delineate between Amish and others. For example,

> Well, like the certain ones that we would terrorize and stuff, they were hypocritical. I mean that is how I felt then. There are regular people who are the same way and I never did it to them. The Amish you know they don't have electricity and they have it coming because they don't believe in electricity but they will sit down and watch TV for 3 hours. And I've had it done, they will come and watch TV at your house for a while. I believe that if you feel that you shouldn't have a TV then you shouldn't watch it, period. I feel that if they do this then they have it coming. (Interviewee 6)

Like the denial of injury, subjects quite readily used the denial of the victim in their neutralizations. For several subjects, the denial of injury was centered on the perception that the Amish were not equal to them (the subjects). Others viewed them as easy targets. Some perceived the Amish as deserving such treatment. Others viewed claping as rightful retaliation toward the Amish due to their hypocritical ways.

Appeal to Higher Loyalties

This social psychological dynamic is complex and multifaceted. This neutralization technique could involve justifying an act of deviance due to loyalty or allegiance to a group. It might also involve beliefs that one should never turn in a coconspirator, "rat," or squeal on a friend. However, loyalty to a group might be demonstrated in different ways.

For example, and as one of our subjects demonstrates, claping with friends was akin to bonding: "To me it brings back more memories of just a bunch of friends being together and doing something. More than a bunch of friends going out to persecute somebody or whatever . . . a bonding" (Interviewee 3).

When probed about his appeal to higher loyalties, this subject said,

> I wouldn't have [when asked if he would squeal on a friend]. Why not? Because those are my friends and we were all in that [acts of claping] together. I would expect the same from them. Not to "rat me out" or whatever. I would have thought that if we were stuck in that situation that we would all just say that we were not doing anything and deny, deny, deny. If that don't work you had better lie. (Interviewee 3)

Another subject, a 24-year-old manual laborer, put this idea the following way:

> Yes . . . it was kind of like male bonding. Some people sit back and smoke cigars and drink beer [legally]. We were under age so we couldn't do that so we just went out and made up our own way of male bonding. We kind of, I would say that it kind of drew us all closer because we went out and did something. I would say that there was always something in it for basically all of us. (Interviewee 4)

Another subject was convinced of his security with the group as the following statement suggests: "Because they are my friends and they wouldn't rat me out. They wouldn't say, 'Yes, he was along too.' They wouldn't do that. I trust that they wouldn't put me in hot water so I wouldn't put them in hot water" (Interviewee 5).

As the following subject stated, the nature of the bond with the group helped him to define the nature of loyalty:

> The group of people that I was with, I would never squeal on. But, I think if I would have been with a group of people, maybe a certain person I didn't like, I don't even know if I would have then but I think I would have been more apt to because I didn't like the person I was with anyway. But, the group of people I was in, we were pretty tight. I wouldn't squeal on them; no. (Interviewee 6)

Finally, and perhaps the most concise response from any subject, the following individual (a college student) stated his beliefs as follows: "Because that is not what type of person I am. I would rather take all the blame and not have my friends get in trouble. . . . That means I wouldn't squeal on them. I would be loyal to them" (Interviewee 7).

Although there is some evidence for the use of this neutralization technique, respondents tended to use it in a certain way. There are two basic ways the technique might be used. First, individuals may appeal to higher loyalties as a justification for engaging in deviant conduct. Second, individuals may appeal to higher loyalties to justify keeping their deviant acts secret, thus not disclosing deviant peers to authorities.

When placed in a dilemma that might call for an appeal to higher loyalties, our subjects did not use the technique to justify acting in the way they did. Rather, the respondent's comments suggest that they would not turn in a friend for claping, they would expect the same in return, and disclosure of such acts to authorities would violate the group's bond.

Condemnation of the Condemners

With this technique, the person neutralizes by redirecting the focus of attention from his or her own behavior to the assumed or actual behavior of those who are doing the accusing. Rather than to accept responsibility, the person attempts to suggest that the person condemning the act is no better, moral, or ethical because he or she may have done something just as harmful and, therefore, has no right to sit in judgment.

For example, the following subject responded quite assertively when he was asked how he would respond if another local from an older generation were to criticize his acts:

> Like you never did it?. . . Like you never did it?! . . . When we were still in high school, I know almost all the cops were still pretty much locals. I would say that they have probably have their fair share of claping or at least making fun of them. . . . Because if they were from around here they would have done either the same thing, felt the same thing, or something of that manner. . . . If they aren't from around here they could be saying that because they view the Amish as being so perfect and close to God and so non-aggressive and all that kind of stuff. (Interviewee 3)

The following subject, a skilled laborer with a new family, said the following with a lot of anger:

> I would tell him to "b— me," and I would probably just turn right around. I would walk right

back out. Tell him to "kiss my a—." You know. I would tell him to go "f— off," and I would be going right back out. If I ever got ratted out, if an Amishman ever told on me that this guy, that this certain young individual is doing this, I would find out who he is. (Interviewee 5)

Going back to one of the subjects who remained in the community, he had an interesting way of determining whether any criticism levied against him would have merit. For example,

> First of all . . . I would ask you how you've treated them. If you say you did the same thing I did, I'd say you're a hypocrite. Now if you would say that I didn't do it anymore then I would have something to listen to. But if you preach at me you best not be doing it yourself. . . . If I ask you, "do you swerve at the Amish when you pass them on the road?" and you say, "yeah," then you don't have any right to say that I shouldn't be swerving at the Amish. What gives you the right to criticize what I'm doing? But if you say no, then I'd ask you why you don't think it's right and they would have something to say. (Interviewee 6)

Indicative of the responses from the interviewees, when asked how they would respond to someone criticizing or condemning them for claping, those subjects who responded did so with bravado. The "condemnation of the condemners" dimension certainly hit a nerve for some respondents. Responses centered on two aspects of accusing the accusers. Respondents indicated that anyone condemning them for their acts had no right to do so. The rationale for this position rested in the perception that if a person grew up in the same community that individual surely either engaged in claping or, if given the opportunity, would have.

Denial of Responsibility

Although not a prominent theme, the following quotations suggest that some interviewees attempted to neutralize their responsibility for hate crimes against the Amish. In neutralizing responsibility, the individual attempts to provide accounts that separate him- or herself from full accountability for the behavior. Ultimately, the use of this technique suggests that responsibility for the behavior may have rested elsewhere.

For example, the following subject, a soon-to-be college graduate with the goal of becoming a teacher, said, "So I think the reason is that we just grew up with them and were used to them. They were just there, and we didn't think anything of it. The harassment was almost common nature" (Interviewee 1).

Another subject seemed to be blaming his socialization. For example, "I don't know, I mean, I would say that that is because of the way that I was raised" (Interviewee 3).

On the other hand, some did not attempt to neutralize their responsibility. That is, there was also the tendency to accept, and be proud of, responsibility for the action. The following subject, who had a long-standing dislike for the Amish going back to his childhood, made this statement: "Fully responsible? . . . Yes. . . . You could say so. Yes. . . . Well as it being my idea, we went out and in my vehicle and we did this and this? . . . I pretty much just meant it. I meant it" (Interviewee 5).

Others felt the same way:

Oh yeah. You can't blame nobody else. That's what I've learned. You got so many people saying, "oh I had a bad childhood." Yeah, there are a lot more people who have had a worse childhood than I have had. But, I feel that I have had a bad one. So, I don't blame anything that happened that I did on anything but me. (Interviewee 6)

Anything that I did, I guess that I am responsible for it. It was my own actions so I would say that I am responsible for it. It is not like my parents brought me up to go out and harass the Amish or hate the Amish. I guess that I am responsible for anything that I did. (Interviewee 8)

By and large, there were two general themes that emerged from the data on the denial of responsibility. First, when responsibility was denied, a softer version of the billiard-ball effect was used. That is, when it came to the person being more "acted on" than "acting," blame was placed on peer pressure. However, such blame was not vehement. An interesting and unexpected pattern emerged in the data. There were several statements made by subjects that were quite the opposite of denials of responsibility. In fact, there was a ready admittance by some respondents that they did it (the claping), and they had no interest whatsoever in denying responsibility for the actions.

Summary and Discussion

Favored Techniques

Although subjects did neutralize their claping behaviors (as motivated by the factors discussed earlier), certain techniques emerged more frequently than others. One could suggest that there was a certain favorability toward some techniques over others. In general, subjects tended to use denial of injury and denial of the victim more often than others (i.e., denial of responsibility, condemnation of the condemners, and appeal to higher loyalties).

Actual Harm

To gauge the amount of actual harm done to Amish victims and the Amish community as a result of claping is difficult to ascertain through absolutes. One key obstacle is the Amish self-perception of harm, and how their views differ from the dominant culture. Although it is likely that the Amish experience the same psychological reactions as others who experience hate crime, their subsequent reactions differ significantly. Given the premium the Amish place on forgiveness of others, this tends to neutralize self-perceived harm. Someone belonging to a different minority group may like to see some type of punishment or retribution for the offender; however, the Amish victim often forgives his or her assailant.

However, there is evidence to suggest that the Amish experienced actual harm at the hands of our subjects. Harm came in the form of intimidation and/or harassment (e.g., name calling), destruction of property (e.g., destruction of mailboxes and outhouses), criminal recklessness or criminal mischief (e.g., swerving at Amish or running Amish off the road), and assault without serious bodily injury (e.g., spraying chicken manure, egg throwing, throwing water balloons, throwing bags of flour—referred to as *flouring* the Amish).

Although there was little remorse expressed by the subjects for the harm they may have inflicted on the Amish, it is clear that the victims would have experienced—at the very least—discomfort, fear, and inconvenience.

Conclusion

One may draw several conclusions from the aforementioned data and discussion. First, in reference to RQ 1, subjects tended to engage in claping to fight boredom and to find excitement. In a word, thrill seeking seemed to be a key motivation. Second, relevant to RQ 2, there was a tendency for individuals who had engaged in claping to use neutralization techniques. Third, subjects used all five of Sykes and Matza's (1957) techniques (RQ 3); however, subjects tended to favor certain neutralization techniques over others (RQ 4). In addition, the subjects were young men who, by and large, did not view their behavior as being harmful.

As with any research, one must address study strengths and limitations. First, it is a strength that this study is quite unique. Two important uniqueness factors are (a) the subject matter of claping, and (b) the ability to access individuals who could share their experiences, reflections, and thoughts. Another strength is the validity of the interview data. The initial informant or gatekeeper attested to the accuracy of all claims and statements without compromising the confidentiality of individual responses. Moreover, responses tended to be quite detailed, and they were shared because of the trust that had been developed with the interviewer. Furthermore, the incidents of claping shared by interviewees were compared with the stories of others, and the accuracy was high. In addition to these factors, validity was also assured through the coding and analysis processes discussed above.

All studies also have limitations. One possible limitation has to do with the study location. That is, the research centered on one particular community. However, this may not constitute a significant drawback considering the exploratory nature of this research, and that gaining access to individuals who have victimized the Amish is no easy task. Moreover, a historically significant act of claping occurred several years ago within that community. Another potential limitation rests with the sample size. However, given the difficulty in accessing such individuals (people who have claped), and the limited number of Amish communities available for study, this limitation does not appear to present any serious threat to the research. Added to this argument is the standard followed here: that qualitative research uses smaller samples coupled with more detailed data from each individual subject.

Future researchers might consider the important roles of gatekeepers and informants. Had it not been for our informant, this research would not have been possible. Future researchers may also wish to consider the perceptions of the Amish toward victimization. That is, studies using Amish subjects would provide an important glimpse into the experiences of those we know little about in terms of victimization. Future researchers may wish to conduct comparison studies of various Amish communities based on both offender and victimization data. Researchers need to continue to strive to learn more about the victimization processes targeted toward specific groups. In addition, future researchers should examine the role neutralizations have in justifying hate crime behavior and reducing personal accountability.

References

Agnew, R. (1994). The techniques of neutralization and violence. *Criminology, 32,* 555–580.

Agnew, R., & Peters, A. (1986). The techniques of neutralization: An analysis of predisposing and situational factors. *Criminal Justice and Behavior, 13,* 81–96.

Baumeister, R., Stillwell, A., & Wotman, S. (1990). Victim and perpetrator accounts of interpersonal conflict: Autobiographical narratives about anger. *Journal of Personality and Social Psychology, 59,* 994–1005.

Berg, B. L. (1995). *Qualitative research methods for the social sciences* (2nd ed.). Needham Heights, MA: Allyn & Bacon.

Byers, B., & Crider, B. W. (1997a, July). *Bias crime against the Amish: A study of claping.* Paper presented at the British Criminology Conference, Belfast, Northern Ireland.

Byers, B., & Crider, B. W. (1997b, March). *Bias crime against the Amish.* Paper presented at the national meetings of the Academy of Criminal Justice Sciences, Louisville, KY.

Gonzales, M. H., Pederson, J. H., Manning, D. J., & Wetter, D. W. (1990). Pardon my gaffe: Effects of sex, status, and consequence severity on accounts. *Journal of Personality and Social Psychology, 58,* 610–621.

Good, M. (1985). *Who are the Amish?* Intercourse, PA: Good Books.

Good, M., & Good, P. (1979). *20 most asked questions about the Amish and Mennonites.* Lancaster, PA: Good Books.

Hamm, M. S. (1994a). *American skinheads: The criminology and control of hate crime.* Westport, CT: Praeger.

Hamm, M. S. (Ed.). (1994b). *Hate crime: International perspectives on causes and control.* Cincinnati, OH: Anderson.

Hazani, M. (1991). Aligning vocabulary, symbols banks, and sociocultural structure. *Journal of Contemporary Ethnography, 20,* 179–203.

Holstein, J. A. (1995). *The active interview.* Thousand Oaks, CA: Sage.

Hostetler, J. A. (1983). *Amish life.* Scottdale, PA: Herald Press.

Hostetler, J. A. (1993). *Amish society* (4th ed.). Baltimore: Johns Hopkins University Press.

Kraybill, D. B. (1989). *The riddle of Amish culture.* Baltimore: Johns Hopkins University Press.

Kraybill, D. B., & Olshan, M. A. (Eds.). (1994). *The Amish struggle with modernity.* Hanover, NH: University Press of New England.

LaBeff, E. E., Clark, R. E., Haines, V. J., & Diekhoff, G. M. (1990). Situational ethics and college student cheating. *Sociological Inquiry, 60,* 190–198.

Levin, J., & McDevitt, J. (1994). *Hate crime training manual,* Federal Law Enforcement Training Center (FLETC). Washington, DC: U.S. Government Printing Office.

Marshall, C., & Rossman, G. B. (1989). *Designing qualitative research.* Newbury Park, CA: Sage.

McCracken, G. D. (1988). *The long interview.* Newbury Park, CA: Sage.

Mitchell, J., Dodder, R. A., & Norris, T. D. (1990). Neutralization and delinquency: A comparison by sex and ethnicity. *Adolescence, 25,* 487–497.

Schwartz, H., & Jacobs, J. (1979). *Qualitative sociology.* New York: Free Press.

Scott, M. B., & Lyman, S. M. (1968). Accounts. *American Sociological Review, 33,* 46–62.

Stamp, G. H., & Sabourin, T. C. (1995). Accounting for violence: An analysis of male spousal abuse narratives. *Journal of Applied Communication Research, 23,* 284–307.

Strauss, A., & Cor ____
research: Grou. ____
niques. Newbury ____
Sutherland, E. H. (1994 ____
J. E. Jacoby (Ed.), C. ____
ed., pp. 225–227). ____
Waveland Press. (Ori_ ____
1947)

Sykes, G. M., & Matza, D. (1_ ____ s of neutralization. *American Soc. ___ Review, 22,* 664–670.

QUESTIONS

1. What are techniques of neutralization? Why did these offenders use these techniques?

2. What are some examples of claping? What were the actual or potential harms to the victims from claping?

3. What were the attitudes of these offenders toward their crimes? Did they accept responsibility for their actions?

4. Which techniques of neutralization were used most frequently by these offenders?

5. Describe some examples of the way these offenders used the "denial of the victim" technique.

6. Describe some examples of the way these offenders used the "appeal to higher loyalties" technique.

7. Describe some examples of the way these offenders used the "condemnation of the condemners" technique.

8. Describe some examples of the way these offenders used the "denial of responsibility" technique.

9. Describe some examples of the way these offenders used the "denial of harm" technique.

10. What reasons did the offenders give for claping?

11. What were the consequences of claping for the victims and the Amish community as a whole?

12. What are the methodological limitations of this study?

11

WHY CAN'T WE JUST GET ALONG?

Interpersonal Biases and Interracial Distrust

JOHN F. DOVIDIO

SAMUEL L. GAERTNER

KERRY KAWAKAMI

GORDON HODSON

Can a person be racist without realizing it? The authors of this article present evidence demonstrating that unconscious, unacknowledged racist attitudes can indeed exist. In fact, such attitudes can be even more damaging than "traditional" overt racism because they are very difficult to combat. If people don't believe they harbor racist attitudes, and in fact they consciously subscribe to egalitarian and tolerant attitudes, they will not be able to recognize the impact of latent racism on those who are affected by it. Consequently, interracial interactions may be perceived quite differently by the participants, with corrosive effects on interracial trust.

Whites and Blacks in the United States have developed widely diverging views on the conditions of racial disparities and perceptions of their causes. Whites greatly underestimate the existence of racial disparities. For instance, despite the compelling evidence of contemporary racial disparities (Blank, 2001), between 40% to 60% of Whites responding to a recent survey, depending on the question asked, viewed the average Black in

EDITORS' NOTE: From Dovidio, J. F., Gaertner, S. L., Kawakami, K., & Hodson, G. (2002). Why Can't We Just Get Along? Interpersonal Biases and Interracial Distrust. *Cultural Diversity and Ethnic Minority Psychology,* *8*(2), 88-102. © 2002 by the Educational Publishing Foundation. Reprinted with permission.

the United States as faring about as well, and often better, than the average White (Morin, 2001). Whites and Blacks also differ substantially in their perceptions of the prevalence and impact of discrimination on the well-being of Blacks. Overall, Blacks perceive racial discrimination to be more pervasive and damaging to Blacks than do Whites (Davis & Smith, 1994; Hochschild, 1995). Blacks view discrimination as a dominant force in their lives. Within the government, 55% of Blacks (and 28% of Hispanics) reported that they believe that discrimination hinders their career advancement (U.S. Merit Systems Protection Board, 1997). Within the military, only 39% of Blacks (compared with 68% of Whites) described race relations as good, and 25% of Blacks described discrimination in performance evaluation as their most bothersome incident in the military (Armed Forces Equal Opportunity Survey, 1999).

In the general public, nearly half of Black Americans (47%) reported on a recent survey (Gallup, 2001) that they were treated unfairly in their own community in at least one of five common situations (while shopping, at work, in restaurants or other entertainment places, in dealing with the police, and using public transportation) during the previous month. Whereas the vast majority (69%) of Whites perceived that Blacks were treated "the same as Whites," the majority of Blacks (59%) reported that Blacks were treated "more badly" than Whites. These differences in perceptions have persisted for over 35 years, with only a modest narrowing of perspectives. Across five surveys conducted in the 1960s that included this item, 67% of Whites felt that Blacks were treated as well as Whites, whereas 72% of Blacks reported that Blacks were treated worse (Gallup, 2001).

Given the magnitude and persistence of these different views held by Blacks and Whites, it is not surprising that current race relations in the United States are characterized by racial distrust. The majority of Blacks in America today have a profound distrust for the police and legal system, and about a third are overtly distrustful of Whites in general (Anderson, 1996). In addition, Blacks commonly believe that conspiracies inhibit the progress of Blacks (Crocker, Luhtanen, Broadnax, & Blaine, 1999; DeParle, 1990, 1991). In the present article, we examine how interpersonal biases can contribute to these different perspectives and ultimately to interracial distrust that can undermine race relations.

We contend that, among other forces, the nature of contemporary biases can shape the everyday perceptions of White and Black Americans in ways that interfere with a foundation of communication and trust that is critical to developing long-term positive intergroup relations. Although we recognize that a variety of historical and social forces are involved, we suggest that the different perspectives and experiences of Whites and Blacks in interracial interaction, which can occur daily and have summative effects over time (Feagin & Sikes, 1994), help to contribute to the climate of miscommunication, misperception, and distrust that characterizes contemporary race relations in the United States. In particular, we propose that there are four aspects of contemporary prejudices held by Whites toward Blacks in the United States that contribute to the divergence of perceptions and interracial distrust in the United States today: (a) Contemporary racism among Whites is subtle, (b) these racial biases are often unintentional and unconscious, (c) these biases influence the perceptions that Whites and Blacks have of these same behaviors or events, and (d) these racial biases have different consequences on the outcomes for Blacks and Whites. These four points are considered in separate sections below.

CONTEMPORARY RACISM IS SUBTLE

Prejudice serves a range of functions: individual (Wills, 1981), group (Sherif & Sherif, 1969), and social (Hechter, 1975). As a consequence, it tends to persist over time within a society, although its nature and expression may be shaped by historical, political, economic, and contextual factors (see Dovidio, 2001; Duckitt, 1992). As we have argued in detail elsewhere (Dovidio & Gaertner, 1998; Gaertner & Dovidio, 1986), due in part to changing norms and to the Civil Rights Act and other legislative interventions that have made discrimination not simply immoral but also illegal, many overt expressions of prejudice have declined significantly over the past 35 years (Dovidio &

Gaertner, 1986, 1998). Whites, for instance, have become substantially more supportive of residential integration and less opposed to interracial marriage over time (Bobo, 2001). Contemporary forms of prejudice, however, continue to exist and affect the lives of people in subtle but significant ways. For these subtle, contemporary forms of prejudice, bias is expressed in indirect ways that can typically be justified on the basis of nonracial factors. Nevertheless, the consequences of these prejudices (e.g., the restriction of economic opportunity) may be as significant for people of color and as pernicious as those of the traditional, overt form of discrimination (Dovidio & Gaertner, 1998; Gaertner & Dovidio, 1986; Sears, 1988; Sears, Henry, & Kosterman, 2000).

Our work has focused on one form of contemporary bias of Whites in the United States: aversive racism (Kovel, 1970). In contrast to "old-fashioned" racism, which is blatant, aversive racism represents a subtle, often unintentional form of bias that characterizes many White Americans who possess strong egalitarian values and who believe that they are nonprejudiced. Because of the central role that racial politics have played in the history of the United States, our work has mainly considered the influence of contemporary racial attitudes of Whites toward Blacks. Nevertheless, we note that many of the findings and principles we discuss extend to Whites' biases toward other groups (e.g., Hispanics) as well (Dovidio, Gaertner, Anastasio, & Sanitioso, 1992). Although we also acknowledge that minority groups may also hold negative attitudes toward majority groups and to other racial or ethnic groups, we have focused on the attitudes of Whites because they have traditionally held a disproportionate amount of political, social, and economic power in the United States. Thus, addressing and improving Whites' attitudes can potentially have a significant effect on social change.

A critical aspect of the aversive racism framework, similar to the position of other types of subtle biases such as modern or symbolic racism (McConahay, 1986), is the conflict between the denial of personal prejudice and the underlying unconscious negative feelings and beliefs. In contrast to traditional approaches that

emphasize the psychopathology of prejudice, however, the negative feelings and beliefs that underlie aversive racism are hypothesized to be rooted in normal, often adaptive, psychological processes (see Dovidio & Gaertner, 1998; Gaertner & Dovidio, 1986). These processes involve both individual factors (such as cognitive and motivational biases and socialization) and intergroup functions (such as realistic group conflict or biases associated with the mere categorization of people into ingroups and outgroups). In contrast to the feelings of open hostility and clear dislike of Blacks, the negative feelings that aversive racists experience are typically more diffuse, such as feelings of anxiety and uneasiness.

Because aversive racists consciously endorse egalitarian values and deny their negative feelings about Blacks, they will not discriminate directly and openly in ways that can be attributed to racism. However, because of their negative feelings, they will discriminate, often unintentionally, when their behavior can be justified on the basis of some factor other than race (e.g., questionable qualifications for a position). Aversive racists may therefore regularly engage in discrimination while they maintain a nonprejudiced self-image. The term *aversive* in this form of racism thus refers to two aspects of this bias. It reflects to the nature of the emotions associated with Blacks, such as anxiety, which lead to avoidance and social awkwardness rather than to open antagonism. It also reflects the fact that, because of their conscious adherence to egalitarian principles, these Whites would find any thought that they might be prejudiced to be aversive.

We have found consistent support for the basic proposition of the aversive racism framework that contemporary biases are expressed in subtle rather than in blatant ways across a broad range of situations (see Dovidio & Gaertner, 1998; Gaertner & Dovidio, 1986; Gaertner et al., 1997). The evidence we present next comes from paradigms involving emergency intervention and employment or admissions decisions.

Emergency Intervention

In one of the early tests of our framework (Gaertner & Dovidio, 1977), we modeled a situation in the laboratory after a classic study by Darley and Latané (1968) of diffusion of responsibility. Darley and Latané's research was inspired by an incident in the mid-1960s in which 38 people witnessed the stabbing of a woman, Kitty Genovese, without a single bystander intervening to help. The researchers reasoned that when a person is the only witness to an emergency, the bystander bears 100% responsibility for helping and 100% of the guilt and blame for not helping. The appropriate behavior in this situation, helping, is clearly defined. If, however, a person witnesses an emergency but believes that somebody else is available who can help or will help, then that bystander's personal responsibility is less clearly defined. Under these circumstances, the bystander could rationalize not helping by coming to believe that someone else will intervene.

As in Darley and Latané's (1968) experiment, we led some of our participants to believe that they would be the only witness to this emergency, while we led others to believe that there would be other people present in this situation who heard the emergency as well. We also introduced a second dimension: We varied the race of the victim. In half of the cases the victim was White; in the other half of the cases the victim was Black. The participants in the study were White, as were the other people who were sometimes presumed to be present.

We predicted that when people were the only witness to the emergency, aversive racists would not discriminate against the Black victim. In this situation, appropriate behavior is clearly defined. To not help a Black victim could easily be interpreted, by oneself or others, as racial bias. We predicted, however, that because aversive racists have unconscious negative feelings toward Blacks, they would discriminate when they could justify their behavior on the basis of some factor other than race—such as the belief that someone else would help the victim (i.e., the ability to diffuse responsibility). Specifically, we expected that Blacks would be helped less than Whites only when White bystanders believed that there were other witnesses to the emergency.

The results of the study supported our predictions. When White bystanders were the only witness to the emergency, they helped very frequently and equivalently for Black and White victims (95% vs. 83%). There was no evidence of blatant racism. In contrast, when White bystanders were given an opportunity to rationalize not helping on the basis of the belief that the other witnesses could intervene, they were less likely to help, particularly when the victim was Black. When participants believed that there were other bystanders, they helped the Black victim half as often as they helped the White victim (38% vs. 75%). Thus, these results illustrate the operation of subtle biases in relatively dramatic, spontaneous, and life-threatening circumstances. Although the bias may be subtle, its consequences may be severe.

We designed subsequent research to extend the work on aversive racism by exploring its potential effects in more everyday situations of potential discrimination, such as on hiring recommendations and college admission decisions for a Black or White applicant. Our primary hypothesis in this research was that bias against Blacks would be more likely to be manifested when the appropriate decision is unclear, for example, because of ambiguous evidence about whether the candidate's qualifications meet the criteria for selection or admission, than when the appropriate response is perceived to be well-defined.

Hiring Decisions

In one study (Dovidio & Gaertner, 2000), we asked participants to evaluate candidates for a position in an ostensibly new program for peer counseling at their university on the basis of excerpts from an interview. White participants evaluated a Black or White candidate who had credentials that we systematically manipulated to represent very strong, moderate, or very weak qualifications for the position. Their responses were supportive of the aversive racism framework. As we predicted, when the candidates' credentials clearly qualified them for the position or the credentials clearly were not appropriate, there was no discrimination against the Black candidate. In the strong-qualifications condition, the Black candidate was recommended for the position 91% of the time, whereas the White candidate was recommended 85% of the time. In the weak-qualifications condition, the Black candidate was recommended 13% of the time, and the White candidate was recommended 6% of the time. However, when candidates' qualifications for the position were less obvious and the appropriate decision more ambiguous, White participants recommended the Black candidate significantly less often than the White candidate (45% vs. 76%) with exactly the same credentials.

These findings suggest that when given latitude for interpretation, as in the moderate-qualifications condition, Whites may give White candidates the "benefit of the doubt," a benefit that is not extended to outgroup members (i.e., to Black candidates). As a consequence, as demonstrated in this study, moderate qualifications are responded to like strong qualifications when the candidate is White but like weak qualifications when the candidate is Black.

The data collected in this study also permitted an examination of potential changes in racism over time. The study involved one group of college students who participated during the 1988–1989 academic year and another group of students from the same institution who participated in the 1998–1999 academic year. Whereas self-reported prejudice was lower for the more recent sample, the pattern of subtle discrimination was equivalent across the samples. Despite reductions in direct expressions of prejudice, the evidence for aversive racism was more persistent.

College Admissions Decisions

We extended this line of research further by exploring more directly how Whites weigh different types of information in making their selection decisions for Whites and Blacks in another context: college admissions decisions. Whereas the previous experiment examined racial biases against job candidates with uniformly strong, moderate, or weak qualifications, this study (Hodson, Dovidio, & Gaertner, 2002) compared racial biases toward college applicants with consistent or mixed (i.e., conflicting) qualifications, specifically: (a) consistently strong Scholastic Aptitude Test (i.e., college board examination) scores and high school performance; (b) consistently weak college board scores and high school record; (c) mixed

qualifications, with strong college board test scores and a weak high school record; or (d) mixed qualifications, with weak college board test scores and a strong high school record. The use of mixed qualifications allowed us to ask White college student participants not only to make their selection decisions but also to provide rankings of the different criteria relevant to their decisions. This procedure enabled us to examine the ways that people weigh applicant information, particularly conflicting information, when assessing Black and White college applications.

As we predicted, and consistent with the earlier research, discrimination against Black applicants relative to White applicants did not occur when the applicants' credentials were consistently strong or weak. However, discrimination in terms of weaker support for admission for Black relative to White applicants with the same qualifications did emerge, mainly for relatively high prejudice-scoring students (who are low-to-moderate in prejudice compared with the general public), when the credentials were mixed and hence ambiguous. Moreover, relatively high prejudice-scoring students weighed the different, conflicting criteria in ways that could justify or rationalize discrimination against Black applicants. In particular, higher prejudice-scoring students tended to weigh college board scores unusually low in importance when the Black applicant had high college board scores but weak scholastic achievement, and they tended to rank high school achievement lower in importance when Black applicants had strong scholastic achievement but weak college board scores. Thus, the higher prejudice-scoring participants weighed application criteria in ways that systematically justified or rationalized the discrimination against Blacks.

Bias and Perceptions of Bias

These three research examples do more than illustrate the pervasive influence that subtle biases may have on the personal, economic, and educational outcomes for Blacks. They also suggest how subtle biases may produce different perceptions of discrimination by Whites and Blacks. To the extent that Whites discriminate against Blacks only when this bias can be attributed to factors other than race and adopt or construct these explanations as the justification for their behavior, they are unlikely to recognize fully that their behavior was racially motivated. For instance, during debriefing in the emergency intervention study described earlier, White participants who did not help a Black victim typically said that they thought that someone else already had or would soon intervene, and thus they thought that their help was not needed. They denied, often vociferously, that race had anything to do with their decision. Yet, experimentally, race was the key determinant of differences in helping. Nevertheless, the ability to justify one's behavior on the basis of factors other than race allows Whites to underestimate the effects of racism and discrimination on the lives of Blacks generally and the effects of racism on their own behavior particularly.

In contrast to these isolated and relatively rare interracial encounters for Whites, Blacks may experience disparate treatment and outcomes more consistently and across a range of situations (see Smelser, Wilson, & Mitchell, 2001). Because the nonracial explanations for different treatment and outcomes vary across these situations, attributions to racial bias may offer the most parsimonious explanation for these disparities from the perspectives of Blacks. Consequently, whereas the subtle nature of contemporary biases may lead Whites to underestimate the impact of racial prejudice, it may lead Blacks and other disadvantaged group members to be particularly attuned to negative behaviors of majority group members that could reveal their prejudice (Shelton, 2000; Vorauer & Kumhyr, 2001). Thus, Whites and Blacks are likely to develop different, and potentially conflicting, views about the roles that racial prejudice plays in their lives.

These divergent views are particularly likely to occur when these biases are unconscious and thus unintentional. We consider this possibility in the next section.

RACIAL BIASES CAN BE UNCONSCIOUS

In the social psychological literature on attitudes and stereotyping, researchers, borrowing from work in cognition more generally, have recently made a fundamental distinction between explicit and implicit processes (Devine, 1989; Greenwald & Banaji, 1995). Explicit attitudes and stereotyping operate in a conscious mode and are exemplified by traditional, self-report measures of these constructs. Implicit attitudes and stereotypes, in contrast, are evaluations and beliefs that are automatically activated by the mere presence (actual or symbolic) of the attitude object. They commonly function in an unconscious and unintentional fashion. Implicit attitudes and stereotypes are typically assessed using response latency procedures, memory tasks, physiological measures (e.g., galvanic skin response), and indirect self-report measures (e.g., involving attributional biases).

In a series of studies, for instance, we used a variety of different response latency procedures to assess the implicit (and presumably unconscious) racial attitudes of Whites toward Blacks (e.g., Dovidio, Evans, & Tyler, 1986; Dovidio & Gaertner, 1993; Gaertner & McLaughlin, 1983). These procedures are based on the assumption that racial attitudes operate like other stimuli to facilitate responses and decision making about related concepts (e.g., doctor–nurse). In general, the greater the associative strength between two stimuli, the faster people can make decisions about them. For example, we have found, using subliminally presented schematic faces of Blacks and Whites as primes, that White participants have faster response times to negative traits after Black than White primes and faster response times to positive traits after White than Black primes (Dovidio, Kawakami, Johnson, Johnson, & Howard, 1997, Study 1; see also Wittenbrink, Judd, & Park, 1997). Convergent evidence has been obtained with a variety of different priming procedures (see Blair, 2001; Dovidio, Kawakami, & Beach, 2001), as well as with other response latency techniques such as the Implicit Association Test (Greenwald, McGhee, & Schwartz, 1998).

Moreover, consistent with the aversive racism framework, Whites' implicit attitudes, which are negative on average, are largely dissociated from their explicit attitudes, which are frequently relatively positive and egalitarian (Dovidio et al., 2001). Implicit and explicit (i.e., self-report) attitudes may thus reflect the components of a system of "dual attitudes." According to Wilson, Lindsey, and Schooler (2000), dual attitudes commonly arise developmentally. With experience or socialization, people change their attitudes. However, the original attitude is not replaced, but rather it is stored in memory and becomes implicit, whereas the newer attitude is conscious and explicit. Because Whites are exposed to negative images of Blacks through the media and to pervasive stereotypes about Blacks through common socialization experiences (Devine, 1989), they may initially develop largely negative attitudes toward Blacks. Later, when as personal and social norms change to become more egalitarian or as an individual is exposed to new normative proscriptions that dictate that people should not have these negative feelings toward Blacks, Whites may adopt explicit unbiased or even positive racial attitudes. Nevertheless, these negative implicit attitudes linger. This combination of explicit egalitarian attitudes and implicit negative attitudes thus characterizes the racial attitudes of aversive racists.

The disassociation between the explicit and implicit attitudes of aversive racists can subtly shape the ways that Whites and Blacks interact and further contribute to the different perceptions that Whites and Blacks develop about their situations. If Whites are unaware of their negative implicit attitudes, they may also be unaware of how their behaviors in interracial interactions may be influenced by these racial biases. In contrast, Blacks, who can observe the negative behaviors of Whites with whom they are interacting, may form very different impressions about whether racial bias is operating and the degree to which it is intentionally determined. Blacks (and other minority groups) may be vigilant to signs of bias and readily attribute these actions to intentional racism. We examine the implications of this aspect of our framework in the next section.

IMPLICIT BIASES
INFLUENCE INTERRACIAL
BEHAVIORS AND PERCEPTIONS

The dissociation between implicit and explicit attitudes that aversive racists experience can have significant, tangible effects on how Whites and Blacks interact in ways that contribute substantially to their divergent perspectives. Implicit and explicit attitudes can influence behavior in different ways and under different conditions (Dovidio & Fazio, 1992; Fazio, 1990; Wilson et al., 2000). Explicit attitudes shape deliberative, well-considered responses for which people have the motivation and opportunity to weigh the costs and benefits of various courses of action. Implicit attitudes influence responses that are more difficult to monitor and control (e.g., some nonverbal behaviors; see Chen & Bargh, 1997; McConnell & Liebold, 2001) or responses that people do not view as an indication of their attitude and thus do not try to control. Thus the relative impact of implicit and explicit attitudes is a function of the context in which the attitudinal object appears, the motivation and opportunity to engage in deliberative processes, and the nature of the behavioral response.

Consistent with the work of other researchers in this area (Fazio, Jackson, Dunton, & Williams, 1995), we have also found evidence in a series of experiments that implicit and explicit attitudes influence different types of race-relevant behaviors of Whites (Dovidio et al., 1997). One study (Dovidio et al., 1997, Study 3), for example, involved two ostensibly unrelated parts: (a) measures of racial attitudes and (b) interaction with a Black and White interviewer sequentially. The measures of racial attitudes included a response latency task and two self-report measures, McConahay's (1986) Old-Fashioned Racism and Modern Racism scales. Measures of deliberative and spontaneous behaviors were assessed during the interaction. As a measure of deliberative behavior, participants were asked to evaluate both other interactants (i.e., the Black and White interviewers) on a series of rating scales. As measures of spontaneous behavior, the nonverbal behaviors of eye contact and blinking were coded from videotapes of the interactions. Higher levels of visual contact (i.e., time spent looking at another person) reflect greater attraction, intimacy, and respect. Higher rates of blinking are related to higher levels of negative arousal and tension. Both of these types of nonverbal behaviors are particularly difficult to monitor and control.

It was predicted that explicit measures of prejudice would primarily relate to bias in the evaluations of Black relative to White interviewers by White participants. In contrast, the response latency measure of implicit negative racial attitude was expected to be the best predictor of nonverbal reactions, specifically higher rates of blinking and less visual contact with the Black relative to the White interviewer.

The results supported the predictions. Bias in terms of more negative judgments about Black than White interviewers was correlated with the two explicit measures of prejudice, old-fashioned racism $(r = .37)$ and modern racism $(r = .54)$, but was uncorrelated with implicit prejudice $(r = .02)$. In contrast, implicit prejudice predicted lower levels of visual contact $(r = -.40)$ and higher rates of blinking $(r = .43)$, but old-fashioned racism $(r \; s = .02, -.04)$ and modern racism $(r \; s = .20, .07)$ did not. Given these conflicting signals, it is not surprising that Blacks are likely to approach interracial interactions with anxiety, guardedness, and underlying mistrust (Hyers & Swim, 1998; Shelton, 2000).

These communication obstacles and interaction problems are exacerbated by the fact that Whites and Blacks have fundamentally different perspectives on the attitudes implied and the actions demonstrated by Whites during these interactions. Whites have full access to their explicit attitudes and are able to monitor and control their more overt and deliberative behaviors. They do not have such full access to their implicit attitudes or to their less monitorable behaviors. As a consequence, Whites' beliefs about how they are behaving or how Blacks perceive them would be expected to be based primarily on their explicit attitudes and their more overt behaviors, such as the verbal content of their interaction with Blacks, and not on their implicit attitudes or less deliberative (i.e., nonverbal) behaviors. In contrast to the perspective of Whites, the perspective of Black partners in these interracial interactions allows them to attend to both the spontaneous (e.g., nonverbal) and the deliberative (e.g., verbal) behaviors of Whites. To the extent that the Black partners attend to Whites' nonverbal behaviors, which may signal more negativity than their verbal behaviors, Blacks are likely to form more negative impressions of the encounter and be less

satisfied with the interaction than are Whites (Shelton, 2000).

To investigate this possibility, we conducted another experiment (Dovidio, Kawakami, & Gaertner, 2002). We assessed perceptions of interracial interactions by Whites and Blacks, and we related these perceptions to White participants' explicit and implicit attitudes. We first assessed the implicit attitudes using Dovidio et al.'s (1997) response-latency priming technique and explicit racial attitudes using Brigham's (1993) Attitudes Toward Blacks Scale. Then we arranged interracial conversations with a Black and a White dyad partner around a race-neutral topic. We videotaped the interactions and subsequently had one set of coders rate the nonverbal and verbal behaviors of White participants and another set of observers rate their global impressions of participants from a videotape recorded from their partners' perspective.

We hypothesized that in these interracial interactions White participants would rely on their explicit, self-reported racial attitudes to shape deliberative behaviors such as their friendliness of verbal behavior toward Black relative to White partners. Explicit racial attitudes and participants' verbal behavior, in turn, were expected to predict Whites' impressions of how friendly they behaved in interactions with the Black relative to the White partner. Implicit racial attitudes, measured with response latencies, and racial bias in White participants' nonverbal behaviors, because they are not easily monitored by the participants, were not expected to predict these impressions.

We also anticipated, based on our previous research, that White participants' implicit racial attitudes would predict biases in their nonverbal friendliness. We further hypothesized that for Black and White partners and independent observers, who could monitor both the White participants' deliberative actions (verbal behaviors) and more spontaneous and subtle behaviors (nonverbal behaviors), perceptions of bias in participants' friendliness would relate significantly to perceptions of bias in participants' nonverbal behaviors and to participants' implicit attitudes. Finally, as a consequence of their different perspectives and their reliance on different cues, we also expected that

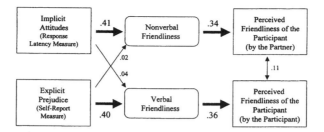

Figure 11.1   The Relationships (correlations) Between Measures of Prejudice and Participant Behavior and Impressions

participants' perceptions of their own racial biases and their partners' perceptions would be only weakly related.

The results, which are summarized in Figure 11.1, are consistent with our predictions. Implicit attitudes predicted nonverbal friendliness $(r = .41)$ but not verbal friendliness $(r = .04)$. Less implicitly biased Whites behaved in a more friendly nonverbal manner. In contrast, the explicit, self-report measure of prejudice predicted verbal $(r = .40)$ but not nonverbal $(r = .02)$ friendliness. Less explicitly prejudiced Whites had more favorable verbal behaviors with the Black partner. Also as anticipated, White participants and Black partners developed very different impressions. As presented in Figure 11.1, more negative impressions of the friendliness of the White participant as judged by the partners were related to his or her non-verbal behavior $(r = .34)$ but not to the White participants' verbal behavior $(r = -.17)$. White participants' impressions of their own friendliness were related more to their verbal behavior $(r = .36)$ than to their nonverbal behavior $(r = -.07)$. Ultimately, the impressions of the friendliness of White participants by themselves and by their partners were essentially unrelated $(r = .11)$. Thus, because of their very different perspectives and reliance on different information, Whites and Blacks left the same interaction with very different impressions.

Our postexperimental discussions with White participants and their Black partners separately provided vivid illustrations of the discordance. White participants typically described that they found the interaction satisfying and

expressed contentment with their contributions. Their Black partners, however, reported being relatively dissatisfied with the exchange and were uneasy about their partners' behaviors. Moreover, both dyad members, when asked, usually assumed that their partner shared the impression of the interaction that they did.

BIASES HAVE DIFFERENT CONSEQUENCES FOR BLACKS AND WHITES

The different and potentially divergent impressions that Blacks and Whites may form during interracial interactions can have significant impact on their coordination and thus their effectiveness in task-oriented situations. Cannon-Bowers and Salas (1999) argued that effective teamwork requires two types of skills, those associated with the technical aspects of the job and those associated with being a member of the team. For this latter factor, team competencies include the knowledge, skills, and attitudes required to work effectively with others. Besides manifesting itself in terms of different impressions and perceptions, contemporary bias can therefore also influence personal relations and group processes in ways that unintentionally but adversely affect outcomes for Blacks.

We propose that for interracial teams, both implicit and explicit racial attitudes are important for effective teamwork. To the extent that explicit attitudes are manifested overtly in less friendly and less supportive actions, interracial interactions involving more highly prejudiced Whites would be expected to be less productive.

To the extent that implicit racial attitudes may also be detected, at least by a Black partner, through more subtle manifestations such as nonverbal behavior, these unconscious biases can erode the trust between group members and negatively affect group performance.

In our research on this issue (Dovidio, in press), White college students were classified on the basis of their self-reported racial attitudes (Brigham's, 1993, Attitudes Toward Blacks Scale) and our response latency measure of bias (Dovidio et al., 1997). A portion of the participants was identified as being low in prejudice on the self-report measure and unbiased on the unconscious (i.e., response latency) measure (nonprejudiced, about 25%). Another group appeared low in prejudice on the self-report measure but had implicit racial biases (aversive racists, about 40%). A third group was relatively prejudiced on the self-report measure as well as biased on the implicit measure (prejudiced, about 20%). (About 15% of the total sample could not be clearly classified into one of these three categories.) We then examined how friendly these participants felt they behaved during an interracial interaction, how friendly and trustful their Black partners perceived them, and how effective the group performed (i.e., how quickly they could decide which items would be most valuable for an incoming student to bring to college).

As we found in our earlier research, Whites' impressions of their behavior were related primarily to their explicit attitudes, whereas Blacks' impressions of Whites were related mainly to Whites' implicit attitudes. Specifically, Whites who appeared low in prejudice on the self-report measure (i.e., nonprejudiced Whites and aversive racists) reported that they behaved more friendly than did those who scored high (prejudiced Whites). Black partners perceived Whites who were unbiased on the implicit, response latency measure (nonprejudiced Whites) to be more friendly than those who had unconscious biases (aversive racists and prejudiced Whites). Blacks were also less trustful of prejudiced Whites and particularly of aversive racists than of nonprejudiced Whites.

Our results further revealed that Whites' racial attitudes were systematically related to the efficiency of the interracial teams. Teams with nonprejudiced Whites solved the problem most quickly. Interracial teams involving prejudiced Whites were next most efficient. Teams with aversive racists were the least efficient. Presumably, the conflicting messages displayed by aversive racists and the divergent impressions of the team members' interaction interfered with the task effectiveness of the team. To the extent that Blacks are in the minority in an organization and are dependent on high-prejudiced Whites or aversive racists on work-related tasks, their performance is likely to be objectively poorer than the performance of Whites who predominantly interact with other Whites. Thus, even when Whites harbor unconscious and unintentional biases toward Blacks, their actions can have effects sometimes even more detrimental than those of old-fashioned racists on interracial processes and outcomes.

CONCLUSION

In this article, we have outlined four ways in which aversive racism can adversely influence interpersonal relations to undermine race relations more generally. First, we argued that contemporary forms of racial bias among Whites, such as aversive racism, are less blatant than the traditional form. Although aversive racists' actions are systematically related to their attitudes, the attitudes of aversive racists are complex, including both conscious egalitarian values and unconscious negative feelings and beliefs. As a consequence, as we demonstrated in our research, aversive racists do not discriminate against Blacks when these actions would be recognized, by others or by oneself, as racially motivated. However, aversive racists do discriminate against Blacks when they can justify their behavior on the basis of factors other than race, and they readily adopt or construct these rationalizations. From the perspective of a casual observer, then, the interracial actions of aversive racists could appear inconsistent and unpredictable, or possibly even dishonest and deceitful. This inconsistency could significantly erode Blacks' confidence in the person's overtly well-intentioned motivations and values, which could then lead to interpersonal and, ultimately, interracial distrust.

Second, because aversive racists may not be aware of their implicit negative attitudes and only discriminate against Blacks when they can justify their behavior on the basis of some factor other than race, they will commonly deny any intentional wrongdoing when confronted with evidence of their bias. Indeed, they do not intentionally discriminate. Nevertheless, because people tend to overattribute intentionality to another person's actions (Jones & Harris, 1967), Blacks who feel discriminated against will likely assume that the White person's behaviors were motivated by conscious, "old-fashioned" racism. An aversive racist's denial of intentionality, although genuine, may then intensify racial conflict and distrust.

Third, because people and their interaction partners have different perspectives and different access to thoughts and observable behaviors, there is significant potential for miscommunication to occur in interactions. This potential is particularly great in interracial interactions involving aversive racists. Even though aversive racists may not consciously endorse or even acknowledge their implicit negative attitudes toward Blacks, this implicit prejudice does significantly influence their behavior. However, as we have shown, implicit attitudes most strongly influence the behaviors that are least controllable and monitorable (e.g., nonverbal behaviors) by the aversive racist. Thus, aversive racists are likely to display mixed messages in interracial interactions while believing that they are behaving consistently appropriately and being confident that they are making the favorable impression that they intended. To the extent that Blacks (Shelton, 2000) and other minority group members (Vorauer & Kumhyr, 2001) may, for historical reasons or personal experience, be particularly sensitive to signs of rejection, dislike, or discrimination, they are likely to weigh the negative signals more heavily than the more positive overt behaviors or even view the communication of mixed messages as evidence of ingenuous or deceitful motivations.

And fourth, in the previous section, we have illustrated how awkward and inefficient interracial communication, which is a consequence of aversive racism, can have a negative impact on group outcomes as well as group processes.

Beyond the substantial differences in social and economic power (Blank, 2001) that can limit the control that Blacks and other minorities can exert over their fate, the simple fact that, because of their numerical minority status, Blacks are more likely to engage in interracial interactions than are Whites makes them more vulnerable to the effects of problems in interracial communication. Whereas Whites may have little opportunity to interact with Blacks and may often be motivated to avoid such interactions (Gaertner & Dovidio, 1986), Blacks commonly must interact with Whites on a regular basis. They are thus susceptible to the cumulative effects of blatant and subtle racism (Feagin & Sikes, 1994) in ways that most Whites do not fully recognize or acknowledge (Morin, 2001).

Although our focus has been on how the racial attitudes of Whites in general and aversive racists in particular can shape racially directed actions and interracial behaviors in ways that contribute to miscommunication and distrust, we conclude by noting that all of the participants in an interaction, Black as well as White, are responsible for the outcomes. Blacks are active participants, and how they react and the actions they take proactively can contribute to more positive race relations. On the one hand, subtle, unconscious biases of one person can systematically affect the responses of others to produce self-fulfilling effects, again without the full awareness of the interactants (Chen & Bargh, 1997). On the other hand, people who are aware of the potential for stigmatization may respond strategically in ways that interfere with this process and produce more positive, individuated, and constructive outcomes (Miller, Rothblum, Felicio, & Brand, 1995). The coordinated roles of both Whites and Blacks in interracial interactions, with greater attention to the explicit and implicit attitudes of Blacks, clearly merit more attention. As Devine and Vasquez (1998) observed, one fundamental limitation

of existing theory is that the previous work has examined majority group members (e.g., whites and heterosexuals) and minority group members (e.g., blacks and homosexuals) separately . . . We have not yet examined carefully and fully the nature of interpersonal dynamics that emerge between majority and minority group members when they are brought together in a specific interpersonal situation. In other words, we do not know what happens when interaction begins. (pp. 240–241)

Finally, as we noted at the beginning of this article, we have focused our efforts at understanding the problem of race relations in the United States by examining one aspect—the influence of the racial attitudes of Whites in interpersonal interracial encounters. Clearly, the problem of race relations involves intergroup, historical, economic, and cultural issues as well. At an interpersonal level, it also encompasses the behaviors and the psychology of Blacks (see Shelton, 2000). Nevertheless, we believe that increasing an understanding and awareness of one particular aspect of this problem, the subtle biases of Whites, may represent a valuable step for creating more open, harmonious, and productive race relations in the future.

REFERENCES

Anderson, J. (1996, April 29 and May 6). Black and blue. *New Yorker*, 62–64.

Armed Forces Equal Opportunity Survey. (1999). Arlington, VA: Defense Manpower Data Center.

Blair, I. V. (2001). Implicit stereotypes and prejudice. In G. B. Moskowitz (Ed.), *Cognitive social psychology: The Princeton symposium on the legacy and future of social cognition* (pp. 359–374). Mahwah, NJ: Erlbaum.

Blank, R. M. (2001). An overview of trends in social and economic well-being, by race. In N. J. Smelser, W. J. Wilson, & F. Mitchell (Eds.), *Racial trends and their consequences* (Vol. 1, pp. 21–39). Washington, DC: National Academy Press.

Bobo, L. D. (2001). Racial attitudes and relations at the close of the twentieth century. In N. J. Smelser, W. J. Wilson, & F. Mitchell (Eds.), *Racial trends and their consequences* (Vol. 1, pp. 264–301). Washington, DC: National Academy Press.

Brigham, J. C. (1993). College students' racial attitudes. *Journal of Applied Social Psychology, 23*, 1933–1967.

Cannon-Bowers, J. A., & Salas, E. (1999). Team performance and training in complex environments: Recent findings from applied research. *Current Directions in Psychological Science, 7*, 83–87.

Chen, M., & Bargh, J. (1997). Nonconscious behavioral confirmation processes: The self-fulfilling consequences of automatic stereotype activation. *Journal of Experimental Social Psychology, 33*, 541–560.

Crocker, J., Luhtanen, R., Broadnax, S., & Blaine, B. E. (1999). Belief in U.S. government conspiracies against Blacks among Black and White college students: Powerlessness or system blame? *Personality and Social Psychology Bulletin, 25*, 941–953.

Darley, J. M., & Latané, B. (1968). Bystander intervention in emergencies: Diffusion of responsibility. *Journal of Personality and Social Psychology, 8*, 377–383.

Davis, J. A., & Smith, T. W. (1994). *General social surveys, 1972–1994: Cumulative codebook*. Chicago: National Opinion Research Center.

DeParle, J. (1990, October 29). Talk of government being out to get Blacks falls on more attentive ears. *New York Times*, p. B7.

DeParle, J. (1991, August 11). For some Blacks, social ills seem to follow White plans. *New York Times*, p. E5.

Devine, P. G. (1989). Stereotypes and prejudice: The automatic and controlled components. *Journal of Personality and Social Psychology, 56*, 5–18.

Devine, P. G., & Vasquez, K. A. (1998). The rocky road to positive intergroup relations. In J. Eberhardt & S. T. Fiske (Eds.), *Confronting racism: The problem and the response* (pp. 234–262). Newbury Park, CA: Sage.

Dovidio, J. F. (2001). On the nature of contemporary prejudice: The third wave. *Journal of Social Issues, 57*, 829–849.

Dovidio, J. F. (in press). On the nature of contemporary prejudice: Outcomes and process. In *Proceedings of the Third Biennial EO/EEO Research Symposium*. Cocoa Beach, FL: Defense Equal Opportunity Management Institute.

Dovidio, J. F., Evans, N., & Tyler, R. B. (1986). Racial stereotypes: The contents of their cognitive representations. *Journal of Experimental Social Psychology, 22*, 22–37.

Dovidio, J. F., & Fazio, R. H. (1992). New technologies for the direct and indirect assessment of attitudes. In J. Tanur (Ed.), *Questions about survey questions: Meaning, memory, attitudes, and social interaction* (pp. 204–237). New York: Russell Sage Foundation.

Dovidio, J. F., & Gaertner, S. L. (1986). Prejudice, discrimination, and racism: Historical trends and contemporary approaches. In J. F. Dovidio & S. L. Gaertner (Eds.), *Prejudice, discrimination and racism* (pp. 1–34). Orlando, FL: Academic Press.

Dovidio, J. F., & Gaertner, S. L. (1993). Stereotypes and evaluative intergroup bias. In D. M. Mackie & D. L. Hamilton (Eds.), *Affect, cognition, and stereotyping: Interactive processes in intergroup perception* (pp. 167–193). Orlando, FL: Academic Press.

Dovidio, J. F., & Gaertner, S. L. (1998). On the nature of contemporary prejudice: The causes, consequences, and challenges of aversive racism. In J. Eberhardt & S. T. Fiske (Eds.), *Confronting racism: The problem and the response* (pp. 3–32). Newbury Park, CA: Sage.

Dovidio, J. F., & Gaertner, S. L. (2000). Aversive racism and selection decisions: 1989 and 1999. *Psychological Science, 11*, 319–323.

Dovidio, J. F., Gaertner, S. L., Anastasio, P. A., & Sanitioso, R. (1992). Cognitive and motivational bases of bias: The implications of aversive racism for attitudes toward Hispanics. In S. Knouse, P. Rosenfeld, & A. Culbertson (Eds.), *Hispanics in the workplace* (pp. 75–106). Newbury Park, CA: Sage.

Dovidio, J., Kawakami, K., & Beach, K. (2001). Implicit and explicit attitudes: Examination of the relationship between measures of intergroup bias. In R. Brown & S. L. Gaertner (Eds.), *Blackwell handbook of social psychology: Vol. 4. Intergroup relations* (pp. 175–197). Oxford, England: Blackwell.

Dovidio, J. F., Kawakami, K., & Gaertner, S. L. (2002). Implicit and explicit prejudice and interracial interaction. *Journal of Personality and Social Psychology, 82*, 62–68.

Dovidio, J., Kawakami, K., Johnson, C., Johnson, B., & Howard, A. (1997). The nature of prejudice: Automatic and controlled processes. *Journal of Experimental Social Psychology, 33*, 510–540.

Duckitt, J. (1992). *The social psychology of prejudice.* Westport, CT: Praeger.

Fazio, R. H. (1990). Multiple processes by which attitudes guide behavior: The MODE model as an integrative framework. In M. P. Zanna (Ed.), *Advances in experimental social psychology* (Vol. 23, pp. 75–109). Orlando, FL: Academic Press.

Fazio, R. H., Jackson, J. R., Dunton, B. C., & Williams, C. J. (1995). Variability in automatic activation as an unobtrusive measure of racial attitudes: A bona fide pipeline? *Journal of Personality and Social Psychology, 69*, 1013–1027.

Feagin, J. R., & Sikes, M. P. (1994). *Living with racism: The Black middle-class experience.* Boston: Beacon Press.

Gaertner, S. L., & Dovidio, J. F. (1977). The subtlety of White racism, arousal, and helping behavior.
Journal of Personality and Social Psychology, 35, 691–707.

Gaertner, S. L., & Dovidio, J. F. (1986). The aversive form of racism. In J. F. Dovidio & S. L. Gaertner (Eds.), *Prejudice, discrimination, and racism* (pp. 61–89). Orlando, FL: Academic Press.

Gaertner, S. L., Dovidio, J. F., Banker, B., Rust, M., Nier, J., Mottola, G., & Ward, C. (1997). Does racism necessarily mean anti-Blackness? Aversive racism and pro-Whiteness. In M. Fine, L. Powell, L. Weis, & M. Wong (Eds.), *Off White* (pp. 167–178). London: Routledge.

Gaertner, S. L., & McLaughlin, J. P. (1983). Racial stereotypes: Associations and ascriptions of positive and negative characteristics. *Social Psychology Quarterly, 46,* 23–30.

Gallup. (2001). *Black–White relations in the United States: 2001 update.* Washington, DC: Gallup Organization.

Greenwald, A., & Banaji, M. (1995). Implicit social cognition: Attitudes, self-esteem, and stereotypes. *Psychological Review, 102,* 4–27.

Greenwald, A., McGhee, D., & Schwartz, J. (1998). Measuring individual differences in implicit cognition: The implicit association test. *Journal of Personality and Social Psychology, 74,* 1464–1480.

Hechter, M. (1975). *Internal colonization.* Berkeley: University of California Press.

Hochschild, J. L. (1995). *Facing up to the American dream: Race, class, and the soul of the nation.* Princeton, NJ: Princeton University Press.

Hodson, G., Dovidio, J. F., & Gaertner, S. L. (2002). Processes in racial discrimination: Differential weighting of conflicting information. *Personality and Social Psychology Bulletin, 28,* 460–471.

Hyers, L. L., & Swim, J. K. (1998). A comparison of the experiences of dominant and minority group members during an intergroup encounter. *Group Processes and Intergroup Relations, 1,* 143–163.

Jones, E. E., & Harris, V. A. (1967). The attribution of attitudes. *Journal of Experimental Social Psychology, 3,* 1–24.

Kovel, J. (1970). *White racism: A psychohistory.* New York: Pantheon.

McConahay, J. B. (1986). Modern racism, ambivalence, and the modern racism scale. In J. F. Dovidio & S. L. Gaertner (Eds.), *Prejudice, discrimination, and racism* (pp. 91–125). Orlando, FL: Academic Press.

McConnell, A. R., & Leibold, J. M. (2001). Relations among the Implicit Association Test, discriminatory behavior, and explicit measures of racial attitudes. *Journal of Experimental Social Psychology, 37,* 435–442.

Miller, C. T., Rothblum, E. D., Felicio, D., & Brand, R. (1995). Compensating for stigma: Obese and nonobese women's reactions to being visible. *Personality and Social Psychology Bulletin, 21,* 1093–1106.

Morin, R. (2001, July). Well-being of Blacks inflated by Whites. *Syracuse Post Standard,* pp. A1, A8.

Sears, D. O. (1988). Symbolic racism. In P. A. Katz & D. A. Taylor (Eds.), *Eliminating racism: Profiles in controversy* (pp. 53–84). New York: Plenum Press.

Sears, D. O., Henry, P. J., & Kosterman, R. (2000). Egalitarian values and contemporary racial politics. In D. O. Sears, J. Sidanius, & L. Bobo (Eds.), *Racialized politics: The debate about racism in America* (pp. 75–117). Chicago: University of Chicago Press.

Shelton, J. N. (2000). A reconceptualization of how we study issues of racial prejudice. *Personality and Social Psychology Review, 4,* 374–390.

Sherif, M., & Sherif, C. W. (1969). *Social psychology.* New York: Harper & Row.

Smelser, N. J., Wilson, W. J., & Mitchell, F. (Eds.). (2001). *Racial trends and their consequences* (Vol. 1). Washington, DC: National Academy Press.

U.S. Merit Systems Protection Board. (1997). *Fair and equitable treatment: A progress report on minority employment in the federal government.* Washington, DC: Office of Policy and Evaluation.

Vorauer, J. D., & Kumhyr, S. M. (2001). Is this about you or me? Self- versus other-directed judgments and feelings in response to intergroup interaction. *Personality and Social Psychology Bulletin, 27,* 706–719.

Wills, T. A. (1981). Downward comparison principles in social psychology. *Psychological Bulletin, 90,* 245–271.

Wilson, T. D., Lindsey, S., & Schooler, T. Y. (2000). A model of dual attitudes. *Psychological Review, 107,* 101–126.

Wittenbrink, B., Judd, C., & Park, B. (1997). Evidence for racial prejudice at the implicit level and its relationship with questionnaire measures. *Journal of Personality and Social Psychology, 72,* 262–274.

QUESTIONS

1. What are the four aspects of contemporary prejudices held by Whites toward Blacks?

2. What is aversive racism? How can the concept of aversive racism help us understand how racism can be perpetuated by people who believe in racial equality and condemn prejudice?

3. How does aversive racism differ from traditional racism?

4. How are the lives of Blacks affected by aversive racism? How does aversive racism contribute to the maintenance of institutional discrimination against Black people?

5. How did aversive racism influence the hiring and college admissions decisions in the experiments reported here?

6. Describe the experiment simulating an emergency situation. Did the results support the theory of aversive racism?

7. How does the subtle nature of aversive racism allow Whites to avoid recognizing their own racial prejudice and its impact on Blacks?

8. How can the influence of aversive racism operating across different contexts shape the perceptions of Blacks about the effect of racial prejudice on their lives?

9. Why might Blacks and Whites leave some interracial interactions with very different impressions of each other's behavior?

10. Have you ever experienced an interaction with another person that reminds you of the awkward situations described in this article? How did you feel after the experience?

11. If "knowledge is power," how can we apply what we've learned about aversive racism to try and improve interracial trust?

12. Do you think you might have implicit negative feelings toward people of another ethnic group? If you discovered that you did, what would you do about it?

12

HATE ONLINE

A Content Analysis of Extremist Internet Sites

PHYLLIS B. GERSTENFELD

DIANA R. GRANT

CHAU-PU CHIANG

The Internet has added a whole new dimension to modern society, and the advantages of cyberspace are particularly attractive to extremists advocating racial or religious superiority. An examination of a varied sample of extremist web sites suggests that extremists are using the Web as a tool to communicate with each other and to package hate propaganda so as to appear more credible and mainstream. Yet beneath the slick appearance of many extremist Web sites, familiar hatreds are difficult to conceal.

Extremist groups were among the very early users of the electronic communication network that eventually evolved into the Internet. In 1985, for example, long before most people had heard about the Internet, Tom Metzger, the leader of the White Aryan Resistance, created a computer bulletin board (Hamm, 1993). Since then, these groups' presence online has been very active (Levin, 2002).

Extremist groups might use the Internet for a variety of purposes. It can be used to communicate with current members, or to recruit new ones. It can be used as a forum for publishing the groups' views, or as an attempt to "educate" the general public. Some of these educational attempts can be intentionally misleading. The extremist web site Stormwatch, for instance, hosts a site about Martin Luther King (http://www.martinlutherking.org) that mimics the site of

EDITORS' NOTE: From Gerstenfeld, P. B., Grant, D. R., & Chiang, C.-P. (2003). Hate Online: A Content Analysis of Extremist Internet Sites. *Analyses of Social Issues and Public Policy, 3*(1), 29-44.

the King Center (http://www.thekingcenter.org). The Internet can also be used to sell merchandise. Resistance Records, the music-selling arm of the white supremacist National Alliance, is estimated to have had about $1 million in sales in 2001 (ADL, 2001).

Although there exists ample literature on hate crimes and hate groups in general, and although the Internet has been used as a means to interview extremists (see, e.g., Glaser, Dixit, & Green, 2002), relatively little scholarly work has focused on the contents and uses of extremist web sites. This is unfortunate, given extremists' heavy use of the Internet. One online directory of hate sites lists 661 web sites, 20 mailing lists, 27 Usenet newsgroups, 45 Internet Relay Chat channels, 131 clubs and groups on Yahoo! and MSN, and 13 electronic bulletin board systems (Franklin, 2001). Another source claims that there are at least 800 hate-related Internet sites (Tsesis, 2001). The Simon Wiesenthal Center estimated that in 2000 there were approximately 2200 extremist web sites (Simon Wiesenthal Center, 2000). These sites are maintained by a variety of people and organizations, ranging from well-known groups such as the Klan and the National Alliance, to relatively obscure groups such as S.T.R.A.I.G.H.T. (an anti-gay group) and La Voz de Aztlan (an anti-Semitic Chicano separatist group), to what appear to be unaffiliated individuals.

Despite extremist groups' frequent use of the Internet, few attempts have been made to examine their web sites in a systematic manner to examine what the sites actually contain, and to determine precisely to what purposes the sites are being put. Burris, Smith, and Strahm (2000) used social network analysis to examine the links between white supremacist sites. Consistent with the expectations discussed above, they found that the movement was decentralized, but that there were no sharp divisions between the groups and that different kinds of groups frequently linked to one another. The researchers also found a number of "soft-core" supremacist sites, which they believed might serve the hard-core groups in their recruitment efforts because they could be "important ports of entry into the movement" (Burris, Smith, & Strahm, 2000, p. 232). Finally, they found evidence that the Internet does assist in the creation of an international virtual extremist community: over two thirds of the links were to international sites (Burris, Smith, & Strahm, 2000).

In another study, McDonald (1999) found that most of the 30 white supremacist sites she examined used sophisticated techniques of persuasion. This supports the hypothesis that these sites are used to recruit, and also gives some support to the claim that the Internet may assist these groups in conveying a respectable image.

To date, the most comprehensive content analysis of extremist web sites was an exploratory analysis conducted by Schafer (2002). Schafer (2002) rated 132 extremist sites. He concluded that these web sites provide a wide range of information, that many of the sites provide groups with the opportunity to sell products, and that the web sites are often used as tools to facilitate communication among members. A number of other issues, however, were not explored in this study, including the number and types of links provided, the degree to which the sites seemed to foster international communication, the images and specific messages conveyed by the sites, and the distinctions between the different types of groups.

Clearly, more research is needed in this area. The current article reports a content analysis of extremist web sites conducted in an attempt to fill this need.

METHODS

As Schafer (2002) points out, conducting content analyses of web sites is problematic because it is impossible to determine the true size and nature of the population. The Internet is in constant flux, and there exists no comprehensive directory of web sites. Therefore, a purposive sampling technique must be used.

For this study, a purposive sample of 215 extremist web sites was compiled from several sources: (1) HateWatch (http://www.hatewatch.org), a non-profit web site devoted to monitoring extremist sites;[1] (2) the Simon Wiesenthal Center's guide to extremist sites, Digital Hate 2000; (3) sites listed under Yahoo's categories of White Pride and Racialism (http://dir.yahoo.com/Society and Culture/Cultures and Groups/

White Pride and Racialism/); and (4) sites prominently and frequently linked to by other extremist sites. Of the 215 sites, many no longer existed or were not available, so the eventual sample consisted of 157 sites.

Although it would be impossible to include every extant extremist site in any analysis, the sample for this study did include all major players in the extremist world, as well as many minor ones. Moreover, it included a wide variety of types of groups. To the extent that the nature of the population can be determined, the sites included within the sample were representative of the population of extremist web sites.

Each site was rated on a number of variables by two independent raters (see Table 12.1). Because many web sites change frequently, and because the raters did not always view the sites on the same day, some inconsistencies in the ratings would be expected. Furthermore, web sites can be very large and complex, and it is quite possible that a single rater might miss a particular item of interest on a particular web site. Therefore, when there was disagreement between the raters on a particular item, the site in question was examined a third time to produce a single response. Interrater reliability correlations were significant for all variables at at least the .05 level.

Data were collected on 157 web sites.[2] Of these, 142 were apparently authored by groups or individuals from the United States; the remaining 15 were internationally based. Initial examination of the sites, as well as the literature on extremist groups, suggested that it made sense to place each site into one of ten broad categories, depending on the predominant nature of the messages conveyed: Ku Klux Klan, Militia, Skinhead, Neo-Nazi, Christian Identity, Posse Comitatus, Holocaust Denial, White Nationalist, Other, and None.[3] Table 12.2 lists the number of sites that were in each category.

The most common category, "Other," was somewhat of a catchall. Included within it were such right-wing groups as the John Birch Society and the Council of Conservative Citizens, "umbrella" sites such as The Freedom Site and Radio White, and non-white supremacist groups

Table 12.1   Variables Recorded for the Content Analysis

Type of Site (Christian Identity, Holocaust Denial, Ku Klux Klan, Militia, Neo-Nazi, Posse Comitatus, Skinhead, White Nationalist, Other)

External Links
  International links
  Links to other types of groups

Content Type
  Non-English content
  Content for children
  Multimedia content
  Mentions economic issues
  Claims to not be racist
  Advocates violence
  Contains racist symbols
  Includes quotes from racist "classics"
  Sells merchandise

Membership
  Includes membership forms
  Includes other means for members to communicate (bulletin boards, listservs, etc.)

such as the Nation of Islam, Radio Islam, and the Jewish Defense League.

The second most common category, White Nationalists, included a variety of groups that espouse white nationalism and separatism. Some of these, such as the American Nationalist Union, are based in the United States, while others (e.g., the British National Party) are not. The remaining categories are fairly self-explanatory and are listed in Table 12.2.

RESULTS

External Links

There were many intergroup links. Most of the sites (126, or 80.3%) contained external links. Skinhead sites were the most likely to contain external links (91.5% did), whereas Neo–Nazi sites were the least likely (58.8% did). Although most sites linked most frequently to other sites within the same category (see Table 12.3), cross-category links were also common. In fact, 49.7% of the sites linked to at least one site in another category (and 62% of

Table 12.2   Number of Rated Sites by Type of
Extremism

Type	Number	Percent of Total
Other	32	20.3
White Nationalist	30	19.1
Skinhead	21	13.4
Christian Identity	21	13.4
Holocaust Denial	20	12.7
Neo-Nazi	17	10.8
Ku Klux Klan	13	8.3
Militia	2	1.3
Posse Comitatus	1	.6

the sites with at least one external link had at least one link to another kind of group). Skinhead sites were the most likely to link to another type (66.7% did), and Klan sites the least likely (38.5%).

Eighty of the sites (51%) contained links to international organizations. Furthermore, if the 31 sites that contained no external links at all are excluded from the analysis, 63.7% of the remaining sites had international links. Table 12.4 lists the percentage of each type of site that contained international links. Klan sites were among those least likely to contain international links, as were Christian Identity sites. Still, a third or more of the sites affiliated with these two groups did contain links to sites in other countries. Fully two thirds of the nationalist sites contained international links.

Extremism makes for some odd bedfellows, and some of the links were a bit unexpected. The Aryan Nations web site, for example, contains links to Radio Islam and Hamas. Conversely, the Radio Islam site contains materials by, among others, David Duke and Louis Farakhan. OurHero.com (the "hero" in question being Adolf Hitler) has a link to the anti-Israeli site Mid-East Realities (http://www.middleeast.org/). The White Survival site links to Qana.net, a site devoted to "The 'Israeli' Massacres against Lebanon." What these seemingly disparate sites have in common is anti-Jewish sentiment. On the other hand, the National Socialist Movement

web site lists under its "Enemies of Humanity" the Nation of Aztlan (http://www.aztlan.org) site, even though the Nation of Aztlan, like the National Socialists, is primarily anti-Jewish in its message (the other "enemies" are the Anti-Defamation League and the American Communist Party).

An interesting phenomenon was that some of the extremist sites also had links to watchdog organizations such as the Anti-Defamation League, the Southern Poverty Law Center, and the Simon Wiesenthal Center. Frequently, the extremist sites claimed that these other groups were the *real* hate groups and that white supremacists are actually victims of this hate.

Content Type

Forty-one of the sites (26.1%) had non-English content.[4] Holocaust denial sites were the most likely to have non-English content (45% did), and Neo-Nazi sites also frequently (41.2%) contained content in languages other than English (most often German). The sites least likely to have non-English content were those in the "other" category (12.9%) and Christian Identity sites (14.3%).

Eleven sites (7%) had some sort of "kids' page." These were generally intended for young children and contained such things as messages from other children, games, music, and "history" lessons. A few sites also had home-schooling curricula.

Seventy-eight of the sites (49.7%) included multimedia materials. Music downloads were particularly common, and some sites also had video downloads, games, and other audio such as sermons and speeches. Again, there was some variation among the types of sites. Nearly 62 percent of Skinhead sites had multimedia content. This may be reflective of the fact that Skinheads tend to be younger than members of other white supremacist groups. On the other hand, only one quarter of the Holocaust denial sites contained multimedia content.

Regardless of the type of site, there was much similarity in content. Seventy-nine of the sites (50.3%) mentioned economic issues, 78 (49.7%) contained racist symbols (such as swastikas or

Table 12.3 External Links Contained Within Each Type of Site[a]

Type of Rated Site	Percentage of Sites That Contained Each Category of Links									
	None	KKK	Militia	Skin-head	Neo-Nazi	Christian Identity	Posse	Holocaust Denial	White Nationalist	Other
Neo-Nazi	47.1	11.8	0	11.8	47.1	11.8	0	23.5	23.5	23.5
KKK	38.5	61.5	0	7.7	23.1	23.1	7.7	0	30.8	15.8
Other	32.3	19.4	9.7	22.6	32.3	29	0	29	29	38.7
White Nationalist	30	30	6.7	26.7	40	30	0	43.3	50	20
Christian Identity	23.8	14.3	14.3	9.5	23.8	66.7	4.8	33.3	14.3	19
Holocaust Denial	20	20	5	10	35	15	0	80	15	25
Skinhead	9.5	28.6	9.5	76.2	33.3	14.3	0	14.3	33.3	28.6

a. Because very few militia sites ($n = 2$) or Posse sites ($n = 1$) were rated, they are excluded from this analysis.

Table 12.4 International Links by Type of Site[a]

Type of Rated Site	Percentage of Sites That Contained International Links
White Nationalist	66.7
Holocaust Denial	60.0
Skinhead	57.1
Neo-Nazi	52.9
Other	45.2
KKK	38.5
Christian Identity	33.3

a. Because very few militia sites ($n = 2$) or Posse sites ($n = 1$) were rated, they are excluded from this analysis.

burning crosses), and 50 of the sites (31.8%) contained quotations from or the entire text of such "classics" of supremacist literature as *Mein Kampf, The Protocols of the Elders of Zion, The Turner Diaries,* or *The International Jew.*

Thirty-four of the sites (21.7%) contained language claiming that the group was not racist or did not hate anyone. For example, David Duke's European-American Unity and Rights Organization claims to stand for equal opportunity for all and also argues that "the real hatred rests within the minority racists," such as the NAACP. The International Third Position claims as one of its principles, "Support for the principles of racial and cultural diversity." The

Knights of the Ku Klux Klan exclaims, "We are not a hate group!"

Of course, these claims are often contradicted by other material on the same web site. The top of the Radio Islam home page states on the left hand side, "No hate. No violence. Races? Only one human race." But on the right-hand side of the same page, it says, "Know Your Enemy! No time to waste. Act now!" The motto of the NAAWP (National Association for the Advancement of White People) is "Equal rights for all, special privileges for none." Yet its site also contains a page titled "The Black War On White Americans: An Overview of United States Crime." The Imperial Klans of America, Realm of Illinois, claims, "We believe everyone has a right to be proud of their race, which means White people have a right to be proud also." However, its web site includes a document titled "The Truth about 'Martin Luther King Jr.'" (which, tellingly, is located at this URL: http://www.k-k-k.com/koon.htm), as well as a variety of anti-Jewish material. Many of the Holocaust denial sites, which often claim to be unbigoted, have links to such overtly racist organizations as Klan and Neo-Nazi groups.

Only 26 (16.6%) of the rated sites specifically urged violence, and many sites actually contained language condemning violence or claiming that the sponsor was nonviolent. This was true even for historically vicious organizations such as the Klan (7.7% of the sites advocated violence) and the Skinheads (28.6% advocated violence). There was a significant correlation between sites encouraging violence and those containing hate symbols ($r^2 = .20$; $p = .012$).

A few of the sites appeared to be deliberately misleading in their titles or content. As already mentioned, the site at www.mlking.org is actually hosted by Stormfront, although this is not obvious. It includes an exhortation to "Bring the Dream to life in your town" by downloading "flyers to pass out at your school." The flyers contain a photo of King, an urging to "learn exciting new facts" about him, and the address of the web site. An example of the "exciting new facts" one can learn on the web site is the following excerpt from an essay titled, "The Beast as Saint: The Truth about 'Martin Luther King Jr.,'" by Kevin Alfred Strom:

> Well friends, he is not a legitimate reverend, he is not a bona fide PhD, and his name isn't really "Martin Luther King, Jr." What's left? Just a sexual degenerate, an America-hating Communist, and a criminal betrayer of even the interests of his own people.[5]

Other examples of misleading sites are the American Civil Rights Review, a number of sites that hide under the guise of mainstream Christianity, and several sites that merely claim to promote freedom of expression or historical accuracy.

Merchandise Sales

Eighty-six of the total sites (54.8%) sell some kind of merchandise, such as books, CDs, videos, clothing, flags, jewelry, or patches. These items presumably help advertise the groups and spread their message, and the income is a benefit to the group as well. There was not a great deal of variation between the types of sites on this variable, but Skinhead cites were the most likely to offer items for sale (66.7% did), and sites in the "Other" category were the least likely (35.5%).

Membership Forms

Forty-eight of the sites (30.6%) included membership forms. If only those 93 sites that obviously belong to organized groups are considered, the percentage including membership forms increases to 44.1. Many sites also offered bulletin boards and electronic mail lists to which interested people could subscribe. Some sites also included photos of the groups' members at meetings, concerts, and other events. One site even featured a "white pride pets" section, with photos of dogs posed in front of racist symbols.

DISCUSSION AND CONCLUSIONS

The sites rated in this study ranged from crude and barely literate to extremely slick and professional appearing. The content varied from a single page containing a few phrases to enormous sites with libraries' worth of information. The language extended from seemingly innocent to wildly inflammatory. The sponsors were anything from single, unaffiliated individuals to large organizations with multiple chapters. Despite this wide variation, however, there are a number of tentative conclusions that can be drawn.

There are several reasons why the Internet might be attractive to extremists. To communicate via the Internet is fast, easy, and inexpensive (Perry, 2000; Whine, 1997). These features make the Internet a much more convenient avenue of expression than more traditional methods like newsletters, flyers, or public speeches. Furthermore, on the Internet, information can be disseminated without compromising the anonymity of the authors, and interactive communication with audience members is easily accomplished. The enormous potential of the Internet as a communication tool is reflected in its increasing use in both commercial and private interactions. For this reason alone, it is not surprising to find extremist groups developing an Internet presence. The very features of the Internet that make it a democratic medium may make it a particularly appealing tool for individuals from marginalized groups to connect with each other. This content analysis suggests several specific benefits the Internet may have to extremist groups.

International Appeal

One feature of the Internet is that it is largely unsupervised and unregulated. Laws that have attempted to restrict electronic hate speech, such as the Communications Decency Act of 1996, have been struck down as unconstitutional in the U. S., or have been largely ineffectual abroad (Siegel, 1999). Moreover, the borderless nature of the Internet makes it particularly attractive to those who want to spread messages that would be banned in print in some countries (Perry, 2000; Whine, 1997). The unregulated nature of the Internet in the United States is so attractive to members of extremist groups that even groups physically based outside the United States appear to be using American-based web sites to communicate with their international audience. Al Qaeda, Hamas, and other terrorist organizations were recently found to be using web sites run from locations such as New York and San Diego (Katz & Devon, 2002). Holocaust denier Ernst Zündel was prosecuted by a Canadian court for violating the Canadian Human Rights Act, and although Zündel was a Canadian resident, the web site in question was actually located on an Internet server in New York.

Although criminal cases have been brought against those involved in spreading hate on the Internet, the prosecutions have been extremely rare and, to say the least, problematic (ADL, 2000; Konkel, 2000; Tsesis, 2001). According to some recent reports, American extremist groups have recently strengthened their ties with their European cohorts (Southern Poverty Law Center, 2001).

We found that frequent attempts were made to appeal to an international audience. Content in languages other than English was common, and international links were present on a majority of the sites. The international approach appeared strongest for certain types of extremists, such as nationalists and Holocaust deniers, but even such seemingly "all-American" groups as the Klan frequently linked to sites outside of the United States.

Recruitment

A second feature of the Internet is that it may make a particularly effective recruiting tool.

Extremist groups do rely heavily on recruitment efforts, in part because members tend to age out of the group, or drop due to other factors (Aho, 1988; Blazak, 2001). McCurrie (1998) found that, whereas traditional gang members sought gang membership for protection or to make money, most white supremacists (62.5% in McCurrie's sample) were recruited in. Many extremist groups focus their recruitment efforts on youths (Blazak, 2001; Turpin-Petrosino, 2002), and the Internet is well suited to this. According to a recent survey, 73% of Americans ages 12 through 17 use the Internet (Pew Research Center, 2001). The Internet permits multimedia approaches that youths find especially appealing (Perry, 2000).

The efficacy of extremists' use of the Internet in recruiting youths is unclear. In a survey of secondary and college students, Turpin-Petrosino (2002) found that only 10 of 567 respondents reported Internet contacts with white supremacist groups, and only four of them claimed to support the groups. In general, word-of-mouth and print contacts were more common and were associated with stronger support of the groups. However, it is possible that some of these students had actually visited extremist web sites without being aware that they were, in fact, extremist (Stormfront's Martin Luther King site would be a good example of this). Leets (2001) found that students did not always recognize the nature of extremist sites. Furthermore, students who visited the sites may have been influenced by some of the groups' dogma without actually supporting the groups in their entirety.

Extremist group web sites frequently proclaim the value of freedom of expression; in fact, some, such as the First Amendment Exercise Machine (www.faem.com) claim this as their raison d'etre. This may be an effective recruiting tool. Cowan, Resendez, Marshall, and Quist (2002) found that when college students were primed with values of freedom of speech, they viewed hate speech as less harmful and the speaker less accountable than did students who were primed with values of equal protection.

The Internet may be particularly attractive to the type of people who are susceptible to hate group doctrines. Some evidence indicates that people who feel lonely or upset might be especially likely to surf the Internet (Sher, 2000). These are precisely the people whom hate groups target in their recruitment efforts (Blazak, 2001; Turpin-Petrosino, 2002).

We found that extremist groups seem to rely heavily on the Internet as a recruiting tool. Attempts are obviously made to appeal to youth, and although specific "kids' pages" are rare, multimedia content is very common, as is merchandise of the type that is likely to attract a younger audience, such as music. For example, on several web sites, one can purchase a video game titled "Ethnic Cleansing." The promotion for this game reads: "The Race War has begun. Your skin is your uniform in this battle for the survival of your kind. The White Race depends on you to secure its existence. Your peoples [sic] enemies surround you in a sea of decay and filth that they have brought to your once clean and White nation. Not one of their numbers shall be spared . . . ." One advertisement for the game (at the National Vanguard web site) declares, "No, you can't shoot those pesky subhumans in real life—but you can in Ethnic Cleansing: The Game! Enter the virtual race war!"

The recruitment possibilities of the Internet are also evident in the relatively large number of sites that include membership forms. Many sites also were willing to mail information packets to interested parties, often for a small fee. Clearly, the Internet offers a convenient way for would-be extremists to get in contact with groups in which they are interested. This is especially true for isolated individuals who have no personal racist contacts to which to turn.

Linking Diverse Groups

A third advantage of the Internet is that it permits small, diverse groups to link to one another. Traditionally, there have been a wide variety of different extremist groups. For example, under the broad umbrella of white supremacism, there are several distinct subgroups. One author (Kleg, 1993) has classified them into five categories: neo-Nazis, skinheads, Klan members, Identity Church members, and members of the Posse Comitatus. To make the list more complete, militias would also have to be added (Cook & Kelly, 1999; Pitcavage, 2001), as would Holocaust revisionists (Levin, 2001). Moreover, each of the subgroups is itself composed of many even smaller groups, and

there are also many groups that don't fit neatly into any of these categories. This situation is the result of historical and geographic differences. It may also be, in part, a response to white supremacists, such as Louis Beam, who have endorsed "leaderless resistance" and "phantom cells" (Levin, 2002; Perry, 2000).

Despite the disjointed nature of extremist groups, the true distinctions between them are minor. Many of them share leadership as well as membership (see, e.g., Ridgeway, 1995), and most of them espouse more or less the same views (Leets, 2001). Numerous authors have noted that the distinctions between the groups are blurry at best (see, e.g., Blazak, 2001; Burris, Smith, & Strahm, 2000; Perry, 2000).

The Internet allows these groups to link to one another, both electronically and logistically. Even geographically isolated groups with only a few members can become part of a collective. Not only does this facilitate the sharing of information and other resources, but it also helps forge a stronger sense of community and purpose. It can, as Perry (2000) argues, create a collective identity. It can help convince even the most ardent extremist that he is not alone, that his views are not, in fact, extreme at all.

Our content analysis suggested that extremists appear to be using the Internet to create a collective identity. Most of the sites link to other sites, and many of them link to groups that are a different type. Indeed, as already mentioned, groups that link to one another can be very different, such as the Aryan Nations (which is affiliated with the Christian Identity movement) and the Hamas. In addition to mutual links, the sites often contained the same borrowed rhetoric, in the form of images (e.g., anti-Semitic cartoons), texts (e.g., *The Protocols of the Elders of Zion*), and so on. Regardless of the sites' nominal affiliations, they frequently espoused the same views: anti-Jewish, anti-immigrant, anti-minority, anti-liberal, and often anti-gay, anti-abortion, anti-feminist, and anti-Communist. Whatever their surface differences, these groups can present a united front with their similar messages. This makes them appear more powerful and less extreme.

Moreover, because of the nature of the Internet, the actual author or sponsor of a site does not always need to be obvious. Therefore, a single individual can claim to be representing a large group, and very few visitors to the page will be the wiser. A webmaster can also bolster the apparent popularity of a site by including a hit counter, which keeps track of the number of visitors to a web page (42 of the sites, or 27%, had hit counters), and perhaps even by artificially inflating the hit count. The Fathers' Manifesto site (http://christianparty.net), for example, a rather obscure site, claims to have had over 12 million hits. CODOH (http://www.codoh.com), a Holocaust denial site, claims over 22 million hits.

Image Control

A final value of the Internet to extremist groups is that it allows them careful control over their own image. In recent years, many extremist groups have shed their white sheets and swastikas in favor of a cloak of respectability (Blazak, 2001; Perry, 2000). The Internet may help them achieve this transformation: slick, professional-looking site design and carefully chosen words can make a web site appear credible and respectable.

Many extremist web sites appear, at first glance, anyway, to reflect fairly mainstream views. The pages frequently contain assertions that the group or web site is nonviolent and not hate-oriented. For example, Bradley R. Smith's Holocaust denial site (http://www.codoh.com) claims that it is meant to "encourage intellectual freedom with respect to the holocaust controversy." The web site called "I Love White Folks" (http://www.ilovewhitefolks.com) includes several assertions that it is not a hate site, but rather a white solidarity site. The Council of Conservative Citizens (http://www.cofcc.org) declares itself the "True Voice of the American Right." One Klan site (http://www.kkkk.net) announces: "The Imperial Klans of America Knights of the Ku Klux Klan are a legal and law abiding organization that will *NOT* tolerate illegal acts of any sort." The web site of the National Association for the Advancement of White People (a group which was founded by David Duke; http://www.naawp.org) states: "The NAAWP is a not for profit, nonviolent, civil rights educational organization, demanding

equal rights for whites and special privileges for none." And the European-American Unity and Rights Organization's site (http://www.white-civilrights.org)—another site affiliated with David Duke—contains this statement: "Do [we] believe in equality? No. We believe that no two individuals or races are exactly equal in their inborn talents and potentialities, but we believe that the best way to determine and reward talent is through equal opportunity and equal rights."

Among the sites included in this analysis, there was infrequent overt support of violence (even by violent groups),[6] and fairly frequent claims that groups were unbiased, not racist, and not hate groups. Indeed, a great many sites were lacking in overt bigotry at all, especially on the home page, although this factor proved difficult to measure objectively.

Usually, the true nature of a site was evident after some exploration of the pages it contained, or of the other groups to which it linked. For example, at the M. L. King site, if one clicks on "Suggested Books," one is taken to a page that includes David Duke's *My Awakening,* and "Historical Writings" links to a page on King's purported plagiarism. Young or inexperienced visitors, however, might not recognize the underlying intent or message of these sites. In one study, most participants did not rate the N.A.A.W.P.'s page as being a hate site (Leets, 2001). One of the authors of the present article taught a freshman honors course in which almost none of the students realized that the King site was written by a white supremacist, even though they were encouraged to critically evaluate its content.

Suggestions for Further Research

These data support the assertions made by several commentators and theorists about extremist groups. They also support the conclusions reached in the few previous content analyses that have been conducted. Further research should be done, however, to answer a number of remaining important questions. For example, precisely what are the messages that are being promoted on these sites? How persuasive are these messages to various potential audiences?

Do the sites, in fact, "convert" new extremists, or do they simply inform and unify existing ones? Who visits these sites and why? Many sites claimed to be unbiased yet also contained latent racist or violent messages. Does this mislead visitors (especially younger ones) and increase the attractiveness of the groups?

The international content of the sites also deserves more attention, both because it confirms the fears of some watchdog organizations that U.S. groups are strengthening their international (especially European) ties, and also because it raises interesting and difficult legal questions. How strong and how deep are these ties? What proportion of extremist web sites' audience is, in fact, international and why? Are people using the Internet to avoid their own countries' restrictions on extremist material? If so, does this partially account for the recent resurgence in the popularity of nationalism in several European countries?

Another issue that was suggested by the data in this study but we did not explore in depth, is the degree to which extremist rhetoric and activities are influenced by particular events. For example, many of the web sites contained references to September 11, often in support of anti-Jewish views. David Duke's home page (http://www.davidduke.org), for instance, has a pop-up window linking to an article on "How Israeli Terrorism and American Treason Caused the September 11 Attacks." Some sites claimed that the attacks were part of a Jewish and/or Israeli conspiracy and that Jews had been forewarned of the impending destruction of the World Trade Center. Other sites had petitions that visitors could sign protesting the American bombing of Afghanistan. Another example of an event that was commented on by many extremist sites was the death on July 23, 2002, of William Pierce, leader of the National Alliance and author of *The Turner Diaries*. Fond memorials to Pierce appeared almost immediately, even on sites with which he was not directly affiliated, such as the Aryan Nations.

Do events like this actually change the message the sites convey or merely serve as a new vehicle for expressing old biases? How accurate is the "news" contained in these sites? Over a year after the actual event, Duke's (undated)

article claimed almost 5000 dead on September 11, one of whom was Israeli. What sorts of events are likely to affect extremist sites? To what extent do these events serve as catalysts for extremist activities and for new membership recruitment?

Finally, this study provides support for the claims that the distinctions between most supremacist groups are tenuous and blurry. While the groups might once have had more separate existences, the Internet allows them to share materials and members with little regard for geographic, linguistic, or other barriers. Furthermore, traditional categories of extremist groups may not be inclusive enough: Nearly 40% of the sites in this study fell in the categories of "White Nationalist" or "Other," neither of which is a traditional category.

On the other hand, this study did find some differences between the groups in web site content, such as use of multimedia and languages other than English. To what extent has the Internet altered the nature of and relationships between extremist groups? What real differences do remain in their membership, their message, or their methods?

As this study demonstrates, the Internet remains a powerful tool for extremists. Without a deeper understanding of the role that the Internet plays for extremists, researchers cannot achieve a true comprehension of the extremists themselves. Moreover, because the Internet itself is changing quickly, it is imperative that the research attempt to keep up with these changes.

Notes

1. As of this writing, Hate Watch itself no longer exists.

2. A complete list of cites is available by contacting the first author at phyllisg@toto.csustan.edu

3. Sites classified as "none" were those in which no extremist content could be found by either rater.

4. It should be noted here that all rated sites, including those based in countries other than the U.S., contained substantial content in English.

5. Even the URL at which one can find this essay is revealing: www.martinlutherking.org/the-beast.html

6. It is unclear whether violence disclaimers are intended to improve the groups' image, to avoid legal liability, or both.

REFERENCES

Aho, J. A. (1988). Out of hate: A sociology of defection from neo-Nazism. *Current Research on Peace and Violence, 11,* 159–168.

Anti-Defamation League (2001). Bigots who rock: An ADL list of hate music groups. Retrieved November 7, 2001, from http://www.adl.org/extremism/bands/default.asp

Anti-Defamation League (2000). Combating extremism in cyberspace: The legal issues affecting Internet hate speech. Retrieved November 26, 2001, from http://www.adl.org/Civil_Rights/newcyber.pdf

Blazak, R. (2001). White boys to terrorist men: Target recruitment of Nazi Skinheads. *American Behavioral Scientist, 44,* 982–1000.

Burris, V., Smith, E., & Strahm, A. (2000). White supremacist network on the Internet. *Sociological Focus, 33,* 215–234.

Cook, W. Jr., & Kelly, R. J. (1999). The dispossessed: Domestic terror and political extremism in the American heartland. *International Journal of Comparative & Applied Criminal Justice, 23,* 246–256.

Cowan, G., Resendez, M., Marshall, E., & Quist, R. (2002). Hate speech and constitutional protection: Priming values of equality and freedom. *Journal of Social Issues, 58,* 247–263.

Franklin, R. A. (2001, November 15). The hate directory. Retrieved November 18, 2001, from http://www.bepl.net/~rfrankli/hatedir.htm

Glaser, J., Dixit, J., & Green, D. P. (2002). Studying hate crimes with the Internet: What makes racists advocate racial violence? *Journal of Social Issues, 58,* 177–193.

Hamm, M. (1993). *American Skinheads: The criminology and control of hate crime.* Westport, CT: Praeger.

Katz, R., & Devon, J. (2002, Aug. 11). American servers of terror. *San Francisco Chronicle,* available online at http://sfgate.com/cgibin/article.cgi?file=/chronicle/archive/2002/08/11/IN80216.DTL.

Kleg, M. (1993). *Hate prejudice and racism.* Albany: SUNY Press.

Konkel, M. (2000). Internet indecency, international censorship, and service providers' liability. *New York Law Journal of International and Comparative Law, 19,* 453–478.

Leets, L. (2001). Responses to Internet hate sites: Is speech too free in cyberspace? *Communication Law and Policy, 6,* 287–317.

Levin, B. (2002). Cyberhate: A legal and historical analysis of extremists' use of computer networks in America. *American Behavioral Scientist, 45,* 958–988.

Levin, B. (2001). History as a weapon: How extremists deny the Holocaust in North America. *American Behavioral Scientist, 44,* 1001–1031.

McCurrie, T. F. (1998). White supremacist gang members: A behavioral profile. *Journal of Gang Research, 5*(2), 51–60.

McDonald, M. (1999). CyberHate: Extending persuasive techniques of low credibility sources to the world wide web. In Schumann, D. W., & Thorson, E. (Eds.), *Advertising and the world wide web,* pp. 149–157. Mahwah, NJ: Lawrence Erlbaum Associates.

Perry, B. (2000). "Buttondown terror": The metamorphosis of the hate movement. *Sociological Focus, 33,* 113–131.

Pew Research Center (2001). The Internet has a pivotal role in the lives of American teenagers. Retrieved November 21, 2001 from http://www.pewInternet.org/reports/reports.asp?Report=36&Section=ReportLevel1&Field=Level1ID&ID=143

Pitcavage, M. (2001). Camouflage and conspiracy: The militia movement from Ruby Ridge to Y2K. *American Behavioral Scientist, 44,* 957–981.

Ridgeway, J. (1995). *Blood in the face* (2d ed.). New York: Thunders Mouth Press.

Schafer, J. A. (2002). Spinning the web of hate: Web-based hate propagation by extremist organizations. *Journal of Criminal Justice and Popular Culture, 9*(2), 69–88.

Sher, L. (2000). The Internet, suicide, and human mental functions. *Canadian Journal of Psychiatry, 45,* 297.

Siegel, M. L. (1999). Hate speech, civil rights, and the Internet: The jurisdictional and human rights nightmare. *Albany Law Journal of Science and Technology, 9,* 375–398.

Simon Wiesenthal Center (2000). *Digital Hate 2001.* [CD] Los Angeles: Author.

Southern Poverty Law Center (2001). The ties that bind. *The Intelligence Report.* Retrieved November 27, 2001, from http://www.splcenter.org/intelligence project/ip4s1.html

Tsesis, A. (2001). Hate in cyberspace: Regulating hate speech on the Internet. *San Diego Law Review, 38,* 817–874.

Turpin-Petrosino, C. (2002). Hateful sirens . . .who hears their song?: An Examination of student attitudes toward hate groups and affiliation potential. *Journal of Social Issues, 58*, 281–301.

Whine, M. (1997). The far right on the Internet. In B. D. Loader (Ed.), *The governance of cyberspace: Politics, technology, and global restructuring*, pp. 209–227. London: Routledge.

QUESTIONS

1. How do extremist Web sites package their messages so that they appear more credible and mainstream? Would most people see through such attempts to mask hatred and bigotry, or not?

2. What are some of the reasons cyberspace is appealing to extremists as a medium of communication?

3. Why are United States-based Web sites apparently used by extremists from around the globe? What role does the First Amendment play in making American cyberspace particularly attractive to people seeking privacy?

4. Are extremist Web sites appealing primarily to people who are already comfortable with extremist views, or might such sites be successful at attracting new adherents to their views?

5. Do you believe that some unsuspecting viewers might fail to recognize the messages from extremist sites for what they are? If so, what could be done to help Web surfers develop their ability to critically evaluate the information presented on such sites?

6. What type of content did the sample of extremist sites discussed in the article contain? For instance, what are some examples of the multimedia content found?

7. Overall, what proportion of the Web sites examined contained racist symbols? What proportion advocated violence?

8. Describe some examples of Web sites which claimed not to be bigoted yet clearly presented bigoted views nonetheless. Do you think that most viewers of such sites would notice this contradiction or not?

9. Describe the three most surprising things you learned from this article about extremists in cyberspace.

10. Do you believe that cyberspace is an effective tool for extremist groups attempting to attract young people?

11. How can extremist groups use cyberspace to help create a collective identity? Support your answer with examples.

12. What key questions for future research do you consider most important? What other questions would you add to the list?

13

HATE CRIME AND EVERYDAY DISCRIMINATION

Influences of and on the Social Context

Lu-Win Wang

It might be comforting to explain hate crimes as the products of a relatively small number of severely disturbed individuals. Yet as this article demonstrates, resorting to dispositional explanations for hate crimes and discrimination leads to distorted conceptions of these crimes that fail to take into account the situational and societal context in which they occur. Failing to recognize the societal context that permits or even encourages discrimination and hate crimes results in a failure to effectively understand the causes of such crimes and their consequences for targeted individuals and groups. In fact, hate crimes and discrimination do not represent aberrations from societal norms so much as conformity to them; the social context is the key to understanding hate crimes and working to prevent them.

I. INTRODUCTION

I would like to discuss aspects of hate crime that make it somewhat unexceptional. By making these points, I do not in any way mean to imply that hate crime is not a problem worthy of attention in the law. To the contrary, I believe that to point out the unexceptional aspects of hate crimes is to highlight just how important a problem hate crime is, and may help us to develop more effective ways of addressing it. My points are based largely on lessons drawn from social science and historical research on the effects of and motivations behind bias-related violence. Specifically, that literature shows that the way we have tended to think about hate crime—as an extreme, deviant, and isolated phenomenon—greatly oversimplifies

EDITORS' NOTE: Wang, L.-W. (2002). Hate Crime and Everyday Discrimination: Influences of and on the Social Context. *Rutgers Race and Law Review, 4,* 1-31. Used with permission.

the problem. The social science and historical research shows instead that hate crimes are connected to the mainstream social context, for they are strongly influenced by the social environment and in turn exert an influence on that environment.

I also draw on points made by other legal scholars with regard to what might be considered more mundane or "everyday" forms of discrimination, such as racial profiling (particularly "Driving While Black"), consumer discrimination, and street harassment of women. Each of these areas is a context in which, as with hate crimes, the law has tended to exceptionalize the motivations and conduct of perpetrators. It thereby overlooks the extent to which those acts are influenced by the mainstream social context and, in turn, reinforce mainstream society's message that certain social groups have been designated as suitable or appropriate targets for ill treatment.

This chapter identifies and describes the reciprocal influences between the mainstream social environment and the perpetration of both extreme and everyday discrimination, as well as the reciprocal influences among various types of discrimination. The law seldom does but ought to take into account these relationships because, as this chapter also discusses, to exceptionalize discrimination has the ironic effect of "normalizing" or rendering acceptable a range of discriminatory practices that continue to reinforce widespread beliefs, assumptions, and expectations concerning the value and place in society of vulnerable groups.

II. DECONTEXTUALIZING DISCRIMINATION: THE CONVENTIONAL VIEW OF HATE CRIMES

For all of the controversy surrounding penalty enhancement statutes and the differential treatment of hate or bias crimes generally,[1] there seems to be widespread agreement on the motivations that drive the bias crime perpetrator or that should be present for an actor to be labeled a "bias criminal." This view is shared by commentators on both sides of the law and policy debate, as well as by professionals within the criminal justice system who decide what acts will be treated as hate crimes and whose decisions influence society's perceptions of hate crime. Yet, though this view is widely accepted as defining and explaining hate crime, it actually distorts understanding of bias crime—and hence, of the issues surrounding the differential legal treatment of it—by oversimplifying the factors that drive the perpetrator and by considering him in isolation from the social context. In particular, the conventional view overemphasizes the perpetrator's deviance or "bad character" and fails to recognize the importance of the social context in promoting the commission of bias crimes. It fails, in other words, to take account of both the ways in which the cultural ideology inspires and rewards bias crime perpetrators and the ways in which the crimes themselves perpetuate the context in which perpetrators can anticipate receiving those rewards.

The common understanding of the "true" hate crime perpetrator may be attributable to several factors. First, as has been important in other contexts, naming the problem as "hate" crime both raised public awareness of and drew the attention of the federal and state governments to the phenomenon of bias-motivated violence. At the same time, however, the label "hate crime" has contributed to the distortion and oversimplification of the problem that it seeks to describe. Second, the conventional understanding of hate crime seems to be based, in part, on the empirical attributes of the "prototypical" or "paradigmatic" bias crime. The prototypical case is a stranger-on-stranger crime, usually involving multiple perpetrators who target an individual victim who represents a hated social group, inflict on that person extreme, gratuitous violence, and appear to have no goal other than to terrorize, injure, or kill. This popular image is reinforced by the great publicity given to the most extreme and brutal cases, such as the 1998 murders of Matthew Shepard and James Byrd Jr. However, a prototypical example can provide a misleading basis for assessing an entire category, for prototypes often are drawn based upon the most "ideal" or "extreme" features of a category member, yet often do not represent the statistical norm. Further, the conventional understanding of the motivations behind bias crime in particular is skewed in a way that is typical of how we tend to explain group-based discrimination—and, indeed, much of human behavior—in general. That is, it reflects the "most commonly documented bias in social perception": the tendency to attribute another person's behavior to his or her enduring dispositional qualities (such as prejudices or personality traits) and to overlook the influence of situational factors (such as situational constraints or social norms). This "fundamental attribution error" or "correspondence bias" causes us to see a person's behavior as being determined by his or her character, beliefs, or feelings even when that behavior also or primarily is the result of constraints or expectations introduced by the social context. This chapter will show how this bias distorts our understanding of the motivations for committing and the effects of hate crime. It will then elaborate on the reciprocal situational influences that the law ought to take into account.

The common understanding of bias crime incorporates three interrelated assumptions concerning the motivations of the "true" bias crime perpetrator: that his bias is based in his personal hostility toward or "distaste" for the target group; that his bias is deviant, irrational, and not shared by mainstream society; and that his exclusive purpose is to harm a member of the hated target group, rather than being more self-serving—for example, to obtain personal gain.

The first assumption locates the source of the perpetrator's bias within the perpetrator himself. The "true" bias crime perpetrator is assumed to act not, in response to situational factors or the prejudices of others, but out of his own pre-existing beliefs, predisposition, or attitude toward the target group. He does not just discriminate in selecting his victim, but instead seeks to further his strong feelings of hatred or hostility toward the target group.

The second assumption is that the perpetrator's hostile views are not shared by members of mainstream society. Perpetrators are often marginalized and viewed as "deviant or freakish," and have been described as a "bewildering menace" and as "'predators' with a 'pack mentality' who 'feed off each others' hatred and lunacy.'" Perpetrators are viewed as being controlled,

"'driven' or 'blinded' by their hatred toward the target group." Accordingly, this assumption discounts the possibility that a perpetrator might choose his victim from a particular social group upon cool-headed reflection or calculation—for example, because he considers members of that group to be "easier" or "more financially rewarding" targets.

The third assumption brings together the first two and has the greatest practical effect on how "hate" crimes are defined and handled within the legal system. This assumption holds that the perpetrator's hostility toward the target group is so powerful and irrational that it overwhelms all other possible reasons for committing a crime. The perpetrator's hatred is assumed to be unable to coexist, for example, with more self-interested motivations such as the desire for material gain or other personal benefits. Thus, although most bias crime statutes require that the defendant's bias be a "substantial" or "significant" motivation—and therefore allow for mixed motive bias crimes—a "true" bias crime is assumed to occur only when the perpetrator's hatred for the target group serves as his exclusive motivation.

Together, these assumptions influence thinking about all of the "big" issues concerning bias crime. They guide the decisions of law enforcement professionals who must determine which cases qualify for treatment as "hate" crime cases and how to handle those cases that do. One major consequence of the three assumptions is that such professionals tend to apply a very narrow definition of bias crime. They tend to pursue only cases that fit the prototype, overlooking cases that are not sensational, do not involve extreme brutality, or do involve mixed motives such as bias coupled with a desire for pecuniary gain. These law enforcement decisions in turn have the cumulative effect of defining bias crime in the public's mind and thereby of shaping society's perceptions of the nature of the problem itself, as being both easily recognizable and rare. The assumptions also strongly influence the identification of the law and policy issues the problem raises, as well as the terms in which those issues should be debated, for the common understanding of the forces that propel bias crimes determines the assessment of whether the law can or should address bias crime as a special problem and what, if anything, law and policy can do to address that problem. Obviously, supporters of the laws maintain that the law does have a role to play in regulating bias crimes, but they tend to view the problem as one that is narrow in scope, with contours that follow the three assumptions.

Critics, on the other hand, cite the three assumptions to support the following arguments: that hate crimes legislation is unconstitutional because it punishes thoughts or beliefs, in violation of the First Amendment; that the laws will be ineffective in addressing hate crime because criminals cannot be forced to treat all social groups equally; and that the laws will even exacerbate intergroup tensions because they highlight divisions among various social groups. The following section questions the crucial assumptions underlying these arguments.

III. "Suitable Victims" and Feedback Loops: Reciprocal Influences Between Hate Crime and the Social Context

What the three assumptions and hence the conventional understanding of hate crime fail to take into account is that hate crimes are not just deviant and isolated acts committed by individuals at the fringe of society. Instead, hate crimes often are committed by individuals who seek to conform to social norms and whose acts reflect mainstream views of the targeted group. Two themes describe the reciprocal influences between both social context and hate crimes and elucidate how these reciprocal influences are connected to more mundane forms of discrimination. The first theme explains the influence of the social context on the perpetration of hate crimes by illuminating the ways in which the social environment marks members of certain groups as "suitable victims," thereby enabling perpetrators to use violence against them as a means to a variety of goals. The second theme points out the social and cultural "feedback loop" by which the perpetration of hate crimes itself exerts influence on the social context that marks particular groups as "suitable victims."

A. "Suitable Victims": Influence of the Social Context

To assume that hate crimes are perpetrated only by those who are deviant, isolated from mainstream society, and driven by strongly felt prejudice against a particular group is to overlook a large body of evidence to the contrary. Social scientists and historians have demonstrated that hate crimes often are committed by individuals who seek to conform to social norms, to obtain personal gain, or both, and who, furthermore, often deny feelings of personal prejudice against the groups that they target. Even in the context of two "prototypical" hate crimes—anti-gay violence and lynching—these researchers have explained that a perpetrator need not personally "hate" a particular group in order to find reasons to target members of that group for violence. In our society, other motivations can be sufficient because bias-motivated violence can fulfill a wide range of functions for perpetrators. As social psychologist Gregory M. Herek has observed about anti-gay violence in particular, "the primary cause . . . is not always the attacker's own personal prejudice against lesbians and gay men."[2] Instead, researchers have found that committing anti-gay violence can serve a variety of functions for perpetrators, and often brings them psychological, social and material rewards. They are able to reap these rewards because the cultural and social environment has identified gay men as suitable vehicles for achieving these goals.

Some perpetrators—particularly young males who commit anti-gay violence in groups—view gay bashing as a "kind of sport."[3] Their participation feels risky and exciting, draws them closer to other members of their group, and enhances their self-esteem by bringing the group recognition and respect from peers. These perpetrators may give little thought to the effects of their acts on the victim, and often disclaim any feelings of hostility or disapproval toward gays.[4] Instead, they see the gay victim as "fundamentally a dramatic prop," to be used in an almost "recreational" fashion. These young men do not seriously consider the harm they cause, for they regard gay bashing as socially acceptable and gay men as "suitable targets" for their violence. The idea that anti-gay violence is socially acceptable is confirmed when perpetrators receive light sanctions or escape punishment altogether. Perpetrators know that many in our society—including authority figures such as parents, law enforcement officers, political and religious leaders—see anti-gay violence as a "rite of passage" for young men, view gays as deserving of such treatment, and will not treat the violence seriously. School officials, for example, often dismiss their antics as "boys being boys" and decline to discipline them. This attitude is also exhibited by judges who impose light sentences, for anti-gay violence and even murder, sometimes insinuating that the gay victims invited the attack through their own inappropriate behavior.

In addition to "recreational" gay bashing, gay men are especially vulnerable to property crimes such as the "shakedown," blackmail, and robbery. These are all crimes in which the perpetrator extorts money or property from a gay man using the threats of both violence and disclosure of the victim's sexual orientation or sexual practices. Perpetrators of such crimes may desire material or economic rewards instead of or in addition to social rewards, but they also are able to use society's general disregard for gay men to their advantage and in a way that is even more openly calculating. These perpetrators predict that gay men are likely to be fearful of how family members, business associates, and even law enforcement officers would react to news of their sexual orientation and will prefer to hand over their money or property rather than fight back or report the crime and risk revealing that information. Perpetrators also count on the likelihood that police, judges, juries, and others will not take seriously offenses against gays.

Even racial violence during this country's lynching era—1880 to 1930—could rationally have been practiced by individuals who did not personally harbor racial animus, despite its horrendous brutality and the apparent hysteria that it aroused among participants and observers. Certainly the racist ideology that prevailed in the South throughout the lynching era was a key

factor in the frequency of racial violence during that period. However:

> Lynching cannot be explained simply as the result of perpetrators' contempt or distaste for or desire to harm members of another race. Contemporary scholars generally agree that lynching was a response to white southerners' perception that freed blacks posed a threat to white dominance in social, political, and economic arenas.

In particular, an important body of recent historical sociological scholarship indicates that White southerners' desire to maintain their economic and social dominance over Blacks played a major role in driving the violence. Stewart E. Tolnay and E.M. Beck conducted sophisticated, quantitative studies of the historical data on lynching. Their studies support the view that White perpetrators used racial violence primarily as a means of obtaining economic benefits in the form of control over land and labor, the two key resources in that region at that time. Their studies also indicate that, not only were perpetrators often primarily focused on the benefits to themselves that they perceived might derive from racial violence, but they also controlled the level and timing of the violence as it suited their interests, escalating the violence at times when and in places where it would help them to control land and labor, and moderating or even abandoning the violence when and where it was either not necessary or even harmful to White interests. Lynching also helped to maintain solidarity between Whites of different economic classes, a function that appears to have been encouraged by White, landowning employers as a means of maintaining their interests by discouraging interracial solidarity among workers, which might have promoted labor unrest.

The widespread practice and utility of racial violence certainly depended upon a racially hostile climate. However, an important point that emerges from these studies is that, in such an environment, an individual perpetrator did not need to harbor racial animus in order to have reason to lynch. As Tolnay and Beck have explained, "given the Deep South's racial caste structure, whites could harass and assault blacks with virtual impunity. Blacks were considered legitimate, and even deserving, objects for white wrath." That is, one could both benefit from targeting members of that group for violence and get away with it.

The work of social scientists who have studied anti-gay violence and lynching demonstrates the flaws in the conventional understanding of hate crimes. Rather than being driven by personal hostility toward the targeted group, many perpetrators engage in selective victimization in order to obtain a range of benefits for themselves by exploiting the group's social vulnerability. In such cases the selective targeting of vulnerable social groups seems sensible or even rational, because the social environment supports, encourages, and even rewards such targeting.

B. The Feedback Loop: Influence on the Social Context

Although hate crimes can be understood as being responsive to the pre-existing social environment, the influence of the social environment provides neither an excuse nor a justification for the discriminatory practice. Moreover, to fully understand the way in which hate crimes fit into the social context, it is important to recognize their role in contributing to and reinforcing that environment. Social scientists and legal scholars have explained that hate crimes have effects that are both different from and more harmful than those of their non-discriminatory counterparts. The individual victim may experience greater emotional and psychological harm and adopt more extreme defensive behavioral strategies to avoid similar encounters in the future. However, it is the effects that extend beyond the individual victim that most clearly distinguish hate crime from non-bias-motivated crime. In particular, the ways in which hate crime influences the perceptions of observers—both those who identify with the victim and those who are able to distinguish themselves from the victim—serve to reinforce the social context in which racial and other group-based targeting occur, by influencing expectations about how certain groups will be treated.

Members of the victim's social group who have not been targeted for hate crime will nevertheless understand themselves to be vulnerable to such violence due to their shared group status. They, too, may feel isolated or fearful and adopt defensive behavioral strategies in order to avoid becoming targets themselves. These avoidance strategies may require them to suffer substantial burdens and inconveniences, as well as to forgo significant benefits and opportunities. For example, they may avoid going to places where they might "stick out" or decline to engage in activities that might draw attention to them. Some writers have described how their fear of hate crime has influenced their decisions about such seemingly mundane matters as what neighborhoods to drive or run through, what events to attend, and even what vacation spots to patronize.[5] For some target group members, another way to avoid inviting attack may be to engage in behavior that is stereotypically "expected" of one's social group so as to avoid attracting unwanted attention.

Hate crimes also contribute to the general perception that some groups are expected targets for violence. Social psychologists have explained that bias-motivated violence creates the conditions for prejudice and discrimination because it defines the "safe" or expected targets for all manners of ill treatment. Even if non-target group observers condemn the acts and would never engage in such conduct themselves, they may derive some comfort from their ability to differentiate themselves from the victim and target group and thereby to feel comparatively less vulnerable and more in control of their circumstances. Further, even if observers do not believe that the victim's social group status justified the attack, they will recognize that the status prompted the attack, and may attribute responsibility to the victim for having invited the crime by making that status visible. The gay bias crime victim may be blamed for making his sexual orientation "obvious" by wearing certain clothes or behaving in a certain way. Similarly, the African American victim of a racially motivated assault may be blamed for having appeared on the streets of a White neighborhood. Observers recognize the "script" or pattern of bias-motivated violence and understand that members of vulnerable groups are "persons whom the dominant culture considers acceptable to derogate."

IV. RECIPROCAL INFLUENCES BETWEEN HATE CRIME AND "EVERYDAY" DISCRIMINATION

These themes—of particular groups being marked as expected or appropriate recipients of ill treatment and of the cultural and social feedback loop that reinforces the designation and perpetuates such treatment—have implications beyond the debate over the constitutionality, desirability, and proper application of hate crimes legislation. First, a feedback loop runs between hate crimes and everyday discrimination. As described above, hate crimes contribute to an environment that promotes other, often less noticeable, forms of inferior treatment of certain groups. Conversely, those more commonplace experiences also contribute to hate crimes, for it is not just violent crime against certain groups that marks them as suitable victims. As this section elaborates, the less dramatic and less noticed ways in which groups are treated on a daily basis also promote the perception that mistreatment of certain groups is acceptable and contributes to the view that they are suitable targets for violence. For example, African Americans were viewed as suitable targets for racial violence during the lynching era in part because of the bad treatment that they routinely suffered in employment and other everyday settings.

Second, there are striking parallels between hate crime and everyday discrimination, both in the conventional assumptions about the motivations behind them and in reciprocal influences that are evident between the social context and various forms of discrimination. As with hate crimes, everyday discrimination cannot be attributed entirely to deliberate discrimination or group-based animus, but is the result of dynamics that parallel those I have discussed in the hate crimes context.

The same sort of extreme and simplistic assumptions that are evident in discussions of hate crime also strongly influence the way the law addresses discriminatory treatment that is less violent, more subtle, and more commonplace. As several legal scholars have demonstrated in contexts ranging from government action to employment decisions to police practices to the treatment of customers in retail settings—in other words, sites of "everyday" discrimination—the law tends to understand "true" or actionable discrimination as being deliberate, conscious, and motivated by ill will or animus.[6] The "fundamental attribution error" applies here, as well. As with hate crimes, the actor who discriminates is examined in isolation from the context surrounding the questioned decision or action and is viewed as deviant or malicious. The consequences of applying these assumptions are also similar in that they lead the law to miss many cases of discrimination, to overlook the social, behavioral, and cognitive dynamics that contribute to discrimination, and to actually further discrimination by perpetuating biased perceptions of what constitutes "appropriate" treatment of different social groups and biased explanations for why certain groups are treated differently.

A. "Driving While Black"[7]

Recently, the federal and state governments, as well as the general public, have become more aware of, and concerned about, a problem that is faced routinely by people of color in the United States, particularly African American males.[8] This problem, "driving while Black," is a form of racial profiling in which "police officers stop[ ], question[ ], and even search[ ] black drivers who have committed no crime, based on the excuse of a traffic offense." Like hate crimes, the practice of racial profiling strongly reflects the influence of a social environment in which members of certain racial and ethnic groups are viewed as suitable targets for abusive treatment. More specifically, it reflects the "myth of criminal propensity" that stereotypes members of certain racial groups as being prone to deviant or criminal behavior.

The influence of these stereotypes is evident in the commonly expressed view that selective detention or investigation of minority groups in routine cases is simply good police practice. As Professor David A. Harris has explained, "the most common justification offered for the disproportionate numbers of traffic stops of African Americans" is that "Blacks commit a disproportionate share of certain crimes," so "it only makes sense for police to focus their efforts on African Americans." Professor Harris and other legal "scholars have pointed out the faulty reasoning underlying this argument," the wide acceptance of which only emphasizes its racist bent. Nevertheless, the appearance of rationality in discriminatory police practices is supported by a social environment in which race alone can be used as a "surrogate indicator" or "proxy" for criminality.

As Professor Dorothy Roberts has explained, racial profiling reflects cultural stereotypes that divide people into two categories, "law-abiding" and "law-breaking," assumes that police can tell the difference between them on sight, and thereby justifies minimizing the rights of the "visibly lawless."[9] This view is so deeply embedded in our culture that it may not be recognized by the law enforcement officer who engages in racial profiling nor even by those—including courts—who might review her decisions.

Also like hate crimes, racial profiling results in "multi-layered effects" on targets, members of the suspect group, and society at large that perpetuate the conduct and beliefs that promote the discriminatory practice. First, for the individual target the experience can be extremely frightening and embarrassing and result in defensive behavioral strategies similar to those seen in victims of hate crime. Some drivers who are stopped suffer depression, try to hide their experience from others, and withdraw from their normal activities. The Black motorist's sense of fear is heightened by the awareness that such encounters can turn, and often have turned, deadly. Moreover, the frequency with which many Blacks are stopped for traffic violations leads many to feel angry, powerless, and distrustful of the police.

Members of the "target" group for racial profiling respond similarly to those who feel vulnerable to hate crimes. That is, they adopt defensive behavioral strategies, adjusting numerous aspects of their daily lives in order to minimize their chances of being noticed and stopped, or to decrease the likelihood that they will be treated abusively if they are stopped:

> These adjustments may include driving cars that are bland and not "flashy," dressing in drab clothing or avoiding accessories that might make them noticeable, sitting erect at all times while driving, obtaining "vanity" license plates that advertise their educational degrees or professional status, keeping the radio tuned to a classical music station, and scheduling extra time for car trips to allow for the delay involved in a traffic stop. These lessons are passed from one generation to the next when young Black males receive "The Lesson": instructions from their elders on "how to behave when—not if—they are stopped by police."

Another common avoidance tactic is to stay out of areas where Black people would "stand out"—a strategy that further distorts the social world by carving out entire areas where Blacks are perceived as "not belonging."

The distorting effect of racial profiling extends beyond its influence on the behavior of the target group, for the practice also affects societal perceptions of the target group and expectations for how they will (and should) be treated. First, and especially when it faces no legal sanction, racial profiling furthers the myth that certain groups are prone to criminality by allowing police to use skin color as a proxy for criminal propensity. The message that Blackness is equivalent to criminality is transmitted to the general public as the public becomes accustomed to seeing disproportionate numbers of Black motorists being detained by police. This image makes even those who are not consciously racist more likely to see the behavior of a Black person as suspicious, especially when that Black person appears in a neighborhood where he or she is viewed as "not belonging." These stereotypes are then "confirmed" through a process of "self-fulfilling prophecy," as police officers look for—and find—criminal conduct disproportionately among Black drivers, on whom they have focused their attention and resources.

Furthermore, racial profiling operates similarly to hate crimes in the way it promotes discrimination by contributing to the devaluation of members of vulnerable groups. As Professor

Roberts has explained, racial profiling contributes to an environment in which both the infringement of constitutional rights and the imposition of physical suffering on members of certain groups become minimized and expected. First, discriminatory targeting by law enforcement officers reinforces the perception that some groups are "second-class citizens" for whom police surveillance and even arrest are "perfectly natural." In turn, this belief promotes the view that those groups are entitled to fewer liberties and that their rights are "mere 'amenities' that may be sacrificed to protect law-abiding people." Acceptance of this view results in an environment in which a pattern of discriminatory targeting seems benign, for, "when social understandings are so uncontested that they become invisible, the social meanings that arise from them appear natural."

B. Consumer Discrimination

Another common form of racial profiling is practiced by private entities. "Consumer racism" or "consumer discrimination" is "the practice of differential surveillance and treatment of African American shoppers." African Americans of all social and economic classes encounter this practice on a daily basis, and, as with its law enforcement-perpetrated counterpart, it sometimes results in violence against, and even the deaths of, its targets. Consumer discrimination primarily takes the form of differential security measures against members of minority racial groups, but it also includes the provision of inferior or abusive service and charging Blacks higher prices than Whites for the same and sometimes inferior goods and services.[10]

Consumer discrimination reflects influences of the social environment similar to those that promote discriminatory police practices, for consumer discrimination often rests on the stereotype of Blacks as being prone to deviant or criminal behavior: specifically, shoplifting. Moreover, consumer discrimination also reveals additional dimensions of societal stereotypes and devaluation of African Americans. As Professor Deseriee A. Kennedy has explained, consumer discrimination is based on a historical and cultural heritage that includes "the legal and de facto use of segregation in places of public accommodations and retail stores." Historically, segregation rested on "a complex set of beliefs about race" that Professor Charles R. Lawrence III has described as including the belief that Blacks and other non-whites were inferior to Whites and posed a threat to society, and therefore did not deserve full status and participation in American society. By segregating retail spaces, selling goods and services on inferior terms, or even denying Blacks their purchase, Whites were able to distance themselves from Blacks and maintain their position in the racial hierarchy. Though contemporary forms of consumer racism may be less extreme or well institutionalized, and are nominally unlawful, the boundary-policing practices continue today. As Professor Regina Austin has pointed out, Black consumption (and selling) is still regarded as deviant activity to which White store-owners continue to present obstacles.

The similarity between consumer discrimination and racial profiling extends to the effects of the practices on individual victims and society at large, creating a "feedback loop" that further entrenches the practice. Like discriminatory policing, discriminatory treatment of shoppers results in heavy emotional and psychological burdens on its targets, causing them to feel angry, humiliated, frightened, and powerless. Also like racial profiling, consumer discrimination results in daily inconveniences for and limits the freedom of members of the targeted group, for it leads Blacks to develop burdensome strategies for avoiding or navigating racist encounters. Further, consumer discrimination similarly insinuates itself into our expectations of how Blacks should be treated. As Professor Kennedy has explained, "Everyday racism perpetuates itself—it becomes integrated into everyday situations and becomes 'part of the expected, of the unquestionable, and of what is seen as normal by the dominant group.'"

Again, however, consumer discrimination has additional implications, because it also promotes and perpetuates the idea that Blacks are not full or legitimate participants in the economic (as well as the political and social) life of American society. Consumption is not just utilitarian; as Professor Kennedy points out, it also has symbolic importance in establishing social identity and class alliances. Furthermore, consumer discrimination is but one manifestation of economic discrimination in a society that also practices race-based discrimination in services, lending, advertising, and other commercial activities. These forms of "economic exploitation" of Blacks all have the effect of increasing the costs and narrowing the choices of Blacks who want to participate in what, for Whites, are routine activities to which they need not give a second thought. Consumer discrimination thus is not just a minor inconvenience nor a rare and isolated experience for African Americans, but a historically based and systematic means by which a group is denied access to the benefits available to other members of society, and by which the dominant group comes to accept and expect that state of affairs.

C. Street Harassment of Women

Women comprise another large social group that are denied their full rights and privileges as members of society through a routine, often unnoticed, and frequently accepted form of discrimination: street harassment. As Professor Cynthia Grant Bowman has defined it, street harassment of women is the "harassment of women in public places by men who are strangers to them . . . ." It encompasses a wide range of verbal and nonverbal behavior aimed at an individual woman (though the perpetrator often intends that it be overheard or observed by others) that is "objectively degrading, objectifying, humiliating, and frequently threatening in nature." Like hate crimes, racial profiling, and consumer discrimination, street harassment of women is not solely a contemporary phenomenon. However, it does seem to have increased in frequency and severity since the 1970's and 1980's, probably at least in part due to the changes in women's lives that have increased the occasions on which they appear in public unaccompanied by men or children.

The context in which street harassment tends to occur, as well as perpetrators' motivations for engaging in the practice, exhibit striking similarities to the "recreational" form of anti-gay violence discussed above, and likewise reflect a societal view that the vulnerable group is a suitable or appropriate target for such abuse. That is, for many men the harassment of women is a group activity—one that they would not choose to engage in alone, and one that provides a way to "bond" with other males, by "demonstrating solidarity and mutual power." Men who have harassed women on the street have told interviewers "that harassment alleviated boredom, was 'fun,' and gave them a feeling of camaraderie with other men; many added, defensively, that it didn't hurt anybody. Some said it was intended as a compliment." These accounts demonstrate that the harassment of women in public spaces is regarded by many perpetrators as socially acceptable and harmless, and reflect the view that women who appear in public have made themselves available for abuse by invading men's "turf."

The effects on the individual victim of street harassment are much like the effects of the other forms of discrimination discussed above. That is, victims suffer "feelings of invasion, anger, humiliation, and fear" as well as "emotional distress and feelings of disempowerment." Victims of street harassment also respond similarly to victims of hate crime, racial profiling, and consumer discrimination by avoiding activities or places where they expect to be more vulnerable to harassment. This avoidance strategy imposes great costs on women by severely limiting their physical and geographical mobility "in a way that substantially offsets the gains women have made in other spheres." Moreover, women's fear and feelings of disempowerment in response to street harassment have an added dimension, for their apprehension is connected directly to fear of another, specific form of violence against women: rape. (As Professor Bowman notes, this fear is not unrealistic, for street harassment sometimes is a precursor to rape.) In addition, women's fear and humiliation often are connected with a sense of shame about their bodies, for the harassment "reduces women to sexual objects." Street harassment thus "is a way of ensuring that women will not feel at ease, that they will remember their role as sexual beings available to men and not consider themselves equal citizens participating in public life."

As is true with hate crimes, racial profiling, and consumer discrimination, street harassment does not just impose harms on its targets, but also distorts the social world in a way that reinforces the acceptability of and thereby promotes the public harassment of women. Professor Bowman points out that street harassment distorts relationships between women and men by, on the one hand, increasing women's dependence on men to "protect" them from harassment by other men and, on the other hand, contributing to distrust and hostility between men and women who view even the well-intentioned among them with suspicion and fear. Further, just as hate crimes, racial profiling, and consumer discrimination reinforce the racial hierarchy in American society, so does street harassment of women strengthen the rigid gender hierarchy from which it draws inspiration, by conveying the message that women belong in the private sphere (at home), and not in public. Especially when street harassment is—as it often is—dismissed as trivial, unavoidable, and acceptable, the harassment itself reinforces the expectations and assumptions that promote its continued practice.

V. Conclusion

As Professor Randall Kennedy has observed, "One of the great achievements of social reform in American history has involved the stigmatization of overt racial prejudice." Other forms of prejudice, as well—including sexism, ethnocentrism, and anti-gay prejudice—have in contemporary times been subject to searching examination and strong condemnation. Supporting the social ideal of equality are explicit constitutional and legislative protections against racial and other types of discrimination in a wide range of contexts from government action to private contracting (though, to be sure, these express protections are not equally comprehensive for all social groups that are vulnerable to discrimination). Yet the legal reforms have not been as expansive as the letter of the law might suggest. As Professor Martha Chamallas has noted, "The limits of contemporary anti-discrimination law are exceedingly narrow."

Professor Chamallas explains that the legal protections do mandate formal or facial equality—for example, prohibiting explicit racial classifications in legislation and formal policies by private entities that expressly provide different standards for traditionally disfavored groups—but do not extend to less explicit disparate treatment, including many updated and more subtle forms of discrimination.

As this chapter has pointed out, one cause of this deficiency in coverage is the law's need to find a "villain" before it can acknowledge that discrimination has occurred. The dominant view, in other words, is that "real" discrimination is perpetrated only by individuals who are motivated by hostility and seek to do harm to disfavored groups. However, as this chapter also has shown, this view is not entirely accurate, for even extreme and brutal acts of discrimination sometimes are motivated more by the perpetrator's desire to "fit in" or to obtain personal benefits than they are by his or her desire to do harm to the targeted group. The perpetrator's ability to achieve these goals through discriminatory acts in such situations depends upon the existence of a social environment that has marked members of certain social groups as appropriate or acceptable vehicles for the perpetrator's use. In turn, the continuing and accepted targeting of socially vulnerable groups itself reinforces the "suitable target" designation.

Moreover, to ignore the reciprocal and reinforcing relationships between discriminatory acts and the mainstream social context is to construct many common forms of discrimination (when the discrimination is recognized at all, rather than being rendered invisible as it often is) as being rational and even desirable or as regrettable but inevitable. Even worse, it serves to justify discrimination on "moral" grounds. As Professor Charles R. Lawrence III has explained, "If there is no discrimination, there is no need for a remedy; if blacks are being treated fairly yet remain at the bottom of the socioeconomic ladder, only their own inferiority can explain their subordinate position." In combination, these constructions perpetuate discrimination, for they institute the notion that the differential treatment of certain social groups is appropriate; it becomes, in the words of

Professor Deseriee Kennedy, "justified and normalized."

Notes

1. Public debate has focused on questions concerning the constitutionality, legitimacy, wisdom, and proper application of penalty enhancement statutes. See generally James B. Jacobs & Kimberly Potter, Hate Crimes: Criminal Law and Identity Politics (1998); Frederick M. Lawrence, Punishing Hate: Bias Crimes under American Law (1999); Susan Gellman, Sticks and Stones Can Put You in Jail, But Can Words Increase Your Sentence? Constitutional and Policy Dilemmas of Ethnic Intimidation Laws, 39 UCLA L. Rev. 333 (1991); Lu-Win Wang, The Transforming Power of "Hate": Social Cognition Theory and the Harms of Bias-Related Crime, 71 S. Cal. L. Rev. 47 (1997); Lu-Win Wang, The Complexities of "Hate," 60 Ohio St. L. J. 799 (1999).

2. Gregory M. Herek, Psychological Heterosexism and Anti-Gay Violence: The Social Psychology of Bigotry and Bashing, in Hate Crimes: Confronting Violence Against Lesbians and Gay Men, 163 (Gregory M. Herek and Kevin T. Berrill, eds., 1992).

3. Gary David Comstock, Violence Against Lesbians and Gay Men 76 (1990) (quoting observations of police officers familiar with teenage perpetrators).

4. Karen Franklin, Unassuming Motivations: Contextualizing the Narratives of Antigay Assailants, in Stigma and Sexual Orientation: Understanding Prejudice Against Lesbians, Gay Men, and Bisexuals 1, 20 (Gregory M. Herek, ed., 1998) (reporting that "people who have assaulted homosexuals typically do not recognize themselves in the stereotyped image of the hate-filled extremist").

5. See, e.g., Lena Williams, It's the Little Things: the Everyday Interactions That Get Under the Skin of Blacks and Whites 41–43 (2000); john a. powell, Rights Talk/Free Speech and Equality, Ann. Surv. Am. L. 587, 589–90 (1992/1993).

6. See generally Stephen L. Carter, When Victims Happen to be Black, 97 Yale L.J. 420 (1988); Martha Chamallas, Deepening the Legal Understanding of Bias: On Devaluation and Biased Prototypes, 74 S. Cal. L. Rev. 747 (2001); Randall L. Kennedy, McCleskey v. Kemp: Race, Capital Punishment, and the Supreme Court, 101 Harv. L. Rev. 1388 (1988); Linda Hamilton Krieger, The Content of Our Categories: A Cognitive Bias Approach to Discrimination and Equal Employment Opportunity, 47 Stan. L. Rev. 1161 (1995); Charles R. Lawrence III, The Id, the Ego, and Equal Protection: Reckoning with Unconscious Racism, 39 Stan. L. Rev. 317 (1987); Anthony C. Thompson, Stopping the Usual Suspects: Race and the Fourth Amendment, 74 N.Y.U. L. Rev. 956 (1999).

7. This section draws from points I have made previously, in Lu-Win Wang, "Suitable Targets"? Parallels and Connections Between "Hate" Crimes and "Driving While Black," 6 Mich. J. Race & L. 209 (2001) (hereinafter Wang, "Suitable Targets").

8. See David A. Harris, When Success Breeds Attack: The Coming Backlash Against Racial Profiling Studies, 6 Mich. J. Race & L. 237, 237–43 (2001) (discussing the increasing public awareness and steps that legislatures and law enforcement departments have been taking to address this problem).

9. Dorothy E. Roberts, Foreword: Race, Vagueness, and the Social Meaning of Order-Maintenance Policing, 89 J. Crim. L. & Criminology 775, 805–807 (1999).

10. See Regina Austin, "A Nation of Thieves": Securing Black People's Right to Shop and Sell in White America, Utah L. Rev. 147, 148–50 (1994) (describing discriminatory treatment and economic exploitation of black consumers).

Questions

1. In what ways are hate crimes both a reflection of the social environment and an influence on it?

2. What is the "prototypical" bias crime reflected in the popular image of hate crimes? Is this image representative of most hate crimes or not?

3. What is the "fundamental attribution error," and how can it explain our failure to take into consideration the influence of situational factors on behavior?

4. According to the author, what are the common public assumptions about hate crime perpetrators?

5. Discuss the assertion that hate crimes are not deviant acts but in fact are behaviors that reflect conformity to social norms. Can you think of examples that support this argument?

6. If the perpetrators of hate crimes are not necessarily motivated by hatred of the members

of the targeted group, what other motivations might they have?

7. What are some examples of the ways in which hate crime perpetrators receive legal and social messages condoning their behavior?

8. The conventional public understanding of hate crimes fails to recognize the power dimension to hate violence, such as the use of racial violence to maintain economic and social power. What is a historic example of this?

9. What are some examples of what the authors refer to as "everyday discrimination"? How does everyday discrimination set the stage for hate crimes to occur?

10. In what ways can members of targeted groups adopt defensive behavioral strategies? What are some examples of this?

11. How does racial profiling perpetuate the social devaluation of members of minority groups?

12. Describe how street harassment of women functions as a social marker of gender inequality that perpetuates such inequality.

Part V

ORGANIZED HATE GROUPS

A lthough most hate crimes are committed by individuals rather than by groups, organized hate groups play a central role in extremism. Such groups recruit, organize, and sustain hate violence in society by providing ideologies that bigoted individuals can use as a rationale for prejudice, discrimination, and violence. These groups also provide extremists with practical means to communicate with like-minded people and groups. Increasingly, hate groups are working together to move into the political and social mainstream by offering more palatable versions of their ideology for public consumption. The growing network of linkages between extremist groups increases the threat of domestic terrorism.

14

AN ETHNOGRAPHER LOOKS AT NEO-NAZI AND KLAN GROUPS

The Racist Mind *Revisited*

RAPHAEL S. EZEKIEL

This article gives us an inside look at the cultural fringes—hate groups. What kind of youths are attracted to these groups, and why? The author suggests that a primary reason may be the sense of identity that such groups apparently provide to youths who are socially isolated and who have a shaky sense of their own identities and a deep fear of social changes. The author recommends some proactive strategies to reach out to such youths and help them meet their psychological needs by engaging them with society in positive ways.

Americans today often learn about Nazis and the Ku Klux Klan through television clips of rallies or marches by men uniformed in camouflage garb with swastika armbands or in robes. These images often carry commentary implying that the racist people are particularly dangerous because they are so different from the viewer, being consumed by irrationality. The racists and their leaders are driven by hatred, it is suggested, and one can scarcely imagine where they come from or how to impede them.

Over 4 years, the author of *The Racist Mind: Portraits of American Neo-Nazis and Klansmen* (Ezekiel, 1995) met about once a week with the young members of a neo-Nazi group in Detroit, periodically holding semistructured interviews with the members and the somewhat older group leader. Over 3 years, he interviewed at length national and middling leaders in the neo-Nazi and Klan movement and attended and observed movement gatherings such as the Aryan Nations national conclaves in Idaho, the regional Klan assembly at Stone Mountain, Georgia, and cross burnings in Michigan. At these gatherings, the writer talked with participants, listened to their conversations with one another, and listened alongside the participants to the speeches of the

EDITORS' NOTE: From Ezekiel, R. S. (2002). An ethnographer Looks at Neo-Nazi and Klan Groups: *The Racist Mind* Revisited. *America Behavioral Scientist, 46(1)*, 51-71 © 2002 Sage Publications. Used with permission movement leaders. The resulting volume describes leaders, followers, and gatherings and employs lengthy quotations from transcripts to buttress reflections on the White racist movement and the meaning of membership in the militant groups. The first half of this article reviews those findings; the second half, beginning with the discussion of Becoming a Neo-Nazi, considerably extends the book's reflections, particularly suggesting steps that would make youth less susceptible to recruitment by racist organizers. It will close with comments on our own social responsibilities.

The methodological core of this work was candor. I was open with my respondents about my identity: That I was a Jew, a leftist, and a university professor. I was direct about my agenda: That I believe (as I do) that most people build for themselves lives that make sense to themselves, and that in my work, I go to people whose lives seem strange to others and ask them to relate to me in their own words the sense of their lives. I told them that I would be using their own words to let others see their meaning, adding my own thoughts. Most people whom I approached were cooperative. (It is relevant that my skin is Caucasian pale. Although I told them that I was a Jew, I did not resemble their rather medieval image of a Jew.)

MOVEMENT SIZE

The militant White racist movement is far from monolithic; it is a loose confederation of small groups made coherent by the organizing work of major leaders and united by common ideology. The Southern Poverty Law Center (2000a) reported that in 1999, there were 36 Klan organizations (with a total of 138 chapters), 21 neo-Nazi organizations (130 chapters), and 10 racist skinhead organizations (40 chapters). The Klan was once the anchor of the movement and kept its distance from the Nazi organizations as they emerged, but since the 1980s, the two sets of organizations have more or less merged in what some have called the Nazification of the Klan. Concepts and symbols are mixed indiscriminately among the various groups.

Membership estimates were available in 1994 from reliable monitoring organizations: The Center for Democratic Renewal (D. Levitas, personal communication, autumn 1994), the Southern Poverty Law Center (D. Welch, personal communication, autumn 1994), and the American Jewish Committee (K. Stern, personal communication, autumn 1994) estimated hard-core membership in the militant White racist movement at 23,000 to 25,000. Of these, 5,500 to 6,000 belonged to one or another of the Klans; 3,500 were skinheads; and 500 to 1,000 were in Nazi groups or in groups close to the Nazis. The remainder of the hard core was less easily identified; the Center for Democratic Renewal referred to them as the Christian Patriot Movement; they were to be found in politically active churches of the Christian Identity sect and in rural groups scattered across the country. The monitoring groups estimated that 150,000 sympathizers bought movement literature, sent contributions to movement groups, or attended rallies, whereas another 450,000 people who did not actually purchase movement literature did read it. The movement is small but has had impact beyond its size because of a reputation based on a history of violence.

MOVEMENT IDEOLOGY

The movement's ideology emerged as one interviewed leaders, listened to their speeches, and read movement newspapers and pamphlets. Two thoughts are the core of this movement: That "race" is real, and those in the movement are God's elect. Race is seen in 19th-century terms: race as a biological category with absolute boundaries, each race having a different essence—just as a rock is a rock and a tree is a tree, a White is a White and a Black is a Black.

Whites are civilization builders who have created our modern world, both its technology and its art. People of color are civilization destroyers, most characteristically showing their essences in the social pathologies of inner-city populations. The races have separate origins, as explained in the theology of Christian Identity (a major influence throughout the White racist movement)[1]: Whites are the creation of God, who is White; people of color, whom they refer to as "the mud races," have originated in the mating of Whites with animals.

Along with White people and people of color, the world includes a third and very dangerous species, the Jews, who have resulted from the mating of Eve with the Serpent. Whites are actual humans and the children of God; Jews are not human but the children of Satan; and people of color are semihuman. God has created the world, which the humans—Whites—are to rule; the people of color, like cattle in the field, should not be hated but tolerated and set to work to meet the needs of the humans. Satan has created the Jews to destroy the Whites and seize the world for Satan. These two forces, the army of God and the army of Satan—the Whites and the Jews—are to struggle with each other until one is destroyed. The Israelites of the Old Testament were early Aryans, unrelated to modern Jews; Jesus thus was an Aryan, not a Jew (Ezekiel, 1995, p. xxvi; Zeskind, 1986).

Most White people, the ideology states, are uninformed about the real nature of things and believe the soothing and ill-intentioned lies of the "Jew-controlled" media. The Jews have made great strides in their war against God, convincing Whites that they must give up their position of dominance in America and cede privilege and power to the African Americans, the Latinos, the Asians, the feminists, the gays, and immigrants. Through their domination of the media, churches, schools, major corporations, and government, the Jews and their White dupes have succeeded in reducing drastically the power of White people; the White race now faces its extinction. Only the members of the movement have grasped this truth and are working to awaken and mobilize White people to defend themselves before the White race has been destroyed. The movement is a defense organization. Members of the movement are very special people, a minority that is not afraid of the truth, is loyal to God, and is willing to fight the workings of Satan and his Jews. Movement members are, in fact, the Chosen People.

The Jews work to destroy the White race through contamination; they call on Whites to engage in race mixing with Blacks and other races, which will produce a hybrid variety that has lost the White essence and thus the God-given strength and virtue of the pure Whites. The call to self-destruction is carried by the media, the churches, and the government, all controlled by the Jews and their flunkies. Only the White racist movement understands the real meaning of the ongoing changes in society and in the culture, understands that a single hidden aim lies behind those seemingly unrelated changes, and that a single hidden force plans them and brings them about. The Jews, in turn, recognize that only the White racist movement stands between them and success, and so the Jews use their organizations, the media, the churches, and the federal government to attack the White racist movement. To the extent the Jews succeed, Whites are taught to lose their race pride and movement leaders are sent to prison.

The struggle between God's agents and Satan's agents is a war of annihilation; only one side will survive. Any measure is justifiable in this war for survival. If innocent people die, it is unfortunate but a given in a war of survival.

All this is heard repeatedly in leadership presentations, and its apocalyptic energy animates the larger movement gatherings. But one wonders how much of the detail is salient for members on a day-by-day basis. If one listens at length to ordinary members, one hears pieces of this God-and-Devil story. But what comes through as central in the members' thinking is that Whites are losing ground, the world is changing, and the member may not do well in the world. The Whites are losing, and the member is losing. These are people who are scared and who draw important comfort from being members of a group.

Official ideology in the movement speaks extensively about the characteristics of the target Others, and this is what the general public assumes is the core of the movement. But, as I shall show in this article, the members teach us that the actual emotional center of the group is thoughts and feelings about the Self. The group is valued most for what it can do for the member's sense of himself.

GENDER

I say "sense of himself" because this is a men's movement. Some women are around but always in quite traditional supportive roles. They are the girlfriends or wives of members, and at gatherings they can serve the food they have cooked. In my 7 years around the movement, I heard many speeches, but never one by a woman. I never saw a woman in a leadership role. Women were servants and nurturers.

Those were the roles open to real women. The men also had their sexualized fantasies about special women who were imagined as trophies. The drawings in their publications, like their chatter, suggested a junior high school mindset: scantily clad women holding AK-47s below their jutting breasts were "saving their love for real men."

HOMOPHOBIA

Fear of homosexual rape was evident; strong Black men who "wanted to rape White women" might also commit anal rape on the White adolescent members. At a less problematic level, there was buy-in to traditional straight American male attitudes about homosexuality: Gay men and lesbian women were perverts. Contemporary shifts in mainstream attitudes toward understanding were seen as the results of the Jewish campaign to undermine the strength of the White race; through their control of the media, the Jews were able to make it seem as though gay men and lesbian women were ordinary people who should be accepted rather than people who were violating God's design. At movement rallies, people were led repeatedly in the chant, "Praise God for AIDS!"

TARGETS

At the ideological level—in the writings and speeches of leaders—the contemporary Klan has joined the neo-Nazis in identifying the Jews as the prime source of evil. Leadership speeches throughout the movement present "the Jew" as the central enemy, with African Americans, Latinos, and Asians as the rather dumb members of "the mud races" who are pawns of the Jews, as are many brainwashed Whites. The leadership ranks gay men and lesbian women with Jews in the enemies list.

Among the rank and file, the picture is more traditional. Most followers whom I have met exhibited intense prejudice against African

Americans that tended to reflect the general prejudice of their families and neighborhoods. Followers could repeat the party line about the Jews, but my strong impression from interviews and from watching socialization into the Detroit group was that new members arrived with strong antipathy toward Blacks but little interest in Jews. They came in hating Blacks and liking the idea that the movement represented Whites in a struggle against Blacks; after entry, they had to be taught who the Jews are and why they should hate them.[2]

LEADERS

There is no White racist movement without its leaders. There are people who are resentful, people who are needy, people who are adventurers, but by themselves they are not a movement. The leaders, themselves a particular kind of adventurer, combine charisma, ideology, and organizational capacity to create White racist groups and, from the groups, the movement.

Racist leaders rise through their own talents. The life stories they tell in the interviews speak of an initial time of puzzlement and casting about, a point of enlightenment, a discovered capacity to draw followers, and a determined struggle to bring the truth forward. Some have college degrees, but in essence all are self-educated with the certainty and the blind spots this entails. The utter certainty is a great deal of their power. The march to prominence has taken place in a context of competition; the racist organizations are in a constant competition with one another, and a leader gains importance as his capacity to attract members and media attention grows. The power to attract members comes from the leader's certainty and his capacity with words and body to be the living expression of the resentment and anger of the listeners. Moreover, he can make his listeners feel that they are part of something that is happening, that these are not empty words.

In many ways, the leader is operating in a vacuum: Middle-class politicians and clergy do not speak to this audience. The audience surmises, accurately, that the Establishment does not see them. The good life seen in advertisements will not be coming to them; their spokespeople are not on the talk shows; their futures will have little wealth and less glory. They do not feel respected.

The leader works with this raw material. The leader radically differs from the media's depiction of him. He is not irrational, and his primary motivation is not race hatred. He is rational and, in many cases, intelligent. He has a flaw: Within his self-education, he has rejected mainstream explanations of the social world and sees himself as one of those original thinkers who is at first scorned but later will be proven correct; this enables him to ignore pieces of personal experience that might disconfirm his ideas.

Because his own life course and thinking are fairly unbound by mainstream assumptions and he is basically self-defined, conspiracy theories are congenial. Within his self-education, he has rejected a sense of the world as tediously complicated, as a result of manifold complex interacting forces. He pictures himself as atomistic and self-determined, and it is logical then that he can believe great effects are caused by tiny groups of hidden men through hidden instrumentalities.

In most cases, the leader is not extremely racist. Racism is comfortable for him, but not his passion. At core, he is a political organizer. His motive is power. Racism is his tool. He feels most alive when he senses himself influencing men, affecting them.

The interviews with national leaders were lengthy—2 or 3 hours, repeated two, three, or more times. As we sat in interview, the respondent would take calls on the phone from lieutenants and would also speak to them in person. From those interactions and from the interviews, a pattern emerged. The leader, usually, is a man who is clever, who is shallow, and who does not respect people. He thinks almost all people are dumb and easily misled. He thinks almost all people will act for cold self-interest and will cheat others whenever they think they will not be caught. His disrespect includes his followers. He respects only those, friend or foe, who have power. His followers are people to be manipulated, not to be led to better self-knowledge. He loves, in abstract words, those whom he feels are disadvantaged. He loves, to this listener's perception, an idea of himself.

As I recall the stories the leaders told me and the things they said to their followers, everything that comes to mind is masculine: The actors in the stories are masculine; the stories are about combat, domination, and subjugation; the stories are not about nurturance or about cooperative effort that adds new elements, not about creativity or about tenderness. In a very fundamental way, the world of the leaders and the followers is an only-masculine world, a world impoverished of half the range of human feeling and thought—like the Army, like prison.

FOLLOWERS

The first years of research were with a Detroit neo-Nazi group that I will call the Death's Head Strike Group. The 1995 book tells how I made the contact with the group and gives portrayals and reflections in depth. The conception of followers that grew from this one group of followers was not contradicted as I met others at movement gatherings.

The members of the Death's Head Strike Group were all male, other than the cell leader's very young lover, who soon left, and several other women who later chanced by briefly. The group was small, with a nucleus of 7 to 10 members and 10 or 15 others in a looser connection. Still another 10 or 15 friends could be mobilized for a specific action. Members were young, ranging from 16 to 30, with a median age of 19. They had come to the group in batches based on friendship clusters. The majority had come from one of three distinct Detroit neighborhoods. People in two of these neighborhoods were extremely poor; the neighborhoods had once been White but now only two or three White families to a block remained, the other families being African American. The third neighborhood was half White and half Black, with families ranging from working-class downward—a struggling but not destitute neighborhood.

Almost every Strike Group member (18 of 20 who were interviewed) had lost a parent when young; usually the loss was of a father (16 of 18). Most of the losses (15 of 18) were due to divorce or separation. The other 3 were due to death or to causes that had never been revealed to the child. The median age at time of loss was 7. The fathers had been working men. After leaving, they maintained no contact with the child or the family and did not send money to the home. Stepfathers or transient boyfriends of the mother tended to be cold, rough, and abusive. Several members had spent portions of their childhood in foster homes.

A few members spoke spontaneously of parental alcoholism or violence; a few others were responsive when I asked questions. Seven members reported alcoholism, six reported family violence. Seven members spontaneously mentioned serving time at detention centers, jails, or prisons. I suspect, from the stories involving street fights and the hints about drug use and pilfering, that there was more undisclosed penal time.

There was little money in the homes. Most of the mothers worked as cooks or waitresses in small eating places or drew disability payments. Most of the members had no jobs and no prospect of work. A couple had steady work at low wages; a few found occasional work in the neighborhood, for example, tearing down a shack for someone. Industrial employment in Detroit was shrinking rapidly, and the prospects for these young men were very poor, especially because they had little work experience or education. They had left school early. The school history of 16 members is known. Six had quit school in the 9th grade, 3 in the 10th, and 4 in the 11th. The 3 who had graduated from high school had each taken a semester or two at a community college.

These young men were living in startling social isolation. The impact of parental loss and poverty depends on the sort of parenting by the remaining parent and on the quality of other social supports. Aside from their mothers, about whom little is known, social supports were minimal. Ties to siblings tended to be weak or nonexistent, and only one member spoke of someone from the extended family who had played a role in his life. None ever mentioned a teacher who had been important to him, or a coach or scout leader, or anyone from a church, the neighborhood, or a social agency.

The members had grown up in neighborhoods in which they had to fight a lot. This would have not been easy because most of them were fairly slim, rather slight. They depended on fighting real hard, once something broke out. They were wiry and tough, but preoccupied with their thinness.

They were not good physical specimens. A surprising number had been born with a childhood disease or deficiency, such as being born a blue baby or "born with half a liver." There are a lot of hospital stories in the interviews.

Very early in the interviewing, I sensed an underlying theme of fear. At an unspoken but deep level, the members seemed to feel extremely vulnerable, that their lives might be snuffed out at any time like a match flame in the wind. This makes the appeal of the Nazi symbols understandable. When I asked them what they knew about Nazism, they referred to late-night movies on television. If you are afraid that you will disappear, how appealing are the symbols of a force that was hard, ruthless, even willing to murder to achieve its goals.

None of the members could establish a long-term intimate relationship. Several had caused pregnancies, but neither they nor the cell leader was able to establish a fathering role. Eventually, two of the members did become seriously involved with women, one of them fathering a child; each of these young men drifted from the group as he became involved. One of them soon was living with his woman friend and held down both a full-time job and a part-time job, where he began to have friendly bonds with some of his African American coworkers; he abandoned the Strike Group.

The group did not have conventional meetings; rather, the members hung out at the leader's apartment. Periodically, they were transported in the windowless rear of a rented Ryder van to some outlying town where they would put on a rally for a few minutes until counterdemonstrators drove them away. I think this action also assuaged their fears. If you are not quite sure that you are alive, how reassuring to stand shoulder to shoulder with your comrades, withstanding for a few minutes the taunts, threats, and hurled snowballs, chunks of ice, and flashlight batteries of the counterdemonstrators. When the police quickly shepherded them safely back to their van, they rode back to Detroit, and, that afternoon and for weeks thereafter, rejoiced in rather inflated memories of their courage, feasting their eyes repeatedly on newspaper photos.

Presence of Racist Group		Differential Outcomes, such as:
Social Dislocation		ordinary coping
Economic Pressure (?)		numbness
Social Isolation		malaise
Racist Ideology	Family	alcoholism
	Dynamics, Personal	chronic anger
Macho Ideology	Psychodynamics	individual violence
		racist activism
Absence of Democratic Ideology		
Absence of Cross-Cutting Loyalties		

Figure 14.1 Schematized Representation of Suggested Factors Influencing a Youth Becoming a White Racist Activist

BECOMING A NEO-NAZI

How does a working-class kid in Detroit become a neo-Nazi? What are the factors that make adolescents vulnerable to recruitment by racist organizers? Figure 14.1 is a schematized representation of factors suggested by the interviews. Social factors, listed on the left, intersect with personal and family psychodynamics. A range of alternative outcomes, shown on the right, may follow.

The tally of social factors begins by noting the *presence of a racist group.* Where there are no groups and where there is no effort at recruitment, recruitment is probably unlikely. Every young person who has been recruited stands for hundreds of others who just as readily might have been recruited if there had been an organization on the scene.

Many of the Detroit youths I met with had written away for membership cards in the Klan when they were in junior high school. This was a mail transaction that gave them a card to carry in their back pockets, with whatever boost that gave their egos as they moved about in the racially mixed schools in which they were the minority. They could not recall how they had found out about this mail-order opportunity. They later heard about the

Detroit neo-Nazi group because it got a lot of publicity on Detroit television. Occasional placards shown on the video clips included the group's phone number, so they could call its leader. After meeting with him a few times, they would start coming around regularly. When one joined, a couple of friends usually followed.

The growing number of White racist Web sites on the Internet make racist propaganda widely accessible. Monitoring organizations fear that this will aid recruitment (Southern Poverty Law Center, 2000b, 2001a; Weitzman, 1998, 2000). Data are absent, and some are skeptical (Southern Poverty Law Center, 2001b).

The diagram's second social factor is *social dislocation.* Widespread changes in American society mean that previous status hierarchies are disrupted or threatened. (Note parallels to developments in Weimar Germany [Kershaw, 1998].) Most members of the American White racist movement believe that they, as White men, are members of an endangered species. Very little about their futures can be taken for granted. Many cues tell them that old values, which they have assumed would benefit them for life, are challenged by new values. Real social change is involved here, as well as exaggerated perceptions of change and endangerment.

White Americans have made only an awkward accommodation to the increased political strength of African Americans. The work of Howard Schuman and his associates addresses the complexity of this issue: Looking at surveys of probability samples over decades, they found White Americans verbally endorsing some egalitarian values, while steadfastly opposing concrete steps that would implement those values (Schuman, Steeb, Bobo, & Krysan, 1997).

In early versions of this diagram, I listed *economic pressure* as a social factor. People that I met seemed to come from families with incomes below the median and sometimes well below the median. I am no longer confident that my impressions justify a claim linking economic factors to membership in racist groups. Several lines of research challenge this assumption. First, Leonard Zeskind (personal communication, autumn 1994), whom I consider the most astute political observer of the White racist movement, believes that the movement is a representative cross-section of American society. Second, James Aho (1990), in a careful study of the movement in Idaho, found educational levels that did not suggest economic pressures. (Interestingly, he noted that respondents in the more extreme portion of the sample "seem either to be college graduates or high school dropouts" p. 141.)

Finally, a strong set of new studies from Yale casts doubt on a linkage between economic status and racist group membership or racist crime. The most impressive of the Yale studies (Green, Strolovitch, & Wong, 1998) demonstrated that the number of bias-crime incidents in New York City neighborhoods between 1987 and 1995 was not related to neighborhood economic status (unemployment rate, poverty rate, or median income) but to turf patterns: Racially motivated crime rose when there was a rise in non-White migration into neighborhoods in which Whites had for a long time enjoyed a large majority. A second study (Green, Abelson, & Garnett, 1999) examined responses from a probability sample of North Carolinians about political and economic matters. Elegant procedures permitted the inclusion of an identified subsample composed of members of White supremacist groups and of hate crime perpetrators. (Unfortunately, this subsample is small.) Although the two

populations differ predictably in political views, the subsample's more negative view of the economic condition and prospects of their communities differs from the general population's assessment to a degree that is only "small to moderate" (p. 447). A third study (Green, Glaser, & Rich, 1998) readdresses, with more sophisticated techniques, historical data on lynchings and economic changes and found "little robust support" for a frustration-aggression hypothesis. Interestingly, the ensuing discussion highlights a more nuanced conception of the linkage of economics and racist activity: The authors point to historical periods in which propagandists from the political, business, or labor communities mobilized racial hostility by identifying a racial group as the cause of economic problems—an analysis that parallels this article's characterization of the White racist leaders as people who are fundamentally political beings.

Despite the power of the Yale studies, this issue may not be conclusively settled. We are dealing with groups with secret memberships, and the historical record in Weimar Germany dramatically commands attention (Kershaw, 1998).

The third social factor is *social isolation,* which has been discussed at length above. The importance of social support has been widely studied; see, for example, the discussion of social support in Cohen and Herbert's 1996 review of health psychology. The young men in the Strike Group may or may not have been close to their mothers, but the lack of other meaningful adults meant unusual vulnerability. The racist group offered comradeship, authority figures, and a home to young people who lived in what might be termed *spiritual poverty.*

The fourth and fifth social factors are *racist ideology* and *macho ideology.* These help determine the direction that the conversion process takes. The ideology of racism, which was passed on to the new member by the group leader and reinforced in conversations with other members, gives the new recruit a continuing sense that there is an important reason for the group to exist. This is more than a casual friendship group. The movement makes its claim, in the ideology, to a turf and declares its role as defending that turf. The members struck me as people who felt rather orphaned, and the racist ideology permits the member to construct in his mind a new family, the mythologized White race. In the member's conversations, we hear the fantasy that someday this great White family will realize what he has done for them and then they will embrace him.

Macho ideology is a familiar presence in authoritarian movements (Adorno, Frenkel-Brunswik, Levinson, & Sanford, 1950; Smith, 1965; Stone, Lederer, & Christie, 1993). This is an ideology of pseudomasculinity, an ideology that glorifies toughness and fears tenderness or nurturance as weakness. This stance buttresses the ego of shaky male individuals; it can be especially important to adolescents, and in this case, we are speaking of particularly fearful adolescents.

The listing of social factors concludes by noting absences: the *absence of democratic ideology* as a real part of the mental life of the youths, and the *absence of cross-cutting loyalties* that might make exclusivist appeals uncomfortable. Research relevant to the latter appears in Urban and Miller (1998) and Marcus-Newhall, Miller, Holz, and Brewer (1993). The two absences become apparent when one asks how it can be that these young people do not experience revulsion when presented with the authoritarian and racist worldviews that are the center of the recruitment process. What is not there that one might expect? The absences, as we shall see, have direct implications for prevention of recruitment.

The diagram assumes that the impact of the social forces depends on the particular characteristics of the individual's psyche and the dynamics in the individual's family. Psychodynamics are examined by Dunbar (2000), Dunbar, Krop, and Sullaway (2000), Hopf (1993), Staub (1989), and Sullivan and Transue (1996). Staub covered historical and social issues as well as psychodynamics. Dunbar et al. (2000) compared men convicted of racist homicide to men convicted of nonracist homicide.

Hopf's (1993) review of qualitative and clinical work on authoritarians and their families yields psychological portraits that fit the neo-Nazi youth of the Strike Group to a startling degree. On pages 128 to 130, she reconstructs Ackerman and Jahoda's 1950 study. Ackerman and Jahoda interviewed psychoanalysts at length about anti-Semitic non-Jewish patients in their caseloads. The following characteristics were described as universal for these anti-Semitic patients:

1. A vague feeling of fear, linked to an inner picture of the world around them that appears to be hostile, evil, and difficult to master;

2. A shaky self-image, identity problems, and fluctuations between overestimation of self and self-derogation;

3. Difficulties in interpersonal relationships manifested in part in a high degree of isolation and hidden in part behind functioning facades. "But at best such disguises deceive the outer world and sometimes the self; they never lead to the establishment of warm, human relationships" (Ackerman & Jahoda, 1950, p. 33);

4. The tendency to conform and fear of attracting attention;

5. Problems in coping with reality; often there are weak bonds not only to other persons but also to external objects (content of work, occupation in leisure time, and so forth);

6. Problems in the development of an autonomous set of ethics.

Hopf's review leads one back to the qualitative chapters of *The Authoritarian Personality* (Adorno et al., 1950). Indeed, the entire Stone et al. volume and Smith's 1965 data argue for readdressing the central concepts of the Berkeley research (also see Smith's 1997 review). Note, on the other hand, a strong, recent dissent by Martin (2001), who argued that even in the qualitative sections, the members of the Berkeley group were fatally naive in their methodology, fell into systematic error because they had reified scale positions as existing human types, and consistently misinterpreted data in a self-serving fashion.

In either case, the psychological has consequence. The diagram proposes that in the presence of the stipulated social factors, some people of particular personal and family psychological patterns will enter into a period of activism in the White racist movement. The diagram proposes as well that small differences in the social and individual inputs will result in quite a range of possible outcomes. One can well imagine people who might become lonely cranks, or drunkards, or even quite ordinarily competent adults. The devil, as always, is in the details.

PREVENTION

Personal Connection

What would make individual White adolescents less vulnerable to the recruitment efforts of neo-Nazi and Klan organizers? Recall the social isolation of the Detroit youths. During those repeated interactions, I became aware that warmth was increasing between us, despite my identifying myself as a Jew and a progressive.

I had my own personal issues. On a pivotal afternoon very early in the project, I was driving to Detroit to continue our conversations and thinking about the life of one of the young men. I had been getting a sense of what his life had been and what its onward trajectory was likely to be. What could be done, I asked myself, that would help him have a more competent sense of himself, that would encourage him to take a firmer grasp on his life—to begin to understand that his life mattered and that it could be directed in a hopeful way? I pondered and abruptly shook myself: "What am I doing, worrying about a Nazi?" I thought about it. And then from my gut came the reply: "He is also a kid. It cannot be wrong to be concerned about a kid."

The neo-Nazi youths were reacting to me as well. Their greetings, their remarks, and their bearing showed that I was becoming a person who mattered to them. That made sense. I would sit and speak with an individual for a long time, talking with him about his life, taking his life seriously, looking into his eyes as we spoke. This happened again and again. Probably no one had acted that way with these youths for a long time.

This sort of interaction may be a critical ingredient in programs that address the needs of disadvantaged kids. Every child needs an adult who *sees* him or her: an adult who does not disappear, who shows by attention and action over time that he or she takes the child seriously and that the child matters.

This is not an elegant formula. It is labor-intensive and lacks multiplier effects. But it may be fundamental. In addition to macro-economic changes, perhaps we need direct personal action if we are to reduce the amount of youth violence, of teenage pregnancy, of youthful gang activity, of racist activity, and of all the other ways that disadvantaged youths hurt themselves and others. We perhaps should tithe ourselves—a tithing of time for children in need of relationships. See in this connection the discussions of mentoring in Freedman (1993) and in Tierney and Grossman (2000).

Community

Complementary ways in which we could address the social isolation of youths such as these tie to the word *community*. Research with the Peace Corps and experience in teaching have convinced me of the power of context: Given a meaningful challenge that is difficult but not insuperable, within an artful combination of structure and freedom, young people can mature and become competent to a degree that would not be predicted from a simple examination of their past (Ezekiel, 1969; Smith, 1966). These lessons were in my mind as I interacted with the neo-Nazi youth and asked myself about alternative scenarios that could have been played out in their lives. They were neither mindless nor hate-filled. They were poorly educated and fearful at the core. What they wanted profoundly was to have close relationships and to feel that their lives mattered.

The Nazi group offered them this feeling to a degree and for a while, but other endeavors could probably have done this as well or better. I thought I probably could have led many of them away from their leader (because I was a warmer person and cared more for them) to some other group. But what other group would fit their needs? The best fit, I felt, would be a radical environmental group such as Earth First. Such a group would have given them adventure and a chance to shock the Establishment, while doing something of intrinsic value and enjoying camaraderie. Earth First's goals would have jibed with the anticorporate bias of the youths and with their romanticism about the outdoors. Working in that organization would not have particularly affected the racial prejudice these kids harbored, but it would have met their need to act out in a shocking and socially relevant fashion while gaining group affection. The youths probably would have remained racist— but so would their peers who did not wear swastikas. The point is that these young people seemed to have no intrinsic need to act out their racism but did have needs to have companionship, to be shocking, and to feel that their lives had meaning.

Community organizations could build much more broadly on the similar hungers of great numbers of kids, who could learn community in contexts of challenge. Our culture tends to relegate young people to roles that are neither meaningful nor honorific. What is the significance of being overindulged or socialized to see oneself primarily as a consumer? What scope do we offer an adolescent who wishes to prove his or her significance in the world? Churches, synagogues, mosques, neighborhood organizations, scouting organizations, and political or ethnic organizations could begin to build youth groups in which there was serious challenge; there are plenty of hard and meaningful tasks to be taken on. A critical need, again, would be for adult leadership that would not fade out.

❧ Schools, Democracy, Antiracist Education

Schools, like community groups, may play a role. The youths I met had first become involved in racist activity in junior high school. Their prior (and subsequent) schooling had not led them to harbor a concept of community. The classroom had seldom been shaped as a community in which class members had felt mutual responsibility for one another. On the contrary, the classroom probably had reflected the desperation and the atomization of the society outside the school.

Equally, the schools had left no feel for democracy. The youths had no positive association to the word, which seemed to them a meaningless term used by adults for hypocritical purposes. School had afforded little chance for real impact on decisions that mattered, opportunities to learn in action the meaning of the word democracy. Both community and democracy can be taught through experience in the classroom, when schools consider these goals part of the curriculum and invest energy in building related skills.

For the neo-Nazi youths, the teaching in school of multiculturalism had been another adult exercise in hypocrisy. Black History Month was an annual annoyance. It is easy for an adult-led discussion to seem like sermonizing. I would suggest that education about racism should begin with respect for the constructs and emotions that the students bring with them into the classroom. The students have ideas and emotions about race that are the product of their own lives. They have heard their parents, their neighbors, and their friends, and they have had their own experiences. To ignore their emotions and constructs around race is to ignore the sense that they make of their own experiences.[3]

Teaching about racism, I want to suggest, is a subtopic of teaching about identity. Perhaps the first step is to help the student think through his or her own sense of identity and to look for its roots. What was the life of your grandparents and what does that life tell you about yourself? What are the legends or myths in your family— why is it special to be a Kelly or a Krueger? What has been the experience of religion that you have heard about from your parents, and what has been your own experience—how have these helped to make you the person you are? Young people, regardless of race or ethnicity, should be helped to see where their own sense of identity comes from and how it affects their own lives. And to see its many different facets. Only then can the student begin to acknowledge that other people also have a sense of identity, and that it also had multiple roots. And also plays a role in their lives.

HOW DO WE RESEMBLE THEM? HOW DO WE DIFFER?

It is fashionable to repeat Walt Kelly's *Pogo:* "We have met the enemy, and they are us." And it is worth noting that the neo-Nazis are not totally alien to White Americans. A social attitude does not exist in the mind as an isolated single entity. Real attitudes, or orientations, are laid down throughout life in layer after layer. If you visited South Africa and spoke with older White South Africans, you would expect to find their minds affected by having grown up in a society that was intensely racist. White Americans grow up in a society in which race has been and is profoundly important.

If I grow up living next to a cement factory and inhale cement dust every day, cement dust becomes part of my body. If I am White and grow up in a society in which race matters, I inhale racism, and racism becomes part of my mind and spirit. (I do not presume to speak here for the experience of people of color.) There will always be layers of myself that harbor racist thoughts and racist attitudes. This is not to say that those must remain the dominant parts of my mind and spirit. It is to say that it is mistaken to presume that I have no traces of racism in me.

The task is to get acquainted with those layers of oneself—to learn to recognize them and not be frightened by them. It is not a disgrace to have absorbed some racism. It is a disgrace not to know it and to let those parts of ourselves go unchecked.

I overcome those layers of myself by getting acquainted with them and by adding additional layers that are not racist. How do I do that? By action: I try to behave in a nonracist fashion or an antiracist fashion in the external world and absorb this experience as another layer of myself.

There is perhaps a parallel in clinical work. In therapy, I may learn to recognize the parts of me that were shaped by early experience with my parents (or, rather, what my childish mind thought was early experience with my parents). I learn to understand that in some circumstances—for example, in a disagreement with a superior—pieces of those early attitudes are likely to get activated. I can learn to think about this before going into the boss's office, and prepare myself not to be blindsided by infantile parts of myself that are not relevant to the situation at hand. And, over time, I can add layers of nondefensive experience to my psyche.

If, then, those of us who are White have grown up in the same society as the racists and have absorbed some of the same cement dust, are we the same as them? The organized White racist movement rests on the following four axioms: that race is real, that White is best, that the language of human interactions is power, and that society's surface conceals conspiracy.

We European Americans have layers of ourselves that also hold the first two of those axioms. We may have been taught in school that race is merely a social construct and that White superiority is a myth. But that teaching runs up against what we are taught by our lives, every day. Race does matter in America. And White ends up on top.

We can learn to not be captive to the layers of ourselves that are racist. "Am I racist?" is not the question. The question is, To what degree am I racist in what situations? And the more important question, What are the concrete effects of my actions (or inactions)? In the 1970s, my interviews with African American families in the Detroit inner-city included interactions with a woman named Ruby and her children (Ezekiel, 1984). Ruby lived on 12th Street (as it was then named), and her children had cornflakes with water for their daily breakfast. Ruby and her children were real; the contrasts between their lives and mine were painful. I learned to ask myself, when people spoke on the radio or at the university about a program or a policy, how it would affect Ruby's children: Would it help them to have milk with their cornflakes, or would they keep on eating cornflakes with water?

THE GUILT OF THE ORGANIZED RACISTS

Between Reconstruction and 1945, 3,000 to 5,000 African American men and women were tortured and killed by lynch mobs. The Ku Klux Klan was a dominant force behind those killings. Local officials were often themselves Klansmen but, in any case, did not obstruct the Klan. During the civil rights struggles of the 1950s and 1960s, Klansmen instigated mob assaults on Freedom Riders and the like, and carried out bombings and murders of activists—or of little girls in a church—under cover of darkness. Organized White racism has a long and bloody history. Its goal has been to preserve White domination in America. Its primary weapon has been terror.

The Klan and neo-Nazi groups hold a different position today. Town and county officials are much less likely to be secret members and are much less likely to be cowed by overt White racist demands. To this writer's perception, White racism remains a major strand in American culture, but as a political force, it has expressed itself more often as a covert message within mainstream politics. Major presidential candidates have not hesitated to win support by suggesting that too much is being done for the undeserving poor, a code word for African Americans. Demonization of the poor has proceeded apace, buttressed by an almost unspoken assumption (a statistically inaccurate assumption) that most of the poor are non-Whites. This demonization may have served as a distracting cover for a reapportionment of wealth from middle-income families upwards (Collins & Yeskel, 2000).

Probably the greatest effect of White racism today is its capacity to slow institutional change. Policies that help institutional racism to continue to flourish do much more to hurt minority people than do hate crimes. High infant mortality rates in the inner cities and policies that let them continue are more dangerous than the Klan.

Actual hate crimes, for the most part, are committed by people who are not members of organized White racist groups (Dunbar, 2000; Dunbar et al., 2000). Deep racial distrust and antipathy mark our culture and would exist without the dramatic statements and demonstrations of the White racist groups. But the statements and the rallies of those groups increase the temperature, and the advocacy of specific steps pinpoints actions that perpetrators can take.

The leaders and the lieutenants of those groups are morally responsible to a nontrivial degree for racial violence in the United States (a responsibility they gladly claim in private conversation). Indeed, the future for which they avowedly work is one in which racial violence increases until the long predicted race war erupts and White America wins back its God-ordained dominance. The followers in the groups, the willing actors in the theater produced by the leaders, share in that moral responsibility. And of course, where leaders or followers have committed crimes, they are fully responsible.

Racism, Hate Crimes, and Responsibility

I chose to talk with members and leaders of White racist organizations as part of a broader project of understanding White racism in

America. I have gained the impression, since publication of *The Racist Mind,* that more and more of the general public and the educated public are letting the task of talking about hate crimes displace from the agenda the task of thinking about racism.

Perhaps this is not surprising. You and I do not commit racial assaults, and no one we know does. It is interesting and unthreatening to imagine the world of those other people, whoever they may be, who engage in racist violence. And how nice if that form of contemplation can also be the only price White people have to pay for living in an unjust society. So that the more indignant and outraged I can be about the evils of the Klan and neo-Nazis, the more virtuous I can feel. And the more virtuous I feel about their misdeeds, the less I need to listen to tiresome critics who talk about racism and the need for institutional changes.

If I were to think about the true and continuing effects of racism, I would have to think about the ongoing social order, in which I am a part and for which I have responsibility. All of us are ready to say that Klan murders are evil. But what are we ready to do, today, about the continuing racially based maldistribution of health, of wealth, and of hope?

Notes

1. A recent report suggested that the influence of Christian Identity in the movement is in decline, being replaced, especially among young members, by racial Odinism (Southern Poverty Law Center, 2001c).

2. In interviews, speeches, and conversations, nothing was said about Catholics or the Catholic Church.

3. The teacher must proceed, I think, with some humility. It is not unreasonable for a White American kid to have absorbed some racism. That young person is growing up in a fairly racist society—that is, a society in which race strongly affects life chances (health, longevity, income, wealth). He or she hears on all sides conversations in which race is an emotionally charged subject. He or she lives, often, in a neighborhood that is segregated by race. This young person learns over and over that race matters in America. To preach to an adolescent that race does not matter, or that we should act as though it does not matter, rightly invites skepticism. Teachers need to wrestle in their own minds and guts with these issues before trying to

educate others. Are teachers ready to be honest with children about the actual state of our society and to talk honestly about the steps that may need to happen for the society to be less racist? This may require talking about economics, the great unspeakable in our culture. Teachers may need to spend time in protected settings, working through their own understanding; they may also need to do a fair amount of reading. Simple preaching is not going to accomplish the task (Ezekiel, 1998, 1999a, 1999b, 1999c).

REFERENCES

Ackerman, N. W., & Jahoda, M. (1950). *Anti-Semitism and emotional disorder: A psychoanalytic interpretation.* New York: HarperCollins.

Adorno, T. W., Frenkel-Brunswik, E., Levinson, D., & Sanford, R. N. (1950). *The authoritarian personality.* New York: HarperCollins.

Aho, J. A. (1990). *The politics of righteousness: Idaho Christian patriotism.* Seattle: University of Washington Press.

Cohen, S., & Herbert, T. (1996). Health psychology: Psychological factors and physical disease from the perspective of human psychoneuroimmunology. *Annual Review of Psychology, 47,* 113–142.

Collins, C., & Yeskel, F. (2000). *Economic apartheid in America: A primer on economic inequality and insecurity.* New York: New Press.

Dunbar, E. (2000). *Toward a profile of violent hate crime offenders: Behavioral and ideological signifiers of bias motivated criminality.* Manuscript submitted for publication.

Dunbar, E., Krop, H., & Sullaway, M. (2000). *Behavioral, psychometric, and diagnostic characteristics of bias-motivated homicide offenders.* Manuscript submitted for publication.

Ezekiel, R. (1969). Setting and the emergence of competence during adult socialization: Working at home vs. working "out there." *Merrill-Palmer Quarterly of Behavior and Development, 15*(4), 389–396.

Ezekiel, R. (1984). *Voices from the corner: Poverty and racism in the inner city.* Philadelphia: Temple University Press.

Ezekiel, R. (1995). *The racist mind: Portraits of American neo-Nazis and Klansmen.* New York: Viking Penguin.

Ezekiel, R. (1998). *Anti-bias education with 5th- and 6th-graders.* Unpublished paper for the Museum of Tolerance, Simon Wiesenthal Center.

Ezekiel, R. (1999a). *Teaching tolerance: Today, tomorrow, five years from now.* Unpublished paper for the Museum of Tolerance, Simon Wiesenthal Center.

Ezekiel, R. (1999b). *Teaching tolerance: Self-examination.* Unpublished paper for the Museum of Tolerance, Simon Wiesenthal Center.

Ezekiel, R. (1999c). *Teaching tolerance: Learning from history.* Unpublished paper for the Museum of Tolerance, Simon Wiesenthal Center.

Freedman, M. (1993). *The kindness of strangers: Adult mentors, urban youth, and the new voluntarism.* Cambridge, United Kingdom: Cambridge University Press.

Green, D., Abelson, R., & Garnett, M. (1999). The distinctive political views of hate-crime perpetrators and white supremacists. In D. Prentice & D. Miller (Eds.), *Cultural divides: Understanding and overcoming group conflict* (pp. 429–464). New York: Russell Sage.

Green, D., Glaser, J., & Rich, A. (1998). From lynching to gay bashing: The elusive connection between economic conditions and hate crime. *Journal of Personality and Social Psychology, 75,* 82–92.

Green, D., Strolovitch, D., & Wong, J. (1998). Defended neighborhoods, integration, and racially motivated crime. *American Journal of Sociology, 104,* 372–403.

Hopf, C. (1993). Authoritarians and their families: Qualitative studies on the origins of authoritarian dispositions. In W. Stone, G. Lederer, & R. Christie (Eds.), *Strength and weakness: The authoritarian personality today* (pp. 119–143). New York: Springer-Verlag.

Kershaw, I. (1998). *Hitler: 1889–1936: Hubris.* New York: Norton.

Marcus-Newhall, A., Miller, N., Holz, R., & Brewer, M. B. (1993). Cross-cutting category membership with role assignment: A means of reducing intergroup bias. *British Journal of Social Psychology, 32,* 125–146.

Martin, J. (2001). The authoritarian personality, 50 years later: What lessons are there for political psychology? *Political Psychology, 22,* 1–26.

Schuman, H., Steeb, C., Bobo, L., & Krysan, M. (1997). *Racial attitudes in America: Trends and interpretations* (Rev. ed.). Cambridge, MA: Harvard University Press.

Smith, M. B. (1965). An analysis of two measures of "authoritarianism" among Peace Corps teachers. *Journal of Personality, 33*(44), 513–535.

Smith, M. B. (1966). Explorations in competence: A study of Peace Corps teachers in Ghana. *American Psychologist, 21,* 555–566.

Smith, M. B. (1997). The authoritarian personality: A re-review 40 years later. *Political Psychology, 18,* 159–163.

Southern Poverty Law Center. (2000a, winter). Active hate groups in the U.S. in 1999. *Intelligence Report, 97,* 30–35.

Southern Poverty Law Center. (2000b, winter). Hate groups on the Internet. *Intelligence Report, 97,* 36–39.

Southern Poverty Law Center. (2001a, spring). Active hate sites in the Internet in the year 2000. *Intelligence Report, 101,* 40–43.

Southern Poverty Law Center. (2001b, spring). Cyberhate revisited. *Intelligence Report, 101,* 44–45.

Southern Poverty Law Center. (2001c, spring). The new Romantics. *Intelligence Report, 101,* 56–57.

Staub, E. (1989). *The roots of evil: The origins of genocide and other group violence.* Cambridge, United Kingdom: Cambridge University Press.

Stone, W., Lederer, G., & Christie, R. (1993). *Strength and weakness: The authoritarian personality today.* New York: Springer-Verlag.

Sullivan, J., & Transue, J. (1996). The psychological underpinnings of democracy: A selective review of research in political tolerance, interpersonal trust, and social capital. *Annual Review of Psychology, 47,* 625–650.

Tierney, J., & Grossman, J. (2000). *Making a difference: An impact study of Big Brothers/Big Sisters.* Philadelphia: Public/Private Ventures.

Urban, L., & Miller, N. (1998). A theoretical analysis of crossed categorization effects: A meta-analysis. *Journal of Personality and Social Psychology, 74,* 894–908.

Weitzman, M. (1998, October). *The inverted image: Anti-Semitism and anti-Catholicism on the Internet.* Paper presented at the fifth biennial Conference on Christianity and the Holocaust, Princeton, NJ.

Weitzman, M. (2000). Workshop 4 on education: Use and misuse of the Internet. In *Proceedings: The Stockholm International Forum on the Holocaust* (pp. 250–253).

Zeskind, L. (1986). *The "Christian Identity" movement: Analyzing its theological rationalization for racist and anti-Semitic violence.* Atlanta, GA: Center for Democratic Renewal.

QUESTIONS

1. What are the two themes of the white racist movement that the author learned about from his research? How does movement ideology reflect an absolutist, dichotomous view of the world?

2. How do white racist movement beliefs illustrate a "defensive" posture, according to the author?

3. How does the movement draw on members' concerns about their identity and their place in the modern world? Discuss examples.

4. Why are the movement leaders' charisma and certainty key aspects of the movement?

5. What were the main motivations of the movement leaders the author studied? What kind of person is a white racist movement leader? Why does the author say that these leaders are not necessarily extremely racist?

6. What were the typical family and social backgrounds of the white racist group followers the author studied? Describe the psychological and demographic characteristics of the followers.

7. How did perceived social and economic dislocation play a role in the recruitment of white racist group members?

8. In the author's view, what is the relationship between economic factors and racist group membership activity?

9. What are the factors that make teenagers vulnerable to being recruited by white racist movements? Which of these factors do you believe is probably most influential, and why?

10. Why is providing a sense of community and developing an understanding of the democratic process important in helping reach at-risk teenagers susceptible to racist group recruitment?

11. What role can mentors play in providing alternatives to the kind of young people described in this research? What kind of organization might be a suitable place for such youths to engage proactively with society? What did you think of the author's suggestion of Earth First?

12. According to the author, what can we do to help provide an effective "antiracist" education for youth? How will this involve helping youth explore their identities and structural inequalities in society?

15

HISTORY AS A WEAPON

How Extremists Deny the Holocaust in North America

BRIAN LEVIN

How can someone deny the fact of the Holocaust? This article discusses the tactics Holocaust deniers employ to deny the realities experienced by millions of Holocaust dead and survivors. The facts of the largest genocide in human history are distorted and denied by extremists for political purposes. The old denial strategies were blatant and crude, but newer ones are relatively sophisticated pseudo-scientific techniques supported by a few credentialed "experts." Deniers use these newer strategies to pursue an agenda of anti-Semitism while attempting to unite extremist groups and influence mainstream public opinion.

If the international Jewish financiers in and outside of Europe should succeed in plunging the nations once more into a world war, then the result will not be the bolshevisation of the earth, and thus the victory of Jewry, but the annihilation of the Jewish race in Europe!

—Adolf Hitler (speech before the German Reichstag,
January 30, 1939, quoted in Stern, 1993, p. 62)

I shall speak to you here with all frankness of a very serious subject. We shall now discuss it absolutely openly among ourselves, nevertheless we shall never speak of it in public. I mean the evacuation of the Jews, the extermination of the Jewish race. It is one of those things which is easy to say. "The Jewish race is to be exterminated," says every party member. "That's clear, it's part of our program, elimination of the Jews, extermination, right, we'll do it."

—Heinrich Himmler (October 4, 1943,
quoted in The History Place, 2000)

EDITORS' NOTE: From Levin, B. (2001). History as a Weapon: How Extremists Deny the Holocaust in North America. *American Behavioral Scientist, 44*(6), 1001-1031. © Sage Publications. Used with permission.

Total consensus in historical analysis, as in science or law, is elusive and probably not particularly beneficial to a society's advancement. Intellectual advancement, as a matter of necessity, requires the testing of older theories and the critical analysis of new evidence. Varying interpretations of history between groups are inevitable to some extent because different groups can be affected differently by the same event. Interpretive bias can occur because different groups played different roles in the formation of disputed events; had different stakes in their outcomes; had different cultural, religious, and informational traditions; and had different levels of access to credible and timely primary source information.

Some interpretive differences, however, are not merely the result of innocent, passive bias. For centuries, ideologues have used contorted legal, scientific, or historical conclusions to serve their own bigoted ends. The pseudoscientific notion of racial inferiority was promoted by those who benefited economically, socially, and politically from the preservation of slavery and segregation. Both the Bubonic plague and later the fictional *Protocols of the Elders of Zion* were exploited to promote false, anti-Semitic conspiracy theories by those who benefited from the persecution or mistreatment of Jews.

Extremist political and terrorist movements, like mainstream political ideologies, rely not only on unifying interpretations of contemporary actors and events but on a unified vision of historical actors and events as well. Seemingly irrational present-day acts of hatred and violence are justifiable to those ideologues who view their conduct as vindication of a past claim or retaliation for a past injustice. One person's terrorist is often another's freedom fighter. For ideologically motivated terrorists, including neo-Nazi skinheads and other hard-core domestic hate crime offenders, variant historical interpretations are often defining components of their belief systems.

For this essay, an extremist is somewhat flexibly defined as someone who for ideological reasons advocates a contention as fact that an unbiased reviewer would regard as wholly or materially unsubstantiated, or someone who, while advocating a particular ideological theory, relies on violence and criminality as a primary means for promoting that position.

One of the most notable attempts by extremists to exploit a historical event for bigoted ends is that of the self-styled Holocaust "revisionists" who question the existence or scope of Hitler's extermination program. What separates revisionists (or, more aptly put, Holocaust deniers) from others who still doubt facts such as the moon landings, a spherical Earth, or the death of Elvis Presley is that denial has been promoted and financed in substantial part by powerful extremists with a distinct political agenda. Although some deniers are in fact merely ill-informed iconoclasts, conspiracy theorists, contrarians, or skeptics, many of the most influential are anti-Semitic ideologues or Third Reich sympathizers attempting to promote anti-Semitism and a rehabilitation of Nazism.

Holocaust denial in North America is an important area of analysis in an overall study of extremism. Although denial certainly stands on its own as an ideological movement, it also plays a crucial role in broadly promoting anti-Semitism. Because the "Jew is a transnational figure of hate" for right-wing extremists throughout the world, denial has a unique power to influence and bond a vast array of autonomous ethnic and political anti-Semites (Back, Keith, & Solomos, 1998, p. 90).

Denial's broad appeal to right-wing, racist extremists also relates to the fact that it promotes two related but independent false ideological axioms. Denial is obviously appealing to those who vigorously promote a theory of secretive, far-reaching, abusive, Jewish conspiratorial power. It is also appealing, however, to those who subscribe to a more broad conspiracy theory that involves the collusion of various governments, political leaders, and Jews, who concocted the Holocaust for their own individual purposes.

However, denial must be examined distinctly because it is more stealthy and potent than some of the other more gutter-level theories used to promote acceptance of anti-Semitism and conspiracies. At face value, Holocaust denial provides a level of credibility to a vast array of less sophisticated extremists who can point to a resource base that includes a small cadre of seemingly credentialed scholars and apparently detailed objective research and documentation. Some deniers also expand their focus to the more broad issue of World War II so they do not appear to be fixated on and biased toward only the Holocaust.

The North American denial movement in particular is important for a variety of reasons. First, the most influential and far-reaching denial organizations are located in North America. Second, the U.S. legal system, unlike those of many other Western nations, provides complete First Amendment protection for both denial and hate speech as long as it does not threaten, defame an individual, financially defraud someone, or incite lawlessness (Levin, 1997). Third, North American denial now heavily relies on the Internet to promote itself worldwide to countries where it would otherwise be inaccessible.

After a brief examination of the Holocaust, I will examine the historical and contemporary ideas and relationships of some of the key figures alleged to have ties to the denial movement.

THE HOLOCAUST

The Holocaust was the largest and most recent coordinated genocidal attack against Jewry in world history.[1] At its conclusion, between five million and six million men, women, and children of Jewish ancestry or religious affiliation were killed by the Nazi regime (see Tables 15.1 and 15.2).

However, the Holocaust did not start spontaneously with bullets or gas chambers in the 1940s but rather with a carefully sculpted campaign of bigoted rhetoric and direct action that escalated throughout the 1930s.

The official Nazi propaganda bureaucracy orchestrated a systematic effort to make Jews the scapegoats for Germany's military, diplomatic, and economic defeats. Media campaigns labeled Jews rodents or vermin unfit for inclusion in an Aryan society. Nazi laws worked hand in glove with economic deprivation and social castigation to remove Jews from meaningful participation in German society.

On November 9, 1938, a 2-day attack of coordinated hate crimes committed by roving bands of Nazi mobs commenced across Germany and Austria, resulting in the death of

96 Jews and the illegitimate arrest of 30,000 more. Arson, vandalism, and looting destroyed thousands of Jewish businesses, homes, and synagogues. As correspondent Otto Tolishus reported in the *New York Times,* "by nightfall there was scarcely a Jewish shop, cafe, office or synagogue in the country that was not either wrecked, burned severely, or damaged." The combination of government complicity and the lack of any meaningful public condemnation in Germany of this initial violent salvo is widely regarded as a crucial turning point for the even greater atrocities that followed (Anti-Defamation League, 1991, p. 7; Berenbaum, 1993, p. 54).

The final stages of the Nazi atrocities involved the complete isolation of Jews from society. Victims were stripped of their belongings and forcibly removed from their homes. In violation of Judaic law, victims were tattooed with identification numbers on their forearms. They were transported in sealed railroad cattle cars to cramped, unsanitary slave labor camps ringed by electrified fences, guard towers, and armed soldiers.

Most of the Jewish deaths during the Nazi regime occurred at 17 major concentration camps spread across Eastern Europe from 1942 to 1945. Although most died from gassings involving either the insecticide Zyklon B or carbon monoxide, a smaller number died from shootings, beatings, anatomical experimentation, and disease (Berenbaum, 1993, p. 123; O'Brien & Palmer, 1993, p. 68).

These concentration camps were the most efficient killing machines ever developed in human history. Those who were infirm, elderly, or too young for forced labor were immediately segregated and executed on arrival. All others, except the few liberated by the Allies, were killed after a period of forced labor. At the conclusion of their periods of forced labor, most victims were stripped and herded into large enclosures where they faced painful deaths from asphyxiation caused by poison gas. Contrary to Judaic law, the bodies of the victims were cremated and reduced to ash in a mass collection of superheated, black, industrial iron ovens located on the premises.

In disputed Soviet territory, roaming Nazi Schutzstaffeln (SS) and police killing squads

Table 15.1   Estimated Numbers and Percentages of Jews Killed in the Holocaust

Country	Number of Jews Killed	Percentage of Jewish Population Killed
Poland	3,000,000	90
SSR Ukraine	900,000	60
Hungary	450,000	70
Romania	300,000	50
SSR Russia	245,000	65
Baltic states	228,000	90
Germany/Austria	210,000	90
Other	600,900	
Total	5,933,900	67

SOURCE: Dawidowicz, 1975, p. 402.
NOTE: SSR = Soviet Socialist Republic.

Table 15.2   Estimated Numbers of Jews Killed in the Holocaust

Nation	Number of Jews Killed
Poland	Up to 3,000,000
USSR	More than 700,000
Romania	270,000
Czechoslovakia	260,000
Hungary	More than 180,000
Lithuania	Up to 130,000
Other	560,000
Total	5,100,000

SOURCE: Hilberg, 1985, p. 1220.

called Einsatzgruppen summarily executed entire communities of Jews. Approximately 25% of the Jews killed during the Holocaust were actually executed by the Einsatzgruppen (Berenbaum, 1993, p. 95). Nearly all the Jews who failed to escape European countries under Nazi domination during that period perished in concentration camps. One third of the world's Jewish population and nearly all of mainland European Jewry was obliterated (Berenbaum, 1993, p. 95; O'Brien & Palmer, 1993, pp. 68–69). Others systematically executed included devout Christians, gypsies, gays, intellectuals, and the disabled.

Notwithstanding wartime chaos and the Nazis' intentional attempt to hide the nature and extent of their brutality, the Holocaust is one of the most thoroughly documented events in human history. After Hitler's initial proclamation in 1939 authorizing the extermination of the disabled, explicit official documentation of extermination was still extensive but involved the use of code words (Berenbaum, 1993, p. 65). After the liberation of the concentration camps by the Allies, various members of Congress, the military, survivors, and the press helped document the atrocities. The 1946 trials at Nuremberg presented exhaustive proof of the Nazis' extermination plan against European Jewry. During the trial, the defendants did not deny the atrocities but rather claimed that they were merely obeying commands. Among the damning evidence was Rudolf Hoess's admission to English interrogators on March 16, 1946, that he "personally arranged on orders received from Himmler in May 1941, the gassing of two million persons between June-July 1941 and the end of 1943, during which time I was Commandant of Auschwitz" (Stern, 1993, p. 69).

THE CHARACTERISTICS OF THE DENIAL MOVEMENT

Following on the heels of the Nazi regime's unsuccessful attempt to disguise its atrocities is a more modern attempt to deny them after the fact. According to Professor Robert Evans of Cambridge University, Holocaust deniers generally, in varying degrees, subscribe to all or some of the following beliefs (*Irving v. Penguin Books Ltd. and Lipstadt,* 2000, § 8.4):

> that Jews were not killed in gas chambers or at least not on any significant scale; the Nazis had no policy and made no systematic attempt to exterminate European Jewry and . . . such deaths as did occur were the consequence of individual excesses unauthorised at senior level; that the number of Jews murdered did not run into millions and . . . the true death toll was far lower; that the Holocaust is largely or entirely a myth invented during the war by Allied propagandists and sustained after the war by Jews in order to obtain financial support for the newly-created state of Israel.

According to Professor Deborah Lipstadt, a noted authority on denial,

> Modern Holocaust denial draws inspiration from a variety of sources. Among them are a legitimate historical tradition that was highly critical of government policies and believed that history was being used to justify those policies; an age-old nexus of conspiratorial scenarios that place a neat coherence on widely diverse developments; and hyperbolic critiques of government policies which, despite an initial connection to reality, became so extreme as to assume a quality of fantasy. (Lipstadt, 1993, p. 31)

In 1991, the leading academic group representing American history scholars, the American Historical Association, without dissent issued a declaration stating, "No serious historian questions that the Holocaust took place." In 1994, the organization further maintained that it would "not provide a forum for views that are, at best, a form of academic fraud" (Anti-Defamation League, 1994, pp. 8–9).

EARLY ROOTS AND FIGURES

The denial movement has its roots in Western Europe beginning in the post–World War II period. French fascist and anti-Semite Maurice Bardeche was the first public figure to challenge the veracity of photographic and documentary evidence of the concentration camps and to suggest that gas chambers had a hygienic rather than homicidal purpose (Lipstadt, 1993, p. 50). This approach would be co-opted by deniers in decades to come. Interestingly, another prominent early denier was fellow Frenchman Paul Rassinier, a concentration camp survivor and Nazi apologist who ultimately denied the existence of gas chambers (Lipstadt, 1993, pp. 51–65).

The two most notable early American deniers were Professors Harry Elmer Barnes and Austin App. App's career as a steadfast Holocaust denier was preceded by his efforts as a Nazi apologist during World War II. App, a Pennsylvania English professor, was known more for his nonacademic pursuits, namely his leadership in various German-American organizations and his frequent rhetorical attacks on Jews and the Holocaust "hoax" (Lipstadt, 1993, p. 92). App is credited with creating eight central axioms that are still used today by the main promoters of Holocaust denial. Some of the primary themes of these false axioms are as follows: the Nazis merely wanted Jews to emigrate; Jews were not gassed in Germany, and the alleged gas chambers at Auschwitz were used for other purposes; most of the Jews who were unaccounted for were under Soviet jurisdiction; most of the Jews who were killed by the Nazis were criminals, partisan enemies, or spies; Israel and others knowingly refuse to provide evidence for research because it would undermine Jewish efforts to persecute their perceived enemies; Jews and the media exploit the Holocaust without any evidence; Jewish exploitation is a myth to receive huge financial rewards; and disagreements between Jewish scholars themselves show that the Holocaust is a myth (Lipstadt, 1993, pp. 99–100).

The other influential early American denier was controversial scholar and Nazi apologist Harry Elmer Barnes. In contrast to App, Barnes was slightly less extreme and much better known in mainstream academic circles for his scholarship. At one time, Barnes's Western civilization texts were used at major American universities. Barnes went from being a staunchly pro-Allies partisan during World War I to an isolationist and Nazi sympathizer thereafter. Although his initial analysis of World War I was favorably received, his credibility in the scholarly world waned because of his acerbic attacks on other scholars, his embrace of conspiracy theories, and his dismissal of Nazi atrocities. An example of his apologist rhetoric is as follows:

> But not a day goes by without one or more sensational articles in the daily papers about the exaggerated National Socialist savagery which required our entry into the war; the leading weekly and monthly journals, especially *Look* and the *Saturday Evening Post* . . . never miss their quota of this lurid prose; the radio has it on the air daily; expensive moving pictures are devoted to it; not a week goes by without several inciting television programs revolving around this propaganda, and sensational books pour forth at frequent intervals. (Barnes, 1980)

Barnes (1980) also made the remarkable assertion that "there had been no systematic extermination in [the] camps" inside Nazi Germany. He further maintained that "the National Socialist 'final solution' was a plan for the deportation of all Jews in their control at the end of the war, Madagascar being one place considered." Despite his diminished academic stature, Barnes's position as a historian lent credibility to the variant new ideology.

Notwithstanding the foundational work of App and Barnes, the fledging denial movement of the 1950s and 1960s suffered because many Americans who lived through the World War II period simply found the deniers' portrayal of events inconsistent with their own memories. Furthermore, except for Barnes, most deniers lacked the sophistication to sculpt their message to reach beyond a small fringe of anti-Semites and those who believed that Germany was unfairly treated.

Still, for the notorious and influential anti-Semites of the day, Holocaust denial was an important part of their ideology. George Lincoln Rockwell, the head of the American Nazi Party, labeled the Holocaust a "monstrous and profitable fraud." He further maintained that the millions of exterminated Jews actually lived in luxury in the United States (Lipstadt, 1993, p. 66).

Another highly influential American Nazi, Gerald K. Smith, relied on Holocaust denial to legitimize anti-Semitism and rehabilitate the Third Reich. In an influential article titled "Into

the Valley of Death Rode the Six Million. Or Did They?" published in 1959 in his anti-Semitic periodical *The Cross and the Flag,* Smith repeated a common denial theme: that murdered European Jews were actually living comfortably in the United States (Lipstadt, 1993, p. 66).

Until his death in the 1970s, Smith was one of the nation's primary purveyors of outlandish, anti-Semitic conspiracy theories, including those involving the Holocaust. Although his primary avocation was anti-Semitism in general rather than denial specifically, Smith was particularly important to other deniers because of his long-lasting, substantial influence on other important bigoted American extremists.

Journalist and extremism expert James Ridgeway (1995, pp. 62–64) labeled Smith "the chief link between the fascism of the 1930s and the White resistance groups of today." Smith was formerly an active member of the American Nazi Silver Shirts. They were the American analogue of Hitler's Brown Shirts, and their proclaimed goal was to further the "work of Christ militant in the open." The Silver Shirts were led by William Pelley, a conspiracy theorist, Hitler fanatic, and virulent anti-Semite, who had accused President Herbert Hoover of being a puppet of international Jewish bankers who had crafted the Great Depression. The Silver Shirts peaked in the mid-1930s with about 15,000 members, but the advent of World War II and several high-profile espionage convictions resulted in the organization's dissolution.

Smith is considered a patriarch to succeeding generations of right-wing, racist extremists. He was initially a fundamentalist Christian minister. After he became an anti-Semitic populist, Smith was a close advisor to another controversial populist, Senator Huey Long of Louisiana, until the senator's rising political career abruptly ended in assassination in 1935. Smith, like his mentor Pelley, railed against the threat of an international Jewish conspiracy for most of his life. Among Smith's associates were fellow Silver Shirt Richard Butler, Christian Identity founder Wesley Swift, and the anti-Semitic, depression-era radio personality Father Charles Coughlin. Now 82 years old, Butler headed Aryan Nations, a notorious Christian

Identity hate group headquartered in Hayden Lake, Idaho, until a lawsuit forced its dissolution in September 2000. Christian Identity is the progeny of British Israelism, a 19th-century belief that White Christians are the real Israelites. Under traditional Identity theology, Jews are the spawn of Satan, and people of color are subhuman "mud people," the products of a faulty first creation. American Identity liturgy preaches that America is a divinely bestowed White Christian homeland to be won in an apocalyptic battle against the Jewish-dominated U.S. government, race traitors, and minorities. Because Identity's conspiratorial, anti-Semitic premises are coextensive with those present in Holocaust denial, it is not unusual to see Identity followers espouse denial as well (Levin, 1998, pp. 129–130; Schwartz, 1996, p. 17).

THE MODERN DENIAL MOVEMENT

By the 1970s, the denial movement had undergone a transformation, in part as a response to greater efforts in society to understand the Holocaust's meaning. The older, blatantly anti-Semitic tactics of deniers failed to appeal to a new generation of Americans who were less anti-Semitic than those of previous generations. As Lipstadt observed,

> Only in the 1970s, when they finally began to recognize the futility of trying to justify Nazi anti-Semitism, did deniers change their methods. They saw that from a tactical perspective, the proof of Nazi anti-Semitism was so clear that trying to deny it or justify it undermined their efforts to appear credible. (Lipstadt, 1993, p. 52)

Moreover, the Holocaust was given renewed attention in mainstream academia, popular culture, mass media, and theology. Schools and universities tackled the subject with renewed vigor, as did prime-time network television. The ascension of Pope John Paul II, who lived through the Holocaust era in Poland, marked the beginning of a period of both renewed theological examination of the Holocaust and interdenominational dialogue.

Denial promoters attempted the difficult task of diversifying their message for both mainstream and extremist audiences. In the extremist world, the new Ku Klux Klan (KKK) was smaller, less influential, and more willing to work together with Nazis against their common enemies. For the first time, these groups began appearing in public together and even used each other's hateful symbols. The younger, new, "Nazified" Klan did not share its previous leaders' distrust of neo-Nazis and were thus more susceptible to the denial message. An article in a 1980 issue of the Klan's periodical *Crusader* stated, "It's easy to understand why 'Holocaust' was shoved down the throats of the American people." It continued, "The one fly in this powerful Jewish ointment is the fact that many courageous men in academia are beginning to seriously question the Holocaust theory" ("Special Holocaust Edition," 1980, p. 1).

Thus, the old KKK of the 1950s and 1960s yielded to a new generation of bigots. Beginning in the 1970s, the KKK lost membership and influence to a growing number of extremist splinter groups, including Christian Identity, neo-Nazis, and antitax and antigovernment groups. Klan membership bounced from a low of about 1,100 in 1974 to about 11,000 in 1981 before settling at the current figure of about 5,000 (Baudouin, 1997, p. 42). A leadership void opened in the Klan as some older leaders died or retired. Furthermore, younger leaders were ineffective, in legal trouble, or defecting to other groups. California KKK leader Tom Metzger and Louisiana Klansman David Duke founded their own racist organizations, White Aryan Resistance and the National Association for the Advancement of White People, respectively. Texas Klan leader Louis Beam became involved with Butler's Aryan Nations and later the antigovernment "militia" movement. Although African Americans were still disdained, Jewish and antigovernment conspiracy theories once again took center stage among America's bigoted extremists. Against this backdrop, denial had a fertile, if somewhat disjointed, audience among domestic hate mongers. Newer racist figures such as Duke, Metzger, Identity promoter Richard Kelley Hoskins, and others vigorously promoted their own extreme versions of denial (Hoskins, 1990, pp. 311–313; Ku Klux Klan, 1980; Mann, 1995, p. 8).

MODERN DENIAL FIGURES

Arguably the most powerful purveyor of denial over the past quarter century is a shadowy and controversial figure named Willis Carto.

Carto is the founder of and main leader behind the Washington, D.C.–based extremist group Liberty Lobby and its offshoots the Noontide Press and the most well-known denial organization, the Institute for Historical Review (IHR). These entities are all part of myriad projects created by Carto to promote bigotry and extremism in North America. Although Carto is listed as the Liberty Lobby's treasurer, it is widely known that he is the dominant economic and political force behind the group. The IHR, a pseudoacademic entity devoted to "revisionism," was founded by Carto in 1979 but has been independent of him since a bitter 1993 dispute with staffers.

Carto was born on July 19, 1926, in Indiana but spent most of his early life in neighboring Ohio. During World War II, Carto served in the U.S. Army and subsequently obtained his undergraduate degree from Denison University. A former employee recently stated that Carto did not become "racially conscious" except (allegedly quoting Carto) "for the normal stuff, like hating niggers" until the early 1950s, when his position as a bill collector caused him to encounter Jews (Southern Poverty Law Center, 2000, p. 55). During that decade, Carto held a number of positions with assorted far-right-wing organizations, including the John Birch Society. By 1955, he had laid the groundwork for the precursor organization to what is now the anti-Semitic Liberty Lobby. Carto was heavily influenced by Frances Yockey, an unstable Hitler supporter who killed himself while serving time in prison for a fraud offense (Caplan, 1993, p. 5; Schwartz, 1996, pp. 21–26).

Carto founded another group in the late 1960s to support segregationist George Wallace's presidential bid and Yockey's Hitlerian philosophy among young people. The leadership of the group was eventually turned over to a rival neo-Nazi, Dr. William Pierce, a former close associate of George Lincoln Rockwell and another promoter of denial. The now independent, West Virginia–based National Alliance (NA) is the most prominent neo-Nazi group in the United States (Schwartz, 1996, pp. 21–26).

THE POPULIST PARTY

In 1983, Mr. Carto founded yet another offshoot group, a far-right political party called the Populist Party. The Populist Party is best known for its conspiracy theorist, bigoted newspaper, the *Nationalist Times,* and for its 1988 presidential candidate, former Klansman David Duke. Populist Party National Director Don Wassall wrote about the party's embrace of the extreme in the February 1987 issue of the *Nationalist Times:*

> The first factor is the healthy alienation one feels when he understands the essential corruption and unjustness of the present system, and through enlightenment is able to cut himself away from the values, mores, and thought patterns of the Establishment. . . . Many populists have realized that our disgust at present trends is not because of alienation per se, but because our souls rebel at the deliberate destruction of the highest, fairest most progressive way of life ever known to man. (quoted in *The Nationalist Times,* 1997)

In that same issue, commentator John Bryant explained the benefits of extremism:

> While the great mass will remain unmoved by events outside their immediate lives, and will thus continue to "carry on the world's work" no matter what the external situation, others—the so-called extremists—will be greatly moved. From this we see that "extremists," far from being "outside the mainstream" as they are generally depicted, are actually those who provide leadership to the social body, and in so doing direct the course of history. (Bryant, 1997)

Carto's long-time professional anti-Semitism and extremism are extensively documented in the United States. On June 25, 1986, the U.S. Supreme Court affirmed a trial court's dismissal of a defamation suit filed by Carto's Liberty Lobby against prominent American journalist Jack Anderson. Anderson had called Carto a "Hitler fan" and the "leading anti-Semite in the country." Carto's Liberty Lobby lost another defamation lawsuit against the *Wall Street Journal,* in which the group was referred to as the "far right anti-Semitic Liberty Lobby." The U.S. Court of Appeals for the District of Columbia, in a unanimous opinion affirming dismissal of the Liberty Lobby defamation suit, stated, "If the term anti-Semitic has a core factual meaning, then the truth of the description was proved here" (*Liberty Lobby, Inc. v. Dow Jones & Co.,* 1988).

U.S. Court of Appeals Judge Robert Bork observed in a footnote to the Court's holding,

> Since its inception, Liberty Lobby has been an outspoken, often vicious critic of Jewish groups and leaders, and of the United States domestic and foreign policy in regard to Jewish issues. In a letter to subscribers to *The Spotlight,* Liberty characterized "political Zionism" as the "most ruthless, wealthy, powerful and evil political force in the history of the Western world." *The Spotlight* has given extensive publicity to the fantastic claim that the Holocaust, the extermination of 6,000,000 Jews by Nazi Germany, never occurred. (*Liberty Lobby, Inc. v. Dow Jones & Co.,* 1988, Note 7)

In a 1981 *National Review* article, well-known conservative commentator William F. Buckley labeled Carto someone "who poisons the wells of polemical discourse" and his Liberty Lobby as a "hot bed of anti-Semitism" (quoted in Caplan, 1995, p. 39). Another prominent conservative, R. Emmet Tyrell, Jr., publisher of the *American Spectator,* wrote,

> Liberty Lobby was founded in the mid-1950s by Willis Carto. Carto remains to this day its mainspring and its devoted treasurer. It has always had a colorful collection of bigots and simpletons around it practicing the solitary vice of political extremism—namely, applying conspiracy theories to every vexatious public problem. (quoted in Caplan, 1995, pp. 39–40)

Two of the most prominent civil rights monitoring organizations in the United States, the Southern Poverty Law Center and the Anti-Defamation League, have chronicled Carto and his organizations for many years. Carto was described by the Anti-Defamation League, a Jewish civil rights organization, as "perhaps the most influential professional anti-Semite in the United States" (Schwartz, 1996, p. 21).

Carto's Liberty Lobby organization has distributed a variety of anti-Semitic and racist periodicals and publications over the decades. The most enduring of his publishing activities are the weekly bigoted newspaper the *Spotlight,* the publisher Noontide Press, and the pseudoacademic *Journal of Historical Review* (*JHR*). All Carto's publications promote denial, but *JHR* has devoted most of its content to denial related issues.

The *Spotlight*

The *Spotlight* is arguably the most circulated racist and conspiracy theorist periodical in the United States today. Its articles often relate to conspiracies concocted by Zionists and allegedly Jewish-controlled entities such as the Trilateral Commission, the Rockefeller family, bankers, the United Nations, the U.S. Federal Reserve Board, and communists. It also devotes space to offbeat news and unorthodox health remedies. Since its founding in 1975, the weekly *Spotlight* has slightly altered its methods. In the past, its bigotry and anti-Semitism were much more blatant and overt than they are today. A lengthy 1979 special supplement featured articles titled "Were Six Million Jews Exterminated?" and "Famous 'Gas Chamber Victims' Living Well," while another issue featured such headlines as "White Race Becoming an Endangered Species" and "Israel Murders Americans" (Caplan, 1995, p. 1).

Although still virulently anti-Semitic, today's *Spotlight* prefers anti-Semitic and "patriotic" code words as part of a probable strategy to increase circulation among militia ideologues in the United States who distrust the government. In recent years, the *Spotlight* has become a vehicle for a fringe subset of right-wing militia extremists who think America has been corrupted by Jews and international conspiracies aimed at instituting a one-world government. The newspaper regularly features advertisements involving extremists. Convicted Oklahoma City bomber Timothy McVeigh placed an advertisement for a rocket launcher using his alias, Tim Tuttle, in the August 16, 1993, issue. A recent article in the March 29, 1999, issue entitled "Have the Zionists Flexed

Too Much Muscle?" asks, "Want to make it in the Big Apple [New York]? Discover you're a Jew." The March 22, 1999, front page featured a photograph of Alan Greenspan under the headline "You Beat the Fed [Federal Reserve Board] Spying Reg." The February 8, 1993, issue urged its readers to "make hundreds of copies to hand out" of a front-page article from the previous week's issue entitled "Bush Said to Take Bribe to 'Get' Saddam Hussein." The article alleged that President George Bush escalated the Gulf War against Iraq in its final days because he was given an $80 million bribe by King Fahd of Saudi Arabia. The standoff at Waco, Texas, and the Central Intelligence Agency are also themes for the *Spotlight*.

The *Spotlight* has rallied around antigovernment extremists for years. The February 1, 1993, issue contained a two-page centerfold expose on the so-called cover-up of the "murder ... by police" of "political dissident" Gordon Kahl. Posse Comitatus adherent Gordon Kahl was a federal ex-convict who violated his parole on tax evasion charges. In 1983, Kahl murdered two federal marshals in North Dakota and later an Arkansas sheriff who attempted to arrest him before dying himself in a fire caused by a police smoke bomb hurled during a gun battle. The forerunner of the 1990s Freemen movement, Posse Comitatus is an anti-Semitic, antitax, extremist organization founded in 1969.

Noontide Press

Noontide Press is arguably the most well-established publishing house catering to American bigots and extremists. It has published and sold material promoting Holocaust denial, bigotry, and bomb making. Its selection includes works such as the anti-Semitic *Protocols of the Elders of Zion, International Jew,* and *Mein Kampf,* the Holocaust denial tract *The Hoax of the Twentieth Century,* and *The Road Back,* a terrorist manual with an ideological bent, popular among antigovernment militias in the United States (Noontide Press, 1983).

The Institute for Historical Review

Carto founded the IHR in 1979 and was extensively involved in its operations until a

putsch ousted him in 1993. The IHR is still the most prominent Holocaust denial organization in the United States. The inaugural issue of the IHR's slickly produced *JHR*, published in 1980, included the following articles by some of the leading figures in the denial movement:

- "The 'Holocaust' Put in Perspective," Austin App
- "The International 'Holocaust' Controversy," Arthur R. Butz
- Hellmut Diwald, *Geschichte der Deutschen* [History of the Germans], reviewed by Charles E. Weber
- "The Mechanics of Gassing," Robert Faurisson
- "Auschwitz Notebook: Certain Impossibilities of the 'Gerstein Statement,'" Ditlieb Felderer
- "Hidden Aspects of the Katyn Massacre: 'The Lost 10,000,'" Louis FitzGibbon
- "The Fake Photograph Problem," Udo Walendy

Shortly after its founding, an IHR stunt backfired on the organization in 1980 when it offered a $50,000 reward to anyone who could substantiate the position that the Holocaust took place. A Holocaust survivor who offered proof and was denied payment by the IHR sued. In 1985, the IHR was forced to pay $90,000 in a court-approved settlement that included an admission by the IHR that Jews were gassed by the Nazis and an apology to Holocaust survivors (Stern, 1993, p. 17).

Time subsequently proclaimed the IHR a "Holocaust denial group" and the denial-oriented *JHR* a "pseudointellectual journal" (Jaroff, 1993, p. 83). Although the IHR and its supporters promoted themselves as being victims of Jewish-sponsored censorship, most were regarded in academic and other circles as being a discredited cadre that manipulated history, generally for extremist political causes. With a scant few notable exceptions, the IHR's publications and conferences under scholarly veneer present an assortment of individuals whose objectivity and historical expertise are suspect.

A representative and pivotal IHR conference was the Fifth Annual International Revisionist Conference in Anaheim, California, in September 1983. The conference was opened and its theme set by Willis Carto, the IHR's founder. For Carto (1984), the IHR and its activities were not part of a scholarly process, but rather part of an overall political strategy to concoct certain "truths" to achieve extremist political goals at the expense of his enemies: "The purpose of history, as I see it, is to uncover the forces which move the pawns of the chess board of the world" (p. 10). Carto saw history less as an academic discipline than as a political and economic tool used by an alliance of evildoers to write truth in a way that promotes their own self-interest:

> The fact is that all great historical events in a so-called "democracy" are produced by an alliance. Alliances are the very warp and woof of politics. There is no one pressure group strong enough to dominate all of the others. (p. 11)

According to Carto, revisionists should not have "monodiabolistic theories" that fail to recognize "other devils" (p. 12). It is unnecessary to put any one "devil" in control, Carto contends, thus making it faulty to try "to prove all supercapitalists are Jews." Historians must instead concentrate on "the reality of the political alliance of Zionism, communism and supercapitalism" (p. 12).

Carto (1984) concludes,

> This Establishment false history not only omits and distorts facts which expose its own wickedness, greed, and corruption—it invents other facts to prove its righteousness. This thing is all-pervasive and can only be successfully combated by challenging it [at] all levels it is to be found. It is not merely a political problem, it has monetary and economic and social dimensions as well. (pp. 13–14)

William Lindsey's conference presentation offered a defense of Dr. Bruno Tesch, who was accused in a 1945 military trial of crimes against humanity for supplying poison gas to the concentration camps. Robert John spoke about the interplay of Jewish conspiracy, finance, and a "founding myth" relating to the Holocaust as a means for achieving Israeli statehood. Another speaker, Friedrich Berg, delivered an address called "Diesels, Gas, Wagons, and Zyklon B" in an attempt to deny the murder by asphyxiation of concentration camp prisoners. Previously, Berg had unsuccessfully petitioned the National Broadcasting Company for equal airtime to respond to the popular miniseries *Holocaust* (IHR Release, 1983). IHR Advisory Board member Wilhelm Staeglich, a German World War II veteran, talked about his book, *Der Auschwitz Mythos* [*The Auschwitz Myth*] and its negative reception in Germany, where it was banned. Staeglich's positions caused him to be removed from the judicial bench, and his alma mater voided his doctorate. Staeglich contends that he saw "well nourished" internees and no evidence of mass extermination (Staeglich, 1984, p. 47). James Martin gave a tribute lecture to another Holocaust denier named Francis Nielson. Martin Larson talked about how bankers, in anti-Semitic circles often a code word for Jews, perpetrated various crimes against Americans. H. Keith Thompson discussed how Hilter's immediate successor, Karl Dolentz, was allegedly "railroaded" at the Nuremberg trials (IHR Release).

Perhaps the most important speech at the conference was given by controversial British historian David Irving, innocuously titled "The Travails of a Transatlantic Writer." Irving, the son of a British naval officer, was born in England in 1938. After a 1-year scholarship to Imperial College, Irving became curious about British fascist Oswald Mosey. After a failed attempt to join the Royal Air Force, Irving moved to Germany to work at a steel factory, where he got the idea for a book on the Allied bombing of Dresden. That book, *The Destruction of Dresden*, became Irving's first best-seller in 1963. In 1977, Irving published *Hitler's War*, a controversial best-seller in England that attempted to rehabilitate Hitler. Irving, not yet a denier in 1977, wrote,

> the burden of guilt for the bloody and mindless massacre of the Jews rests on a large number of Germans, many of them alive today, and not just on one "mad dictator," whose order had to be obeyed without question. (Guttenplan, 2000, p. 50)

In April 1983, Irving gained notoriety for challenging the veracity of the bogus Hitler diaries, which had been accepted for publication by some of the world's most prominent newspapers and journals. Irving also gained publicity over a $1,000 offer he made to anyone able to produce evidence of Hitler's culpability for Jewish extermination (Guttenplan, 2000, pp. 48–51).

The Englishman's speech marked a milestone because it was the beginning of a lengthy, public, and increasingly close relationship between Irving, the IHR, and other North American extremists. Irving's (1984) conference speech was published in *JHR* under the title "On Contemporary History and Historiography."

Irving's speech (and subsequent *JHR* article) dwelled on four primary themes that he would repeat and intensify in years to come. These themes are as follows:

1. a defense and minimization of Hitler's role in anti-Semitic atrocities,

2. a minimization of anti-Semitic atrocities and ultimately a denial of the Holocaust,

3. anti-Semitic remarks and statements relating to Jewish conspiracies, a device commonly used by anti-Semites, and

4. a self-absorbed presentation of his role as a persecuted standard bearer for truth who has been targeted by Jews.

Irving (1984) summed up one position as "claiming that Adolf Hitler didn't know what was going on, in short, that Adolf Hitler didn't know about Auschwitz and so on" (p. 263).

Irving (1984) referred to Hitler as a man of "intellectual honesty" (p. 263). He further contended, "This evidence all goes to support my theory that probably the biggest friend the Jews had in the Third Reich, certainly when the war broke out, was Adolf Hitler" (pp. 274–275).

In his initial public statements to revisionists, Irving employs a variety of his trademark literary devices. Through muted disclaimers, attempts at humor, code words, and careful, lengthy sentence construction, he finesses a niche of independence from other, more crude and direct deniers. Irving's strategy also craftily and delicately concedes the existence of various less important contentious historical facts to shield his central suppositions. Although conceding that Hitler "uncorked the bottle" of anti-Semitism, in the following selection, Irving

(1984) employs many of his usual polemical tactics in defense of Hitler and the Nazi regime:

> There is a whole chain of evidence from 1938 right through to October 1943, possibly even later, indicating that Hitler was completely in the dark about anything that may have been going on. And I use the words very closely. I am sure you realize that I take a slightly different line from several people here. I would specify as follows: I would say I am satisfied in my own mind that in various locations Nazi criminals, acting probably without direct orders from above, did carry out liquidations of groups of people including Jews, gypsies, homosexuals, mentally incurable people and the rest. I am quite plain about that in my own mind. I can't prove it, I haven't gone into that, I haven't investigated that particular aspect of history from the documents I have seen. (p. 274)

In the next selection from the same speech, Irving (1984) employs a theme he would repeatedly and selectively use in his public talks in the years that followed. Often invoking code words, he paints Jews with both personal contempt and conspiratorial overtones while reveling in his own "persecution" by them:

> I'm always running into problems with my critics of a certain persuasion. It's not a battle of my choosing.
>
> I am not anti-Jewish, I am not anti-Semitic. I have employed Jewish staff: my lawyer, my attorney in London for the last 26 years has been the firm of Michael Rubinstein; they've lost every case they've fought for me but I've stood loyal to them. (p. 274)

Irving (1984) referred to communist aggressors of Hungary as follows:

> This Jewish camarilla, this four-headed monster which descended on the Hungarian people, bore down on them from Moscow, had been in Moscow throughout the war years and was imposed on them as the post war government, obtaining power by quite illegal and undemocratic means, and exercising that power with brutality and ruthlessness. (p. 266)

Irving ended his speech to a standing ovation (Kuesters, 1984, p. 318).

By October 1983, the IHR was selling tapes of Irving's conference lecture, noting, "Irving's powerful presence and masterful speaking ability make this one of the most exciting lectures the IHR has ever had the pleasure to put on tape" (Institute for Historical Review, 1983).

One day after Irving's talk, Robert Faurisson, a notorious hard-core denier, offered a vigorous retort to Irving's comparatively muted conclusions. Faurisson coupled his criticism with a challenge to Irving to examine and harden his denial convictions, a challenge to which Irving ended up succumbing. The IHR conference was the first time the two had met (Faurisson, 1984, p. 289).

Faurisson, a member of the IHR board and controversial former associate professor of literature at the University of Lyon, was the subject of two civil suits and one criminal suit in France relating to his denial work. After that conference, Faurisson faced two more denial-related criminal charges in France, with one resulting in conviction (Caplan, 1993, pp. 41–42).

He was also relieved of his teaching duties (Caplan, 1993, p. 319). On December 17, 1980, Faurisson summarized his position on a European radio station:

The alleged Hitler gas chambers and the alleged genocide of the Jews form one and the same historical lie, which has opened the way to a gigantic political financial hoax of which the principal beneficiaries are the State of Israel and International Zionism, and of which the principal victims are the German people—but not their leaders—and the Palestinians. (quoted in Caplan, 1993, p. 41)

At the IHR conference, Faurisson criticized Irving's position and asked him to more fully review the facts of the "alleged physical extermination of the Jews" (Faurisson, 1984, pp. 303–305).

Numerous other controversial figures have been associated with the IHR over the years. The late Dr. Revilo Oliver was a former classics professor from the University of Illinois with a record of bigotry dating back several decades with various groups. Oliver was a long-standing member of the *JHR* Advisory Board and also of the Advisory Board of the neo-Nazi National Youth Alliance during the 1970s. Later, he was a regular contributor to the racist magazine *Liberty Bell.* In the December 1993 issue of *Liberty Bell,* Oliver wrote,

The sheenies used pictures of the bodies of German civilians, killed when the Anglo-American barbarians incinerated Dresden, and claimed they were pictures of God's children who had been slain by the Germans in the great Holohoax. . . . Years ago, when a horde of vicious niggers accompanied by white degenerates swarmed into the small town of Selma, Alabama . . . many of our jewspapers printed a photograph that showed nasty white policeman in the act of brutalizing an oversized female nigger. . . . I shall not be astonished if a pack of pictures that show . . . Nazis . . . asphyxiating, gassing, incinerating, or vaporizing saintly Sheenies is discovered in the "secret archives of the KGB." (quoted in Caplan, 1993, pp. 72–73)

Oliver also was a contributor to *Racial Loyalty,* the monthly magazine of the now defunct White supremacist Church of the Creator (COTC). The original COTC was founded by anti-Semite and White supremacist Ben Klassen, who killed himself in 1993. The COTC's successor promotes "RAHOWA" (an acronym for "racial holy war") against a list of enemies including Christians, Jews, and non-White minorities. RAHOWA is now a common pledge among skinheads and other neo-Nazis in the United States. COTC followers have been implicated in various crimes, including the murder of an African American Gulf War veteran in 1991 and a murderous shooting spree in the Midwest in 1999 (Caplan, 1993; Schwartz, 1996, p. 198).

Another controversial IHR advisory member is Dr. Arthur Butz, an associate professor of electrical engineering and computer science at Northwestern University in Evanston, Illinois. He first joined the *JHR* Advisory Board in 1980. Although he lacks a background in history, his 1976 book *The Hoax of the Twentieth Century: The Case Against the Presumed Extermination of European Jewry* is a mainstay of the denial movement in the United States. It is published in the United States by the Noontide Press. In his book, Butz maintains that the trials at Nuremberg were corrupted by forgery and torture. He also refutes Jewish deaths in concentration camp gas chambers. Top university officials have criticized him for his promotion of Holocaust denial. Butz was a featured speaker at the Nation of Islam's 1985 convention in Chicago (Caplan, 1993; Institute for Historical Review, 1999a). The Nation of Islam distributes anti-Semitic materials that promote conspiracy theories and blame Jews for a variety of things including the slave trade (Stern, 1993, pp. 19–20).

Most of the IHR's executive staffers have controversial backgrounds as well, including some with deep ties to prominent hate groups. Racist "Lewis Brandon" was an early director of the IHR. Brandon was the alias of Northern Ireland expatriate extremist David McCalden. McCalden founded the British National Party in 1975 out of the racist, neo-Nazi National Front. His bigoted views caused the British Nationalist Union of Journalists to reject his membership. McCalden also served as office manager for Noontide Press (Caplan, 1993, pp. 16–18).

McCalden continued his Holocaust denial work after departing from the IHR in 1982 following a dispute with Willis Carto. In 1989, McCalden's anti-Semitic activities culminated with his arrest on charges of assault with a deadly weapon, property destruction, and civil rights violations after he went on a rampage at a Los Angeles synagogue. McCalden died in 1990 from AIDS-related complications (Caplan, 1993, pp. 16–18).

Longtime staff member Mark Weber eventually became the IHR's director. Weber received his masters in history from Indiana University. In 1978, he became the editor of the NA's magazine, the *National Vanguard*. During the 1980s, Weber continued his affiliation by serving as treasurer for the NA's racist Cosmotheist Church, an unsuccessful attempt to gain tax-free status as a religious organization for the NA. By 1979, Weber had become a frequent contributor to the *Spotlight*. Over the next several years, he became a fixture at the IHR, editing its newsletters, serving on its editorial board, and presiding over its annual conferences.

In 1987, Weber joined another revisionist, Bradley Smith, to codirect the new Committee for Open Debate on the Holocaust (CODOH). CODOH is best known for its regular attempts to buy revisionist advertisements in college newspapers across the United States. These attempts attract publicity even when college newspapers refuse to carry the advertisements. Smith subsequently handled media relations at the IHR. Previously, Smith had published his own denial newsletter, entitled *Prima Facie,* and marketed Holocaust denial talks to American radio stations (Anti-Defamation League, 1993).

After contributing articles to *JHR,* Weber was named its editor in 1992 and was later named director of the IHR. Following the internal IHR dispute with Carto in 1993, the newly independent IHR, Weber, and another one-time *JHR* editor Ted O'Keefe were defended by their former leader, William Pierce, against attacks from Carto in the neo-Nazi *National Alliance Bulletin* in March 1994:

> Among the new people at IHR were two former National Alliance members, Mark Weber and Ted O'Keefe. . . . Both he [Weber] and O'Keefe have their weaknesses, like all of us, but their competence, sincerity and commitment to the cause have never been in doubt. . . . The IHR is not controlled by the Jews, and we will continue to distribute books published by the IHR. . . . The IHR and the Alliance have a good working relationship. (National Alliance Bulletin, March 1994, p. 4)

The Southern Poverty Law Center (1999) observed that

> Pierce appears to have friends within the Institute for Historical Review. . . . Mark Weber, the editor of the IHR's Journal of Historical Review who has for years been in a legal battle with Carto of a multimillion-dollar bequest, was once a key Pierce protégé and staff member and now appears to be again drawing close to his mentor. (p. 12)

ZÜNDEL'S TRIAL

The most significant event in the denial movement in the late 1980s, however, involved German expatriate Ernst Christof Friedrich Zündel, arguably Canada's most famous neo-Nazi extremist and Holocaust denier. In 1988, Zündel faced a criminal retrial related to his denial activities. Zündel was awarded a retrial following an initial 1985 conviction for disseminating "false news" about the Holocaust and other subjects. His 1988 retrial was one of various trials, appeals, and retrials Zündel faced from the mid-1980s onward. His 1988 retrial related to his violation of a Canadian law, Criminal Code § 177, which outlawed the promotion of intolerance by spreading false information.

Canada, like various European countries, has criminalized Nazi propaganda and Holocaust denial under certain circumstances. In the early 1980s, before his false news trials, Zündel had been sanctioned by Canadian authorities for mailing illegal bigoted material to West Germany (Schwartz, 1996, pp. 172–175).

Zündel was born on April 24, 1939, in Calmbach in Germany's Black Forest. Zündel moved to Canada in 1957 (Schwartz, 1996). His company, Samisdat Publishers Ltd., is one of the world's primary producers and distributors of neo-Nazi and racist material. His Web site proclaims the following:

> It bears repeating: 1) Adolf Hitler never gave an order to eradicate the Jews; 2) there were no homicidal gas chambers in any German concentration camps set up specifically to kill human beings, and 3) not nearly as many Jews died or were killed as a result of German policies as is now widely and ever more viciously claimed. Jews were a vocal small minority in a global struggle involving many nationalities. It is deceptive to portray them as prime "victims" of a non-existent German genocidal policy.

Initially, Zündel penned materials under the pseudonym Christof Friedrich. His two most prominent works under that name were *UFO's: Nazi Secret Weapon* and *The Hitler We Loved and Why.* The latter work begins with the following explanation:

> At no time in recorded history has a leader, a wielder of power in human terms, not a popular figurehead or celebrity, had such a closeness to his followers, his entire people, as did Adolf Hitler. It can only be called a love relationship. . . . What other than love, can explain the fact that those who remember him love him still. (Friedrich & Thomson, 1977, p. 1)

Later in the book, Zündel writes,

> Hitler taught us Nature's Way of Preserving our race by having large families. Thus, Nature could

help us in the fulfillment of our racial destiny by selecting of us our best. So-called experts on human genetics claim today that man is not a part of Nature when it comes to heredity! Healthy animals can mate, but healthy humans are something else entirely. These "experts" . . . can no longer distinguish cripples from accomplished athletes and idiots from geniuses. (Friedrich & Thomson, 1977, p. 84)

Zündel also has long-standing ties to other prominent Nazi supporters. He was an editorial staff member of and contributor to the now defunct *American White Power Report,* published by West Virginia resident and native German George Dietz. Although Dietz no longer publishes the *American White Power Report,* he has for years published the blatantly anti-Semitic *Liberty Bell,* a monthly periodical. Zündel's material has been published in the United States by Dietz's White Power Publications, and his work has been promoted in *Liberty Bell* (Schwartz, 1996, pp. 172–176).

For Zündel's 1988 retrial, David Irving joined other prominent deniers Fred Leuchter, Mark Weber, Bradley Smith, and Robert Faurisson as defense experts. For Irving in particular, the trial became a pivotal moment. After his involvement with the trial, his denial views hardened, and his associations with extremists grew closer. *JHR* categorized Irving's "startling" testimony this way:

> He stunned the completely packed Toronto courtroom by announcing that he had changed his mind about the Holocaust story. During three days on the stand, he explained in detail why he now endorses the revisionist view of the extermination story. (Weber, 1993a, p. 5)

Although Zündel was convicted, the Canadian Supreme Court overturned the law on which his conviction was based in 1992 (Schwartz, 1996, pp. 172–176).

Irving credited Fred Leuchter, a Zündel defense "expert," with influencing him to take a hardened line on his views about the Holocaust:

> I was called as an expert witness as a historian to give evidence at the Ernst Zündel case, where Zündel's researchers showed me the Leuchter Report, the laboratory tests on the crematoria and

the gas chambers. As a person who, at the University in London studied chemistry and physics and the exact sciences, I knew that this was an exact result. There was no way around it. And suddenly all that I'd read in the archives clicked into place. You have to accept that, if there is no evidence anywhere in the archives that any gassings were going on; that if there's not one single German document that refers to the gassings of human beings—not one wartime German document; and if there is no reference anywhere in the German archives to anyone giving orders for the gassing of people, and if, on the other hand, the forensic tests of the laboratories, of the crematoria, and the gas chambers at Auschwitz and so on, show that there is no trace, no significant residue whatsoever of a cyanide compound, then this can only mean one thing. . . . Well, the answer is: we have been subjected to the biggest propaganda offensive that the human race has ever known. (Irving, 1990, p. 490)

Leuchter, of Malden, Massachusetts, graduated in 1964 from Boston University with a B.A. in history (Caplan, 1993, pp. 8–9; Institute for Historical Review, 1999b). Despite his lack of engineering credentials, Leuchter maintained a business that marketed execution devices to various states that imposed the death penalty. Despite the fact that Leuchter fervently denies revisionist leanings, he is a frequent speaker at IHR and similar functions and is a celebrity in the movement.

After the trial, both Irving and Zündel published the results of Leuchter's trial research as *The Leuchter Report: The End of a Myth,* despite the fact that the court rejected both the report and Leuchter's testimony. The report alleges that scientific evidence establishes that gassings did not take place at Nazi concentration camps. The discredited report is popular in the Holocaust denial movement, and one edition features a foreword by Irving.

Focal Point Publications (1989), Irving's publishing company, published *The Leuchter Report* in the United Kingdom. At a press conference in June 1989 to promote the report, Irving informed journalists that no extermination gas chambers existed at Auschwitz or Majdanek (Weber, 1993a, p. 5). His press release of June 23, 1989, stated,

Irving, controversial—but always right . . . has placed himself at the head of a growing band of historians, worldwide, who are now skeptical of the claim that at Auschwitz and the other camps that were "factories of death" in which millions of innocent people were systematically gassed to death.

Irving has a record of exposing fakes and swindles. . . . Now he is saying the same thing about the infamous "gas chambers" of Auschwitz, Treblinka and Majdanek. They did not exist—ever—except, perhaps, as the brainchild of Britain's brilliant wartime Psychological Warfare Executive (PWE). The tragic "eye-witness" testimony must have been to use no harsher word, mistaken. The survivors of Auschwitz are themselves living testimony to the absence of an extermination programme. (Irving, 1989)

Despite Leuchter's popularity within the denial movement, he faced various obstacles in his business when questions arose about his methods and credentials (Hinds, 1990, p. 1). According to a 1990 *Newsweek* article,

an Alabama assistant attorney general wrote a memo to colleagues in other states alleging that Leuchter was running a death-row shakedown scheme: if a state didn't purchase Leuchter's execution services, he would testify at the last minute for the condemned man that the state's death chamber might malfunction. (Kaplan, 1990, p. 64)

On June 11, 1990, Leuchter avoided a Massachusetts court trial and possible incarceration for illegally practicing engineering without a license by settling with authorities. Leuchter admitted that he lacked the credentials of an engineer but that he nevertheless represented himself as such to various states. He also agreed to stop circulating reports that identified him as an engineer, including *The Leuchter Report* (Daly, 1991, p. A6; Hart, 1990, p. 17).

THE 1990s

In the 1990s, Ernst Zündel continued his association with other controversial figures. The IHR gave Zündel its 1992 George Orwell Free Speech Award at around the same time he prevailed before the Canadian Supreme Court. In 1993, he collaborated on a denial video with another unusual denial figure named David Cole. Cole, a California atheist claiming Jewish ancestry, briefly became known as a rising star in the denial movement before leaving it. Zündel also extended his denial activities to the advertisements in college newspapers (Schwartz, 1996, p. 175). Zündel's supporters, David Irving, and the IHR also expanded denial promotion to the Internet.

Two legal disputes during the 1990s dealt severe blows to the denial movement. In the fall of 1993, Carto was ousted from the IHR in a dispute over dubious financial practices, his leadership, the proceeds from a multimillion-dollar bequest, and the editorial direction of *JHR*. Carto and other IHR employees were arrested after a fight broke out at the organization's offices, and Carto eventually lost a civil case for control of the company. In 1994, Carto formed a competing journal called the *Barnes Review* that focuses more directly on articles promoting racism, anti-Semitism, and conspiracy rather than on denial. Interestingly, Carto now believes that his former employees are part of a conspiracy against him orchestrated by Jews and the Church of Scientology (Kaufman, 1994, p. 6).

During the 1990s, Irving emerged as the most famous promoter in the denial movement and the most identifiable figure associated with the IHR, even though he had no official position with the group. In 1993, the IHR summed up their relationship this way: "The best selling British historian is also a good friend of the Institute [IHR] who has delighted attendees at four IHR conferences" (Weber, 1993b, p. 3). By the end of the decade, *JHR* had published more than two dozen articles by or about Irving. The IHR sold videotapes and audiotapes of his statements at IHR functions, an alleged documentary on his "persecution," and books he authored. His biography on the IHR Web site was the longest and the only one to feature a photograph. It reads, "as a kind of one-man IHR, David Irving has made highly successful speaking and promotional tours in West Germany, Canada, Australia, South Africa, the United States and other countries" (Institute for Historical Review, 1999c).

Irving's feelings were mutual:

I warmly endorse the IHR Journal: it is sincere, balanced, objective, and devoid of polemics. It presents the enemies of the truth with a serious opponent. Having said that, it is clear that I also have confidence in each and every member of the current team behind this achievement: long may they, and the Journal, stay unchanged—staunch and unflinching soldiers in what our brave comrade Robert Faurisson has called "this great adventure." (Institute for Historical Review, 1999c).

Although he vacillated on occasion, Irving's pronouncements became increasingly vitriolic and his associations more extreme:

[Calgary, Canada, September 29, 1991]: And I'm in deep trouble for saying this around the world, that the eye-witnesses in Auschwitz who claim, like Elie Wiesel to have seen the gassings going on and the subsequent cremations, that they are liars. . . . He's a liar. And so are the other eye-witnesses in Auschwitz who claim they saw gassings going on because there were no gas chambers in Auschwitz, as the forensic tests show. And I've got into a lot of trouble saying this.

And there are so many survivors of Auschwitz now, in fact, that I get very tasteless about all of this. I don't see any reason to be tasteful about Auschwitz. It's baloney, it's a legend. Once we admit the fact that it was a brutal slave labour camp and large numbers of people did die, as large numbers of innocent people died elsewhere in the War, why believe the rest of the baloney? I say quite tastelessly, in fact, that more women died on the back seat of Edward Kennedy's car at Chappaquiddick than ever died in a gas chamber in Auschwitz. [Laughter] Oh, you think that's tasteless, how about this? There are so many Auschwitz survivors going around, in fact the number increases as the years go past, which is biologically very odd to say the least. Because I'm going to form an Association of Auschwitz survivors, survivors of the Holocaust and other liars, or the A-S-S-H-O-L-S. (*Irving v. Penguin Books Ltd. and Lipstadt*, 2000, § 8.17)

[11th IHR Conference, October 11, 1992]: Now you probably know that I'm a Revisionist to a degree, but I'm not a Revisionist to the extent that I say that there were no murders of Jews. I think we have to accept that there were My Lai-type massacres where SS officers—the *Einsatzkommandos*—did machine-gun hundreds if not thousands of Jews into pits. On the Eastern Front, at Riga, at Minsk, and at other locations, this kind of thing did happen. Most of these SS officers—the gangsters that carried out the mass shootings—were, I think, acting from the meanest of motives. . . . And two days later the order comes back from Hitler, "These mass shootings have got to stop at once." So Hitler intervened to stop it. (*Irving v. Penguin Books Ltd. and Lipstadt*, 2000, § 8.19)

[Tampa, Florida, October 6, 1995]: Mrs. Altman, how much money have you made out of that tattoo since 1945? [Laughter] How much money have you coined for that bit of ink on your arm, which may indeed be real tattooed ink? . . . But I said to this man . . . "it's your own fault, everything that's happening to you. You were disliked, you people. You have been disliked for 3000 years. You have been disliked so much that you have been hounded from country to country from pogrom to purge, from purge back to pogrom. . . . It would never occur to you to look in the mirror and say 'why am I disliked, what is it that the rest of humanity doesn't like the Jewish people, to such an extent that they repeatedly put us through the grinder?'" And he went berserk, he said, "are you trying to say that we are responsible for Auschwitz, ourselves?" and I said, "well the short answer is 'yes.'" (*Irving v. Penguin Books Ltd. and Lipstadt*, 2000, § 8.17, § 9.5)

[September 17, 1994, diary entry in which Irving states that he recites the following song to his 9-month-old daughter during walks in the park] when half-breed children are wheeled past:

I am a Baby Aryan
Not Jewish or Sectarian
I have no plans to marry-an
Ape or Rastafarian

Bente [the girl's mother] is suitably shocked. (*Irving v. Penguin Books Ltd. and Lipstadt*, 2000, § 9.6)

In addition to the IHR, Irving's lecture sponsors in the United States included KKK Grand Dragon Kim Badynski, the NA, and other racists (Coalition for Human Dignity, p. 1; *Irving v. Penguin Books Ltd. and Lipstadt*, 2000, § 10.32; National Alliance, 1998).

One Irving lecture sponsor, the NA, is based in Hillsborough, West Virginia, and presided over by William Pierce. It is the largest and one of the most influential neo-Nazi groups in the United States. According to the Southern Poverty Law Center (1999), the group had 35 chapters across the United States at the end of 1998 (pp. 10–14). The NA has sponsored various presentations by Irving in the United States and promoted them in its publications and on a racist radio show. It has referred to Irving as a revisionist of "stature" whose statements are received "enthusiastically" (National Alliance, 1994, p. 8, 1995, pp. 4–5). The NA also has sales divisions that sell a variety of books, stickers, rock music CDs, and other memorabilia devoted to anti-Semitism, Hitler, and Nazism.

The NA grew out of a youth organization established by Willis Carto to support Hitlerian philosophy and the 1968 presidential candidacy of noted segregationist and former governor of Alabama George Wallace. In 1970, William Pierce left his position at the American Nazi Party to assist in the development of the National Youth Alliance. Pierce wrested control of the group from Carto. In 1971, hostilities between Pierce and Carto became public following a dispute over mailing lists.

Originally from Atlanta, Georgia, Pierce received his Ph.D. in physics in 1962 from the University of Colorado. Pierce taught physics at Oregon State University for 3 years. Following a short-lived scientific job, he joined the American Nazi Party under the stewardship of firebrand extremist George Lincoln Rockwell. Following Rockwell's murder in 1967 at the hands of another Nazi, Pierce became a leader in the American Nazi Party.

In 1974, 4 years after taking control of the organization, Pierce changed the name of the fledgling organization to the National Alliance. In 1978, the Internal Revenue Service rejected Pierce's attempt to gain tax-exempt status for the NA as an educational organization.

That same year, Pierce published *The Turner Diaries* under the pseudonym Andrew MacDonald. The book is a glorified fictional account of an antigovernment race war by a band of White supremacists who perpetrate atrocities against government officials, Jews, intellectuals, and Blacks. After Pierce proclaimed the novel a "handbook for White victory," American neo-Nazis embraced the book as a call to action.

A group of neo-Nazis including NA and Aryan Nations members from the Northwest organized the terrorist group The Order, named for the fictional protagonist criminal group featured in *The Turner Diaries*. The real group, led by the NA's Pacific Northwest leader, Robert Mathews, issued a "declaration of war" against American society that culminated in the largest armored car heist in American history and the assassination of a prominent antiracist radio personality, Alan Berg, in 1984.

In December 1984, Robert Mathews died in a fire ignited after a pitched battle with federal authorities in Washington State. The surviving Order members were captured and convicted on federal charges, although millions of dollars from the armored car heist were never recovered. It is alleged by authorities, but not proven, that the money was circulated among prominent American White supremacists. After the heist, Pierce paid $95,000 in cash for 346 acres of land in rural West Virginia for the new site of the NA's headquarters (Southern Poverty Law Center, 1999, p. 15).

Over the next several years, Pierce continued regular publication of newsletters, periodicals, and books. The March-April 1989 issue of the *National Vanguard* featured a full-page cover photo of Adolf Hitler and proclaimed him "the greatest man of our era." Pierce's follow-up racist novel was dedicated to Joseph Paul Franklin, a violent racist felon who assassinated two innocent Black joggers in Salt Lake City, Utah.

In 1995, Dr. Pierce received more publicity when it was revealed that convicted Oklahoma City bomber Timothy McVeigh was obsessed with *The Turner Diaries* and had made calls to the NA in the period before the bombing. Part of the book glorifies an antigovernment terrorist who blows up a federal building in an early morning truck bomb blast. In 1996, an NA member, Todd Vanbiber, was implicated in three bank robberies after police responded to an accidental bomb blast at his home. It is alleged in court testimony that Pierce was to have received at least $2,000 in proceeds from Vanbiber's criminal gang (Southern Poverty Law Center, 1999; Schwartz, 1996, pp. 106–112).

Pierce's promotion of a plan for a White revolution against Jews, minorities, and other enemies is illustrated by his statements in his January 1994 newsletter:

> The Christians who now talk about the impiety of opposing Jews because they are God's chosen people can be made to talk instead about the impiety of collaborating with Jews because they are the spawn of Satan. . . . All the homosexuals, racemixers, and hard-case collaborators in the country who are too far gone to be re-educated can be rounded up, packed into 10,000 or so railroad cattle cars, and eventually double-timed into an abandoned coal mine in a few days time. All of these people simply don't count, except as a mass of voters. . . . Those who speak against us now should be looked at as dead men—as men marching in lockstep toward their own graves—rather than as people to be feared or respected or given any consideration. (Pierce, 1994, p. 5)

It was also reported that Irving maintained a "long acquaintance" with racist David Duke, also a prominent denier. The *Atlantic Monthly* reported that Duke even received Irving's editorial assistance on the Holocaust and other issues for his 1998 racist tract *My Awakening* (Guttenplan, 2000, p. 64).

Irving's denial activities also resulted in banishment from or criminal charges by Austria, Germany, Canada, Italy, and other countries where Holocaust denial is punishable ("Nature of the Beast," 1997, p. 4). As his reputation became more extreme, he also became professionally isolated as an author and an expert. Among those he blamed for his professional decline was Emory University religious studies professor Deborah Lipstadt (1993), author of *Denying the Holocaust: The Growing Assault on Truth and Memory* (Guttenplan, 2000, p. 66).

In September 1996, Irving sued Lipstadt and her publisher, Penguin Books Ltd., maintaining that Lipstadt's book defamed him by labeling him a dangerous promoter of Holocaust denial who admired Adolf Hitler and who knowingly consorted with those who further Holocaust denial, anti-Semitism, and anti-Israel positions. Irving and the Holocaust denial movement were dealt a crushing blow in April 2000 when British judge Charles Grey ruled for the defendants, stating,

Irving, for his own ideological reasons persistently and deliberately misrepresented and manipulated historical evidence; that for the same reasons he has portrayed Hitler in an unwarrantedly favourable light, principally in relation to his attitude toward and responsibility for the treatment of the Jews; that he is an active Holocaust denier; that he is anti-Semitic and racist and that he associates with right wing extremists who promote neo-Nazism. (*Irving v. Penguin Books, Ltd. and Lipstadt*, 2000, § 13.167)

Although British defamation law puts a higher burden of proof on the defendant, it also allows the prevailing party to collect trial expenses. The loss likely means that Irving will be forced into bankruptcy because his opposition incurred more than £1 million in mounting their trial defense.

CONCLUSION

Despite the efforts of the IHR and Irving, the denial movement has failed to make any significant inroads into changing mainstream opinion. Notwithstanding the occasional flirtation of a public figure such as politician Pat Buchanan, a recent Gallup poll indicated that "only 2% said the Holocaust probably did not happen, and 1% said it definitely did not happen, while 83% said it definitely did happen and 13% said it probably occurred" (The Gallup Organization, 1999). However, denial has become a staple for American bigoted extremists, who regularly feature it in their literature. As Northeastern University sociology and criminology professor Jack Levin states,

Neo-Nazis, the Ku Klux Klan, unaffiliated white supremacists and Christian Identity followers now consistently feature denial in their propaganda as part of an attempt to further stereotype Jews as enemies and rob them of their victimization. It is no coincidence that alleged anti-Semitic hate crime felons like Bufford Furrow, Benjamin Smith, and the Williams brothers found inspiration in propaganda from the same extremist groups that keep Holocaust denial in their arsenal of hateful rhetoric. (J. Levin, personal communication, June 3, 2000)

Denial does not take place in a vacuum. It is a stealthy form of anti-Semitism that connects and strengthens a broad spectrum of extremists. The threat from the extremist denial movement in bastardizing history and fomenting hate does not involve an immediate victory today but rather an incremental one tomorrow, when the voices of the World War II generation finally fall silent.

NOTE

1. The term *holocaust* is defined by *Webster's New World Dictionary* as "great destruction of life, esp. by fire" and the Holocaust as "the killing of millions of European Jews by the Nazis."

REFERENCES

Anti-Defamation League. (1991). *The record: The Holocaust in history*. New York: Author.

Anti-Defamation League. (1993). *Mark Weber: A career in bigotry*. New York: Author.

Anti-Defamation League. (1994). *Holocaust denial: A pocket guide*. New York: Author.

Back, L., Keith, M., & Solomos, J. (1998). Racism on the internet. In J. Kaplan & T. Bjorgo (Eds.), *Nation and race: The developing Euro-American racist subculture*. Boston: Northeastern University Press.

Barnes, H. E. (1980). The public stake in revisionism. *Journal of Historical Review, 1*, 205–230.

Baudouin, R. (1997). *The Ku Klux Klan: A history of racism & violence* (5th ed.). Montgomery, AL: Southern Poverty Law Center.

Berenbaum, M. (1993). *The world must know: The history of the Holocaust as told in the United States Holocaust memorial museum*. New York: Little, Brown.

Caplan, M. (1993). *Hitler's apologists: The anti-Semitic propaganda of Holocaust "revisionism."* New York: Anti-Defamation League.

Caplan, M. (1995). *ADL research report: Liberty Lobby—Hate central*. New York: Anti Defamation League.

Carto, W. (1984). Toward history. *Journal of Historical Review, 5*, 7–14.

Coalition for Human Dignity. (1995, October 15). *Northwest Update* [Newsletter], p. 1.

Daly, C. (1991, June 18). Holocaust revisionist admits he is not engineer. *The Washington Post*, p. A6.

Dawidowicz, L. S. (1975). *The war against the Jews, 1933–1945.* New York: Holt, Rinehart & Winston.

Faurisson, R. (1984). A challenge to David Irving. *Journal of Historical Review, 5,* 289–306.

Focal Point Publications. (1989). *The Leuchter report: The first forensic examination of Auschwitz.* London: Author.

Friedrich, C., & Thomson, E. (1977). *The Hitler we loved and why.* Reedy, WV: White Power Publications.

The Gallup Organization. (1999, December 6). *The most important events of the century from the viewpoint of the people* [Online]. Available: http://www.gallup.com//poll/releases/pr991206.asp

Guttenplan, D. (2000, February). The Holocaust on trial. *Atlantic Monthly, 285,* 45–66.

Hart, J. (1990, October 1). Death machine builder under scrutiny for Nazi gas report. *The Boston Globe,* p. 17.

Hilberg, R. (1985). *The destruction of European Jews.* New York: Homes & Meier.

Hinds, M. D. (1990, October 13). Making execution humane (or can it be?). *The New York Times,* p. 1.

The History Place. (2000). *Holocaust timeline* [Online]. Available: http://www.historyplace.com/worldwar2/Holocaust/h-posen.htm

Hoskins, R. (1990). *Vigilantes of Christendom: The history of the Phineas priesthood.* Lynchburg: Virginia Publishing.

Institute for Historical Review. (1983, October). Yes—We are rewriting history [Advertisement]. *IHR Newsletter.*

Institute for Historical Review. (1999a). *Biography of Arthur Butz* [Online]. Available: http://www.ihr.org/bios/butz.html

Institute for Historical Review. (1999b). *Biography of David Irving* [Online]. Available: http://www.ihr.org/bios/irving.html

Institute for Historical Review. (1999c). *Biography of Fred Leuchter* [Online]. Available: http://www.ihr.org/bios/leuchter.html

Irving, D. (1984). On contemporary history and historiography. *Journal of Historical Review, 5,* 251–288.

Irving, D. (1989, June 23). *Press statement.* London: Focal Point Publications.

Irving, D. (1990). Battleship Auschwitz. *Journal of Historical Review, 10,* 490–508.

Irving v. Penguin Books Ltd. and Lipstadt, High Court of Justice, Queen's Bench Division 1996-I-1113 (April 11, 2000).

Jaroff, L. (1993, December 27). Debating the Holocaust: Those who deny the Nazi atrocities are finding a platform in college newspapers and raising a First Amendment ruckus. *Time,* 83.

Kaplan, D. (with Picker, L.). (1990, October 22). The executioner's handyman. *Newsweek,* 64.

Kaufman, R. (1994). *ADL special report: Embattled bigots: A split in the ranks of the Holocaust denial movement.* New York: Anti-Defamation League.

Kuesters, E. (1984). Encountering the revisionists. *Journal of Historical Review, 5,* 307–324.

Levin, B. (1997). A false dilemma: Civil rights v. civil liberties in the debate over hate & dissent. In E. Ward (Ed.), *The second American revolution: State rights, sovereignty, and power of the county* (pp. 29–61). Seattle: Peanut Butter Press.

Levin, B. (1998). The patriot movement: Past, present & future. In H. Kushner (Ed.), *The future of terrorism: Violence in the new millennium* (pp. 97–131). Thousand Oaks, CA: Sage.

Liberty Lobby, Inc. v. Dow Jones & Co., 838 F. 2d 1287, 1297 (D.C. Cir. 1988).

Lipstadt, D. (1993). *Denying the Holocaust: The growing assault on truth and memory.* New York: Penguin.

Mann, A. W. (1995, July). A day in the life of Tinki Rabinowitz. *WAR,* p. 8.

National Alliance. (1994, March). *National Alliance Bulletin,* p. 4.

National Alliance. (1995, October). Cleveland activity. *National Alliance Bulletin,* pp. 4–5.

National Alliance. (1998, August 23). *Irving to speak in Texas tomorrow* [Press release].

The Nationalist Times. (1997, May).

Nature of the beast. (1997, April 6). *Independent,* p. 4.

Neufeldt, V., & Sparks, A. (Eds.). (1990). *Webster's new world dictionary, third edition.* New York: Simon & Schuster/Warner Books.

Noontide Press. (1983). *Catalogue.* Costa Mesa, CA: Author.

O'Brien, J., & Palmer, M. (1993). *The state of religion atlas.* New York: Simon & Schuster.

Pierce, W. (1994, January). Reorienting ourselves for success. *National Alliance Bulletin,* p. 5.

Ridgeway, J. (1995). *Blood in the face.* New York: Thunder's Mouth.

Schwartz, A. M. (Ed.). (1996). *Danger: Extremism— The major vehicles and voices on America's far right fringe.* New York: Anti-Defamation League.

Southern Poverty Law Center. (1999, Winter). The alliance and its allies: Pierce builds bridges at home, abroad. *Intelligence Report, 93.*

Southern Poverty Law Center. (2000, Winter). "Paying the price": After four years as a player on the radical right, as Washington, D.C., consultant says he wants to come clean. *Intelligence Report, 97,* 53–56.

Special Holocaust edition. (1980, April). *Crusader.* Metairie, LA: Patriot Press.

Staeglich, W. (1984). "Der Auschwitz mythos": A book and its fate in the German Federal Republic. *Journal of Historical Review, 5,* 47–68.

Stern, K. (1993). *Holocaust denial.* New York: American Jewish Committee.

Weber, M. (1993a). David Irving: Intrepid battler. *Journal of Historical Review, 13,* 4–6.

Weber, M. (1993b). From the editor: A new journal and a new era. *Journal of Historical Review, 13,* 2–3.

The Zündelsite. (1999, May 1). Mission statement [Online]. Available: http://www.zundelsite.org/english/misc/mission.html

QUESTIONS

1. What purposes do revisionist interpretations of history serve for extremist groups?

2. What was the impact of the Nazi extermination program on Jews and others targeted by the Nazis?

3. What are the eight axioms created by Austin App that are used by Holocaust deniers in attempts to discredit evidence of the Holocaust?

4. What is the Institute for Historical Review? What is the Liberty Lobby? What happened when the IHR issued a cash reward to anyone who offered proof of the Holocaust?

5. How have the propaganda efforts of the hate organizations described in this article changed over time as they attempted to increase their credibility and mainstream appeal?

6. What are some examples of the ways Holocaust deniers attempt to use history as a political tool to achieve their goals?

7. In the United States, false information such as Holocaust denial claims constitute an example of free speech protected by the First Amendment, whereas many European countries censor such material. Should such false information be protected? Why or why not?

8. Describe some examples of the claims that Holocaust deniers have made in their attempts to distort historical facts. What are some of the most extreme denial claims, in your view?

9. Considering the behavior and speech of key Holocaust denial figures, do you believe that they pose a significant terrorist threat?

10. What is the impact of the Holocaust denial movement?

11. What threat does the denial movement pose for the future in terms of societal understanding of history?

12. How much influence do you think the Holocaust denial movement may have had on mainstream public opinions?

16

WHITE BOYS TO TERRORIST MEN

Target Recruitment of Nazi Skinheads

RANDY BLAZAK

Youths who feel isolated, alienated, and threatened by a perceived loss of status in a changing world are susceptible to recruitment by hate groups. Blazak contends that this illustrates Durkheim's concept of "anomie" in action and describes how racist skinheads cultivate hate in such alienated youths. Insecurity in anomic youths translates into terror for those subjected to hate violence by racist skinhead recruits. The article raises an important question: Are some of the young people navigating complex social changes in today's world particularly susceptible to hate group recruitment?

Skinheads in Denver murder a police officer and a Black man waiting for a bus, critically injuring a White woman who tried to help the victim. A Black Texan is dragged to his death behind a truck driven by three members of the Aryan Brotherhood. A member of the World Church of the Creator goes on a shooting spree in Illinois and Indiana, killing two minorities and wounding nine others. The late 1990s saw its share of violence committed by members of hate groups.

According to the Southern Poverty Law Center's (SPLC) (2000a) *Intelligence Report,* the number of hate groups may be on the decline, but their activity is not. "Official" data on hate crimes are becoming more reliable since the implementation of the 1990 Hate Crimes Statistics Acts, but there are still problems. Many police departments are not trained to identify hate crimes or, for various reasons, may choose not to report acts as hate crimes. Several states have no hate crime laws, and those that do have varying definitions of who should be included in the laws' "protected class." Should women, homosexuals, the disabled, and others be protected by hate crime laws? And, of course, there is a great reluctance by many to report hate crimes.

According to the Federal Bureau of Investigation (FBI) data that we do have, most

EDITORS' NOTE: From Blazak, R. (2001). White Boys to Terrorist Men: Target Recruitment of Nazi Skinheads. *American Behavioral Scientist, 44*(6), 982-1000. © 2001 Sage Publications. Used with permission.

hate crimes are committed by young people. In their research, Levin and McDevitt (1993) classified 60% of hate criminals as "youthful thrill seekers." Some of these youth are members of hate groups; most are not. That hate crimes tend to be more vicious and injurious than normal violent crimes only adds to the destructive impact they have on the community. As with other forms of crime, most youthful hate criminals will "age out" of their criminality. But, some will be brought into the fray of terrorist hate groups. These groups may perpetrate or encourage other hate crimes, but more importantly, they create a climate where bias-motivated crime is justified. To groups such as the Aryan Nations, the Ku Klux Klan (KKK, Klan), and the World Church of the Creator, the hate criminal is a hero, doing God's work to save the White race from extinction.

The process by which young people are brought into the shadowy world of White supremacy must be researched for two primary reasons. First, we must be able to identify the macro-level social dynamics that create environments conducive to hate. Hate group membership ebbs and flows. Although some of this may be due to law enforcement policing and the courtroom challenges of legal groups such as the SPLC, it must also be related to shifts in social dynamics, including the economy, immigration, and changes in gender roles. Second, by understanding the root explanations behind hate group recruitment, strategies can be developed to combat youth involvement in adult terrorist groups. Prevention programs on the local level (education, mentoring, etc.) as well as the global level (multicultural curriculums, youth employment, etc.) can feed from the findings of sociological research.

✔ The distinction between hate crimes and hate group activity is an important one. Although official data reflect increases and decreases in their activity, hate groups continue to operate. The SPLC (2000b) reports that in 1998, there were 537 identifiable active hate groups, but in 1999, there were only 457, 80 fewer. Understanding this trend is crucial because a significant part of change is related to the development of more sophisticated recruitment tactics. The reduction in the number of hate groups relates to five key trends:

1. Consolidation: Like corporations in merger frenzy, small hate groups are being swallowed up by larger ones. A Michigan chapter of the neo-Nazi group the American Nationalist Party joined the National Alliance. The New Jersey Confederate Knights merged with the Alabama-based America's Empire of the KKK. Even skinheads who have been fiercely defensive of their autonomy are being brought back into adult racist groups. Most notable is the Hammerskin Nation, which has moved beyond its Texas home to recruit skinheads from Oregon to Russia. According to the SPLC, the group increased in size by 70% in 1999. According to the Center's *Intelligence Report* director, Joseph Roy, the situation is deeply troubling: "Many of the less active groups have joined forces with much more serious players. There is strong evidence that far more people are now in really hard-lined groups like the National Alliance and the Hammerskin Nation" (Southern Poverty Law Center, 2000b, p. 7).

2. Web sites: More than 300 hate sites on the Web allow hate groups to spread their messages to those who might not ever travel to a rally or clandestine meeting. But, Web sites also allow individuals not associated with groups to spread their ideologies. The SPLC reports that 47% of hate sites are not affiliated with active hate groups. But, these sites may be gateways into established hate groups because most provide links to them; just a click away.

3. Leaderless resistance: On October 23, 1992, Christian Identity leader Pete Peters launched the idea of the leaderless resistance into the extreme right. At a meeting of White supremacists who desired to respond to the siege at Ruby Ridge, Idaho, earlier that year, Peters argued that the Klan, militias, and others should move away from the hierarchical organizations of the past because of their tendency to be infiltrated by law enforcement agents. Small cells of terrorists who shared an ideology and agenda (as laid out in *The Turner Diaries,* a fictional manual for starting a race war) would avoid government policing. Timothy McVeigh and Terry Nichols, the 1995 Oklahoma City bombers, represent Peters's concept. As some right-wing extremists consolidate into larger

hate groups, others (perhaps more) join no groups, only the vague leaderless resistance. This includes skinheads. Whereas some merge into the Hammerskin Nation, others claim no affiliation, making it hard for law enforcement and community groups to monitor nameless, small groups of skinheads.

4. Mainstream politics: It should be acknowledged that many right-wing extremists may have found homes in mainstream right-wing politics. Encouraged by the election to the Louisiana State legislature as a Republican of David Duke, the leader of the National Association for the Advancement of White People, others have taken off their Klan hoods and played the mainstream game. Successful campaigns against affirmative action in California, Washington, and Texas, the power of the gun lobby and the antihomosexual lobby, and sizable campaigns to preserve the Confederate battle flag's place in Southern society give right-wingers legitimate opportunities to advance their causes.

5. Recruitment: Like gangs and cults, hate groups have a high turnover rate. Research shows that most members stay in hate groups only as long as the groups meet their personal needs (Ezekial, 1995). Hate groups play the role of subcultural "problem solver" (Cohen, 1955). When they no longer appear to be solving the problem, members move on. Although many hate groups may find new members from the mainstream right-wing community, this research focuses on how skinhead groups specifically target young, "anomic" people. Both skinhead and nonskinhead groups are increasingly skilled in identifying "strained" populations that have gone through some type of ascribed status crisis ranging from factory layoffs to interracial schoolyard fights. Instead of the general recruitment of Whites in the past, skinheads and similar groups now target specific populations from which they are most likely to successfully recruit new members.

These five trends create a three-level environment conducive to right-wing terrorism: (a) stronger, consolidated hate groups with chapters in many states and even nations; (b) an unknown number of leaderless cells that share much of the hate groups' philosophy along with a mandate that supports violence against representatives of the government, abortion, and multiculturalism; and (c) a populace in which bigoted, antigovernment agendas are reinforced and supported. An example of the relationship between these three levels is the case of Eric Rudolph. Rudolph shared the ideology of the large Christian Identity movement. Identity Christians believe that multiculturalism, abortion, and homosexuality are promoted by an evil, Jewish power known generally as the New World Order. The FBI believes that Rudolph led a cell called the Army of God, which was responsible for bombings at the 1996 Olympics, an abortion clinic, and a lesbian bar. In 1997, Rudolph was seen fleeing into the dense North Carolina woods. Among the mainstream people of that region, there is much support for Rudolph, who has become a local folk hero.

SKINHEADS AS TERRORISTS

Skinheads have been affiliated with hate groups in America for more than 15 years. Their roots as a subculture go back to the mid-1960s, when they emerged in London as a working-class response to the hippie phenomenon. Not initially racists (in fact, skinhead style draws heavily from Black "rude boys," Jamaican immigrants), skinheads were reactionary, resenting social forces representing social change (Hebdige, 1979). Skinheads first appeared as a reactionary element of the American punk rock scene, but it was not until the mid-1980s that they began to be recruited by more established racist groups (Blazak, 1995).

As groups such as the Klan, the White Aryan Resistance (WAR), and the New Order (a Nazi group) increased their recruitment of skinheads, skinhead violence also rose. Hundreds of acts of violence and destruction in the late 1980s were attributed to skinhead groups. One of the better known cases was the murder of Mulugeta Seraw in Portland, Oregon, in 1988. The day after an airing of an episode of *Geraldo* that featured skinheads and Nazis violently rioting on TV, Seraw was killed by three skinheads. The skinheads claimed membership in a Portland hate group known as East Side White Pride. In a

1990 civil trial, SPLC founder Morris Dees successfully proved that East Side White Pride members had been recruited by the California-based WAR to become foot soldiers in a violent race war. The trial ended with a $12.5 million judgment against WAR leader Tom Metzger and his son John, head of the Aryan Youth Movement.

Although the judgment may have temporarily sidelined WAR from recruiting skinheads (Metzger's Web site, http://www.resist.com, is now one of the most popular sources of hate propaganda on the Web), skinhead violence continued well into the 1990s. Some of the most violent acts made headlines. In 1990, two Houston, Texas, skinheads killed a Vietnamese teenager whose dying words were "Please stop. I'm sorry I ever came to your country. God forgive me!" (SPLC, 2000a, p. 11). In 1992, three skinheads recruited by Bill Riccio's Aryan National Front stabbed to death a homeless Black man. Two Aryan Nations skinheads killed their parents and brother in 1995 in Allentown, Pennsylvania. Their motivation was that their parents were Jehovah's Witnesses. In 1996, a dozen Nazi skinheads stabbed to death a youth who had ejected them from a party. Denver, Colorado, saw a wave of skinhead violence in 1997 that included two murders. There have also been numerous synagogue and church attacks, random bombings, and malicious harassment cases that police attribute to skinhead groups.

Although the number of skinhead groups may have peaked in 1991, when the SPLC counted 144 groups, they may be more active now in consolidated groups such as the Hammerskins or in unaffiliated small cells. Many racist skinheads share a belief in an inevitable race war in America. Although this race war will lead to an "autonomous Aryan homeland in the Northwest" (as a Volksfront newsletter describes it), the ultimate goal is an America that has been ethnically cleansed of all enemies, including White race traitors. This civil war may require some "sparking," as described in *The Turner Diaries* (which was written by National Alliance leader William Pierce). Acts of violence and terror by skinheads are viewed within the movement as important in speeding the polarization of the public into racial "tribes."

The relatively infrequent attacks by racist skinheads (compared with economically or interpersonally motivated crimes) should not distract observers from the increase in hate group activity. Effective policing on the federal and local levels as well as the willingness of prosecutors to test new hate crime laws may have discouraged some violence. But, recruitment and consolidation, along with the spread of unaffiliated cells, are part of racists' vision of forming armies in preparation for the prophesied racial civil war. This "drawing up of sides" is reflected in a recent statement on the Hammerskin Nation Web site:

> Skinheads are meant to be a visible opposition on the street, but when you're out there, try to earn respect rather than contempt. Even those of us who aren't so visible anymore matter, because people still know who we are. Only with people's respect will we ever gain any public sympathy, which will lead us toward our goals. It takes the few brave souls to lead before the "sheep" will follow. I am reminded of some of the "outlaw" motorcycle clubs who calls themselves "1 percenters" because they are the few who have the courage to "live on the edge" and defy the law. I say Hammerskins are like 1 percenters, except that we are forced to the edge. We are sane people in an insane world. Let us bring that edge inward until our values, morals, honor and glory are the only law and we have won back the minds, hearts and souls of our people! (Hyde, 2000)

STRAIN THEORY AND HATE GROUP RECRUITMENT

From Durkheim and Merton to Passas and Agnew (1997), it has been argued that the effects of macro-level anomie can manifest on the micro level as criminal behavior. Existing as a sense of "normlessness" or as a disjunction between aspirations and expectations, this state is reflected in a form of psychological distress or strain. Whether it is Agnew's (1992) general strain theory or Messner and Rosenfeld's (1994) institutional anomie theory, the human face of strain is the same: frustration, anger, and a need to resolve some perceived inequity.

Much has been written about how strained boys and men end up in gangs as a way to address their blocked goal attainment (Cohen, 1955; Cloward & Ohlin, 1960). Not as evident are data that suggest that strained youth are actually targeted for recruitment by delinquent subcultures. This article explores research on racist skinhead groups and their recruitment targets. Although the criminal activity of skinheads is often seen as a phenomenon separate from street gangs (Blazak, 1998; Hamm, 1993; Levin & McDevitt, 1993), criminologists have referred to skinhead groups as "White gangs." Increasingly, local police departments are including skinheads in their gang-monitoring activities.

Strain as a Red Flag

What does strain look like? How can one tell if someone is experiencing anomie? Agnew (1985) discussed the presentation of "life hassles" coming from the presentation of negative stimuli and the removal of positively valued stimuli as well as blocked opportunities. This "negative affect" generates anger and frustration, and crime becomes a corrective action. Cohen (1955) researched how strained individuals search out subcultural solutions (i.e., gangs) to resolve their strain but not how gangs search out strained individuals to recruit. On the street, strain can manifest in the values seen in Cohen's delinquent boys: nonutilitarianism, maliciousness, and negativism.

This "reaction formation" to dominant conforming values can appear as antisocial behavior (e.g., fighting or vandalism) before the strained individual finds his or her collective solution in either a nonutilitarian gang or, if he or she has the opportunity, in a more goal-oriented gang (Cloward & Ohlin, 1960). Regardless of the path, the individual is exhibiting behavior reflective of his or her psychic stress. Researchers have found evidence of this desire for a group to relieve individual alienation. In Wooden and Blazak's (2000) work on skinheads, graffiti taggers, and skaters, the authors identify anomie as a motivating factor for joining deviant groups.

Although the musical tastes and styles of dress differ from group to group, these adolescents share one commonalty: They are experiencing what sociologists refer to as anomie, a

sense of rootlessness or normlessness. In part, to combat this state, they join groups and assume identities that, for many, become all encompassing, a form of a "master status," the core way of defining themselves. And, embracing or identifying with a specific group—whether a "metaler" clique, a stoner gang, or a tagger crew—provides these "tearaway" teenagers with a way of reducing their anxiety and alienation (Wooden & Blazak, 2000, p. 12).

The logic of anomie theory is that the individual experiences strain, which then leads him or her to group delinquency. Much of the research focuses on the group delinquency (Cloward & Ohlin, 1960) or the presence of strain from noxious stimuli (Agnew, 1985) but not necessarily on the precriminal expressions of strain. There is an assumption that the anomic person is flailing around, frustrated, angry, and inching toward the "criminal solution." High school counselors are skilled at identifying these "at-risk" youth. They exhibit certain characteristics of alienation including maliciousness, rebellious dress, and antisocial attitudes, all of which are red flags.

Other red flags can be the social-structural conditions that create anomie. The disjunction between goals and legitimate opportunities or between aspirations and expectations can take the form of economic blockage, as described in the classic strain theory of Cohen (1955); in more micro-level problems, as described in Agnew's general strain theory (1985); or in the institutional overemphasis on economic success, as described in Messner and Rosenfeld's (1994) institutional anomie theory. In each of these instances, the individual wants something—a car, popularity, wealth—and society has not regulated the means to attain these positively valued goals. There is also evidence that cultural status (Blazak, 1995) and masculinity (Messerchmidt, 1993) may represent goals that when blocked lead to criminal activity. Gangs, for example, may use the lack of opportunity for material wealth and legitimate performances of masculinity in poor urban areas to offer a group solution for those strained boys who need to "be a man and make money."

With regard to the racist skinheads, the negative stimuli can be represented in the presence of threats to class and ascribed status. Skinhead belief is based on the traditional cultural superiority of heterosexual, White men; therefore, anything that could undermine that group's dominance represents a threat. Antiracism, gay rights, feminism, and multiculturalism are all perceived as enemies of the status quo. Therefore, in places where these concepts are a part of the dominant discourse, it can be assumed that a certain segment of heterosexual White men will feel a great deal of strain as their traditional picture of the world and their place in it is threatened.

I theorize that both identifiers of strain are used by skinheads to target recruits. The presence of structural conditions that represent threats to ascribed status first attract the attention of the group to a specific population. An example would be a publicized debate in a school over a gay student group. Second, within that population, strained individuals who exhibit at-risk behavior are purposely recruited. This could be a boy with a reputation for fighting or who dresses differently from the general student population. The skinhead group is then presented as a collective problem solver to the boy (Blazak, 1998). This tactic is evident in the following passage from a Nazi group's *Action Program for Aryan Skinheads:*

> Recruit Skins or covert activists from Punk Rockers and from the group of disaffected White kids who feel "left out," isolated, unpopular, or on the fringe or margin of things at school (outsiders, loners). There are some very effective people among such kids, and working with Nazi skinheads will give them a sense of accomplishment, attainment, success, and belonging. In recruiting, proceed from such "outsiders," inwards toward the mainstream, conventional, average students. (New Order, 1989, p. 6)

Groups such as the New Order teach their recruits the vivid philosophy of White supremacy, including the belief that the United States is manipulated by foreign Jewish interests collectively known as the Zionist Occupation Government (ZOG). With this conspiracy theory, the strain is "explained" (e.g., the Jews are behind multicultural curricula), and the solution is presented: hate crimes and race war.

I hypothesize that racist skinhead groups use these red flags of strain to guide their recruiting activity. Threats to the traditional status quo or "cultural anomie" attract the groups, which then seek out strained individuals. The threats exist in four categories:

1. Threats to ethnic or racial status
   - growth in the minority student population
   - minority student organizations or events
   - shifts to multicultural curricula
   - racial conflict in which the institutions appear to support the minority group

2. Threats to gender status
   - conflict over female participation in male activities
   - feminist activist groups
   - antisexual violence events or programs

3. Threats to heterosexual status
   - sexual minority organizations
   - gay pride events
   - inclusiveness movements or sponsored dialogue

4. Threats to economic status
   - factory layoffs
   - large employer downsizing
   - high competition for manual labor or service sector jobs

The most common scenario involves the transition in secondary schools from Eurocentric curricula to inclusive, multicultural curricula. Here, the representations of ethnic Whites as the "heroes" of civilization (where every month is "White History Month") are replaced with a more balanced picture of social history that presents non-White perspectives that may be seen as vilifying White participation in society. Especially when reluctantly presented by "old-school" White teachers, this new curriculum may be portrayed as attempting to create "White guilt" over issues such as slavery, colonialism, and segregation. A 15-year-old boy, born in the 1980s, without the benefit of firsthand experience of his country's overtly racist past, may wonder why he has been pegged as the bad guy in history. He notices Black, Hispanic, and Asian student groups flourishing, yet he is branded a racist if he asks why there is no White student group. He is in the middle of cultural change without the tools to navigate it. This condition of anomie is exactly what racist groups are looking for.

METHOD

The data to support the theory that culturally strained youth end up in skinhead groups were collected in a 7-year ethnographic study (Blazak, 1995) in which it was found that members of skinhead groups had experienced threats to economic status (usually, their parents had experienced downward mobility), racial status (through the increased integration of White suburbs), gender status (represented in the perceived end of the ability to be "real men" because of feminism), and heterosexual status (fostered by the idea that the gay rights movement was destroying the traditional family). Data on the recruiting goals of the skinheads were retrieved more through guided conversations and anecdotal experiences.

The ethnographic study took place from 1987 to 1995. During this time, participant observation projects were run with groups of skinheads in places such as Orlando, Florida; Atlanta, Georgia; Chicago; and several other cities. Additional research was done firsthand with groups in London and Eastern Europe. Additionally, 65 face-to-face interviews were conducted. The focus of these interviews was on the subjects' own experiences with strain, but many discussions touched on the recruiting practices of the various groups. Most of this information was logged in field notes or on a voice recorder.

After the conclusion of the ethnographic study, a new series of interviews began through a grassroots organization called Oregon Spotlight. Oregon Spotlight monitors hate-group activity in the state of Oregon, counsels convicted hate crime offenders, and runs presentations for middle and high school students on preventing hate crimes. Through Oregon Spotlight, interviews have been conducted with skinhead recruiters as well as with secondary school youth in focus groups on the experience of being recruited. Additional information from school counselors served to verify claims of recruitment activity.

Based on the 65 formal interviews, approximately 200 informal interviews from the ethnographic study, the interview with three skinhead recruiters through Oregon Spotlight, and the additional data from approximately 200 Oregon secondary school students, a theory can be inductively reasoned. Ultimately, future research will test the hypotheses that (a) schools that publicly experience a threat to culturally valued status are targeted for recruitment and (b) individuals expressing the negative affect of strain are targeted for recruitment.

FINDINGS

Of the 65 intensively interviewed skinheads, roughly half admitted being involved in some form of recruitment activities. Usually, these involved getting flyers into high schools or rock clubs. The flyers contained contact addresses or phone numbers for those who were interested. An informal youth network was also used to find out about specific individuals who might be easily recruited. The three skinheads in the Oregon Spotlight research were all active recruiters in the Portland and Eugene areas. All three have also served prison terms for various hate crimes, and one is currently incarcerated for a parole violation.

The Selection of Anomic Populations

Members of organizations such as Youth Corps (the youth wing of the KKK), the Aryan Youth Movement (the youth wing of WAR), and Volksfront (an Oregon Nazi skinhead group) often discussed strategy meetings in which core members would discuss target populations where recruitment activities would have the greatest results. Leafleting was the most common strategy, but members might also stage a violent confrontation with an "enemy" to raise visibility and awareness. There was a manipulation of the power of rumor and the knowledge that young people will quickly spread forbidden information. Trey, a 22-year-old Portland skinhead, said,

There was this fight at [Walker] High School between a Black kid and a White kid and everyone was supporting the Black kid who had been picking on this White forever. Typical bullshit, right? But we knew that there were Whites there who were sick and tired of being called "racists" just for sticking up for themselves. So we went down there one day, right, when school was letting out and beat the shit out of some gangster-looking nigger. The next day everyone at Milwaukee was talking about, "Oh man, did you hear that the skinheads kicked some nigger's ass?" It was the talk of the school so we went back a week later and put up a bunch of flyers and got a bunch of calls from kids wanting to know what they could do.

(This tactic was not uncommon. The skinheads like to view themselves as rescuing the cultural underdogs in a heroic, macho fashion. One of the more common images in skinhead art and tattoos is the Viking warrior who comes to rescue his people from the "evil Jews and sub-human mongrels." During the ethnographic research, one ritual was regularly observed. Racist skinheads would often mix with other youth subcultures at all-ages alternative music clubs. These clubs, where musicians often performed, would attract punk rockers (both left wing and right wing), hippies, minority youth, and mainstream "slummers." The skinheads would stay in the background, drinking beer and talking to girls. But, as soon as any conflict arose, the skinheads bounded into the fray to attack whichever party was the least like the skinheads. Most commonly the victim was a SHARP (Skinhead Against Racial Prejudice), who was seen as a racial traitor, but occasionally, it was an ethnic or sexual minority. The goal was that the skinheads would be seen as "kicking ass" and doing something about the problem of threats to ascribed status. Jack, a 20-year-old Orlando skinhead, said,

> It's a fun Saturday night for us. We go down to [the club] and drink beer, slam dance, and pick up some punk chicks and fight. All it takes is one spic to start something and we just open a can of whoop-ass. It's great for us because we know that half the White kids there are getting harassed by the Hispanics in their school and they are just waiting for someone to stick up for them. I've had these totally straight looking kids come up to me later, maybe a month later, and say, "Hey, that was really cool what you did. I wish you guys would come to my school and kick some ass." It's like a commercial for Youth Corps.

The selection of schools or neighborhoods usually involves two factors. First, are there any racist skinheads already in the school or younger siblings of older skinheads who can be used as contacts? The second factor represents more of the awareness of the value of anomie: Is there any perceived threat to straight, White (male) students that can be manipulated by the racist group? As mentioned, this threat can be economic, racial, or sexual. The following comments represent these categories:

> The easiest place to recruit is around some big layoff, which is pretty common around here [Chicago]. You wait for things to get bad and you go talk to the kids, not the parents and say, "You know why your dad got laid off? It's because the money hungry Jews sent his job to China. They care more about the fucking Chinese than they do about the White workers." You know, they're all fucked up because their world is upside down and here is someone explaining it to them in very simple terms. (Sid, 18, Chicago skinhead)

> The suburbs are the new battle zones. We hardly even go into the city anymore. But the burbs are supposed to be White! I mean, Whites moved out here to get away from all the crime and niggers and shit and here they come. And now we have gangs out here and drugs and these nice clean White kids gettin' jumped. We know that White parents are tired of moving and White teachers are scared to death and the young people are on the front line. (Bryan, 25, Atlanta skinhead)

> The feminists are as bad as the queers are. We try to get our guys to talk to dudes who think feminism is cool. You know, they're into it because they think they'll get laid. But we say, "Hey, you know what happens if the feminists gets their way? No one's gonna listen to you because you're a man and you're gonna be cleaning out the toilet. And even fewer White babies are gonna be born because *if* a chick has sex with you and gets pregnant she's gonna have an abortion so she can keep her paycheck. Do you think the niggers and the Mexicans are having abortions? Hell no!" So then they see feminism as the nail in the coffin. It's like, who wants to be a minority? (Harley, 24, San Francisco skinhead)

> I'll tell ya, as much as I hate all this "gay pride" shit, it's been the best thing for skinheads. Our numbers have tripled since they've been having these (gay pride) rallies in Cobb. It's like fag haters just come out of the woodwork and we just scoop 'em up. We can't print enough flyers. I think people see that our way of life is threatened

and they want to do something. We've got an idea! (Frank, 21, Atlanta skinhead)

Over 15 years, I have heard these stories over and over again: Skinheads leafleting neighborhoods where automobile or textile workers have been laid off, blaming affirmative action and "Jewish capitalism." Skinheads coming to the "rescue" of White youth who have been victimized by minority gangs. Skinheads who present a viable model of masculinity to boys confronted with the "homofication" (a skinhead term) of American culture. But, perhaps the newest recruitment technique is to target schools that are experiencing a curriculum shift toward multiculturalism. As history and social science books are retooled to be more inclusive, the voice that is diminishing is the hegemonic, straight, White male perspective. Without the proper context, this shift can seem to be a conspiracy to write White contributions out of the standard educational curriculum. Several high schools in Oregon have been targeted for recruitment using the backlash against multiculturalism as a way in.

One of the most common skinhead tactics is to attempt to establish a "White student union." This method was pioneered in the 1980s by the Klan in the east and WAR in the west as simply an issue of equality. There is a Black prom queen; there should be a White prom queen. There is an Asian student union; there should be a European student union. There are gay pride stickers; there should be straight pride stickers. There is a Hispanic heritage week; there should be a European heritage week, and so on. The concept of the White student union appeals to the adolescent's need for fairness and balance. Without an understanding of cultural history, in which power has been slanted in the direction of straight, White males, the concept seems just. This is enhanced by the switch to the multicultural curriculum, which further removes the voice of the weakening hegemony.

Sam, 26, who had spent years recruiting high school youth into the Aryan skinhead movement, explained the importance of manipulating the victim mentality.

It's really easy. You find out what's happening in a school and then find out where the kids hang out. You get some stupid conversation going and then you ask them about school. They bitch and moan and you say, "Yeah, it was a lot better in my day when we didn't have gangs and people who can't even speak English and all this multicultural shit." I'd say, "Don't you think it's fucked up that you can have a Black student union but not a White student union? Why are the Blacks allowed to be racist?" And you can see them agreeing. I say, "Did you ever own a slave? Did you ever kill an Indian? So why are they trying to make you feel guilty for being White?" Before they can answer I'd start telling them about ZOG. About how the Jews are behind all this to fuck over the White man. I give them the whole line, multiculturalism, gay rights, affirmative action. These kids don't know shit so they just eat it up. Then I tell them they should hang out with us or start an "unofficial" White student club. They just look at me like I'm Jesus Christ and I just saved them.

Targeting Strained Individuals

As the New Order's (1989) recruitment manifesto illustrates, "disaffected White kids who feel 'left out,' isolated, unpopular, or on the fringe or margin of things at school" (p. 6) are targeted for intensive recruitment, as well as those experiencing strain due to the inability to achieve positively valued goals or who are presented with noxious stimuli. The ethnographic part of this research revealed that Nazi skinheads can serve as "big brothers" or "friends in need" to frustrated boys whose fathers have been laid off or who have been harassed by minority peers. Like the members of cults, skinheads provide a sympathetic ear, a critical explanation of the problem, and an action program that appears to (somewhat) resolve the problem.

Discussion

I found that the skinhead recruiters interviewed were aware of the experience of normlessness among certain youth populations. These populations were targeted because of their desire for structure, a subcultural solution to their anomie, as well as their need for consistent models of authority and masculinity. They were easily manipulated and brought into the fray of right-wing hate groups.

The violent solution that these groups offer (becoming a soldier in a race war) will appeal to a large percentage of anomic young men because of its simplistic reality. Wars are won. Evil conspirators are banished. The mythical past of unchallenged, straight, White male hegemony is restored. For a generation weaned on video games and violent media, the world of Aryan terrorists can be intoxicating.

Sociological research is crucial in unlocking this attraction that makes recruiting so easy. The recruiting process is similar to that used by cults. Young skinheads may also end up in more serious right-wing groups such as Aryan Nations and even militia groups. Additionally, the readiness of the coming youth generation to look for extremist, subcultural solutions must be discussed. Finally, intervention strategies are proposed that will prevent young people from entering the world of racist terror.

Similarities With Cults

Recruitment into hate groups most obviously parallels gang recruitment. Criminological research is replete with examples of how alienated urban youth find homes in gangs. Venkatesh (1997) found that gangs recruit as corporate partners with the urban community, providing both opportunity and service for youth. Davis (1999) has written that gangs are "pseudo communities," attracting interstitial youth who are not reached by other institutions. The gang is primarily a replacement family.

But, unlike economically driven gangs, hate groups have ideological motivations for recruitment. Less obvious are the parallels with the recruitment activities of religious cults. Both hate groups and cults bring their new members into a world filled with evil conspiracies and righteous crusades. They are the "chosen few" who must fight a holy battle against often unseen enemies. The tricks that cults use to attract new members, described in Robert Cialdini's (1993) book *Influence: Science and Practice,* are significant for their use by skinhead groups in approaching strained youth. Cialdini describes six principles of cult recruitment:

1. The rule of reciprocity: Recruiters perform favors for recruits in exchange for a significantly larger favor later. In my research, older skinheads would often "take care of" (i.e., threaten, attack) non-White (or White) bullies of their target and later remind the target of how they had "saved his ass" when it came time to increase commitment levels.

2. Commitment and consistency: Once a recruit takes a stand on a specific issue, there is reinforcement for that person to remain consistent to that idea until it becomes effortless. One of the first questions Klan recruiters ask young targets is "Do you believe in the White race?" Once they have an affirmative answer, the subsequent discussion reinforces that target's belief in his or her race and its crisis.

3. Social proof: Ideology becomes more appealing when others, especially the famous, believe it. When there are degrees of uncertainty and similarity between themselves and recruiters, individuals are more likely to defer to others for context cues. The most common tool of the racist skinhead is White power rock. The presence of numerous bands and active record labels, such as Resistance Records, shows the legitimacy of the ideology to a potential recruit who may be waffling. Additionally, racist, sexist, and homophobic quotations from non–hate group members, such as Atlanta Braves pitcher John Rocker, are offered as evidence of the "normality" of bigotry.

4. Liking: People are more likely to say "yes" to people they like. Physical attractiveness, praise, and sensitivity can be used to manipulate recruits. As mentioned, anomic youth are "lost." They are often lacking father figures or consistent emotional attachments. Skinhead recruiters are very savvy at presenting themselves as attractive macho men who are genuinely concerned about the lives of their targets. They want to be their targets' best friend. This is an incredibly effective tactic when used on confused youth who are looking for someone who cares and listens to them.

5. Authority: Authorities can use symbols such as titles, clothing, or automobiles, to convince others of their knowledge, wisdom, and power. As Stanley Milgram's classic studies

demonstrated, we are more than willing to follow individuals we believe hold power (even if they don't). The skinhead recruiters in this study flaunted bogus titles, such as youth director, and detailed skinhead uniforms to impress potential new members.

6. Scarcity: People assign more value to things that are harder to acquire. The "scarcity principle" works because the availability of an item or experience is seen to reflect its quality, and one perceives a loss of freedom when an opportunity disappears. According to Cialdini (1993), cults often use "limited number" and "deadline" tactics to recruit members. Similarly, skinhead recruiters refer to "time running out" before some inevitable calamity (Y2K, the race war, etc.) when the lines will be drawn. "You gotta get onboard before the shit hits the fan," said Sam, the skinhead recruiter. "After that, you're on your own."

Similarities between cult and skinhead recruiting are subjects of future research. Although cult violence is usually directed inward, as in the 1978 Jonestown massacre or the 2000 mass death of members of The Movement for the Restoration of the Ten Commandments of God in Uganda, the apocalyptic rhetoric is similar. Youth alienated from mainstream institutions, including religion, are prime targets.

Recruitment of Adult Skinheads

Of course, there is a food chain in the hate movement. Despite the terrorist cell approach of leaderless resistance, there is an informal hierarchy, with rabble-rousing skinheads at the bottom and "legitimate" militia groups at the top. When I began my research on skinheads in the mid-1980s, people often asked, "What happens to skinheads when they grow up?" I had no answer then, but now, 15 years later, there are some good ideas. Most experience the skinhead phenomenon as a subcultural phase of their youth, often leaving once they start their own families. Some join adult White supremacist groups and become more involved in the political aspects of White supremacy. But, as research shows, the desire for autonomy that led

them to become skinheads in the first place tends to drive them out of the authoritarian groups that require obedience. Many of these youth become antiracist skinheads to preserve their independence. As one ex-skinhead said, "I went from my parents telling me what to do to the Nazis telling me what to do. I just said, 'Fuck it.'"

But there are those who are content with the reduced autonomy because along with it comes the structure absent in the normless world from which they are retreating. Seasoned skinheads are actively recruited by groups such as Aryan Nations, the World Church of the Creator, and various Klan groups. There, they are used as security agents, sources of weapons, and symbols of the soldiers on the front line of the race war. In the early 1990s, Tom Metzger, leader of the White Aryan Resistance, shaved his head to show his support for the skinheads.

The role skinheads play in the militia movement is yet unclear. That state militias often draw their members from groups such as Aryan Nations and the Klan, who themselves recruit skinheads, leaves one to imagine the inevitable. Skinheads were active in the antigovernment demonstrations during the siege at Ruby Ridge in 1992 and continue to share many of the antigovernment ideas of some militia groups. This research shows that skinheads have adopted the idea of leaderless resistance. The killings in Denver in 1997 were the work of a terrorist cell that killed one of its victims because "he was wearing the enemy's uniform." His skin was black.

Generation Why?

Despite the success of multicultural curriculums in reducing bias among youth, no cohort may be more ripe for recruitment than the current teenage generation. Unlike the culture-shaping baby boomers and the relatively small Generation X, youth born after 1981 face numerous sources of anomie and thus have been dubbed "Generation Why?" (Wooden & Blazak, 2000).

The youth of Generation Why? were born after the experience of overt racism (busing, segregation, etc.) and have always known Black History Month. But, they are also a more racially diverse generation. Thirty-three percent of the high school class of 2000 were members of minority groups. Only 28% of Americans, in general, are minorities (Foster, 1999). The potential for racial unity exists as more youth define themselves as "multiracial," but there is also a potential for conflict as schools and communities become "less White," inciting fears among racists. The 2000 census is expected to reveal that California is the first state where Whites are a minority.

This has been described as a generation in crisis. They are less likely to spend time with their parents or to be known by name to their teachers. Nanette Davis (1999), in her book *Youth Crisis: Growing Up in the High-Risk Society,* points out that all the institutions involved in helping youth make a safe transition from childhood to adulthood are in a state of crisis. These include the family, schools, religion, the juvenile justice system, and the occupational structure. Davis outlines seven of the manifestations of cultural "crisis":

1. Modern life is uncertain.

2. Politicians opt for short-term solutions, ignoring long-term consequences.

3. The emphasis on consumerism.

4. Race, class, age, and ethnic divisions discourage youth from believing in social institutions.

5. There is a lack of adequate child care.

6. Risk reduction attempts do not target the most vulnerable.

7. There is a "cult of individualism." (pp. 14–15)

Davis's (1999) risk model fits right in with the fears of potential skinhead recruits:

1. Modern life involves dramatic shifts in "what was." This includes the perceived secure place for heterosexual, White men in a traditional society.

2. Short-term solutions are also appealing to skinheads who see "bashing" someone as a solution to a social problem.

3. The emphasis on consumerism alienates those who do not share in the current economic prosperity. This is magnified when previously subordinated groups such as African Americans seem to be experiencing dramatic upward mobility.

4. The politics of political correctness also alienate some straight, White males who no longer feel that mainstream institutions such as the business world or higher education represent them.

5. The lack of child care can be attributed to the "unnatural" movement of women into the workforce and away from the home. This may also be a source of resentment for those who did not receive adequate bonding with their parents.

6. At-risk youth are often conceptualized as poor, urban minorities, not products of the socially disorganized suburbs. There is a plethora of programs for gang-affiliated youth, but few for Klan-affiliated youth.

7. Finally, the cult of individualism assures every American of his or her inalienable rights (the right to a cell phone, the right to go to the college of one's choice, the right to maintain one's privileged position in society) without any responsibility. It is this experience of crisis that makes certain youth so attractive to hate groups. (pp. 14–15)

The suicide of rock star Kurt Cobain in 1994 brought the sociological term anomie into the American lexicon. Generation Why? is often in "drift" due to uninvolved parents who can't see the crisis. Five million children under the age of 13 are "latchkey kids," left unattended after school each day (Siegel, 2000). The parents of half of American teenagers are divorced, and 63% of teenagers live in homes where both parents work outside the home (Kantrowitz & Wingert, 1999). According to the Centers for Disease Control and Prevention, cases of teen depression have increased 300% in the past 30 years (Mehren, 1999). For these youth, hate groups and their solution-oriented agendas may be highly attractive.

Prevention Strategies

Considering the proclivity of hate groups to bring young people into their dark world of conspiracy and violence through the skinhead subculture, strategies must be developed to protect youth. Although the life of the terrorist might seem romantic or heroic, the reality is far different. Death in police shoot-outs or from unexpectedly exploding pipe bombs is normative in adult hate groups such as The Order. More likely are long prison terms due to stricter policing by the FBI, the Bureau of Alcohol, Tobacco, and Firearms, and local police, and enhanced sentences mandated by new hate crime laws. The fact that the largest skinhead group, the Aryan Brotherhood, is essentially a prison gang reflects this.

Reducing Cultural Anomie

Reducing cultural anomie on the macro level is no easy task. As long as society values correcting the power imbalances that have given certain categories privilege, straight, White men will feel threatened. No one likes to lose the privileges of power. Riane Eisler advocates the development of institutions based on partnerships (Eisler, Love, & Loye, 1998). The current dichotomous power model (male-female, straight-gay, White-Black) dictates that one group be dominant and the other group subordinate. Here, the advances of the subordinate group are seen as losses by the dominant party in a zero-sum game format. Erasing those boundaries allows all to share in the advancement of any member of society. The gains of women and ethnic and sexual minorities are not seen as threats to men, Whites, and heterosexuals in the partnership model.

Shifting society out of the dominant-subordinate paradigm may be plausible, but I argue here that an achievable macro-level solution is to reduce threats to economic status. The policies of deregulation under Ronald Reagan and the North American Free Trade Agreement under Bill Clinton have propelled the deindustrialization of the American workforce. The Dow Jones industrial average topping 10,000 and the creation of millions of low-wage, service-sector jobs in the 1990s have not prevented a significant portion of Americans from feeling that they have lost out on the American dream. As has been done in other countries, legislation can be passed that protects factory workers from layoffs and white-collar workers from downsizing. Currently, few politicians advocate for the

working class, leaving racists free rein in their interpretations. To them, the lack of legislation is proof that Congress is just a tool of the Jews, who lay off and downsize at will to maximize their wealth.

Think Globally, Act Locally

They might just be Band-Aids compared with large-scale cultural shifts, but local solutions can be effective in reducing bias-motivated violence. Oregon Spotlight, along with many other groups, spends a great deal of time working with young people in hopes of keeping them from moving up the ladder into adult racist movements. The strategy works with three types of youth:

1. Youth who are members of hate groups: These young people can be reached. Most are just looking for a subculture that makes sense of their world. They tend to lack consistent male role models in their lives.

2. Youth who have been arrested for committing hate crimes: Often, the worst scenario is when a young hater is put into a correctional facility where racist gangs such as the Aryan Brotherhood are waiting to indoctrinate them. Within the total institution, racists can resocialize the youth, who, on release, will have been transformed into a warrior for the extreme right. There are diversion programs for young minority gang members. The same can be mandated for hate criminals (as they have by groups such as the Anti-Defamation League in New York).

3. Youth in target populations. Populations that have experienced threats to ascribed or economic status are likely targets for hate group recruitment. Classroom discussions, school assemblies, and programs can teach youth about the tactics of hate groups as well as the value of diversity. Curriculums such as the SPLC's Teaching Tolerance program strive to make multiculturalism meaningful to all, including ethnic Whites.

Each of these groups must be targeted with a program that teaches critical thinking. The illogic of racism and bigotry can be illuminated. Who qualifies as White? Why are there so many contrary examples of stereotypes? What would the world really be like if the extreme right got its way? And, most importantly, what would you give up by not living in a diverse culture? After I had talked to him, one Nazi skinhead called Oregon Spotlight and told me he wanted out of the movement. I asked what turned him around, and he said it was an offhanded comment I had made about peanut butter being invented by George Washington Carver, a Black man. "Man, I love peanut butter and I'm not going to give it up just so I can be a good racist!" he told me.

There are enough angry adults who do not understand what is happening to their world and will seek out hate groups to express their rage. Some may be satisfied with membership in the KKK, and some will join terrorist cells and try to fulfill the hate-filled dictates laid out in *The Turner Diaries*. But, it is clear that hate groups are also recruiting young people. They are the new blood; they are the future. Anomic youth who are looking for answers and big brothers, if they cannot obtain those things from other sources, will follow.

REFERENCES

Agnew, R. (1985). A revised strain theory of delinquency. *Social Forces, 64,* 151–167.

Agnew, R. (1992). Foundations for a general strain theory of crime and delinquency. *Criminology, 30,* 47–87.

Blazak, R. (1995). *The suburbanization of hate: An ethnographic study of the skinhead subculture.* Unpublished doctoral dissertation, Emory University.

Blazak, R. (1998). Hate in the suburbs: The rise of the skinhead counterculture. In L. J. McIntyre (Ed.), *The practical skeptic: Readings in sociology.* Mountain View, CA: Mayfield.

Cialdini, R. B. (1993). *Influence: Science and practice.* New York: HarperCollins.

Cloward, R. A., & Ohlin, L. E. (1960). *Delinquency and opportunity.* New York: Free Press.

Cohen, A. (1955). *Delinquent boys.* New York: Free Press.

Davis, N. J. (1999). *Youth crisis: Growing up in the high-risk society.* Westport, CT: Praeger.

Eisler, R., Love, D., & Loye, D. (1998). *The partnership way: New tools for living and learning.* New York: Holistic Education Press.

Ezekial, R. S. (1995). *The racist mind: Portraits of American neo-Nazis and Klansmen.* New York: Penguin.

Foster, D. (1999, September 12). Y2K generation forced to grow up fast. *Desert Sun,* p. A-3.

Hebdige, D. (1979). *Subculture: The meaning of style.* London: Methuen.

Hyde, H.F.F.H.F. (2000). Retrieved from the World Wide Web: http://www.hammerskins.com/press/whatmakes.html

Kantrowitz, B., & Wingert, P. (1999, October 18). The truth about teens. *Newsweek.*

Levin, J., & McDevitt, J. (1993). *Hate crimes: The rising tide of bigotry and bloodshed.* New York: Plenum.

Hamm, M. S. (1993). *American skinheads: The criminology and control of hate crime.* Cincinnati, OH: Anderson.

Mehren, E. (1999, July 18). Troubled teens' parents desperate for solutions. *Los Angeles Times.*

Messerschmidt, J. (1993). *Masculinites and crime.* Lanahm, MD: Rowman and Littlefield.

Messner, S. F., & Rosenfeld, R. (1994). *Crime and the American dream.* Belmont, CA: Wadsworth.

New Order. (1989). *Action program for Aryan skinheads.* Lincoln, NE: NSDAP.

Passas, N., & Agnew, R. (1997). *The future of anomie theory.* Boston: Northeastern University.

Siegel, L. (2000). *Criminology.* Belmont, CA: Wadsworth.

Southern Poverty Law Center. (2000a, Winter). Bombs, bullets, bodies: The decade in review. *Intelligence Report, 97.*

Southern Poverty Law Center. (2000b, Winter). The year in hate. *Intelligence Report, 97.*

Venkatesh, S. A. (1997). The social organization of street gang activity in an urban ghetto. *American Journal of Sociology, 103*(1–3), 82–111.

Wooden, W., & Blazak, R. (2000). *Renegade kids, suburban outlaws.* Belmont, CA: Wadsworth.

QUESTIONS

1. What are some examples of how hate groups provide a rationale to their members to help them justify hate groups?

2. What are the five key trends related to the decrease in the number of hate groups?

3. Discuss how "leaderless resistance" and mainstreaming make it harder to successfully identify right-wing extremists.

4. What changes in the hate group movement increase the potential for right-wing terrorism?

5. How does the concept of anomie, and strain theory, help us understand why youths join racist skinhead groups?

6. What are some examples of violence committed by racist skinheads? Should violent attacks on members of targeted groups be considered examples of domestic terrorism?

7. What are some examples of red flags indicating that a young person may be feeling alienated?

8. How can social-structural conditions such as lack of legitimate opportunities to reach desired goals lead to feelings of alienation?

9. How do racist skinhead organizers use indications of strain and alienation to target certain youths for recruitment? What kind of perceived "threats" to the status quo do organizers use to help them target potential recruits?

10. According to Blazak, both cults and racist skinhead groups recruit alienated youth by providing them with an alternative perspective on the status quo. What are some examples of this?

11. What are the six principles of cult recruitment? How are these similar to the recruitment tactics used by racist skinhead groups?

12. Why might "Generation Why" youth be especially "ripe for recruitment" by hate groups? Do you agree or not? Why?

Part VI

HATE CRIME VICTIMS

The impact of hate crimes is multidimensional, extending beyond the physical and psychological harm suffered by the direct victims to the fear such crimes create in others who are (or appear to be) members of the group targeted by hate criminals. The articles in this section document both historical and contemporary examples of the ways in which members of targeted groups have been victimized by hate crimes. In addition to describing the nature and impact of hate crimes, the articles in this section further illuminate the social processes by which people come to be characterized as "others" outside the mainstream of society. Examining how some groups are labeled as different from the perceived societal norm is essential to understanding both the impact of hate crimes on victims and the nature of legal and social reactions to hate crimes.

17

HATE CRIMES AGAINST AFRICAN AMERICANS

The Extent of the Problem

SAM TORRES

Despite the difficulties inherent in collecting complete data on the nature and incidence of hate crimes, this article assembles data from a variety of sources to help illuminate the extent of the problem of hate crimes that African Americans experience. The evidence supports the contention that hate crimes are substantially underreported. Hate crimes appear to be increasing in recent years, reflecting changes in societal attitudes that lend support to overt expressions of intolerance and bigotry.

Historically, African Americans were victimized more often than any other minority group by what has come to be defined as hate crimes. In 1996—the most recent year that hate crime statistics were available from the Federal Bureau of Investigation's (FBI) Uniform Crime Reports (UCR)—almost 9,000 hate crimes were reported by more than 11,000 law enforcement agencies in 49 U.S. states and the District of Columbia. Of all the hate crimes reported in 1996, approximately 61% were motivated by racial prejudice, and in these incidents, African Americans were the victims in 66% of the cases reported to police. Despite these alarming statistics, the U.S. Department of Justice (1996) reports that most hate crimes go unreported. Consequently, as a result of such issues as underreporting, individual agency data collection methods, disparate definitions of what constitutes a hate crime, and agency nonparticipation in hate crime data collection, the extent of the problem may be significantly understated—particularly as it affects African Americans.

The purpose of this article is to demonstrate that hate crimes against African Americans

EDITORS' NOTE: From Torres, S. (1999). Hate Crimes Against African Americans: The Extent of the Problem. *Journal of Contemporary Criminal Justice, 15*(1), 48-63. © 1999 Sage Publications. Used with permission.

have increased significantly since 1990. They represent a serious social problem that requires strict enforcement of existing state and federal laws. This article examines what appears to be an increasing intolerance of racial diversity in the United States—especially as it pertains to African Americans. Although there are various other groups that are also victims of hate crimes, including Jews, Latinos, Asian Americans, the disabled, gays, and lesbians, this article focuses on African Americans because they continue to be the most likely victims of racial bigotry. Also, this article examines African American hate crime victimization trends since the passage of the Hate Crime Statistics Act (HCSA) of 1990, the factors that contribute to hate crimes against African Americans, and some of the recommendations that have been put forth to deal with this growing problem.

PROCEDURES

This article stems from an effort to examine the results of hate crimes data gathered pursuant to the HCSA (1990). The HCSA requires the attorney general of the United States to acquire data about crimes that manifest evidence of prejudice based on race, religion, sexual orientation, or ethnicity. Where appropriate, this includes the crimes of murder; nonnegligent manslaughter; forcible rape; aggravated assault; simple assault; intimidation; arson; and the destruction, damage, or vandalism of property. I examine hate crimes against African Americans for the 6 years from 1990 to 1996 that the FBI has been gathering data. I examined scholarly empirical articles on the topic as well as several recently published texts on hate crime. A review of other existing data for this review included a thorough search of approximately 350 Internet Web sites addressing the issue in one form or another. I also reviewed government reports from the U.S. Department of Justice as well as statistics gathered by the FBI's UCR Division, to determine the extent of African American victimization since 1990. Several newspapers were also used to examine recent African American hate crime incidents that have occurred since 1990.

LITERATURE REVIEW

Definition of Hate Crimes

Hate crimes are commonly referred to as bias-motivated crimes. These are offenses prompted by the hatred against a person by virtue of their race, religion, sexual orientation, disability, ethnicity, or national origin. Although this definition appears to be succinct and precise (thus making identification of hate crimes relatively easy), criminal behavior motivated by prejudice can be obscured with forms of expression protected by the Constitution (Bureau of Justice Assistance [BJA], 1997). In *Hate Crimes* (1998), D'Angelo describes hate crimes as a broad range of bias-motivated crimes, from vandalism to murder. The legal definition has been clarified by a number of Supreme Court decisions that differentiate between symbolic hatred and purely verbal expressions from actual behavior. According to D'Angelo, words may be weapons, but they are protected by the First Amendment.

The complexity of defining hate crimes is further exacerbated because states differ regarding what is considered a hate crime and how such crimes should be punished. In addition, some states have specific hate crime statutes and other states have penalty enhancements for crimes that are motivated by prejudice. States that have enacted hate crime statutes may also differ with respect to which groups are identified specifically for protection. At the federal level, there have been three different hate crime laws enacted by Congress. The first federal hate crime law, the HCSA, was passed in 1990. In 1994, the Hate Crime Sentencing Enchancement Act (HCSEA) mandated a revision of the U.S. sentencing guidelines to provide sentencing enhancements of not less than three offense levels for offenses considered hate crimes. A concise, understandable definition is put forth by D'Angelo (1998) who says, "If legal definitions are somewhat elusive, the crucial elements in any hate crime are the offender's motivation in selecting a victim based on that person's membership in a group and the effect the crime has on the group" (pp. 18–19). The degree of harm perpetrated by hate crime offenders is assessed not only by the injury to the specific victim(s) but, perhaps more critically, by the terror and intimidation that affects the entire group or community. After the civil war, the Ku Klux Klan became remarkably effective in preventing African Americans from voting or exercising their civil rights. The lynching of African Americans was common in the South during Reconstruction, and it served to intimidate entire communities from their efforts to overcome poverty, to own real property, to obtain an education, and participate in local politics. Between 1889 and 1918, 1,481 people, mostly African Americans, were lynched in Georgia, Mississippi, Louisiana, Texas, and Alabama (Jacobs & Potter, 1998).

Perhaps one of the most significant Supreme Court cases upholding hate crime statutes is the case of *Wisconsin v. Mitchell* (1993) that states, in part,

> If a person . . . intentionally selects the person against whom the crime . . . is committed or selects the property which is damaged or otherwise affected by the crime . . . because of the race, religion, color, disability, sexual orientation, national origin or ancestry of that person or occupant of that property, the penalties for the underlying crime are increased . . . [by as much as triple].

HCSA

The HCSA was passed in 1990 and, along with its 1994 extension, it requires the U.S. attorney general to collect data on the number of crimes committed each year that are motivated by prejudice based on race, religion, sexual orientation, or ethnicity. The FBI has assumed the responsibility, under the UCR Program, of collecting hate crime data as defined by the HCSA. However, the submission of hate crime data by state and local law enforcement agencies is voluntary.

When the UCR issued its first report on hate crimes in January 1993, only 20% of all of the nation's law enforcement agencies were participating in reporting hate crimes. As of October 1996, almost 60% of the country's law enforcement agencies were providing data on hate

crime. Furthermore, 19 states have now enacted legislation requiring state law enforcement agencies to collect hate crime data. Since the passage of this legislation in 1990, there has been considerable interest in examining the incidence and nature of hate crimes in the United States.

Byers and Zeller (1997) analyzed data obtained from the UCR between 1991 and 1994. They found that the data show exceptional stability when examining both bias motivation and type of offense. They conclude that the official data tend to support findings from previous research: Bias-motivated offenses that are categorized as harassment or intimidation are the most frequently reported, and racial bias is one of the most common reasons for hate crime. However, an earlier study casts doubt on the claim that the United States is experiencing a hate crime epidemic (Jacobs & Henry, 1996). The authors examine the hate crime data collection efforts of the Klanwatch Project and the FBI. They note that figures from these organizations are widely used to confirm the existence of the hate crime epidemic. Jacobs and Henry underscore the political and subjective nature of counting hate crimes, and they offer their observations on the status of hate crimes. They stress the problems associated with collecting hate crime data: defining *hate crime,* establishing a reliable means for determining when an offender's bias should convert an ordinary crime into a hate crime, and deciding which biases are important when counting hate crimes.

In an elaboration on this theme, Jacobs and Potter (1998) argue against the enactment and enforcement of hate crime laws. They conclude that these laws are well intentioned; however, they represent the importation of identity politics into criminal law by seeking to give special recognition to the victimization of members of historically discriminated groups. In their book on hate crimes, Jacobs and Potter again stress the difficulty of counting hate crimes because of their ambiguous, subjective, and contentious nature. They note that attempting to measure hate crime is doomed to failure because of the difficulty of reliably determining the motivation of individual and group offenders. Hate crime data collected and published by the FBI are criticized as fragmentary, nonuniform, and distorted. They conclude that to date these data collection efforts have not contributed to a better understanding of crime, prejudice, or prejudice-motivated crime in American society, nor have the UCR reports contributed to better law enforcement practices. The authors state that the government collections of hate crime data serve to create the false impression that the country is experiencing an epidemic of prejudice-motivated crime, and the long-term consequence may be to simply reinforce a sense of group victimization and grievance. They argue that the criminal justice system's attempt to single out hate crimes for greater punishment is, in effect, an effort to punish some offenders more severely because of their bad beliefs, opinions, or values and, of course, this conflicts with the First Amendment.

Hate Crimes Trends
Against African Americans

Although the federal government has made a substantial effort to initiate a statistical baseline of hate crime in the United States, considerable uncertainty continues regarding whether the hate crime rate is increasing or decreasing.

In 1993, the FBI released the first official hate crime report covering 1991. The data was obtained from 2,771 law enforcement agencies out of a total of about 12,805 in the United States. Only 32 states provided hate crime data this first year. Of the agencies providing hate crime data, 73% reported no hate crime offenses occurring in their jurisdiction the entire year. In 1991, 4,558 hate crime incidents were reported in the United States. As in subsequent years, intimidation was the most frequently reported crime, representing about 33% of all hate incidents. Racial bias was the most frequently reported hate crime when African Americans were the target (Jacobs & Potter, 1998).

Some of the organizations that fought the strongest for passage of hate crime legislation were the most critical when the initial data was released, concluding that the FBI report did not adequately capture the high incidence of hate crimes in the United States. The Klanwatch organization was highly critical of the 1991 Hate Crime Report, indicating that it was "inadequate and nearly worthless" (Welch, 1993, p. 5).

In 1992, 41 states and 6,200 law enforcement agencies participated in reporting hate crime incidents to the UCR. In that year, there were 6,623 incidents and, of these, the highest number, 2,296 (35%) were aimed at African Americans. Intimidation was by far the most frequently reported offense with 2,318 (35%) of all hate crimes, followed by vandalism, simple assault, and aggravated assault (U.S. Department of Justice, 1993).

By 1993, the number of states and law enforcement agencies participating in the collection and reporting of hate crimes had again increased significantly. In that year, the UCR reported a total of 7,587 hate crimes reported by 6,900 law enforcement agencies from 46 states. Intimidation, as in previous years, was the most often reported hate crime. African Americans were targets of hate crimes in 3,559 incidents representing 47% of the total reported for 1993 (U.S. Department of Justice, 1994). In 1994, hate crime dropped precipitously by almost 30% to 5,852, then jumped rather significantly in 1995 to 7,947 offenses—including 20 murders. Hate crimes aimed at African Americans in 1994 represented 42% (2,476) of the overall bias-motivated crimes reported to the police (U.S. Department of Justice, 1995).

Of the 7,947 hate crimes reported in 1995, 61% were motivated by racial bias. Furthermore, of the 6,438 hate crime incidents motivated by racial prejudice, 3,945 or 61% involved African American victims. Although Whites are also victims of hate crimes, their rates of victimization are substantially lower that of African Americans. In 1995, Whites were victims of hate crimes in about 15% of the incidents, and African Americans were victims 61% of the time.

As in previous years, hate crimes in 1995 were usually directed at individuals. Individual victims represented 83% of all reported hate crimes for 1995. Of serious concern is the fact that crimes against persons accounted for 72% of the total number of 9,895 offenses reported, with intimidation accounting for 41% or 4,048 of the total number. The degree of physical violence directed toward hate crime victims is also of serious concern. Of the total number of hate crime offenses (9,895), 31% involved aggravated assault and simple assault. Overall, 78% of hate crime offenses involved intimidation,

Table 17.1

	1992	1993	1994	1995	1996
Total hate crimes reported	6,623	7,587	5,852	7,947	8,759
Anti-African American hate crimes (%)	2,296 (35)	3,559 (47)	2,476 (42)	3,945 (50)	4,600 (52)

SOURCE: U.S. Department of Justice (1993, 1994, 1995, 1996, 1998).

aggravated assault, and simple assault (U.S. Department of Justice, 1996).

Based on the data collected thus far, it appears that the number of hate crime offenses seems to have grown substantially in 1992, increased slightly in 1993, decreased in 1994, and increased in 1995 (BJA, 1997).

In 1996, the most recent year that hate crime statistics were available from the UCR, 8,759 hate crimes were reported in the United States by the 11,354 law enforcement agencies. Although hate crime incidents increased by about 10% from the 7,947 reported in 1995 to 8,759 in 1996, it should be noted that the number of law enforcement agencies participating in data collection increased by 18%. Therefore, rather than observing an increase in hate crimes, we may simply be improving our ability to identify and record the rate of crime that is motivated by bias. Of course, it may also be that in addition to improving our data collection skills and increased law enforcement participation, hate crime in the United States may, in fact, be increasing (U.S. Department of Justice, 1998).

Of the 8,759 hate crimes that were reported in 1996, 61% or 5,396 crimes were motivated by racial prejudice. Of the 7,000 victims of race motivated crime, 4,600, or approximately 66% were attacks against African Americans. This number represents a disturbing increase of 5% more than the previous year. Although the percentage of hate crime motivated by racial prejudice remained stable at 61%, of the total incidents in 1995 and 1996, there has been an increase in the number of African American victims. Despite these alarming numbers, the U.S. Department of Justice (1998) reports that many, if not most, hate crimes go unreported.

In 1996, intimidation accounted for the greatest number of incidents, 3,416, or 39% of the total. This was followed by destruction of property and vandalism at 27%; simple assault, 16%; and aggravated assault, 13%. Also in 1996, 12 murders were related to hate crimes.

African Americans: Primary Targets of Race-Biased Hate Crimes

Data obtained from the UCR Reports and presented in Table 17.1 revealed that African Americans experience a high rate of race-motivated hate crimes. From lynching to cross burning, and most recently, church burning, anti-African American sentiments continue to represent the standard type of hate crime in the United States. It is significant that from 1992 to 1996 there has been a 50% increase in the number of hate crimes reported against African Americans. The intent of the hate crime perpetrator is not only to harm or inflict injury on the African American victim, but also to intimidate an entire group of people.

The recent burning of African American churches has created a great deal of concern because churches have always been the most important independent institution in the African American community, and those who seek to attack and intimidate African Americans often choose to attack their churches. Although the majority of church burnings have taken place in the South, other parts of the country have also been victimized. In Los Angeles in 1994, two members of the Fourth Reich Skinheads were convicted and sentenced to federal prison for planning to attack the First African Methodist Episcopal Church ("Skinheads Get Prison," 1994).

Since 1995, 73 African American churches have been burned or desecrated. Most of those who have been arrested and convicted for burning African American churches since 1990 have been White males between the ages of 14 and 45. Since 1995, 39 people have been arrested and charged with arson in the burning of African American churches. Of the 39, 26 were White, and 13 were African American. As with hate crimes against other minority groups, acts of intimidation and violence against African Americans have not been restricted to the burning of churches. Examples of recent hate crimes against African Americans include the following:

On December 7, 1995, two African American residents of Fayetteville, North Carolina, were brutally and senselessly murdered by three soldiers who apparently identified themselves as neo-Nazi skinheads. Police said the soldiers were looking for Black people to harass and shot the victims as they were walking down the street. A federal investigator later said, "this [crime] gives new meaning to the definition of a hate crime" ("Three White Soldiers," 1995).

In Fairfax County, Virginia (an affluent community near Washington, D.C.), in 1993, a 41-year-old Black woman heard the doorbell ring at the home where she was house-sitting. When she looked out the window, she saw a cross burning 10 feet from the front door ("Increase in Hate Crime," 1994).

In South Gate, California (near Los Angeles) in 1994, the White neighbors of a Black woman burned a cross on her lawn, kicked her children, hanged and gassed her puppies, and placed a "White Power" sign on her property (Los Angeles County Commission on Human Relations, 1995).

In Orland Park, Illinois, in 1995, a Black man who was talking with a White woman was attacked by a 25-year-old White male who yelled racial slurs during the attack (Welch, 1993, p. 16).

In Harper Woods, Michigan, a Black couple was threatened by a White man who said he would kill and dismember them if they moved into his neighborhood (Welch, 1993, p. 16).

One of three white men accused in a beating that left a Black 13-year-old severely brain damaged was acquitted of attempted murder. Frank Caruso, 19, instead was convicted of hate crimes against both the beaten boy, Lenard Clark, and one of the boy's friends, Clevon Nicholson, 14. He also was convicted of aggravated battery against Lenard Clark. Caruso was identified in court as the instigator of the March 21, 1997, attack that left Clark

crumpled and unconscious in a street a few blocks north of Comiskey Park, home of the Chicago White Sox. The incident stunned Chicago and brought a denunciation of racial hatred from President Clinton ("Man Acquitted," 1998).

The most recent and brutal hate crime directed at an African American that appears to have been motivated solely by the victim's race occurred in 1998 in Jasper, Texas. Three men with reported ties to White supremacist groups were charged with chaining a Black man to a pickup truck and dragging him 2 miles, tearing off his head, part of his neck, and his right arm. According to newspaper reports,

> Don Clark, special agent in charge of the FBI's Houston office, told a news conference today the slaying was "clearly a racially motivated crime," but a 30-day review will determine if federal charges are warranted. The suspects are Shawn Allen Berry and John William King, both 23, and 31-year-old Lawrence Russell Brewer. They are charged with first-degree murder, and are held without bail in the Jasper County Jail. An arrest affidavit states King referred to *The Turner Diaries,* a White supremacist novel in which Blacks are slaughtered, as he drove the truck that allegedly dragged 49-year-old James Byrd, Jr. to his death last Sunday. ("Prosecutor Considers," 1998)

As for the people who commit hate crimes, a substantial number tend to be young thrill seekers, rather than hardcore haters. A study conducted by Northeastern University in 1993 found that 60% of offenders committed hate crimes for the "thrill associated with the victimization" (B. Levin, 1993, p. 9). Most of the time these youthful offenders believe that their participation in crime will earn them respect from their friends.

The second most common type of offender of hate crimes is the reactive offender who feels that he is responding to an attack or insult by the victim, such as interracial dating, an African American family moving into the neighborhood, or his wife's decision to leave. The least common type of hate crime offender is the hardcore fanatic who is filled with an ideology of racial hatred, and is often a member of an extremist organization (Aronson & Height, 1998).

Contributory Factors to African American Hate Crimes

Several factors may contribute to a social and political climate in which people who are prejudiced against African Americans and other racial minorities are prompted to commit a hate crime. Some of these factors include unemployment, poor financial circumstances, racial stereotypes in the media, race-biased advertisement, radio talk show discussions, the use of race-baiting language, and a person's own experiences with African Americans. When some of these factors combine to create a climate of hate, a single incident can cause a hate crime attack on an African American (BJA, 1997).

The U.S. Department of Justice (1997) defines *trigger incidents,* and notes that when the climate for hate crimes is present, all that is required is a high profile racial incident to set off a cycle of retaliatory incidents or even a large scale racial disorder. The videotaping of Los Angeles police officers beating Rodney King in March 1991, and the subsequent acquittal of the four officers who were charged in the case, represented a trigger incident that resulted in large scale public disorder that required the National Guard to restore order. The following month, the number of hate crimes in other areas of the country began to rise. In another case in Howard Beach, New York, a trigger incident was the racially motivated attack on a group of Black men (BJA, 1997).

Racially motivated hate crimes are also sensitive to external circumstances. During the 1980s, when Japanese auto and electronic manufacturers were increasing their share of the U.S. market, there was an increase in the number of hate crime incidents directed at Asian Americans. Attacks on Arab Americans also increased during the Gulf War as a climate of retaliation seemed to spread in the United States (BJA, 1997).

Scapegoating is a common defense mechanism whereby someone who is experiencing a negative life situation—unemployment and/or economic strain—looks around to blame someone for his or her troubles. The scapegoating of African Americans often results in blaming this group for the rise in crime, the welfare state, the drug problem, and the general deterioration in the quality of life. B. Levin (1993) says that "learning to hate is almost as inescapable as breathing" (p. 221). Like everyone else, the hate crime offender grows up in a society that defines people in certain ways. Stereotypes, according to Levin, usually develop in the family during the process of socialization. The African American hater may never have had contact with a Black person, but early in his or her social development they learn negative characteristics associated with this group from parents and significant others.

Scapegoating and stereotyping attitudes and behaviors also are influenced by the cultural climate. Negative racial attitudes today are reflected in the recent changes in music, humor, art, and politics that seem to lead to a conclusion that "hatred is hip." The attitude in the United States today gives rise to a belief that bigotry is no longer politically incorrect, and is once again finding a degree of respectability. The prejudicial attitudes that have always been present in some people have not been manifested because the social and political climate was not conducive to such expressions of bigotry. However, what used to be kept below the surface or whispered behind closed doors about African Americans in now openly flaunted because of a social and political climate now conducive to such expression. Whether this climate was intended by the conservatives to backlash against policies of affirmative action, bilingual education, immigration, and funding of social programs, we appear to be in the midst of a growing culture of intolerance—especially as it affects our African American citizens (B. Levin, 1993).

Generalized resentment also frequently forms the basis for hate crimes against African Americans and other minority groups. Individuals who experience a generalized attitude of resentment feel that they are being left out and abused, that their way of life is being destroyed, and that their rights are gradually being eroded by racial minorities who receive preferential treatment. These people see themselves as victims of a society that is out of control and has highly distorted priorities. They believe that society is looking for someone to blame. People who are prejudiced and prone to commit hate crimes possess a tendency toward ethnocentricity—an attitude of hostility toward groups that are different (B. Levin, 1993).

Committing a hate crime "for the thrill of it" is motivated by the exhilaration of seeing someone else suffer. Young offenders receive the social approval from their friends. As noted earlier, another reason for race-motivated hate crime is a reaction to a personal threat. These offenders attack an African American because they (African Americans) threaten their community, livelihood, their women, or their way of life. However, the most atypical type of hate crime offender is the one who attacks an African American as part of his or her mission. These perpetrators want to rid the world of evil by attacking or getting rid of African Americans. From this viewpoint, the African American is seen as a subhuman who is intent on destroying the offender's way of life, taking away jobs, or simply polluting the White race (B. Levin, 1993).

DISCUSSION

In recent years, hate crimes have come to be viewed as constituting a serious problem in the United States. The serious concern about the growing incidence of hate crime rests on the belief that these offenses have an intense impact on African American victims that causes them to experience apprehension and terror. As a result of what is felt to be an increase in the incidence of such crimes, local, state, and federal officials are taking a tough stance on crimes motivated by prejudice. Although this increase is very disturbing and does not bode well for race relations in this country, there are some reasons for optimism. As noted, public officials at all levels have moved aggressively to address this problem. Furthermore, communities throughout the United States are becoming involved to further pressure agencies of the criminal justice system to move forcefully to investigate hate crimes and to punish harshly those offenders who are convicted of race-biased crimes. As a result of community pressure, many law enforcement agencies and courts are determined to send a strong message that hate crimes will not be tolerated (J. Levin & McDevitt, 1993).

Arriving at definitive conclusions based on the statistical data available is problematic for several reasons. Hate crime statistics released by the FBI for the past 6 years have differed significantly from information obtained by private organizations like the Anti-Defamation League, Klanwatch, Southern Poverty Law Center, and the Center for Criminal Justice Policy Research Center. This is because the FBI gathers data on actual crimes reported to the police, and private organizations tend to gather information on all incidents that are reported regardless of whether they represent a crime. In addition, although the number of police agencies voluntarily participating in data collection has increased, there are still a substantial number that do not. As of October 1996, 40% of law enforcement agencies in the United States were not providing hate crime data to the FBI. Many agencies simply do not have the staff needed to obtain and record this type of data. Other agencies have neither the technical expertise nor the inclination to gather hate crime information. Public officials in many communities also are concerned about potential social and economic repercussions by admitting the existence of hate crimes in their communities (BJA, 1997).

However, Jacobs and Potter (1998) have argued that to date, data collection efforts have not contributed to a better understanding of crime, prejudice, or prejudice-motivated crime in the United States, nor have the UCR reports contributed to better law enforcement practices. The government collections of hate crime data serve to create the false impression that the country is experiencing an epidemic of prejudice-motivated crime, and the long-term consequence may be to reinforce a sense of group victimization. Jacobs and Potter underscore the political and subjective nature of counting hate crimes, and they stress the problems associated with collecting hate crime data, such as defining hate crime, establishing a reliable means for determining when an offender's bias should convert an ordinary crime into a hate crime, and deciding which biases are important when counting hate crimes. As a result of these problems, Jacobs and Potter argue against the enactment and enforcement of hate crime laws. They conclude that although these laws are well intentioned, they represent the importation of identity politics into the criminal law by attempting to give special recognition to the victimization of members of historically discriminated groups. They note that attempting to measure hate crime is doomed to failure because of the difficulty of reliably determining the motivations of both individual and group offenders. They conclude that the FBI hate crime data is fragmentary, nonuniform, and distorted.

Although Jacobs and Potter present persuasive arguments against the enactment of hate crime statutes, the official response has clearly been in the direction of establishing laws that punish hate-motivated crime more severely. One can debate the extent of the problem; however, it seems rather evident that race-motivated attacks on African Americans are occurring with greater frequency, as is the violence associated with such crimes. The climate in the United States has become increasingly less tolerant of racial diversity issues. This is reflected by a reaction against affirmative action, bilingual education, and immigrant rights. Long held racial attitudes, heretofore suppressed and kept below the surface, are no longer politically incorrect, and they find a disturbing degree of respectability. In my view, the fact that racial bigotry is no longer viewed as contemptuous by many is fueled by the racial politics of the 1980s and 1990s—when some politicians sought to capitalize on the fears and prejudices of the electorate.

The deficiencies that exist in current hate crime statistics makes analysis of the problem difficult, if not almost impossible. Nonetheless, the raw data collected by the FBI should give grounds for serious concern. Rather than a problem with overreporting, it seems reasonable to conclude that the data currently available significantly underestimates the number of bias-related crimes that occur in the United States. Many victims of hate crimes do not report the incidents to the police, and have little confidence that officials can or will do anything to apprehend the persons responsible. Distrust of the police by African Americans also makes them reluctant to report hate crimes to the police, and others may fail to report hate crimes to the police because they wish to avoid the embarrassment of relating the circumstances of the episode. The aforementioned data collection problems also contribute further to the underreporting—rather than the overreporting—of hate crimes. Although the data presented in Table 17.1 is disturbing, it is likely that the incidence of hate crimes against African Americans is much greater.

Based on the data presented by the FBI, African Americans are most often the victims of race-motivated crimes. It is significant to observe that from 1992 to 1996 there has been a significant increase in the number of hate crimes reported against African Americans. Whether one is of the opinion that hate crime laws serve to address the problem or, conversely, that existing criminal statutes adequately address the matter, there should be little doubt that racial intolerance is again rearing its ugly head in America. What follows are some of the proposals that have been put forth to deal with this disturbing social problem.

POLICY IMPLICATIONS

The two schools of thought on the issue are whether or not the United States should gather hate crime statistics. However, as noted earlier, this debate seems to have been largely settled because the federal government and many states have enacted laws requiring the collection of hate crime statistics. However, those that are opposed to hate crime statutes and data collections make several recommendations on the issue. First, hate crime reporting statutes should be repealed because hate crime cannot be counted accurately given the ambiguous, subjective, and contentious concept of prejudice. Accurate data collection is doomed by the difficulty of trying to reliably determine an individual's motivation for the crime.

Second, hate crime sentence enhancement statutes also should be repealed because hate crimes are no more morally wrong than other crimes that result in injury to victims. Last, judicially imposed enhancements are just as offensive as legislatively imposed enhancements. Proponents of this view hold that judges possess sufficient discretion to either reduce or increase specific sentences based on aggravating and mitigating factors. As such, there is no need for statutes enhancing hate crimes (Jacobs & Potter, 1998).

Perhaps the most significant official action based on a belief that hate crimes are particularly injurious to society was the passage of the HCSA on April 23, 1990. Furthermore, as of 1995, 39 states have enacted laws that address bias-motivated violence and intimidation, and 19 states have passed laws requiring the collection of hate crime data. Also, many law enforcement agencies in the United States have implemented policies that specifically address crimes motivated by racial prejudice. These policies and procedures were generally developed through the use of model policies created by the International Association of Chiefs of Police and the National Organization of Black Law Enforcement Executives (BJA, 1997).

In the past 6 years, Congress and the U.S. Department of Justice have implemented numerous initiatives to combat crime and violence, and they have provided considerable funding for such projects. In addition, the government and private organizations have cooperated to develop hate crime legislation, improve the enforcement of existing hate crime laws, prosecute and track hate crime offenses, and prevent the further spread of hate crimes (BJA, 1997).

After recognizing an increasing climate of racial hatred in the United States, the administration sought to address the problem after President Clinton's reelection in 1996. Early in 1997 the administration offered two alternatives for a race-study group. The first was to appoint an independent commission that would evaluate the racial climate in the United States and would make formal recommendations to the president. The second alternative was to assign the race study to the White House domestic policy team (which seemed ill equipped to take on a task of this magnitude). The final decision was a compromise that resulted in the formation of a task force to be headed by a respected individual. Ultimately, Judith A. Winston, a former education department official with strong ties to the civil rights community, was appointed as executive director ("Panel on Race," 1998a).

However, after 15 months, 3 presidential town meetings, 11 board meetings, and more than 300 public hearings nationwide, the final

recommendation submitted by the commission was, according to the *Los Angeles Times,* simply to "just keep talking." The report concluded that, "if we are to succeed in the mission to create a more just nation, the initiative's work must continue," and "not only must it continue in name but it must continue in the spirit with which it began." This conclusion fell far short of the president's mandate when he said, "if we do nothing more that talk, it will be interesting— but it won't be enough" ("Man Acquitted," 1998, p. A31).

Given the current political atmosphere, it is unlikely that any significant progress will be made at this time. However, one thing is certain: The current racial climate in the United States is not healthy. Although controversy regarding the need for additional legislation to combat hate crime still remains, there does exist considerable protection under existing law. I believe the problem does not stem from a deficiency in the law to protect against hate crimes; rather, it is from a failing to give sufficient priority to the problem. Discrimination based on prejudice was not tolerated in the 1970s, and such attitudes, although no doubt present, did not often surface because the social and political climate did not provide a supportive atmosphere for their expression. However, the conservative climate of the 1980s and 1990s has contributed to an atmosphere in which expressions of such prejudices are once again finding respectability, and African Americans are increasingly the victims of such racial hatred.

REFERENCES

Aronson, A., & Height, D. I. (1998, August 25). *Cause for concern: Hate crimes in America* [Online]. Available: http://www.civilrights.org/lcef/hate//p6.html.

Bureau of Justice Assistance (BJA). (1997). *A policymaker's guide to hate crimes.* Washington, DC: U.S. Department of Justice.

Byers, B., & Zeller, R. A. (1997). Examination of official hate crime offense and bias motivation statistics for 1991–1994. *Journal of Crime and Justice, 20*(1), 91–106.

D'Angelo, L. (1998). *Hate crimes.* Philadelphia: Chelsea House.

Hate Crime Sentencing Enhancement Act (HCSEA) of 1994. Pub. L. No. 103-322, 108 Stat. 1796, H.R. 1796.

Hate Crime Statistics Act (HCSA) of 1990. Pub. L. No. 101-275, 28 U.S.C. 534, H.R. 1048.

Increase in hate crime reports has Fairfax on guard. (1994, July 14). *The Washington Post,* p. 4.

Jacobs, J. B., & Henry, J. S. (1996). Social construction of a hate crime epidemic. *Journal of Criminal Law & Criminology, 86*(2), 366-391.

Jacobs, J. B., & Potter, K. (1998). *Hate crimes: Criminal law and identity politics.* New York: Oxford University Press.

Levin, B. (1993). A dream deferred: The social and legal implications of hate crimes in the 1990s. *Journal of Intergroup Relations, Fall, 9.*

Levin, J., & McDevitt, J. (1993). *Hate crimes: The rising tide of bigotry and bloodshed.* New York: Plenum.

Los Angeles County Commission on Human Relations. (1995). *A report to the Los Angeles County Board of Supervisors.* Los Angeles: County of Los Angeles.

Man acquitted in black teen's beating. (1998, September 19). *Los Angeles Times,* p. A31.

Panel on race urges nothing but more talk. (1998, September 18). *Los Angeles Times,* p. A1.

Prosecutor considers capital murder. (1998, June 19). *Dallas Times,* p. 1.

Skinheads get prison for bombing plot. (1994, January 14). *Los Angeles Times,* p. B1.

Three white soldiers held in slaying of black couple. (1995, December 9). *The Washington Post,* p. A1.

U.S. Department of Justice. (1993). *FBI press release: Hate crime statistics, 1992.* Washington, DC: Author.

U.S. Department of Justice. (1994). *Federal Bureau of Investigation, Criminal Justice Information Services (CJIS) Division, uniform crime reports: Hate crimes, 1993.* Washington, DC: Author.

U.S. Department of Justice. (1995). *Federal Bureau of Investigation, Criminal Justice Information Services (CJIS) Division, uniform crime reports: Hate crimes, 1994.* Washington, DC: Author.

U.S. Department of Justice. (1996). *Federal Bureau of Investigation, Criminal Justice Information Services (CJIS) Division, uniform crime reports: Hate crimes, 1995.* Washington, DC: Author.

U.S. Department of Justice. (1998). *Federal Bureau of Investigation, Criminal Justice Information Services (CJIS) Division, uniform crime reports: Hate crimes, 1996.* Washington, DC: Author.

Welch, D. (1993, February). *Klanwatch intelligence report* (p. 5). Washington, DC: Klanwatch.

Wisconsin v. Mitchell. 113 S. Ct. 2194 (1993).

QUESTIONS

1. What are some of the reasons that hate crimes are underreported by both victims and law enforcement agencies charged with gathering data on hate crimes?

2. What is the extent of the problem of hate crimes suffered by African Americans? What evidence suggests that such crimes have increased since 1990?

3. Describe some historical examples of how hate crimes have been used to try to prevent African Americans from exercising their civil rights.

4. What are the difficulties associated with collecting complete and accurate data on the nature and extent of hate crimes?

5. What crimes are included in the FBI's list of designated hate crimes? What is the most common hate crime reported in the Uniform Crime Reports?

6. What are some examples illustrating that African Americans experience a comparatively high rate of hate crimes?

7. Describe some recent examples of hate crimes against African Americans. What other current examples have you heard recently reported in the news?

8. Why are church burnings an especially significant type of hate crime against African Americans in terms of the impact on the community?

9. What was the outcome in the case against the killers of James Byrd, Jr.? Do you think this case raised public awareness of hate crime?

10. What factors may contribute to hate crimes against African Americans? Describe these factors and discuss which ones you believe are particularly important and why.

11. What are some examples of how the cultural climate has become increasingly receptive to expressions of prejudice and intolerance?

12. How does the cultural climate contribute to the occurrence of hate crimes against African Americans (and others)?

18

Hate Crime Victimization Among Lesbian, Gay, and Bisexual Adults

Prevalence, Psychological Correlates, and Methodological Issues

Gregory M. Herek

J. Roy Gillis

Jeanine C. Cogan

Eric K. Glunt

What kinds of antigay crimes are experienced by gay, lesbian, and bisexual people, and how prevalent is such victimization? This article reports research using self-report questionnaires and interviews to examine the nature of antigay hate crimes and the psychological impacts of such crimes on the victims. Consistent with prior research, the results revealed that antigay victimization was a common experience and that the psychological consequences included depression, posttraumatic stress disorder, and decreased belief in the benevolence of the world and other people.

I n the past decade, the problem of criminal victimization based on an individual's perceived sexual orientation—commonly referred to as antigay *hate crimes* or *bias* crimes—has received increasing attention from policy makers and social scientists (e.g., Comstock, 1991; Herek, 1989; Herek & Berrill, 1992a; Jenness, 1995). The available data

EDITORS' NOTE: From Herek, G. M., Gillis, J. R., Cogan, J. C., and Glunt, E. K. (1997). Hate Crime Victimization Among Lesbian, Gay, and Bisexual Adults: Prevalence, Psychological Correlates, and Methodological Issues. *Journal of Interpersonal Violence, 12*(2), 195-215. © 1997 Sage Publications. Used with permission.

indicate that many lesbians and gay men in the United States have suffered physical violence, intimidation, and harassment because of their sexual orientation (Berrill, 1992; Hershberger & D'Augelli, 1995).

Unfortunately, previous studies of antigay hate crimes have varied widely in the quality of their data-collection and reporting procedures. This variability is evident in the most thorough review of prevalence research to date (Berrill, 1992). Although some studies reviewed by Berrill were published in peer-reviewed scientific journals (e.g., Comstock, 1989; D'Augelli, 1992; Herek, 1993), information about others was available only in a brief press release from a community organization. Consequently, critical evaluation of many surveys' methodology was not possible, and important details—including question wording, data collection procedures, and sample size—sometimes were not reported. Thus empirical data about antigay violence still are needed from studies that meet rigorous methodological standards (Herek & Berrill, 1992b).

Whereas some prevalence data for antigay victimization are available, the psychological consequences of such crimes remain largely undocumented. A notable exception is the structural equation analysis conducted by Hershberger and D'Augelli (1995; see also Pilkington & D'Augelli, 1995) with a sample of 165 lesbian and gay youths (mean age = 19 years) recruited through community centers in 14 different U.S. cities. The authors found that victimization affected mental health both directly and indirectly, the latter through its effects on family support and self-acceptance. Moderate correlations (ranging from .21 to .28) were observed between general psychological distress and three different measures of victimization.

The study by Hershberger and D'Augelli (1995) provides a valuable starting point for understanding the association between victimization and mental health. Data are lacking, however, from comparable adult samples. Adult survivors of antigay hate crimes face two sources of negative psychosocial consequences (Garnets, Herek, & Levy, 1990). First, they are likely to experience the same types of psychological distress as other crime victims, including depression, anxiety, and symptoms resembling posttraumatic stress disorder (PTSD). Any crime experience can also challenge victims' beliefs about their personal safety and invulnerability and their own self-worth. Alterations in such beliefs, in turn, may affect survivors' subsequent psychological distress (see Bard & Sangrey, 1979; Janoff-Bulman & Frieze, 1983a, 1983b; Kilpatrick et al., 1985).

Second, lesbian, gay, and bisexual survivors of bias crimes face added challenges because of their stigmatized status in American society. Because antigay hate crimes represent attacks on victims' gay identities and their community, it is likely that such crimes affect victims' feelings about themselves as gay individuals and their feelings toward the gay community. If a victim's homosexuality becomes directly linked to the heightened sense of vulnerability that normally follows victimization (Norris & Kaniasty, 1991), for example, being gay consequently may be experienced as a source of danger, pain, and punishment rather than intimacy, love, and community.

The present article describes results from the pilot-testing phase of an ongoing investigation of the prevalence, nature, and psychological consequences of antigay crimes. The data reported here were collected in the project's initial phase through self-administered questionnaires, with additional information obtained through follow-up interviews with a subset of the questionnaire sample. The article addresses three principal goals. First, prevalence data on criminal victimization and noncriminal harassment are reported. We recognize that these results—obtained from a convenience sample—cannot be reliably generalized to a larger population. In the absence of data from probability samples, however, findings from multiple studies with convenience samples provide a starting point for estimating population prevalence. Accordingly, we compare our findings to those of other studies of hate crimes that also employed convenience samples (e.g., Berrill, 1992).

Second, psychological correlates of victimization are identified. We hypothesized that lesbians, gay men, and bisexuals who had experienced victimization or harassment based on their sexual orientation would report higher levels of psychological distress than nonvictims or victims of nonbias crimes. We also hypothesized that survivors of bias crimes based on sexual orientation would be more likely than others to perceive the world as malevolent and unsafe, display lower self-esteem, and feel personally vulnerable to future victimization.

Third, the study addressed several methodological issues, including the cross-modal consistency of self-reports and the strategies that respondents use for deciding that a crime was based on their sexual orientation. As noted above, most published studies of antigay hate crimes have relied on data from self-administered questionnaires. Questionnaire studies permit efficient and relatively inexpensive data collection from large samples, but they also have potential validity problems resulting from memory limitations, variations in question interpretation, and the inherent constraints of self-administered questionnaires for utilizing complex item-skip patterns. Lacking the memory cues and probes that are routinely included in face-to-face interviews, for example, questionnaire respondents may fail to report experiences that are relatively inaccessible to memory, including minor victimization experiences (e.g., small-scale property crimes) or those that occurred in the distant past. Alternatively, questionnaire studies may be biased by overreporting of victimization experiences because of problems with question interpretation. In particular, respondents to a questionnaire may broadly interpret terms such as *crime, attack,* or *antigay/anti-lesbian* to include experiences that were not crimes (e.g., another person's use of derogatory language or expression of hostile attitudes toward gay men and lesbians generally) or that were not motivated primarily by antigay/-lesbian prejudice (i.e., they were based on the victim's specific circumstances rather than sexual orientation). By directly comparing self-reports of victimization in questionnaires and in follow-up interviews, we sought to develop a preliminary understanding of the consistency of such reports across data collection modes. Furthermore, by asking respondents why they believed their victimization was based on sexual orientation, we hoped to shed light on the attributional processes that underlie self-reports of antigay and anti-lesbian victimization.

METHOD

Sample and Procedure

Participants were 75 women and 75 men recruited in September of 1993 at a large lesbian/gay/bisexual street fair in Sacramento, California, sponsored by the Lambda Center, the city's gay and lesbian community center. Attendance at the 1993 festival was estimated by organizers to have exceeded 4,000. The research team rented a booth at the fair, from which participants were recruited. Volunteers were paid $5, offered a soft drink, and provided space in a shady area to complete the questionnaire, which required approximately 40 minutes. Of the 150 questionnaires, 3 were discarded because of excessive amounts of missing data. This left 147 questionnaires, 74 from women and 73 from men.

Follow-up interviews were later conducted with a subsample of respondents ($n = 25$ women, 20 men). These individuals had provided their name and contact information, could be successfully recontacted approximately 6 months after the questionnaire study, and were willing at that time to be interviewed. Interviews were conducted in a location convenient for the participant, usually her or his home. Respondents and interviewers were matched for gender in all but three interviews (three males were interviewed by a female). At the beginning of the interview, the interviewer explained the study procedures, obtained informed consent, and paid the participants a $10 honorarium.

Self-Administered Questionnaire

Victimization Experiences

Based on previous questionnaires used in studies of antigay victimization (Herek & Berrill, 1992b), respondents were asked whether they had ever experienced each of 10 different events in two time periods: (a) since the age of 16, and (b) in the past year. The events included crimes against the person (assault, sexual assault, assault with a weapon, robbery/mugging), property crimes (burglary/theft, vandalism), attempted crimes (attempted assault, attempted sexual assault, attempted theft/vandalism), and witnessing the murder of a loved one. The items were presented with response options of "yes" or "no" for each time period.

Two versions of the victimization questionnaire were randomly distributed to ascertain whether respondents' self-reports of hate-crime victimization would be affected by first responding to questions about their experiences with random (nonbias) crimes. Version 1 first posed the questions about respondents' experiences with any sort of crime victimization; on the next page, respondents were asked if any of the events they reported on the previous page had occurred because of their sexual orientation. Version 2 asked first about victimization experiences related to respondents' sexual orientation; these questions were followed on a separate page by a series of items about respondents' experiences with crime *not* related to their sexual orientation. All other measures were the same for both questionnaire versions. Because no differences in the frequency of bias-related victimization were observed for the two questionnaire conditions, the data are combined in the remainder of this article.

Psychological Distress

Four different aspects of psychological distress during the previous 30 days were measured. The response alternatives for all items were *never, almost never, sometimes, fairly often,* and *very often.* Depressive symptoms were assessed with the 20-item Center for Epidemiologic Studies Depression scale (CES-D; Radloff, 1977; $\alpha = .93$ for women and .94 for men).[1] Symptoms of crime-related PTSD were assessed with 20 items formulated by Kilpatrick et al. (1989) based on DSM-III diagnostic criteria for posttraumatic stress; they were adapted for a self-administered questionnaire. Examples of items are "I had trouble concentrating, even when I tried to concentrate," and "Disturbing memories kept coming into my mind whether I wanted to think of them or not" ($\alpha = .96$ for women and .94 for men). State anxiety and state anger were measured with items taken from the

short versions of Spielberger's scales for these two constructs: for the 6-item anxiety scale (Marteau & Bekker, 1992), $\alpha = .81$ for women and .82 for men; for the 10-item anger scale (Spielberger, Jacobs, Russel, & Crane, 1983), $\alpha = .93$ for women and .95 for men.

Victimization-Related Beliefs

The experience of crime often increases victims' sense of vulnerability, altering their beliefs about the benevolence of the impersonal world, the benevolence of people, personal safety, and self-worth. Beliefs about the benevolence of the impersonal world and of people were assessed with items from Janoff-Bulman's (1989) measures (for the 4-item Benevolence of World Scale, $\alpha = .83$ for women and .74 for men; for the 4-item Benevolence of People Scale, $\alpha = .71$ for women and .63 for men). Beliefs about personal safety were assessed with 8 items from the Fear of Crime measure developed by Norris and Kaniasty (1991), supplemented with 3 new items specific to Sacramento lesbians and gay men ("I worry about being the victim of an anti-lesbian/anti-bisexual [for men: antigay/anti-bisexual] hate crime"; "I worry about being attacked at a Sacramento gay/lesbian community event"; and "I feel safe from crime in Sacramento" [reverse-scored]; $\alpha = .86$ for women and .81 for men). Global self-esteem was assessed with Rosenberg's (1965) 10-item scale ($\alpha = .87$ for women and .90 for men). All of these measures were administered with a 5-point response scale ranging from *disagree strongly* to *agree strongly.*

Perceived vulnerability to crime was assessed with 4 items concerning respondents' estimation of their own risk for future criminal victimization (e.g., "How likely do you think it is that you will be the victim of any sort of crime during the next 12 months?"). For each question, respondents used a 10-point response scale, with higher scores indicating greater perceived likelihood ($\alpha = .86$ for women, .89 for men).

Face-to-Face Interviews

Three sets of questions from the interview are relevant to the present article. First, respondents were asked to recount their life history of victimization, including victimizations based on their sexual orientation. This information provided a consistency check for the incidents described in the self-administered questionnaire. Second, respondents who had experienced one or more attacks or harassment events based on their sexual orientation were asked to describe the incident, including characteristics of the perpetrators and the setting. (Interviewees who reported more than one antigay crime were asked to describe the crime in which they felt they were in the greatest physical danger.) Finally, respondents who had been victimized were asked to explain how they had decided or realized that the attack was based on their sexual orientation.

RESULTS

Sample Characteristics

Except as noted below, gender differences were not observed in demographic characteristics. The full sample ($N = 147$) was predominantly White (82%), with another 7% Latino, 1% African American, 2% Asian/Pacific Islander, and 1% Native American. The remaining 7% classified themselves as "other," most of them reporting mixed ancestry. Respondents ranged in age from 16 to 68 years ($M = 33$ years). The sample was highly educated, with 47% having earned a bachelor's or higher degree. Only 8% had not completed any formal education beyond high school. Respondents' median annual income was in the range of $15,000 to $25,000. Twenty-five percent reported earning $35,000 or more, whereas 35% reported income of $15,000 or less. Women were more likely than men to report that they were currently working at a job for pay (85% vs. 72%; $\chi^2 [1, N = 145] = 3.82$, $p = .05$). Most respondents (86%) identified their sexual orientation as lesbian or gay, with another 11% identifying as "bisexual" or "bisexual, mostly lesbian/gay" and 3% identifying as "bisexual, mostly heterosexual." Most (78%) had never been married heterosexually, but 19% had once been married, and one respondent was currently married. One tenth of the respondents had at least one child. A majority

(60%) reported that they were currently in a long-term, committed relationship.

Compared to the full sample, the interview subsample was slightly older (mean age = 36 years) and more likely to be White (91% were White); for both comparisons, $p < .05$, using χ^2. They did not differ significantly from the full sample on other demographic variables.

Descriptive Data About Victimization

Prevalence

As shown in Table 18.1, respondents reported 86 antigay/anti-lesbian incidents for the previous year, and another 213 such incidents prior to the previous year. Because each respondent could report multiple forms of victimization within the same time period, the categories in Table 18.1 are not mutually exclusive. Counting each respondent only once, we found that 20% of the sample reported an antigay/anti-lesbian crime against their person (7% of the sample) or property (13% of the sample) that had occurred in the previous year. Another 5.5% reported an attempted antigay/anti-lesbian crime against them in the previous year. Another 21% did not experience antigay/anti-lesbian criminal victimization in the previous year, but reported a bias victimization experience since age 16 (15% reported assaults and 6% reported property crimes). Another 4% reported an attempted antigay/anti-lesbian crime against them since age 16 (but not in the previous year). In summary, half of the respondents had experienced at least one crime or attempted crime that they believed was based on their sexual orientation.

Description of Crime Incidents

Information about perpetrators and crime settings was obtained from the interview subsample. Because of the subsample's small size and highly select nature, we focus here on simple descriptions of patterns rather than statistical significance tests. More than one half of those interviewed (14 women and 12 men, or 58% of the sample) had experienced an antigay hate crime at some time in their life. Most described an antigay assault ($n = 16$) or attempted assault ($n = 4$); the remainder described a property

Table 18.1   Frequency (and Proportion) of Reports of Victimization Based on Sexual Orientation

| | In Past Year | | Since Age 16 | |
Type of Victimization	Females	Males	Females	Males
Assault with weapon	4 (5.4%)	1 (1.4%)	11 (14.9%)	5 (6.8%)
Sexual assault	5 (6.8%)	1 (1.4%)	15 (20.3%)	10 (13.7%)
Other assault	3 (4.1%)	1 (1.4%)	11 (14.9%)	9 (12.3%)
Attempted sexual assault	5 (6.8%)	3 (4.1%)	12 (16.2%)	11 (15.1%)
Attempted other assault	6 (8.1%)	2 (2.7%)	14 (18.9%)	15 (20.5%)
Robbery/mugging	4 (5.4%)	2 (2.7%)	6 (8.1%)	6 (8.2%)
Burglary/theft	8 (10.8%)	10 (13.7%)	18 (24.3%)	16 (21.9%)
Vandalism	7 (9.5%)	10 (13.7%)	11 (14.9%)	14 (19.2%)
Attempted property crime	6 (8.1%)	5 (6.8%)	8 (10.8%)	10 (13.7%)
Witnessed murder of loved one	2 (2.7%)	1 (1.4%)	5 (6.8%)	6 (8.2%)

NOTE: Percentages are based on the 71 females and 71 males who provided complete data for this section of the questionnaire.

crime ($n = 5$) or witnessing the violent death of a loved one ($n = 1$).

Nearly all of the perpetrators described by interviewees were males, both for male victims (96%) and female victims (91%). A plurality of perpetrators were White (49%), with most of the remainder either Hispanic (26%), or Black (23%). The modal estimated age of perpetrators was between 19 and 25 years (61% of perpetrators), with most of the remainder (19%) estimated between 26 and 40 years. Whereas men were equally likely to report a victimization by a single perpetrator or by a group, women were more likely to describe an attack by one perpetrator (64%, compared to 36% who were victimized by a group). A majority of women (77%) were attacked by someone they knew, whereas the majority of men (58%) were attacked by one or more strangers.

The location of the incident could be ascertained for 25 of the 26 interview respondents who reported an antigay attack. A majority of the women (8, or 62% of the female hate crime survivors in the interview sample) described an attack that occurred in a private setting, either their own home (5 respondents) or the perpetrator's home (3 respondents). In contrast, most men (9, or 75% of the male hate crime survivors) reported an attack that occurred in a public setting; these incidents included vandalism of the respondent's property (e.g., car or

house). Of the 14 incidents that were described as occurring in public settings, 4 (29%) occurred in proximity to a gay bar or other gay-identified location; the remainder occurred in neutral or non-gay-identified settings.

The gender differences observed here in number of perpetrators, familiarity to the victim, and crime location appeared to be due primarily to the high prevalence of sexual assault among women. Half of the women interviewees reporting an antigay crime (7 of 14) had been sexually assaulted, compared to one of the men (one other man reported an attempted sexual assault). Sexual assaults tended to differ from other hate crimes in that they were usually committed in a private setting by a lone assailant who was known to the victim.

Psychological Correlates of Victimization

Psychological Distress

To assess the relationship between victimization experiences and psychological distress, we categorized respondents hierarchically into one of five groups: (a) those who reported *both* bias-related crimes against their person *and* nonbias crimes against their person (9.5% of the sample); (b) those who reported at least one bias-related person crime, but no non-bias-related person crimes (17%); (c) those who reported at

Table 18.2   Mean Scores for Psychological Distress Among Victimization Groups

Group	CES-D[a]	PTSD[b]	Anxiety	Anger
Bias person crime only	33.76$_a$ (15.45)	27.19$_a$ (19.31)	10.74$_a$ (5.02)	15.30 (11.26)
Both bias and nonbias person crimes	30.08 (18.03)	26.75 (16.13)	10.00 (4.89)	12.54 (9.51)
Nonbias person crime only	26.09 (15.25)	16.26 (14.63)	8.13 (4.46)	12.83 (7.03)
Property crime only (bias or nonbias)	20.79$_b$ (11.09)	13.44$_b$ (11.59)	7.33$_b$ (3.38)	10.58 (6.90)
No victimization	25.89 (15.17)	17.86 (18.28)	7.89 (4.39)	10.62 (9.27)

NOTE: Standard deviations are shown in parentheses. Within each column, means with different subscripts are significantly different, based on Student Newman Keuls comparisons ($p < .05$).
a. CES-D = Center for Epidemiologic Studies Depression Scale.
b. PTSD = Posttraumatic Stress Disorder.

least one non-bias-related person crime, but no bias-related person crimes (16.3%); (d) those who reported at least one property crime of either type, bias or nonbias (27.2%); and (e) those who reported no criminal victimization or only attempted victimizations (19.7%). We were unable to classify 15 of the 147 respondents, either because of missing data or because of limitations inherent in the version of the survey that they completed.[3]

Table 18.2 reveals a consistent pattern in scores for psychological distress among the victimization groups: Individuals who experienced a bias crime scored highest, followed closely on three of the four measures by individuals who reported both bias and nonbias person crimes. Individuals reporting property crimes consistently scored lowest on psychological distress, although their difference from the nonvictimized group was minuscule for anxiety and anger scores. ANOVA indicated that the differences among victimization groups were statistically significant for depressive symptoms ($F[4,117] = 3.02$, $p < .05$), anxiety ($F[4,124] = 2.92$, $p < .05$), and PTSD symptoms ($F[4,119] = 3.56$, $p < .01$). The differences for anger were not statistically significant, although the pattern of scores was similar to other groups. Student Newman Keuls comparisons indicated that the group reporting bias-related person crimes consistently scored significantly higher than the group reporting property crimes ($ps < .05$).

Beliefs About the World and Personal Safety

Using a similar analytic procedure, we compared respondents' beliefs about the benevolence of the impersonal world and of people, personal safety, vulnerability to crime, and self-worth. As shown in Table 18.3, intergroup differences were less pronounced than with the measures of psychological distress. In general, individuals in the two groups encompassing bias-related person crimes scored higher than others for fear of crime and perceived vulnerability, but lower than others for self-esteem, beliefs in the benevolence of the impersonal world, and beliefs in the benevolence of people. However, many of these differences were of small magnitude. ANOVA revealed a significant difference only for beliefs about the benevolence of people ($F[4,124] = 3.48$, $p = .01$) and marginally significant effects for perceived likelihood of victimization ($F[4,119] = 2.33$, $p = .06$) and beliefs about the benevolence of the world ($F[4,124] = 3.48$, $p = .07$).

Consistency Between Questionnaire and Interview Responses

Comparison of self-reports across modes of data collection—between self-administered questionnaires and face-to-face interviews—necessarily required caution because multiple

Table 18.3   Mean Scores for Beliefs Among Victimization Groups

Group	Benevolence of World	Benevolence of People	Fear of Crime	Self-Esteem	Perceived Vulnerability
Bias person crime only	14.08 (4.06)	13.17$_a$ (3.45)	30.52 (9.16)	39.04 (8.31)	15.86 (9.43)
Both bias and nonbias person crimes	13.00 (2.22)	13.71 (2.46)	28.21 (7.54)	40.50 (7.57)	15.36 (6.98)
Nonbias person crime only	16.00 (2.73)	15.27$_b$ (2.60)	27.76 (8.06)	42.38 (7.83)	14.25 (6.12)
Property crime only (bias or nonbias)	14.75 (2.77)	15.43$_b$ (2.21)	28.23 (8.66)	43.58 (6.07)	12.03 (6.93)
No victimization	14.14 (4.07)	14.97$_b$ (2.73)	25.31 (7.88)	42.39 (8.05)	10.42 (6.95)

NOTE: Standard deviations are shown in parentheses. Within each column, means with different subscripts are significantly different, based on Student Newman Keuls comparisons ($p < .05$).

factors could have influenced response consistency. In addition to the effects of different modes of data collection, observed differences might have been caused by the passage of time between completing a questionnaire and participating in an interview (in some cases, 7 months separated the two data collection points). This lag could have introduced memory problems (e.g., an incident that was relatively recent at the time of questionnaire completion might have faded in memory by the time the interview was conducted) and might also have created confusion about the time frame for incidents (e.g., events that were appropriately reported as having happened "in the past year" on the questionnaire might have been appropriately reported as happening more than 1 year ago in the interview). When we compared the two response modes, we excluded incidents reported during the interview that appeared to have occurred after the questionnaire was completed (researcher judgments in this regard were sometimes necessary because respondents did not always recall the exact date of a victimization).

Of the 45 respondents who completed questionnaires and interviews, 3 failed to complete all of the violence items on the questionnaire, and another 3 failed to follow directions or provided uninterpretable questionnaire responses (e.g., multiple responses to a single item). Of the remaining 39 respondents, 20 (51%) were consistent across data collection modes in reporting bias crimes: 11 reported a bias incident in both their questionnaire and interview, whereas 9 reported

no bias incidents in either mode. The remaining 19 respondents (49%) were inconsistent in their self-reports. In most cases (4 person crimes and 7 property crimes), a crime was reported in the interview that had not been reported in the self-administered questionnaire. In the remainder (3 person crimes and 5 property crimes), a crime that had been reported in the questionnaire was not subsequently reported in the interview.

Judgments About Motivations for Attacks

Four different strategies were identified from respondents' answers to the open-ended question about how they decided that their victimization experience was based on their sexual orientation. Intercoder reliability for categorizing responses into one of these categories was acceptably high (96% agreement between two coders). Although the interview subsample was not representative of a larger population, their answers suggest at least some of the ways in which lesbians and gay men make judgments about their attackers' motivations.

Verbal Cues

Almost half of the respondents (12, or 46% of those who experienced a hate crime) based their judgment on verbal statements made by their attacker(s). Eight women and four men cited the attacker's explicit antigay or anti-lesbian remarks. One female respondent, for example, said that she believed the attack was based on her sexual orientation because "They told me. The two men that raped me said, as they held the gun to my head, they wanted to get me, that they thought about killing me. They said, 'We thought of different ways of harming you, even killing you,' as they held the gun to my head, 'but raping you as a lesbian, we felt, would be the best way to get to you.'" Another example was provided by a male respondent who based his attribution on the assailant "screaming, 'you dirty mother-fucking faggot.'"

Visibility Cues

A second way that respondents decided that a crime was based on their sexual orientation was if it occurred in a gay-identified location or situation. Three respondents (12% of those who experienced a hate crime) described incidents that occurred in specific gay-identified settings, such as outside a gay bar. One male respondent, for example, believed his attack was bias-motivated "Because it happened in front of a gay bar. Considering there was no demand for money or anything else, I concluded that it is based only on who you were."

Four other respondents (15% of those who experienced a hate crime) based their decision on the fact that the attack occurred immediately after they (or others with them) had behaved in a way that made their gay or lesbian identity apparent to others. For example, a female respondent described the context in which some males attacked the vehicle she was riding in: "Because the guys double-look at you, and look disgusted. They saw the two guys in [our] back seat hugging and kissing. The attackers were laughing while trying to run us off the road."

Contextual Inference

Four respondents (15% of those who experienced a hate crime) based their judgment on a hunch or inference, rather than on the perpetrators' overt behavior. Such hunches often were based on the timing of the incident or a belief that the perpetrators recognized the respondent's sexual orientation. One male respondent whose home was vandalized, for example, said

"I guess it's because it happened on gay pride Saturday and someone decided to mark the front of my house while I'm gone. It seemed just a bit too much of a coincidence." Another male respondent said that his attribution was based on "Just the teenage and younger kids yelling names at people prior to that. It was almost as if they realized—it clicked—that my partner and I were gay, and that's when it started."

Nonbias Crimes

Finally, three people (12%) described an incident that did not conform to the research team's definition of a hate crime. In these cases, respondents categorized the incident as based on their sexual orientation solely because both they and the perpetrators were gay or lesbian. The crime, however, did not appear to have been directed at the victim primarily because the perpetrator wanted to attack a gay or lesbian person.

Other Experiences With Harassment and Threat of Victimization

Although the focus of the present research was criminal victimization, the self-administered questionnaire also included questions about other types of harassment based on sexual orientation. As shown in Table 18.4, verbal harassment in the past year was reported by roughly one half of the sample (57% of women and 49% of men); the vast majority of respondents (75% of women and 88% of men) had experienced such harassment since age 16. Threats of violence also were common. In the past year, such threats had been experienced by approximately one fifth of the women and one third of the men, with lifetime prevalence increasing to more than one third of the women and more than one half of the men. Chi-square analyses indicated that men were significantly more likely than women to report verbal harassment since age 16 (χ^2 [1, $N = 142$] = 4.05, $p < .05$), threats of violence since age 16 (χ^2 [1, $N = 141$] = 4.37, $p < .05$), and having objects thrown at them since age 16 (χ^2 [1, $N = 142$] = 7.53, $p < .01$). Women were more likely than men to report having been spat upon in the previous year (χ^2 [1, $N = 134$] = 3.77, $p = .05$).

Table 18.4   Frequency (and Proportion) of Reports of Other Types of Harassment

	In Past Year		Since Age 16	
Type of Victimization	*Females*	*Males*	*Females*	*Males*
Threat	15 (21%)	18 (29%)	26 (36%)	37 (54%)
Verbal harassment	40 (57%)	33 (49%)	55 (75%)	61 (88%)
Spat upon	4 (6%)	0 (0%)	11 (15%)	5 (7%)
Objects thrown	7 (10%)	11 (17%)	16 (22%)	30 (43%)
Chased/followed	10 (14%)	12 (18%)	18 (25%)	27 (39%)

NOTE: Because of missing data, *n* varies across questions. The minimum *n* on which any percentage is based is 74 females and 73 males.

Table 18.5   Comparison of Sacramento Data to Other Studies of Victimizations Since Age 16 (in Percentages)

Type of Victimization	*Sacramento Adults*	*National Adults*[a]	*National Youth*[b]
Assault with weapon	11	9	9
Assault	14	17	18
Vandalism	17	19	23
Threat	45	44	44
Chased	32	33	31
Objects thrown	33	25	33
Verbal abuse	82	80	80

NOTE: Percentages for Sacramento are based on a sample of *n* = 142.
a. Medians from 24 studies reviewed by Berrill (1992).
b. Proportions from a sample of 193 lesbian, gay, and bisexual adolescents and young adults from 14 U.S. cities (Pilkington & D'Augelli, 1995). For additional details about this sample, see Hershberger and D'Augelli (1995).

Comparisons to Other Studies of Prevalence

As noted earlier, systematic prevalence data concerning violence against lesbians and gay men are limited. Berrill's (1992) review and the study by D'Augelli and his colleagues (Hershberger & D'Augelli, 1995; Pilkington & D'Augelli, 1995), however, provide a basis for tentative comparison of the present prevalence findings to reports from other communities. As shown in Table 18.5, the results from our Sacramento-area sample are strikingly similar to the findings of the other studies. In most cases, they are within a few percentage points. Because data were not reported separately for male and female respondents in many of the studies reviewed by Berrill (1992), data from the present study have been collapsed across genders in Table 18.5.

DISCUSSION

The present study has both substantive and methodological implications for research on antigay and anti-lesbian hate crimes. The data indicate that, as in other parts of the United States, antigay victimization is a common experience for gay men, lesbians, and bisexuals in the Sacramento area. In the present sample, roughly one fifth of the respondents had experienced an antigay assault at some time in their lives, and another one fifth had experienced an antigay property crime. Verbal harassment and threats were even more prevalent, with approximately one half of the respondents experiencing at least one incident in the previous year, and most of the sample reporting at least one such incident since age 16.

Furthermore, individuals who experienced physical assault because of their sexual orientation appeared to have higher levels of psychological distress than did others. Bias crime assault survivors were more anxious and angry than others, and experienced more symptoms of depression and PTSD. They also displayed less willingness to believe in the general benevolence of people and rated their own risk for future victimization somewhat higher than did others. Although the magnitude of these differences was modest, the present findings are consistent with Garnets et al.'s (1990) hypothesis that hate crimes—by attacking the victim's identity as well as her or his person or property—can inflict psychological damage beyond that associated with nonbias crimes.

The interview data underscore the importance of recognizing that antigay crimes take a variety of forms and probably manifest many different patterns. Among interviewees, antigay sexual assaults differed from other hate crimes in the typical number of perpetrators (a single assailant in sexual assaults compared to multiple assailants in other crimes), the attacker's relationship to the victim (perpetrators of sexual assaults tended to be known by the victim whereas other perpetrators were not), and the location of the crime (antigay sexual assaults tended to occur in private settings whereas other hate crimes often occurred in public settings). Because the interview sample was small and nonrepresentative, generalizations from these observations are necessarily tentative. Future research with larger samples is needed to replicate the present findings and to explore other possible differences in crime patterns (e.g., between male and female sexual assault victims, and between the victims of property crimes and person crimes).

In other respects as well, the results reported here must necessarily be regarded as preliminary. Although larger than the interview subsample, the questionnaire sample was itself relatively small and recruited through a single venue in which individuals who are publicly identified as gay, lesbian, or bisexual (and thus possibly at greater risk for victimization) were likely to have been overrepresented. In addition, the methodological analyses point to at least two important limitations on the present findings. First, the comparison of self-reports in interviews and self-administered questionnaires indicates that prevalence data might be affected by the mode of data collection. Discrepancies were observed between the questionnaire and interview responses of nearly half of the interviewees. Most such discrepancies involved respondents reporting an incident in the interview but not in the questionnaire. This pattern is important but perhaps not surprising in light of the many memory cues and prompts included in the interview. It suggests that exclusive reliance on self-administered questionnaires may result in undercounting of some types of victimization experiences. At the same time, approximately 40% of the inconsistencies resulted from incidents—most of them property crimes—that were reported in the questionnaire but not in the interview. Given the time lag between questionnaire completion and interviews, respondents may have forgotten about relatively minor thefts or vandalisms between the two data collection points. Another possibility is that respondents reinterpreted their experiences between the questionnaire and interview sessions, with some reclassifying an experience as a hate crime that previously was assumed to be unrelated to their sexual orientation, and others reclassifying their experiences in the opposite direction.

The possibility that experiences were recategorized over time underscores the importance of understanding the cognitive processes whereby lesbians, gay men, and bisexuals decide that their victimization experiences are (or are not) linked to their sexual orientation. The interview data suggest that most respondents decided that a crime was based on their sexual orientation because of explicit statements by the perpetrator or their own visibility as a gay or bisexual person at the time of the incident. Others classified an incident as linked to their sexual orientation on the basis of a hunch. Still others described a crime as having occurred because of their sexual orientation simply because both they and the perpetrator were gay or lesbian. This last criterion was at odds with our own working definition of a hate crime, and suggests that prevalence data from questionnaire studies using similarly worded items may incorrectly label some nonbias victimizations as hate crimes. These findings highlight the importance for researchers of clearly defining what is meant by terms such as *antigay, anti-lesbian,* or *crime based on your sexual orientation* in studies of victimization.

In addition to answering our a priori methodological questions, the research described here also provided three additional insights that warrant comment. First, our questionnaire instrument did not permit adequate examination of the longitudinal effects of victimization. Following previous research (Berrill, 1992; Herek & Berrill, 1992b), it asked about victimization within the past year and since age 16. The lack of differences in psychological functioning between respondents reporting victimization in these two periods indicates that trauma associated with hate crime victimization probably lasts longer than 1 year. In future research, it would be beneficial to ask respondents to report the specific year(s) in which their victimization experiences occurred, thereby permitting recency of victimization to be directly considered as a variable.

A second problem with the questionnaire used in the present study (and with most previous questionnaires) is that its checklist format did not allow us to determine whether respondents who reported several types of victimization had experienced them in a single incident or in multiple incidents. For example, if a respondent reported having been sexually assaulted, assaulted with a weapon, and robbed, we were unable to ascertain whether these were three separate attacks or part of a single victimization. This limitation is important for at least two reasons. First, incidents that included multiple types of victimization could be counted more than once, thereby distorting prevalence estimates. Second, a single incident that includes multiple types of victimization may be more traumatic than an incident that includes only one kind of victimization (the former, for example, may be perceived as more life-threatening), and consequently may have a more negative effect on psychological functioning. Alternatively, multiple victimization incidents may exert a cumulative negative effect on mental health. In either case, ascertaining how many separate hate crimes individuals have experienced, as well as the variety of types of victimization that occurred in each crime, will be

important for better understanding the prevalence and consequences of hate crimes. We now ask respondents in our ongoing study to describe each crime separately, reporting all forms of victimization (assault, robbery, etc.) that occurred in each incident.

Finally, the interview responses made clear the importance of considering childhood victimization experiences in examining the psychological impact of adult victimization. Consistent with most other studies in this area (but see Hershberger & D'Augelli, 1995; Pilkington & D'Augelli, 1995), our focus has been on antigay/anti-lesbian victimization experiences that occurred during adulthood (defined as since age 16). During the interviews, however, questions about lifetime victimization experiences yielded a large number of reports of assault or sexual abuse during childhood or early adolescence. Almost half of the respondents (56% of females, 40% of males) reported some type of childhood victimization or attempted victimization. Most incidents involved sexual abuse. Approximately one third of all interview respondents (48% of females and 15% of males) reported childhood sexual victimization (i.e., a sexual assault or abuse incident that occurred before age 16) and another 9% (4% of females and 15% of males) reported an attempted sexual victimization. The small size of the interview sample makes it inadvisable to generalize or draw conclusions from these patterns. Because such experiences may be relevant to understanding the mental health consequences of adult victimization, however, we strongly recommend that researchers include questions about preadult victimization in their interview protocols.

Despite its limitations, the present study shows that criminal victimization based on sexual orientation is a fact of life for many lesbians, gay men, and bisexuals in the United States. Such victimization may have long-term negative effects on mental health. The need is clear for programs to prevent such violence and to respond to the needs of survivors (e.g., Wertheimer, 1992). In addition, more social science research clearly is needed on the prevalence and consequences of antigay/anti-lesbian hate crimes, as well as on the social and psychological factors that mitigate their impact.

NOTES

1. To maintain consistency throughout the questionnaire, CES-D items were administered with a 5-point response scale (rather than the 4-point scale on which published scale norms are based).

2. The 5-category classification scheme was based on observations of three principal patterns in preliminary analyses. First, contrary to expectations, victimizations within the past year were not associated with higher levels of distress than earlier victimizations. Indeed, in some cases, we observed greater psychological distress among individuals who reported a victimization prior to the past year. (See the Discussion section for comment on the importance of directly assessing the recency of victimization in future studies.) Consequently, we collapsed across recency of victimization. Second, psychological distress was substantially lower among respondents who reported property crimes exclusively than among those who reported any person crimes (bias or nonbias). Hence, we grouped all victims reporting exclusively property crimes in the same category. Third, levels of psychological distress did not differ substantially between nonvictims and respondents who reported one or more attempted victimizations (but no completed victimizations). Consequently, these respondents were grouped together. Because these patterns may be specific to the current sample, we caution researchers to assess the patterns in their own data before adopting this classification scheme.

3. Unfortunately, we could not determine whether reports of the same category of crime (e.g., physical assault) on both pages indicated the experience of one crime or multiple crimes for respondents who first completed the questionnaire page about random (nonbias) victimization, followed by the page about antigay/anti-lesbian victimization.

REFERENCES

Bard, M., & Sangrey, D. (1979). *The crime victim's book.* New York: Basic Books.

Berrill, K. T. (1992). Antigay violence and victimization in the United States: An overview. In G. M. Herek & K. T. Berrill (Eds.), *Hate crimes: Confronting violence against lesbians and gay men* (pp. 19–45). Newbury Park, CA: Sage.

Comstock, G. D. (1989). Victims of anti-gay/lesbian violence. *Journal of Interpersonal Violence, 4,* 101–106.

Comstock, G. D. (1991). *Violence against lesbians and gay men.* New York: Columbia University Press.

D'Augelli, A. R. (1992). Lesbian and gay male undergraduates' experiences of harassment and fear on campus. *Journal of Interpersonal Violence, 7,* 383–395.

Garnets, L., Herek, G. M., & Levy, B. (1990). Violence and victimization of lesbians and gay men: Mental health consequences. *Journal of Interpersonal Violence, 5,* 366–383.

Herek, G. M. (1989). Hate crimes against lesbians and gay men: Issues for research and policy. *American Psychologist, 44,* 948–955.

Herek, G. M. (1993). Documenting prejudice against lesbians and gay men on campus: The Yale Sexual Orientation Survey. *Journal of Homosexuality, 25*(4), 15–30.

Herek, G. M., & Berrill, K. T. (Eds.). (1992a). *Hate crimes: Confronting violence against lesbians and gay men.* Newbury Park, CA: Sage.

Herek, G. M., & Berrill, K. T. (1992b). Documenting the victimization of lesbians and gay men: Methodological issues. In G. M. Herek & K. T. Berrill (Eds.), *Hate crimes: Confronting violence against lesbians and gay men* (pp. 270–286). Newbury Park, CA: Sage.

Hershberger, S. L., & D'Augelli, A. R. (1995). The impact of victimization on the mental health and suicidality of lesbian, gay, and bisexual youth. *Developmental Psychology, 31,* 65–74.

Janoff-Bulman, R. (1989). Assumptive worlds and the stress of traumatic events: Applications of the schema construct. *Social Cognition, 7,* 113–136.

Janoff-Bulman, R., & Frieze, I. H. (Eds.). (1983a). Reactions to victimization [Special issue]. *Journal of Social Issues, 39*(2).

Janoff-Bulman, R., & Frieze, I. H. (1983b). A theoretical perspective for understanding reactions to victimization. *Journal of Social Issues, 39*(2), 1–17.

Jenness, V. (1995). Social movement growth, domain expansion, and framing processes: The gay/lesbian movement and violence against gays and lesbians as a social problem. *Social Problems, 42,* 145–170.

Kilpatrick, D. G., Best, C. L., Veronen, L. J., Amick, A. E., Villeponteaux, L. A., & Ruff, G. A. (1985). Mental health correlates of criminal victimization: A random community survey. *Journal of Consulting and Clinical Psychology, 53,* 866–873.

Kilpatrick, D. G., Saunders, B. E., Amick-McMullan, A., Best, C. L., Veronen, L. J., & Resnick, H. S. (1989). Victim and crime factors associated with the development of crime-related post-traumatic stress disorder. *Behavior Therapy, 20,* 199–214.

Marteau, T. M., & Bekker, H. (1992). The development of a six-item short form of the state scale of the Spielberger State-Trait Anxiety Inventory. *British Journal of Clinical Psychology, 31,* 301–306.

Norris, F. H., & Kaniasty, K. (1991). The psychological experience of crime: A test of the mediating role of beliefs in explaining the distress of victims. *Journal of Social and Clinical Psychology, 10,* 239–261.

Pilkington, N. W., & D'Augelli, A. R. (1995). Victimization of lesbian, gay, and bisexual youth in community settings. *Journal of Community Psychology, 23,* 33–56.

Radloff, L. (1977). The CES-D Scale: A self-report depression scale for research in the general population. *Applied Psychological Measurement, 1,* 385–401.

Rosenberg, M. (1965). *Society and the adolescent self image.* Princeton: Princeton University Press.

Spielberger, C. D., Jacobs, G., Russel, S., & Crane, R. S. (1983). Assessment of anger: The State-Trait Anger Scale. In J. N. Butcher & C. D. Spielberger (Eds.), *Advances in personality assessment* (Vol. 2, pp. 161–189). Hillsdale, NJ: Lawrence Erlbaum.

Wertheimer, D. M. (1992). Treatment and service interventions for lesbian and gay male crime victims. In G. M. Herek & K. T. Berrill (Eds.), *Hate crimes: Confronting violence against lesbians and gay men* (pp. 227–240). Newbury Park, CA: Sage.

QUESTIONS

1. What are the two sources of negative psychosocial consequences that victims of antigay hate crimes experience?

2. What are some examples of how victims of antigay hate crimes face additional sources of stress associated with victimization because of their sexual orientation?

3. According to the results in this study, how common was antigay victimization?

4. How did the nature and circumstances of the antigay crimes reported by female victims differ from those reported by male victims? Which difference surprised you the most?

5. How were the different types of victimization studied in this research associated with different patterns of psychological distress?

6. Describe the four strategies that victims used to decide whether their victimization was based on their sexual orientation. What were some examples of each strategy?

7. What factors may have influenced the consistency of victims' responses on the questionnaire and in the interview?

8. What proportion of victims in this research reported experiences with harassment and threats of violence?

9. Describe the types of psychological distress experienced by victims of antigay hate crimes.

10. Why are hate crimes, which represent an attack on the victim's identity, potentially more harmful psychologically than nonbias crimes?

11. What are the methodological strengths and limitations of this research?

12. Can you think of an example of an antigay hate crime recently reported in the news? How do you think the crime affected both the victim and other lesbian, gay, and bisexual people who heard about the crime?

19

HATE VIOLENCE AS BORDER PATROL

An Asian American Theory of Hate Violence

TERRI YOUH-LIN CHEN

What does it mean to be an "American"? This article demonstrates how Asian Americans and other people of color are perceived as foreigners whose presence is marked and monitored by actions that essentially constitute a form of "border patrol." Hate violence is used by both government actors and private individuals to support an exclusivist vision of America as a white nation. Routine "border patrol" activities include hate crimes that are used to defend white cultural boundaries in the name of preserving "American-ness." In this monochromatic conception of America, Asian Americans are permanently marked as foreigners and thus targeted for hate crimes.

CHICO, CALIFORNIA 1877 Arsonists of the Order of Caucasians, a white supremacist group that blamed Chinese immigrants for all the economic sufferings of white workers, tried to burn down the Chinatown in Chico and murdered four Chinese men by tying them up, dousing them with kerosene, and setting them on fire.

ROCK SPRINGS, WYOMING 1885 A mob of white miners massacred twenty-eight Chinese laborers, wounded fifteen, and chased several hundred out of town. The white miners opened fire at a crowd of unarmed Chinese, burned their huts to the ground, and threw the bodies of the dead Chinese as well as the wounded Chinese who were still alive into the flames. A grand jury did not indict a single person.

EDITORS' NOTE: From Chen, T. (2000). Hate Violence as Border Patrol: An Asian American Theory of Hate Violence. *Asian Law Journal, 7,* 69-101. © 2000 by *Asian Law Journal.* Reprinted by permission of *Asian Law Journal.*

DETROIT, MICHIGAN 1982   Vincent Chin was a Chinese American male beaten to death a few days before his wedding with a baseball bat by two white laid-off autoworkers who screamed during the killing that the "Japs" were taking all the jobs. The killers were fined less than $4,000 each and sentenced to three years of probation.

Denver, Colorado 1984   Helen Fukui, a fifty-two-year-old woman, disappeared in Denver on December 7, 1984. Her decomposed body was found weeks later. The fact that she disappeared on Pearl Harbor Day when anti-Asian speech and incidents heightened racial tensions was considered significant in the Asian American community, but the case was not investigated as a hate crime. No suspects were ever arrested.

NEW YORK CITY, NEW YORK 1985   Ly Yung Cheung, a nineteen-year-old seamstress in New York's Chinatown, was waiting for a subway train when she was pushed into the path of a train by a man claiming to have a psychotic "phobia about Asians." Cheung was decapitated by the oncoming train. She was seven months pregnant at the time.

JERSEY CITY, NEW JERSEY 1987   A Jersey City gang who called themselves the "Dotbusters" (a reference to the red bindi that some South Asian women wear as a sign of marital fidelity) published a letter in the paper stating that they would take any means necessary to drive the Indians out of Jersey City. Numerous racial incidents from vandalism to assault followed. Later that month, the Dotbusters used bricks to bludgeon and beat Navroze Mody, a South Asian male, into a coma. No bias charges were brought against the killers.

STOCKTON, CALIFORNIA, JANUARY 1989   A gunman dressed in military clothes entered the schoolyard of Cleveland Elementary School in Stockton and opened fire with an AK47 assault rifle. He killed one Vietnamese and four Cambodian children: Raphanar Or, age 9; Ram Chun, age 8; Thuy Tran, age 6; Sokhim An, age 6; and Ocun Lim, age 8. The killings were driven by the gunman's hatred of Southeast Asians because of the Vietnam War.

HOUSTON, TEXAS, AUGUST 1990   Hung Truong, a fifteen-year old Vietnamese American teenager, was walking down the street with three friends when they were accosted by persons in two cars that stopped alongside them. Two men stepped out of one car with a club and began to chase Truong, who was separated from his friends. While shouting "white power," the two men kicked and beat Truong. Truong begged them to stop and said "God forgive me for coming to this country. I'm so sorry." After they left him bleeding on the ground, Truong's friends called the paramedics who claimed that Truong seemed well enough to go home. Truong died the next morning.

ALPINE TOWNSHIP, MICHIGAN, JUNE 1995   Thanh Mai, a 23-year-old Vietnamese American, visited a teen nightclub with two of his friends in Alpine Township, Michigan, on June 18, 1995. Mai was sitting alone and was accosted by three young white males who taunted Mai with racial slurs, including "What the f—k are you looking at, gook?" Mai tried to walk away from the situation, but when his attention was diverted, one of the white men surprised Mai by hitting him in the face. Mai fell to the concrete ground with such force that his skull split open, sending him into convulsions. Mai died five days later from major head trauma.

SOUTHERN CALIFORNIA, AUGUST 1999   Joseph Ileto, a Filipino postal worker, was gunned down by a white supremacist on a shooting rampage in Southern California, which included opening fire in a Jewish community center. The killer shot Ileto nine times in the chest and later confessed that he killed Ileto because he looked Asian or Latino. The media initially invisibilized the murder of Joseph Ileto and characterized the rampage as a solely anti-Semitic one.

INTRODUCTION

Violence has been an integral part of the histories and experiences of Asian Americans in the United States from our arrival in this nation to the present. Anti-Asian violence can occur at any given moment, but it is especially prevalent during periods of anti-immigrant sentiment. Most hate crimes committed against Asian Americans draw upon notions of Asian Americans as perpetual foreigners who do not belong in this society.[1] Indeed, Victor Hwang notes how violence based on notions of foreignness has been an integral theme in Asian American history when he writes:

> The Asian American community is based on an understanding and appreciation for the fact that we have struggled for nearly two centuries against this violence and exclusion in the plantations, in the courts, and on the battlefields. . . . It is in our struggle against this pattern of violence and its underlying message of physical, political, and historical exclusion that we find ourselves as Asian Pacific Americans.[2]

In the United States, wherever there is foreignness, there is also a negative reaction to foreignness. This negative reaction includes setting up borders and expelling foreigners. Robert S. Chang and Keith Aoki note, "in the same way that the cell wall or membrane serves a screening function, the border operates to exclude that which is dangerous, unwanted, undesirable."[3] The United States guards its borders seriously and marks foreigners within its physical borders according to race. Not all foreigners are treated the same by the United States. Angelo Ancheta uses the term "outsider racialization" to describe the construction of Asian Americans and other non-whites as foreigners. Outsider racialization operates on two different levels:

First, Asian Americans, Latinos, and Arab Americans are racially categorized as foreign-born outsiders, regardless of actual citizenship status. Racialization operates on multiple levels: through psychological cognition and learning,

social and political discourse, and institutional structures. Second, ostensibly race-neutral categories such as "immigrant" and "foreigner" are racialized through the same social processes. Just as Asian Americans, Latinos, and Arab Americans are presumed to be foreigners and immigrants, foreigners and immigrants are presumed to be Asian, Latino, or Arab.[4]

Thus, some immigrants are able to cross the border into the United States and gain immediate acceptance as un-foreign because of their white appearance. Racialized others may physically enter the country, but not without foreignness stamped on their faces through their racial uniforms. Accordingly, hate crimes against Asian Americans take on the unique dimension of operating as a form of border patrol and protection of the nation against the foreign "alien." An analysis of anti-Asian hate violence must recognize the social context of foreignness in which the violence manifests as well as the reactions that foreignness triggers from the state and from private actors.

Part I of this chapter briefly examines violence as a form of systemic oppression against people of color throughout history and its prevalence in particular against the Asian American community. Part II addresses how perceptions of Asian Americans have always been and continue to be informed by stereotypes grounded in foreignness and focuses on the treatment of Asian Americans by the state. Part III explores white American national identity in the context of immigration, white American anxiety over cultural security and over maintaining borders as a way to deal with the resulting identity crisis. This section also focuses on popular and cultural perceptions of Asian Americans as foreigners. Part IV builds upon the notion of Asian Americans as perpetual foreigners and analyzes how perceptions of foreignness cause Asian Americans to be subject to both official state and unofficial private forms of border patrol. Hate violence is examined as constituting a form of border patrol by both state and private actors. Finally, this section considers how the construction of individual hate crimes as the sole problem ignores the border patrol function of hate violence and the role of the state in perpetrating hate violence.

I. VIOLENCE: THE AMERICAN WAY

I believe in revolution
because everywhere the crosses are burning,
sharp-shooting goose-steppers round every
corner,
there are snipers in the schools . . .
(I know you don't believe this.
You think this is nothing
but faddish exaggeration. But they
are not shooting at you.)[5]

A. The Face of Oppression: Violence

Group-based violence has been a means of maintaining dominant power relationships throughout the history of the United States. Violence played a major role in the initial colonization of North America and genocide of Native Americans, the subjugation of African Americans into slavery, the conquest and annexation of Mexico and its people, and the exclusion of Asian Americans. It has been used strategically to circumvent any protective laws and to suppress any rebellion from the subordinated. One representation of such violence is evident during the reign of terror when the Ku Klux Klan commanded during Reconstruction to prevent the Thirteenth, Fourteenth, and Fifteenth Amendments from being effectively implemented. Physical violence and the psychological terror that accompanies it have been some of the most effective tools of the state to oppress people of color, and they are tools that the private citizenry has utilized fully. Violence by private individuals and by organized white supremacist groups like the Ku Klux Klan has a long history and continues today as a major threat to targeted groups, especially with new media such as the Internet available to spread its message of terror.

While oppression occurs in many different forms, violence is one of its oldest and most pervasive forms. Iris Young explains:

What makes violence a face of oppression is less the particular acts themselves, though these are often utterly horrible, than the social context surrounding them, which makes them possible and even acceptable. What makes violence a phenomenon of social injustice, and not merely an individual moral wrong, is its systemic character, its existence as a social practice.[6]

Thus, the violence that people of color experience is not simply a random, individual act, but a widespread and systematic act of domination with all institutions of society in complicit support of the violence. Young further describes:

Violence is systemic because it is directed at members of a group simply because they are members of that group. . . . The oppression of violence consists not only in direct victimization, but in the daily knowledge shared by all members of oppressed groups that they are *liable* to violation, solely on account of their group identity. Just living under such a threat of attack on oneself or family or friends deprives the oppressed of freedom and dignity, and needlessly expends their energy.

Consequently, people of color understand that violence is a part of racial oppression which must be struggled against in the quest for liberation.

Violence is a tool of the state as well as a tool of individuals over oppressed groups. The two forms of manifested violence are interrelated: violence by the state is approved and supported by the private citizenry, and violence by private actors is tolerated and encouraged by the state. Thus, violence by police officers, border patrollers, and the military are all state forms of violence supported by the citizenry, and the state's condoning and ignoring violence by private actors by failing to prosecute such behavior is a form of state complicity with private acts of violence.

B. Pervasiveness of Hate Violence Against Asian Americans

For this paper, I define hate violence according to how it is defined by the National Asian Pacific American Law Consortium (NAPALC). Under this approach, hate violence includes:

any verbal or physical act that intimidates, threatens, or injures a person or person's property because of membership in a targeted group. That membership can be based on actual or perceived race, ethnicity, national origin, immigration status, religion, gender, sexual orientation, or age. Such acts may include verbal or written threats, harassment, graffiti, property damage, and physical assaults, some of which result in serious injury or death.

This definition is broader than the legal definition of a hate-motivated crime used by the Federal Bureau of Investigation (FBI) in collecting its statistics. Under the FBI's approach, hate crimes only consist of criminal offenses motivated by a person's race, religion, ethnicity, or sexual orientation. In addition, the FBI requires more than the mere utterance of racial epithets as evidence of bias motivation in order to consider an incident as a hate crime. NAPALC's broader definition "recognizes the role of racist language in dehumanizing, humiliating, and ultimately creating an atmosphere that both fosters and condones violence against racial minorities." The more inclusive definition also reflects the common occurrence of racial slurs that escalate into physical violence. The effects of hate violence reach far beyond the physical consequences, as the psychological, sociological, and political costs of hate violence reverberate throughout the larger Asian American community as well as other oppressed communities of color.[7]

Hate crimes are committed against all subordinated groups in the United States, but they exist as particular forms of control over people of color who are perceived as foreign. Victor Hwang, staff attorney at the Asian Law Caucus in San Francisco and head of its Race Relations: Hate Violence Project, states that most hate crimes against the Asian American community reflect the notion of Asians as foreigners who need to be expelled from the country. Asian Americans are the fourth most likely group to be hate crime victims, yet are only 3% of the U.S. population.[8] In fact, hate violence against Asians has increased at a faster rate than for any other ethnic group.

The Asian American civil rights community recognizes the prevalence of violence as a major civil rights issue for Asian Americans. In 1993, the National Asian Pacific American Legal Consortium began to track hate incidents and published its first annual report on anti-Asian violence. It was the first comprehensive, nationwide, non-governmental attempt to collect and assess data on anti-Asian violence. However, it is critical to note that severe underreporting problems exist for a variety of reasons. Not all law enforcement agencies collect data on hate crimes, and although the federal Hate Crimes Statistics Act, enacted in 1990, sought to develop a uniform system of data collection, reporting is only voluntary for law enforcement agencies. Furthermore, there is widespread underreporting of hate crimes against Asian Americans because of linguistic barriers between victims and police and the lack of bilingual law enforcement personnel, a lack of knowledge on the part of Asian Americans regarding hate crime laws and civil rights protections, a mistrust of the police and thus a reluctance to report hate crimes, and finally, shame or embarrassment of being a victim. Even when racially motivated incidents are reported to the police, law enforcement may still fail to classify the incident as a hate crime, sometimes deliberately to avoid further investigation and additional paperwork. Even with severe underreporting, the statistics are alarming because they reveal that Asian Americans are twice as likely to be assaulted than harassed and thus more likely to be physically injured during a hate crime.

II. THE PERPETUAL FOREIGNERS: STATE TREATMENT OF ASIAN AMERICANS AS FOREIGNERS

"Mrs. Hammerick . . . Boiling Spring Elementary School . . . I was scared of her like no dark corners could ever scare me. You have to know that all the while she was teaching us history . . . she was telling all the boys in our class that I was Pearl and my last name was Harbor. They understood her like she was speaking French and their names were all Claude and Pierre. I felt it in the lower half of my stomach, and it throbbed and throbbed until I thought even you sitting three rows away could hear it . . . It would be so many years . . . I would understand that Pearl Harbor was not just in 1941 but in 1975."[9]

The state has historically classified Asian Americans as foreigners and has treated Asian Americans as threats to U.S. solidarity and security. In this section, I will explore three specific examples of how Asian Americans were perceived as foreign by the state and the impact of such perceptions.

A. Chinese Exclusion

The fear of non-white immigration can be seen in the Chinese Exclusion laws of the 1880s and 1890s. In fact, U.S. immigration law is fundamentally based on the exclusion of Chinese immigrants. In 1882, 1884, 1888, and 1892, Congress passed the Chinese Exclusion laws, which were the first set of federal immigration laws to be challenged in the judicial system. In the Chinese Exclusion Case, *Chae Chan Ping v. United States*, 130 U.S. 581 (1889), the Court worried about the refusal of Chinese immigrants to assimilate and feared that Chinese immigrants presented a "great danger" because "at no distant day that portion of our country would be overrun by them [Chinese], unless prompt action was taken to restrict their immigration." Justice Field, writing for a unanimous Court, stated that "it seemed impossible for them [Chinese] to assimilate with our people, or to make any change in their habits or modes of living." He also referred to Chinese immigrants as an "Oriental invasion" and as a "menace to our civilization."

In *Chae Chan Ping*, the Supreme Court sought to answer for the first time the question of which branch of government had the authority to set immigration policy and invented the plenary power doctrine. The Constitution does not grant authority to Congress to regulate immigration. Despite the idea that the United States is a government of enumerated powers, the Supreme Court declared that the power of the United States to regulate immigration and control its borders was so basic that it was inherent in the sovereign power of the state. This plenary power doctrine defies the constitutional structure of delegated powers and allows the power to exclude foreigners to remain unchecked by the Constitution. The doctrine of plenary power has continued to dominate immigration law and virtually exempts it from judicial review. Consequently, judges are very reluctant to intervene and usually defer to the legislative branch instead. Although Chinese Exclusion was later modified by legislation, *Chae Chan Ping* is not merely an ugly remnant of the past. In fact, *Chae Chan Ping* is valid precedent as the case has never been modified or reversed and continues to be cited by modern courts to support the plenary power doctrine.

The states have also sought to exclude Chinese immigrants from entering its borders. California's State Constitution, for example, included an entire section devoted to how Chinese must be excluded from sectors such as corporations and public works. As declared in the constitution: "No corporation now existing or hereafter formed under the laws of this state shall, after the adoption of this constitution, employ, directly or indirectly, in any capacity, any Chinese or Mongolian. The legislature shall pass such laws as may be necessary to enforce this provision." The next section stated, "no Chinese shall be employed on any state, county, municipal, or other public work, except in punishment for crime." In referring to Chinese immigrants, the state constitution also stated, "the presence of foreigners ineligible to become citizens of the United States is declared to be dangerous to the well-being of the state, and the legislature shall discourage their immigration by all the means within its power."

B. Alien Land Laws

Even for the Asian Americans exempted from the Chinese Exclusion laws, the alien land laws ensured their subordinate position in society by denying them the right to own land. The California legislature began to discuss proposals to prohibit land ownership by Japanese immigrants in 1907 and introduced such bills within the next few sessions.[10] In 1913, the California legislature passed the first Alien Land Law, which restricted land ownership to U.S. citizens. It stated that only "aliens eligible to citizenship may acquire, possess, enjoy, transmit, and inherit real property or any interest therein."[11] Since the federal 1790 Naturalization Act prohibited non-whites from becoming naturalized citizens, only white immigrants could satisfy the phrase 'aliens eligible to citizenship,' thus effectively precluding Asians from owning land. The proponents of the legislation openly acknowledged the racially discriminatory intent of the law and claimed that it was necessary to combat the Japanese threat. State Attorney General Ulysses Webb maintained that the concern of "race undesirability" prompted the bill since Japanese individuals would probably not immigrate and remain in the United States if they could not acquire land and settle here.

Other states were quick to follow California's lead and soon a multitude of alien land laws spread rapidly in the early 1900s. Arizona passed one in 1917, Washington and Louisiana in 1921, New Mexico in 1922, Idaho, Montana, and Oregon in 1923, and Kansas in 1925. These laws were facially neutral and survived constitutional challenge but were targeted towards Asian immigrants as a group because the racial bar on naturalization made them ineligible for citizenship. The alien land laws diminished the ability of Chinese, Japanese, Korean, and South Asian immigrants to earn a living in agriculture. Although California's 1913 Alien Land Law was not enforced by prosecutors much during World War I due to the need for food production, once the war was over Californians passed a ballot initiative in 1920 to eliminate the ability of Asian non-citizens to lease farm land completely. In 1923, an amendment made sharecropping agreements between landowners and Asian non-citizen farmers illegal even though technically no legal interest in the land itself was conferred.

While the Chinese community focused on the legal challenges to the exclusion laws, the Japanese community challenged the validity of the alien land laws. Four landmark cases were heard by the U.S. Supreme Court in 1923, all of which eliminated any rights the Japanese farmers may have previously exercised. The Court upheld Washington's and California's alien land laws in *Terrace v. Thompson* and *Porterfield v. Webb.* In *Webb v. O'Brien,* the Court held that sharecropping agreements were illegal, and in *Frick v. Webb,* the Court upheld laws prohibiting non-citizens from owning stocks in corporations formed for the purpose of farming. It was not until *Oyama v. California* in 1947 that California's alien land law was finally struck down.

C. Japanese American Internment

The construction of Japanese Americans as foreigners began long before the Pearl Harbor bombing, as evidenced by the alien land laws and the anti-Japanese hysteria that shrieked for the removal of Japanese Americans. The Los Angeles Times editorialized, "[a] viper is nonetheless a viper wherever the egg is hatched—so a Japanese American, born of Japanese parents—grows up to be a Japanese, not an American." Henry McLemore, a prominent syndicated columnist for the Hearst papers, called for the internment of Japanese Americans:

> I am for immediate removal of every Japanese on the West Coast to a point deep in the interior. I don't mean a nice part of the interior either. Herd 'em up, pack 'em off and give 'em the inside room in the badlands. Let 'em be pinched, hurt, hungry and dead up against it. . . . Personally, I hate the Japanese. And that goes for all of them."

This anti-Japanese rhetoric was also present in governmental documents. General DeWitt, military commander for the western states, stated in his formal recommendation for removal, "In the war in which we are now engaged racial affinities are not severed by migration. The Japanese race is an enemy race and while many second and third generation Japanese born on United States soil, possessed of United States citizenship, have become 'Americanized,' the racial strains are undiluted."

Japanese American Internment exemplified the fear of the "alien" within our borders and the need to expel the foreigner. Neil Gotanda writes, "It is within this dynamic—the evolution of the treatment of Other non-whites—that the concentration camp cases are best understood. . . . these cases were crucial steps in the development of the complex links of the social and legal categories of race and alienage. Most important in this development has been the persistence of the view that even American-born non-Whites were somehow 'foreign.'"[12] In *Korematsu v. United States,* the Court upheld the internment of Japanese Americans even under its own strict scrutiny test because internment supposedly constituted a military necessity. The Court insisted that it was not merely looking at race but the issue of military necessity and "national security": "To cast this case into outlines of racial prejudice, without reference to the real military dangers which were presented, merely confuses the issue. Korematsu was not excluded from the Military Area because of hostility to him or his race. He *was* excluded because we are at war with the Japanese Empire." However, white immigrants like German and Italian Americans were not interned like the Japanese Americans because they did not seem foreign in the same way; unlike the foreign and "otherized" Japanese Americans, German and Italian Americans did not threaten the existence of a white national identity or its security.

III. THE PERPETUAL FOREIGNERS: IDENTITY AND BORDER CRISIS

"excuse me, ameriKa,
I'm confused.
You tell me to lighten up,
but what you really mean is whiten up.
You wish to wash me out,
melt me into your cauldron.
Excuse me, if I tip your melting pot,
spill the shades onto your streets."[13]

A. White American National Identity and Immigration

In order to fully understand the dynamics occurring in anti-Asian hate violence, we must examine the role that race and foreignness play in the construction of white American identity. American national identity is defined as a white one, and thus, anyone not white is "otherized." The status of being the "Other" implies being "other than" or different from the assumed norm of white national identity. Because America sees color as fundamental to its very core identity and existence, it needs to label and drive out the "Other" to preserve this color of white. This dynamic is reflected in American immigration history.

After over a century of Asian exclusion, the Immigration and Nationality Act of 1952 (McCarran-Walter Act) nullified the 1790 Naturalization Act restricting naturalization to whites, finally allowing Asian Americans to naturalize, and technically ended exclusion by allowing a small number of immigrants from South and East Asia. However, it was post-1965

immigration that really changed the landscape for Asian immigration. The 1965 Immigration Act was framed as an amendment to the McCarran-Walter Act of 1952, but it substantially changed the immigration system by reforming the "national origins quotas" as the basis for immigration. The 1965 Act provided for an annual admission number from the eastern and western hemispheres and enacted a new preference system for immediate family members and skilled laborers.

The 1965 Act changed immigration patterns and demographics more dramatically than the proponents of the legislation could have imagined. Although the original supporters of the Act had predicted that European immigration would continue to predominate, in actuality, Asian immigration has dominated, behind only Mexico. The proponents appeased nativist groups opposing the legislation by arguing that Asian immigration could only increase slightly because the number of Asian citizens in the United States was too small to really take advantage of the family preference system for reunification of immediate family members. However, because of the 1965 reforms, Asian immigration has increased steadily. The Philippines, Korea, China, and Vietnam rank as the second through fifth largest sending countries of immigrants to the United States, behind only Mexico which sends the highest number of immigrants. Prior to 1965, immigration had been predominately European and from the western hemisphere.

Differential racialization of immigrants is obvious when examining the treatment and acceptance of white immigrants as compared to immigrants from Africa, Asia, the Caribbean, and Latin America. Chang and Aoki explain, "Fear of immigration, often discussed in generalized terms, is colored so that only certain immigrant bodies excite fear. . . . The 'problem' of legal and illegal immigration is colored in the national imagination: fear over immigration is not articulated solely around foreignness per se; it includes a strong racial dimension." The ability to label a group of people as foreigners enables white America to define itself in opposition to the foreigners, because white Americans are not foreign. Different non-white groups experience being the "Other" as a foreigner outside of white American national identity in different ways. Obviously no group of color fits the definition of white American national identity, but the specific ways in which foreignness may be constructed and experienced varies across different communities of color. For Asian Americans, the image of the perpetual foreigner is a pervasive stereotype, which informs our experience as the "Other."

The process of "othering" necessarily involves a relational system of defining identity in a social and historical context of domination and subordination. Thus, "othering" involves the categorization of people in terms of their difference from one another so that one derives its meaning only in relation to the other. Patricia Collins explains, "for example, the terms in dichotomies such as black/white, male/female, reason/emotion, fact/opinion, and subject/object gain their meaning only in *relation* to their difference from their oppositional counterparts." In this relational system, American national identity is inextricably tied to non-American (foreign) identity. The positive, superior American national identity is white, good, patriotic, and belonging; the negative, inferior non-American identity (foreign) is non-white, bad, treacherous, and invasive.

Edward Said's work on "Orientalism" examines how the western colonial gaze constructed "the Orient" in opposition to itself, "the Occident" so that its self-identity relied on a negation: what we are, they are not; what they are, we are not.[14] Keith Aoki elaborates on Said's notion of "Orientalism" by analyzing a particular strand of "American Orientalism" which explains the process of "othering" for Asian Americans in the context of foreignness:

the national identity of the United States has been constructed in opposition to racialized 'Others' like Asian immigrants and Asian Americans. 'American Orientalism' also carries a significant additional component: the idea of 'foreignness,' which refers to the construction of the American nation-state that involves categorization of persons as 'citizens' or 'foreigners.' . . . In a complex fashion, the American 'Orientalist' gaze deeply inscribes 'otherness' on Asian Americans and Asian immigrants as simultaneously 'racialized' as 'non-white' and 'foreign and unassimilable.'[15]

Thus, Asian Americans are "otherized" as non-whites, but are also "otherized" as foreign.

B. White American National Identity Crisis and Cultural Insecurity

The desire to protect white national identity has often been framed in terms of "national security." However, this term must be distinguished from cultural insecurity on the part of anxious whites. Often, "national security" points to cultural insecurity and the preservation of a white, Eurocentric national identity. This is exemplified by Pat Buchanan's statement, "if we had to take a million immigrants in, say, Zulus, next year or Englishmen and put them in Virginia, what group would be easier to assimilate and would cause less problems for the people of Virginia? There is nothing wrong with us sitting down and arguing that issue, that we are a European country."[16]

Multiculturalism and people of color are perceived as threats to this illusory notion of a cohesive white cultural security. Consequently, it does not take a large number of Asians to trigger the perceived threat to cultural security. The mere presence of Asians in America and their impact on the national culture, in terms of, for instance, languages other than English being spoken, is enough. Immigration policy has historically reflected such fears. Enid Trucios-Haynes explains, "The current immigration debate fully illustrates that U.S. society will accept only a multiracial population that is subordinate and non-threatening to the dominant Western European culture."[17] Fears that Chinese immigrants would be unable to assimilate and would challenge the cultural/"national security" were certainly reflected in the Chinese Exclusion legislation. The Court in *Chae Chan Ping* articulated concern over the unassimilability of the Chinese, but it was really trying to protect American cultural/"national security" from an "Oriental invasion." Ruben J. Garcia notes, "Assimilationism is also proxy for the fear of shifting demographics which will make whites the minority in some areas of the country."[18] Indeed, efforts to either expel or assimilate Asians in this country have always had roots in white cultural insecurity.

C. Nativistic Racism and Figurative Borders

The interplay of racialized foreignness results in what Chang and Aoki term "figurative borders":

> Foreignness is inscribed upon our bodies in such a way that Asian Americans and Latinas/os carry a figurative border with us. This figurative border, in addition to confirming the belonging-ness of the 'real' Americans, marks Asian Americans and Latinas/os as targets of nativistic racism. It renders us suspect, subject to the violence of heightened scrutiny at the border, in the workplace, in hospitals, and elsewhere.

Asian Americans and Latinas/os are threatening to whites as we have crossed the physical border and have "penetrated" into the interior. Despite being physically inside the border, we can still be marked with figurative borders.

These figurative borders have serious consequences because "violence operates to regulate boundaries." Borders have historically been places of violence, and those marked as foreign are likely to experience violence. Chang and Aoki explain:

> This violence is spurred on by certain narratives of America which permit and perhaps encourage the pathological impulse toward nativistic racism. This violence is not confined to the geo-political periphery; it may explode anywhere that there is a border (and remember: the border is everywhere). This has serious consequences for those who carry a figurative border on our bodies. Asian Americans and Latina/os, as perpetual internal foreigners, allow "real" Americans to reassure themselves that the national community begins and ends with themselves, ensuring, at least momentarily, a stable notion of the national community and the fiction of a homogeneous American identity.

This ability to mark non-whites with figurative borders allows white Americans to believe in cultural security and temporarily stabilizes the white American national identity crisis.

D. Stereotypes of Asian Americans: Threats to Cultural Security

Stereotypes of foreignness abound in the popular imagination, mostly with Asian Americans and Latinas/os as the epitome of foreignness. Stereotypical portrayals of Asian Americans are very much informed by foreignness. Both the "model minority" and the "yellow peril" stereotypes have elements of foreignness embedded in them. Gary Okihiro describes, "the yellow peril and the model minority are not poles, denoting opposite representations along a single line, but in fact form a circular relationship that moves in either direction."[19]

The characterization of foreignness of Asian Americans is what allows dominant society to move freely between these two seemingly contradictory stereotypes. The underlying constant of foreignness provides the continuity needed to transform from positive to negative to positive. Natsu Taylor Saito notes the slipperiness and interconnectedness of the traits: "The positive versions of these stereotypes include images of Asian Americans as hardworking, industrious, thrifty, family-oriented, and even mysterious or exotic. It is striking that the negative images almost invariably involve the same traits. Hardworking and industrious become unfairly competitive; family-oriented becomes clannish; mysterious becomes dangerously inscrutable."

These stereotypes of Asian Americans as foreigners and the enemy are reinforced through the media, educational, and political institutions of dominant society. An almost infinite number of examples exist which perpetuate Asian Americans as foreigners and as the enemy. Anti-immigrant scapegoating is often triggered by current events, which portray Asian Americans as negative foreigners. In June of 1993, a freighter (the *Golden Venture*) carrying 300 Chinese indentured servants ran aground in Queens, New York. The resulting media coverage perpetuated negative stereotypes of Asians as foreign illegal smugglers (specifically, Chinese as undocumented immigrants) and fueled anti-immigrant sentiment across the nation. In reality, Italians were the largest group of undocumented immigrants in the state of New York in 1993. Next on the list were undocumented immigrants from Ecuador and Poland. In fact, illegal Chinese did not even make the top ten list of groups of undocumented immigrants in the state of New York. The *Golden Venture* incident ignited serious backlash, which had ramifications for the Asian American community, including unwarranted detention of Asian Americans at international airports, searches for undocumented immigrants at Asian American homes, and a flood of hate mail to Asian Americans. One letter sent in East Brunswick, New Jersey in July 1993 was signed by the "Ping Pong Exterminators." The letter stated:

> Enough is Enough. It is now time to send these illegals and slave traders to where they come from. We will get rid of Chinese from the Garden State beginning one month from July 4th. They are criminals hiding behind their BMW's, Benz and use their laundry, restaurant and massage parlors to cheat this country. They are infiltrating into safe communities of the Garden State and bringing big city criminal gangs with them. Look what happened in Teaneck. We will start with Edison and East Brunswick, two of the safest communities these Chinese gangs have picked to infiltrate. If you think what is happening in Germany is violent, you ain't seen nothing yet. There will be Chinese blood and bones all over if they don't quit voluntarily by August 5th. God save and bless America. God bless the Ping Pong Exterminators.

The backlash also resulted in increased efforts to pass restrictive immigration laws and to dismantle political asylum. The National Asian Pacific American Legal Consortium notes, "Anti-immigrant sentiment has become legitimized in that it is permissible to openly discriminate against people who look different, speak a language other than English, have a non-Anglo name or appear otherwise 'foreign.'"

Other recent examples of Asian Americans as the perpetual foreigner include the portrayal of the Chinese boat people in *Lethal Weapon 4* (which was the top-grossing film the first week it was released), the MS-NBC headline reporting on Tara Lipinski winning the gold medal over Michelle Kwan's silver as "American Beats Kwan," and the Democratic political donations scandal portraying Asians taking over the American government with dirty money. Being the perpetual foreigner has serious ramifications for Asian Americans in the context of anti-Asian hate violence.

IV. HATE CRIMES AS BORDER PATROL

La Migra

I

Let's play La Migra *I'll be the Border Patrol. You be the Mexican maid. I get the badge and sunglasses. You can hide and run, but you can't get away because I have a jeep. I can take you wherever I want, but don't ask questions because I don't speak Spanish. I can touch you wherever I want but don't complain too much because I've got boots and kick—if I have to and I have handcuffs. Oh, and a gun. Get ready, get set, run.*

II.

Let's play La Migra *You be the Border Patrol. I'll be the Mexican woman. Your jeep has a flat, and you have been spotted by the sun. All you have is heavy: hat, glasses, badge, shoes, gun. I know this desert, where to rest, where to drink. Oh, I am not alone. You hear us singing and laughing with the wind,* Agua dulce brota aqui, aqui, aqui, *but since you can't speak Spanish, you do not understand. Get ready.*

excuse you, ameriKa

excuse you, ameriKa, While I scratch your name with 3 'K's, mark 'X' for your xenophobic tendencies, scrape the violence off your skulls, and ask you why. Why are you so angry, ameriKa? You whip out wisecracks, attack the defenseless, flashing the superior color of your badge. You beat us down, blameless as victims, who remain nameless. Bashing the heads of all our Vincent Chins, you serve violence, a beating for culture's sake, fist fights that finish a Denny's meal. You dig graves for forgotten faces, steal lives for petty skin crimes, bury our dead with bullet wounds, slay the living with foreign stares. Why don't you stop hating me? Why don't you stop killing me?

Those who are marked as foreign are forever subject to border checks, both officially and unofficially. Border patrols occur all the time, everywhere, and in all different forms by both state and private actors. Hate violence is one such form of border patrol and can also be executed by either state or private actors.

A. State Forms of Border Patrol

Officially, the state controls the border carefully through a complex web of institutions and legal restrictions on non-citizens. The enforcement function of the Immigration and Naturalization Service (INS) consists of four different programs, which include Inspections, Investigation, Detention and Deportation, and Border Patrol. The mission of the Border Patrol is to police the border and stop illegal immigration into the United States. However, border patrol does not exist just on the border. For instance, the INS border checkpoint on Interstate 5 is located approximately halfway between San Diego and Los Angeles, many miles away from the literal United States-Mexico border.

The anxiety of whites has led to an intense anti-immigrant hysteria and has spurred a renewed policing of the border with Asians and Latinas/os as the special targets of the INS and Border Patrol. Both the Asian American and the Latina/o communities are perceived to be perpetual foreigners to the United States. The similarities between these two groups have increased even more as an anti-immigrant climate has led to both communities being seen as illegal immigrants. At the same time, the INS has stepped up efforts against these two groups. For Asians, the focus now is on accusing Asian immigrants of being smuggled through the Mexico-United States border. The INS has described the problem as one of multilingual smugglers in a global network who are bringing in an influx of Chinese into the United States. The concern of the INS has prompted President Clinton to announce the creation of a multi-agency federal offensive against the trafficking of immigrants.

Such border patrol targeted against Asians has also intensified along the U.S.-Mexico border along the Rio Grande. In 1993, the Border Patrol launched "Operation Hold the Line" (originally named "Operation Blockade") in El Paso, Texas, which stationed 450 agents (three times the normal number) on an around-the-clock watch along the twenty miles of the Rio Grande River separating El Paso, Texas from Ciudad Juarez in Mexico. This new strategy was to saturate the border with agents instead of the old strategy of allowing movement across the border and then apprehending illegal immigrants once they were on United States soil.

Following the implementation of "Operation Hold the Line" in Texas, the Border Patrol instituted "Operation Gatekeeper" in Southern California and "Operation Safeguard" near Nogales, Arizona in 1994. These operations also saturated the border with agents and erected new fences and lights. However, even before "Operation Gatekeeper," the INS had already replaced the traditional chain-link fencing with "solid metal fencing, fashioned from obsolete military landing mats used for temporary runways." In 1994, the INS also added new computerized fingerprinting technology, which would identify repeat illegal crossers. Doris Meissner, commissioner of the INS, attributes the increased smuggling of Asians through Mexico to the heightened crackdown on maritime smuggling that followed the 1993 *Golden Venture* incident. Thus, with respect to Asians, the Border Patrol now focuses on the United States-Mexico land border in addition to maritime and airport patrol. Asian Americans are increasingly being targeted as part of a crackdown on smuggling rings involving Asian and Latina/o members. This demonstrates how Asians and Latinas/os are being linked together in Border Patrol raids and operations. In November 1998, federal officials were involved in a yearlong investigation called "Operation Seek and Keep" to catch smuggling cartels of Asian immigrants who attempted to illegally enter the U.S. through Russia, Cuba, and Latin America. "Operation Seek and Keep" was the first investigation authorized to use new wiretap technology in illegal immigrant smuggling cases that was approved by Congress in 1996.

The state takes its duties of border control seriously and supports this with the necessary funding. Border Patrol funding increased from 374 million dollars in 1994 to 631 million dollars in 1997. In addition, Congress has authorized increased funds for additional Border Patrol employees. In November 1999, the INS Border Patrol website contained a recruitment list of 2000 open INS agent positions. Over 90% of Border Patrol agents are concentrated on the Southwest border where the number of border agents has jumped from 3,300 in 1994 to 6,200 in 1997. Furthermore, the number of prosecutions brought by U.S. attorneys in the Southwest for immigration-related violations has increased threefold between 1994 and 1997.

The last decade's intensification of immigration control has been accompanied by a climate of anti-immigrant hysteria. This hysteria has further encouraged law enforcement and private actors to discriminate against foreigners. Because so much of their job is based on discretionary judgments, Border Patrol agents possess a very powerful tool against anyone they perceive to be foreign. Border Patrol agents can subjectively determine whether reasonable suspicion exists that someone entered the U.S. illegally and have the right to stop and question a person solely to discern if the person has the right to be in the United States. Such discretion allows Border Patrol agents to target Asian Americans driving across the border or arriving on international flights and to question them more aggressively.

While such harassment by INS agents may simply lead to inconvenience, it can also result in more tragic consequences. The Hwang case is one example of such tragedy. Stephen Hwang contends that "some immigration officers are overly aggressive when they question immigrants, Asians in particular, seeking re-entry into the United States."[20] Unfortunately, Stephen Hwang knows this from personal experience. His sixty-six-year-old mother, Chen Seu-Ing Hwang, collapsed on the floor in customs at Los Angeles International Airport while being harassed by an immigration inspector. She suffered a stroke, which left her partially paralyzed, and died a few weeks later. Stephen Hwang filed suit against the INS and inspector Craig Porter.

The suit charges that the stroke Chen Seu-Ing Hwang suffered was the result of undue harassment by Porter, who had been aggressively questioning her in customs. An airline employee who was translating for Mrs. Hwang in customs said that Porter had tried to get Mrs. Hwang to admit that she had been out of the country for longer than 12 months, in violation of her permanent residency status. In fact, Mrs. Hwang had originally traveled to Taiwan to meet her husband who was undergoing eye surgery. However, he suffered chest pains after the surgery and died after a heart bypass operation. Mrs. Hwang stayed in Taiwan to take care of her late husband's affairs, which led her to be absent from the United States longer than anticipated. Stephen Hwang believes that Porter did not give Mrs. Hwang a chance to explain her circumstances and instead, harassed her and tried to bully her into admitting she had done something wrong.

Linda Wong, an immigration attorney formerly with the Mexican American Legal Defense and Education Fund, has said that many non-white permanent residents have had problems with airport immigration inspectors. Wong has encountered numerous complaints of agents targeting permanent residents at the airport and at the U.S.-Mexico border. Agents ask more aggressive questions, and even try to entrap non-white immigrants into saying that they have been out of the country for so long that they have abandoned their residency.

B. Legal Restrictions for Non-Citizens

Legally, non-citizens, or permanent residents, are an incredibly vulnerable class because they have limited rights and increasingly fewer constitutional protections. Since non-citizens are disenfranchised, they cannot participate in the political process and have no political clout. Even though "immigrant rights [groups] and some ethnic groups lobby aggressively for immigrants, their pull with politicians naturally is restricted by the electoral powerlessness of their constituency."[21] Hence, it is easy for politicians to trample on them since their voices cannot be heard at the election booth. Permanent residents' lack of input in the political process is exacerbated by the plenary power doctrine. The doctrine compels the judiciary to defer to the other political branches when reviewing immigration policies. Thus, the political branches which immigrants have little influence over are given significant freedom by the judiciary in immigration matters.

Although permanent residents are obliged to pay taxes and serve in the United States military if called upon, they do not have the right to vote or to serve on juries. Permanent residents are now ineligible for most benefits, especially since the passage of the 1996 Welfare Reform Act, which made permanent residents ineligible for Social Security Insurance (SSI) and food stamps. The plenary power doctrine gives the legislature broad latitude to restrict federal public benefits for permanent residents. For example, a challenge to the 1996 Welfare Act brought in New York district court was struck down in *Abreu v. Callahan.* The court in that case upheld the Welfare Act denying SSI benefits to lawful permanent residents who would have been eligible before the 1996 Act. The court found the government's interests legitimate and rationally related to the statute.

In the employment arena, all sorts of restrictions exist which make an already vulnerable class even more susceptible to exploitation. The 1986 Immigration Reform and Control Act permits discrimination based on one's citizenship status if required by state or local governmental authority. For instance, states can make citizenship mandatory as a job requirement in certain professions such as state troopers, public school teachers, and deputy probation officers. In addition, employers may give preference to a citizen over a legal permanent resident if the two are "equally qualified." The rights and privileges of citizenship are not fixed. The plenary power doctrine allows the executive and legislative branches to determine which rights to attach based on citizenship. For example, during the nineteenth century, some states granted non-citizens the right to vote, partly to increase the number of white male voters. Some cities have also permitted non-citizen parents to vote in school board elections. However, the overwhelming trend is to deny rights to non-citizens, not to extend them.

C. Private Forms of Border Patrol

The state engages in various forms of border patrol, but it does not end with the state, for the citizenry also performs border patrol in its own way. Every time people who are marked as foreign are asked how long they have been here or where they are from with the assumption that they must not be from the U.S., how they learned to speak English so well, or told to go back to another country, that is a type of unofficial border check. By relying on popular notions of foreignness, individuals participate in border patrol when they mark others as foreign and ask questions or make comments implying that the others must be foreigners. As signals of foreignness, accent discrimination and racial discrimination are forms of unofficial border patrol.[22]

Because the American national identity is defined by whiteness, border patrol is practiced within the physical borders of the United States. Those individuals inscribed with figurative borders will be subject to internal policing mechanisms of foreignness.

A group in San Diego called "Light Up the Border" exemplifies private individuals taking border patrol into their own hands and performing their own border checks. In 1989, a group of private residents started a campaign where more than 1,000 volunteers parked their cars along the U.S.-Mexico border and shined their headlights toward Tijuana. Critics claim that "Light Up the Border" has heightened racial tensions and fueled anti-immigrant and anti-Latino sentiments. Since the group began its vigilante campaign, the U.S. Border Patrol has placed lights on the U.S.-Mexico border and the California National Guard has begun to improve the dirt roads that the Border Patrol drives on in its patrols. The "Light Up the Border" group highlights private actors attempting to informally participate in border patrol.

In addition to the annoying questions regarding birthplace, shining lights on the border, and accent and racial discrimination, those inscribed with figurative borders must also worry about a more dangerous form of private border patrol. Hate violence has become a way of protecting cultural security and a form of border patrol over people marked as foreign which the private citizenry has taken upon itself to perform. Hate crimes are a manifestation of this border control on a much more physical and extreme level. Most hate crimes against Asian Americans involve anti-immigrant, nativistic racism and place Asian Americans in the context of foreignness.[23] One of the most well-known hate crimes against Asian Americans occurred in 1982 when Vincent Chin, a Chinese American, was killed in Detroit, Michigan by two white laid-off autoworkers who yelled "you Japs are taking all our jobs" while beating Chin with a baseball bat. During the early 1980s, anti-Asian sentiment in the United States was intensely heightened, especially against Japan. Paula Johnson describes this sentiment as "particularly acute in Detroit, Michigan, where the heart of the American auto industry was economically depressed and Japanese auto imports gained in sales and popularity in this country." Bumper stickers saying "Unemployment— Made in Japan" and "Toyota-Datsun-Honda-and-Pearl Harbor" were popular in Detroit and other areas of the country. Johnson explains, "It was within this social climate and other social contexts that the killing of Vincent Chin occurred, bringing national and international attention to the issue of racially motivated violence against Asian Americans in the United States."

The Vincent Chin murder must be seen in this context of foreignness and border patrol. Although this case involved two private individuals, they were supported and implicitly condoned by a legal system, which did not bring any justice to Vincent Chin. Neither killer served any time in prison for the murder. They each instead received small fines and only three years of probation. Robert Chang recognizes the context of the murder of Vincent Chin in terms of borders when he writes, "The border and the color line are inscribed on his body, marking him as a foreign and racial other, a legitimate target for nativistic racism. Through his construction as a foreigner, he and others who look like him, help define America."

Nativistic racism also manifested itself in the tragic death of Navroze Mody in Hoboken, near Jersey City, and is another incident of hate violence as a form of border patrol by private actors. On September 27, 1987, Mody, a 30-year-old South Asian, was "bludgeoned with bricks, punched, and kicked into a coma" by a gang of eleven youths who shouted "Hindu! Hindu!" during the attack. Mody's white friend who was walking with him that night was not harmed. No bias charges were brought, and the jury convicted four of the attackers on assault charges. No one was found guilty of murder or even manslaughter. This case must also be placed in its social and historical context to fully understand what occurred.

In the weeks before Mody's death, racial tensions and anti-South Asian sentiment were heightened after a racist group called the "Dotbusters" (referring to the red bindi worn by South Asian women on their foreheads as a sign of marital fidelity) published a letter in the *Jersey Journal* stating that their mission was to drive all South Asians out of Jersey City. A campaign of racial harassment, vandalism, and assault was launched against the South Asian community. Three days after Mody's attack, another South Asian man, Dr. Kaushal Sharan, was severely beaten while walking home. For at least a year after Mody's violent death, anti-South Asian incidents continued to occur in the Jersey City area. In this case, private actors banded together to form their own border patrol gang, the "Dotbusters," to expel South Asians through the use of hate violence. The police failed to protect the South Asian community, and the legal system failed to render justice to Mody's life. Mody's family later brought a civil rights action against the city of Hoboken for racial discrimination in failing to protect the South Asian community and in failing to prosecute Mody's attackers in earlier assaults on other South Asians. However, a federal judge dismissed the suit, claiming that there was no evidence of racial bias and at worst, there was only negligence on the part of the police.

These attacks involve more than just the message of hatred but also include the message of hatred based on xenophobia, immigrant scapegoating for economic woes, and a sense of border control. Although the deaths of Vincent Chin and Navroze Mody are widely known examples of anti-Asian hate crimes, there are countless others who have suffered the same type of hate violence as border patrol.

Hate violence by private actors has escalated along with the increase in immigration from Asian and Latin American countries. Demographic changes between 1970 and 1990 have certainly fueled the perception that there has been an influx of Asians who are taking over the country. Between 1970 and 1990, the United States population experienced a total growth of 22.4%. The African American population increased by 33% and comprised 12.1% of the total population. The Native American population grew from 0.4% of the population to 0.8%. However, it is the Asian American and Latina/o populations, which have increased the most dramatically. The Asian American population grew by 384.9% to reach 2.9% of the population while the Latina/o population grew by 141% to reach 9% of the population.[24] During the period from 1970 to 1990, approximately nine million immigrants entered the United

States from Asian and Latin American countries.

One popular perception is that the country is being overrun with immigrants of color, and studies have revealed that most whites believe that the United States is being taken over by people of color and that whites are the new minority in the United States. For instance, a recent *New York Times* poll showed that whites believed that African Americans comprised 23.8% of the population, Asian Americans 10.8%, Latinas/os 14.7%, and whites only 49.9% when in reality, African Americans are 11.8% of the population, Asian Americans 3.1%, Latinas/os 9.5%, and whites 74%. The dramatic gap between reality and perception reflects the anxiety of whites that the "invasion" has begun.

On a state level, by 2001, the state of California will be officially majority non-white. This demographic has frightened many whites into action, spawning an onslaught of conservative ballot initiatives in the 1990s attacking immigration, affirmative action, and bilingual education. These initiatives were supported by the majority of white California voters.

D. Blurring of State and Private Border Patrol: Proposition 187

Proposition 187, passed by California voters in November 1994, collapsed the distinction between state and private border patrol by effectively transforming private citizens into state agents. Proposition 187 restricted undocumented immigrants from public benefits, public education, and non-emergency health care and created serious criminal penalties for the sale or use of false citizenship papers. Proposition 187 also requires employees in social services, health care, and education to report any persons who are "reasonably suspect" of being undocumented to the State Director of Social Services, the Attorney General of California and the United States, and the Immigration and Naturalization Service. Thus, private actors are basically made to assume the duties of an INS agent. Proposition 187 creates a police state mentality by forcing public officials to report anyone who they "suspect" of being illegal. Proposition 187, however, does not define what

constitutes proper suspicion, thereby increasing the probability of discrimination occurring. Linda Bosniak notes different bases for suspicion: "Will the suspicion be based on the way you speak? The sound of your last name? The color of your skin?"[25] As Chang and Aoki describe Proposition 187, "Foreign-ness then becomes a proxy for questionable immigration status. Foreign-ness triggers further scrutiny." This police state would regulate the borders with the participation of the state and its citizens. Racist literature supporting Proposition 187 stuffed into mailboxes in Los Angeles demonstrates citizen border patrol occurring: "WE NEED A *REAL* BORDER, FIRST WE GET THE SPICS, THEN THE GOOKS, AND AT LAST WE GET THE NIGGERS. *DEPORTATION* THEY'RE ALL GOING HOME."

The Proposition 187 campaign was premised on the idea of immigrants as "aliens" who needed to be taught a lesson. Proposition 187 represented a new chapter in the history of nativism in California and the nation. Proponents of Proposition 187 staunchly maintained that the issue was not race but immigration and saving America, but the immigration problem was definitely framed in racialized terms. There was no mention of the Immigration Act of 1990, which had just increased dramatically the number of immigrants from Northern Europe, particularly Ireland. Instead, the focus was on portraying illegal "aliens" as Mexicans running across the border and of Chinese boat people. Stop Immigration Now founder Ruth Coffey could only explain her position on the immigration issue in a racial manner when she said, "I have no intention of being the object of 'conquest,' peaceful or otherwise, by Latinos, Asians, Blacks, Arabs or any other group of individuals who have claimed my country."

Especially after Proposition 187 passed, those individuals inscribed with figurative borders and marked as foreigners regardless of citizenship status or length of residence in the United States experienced intensified discrimination and increased hate violence. The rhetoric permeating the debate over Proposition 187 created an environment that encouraged discrimination and intolerance for anyone who was marked with figurative borders. Both the Latina/o and the Asian American communities suffered increased discrimination in places of business, increased hate crimes and hate speech, and increased police brutality. Anti-Asian hate violence more than doubled in Northern California and increased by 40% in Southern California in 1994 from the previous year. The dramatic rise in anti-Asian violence in California was attributed to anti-immigrant sentiment supporting Proposition 187. The Coalition for Humane Immigrant Rights of Los Angeles (CHIRLA) set up a hotline after the passage of Proposition 187 to document the rise in incidents against the Latina/o community. Hundreds of phone calls poured in on the first day of the hotline describing people not being allowed to cash a check unless they showed passports, police demanding documents while beating those who they called "aliens," and Latina/o households being burned by arsonists who spray painted "white power" and "Mexico" with an "X" through it. Essentially, Proposition 187 gave citizens a license to carry out their own border checks against anyone who looked foreign. The National Asian Pacific American Legal Consortium reported that in the months leading up to the passage of Proposition 187, there was a significant increase in incidents which included references to "go home" and get out of America. There was an unprecedented number of hate fliers stuffed into grocery bags, home mailboxes, and student lockers. The fliers referred to the 'invasion' of the 'Gooks' and demanded that they 'had to go.' Most references in the fliers were to 'genocide' and to taking back America. The result is that anti-immigrant sentiment has become legitimized and legalized so that it is acceptable to openly discriminate against people who are marked as foreign. This includes border checks from questions regarding citizenship status to hate speech and hate crimes manifesting this anti-immigrant sentiment in a more physical manner. Proposition 187 authorized private actors to perform border patrol and gave them the legitimacy and power of the state to do so.

A group in San Diego formed after the passage of Proposition 187 demonstrates just how much authority civilians believe they possess to conduct border patrol. In 1996, Win Housley and 200 other private citizens formed a band of vigilantes into the "Airport Posse" and began to patrol the San Diego International Airport to find undocumented immigrants. The group roams the airport in blue shirts that read "U.S. Citizen Patrol," imitating government uniforms with the belief that the government has failed in its duty to end illegal immigration. Jose Luis Perez Canchola of Mexico's National Commission on Human Rights reported an incident in which the posse had confronted a group of 22 individuals and demanded proof of citizenship. He said, "They are civilians assuming the role of an immigration officer." In response to criticism that it is difficult to identify illegal immigrants, "Airport Posse" leader Housley insists that they are easy to spot. He explains, "They're nervous. They're in out-of-style clothing. When they talk to one another, it's always in Spanish. They're all, as I said, real nervous." Obviously the "Airport Posse" is relying on their notions of foreignness as proper suspicion and targeting those with inscribed figurative borders.

E. Blurring Continued: State Engages in Hate Violence

Border patrol is clearly performed by both the state and non-state actors as the divisions have become blurred. As a form of border patrol, hate violence necessarily involves both state and private actors. However, hate violence has been constructed as a private problem of individual perpetrators. So construed, hate violence seems easily controlled under the traditional view advocated by law enforcement, the media, and mainstream society: that the law will protect subordinated groups if they would just let the system work. The problems with this approach are numerous, including what happens when law enforcement does not react to a hate crime or when law enforcement is the perpetrator of a hate crime. Victor Hwang, in his experience with the Race Relations: Hate Violence Project at the Asian Law Caucus, finds that law enforcement generally does not take hate crimes seriously. This is confirmed by the fact that although almost 9,000 hate crimes were reported to the FBI in 1996 (with reporting by law enforcement agencies covering only 84% of the U.S. population), only 38 of these resulted in prosecution by the Department of Justice. Thus, the state implicitly sends a message condoning hate violence by failing to prosecute hate crimes. The recent failure to pass the federal Hate Crimes Prevention Act (HCPA) also demonstrates an unwillingness on the part of the state to recognize the need for protection from hate crimes and the need to send an unequivocal message that hate violence will not be tolerated. The HCPA would have given the federal government a strong, uniform statute on which to prosecute hate crimes and would have closed the gaps in existing federal hate crime laws. The HCPA would have authorized the Department of Justice to prosecute hate crimes based on sexual orientation, gender, and disability, which are currently not covered by federal hate crime laws. Furthermore, under current law, federal prosecutors may only file hate crime charges if the victim was exercising a federally protected right such as voting or attending school when attacked, leaving a loophole for a situation where a victim is killed in her/his home. The new statute would have allowed the Department of Justice to prosecute hate crimes involving bodily injury or death regardless of whether the victim was exercising a federally protected right.

The violent death of Kuanchung Kao exemplifies the participation of the state in hate violence and in policing the perceived foreign enemy who can and will attack with his martial arts skills. Kuanchung Kao, a 33-year-old father of three, was shot to death by Rohnert Park police on April 29, 1997. Earlier that evening, Kao had been drinking after being racially harassed in a separate incident. He returned home and began crying and screaming for help in front of his house. Officer Jack Shields and Officer Mike Lynch responded to a disturbing-the-peace call at the Kao residence. Within 34 seconds of their arrival, the officers shot Kao in the chest from at least 7 feet away, killing him. Officer Shields claimed that Kao was waving a stick he was holding in a threatening and "martial arts" like manner and that he had to shoot because he did not know where Mr. Kao was from and feared him to be an expert in martial arts. Certainly the fact that Mr. Kao was Asian American informed the officers in their fear and judgment that Mr. Kao must know martial arts and their quick decision to shoot and kill him. Mr. Kao died on the front lawn and police

would not allow Mrs. Kao, a registered nurse, to attend to her husband or to call for help. The District Attorney cleared the officers of any wrongdoing, mainly because one of the officers claimed self-defense. This was the same officer who had been demoted by his own police department after being convicted of falsifying records the year before. The U.S. Department of Justice also refused to file federal civil rights charges in this case. Thus, the state is just as capable of committing hate violence based upon racial stereotypes of the foreigner as individual citizens are in the private sphere.

In fact, the National Asian Pacific American Legal Consortium's 1994 audit of anti-Asian violence found that the main perpetrator of racially motivated violence against Asian Americans in New York City was the police. The data reveals that the New York City police committed 50% of the total number of anti-Asian violent incidents in 1994. In over half of these incidents involving police brutality, racial slurs such as "Go back to China," "F—ing Orientals," "Go back to Pakistan," and "This is not f—ing Pakistan" were uttered. Many of these incidents involved South Asian American taxi drivers whose police encounters ranged from racial slurs to assaults. The police also issued false traffic violations in retaliation for civilian complaints the South Asian American taxi drivers have filed against the police officers for their discriminatory treatment. Two years later, the 1996 National Asian Pacific American Legal Consortium report on anti-Asian violence again noted that police brutality continued to be a problem in New York City.

F. A Community Response to Hate Violence

With the collapsing of state and non-state forms of border patrol into the same capacity, we must realize the potential for hate violence by anyone in the private or public sector. The narrow construction of hate crimes focuses on the individual actor who perpetrates hate crimes and obscures the legalized aspects of border patrol, which are also drawing on the same notions of foreignness and result in anti-Asian violence. However, by focusing only on the individual aspect, we ignore the state's role in border patrol as well as the historical context behind the systematic oppression of people of color through violence. Violence occurs in our social and historical system of domination and subordination and not in a vacuum. Even if law enforcement did take hate crimes against Asian Americans more seriously, the issue still remains with legalized hate violence in the form of border patrol. As previously discussed, border patrol exists officially and unofficially with the blurring of the two by laws such as Proposition 187 so that individual hate violence perpetrators are working in compliance with the state to protect white American national identity and cultural security.

Because anti-Asian violence may come from both state and private actors, solutions to anti-Asian violence must be pursued on multiple fronts. We must turn inwards for strength, community education, and empowerment and not rely on the state and law enforcement agencies to meet our needs. Victor Hwang explains that because hate crimes are social-political crimes, Asian Americans should look beyond the strictly legal aspect and concentrate on political and community pressure in order to be taken more seriously by law enforcement. Thus, we must turn to the community for solutions and not solely rely on the state to protect us.

Conclusion

This chapter has attempted to place hate violence against Asian Americans as part of a larger context of increased border patrol. Asian Americans are marked with figurative borders, which has serious consequences, especially in the present anti-immigrant climate. Hate violence has become another way to patrol the borders of the nation which both state and private actors can participate in to preserve a white national identity and cultural security. As a community, we must turn inwards for strength rather than depend on the State to protect us. Anti-Asian violence has been a part of the Asian American community from the moment we arrived in this country and will unfortunately, continue into the future. It is through our collective struggle against violence and exclusion that we ensure our survival.

Notes

1. Jerry Kang, *Racial Violence Against Asian Americans,* 106 HARV. L. REV. 1926 (June 1993); National Asian Pacific American Legal Consortium, Audit of Violence Against Asian Pacific Americans: Continuing the Campaign Against Hate Crimes, Fifth Annual Report (1997).

2. Victor Hwang, The Interrelationship Between Anti-Asian Violence and Asian America, 22 CHICANO-LATINO L. REV. 18, 19 (2000).

3. Robert S. Chang and Keith Aoki, *Policy, Politics and Praxis: Centering the Immigrant in the Inter/National Imagination,* 85 CAL.L.REV. 1395, 1411 (1997).

4. Angelo N. Ancheta, RACE, RIGHTS, AND THE ASIAN AMERICAN EXPERIENCE 64 (1998).

5. Lorna Dee Cervantes, *Poem for the Young White Man Who Asked Me How I, an Intelligent, Well-Read Person, Could Believe in the War Between Races, in* UNSETTLING AMERICA, AN ANTHOLOGY OF CONTEMPORARY MULTI-CULTURAL POETRY 248, 248–49 (Maria Mazziotti Gillan and Jennifer Gillan eds., 1994).

6. Iris Young, JUSTICE AND THE POLITICS OF DIFFERENCE 61–62 (1990).

7. *See* Richard Delgado, *Words that Wound: A Tort Action for Racial Insults, Epithets, and Name Calling,* 17 HARV. C.R.-C.L. L. REV. 133 (1982).

8. *See* Jerry Kang, *Racial Violence Against Asian Americans,* 106 HARV. L. REV. 1926 (1993) (citing ORGANIZATION FOR CHINESE AMERICANS, IN PURSUIT OF JUSTICE 2 (1992)).

9. Monique Thuy-Dung Truong, *Kelly, in* ASIAN AMERICAN LITERATURE: A BRIEF INTRODUCTION AND ANTHOLOGY 288, 289 (Shawn Wong ed., 1996).

10. *See* Ronald Takaki, STRANGERS FROM A DIFFERENT SHORE: A HISTORY OF ASIAN AMERICANS 203 (1989).

11. Bill Ong Hing, MAKING AND REMAK-ING ASIAN AMERICA THROUGH IMMIGRA-TION POLICY 1850–1990 30 (1993).

12. *See* Neil Gotanda, *Other Non-Whites in American Legal History: A Review of Justice at War,* 85 COLUM. L. REV. 1186 (1985).

13. Anida Rouquiyah Yoeu Esguerra *of* I WAS BORN WITH TWO TONGUES, *excuse me, ameriKa, on* BROKEN SPEAK (Fist of Sound Records 1999) (transcribed by the author).

14. *See* Edward W. Said, ORIENTALISM (1978).

15. Keith Aoki, *"Foreign-ness" and Asian American Identities: Yellowface, World War II*

Propaganda, and Bifurcated Racial Stereotypes, 4 UCLA ASIAN PAC. AM. L.J. 1, 6–9 (1996).

16. Bill Ong Hing, *Beyond the Rhetoric of Assimilation and Cultural Pluralism: Addressing the Tension of Separatism and Conflict in an Immigration Driven Multiracial Society,* 81 CAL. L. REV. 863, 863–64 (1993) (citing Patrick Buchanan on *This Week With David Brinkley,* ABC News television broadcast, Dec. 8, 1991).

17. Enid Trucios-Haynes, Symposium, *Citizenship and Its Discontents: Centering the Immigrant in the Inter/National Imagination (Part I): Section One: Race, Citizenship, and Political Community Within the Nation-State: Article: The Legacy of Racially Restrictive Immigration Laws and Policies and the Construction of the American National Identity,* 76 OR. L. REV. 369, 377–78 (1997).

18. Ruben J. Garcia, *Critical Race Theory and Proposition 187: The Racial Politics of Immigration Law,* 17 CHICANO-LATINO L. REV. 138 (1995).

19. Gary Y. Okihiro, MARGINS AND MAINSTREAMS: ASIANS IN AMERICAN HISTORY AND CULTURE 142 (1994).

20. David Reyes, *Son Says Intent in Suing INS Is to Give Value to Mother's Death,* L.A. TIMES, Sept. 19, 1989, at Metro 3.

21. Kevin R. Johnson, *Symposium on Immigration Policy: An Essay on Immigration Politics, Popular Democracy, and California's Proposition 187: The Political Relevance and Legal Irrelevance of Race,* 70 WASH. L. REV. 636 (1995).

22. It is important to note that only accents of certain groups are considered to be foreign in this negative way. For instance, while a French or British accent may appear to be intellectual, an Asian or Spanish accent is perceived to be an indicator of foreignness and/or ignorance. For an excellent discussion of accent discrimination, see Mari Matsuda, *Voices of America: Accent, Antidiscrimination Law, and a Jurisprudence for the Last Reconstruction,* 100 YALE L.J. 1329 (1991).

23. *See* Paula C. Johnson, *The Social Construction of Identity in Criminal Cases: Cinema Verite and the Pedagogy of Vincent Chin,* 1 MICH. J. RACE & L. 347 (1996) for a detailed analysis of the legal case.

24. *See* Bill Ong Hing, *Beyond the Rhetoric of Assimilation and Cultural Pluralism: Addressing the Tension of Separatism and Conflict in an Immigration Driven Multiracial Society,* 81 CAL. L. REV. 863, 865 (1993).

25. Linda S. Bosniak, *Opposing Proposition 187: Undocumented Immigrants and the National Imagination* 28 CONN. L. REV. 555, 561 n.9 (1996).

QUESTIONS

1. How do the examples in this article illustrate racial "essentialism"—the notion that race/ethnicity is the most important defining characteristic of a person?

2. How is white cultural insecurity related to national security concerns? What are some examples of this?

3. How does the characterization of Asian Americans as "foreign" serve as a connector between positive and negative stereotypes about Asians?

4. What role does marking Asian Americans as "foreign" play in maintaining the white American national identity?

5. What are some examples of "border patrol" carried out by private individuals? How are hate crimes manifestations of "border patrol"?

6. What was the societal context surrounding the murders of Vincent Chin and Navroze Mody? What messages do you think the legal outcomes in these cases sent?

7. How have demographic changes in California resulted in a conservative backlash? How did Proposition 187 illustrate this?

8. What was the official rationale given in *Korematsu v. United States* for the internment of Japanese Americans during World War II? What were the flaws in this rationale, and what was the ultimate legal outcome of the internment issue?

9. How does police brutality illustrate hate-based violence by the state? What are some examples involving Asian Americans?

10. Why is it essential to consider the historical, legal, and societal context in which hate crimes occur? Discuss using examples to illustrate.

11. How does marking non-white Americans as "others" present a contrast that functions to preserve a sense of cultural security for white Americans?

12. What are some historic and current examples of how immigration control policies reflect nativist sentiment, racial bigotry, and anti-immigrant hysteria?

20

Examining the Boundaries of Hate Crime Law

Disabilities and the "Dilemma of Difference"

Ryken Grattet

Valerie Jenness

Does fairness require that all individuals be treated the same, regardless of their individual characteristics? Or does fairness sometimes require taking individual differences into account? This article explores the "dilemma of difference" in relation to the policy issue of whether hate crime laws should include disability as a protected legal status. What are the legal and social implications of recognizing "difference" by including disability along with other statuses (such as ethnicity and race) that are included in hate crime laws, versus failing to include disability as a protected status? Regardless of which policy response is chosen, this question has important consequences for both people with disabilities and for our understanding of the boundaries of hate crime law.

Introduction

Although anyone is potentially a victim of crime, some groups are particularly susceptible to victimization because of their vulnerability, social marginality, or invisibility. Some criminals use a victim's minority group membership as a means of gauging the victim's level of guardianship and the degree to which society cares about what happens to the victim. They often expect—with good reason—that the criminal justice system will share the view that such

EDITORS' NOTE: From Grattet, R., & Jenness, V. (2001). Examining the Boundaries of Hate Crime Law: Disabilities and the "Dilemma of Difference." *Journal of Criminal Law & Criminology, 91,* 653-697. Reprinted by special permission of Northwestern University School of Law, *Journal of Criminal Law and Criminology.*

victims are unworthy of vigorous enforcement of the law. The stereotypes and biases upon which these views are based are, in turn, residues of historical relations of subordination, inequality, and discrimination, which criminals capitalize upon and reinforce. Moreover, like the schoolyard bully who preys upon the small, the weak, and the outcast, crimes against the disadvantaged are increasingly understood to possess a distinct moral status and evoke particular policy implications.

For students of public policy, advocacy groups, and legislators alike, questions about how law can best respond to the criminal victimization of minorities and others who are systematically disadvantaged presents a pressing, yet familiar, problem. This problem is often stated as a question: should those interested in enhancing the status and welfare of minority groups pursue policies that provide "special" treatment for minorities; or, alternatively, should they pursue policies that ignore the unique social location, special qualities, and socially structured obstacles faced by minorities and work solely towards improving the social and legal resources available to all victims of crime, regardless of their social characteristics or group membership? Stated more succinctly, should all victims of crime be treated the same or should some victims of crime, namely people who face unique barriers when accessing the criminal justice system and pursuing justice, be distinguished and treated differently? Historically and in the current era, policymakers, especially lawmakers, and advocates for minorities have had to respond to this question. And, how they have responded and continue to respond to this question is consequential for the making of criminal law and the delivery of social justice in the United States. This article addresses this concern by examining the contours of and justifications for status provisions, especially "disabilities," in American hate crime law.

There are costs and benefits associated with both choices to policymaking. Policies that emphasize the "special" needs of minorities, such as affirmative action policies and anti-discrimination laws, can reinforce cultural distinctions between "minorities" and "normals." Such policies can render minorities different from normals, underscore their "incapacities" and special needs as the defining feature of their identities and, ultimately, place them in subordinate positions within both the public and privates spheres of social life. Arguably, one of the unintended consequences of social policies that single out subpopulations for "special" protections and treatment is the reinforcement of the idea that people of color, women, gays and lesbians, the poor, immigrants, those with disabilities, and non-Christians, for example, are more vulnerable members of society, less capable of responding to real and perceived vulnerabilities, and ultimately less credible participants in an array of social activities, especially those interfacing with the criminal justice system.

In contrast, policies that ignore differences between types of victims risk being insensitive to the increasingly well-documented institutional, organizational, and interactional disadvantages faced by minorities, including those who find themselves confronting a criminal justice system with ideologies and structures that were enacted without them in mind.[1] Treating minorities the same as other crime victims does little to challenge the biases and stereotypes with which criminal justice officials often operate. A sizeable body of evidence suggests that ignoring social difference seldom is enough to produce equality, especially in the criminal justice system.[2] Indeed, as many advocates for people of color, Jews, women, gays, lesbians, and persons with disabilities have recently pointed out, crimes against minorities are often unrecognized or ignored by law enforcement.[3] Failing to acknowledge the differences around which systematic injustices revolve, the argument goes, allows state officials to continue to do business as usual and does little to remedy systematic inequality.

The choice between whether or not to emphasize and delineate social difference in social policy, especially law, has been astutely characterized by Harvard Law Professor Martha Minow as the "dilemma of difference."[4] As Minow details in her book *Making All the Difference: Inclusion, Exclusion, and American Law*, the dilemma of difference is a philosophical, legal, and strategic issue that has implications for an array of social issues ranging from affirmative action to maternal leave policies to gay marriage to discrimination in the workplace against persons with disabilities. As Minow writes:

> The stigma of difference may be recreated both by ignoring and by focusing on it. Decisions about education, employment, benefits, and other opportunities in society should not turn on an individual's ethnicity, disability, race, gender, religion, or membership in any other group about which some have deprecating or hostile attitudes. Yet refusing to acknowledge these differences may make them continue to matter in a world constructed with some groups, but not others, in mind. These problems of inequality can be exacerbated both by treating members of minority groups the same as members of the majority and by treating the two groups differently.

Often summarized as a tension between "same" versus "different" treatment policies, the dilemma of difference is routinely confronted by advocates for minority constituencies, most notably those supporting or opposing the agendas of the contemporary civil rights movement to enhance the status and welfare of people of color, the modern women's movement to enhance the status and welfare of girls and women, the gay and lesbian movement to enhance the status of nonnormative sexualities, and the disabilities rights movement to enhance the status and welfare of persons with disabilities. Regardless of the vast differences among these groups, their constituencies, and the issues they confront, the value of considering the dilemma of difference is that it forces activists, policymakers, and members of the morally concerned citizenry to 1) anticipate the negative consequences of reforms based upon creating "special" treatment where such treatment directly or indirectly reproduces stereotypes about minorities and 2) acknowledge the drawbacks of ignoring the differences that define minorities of all sorts. Of course, being cognizant of the dilemma of difference does not necessarily ensure that it is resolved; rather, it only sensitizes advocates and policymakers to the costs associated with pursuing one kind of policy approach over another.

With the dilemma of difference in mind, this chapter addresses a core question in the study of contemporary public policy in general and lawmaking in particular: when, how, and why should minority status be emphasized in public policy, especially criminal law? To address this broad question, we direct specific attention to the making of hate crime law in the United States, with a particular focus on the place and viability of "disabilities" within this body of law. First, we describe the history of state and federal hate crime lawmaking as a recent, innovative, and distinct policy response to age-old human behavior: violence motivated by bigotry and manifest as discrimination. Then, we argue that an empirical focus on the inclusion/ exclusion of "disabilities" provisions in this body of law provides a useful, if not ideal, window through which we can examine a legal basis for including some status provisions (i.e., race, religion, ethnicity, sexual orientation, etc.) and not others (i.e., age, gender, marital status, class, occupation, etc.) in hate crime law. Once our analytic focus on disabilities is indicated, we discuss the parameters of "disabilities" provisions in hate crime law as a precursor to identifying a set of social and legal criteria for resolving the dilemma of difference relative to hate crime law. Consistent with the original motivation for writing this paper, this is the first article to systematically consider the legal basis and policy implications of treating crime victims with disabilities as victims and survivors of hate crime. This paper uses sociological data and research to consider the degree to which the deployment of hate crime law is a viable venue through which the status and welfare of minority groups—in particular persons with disabilities—can be enhanced.

I. Hate Crime Law: An Innovative Response to "Bias Violence"

The National Law Journal recently noted that the 1990s may go down in history as "the decade of hate—or at least of hate crime."[5] Although it remains questionable whether the United States is actually experiencing greater levels of hate-motivated conduct than in the past,[6] it is beyond dispute that the ascendance of the concept of "hate crime" in policy discourse has focused attention on violence motivated by bigotry and manifest as discrimination in a new way. As we have argued elsewhere, what is now commonly understood as "bias" or "hate" crime is an age-old problem approached with a new conceptual lens and sense of urgency.[7] Despite a well-documented history of violence directed at minorities, during the 1980s and 1990s multiple social movements began to identify and address the problem of discriminatory violence directed at minorities: federal, state, and local governments instituted task forces and commissions to analyze the issue; legislative campaigns sprang up at every level of government; new sentencing rules and categories of criminal behavior were established in law; prosecutors and law enforcement developed special training policies and specialized enforcement units; scholarly commentary and social science research exploded on the topic; and the United States Supreme Court weighed in with its analysis of the laws in three highly controversial cases. As a result of these activities, criminal conduct that was once undistinguished from ordinary crime has been parsed out, redefined, and condemned more harshly than before. And "hate crime" has secured a place in the American political and legal landscape.

These extraordinary developments attest to the growing concern with, visibility of, and public resources directed at violence motivated by bigotry, hatred, or bias. They reflect the increasing acceptance of the idea that criminal conduct is "different" when it involves an act of discrimination. More importantly, for the purposes of this article, it is clear that the law has become the primary institution charged with defining and curbing hate or bias-motivated violence. Legal reform has been one of—if not the most—dominant response to bias-motivated violence in the United States. During a congressional debate on hate crime, Representative Mario Biaggi said it most succinctly when he argued, "the obvious point is that we are dealing with a national problem and we must look to our laws for remedies." Concurring, Representative John Conyers, Jr. explained that the enactment of hate crime legislation "will carry to offenders, to victims, and to society at large an important message, that the Nation is committed to battling the violent manifestations of bigotry." These views reflect a general agreement among state and federal legislators that "hate crimes, which can range from threats and vandalism to arson, assault and murder, are intended not just

to harm the victim, but to send a message of intimidation to an entire community of people."

With this solidified view of discriminatory violent conduct in hand, in the 1970s and early 1980s, lawmakers throughout the United States began to respond to what they perceived as an escalation of violence directed at minorities with a novel legal strategy: the criminalization of discriminatory violence, now commonly referred to as "hate crime." As result, by the turn of the century, "in seemingly no time at all, a 'hate crimes jurisprudence' had sprung up."[8]

A. State Hate Crime Law

In the last two decades almost every state in the United States has adopted at least one hate crime statute that simultaneously recognizes, defines, and responds to discriminatory violence. Hate crime statutes have taken many forms throughout the United States, including statutes proscribing criminal penalties for civil rights violations; specific "ethnic intimidation" and "malicious harassment" statutes; and provisions in previously enacted statutes for enhanced penalties if an extant crime is committed for bias or prejudicial reasons. These laws specify provisions for race, religion, color, ethnicity, ancestry, national origin, sexual orientation, gender, age, disability, creed, marital status, political affiliation, age, marital status, involvement in civil or human rights, and armed service personnel. In addition, a few states have adopted statutes that require authorities to collect data on hate (or bias) motivated crimes; mandate law enforcement training; prohibit the undertaking of paramilitary training; specify parental liability; and provide for victim compensation. Finally, many states have statutes that prohibit institutional vandalism and the desecration or the defacement of religious objects, the interference with or disturbance of religious worship, cross burning, the wearing of hoods or masks, the formation of secret societies, and the distribution of publications and advertisements designed to harass select groups of individuals. This last group of laws reflects a previous generation of what, in retrospect, could be termed "hate crime" law.[9]

Across the United States, state hate crime laws vary immensely in wording. Some laws employ a language of civil rights. For example, in 1987 California adopted an "Interference with Exercise of Civil Rights" statute that states:

> No person, whether or not acting under the color of law, shall by force or threat of force, willfully injure, intimidate, interfere with, oppress, or threaten any other person in the free exercise or enjoyment of any right or privilege secured to him or her by the constitution or laws of this state or by the Constitution or the laws of the United States because of the other person's race, color, religion, ancestry, national origin, or sexual orientation.

In contrast, some states employ the language of "ethnic intimidation or malicious harassment." In 1983, for example, Idaho adopted a "Malicious Harassment" law that declares:

> It shall be unlawful for any person, maliciously and with the specific intent to intimidate or harass another person because of that person's race, color, religion, ancestry, or national origin to: (a) Cause physical injury to another person; or (b) Damage, destroy, or deface any real or personal property of another person; or (c) Threaten, by word or act, to do the acts prohibited if there is reasonable cause to believe that any of the acts described in subsections (a) and (b) of this section will occur. For purposes of this section, "deface" shall include, but not be limited to, cross-burnings, or the placing of any word or symbol commonly associated with racial, religious, or ethnic terrorism on the property of another person without his or her permission.

Finally, some statutes simply increase the penalty for committing an enumerated crime if the defendant committed a criminal act that "evidences" or "demonstrates" prejudice or bigotry based on the victim's real or imagined membership in a legally recognized protected status. For example, in 1989 Montana adopted a "Sentence Enhancement" law that states:

> A person who has been found guilty of any offense, except malicious intimidation or harassment, that was committed because of the victim's race, creed, religion, color, national origin, or involvement in civil rights or human rights activities or that involved damage, destruction, or

attempted destruction of a building regularly used for religious worship, in addition to the punishment provided for commission of the offense, may be sentenced to a term of imprisonment of not less than 2 years or more than 10 years, except as provided in 46–18–222.

Despite variation in wording, these laws have criminalized select forms of bias-motivated violence.

B. Federal Hate Crime Legislation

Following the states' lead, the United States Congress has passed three laws specifically designed to address bias-motivated violence and it continues to consider additional legislation. In 1990, President Bush signed the Hate Crimes Statistics Act, which requires the Attorney General to collect statistical data on "crimes that manifest evidence of prejudice based on race, religion, sexual orientation, or ethnicity, including where appropriate the crimes of murder; non-negligent manslaughter; forcible rape; aggravated assault, simple assault, intimidation; arson; and destruction, damage or vandalism of property." As a data collection law, the Hate Crimes Statistics Act merely requires the Attorney General to gather and make available to the public data on bias-motivated crime, which has been done every year since 1991. It does not, in any way, stipulate new penalties for bias-motivated crimes, nor does it provide legal recourse for victims of bias-motivated crime. The rationale for the Hate Crimes Statistics Act was to mandate the collection of empirical data necessary to develop effective policy. Those supporting it argued that involving the police in identifying and counting hate crimes could help law enforcement officials measure trends, fashion effective responses, design prevention strategies, and develop sensitivity to the particular needs of victims of hate crimes.

In 1994, Congress passed two more hate crime laws. The Violence Against Women Act specifies that "all persons within the United States shall have the right to be free from crimes of violence motivated by gender." The Violence Against Women Act allocated over $1.6 billion for education, rape crisis hotlines, training of justice personnel, victim services (especially shelters for victims of battery), and special units of police and prosecutors to deal with crimes against women. The heart of the legislation, Title III, provides a civil remedy for "gender crimes."

In essence, Title III entitles victims to compensatory and punitive damages through the federal courts for a crime of violence if it is motivated, at least in part, by animus toward the victim's gender. This allowance implicitly acknowledges that some, if not most, violence against women is not gender-neutral; instead, it establishes the possibility that violence motivated by gender animus is a proper subject for civil rights action. In so doing, it defined the term "hate crime" as "a crime of violence committed because of gender or on the basis of gender, and due, at least in part, to animus based on the victim's gender." Although this law was recently ruled unconstitutional, it was predicated upon and promoted the inclusion of gender in the concept of a hate crime. Also in 1994, Congress passed the Hate Crimes Sentencing Enhancement Act. This law identifies eight predicate crimes—murder; nonnegligent manslaughter; forcible rape; aggravated assault; simple assault; intimidation; arson; and destruction, damage, or vandalism of property—for which judges are allowed to enhance penalties of "not less than three offense levels for offenses that the finder of fact at trial determines beyond a reasonable doubt are hate crimes." For the purposes of this law, "hate crime" is defined as criminal conduct wherein "the defendant intentionally selected any victim or property as the object of the offense because of the actual or perceived race, color, religion, national origin, ethnicity, gender, disability, or sexual orientation of any person." Although broad in form, this law addresses only those hate crimes that take place on federal lands and properties.

Finally, the Hate Crimes Prevention Act was introduced in the Senate and House of Representatives. If signed into law, this legislation would

Amend the Federal criminal code to set penalties for persons who, whether or not acting under the color of law, willfully cause bodily injury to any person or, through the use of fire, firearm, or explosive device, attempt to cause such injury, because of the actual or perceived: (1) race, color, religion, or national origin of any person; and (2) religion, gender, sexual orientation, or disability of any person, where in connection with the offense, the defendant or the victim travels in interstate or foreign commerce, uses a facility or instrumentality of interstate or foreign commerce, or engages in any activity affecting interstate or foreign commerce, or where the offense is in or affects interstate or foreign commerce.

Although not yet law, this pending legislation broadens the reach of the Hate Crimes Sentencing Enhancement Act.

The state and federal laws described above show that many contemporary advocates share a commitment to using the law,[10] law enforcement,[11] and the criminal justice system[12] as vehicles to enhance the status and welfare of minority constituencies deemed differentially vulnerable to violence motivated by bigotry. Despite variation in their wording and content, criminal hate crime statutes are laws that criminalize, or further criminalize, activities motivated by bias toward individuals or groups because of their real or imagined characteristics. Drawing from Grattet, Jenness, and Curry, this definition consists of three elements. First, the law provides a new state policy action, by either creating a new criminal category, altering an existing law, or enhancing penalties for select extant crimes when they are committed for bias reasons. Second, hate crime laws contain an intent standard. In other words, statutes contain wording that refers to the subjective intention of the perpetrator rather than relying solely on the basis of objective behavior. Finally, hate crime laws specify a list of protected social statuses, such as race, religion, ethnicity, sexual orientation, gender, disabilities, etc. These elements of the definition of hate crime law capture the spirit and essence of hate crime legislation designed to punish bias-motivated conduct.

The emergence and proliferation of hate crime law marks an important moment in the history of crime control efforts, the development of criminal and civil law, the allocation of civil rights, and the symbolic status of select minorities in the United States. As such, the emergence and proliferation of hate crime laws invites an examination of the place and prominence of status provisions—what Soule and Earle call "target groups"[13]—in hate crime law. This, in turn, sets the stage for an assessment of the bases upon which some status provisions are included in hate crime law, while others are not.

II. "DISABILITIES" AS AN ANALYTIC FOCUS

Our review of hate crime law leads to two interrelated questions about hate crime law as a policy response to discriminatory violence and its relationship to select minority groups. First, to what degree have lawmakers recognized some minority populations, and not others, as potential and actual victims of bias-motivated conduct? Second, upon what basis should particular constituencies be considered for inclusion in hate crime law? To address these interrelated questions, we focus on the case of "mental and physical disabilities" as a status provision and "persons with disabilities" as a target population.[14] Although our focus on disabilities and persons with disabilities is primarily for analytic purposes, there are at least three good reasons for choosing this particular example.

First, persons with disabilities represent one of the largest minority groups in the United States. According to a 1997 Census Bureau report, about fifty-four million, or twenty percent, of Americans qualify as having some level of disability and half of those have a "severe" disability.[15] Moreover, literally anyone can become disabled at some point in their life; after all, some disabilities are ascribed and some are achieved. With regard to the latter, as the life expectancy for Americans increases, the population as a whole continues to age. And, as the population gets older and older, we can continue to expect more and more people to acquire debilitating conditions in ways that accompany the aging process itself.

Second, recent research suggests that the multitude of ways that persons with disabilities are victimized is pronounced and, according to some, increasing.[16] In particular, there is growing agreement that the criminal justice system currently does not serve the needs of people

with disabilities particularly well; thus, a variety of organizational and procedural reforms have been envisioned and proposed by various groups concerned about persons with disabilities and their relationship to crime, the criminal justice system, and the pursuit of justice. The bulk of these proposals for reform have been itemized and articulated by the Office of Victims of Crime in a recently released bulletin on "Working with Victims of Crime with Disabilities."[17] Sponsored by the Department of Justice, this publication suggests an array of specific policy recommendations, including increasing the accessibility of the criminal justice system through everything from architectural changes to the introduction of communication technologies;[18] the creation of training measures for sensitizing law enforcement officials to the needs of persons with disabilities; fostering relations with disability service and advocacy organizations within the community; improving data collection efforts; and introducing specific protocols to assist the participation of persons with disabilities in the criminal process and to protect them from retaliation. Finally, and perhaps most notably for the purposes of this chapter, a single recommendation put forth, almost in passing, by the Office of Victims of Crime indicates that hate crime law should be applied to crimes against persons with disabilities. To be exact, "prosecutors should invoke hate crime statutes, if indicated, when prosecuting crimes against people with disabilities. Judges should apply equal sentencing or sentencing enhancements, when allowed, for offenders who victimize people with disabilities." Interestingly, from the point of view of the dilemma of difference, all of these proposals assume, in one way or another, that persons with disabilities are differentially subject to bias-motivated violence, have special needs, and face unique barriers when it comes to accessing the criminal justice system and pursuing justice if or when they are victims of violence.

Third, despite their numbers and an increasingly well-documented connection to violence, persons with disabilities have been largely overlooked by social scientists and sociolegal scholars interested in the nexus between violence, law and minority rights, as well as policymakers interested in responding to violence in particular and systematic inequalities more generally.[19] The vast majority of the sociolegal literature focusing on the intersection of law and violence, and minority status or rights, focuses on race, religion, ethnicity, gender, and sexual orientation as the prime categories of civil rights law. In large part, this no doubt reflects the relative newness of "disabilities" as a recognizable axis of discrimination. The Americans with Disabilities Act of 1990 is relatively new compared to other notable civil rights laws, such as the Civil Rights Act of 1964. Accordingly, and as we detail below, the term "disabilities" has had a less developed history in legal and public lexicon; moreover, the term "disabilities" in hate crime law is, at best, a second-class citizen insofar as it is peripheral to the core of hate crime legislation in the United States. Thus, it remains one of the most overlooked and occasionally negotiable status provisions in hate crime law.

Surprisingly, a critical discussion of the relationship between crimes against persons with disabilities and the parameters of hate crime law has yet to be developed. In particular, it is useful to first evaluate the place of "disabilities" in federal and state hate crime law, and then examine the bases for including "disabilities" alongside race, religion, ethnicity, gender, and sexual orientation in United States hate crime law. To do so creates a venue through which a social and legal justification for the formulation of hate crime law can be articulated and advanced.

III. The Place and Prominence of "Disabilities" in Hate Crime Law

The most direct way to assess the degree to which state lawmakers have recognized persons with disabilities as a constituency particularly vulnerable to violence and worthy of legal and social recognition as hate crime victims is to examine the "status provisions" currently referenced in hate crime law. Accordingly, in this section we do so by first focusing on the distribution of status provisions in state hate crime law and then focusing on the place of "disabilities" in the evolution of federal hate crime law.

A. The Status of "Disabilities" in State Hate Crime Law

In 1988, the most common status provisions were for race, religion, color, and national origin. These provisions represented a legal response to the most visible, recognizable, and stereotypical kinds of discriminatory behavior:[20] bias-motivated violence directed at blacks, immigrants, and Jews. While other categories of discriminatory violence—like those organized around gender, ancestry, sexual orientation, creed, age, political affiliation, marital status, and disabilities—are sometimes recognized in the early period of lawmaking, they appear infrequently enough to cause one to conclude that they were not part of legislators' conceptions of the "normal" axes along which discriminatory violence routinely occurs. Most notably, only five out of the nineteen states that had passed laws by 1988 included disability in those laws.

By 1999, however, a second tier of categories emerged and sexual orientation, gender, and disabilities became increasingly prominent in state hate crime law. Disability, in particular, rose from being included in about one-quarter of the states to one-half of the states. Currently, twenty-one states have laws covering disability, and that number continues to grow. While less stereotypical than their predecessors (i.e., race, religion, and national origin), sexual orientation, gender, and disability are categories that have become increasingly recognized as axes along which hate-motivated crime occurs.[21]

The respective unfolding of these clusters of statuses—the core and the second tier—reflects the history of various post-1960s civil rights movements in the United States.[22] Race, religion, color, and national origin reflect the early legal contestation of minorities' status and rights. Thus, there is a more developed history of invoking and then deploying the law to protect and enhance the status of blacks, Jews, and immigrants. Because the gay and lesbian movement, the women's movement, and the disability movement reflect a "second wave" of civil rights activism and "identity politics," sexual orientation, gender, and disability, respectively, have only recently been recognized by policymakers responsible for the formulation of hate crime law as legitimate axes around which hate crime occurs. Therefore, these statuses remain less embedded in hate crime law, resulting in gays and lesbians, women, and people with disabilities remaining less visible than other minority groups (e.g., blacks, Jews, and immigrants) and yet more visible than other groups (e.g., union members, the elderly, children, police officers, etc.).

B. The Status of "Disabilities" in Federal Hate Crime Law

Consistent with the patterns revealed in the previous section, a review of the legislative histories of federal hate crime law reveals how the substantive character of federal hate crime law was shaped—at first by minorities' advocates and social movements and later by processes of institutionalization—such that those with disabilities were recognized as victims of hate crime only in the latter phases of federal lawmaking around the issue.[23] As Jenness documents, early advocacy work sponsored by an array of local, regional, and state level organizations comprising the Coalition on Hate Crimes focused solely on the scope and consequences of race, religion, and ethnicity-based violence. Growing awareness of this type of violence became grounds for promoting federal hate crime legislation by a limited number of advocates, none of whom represented the interests of persons with disabilities. This advocacy successfully solidified a trio of statuses—"race, religion, and ethnicity"—as the anchoring provisions of all hate crime law. This solidification occurred without protest from federal legislators over the appropriateness of these provisions, which had already been legitimated by prior decades of civil rights organizing and changes in law.

The character of hate crime law was reshaped when the domain of the law expanded to include additional provisions. Shortly after federal hate crime law was envisioned, gay and lesbian advocates developed and promoted proposals to further differentiate hate crime victims by adding "sexual orientation" to the list of provisions in federal hate crime law. Through direct and sustained testimony, gay and lesbian advocates were able to bestow empirical

credibility upon the violence connected with this provision (i.e., antigay violence). In addition, they successfully engaged in discursive tactics that rendered the meaning of sexual orientation more similar to (rather than dissimilar from) the meanings already attached to race, religion, and ethnicity. By successfully engaging in these linking strategies of persuasion, advocates representing gays and lesbians proved crucial to the expansion of hate crime law to cover sexual orientation, thereby ensuring that gays and lesbians are routinely recognized as victims of bias crime.

In contrast, other status provisions initially recommended for inclusion in the law, but not added to the bill prior to its passage, did not attract significant, sustained advocacy and social movement mobilization in congressional hearings. For example, prior to the passage of the Hate Crimes Statistics Act, at least eight Senators argued: "we believe that the measure does not go far enough and include violence by and against union members." Since hearings were not held on this type of bias-motivated violence, there was not a structural opportunity for representatives from unions to establish the empirical credibility of the problem and thus legitimate this provision; as a result, union affiliation was not adopted as a provision in federal hate crime law.

This same pattern applies to claims about children, the elderly, and police officers: all were status provisions proposed early in federal lawmaking but never adopted as core elements of federal hate crime law, in large part because none of these target groups had advocates lobbying Congress to include them in federal lawmaking on hate crime. Representative John Conyers, Jr., the legislator primarily responsible for initiating and sustaining federal hearings on hate crime, conceded the importance of social movement organizations and other activist groups when he explained why, at least early on in federal lawmaking on hate crime, some statuses were included and others were not:

The reason we did not include octogenarians who are assaulted is because there was no testimony that suggested that they ought to be, as awful as the crimes visited upon them are, and the reason we did not account for policemen killed in the line of duty, although police organizations do, is that there was no request that they be separated out from the uniform crime statistics.

Senator Gekas, who opposed the inclusion of sexual orientation being based primarily on the presence and persuasive politics of gay and lesbian advocates, immediately responded to Representative Conyers:

> If the only criterion is to have the gay rights organization have its request acceded to by inclusion in that, I say to the Members that the gentleman should join with me now in a motion to recommit, to put this bill back into committee and allow the inclusion in this bill of statistics to be gathered on the incidence of child abuse, of attacks on the elderly, attacks on policemen, and attacks on other groups which might for one reason or another be victims of such type of crime.

The reverse of this pattern, particular only to the later phase of lawmaking, is further evidenced by the history of the disabilities provision in federal hate crime law. Although "the Congress apparently did not think that disabled people compromised [sic] a 'high risk' group in relation to interpersonal violence" when it first contemplated hate crime legislation, disability was later added to federal hate crime law via the reauthorization of the Hate Crime Statistics Act, the original and final formulation of the Hate Crimes Sentencing Enhancement Act, and the current formulation of the Hate Crime Prevention Act. The changing character of federal hate crime law along these lines occurred despite the fact that federal lawmakers have never held a hearing on violence directed at those with disabilities as a type of hate crime and no protest occurred over this provision. Moreover, the official records of federal level hate crime lawmaking reveal that representatives from the disability rights movement have yet to offer testimony related to federal hate crime legislation. Nonetheless, later in the history of federal lawmaking on hate crime, the inclusion of disabilities in federal hate crime law occurred in light of the fact that disability—like race, religion, and gender—was already a standard subject of federal discrimination law. In large part, this occurred because of the earlier passage of the Americans with Disabilities Act

in 1990, which ensured that "disabilities" had a home in federal civil rights legislation.

C. "Disabilities" as a Second-Class Citizen in Hate Crime Law in the United States

As the above examination of both the federal and state laws reveals, the provision for disabilities has found a home in hate crime legislation, but it remains somewhat in the basement of that home. First, after more than twenty years of lawmaking in response to bias-violence, only half the states have laws that cover disabilities. And while all three of the federal laws now contain provisions for "disabilities," these provisions were only included as afterthoughts.

Second, both the federal and state efforts to collect data on bias crimes directed at people with disabilities have lagged behind efforts to collect data on the other types of bias crimes. For example, as mandated by the Hate Crime Statistics Act, the Federal Bureau of Investigation began to collect bias crime data as part of the Uniform Crime Report in 1990. However, consistent with the late arrival of "disabilities" as a status provision, the FBI only began to report figures for violence against persons with disabilities in 1997. Even then, the FBI reported only thirteen cases of hate crimes directed against people with disabilities nationwide. Given the size of the disability population, it seems highly likely that there is a severe underreporting of the hate crimes committed against this class of people. Similarly, at the state level, reporting efforts have been delayed. For example, California—with more than four and a half million people with disabilities (more than twenty percent of the population) and a fifty-two percent increase in the number of persons classified as having developmental disabilities between 1985 and 1986—has only been publishing hate crime statistics since 1995. Specifically, from 1995–1998, California reported three or fewer cases of hate crimes directed at people with disabilities. Given the marginal status of disability in the laws and the fact that victims of such crimes are frequently unable to garner the full attention of the criminal justice system, it seems highly likely that this number is an underestimate.

Third, police training publications and curriculum at the federal, state, and local level tend to discuss disability-based hate crime only infrequently, if at all. For example, in the definitive national bias-crime training manual for law enforcement and victim assistance professionals, none of the "bias crime indicators" and illustrative cases relate to victims who were selected because of their disabilities. As a result, disability-based hate crime remains largely invisible to front-line law enforcers, who tend to focus mostly on race, religion, sexual orientation, and nationality. This incomplete focus, in turn, results in an underreporting of crimes motivated by someone's disability.

Fourth, there have been no appellate cases dealing with the disability provision. Most of the case law throughout the 1990s dealt with hate crimes based upon race, religion, and national origin—the triad of categories embedded earliest in the law. Later on, appellate courts considered sexual orientation and gender cases. The lack of disability-based hate crime cases may suggest that prosecutors were most concerned with applying the laws to "familiar" kinds of hate crime cases.[24] It may be harder for prosecutors to perceive crimes against persons with disabilities as hate crimes, even though half the state laws in existence cover them. As a result, the special problems the disability status provision might present have not been subjected to judicial scrutiny.

The bottom line is that as both a legislative provision and practical issue, the connection between the legal and conceptual definition of "hate crime" and "disabilities" is tenuous. Disabilities provisions remain less embedded in hate crime law than do the race, religion, ethnicity, sexual orientation, and gender provisions. Yet, while people with disabilities remain less visible as victims of hate crime than the other minority groups (e.g., blacks, Jews, and immigrants) included in the laws, they are still more visible than other groups that have been proposed (e.g., union members, octogenarians, the elderly, children, police officers, etc.).

A comparison along these lines reveals that the inclusion of status provisions in the law is, in the first instance, an outgrowth of social movement mobilization, the presence of interest groups, and the dynamics of lawmaking. As

Jenness and Grattet conclude, "as with other social constructions, especially those imbued with criminal meaning, hate crime can first and foremost be seen as an outgrowth of the interplay between social movement activism, policymakers, the law (i.e., judges, police, and law enforcement), and the meanings they engender." Acknowledging the validity of this statement, it is nonetheless crucial to ask: upon what criteria should the selection of "target groups" for inclusion in hate crime law proceed, especially if it is desirable to have the law reflect something other than mere "identity politics"?

IV. KEY CRITERIA FOR DETERMINING STATUS PROVISIONS IN HATE CRIME LAW

As Laurence Tribe, constitutional law professor at Harvard University, explained to Congress, "nothing in the United States Constitution prevents the Government from penalizing with added severity those crimes directed against people or their property because of their race, color, religion, national origin, ethnicity, gender or sexual orientation, and nothing in the Constitution requires that this list be infinitely expanded." Not surprisingly, then, throughout the history of social movement and legislative activity that has resulted in the enactment of the hate crime laws discussed above, there has been considerable controversy over what groups should be protected by hate crime legislation.

This determination and attendant differentiation is significant. It affects the kinds of people protected, and thus the kinds of violence prosecutors can pursue as hate crimes. It also affects which minority groups are legally recognizable as victims of hate crime. More importantly, it reflects the selection of one choice over another when faced with the dilemma of difference. Specifically, to include a status provision serves—rightly or wrongly, accurately or inaccurately—to demarcate the enhanced vulnerabilities of some types of people and inscribe victim statuses on some minority groups and not others. Here, race is a proxy for non-Whites, religion is a proxy for non-Christians, sexual orientation is a proxy for gays and lesbians, gender is a proxy for girls and women, etc. In contrast, to forego including a status provision serves to render such social differences invisible in both the social and legal lexicon.

To determine what distinctions are to be made in the law, social scientists, legal scholars, and advocates for minority groups have identified many grounds upon which the inclusion of select status provisions can be justified, as well as many grounds upon which the exclusion of select provisions can be justified. Continuing with our focus on "disabilities," a systematic consideration of key criteria is useful for assessing the viability of orienting toward any form of group membership as an axis along which bias-motivated violence occurs and is thus legally recognized as a "hate crime."

Frederick Lawrence distinguishes bias crimes from other crimes—what he refers to as "parallel crimes"—by arguing that the former are far worse than the latter because "a bias crime occurs not because the victim is who he is, but rather because the victim is what he is." With this distinction as a starting point, in his book Punishing Hate: Bias Crime Under American Law, Lawrence addresses the question of which status characteristics should be written into hate crime law and which ones should be excluded. He proposes a "proper methodology for going about constructing such a list." This methodology hinges upon moving beyond simply identifying select constituencies victimized by violence and toward an assessment of multiple factors associated with candidate constituencies, including the presence of a group identity, evidence of historical discrimination, and distinctions between types of discrimination and bias motivations. An examination of the way in which these factors contextualize crime provides a lens through which the inclusion of disabilities in hate crime law can be understood and assessed as a policy response to violence directed towards people with disabilities and the dilemma of difference more generally.

A. Presence of a Group Identity

Lawrence's methodology is attentive to "self-regarding groups" and not "random collections of people." That is, for a group to be recognized in hate crime law requires that some portion of society view such a collection of people as an identifiable group of persons who, to some degree, maintain a collective identity.[25] Two of the most cited scholars on the topic, sociologists Taylor and Whittier, describe a collective identity as "the shared definition of a group that derives from members' common interests, experiences, and solidarity." For social psychologists and social movement scholars alike, "individuals see themselves as part of a group when some shared characteristic becomes salient and is defined as important, resulting in a sense of 'we-ness.'"[26] This "we-ness," in turn, often implies opposition to other groups and/or the dominant social order. To be concrete, various groups of people of color, Jews, people from other countries with non-American identities, gays and lesbians, and girls and women qualify along these lines, but blue-eyed people, people who prefer casual dress to formal dress, and people who come from one-parent families do not.

Two sources of evidence suggest that persons with disabilities comprise a "self-regarding group." First, survey data suggests that persons with disabilities do, indeed, feel a common identity with one another and see themselves as minorities in the same sense as people who are black or Hispanic.[27] Second, persons with disabilities have, over the last two decades, emerged to comprise no small sector of the modern civil rights movement. Shapiro's book, No Pity: People with Disabilities Forging a New Civil Rights Movement, demonstrates that people with disabilities have done so by constituting a "self-regarding group" in the form of a distinct political entity. Much like people of color, gays and lesbians, and women, people with disabilities constitute an identifiable sector of a larger civil rights movement in the United States that has increasingly made demands on the political system as people with disabilities. As Shapiro details:

. . . it did not matter if disability came at birth or later, whether the person was rich or poor, or even if it did not interfere with one's accomplishments. To be disabled meant to fight someone else's reality. Other people's attitudes, not one's own disability, were the biggest barrier. This frustration gave rise to the ardor behind the disability rights movement.

Representative Tony Coelho of California argued that "the strength of the disability movement came from a 'hidden army' of people who had an instinctive understanding of the stigma of being disabled.

B. Evidence of Historical Discrimination

Every "self-regarding group," however, is not an equally viable contender for inclusion in hate crime law. Rather, those constituencies sharing a characteristic that implicates "classic societal fissure lines" or "divisions that run deep in the social history of a culture" are prime candidates. Indeed, the dominant conception of hate crimes, evident in congressional debates, popular media sources, and the testimony of interest group actors, is one in which the targets of hate crimes are minorities of one kind or another and who historically have been victims of racism, nativism, heterosexism, and religious persecution—blacks, Mexicans, gays and lesbians, and Jews, respectively.

In sharp contrast to the research conducted on the other categories included in hate crime laws and for which there is ample evidence of a long term pattern of discrimination and violence, historians, criminologists, activists, and various state agencies have only recently begun to document the influence of disabilities as a predisposing factor in discriminatory violence. Although most violence against persons with disabilities is hidden from view, researchers have begun to document a variety of forms of violence directed towards persons with disabilities, from symbolic to fatal assaults involving a range of perpetrators, and from intimates to strangers to institutions such as the state and medicine. This includes "assisted suicides" of severely disabled people, parental participation in the starvation of disabled newborns in hospitals, sexual abuse in the isolation of the nuclear family, routine physical abuse in institutional settings, and an array of medical practices legitimized as necessary, such as electro-convulsive therapy, psychosurgery, eugenic sterilization, medical experimentation, and extensive medicating and adverse behavioral modification. It also includes seemingly "random violence" in the public sphere.

With the passage of the Americans with Disabilities Act in 1990, the United States government recognized that disabled persons have been "subjected to a history of purposeful unequal treatment." Harlan Hahn's work suggests that, at least in part, this unequal treatment resulted because both historically and in the current era, people with disabilities have been positioned as inferior, thereby leading to centuries of systematic discrimination. In perhaps the most cited work on the topic, Dick Sobsey points to the cultural exosystem—the cultural and social beliefs about disability—that has contributed to the differential treatment of people with disabilities, as well as patterned and predictable violence against those with disabilities for centuries.[28] With regard to the latter, Petersilia's recent work corroborates this view. She found that people with developmental disabilities are four to ten times more likely to be crime victims than people without a disability. Moreover, children with any kind of disability are more than twice as likely as nondisabled children to be physically abused and almost twice as likely to be sexually abused. Consistent with these findings, Waxman observed that "disabled people face a pattern of oppressive societal treatment and hatred, much as women face misogyny [sic], gay men and lesbians face homophobia, Jews face antisemitism, and people of color face racism."

Taken together, this research suggests that the visibility of violence against persons with disabilities is where the visibility of violence directed at people of color, girls and women, and gays and lesbians was not so long ago. That is, what was once invisible is becoming increasingly recognized. Private pain and violence are increasingly being perceived as public problems, requiring governmental response. Moreover, violence is being increasingly seen as not merely epiphenomenal to the subordination of persons with disabilities, but as central to its maintenance.

C. Distinguishing Between Types of Discrimination and Bias Motivations

To simply document how different groups—racial, religious, and ethnic minorities, as well as gays and lesbians, women, and people with disabilities—are differentially vulnerable to crime does not, in and of itself, constitute prima facie evidence of hate crime. To further demarcate how bias crimes are different from parallel crimes, Berk, Boyd, and Hamner make a useful distinction between actuarial and symbolic crimes. In their words:

> Perhaps the best place to begin is with the broad observation by Grimshaw (1969b), Sterba (1969), and Nieburg (1972) that one key ingredient in hate-motivated violence is the 'symbolic status' of the victim. Thus Grimshaw (1969b, p. 254) speaks of violence as 'social' when 'it is directed against an individual or his property solely or primarily because of his membership in a social category.' A social category is defined by one or more attributes that a set of individuals share, which have implications for how the individuals are perceived or treated.

Accordingly, symbolic crimes are best envisioned as social crimes because the victims are selected precisely because of what they symbolize. The crime is committed for expressive reasons. The most vivid historical example of this is perhaps the lynching of blacks where the corpses were then displayed in communities to send a message to other blacks and whites who sympathized with the plight of the blacks.[29] A more recent example is the incident that occurred in Laramie, Wyoming, where Matthew Shepard, a young gay man, was robbed, pistol-whipped, tied to a fence, and left to die by two young men who were offended by his homosexuality. In each case, the individual had been victimized in order to convey a message to the larger community. As Representative Conyers explained when trying to convince his fellow legislators of the importance of hate crime legislation,

> Hate crimes, which can range from threats and vandalism to arson, assault, and murder, are intended to not just harm the victim, but to send a message of intimidation to an entire community of people. [Because of this added element] Hate crimes are extraordinary in nature and require a special government response.

In contrast to symbolic crimes, actuarial crimes involve the selection of a victim based on his/her real or imagined social characteristic(s), but not for expressive or symbolic reasons. Rather, actuarial crimes are done for instrumental reasons. As Berk, Boyd, and Hamner explain, "people routinely make lay estimates of central tendencies associated with particular social categories." These assessments play into all sorts of choices criminals make prior to engaging in criminal conduct. For example, a group of perpetrators may purposely assault and rob a gay man not because of what his sexual orientation represents to them, but because they apply a stereotype to him that is anchored in the notion that gay men are effeminate and thus less inclined to resist assault. Alternatively, a group of perpetrators may purposely assault and rob a Jewish man not because of what Jewishness represents to them, but because they apply a stereotype to him that is anchored in the notion that Jews have more money than gentiles, thus they are more likely to "pay-off" than random victims of assault and robbery. In a similar fashion, a group of perpetrators may purposely assault and rob a person in a wheelchair not because of their antipathy toward persons with disabilities, but because they apply a stereotype to him that is anchored in the notion that persons with disabilities are less inclined to resist, unable to seek assistance, unlikely to evoke the attention of authorities, and/or unable to testify about victimization when authorities are attentive. In each of these examples, the victim's symbolic status is used to retrieve relevant "factual" information about him/her as a likely crime victim, not as a member of a social category held in ill-repute. In other words, it is this factual information, mediated through some imagined actuarial table, that motivates the crime, not bigotry. "This distinction between symbolic and actuarial crimes suggests a potentially useful boundary between hate-motivated crimes and other offenses," even though in many cases making clear empirical distinctions can be difficult. Nonetheless, Berk, Boyd, and Hamner conclude that "perhaps the essential feature of hate-motivated crimes is their symbolic content. Crimes motivated solely by the victim's actuarial status would seem best included in another category."

Related to the distinction between symbolic and actuarial crimes, a distinction can be made between "two analytically distinct, but somewhat overlapping [statutory] models of bias crimes": the discriminatory selection model and the racial animus model. Each of these models assumes the presence of discrimination in the selection of crime victims. Each model, however, posits different criteria for assessing what does and does not equal bias or hate crime. Accordingly, each model is relevant to the consideration of persons with disabilities as victims of hate crime.

The discriminatory selection model defines hate crime solely on the basis of the perpetrator's discriminatory selection of a victim, regardless of why such a selection was made. For example, like girls and women, people with disabilities may be targeted simply because they are perceived to be more vulnerable victims. Consistent with the development of sexual harassment law, the reasons or motivations for the discrimination—in this case, differential selection—are irrelevant to the applicability of the law. As the Court of Appeals of Florida has stated in regard to Florida's hate crime law,

> It does not matter why a woman is treated differently than a man, a black differently than a white, a Catholic differently than a Jew; it matters only that they are. So also with section 775.085 [Florida's hate crime statute]. It doesn't matter that Dobbins hated Jewish people or why he hated them; it only mattered that he discriminated against Daly by beating him because he was Jewish.

With this view, victim selection based upon vulnerability would be punished the same as a situation where a victim was selected to express hatred. In other words, the discriminatory selection model does not distinguish between symbolic and actuarial crimes. It is inclusive of both kinds. It is also the most popular form of the law, with roughly two-thirds of the state laws and the existing and proposed federal laws based upon it. Finally, this form of the law was legitimated in 1993 in Wisconsin v. Mitchell, the first case in which the Supreme Court expressly sustained a modern bias crime law.

In sharp contrast, the racial animus model focuses attention on the reason for the discriminatory selection of victims. This approach assumes that the motivation for the selection of a victim is less instrumental and more expressive; perpetrators use the act of victimization to express animus toward the category of persons the victim represents (i.e., a person of color, a homosexual, a Jew, a disabled person, etc.). As such, the racial animus model follows the distinction between actuarial and symbolic crimes by defining the former as beyond the domain of the law and the latter within the desirable domain of hate crime law. As Lawrence explains,

> This model is consonant with the classical understanding of prejudice as involving more than differential treatment on the basis of the victim's race. This understanding of prejudice, as reflected in the racial animus model of bias crimes, requires that the offender have committed the crime with some measure of hostility toward the victim's racial group and/or toward the victim because he is part of that group.

Interestingly, this model of bias crime is evident in the regulations promulgated by the FBI to implement the Hate Crimes Statistics Act. These regulations define bias crime conduct as that which is motivated, in whole or in part, by a "preformed negative opinion or attitude toward a group of persons based on their race, religion, ethnicity/national origin, or sexual orientation."

By definition, all cases falling under the rubric of the racial animus model are also cases that fall under the rubric of the discriminatory selection model, but not vice-versa. Thus, the racial animus model implies a more stringent approach to hate crime than does the discriminatory selection. From Lawrence's legally and politically strategic point of view, the discriminatory selection errs on the side of over-inclusion. He argues that a focus on the racial animus model is preferable precisely because of the type bigotry it implicates and the harm it encapsulates. With regard to the latter, Lawrence argues that "bias crimes ought to receive punishment that is more severe than that imposed on parallel crimes" because "they cause greater harm than parallel crimes to the immediate victim of the crime, the target community of the crime, and the general society." This argument draws on an array of ideas from theories of punishment to posit that there are two elements of a crime that describe its seriousness: culpability of the offender and harm caused by society.

Compared to the discriminatory selection model, however, the racial animus model has had a considerably more difficult time marshaling appellate court approval. The United States Supreme Court and the supreme courts of Washington and New Jersey have struck down laws, in whole or in part, because they relied on phrasing that went beyond mere bias intent. In addition, in State v. Stadler the Florida Supreme Court stated that its law, which required "evidence of prejudice," should be interpreted as a discriminatory selection law, regardless of the specific wording of the statute. Thus, while the animus model is desirable insofar as it targets bigotry directly, its weaker jurisprudential foundation in antidiscrimination principles renders it more vulnerable to constitutional challenges.

Both the discriminatory selection model and the racial animus model can be applied to the case of violence against persons with disabilities. With regard to the latter model, some evidence suggests that persons with disabilities face higher rates of victimization not because perpetrators harbor ill-will toward those with disabilities, but because people with disabilities are in vulnerable situations. According to the Office for Victims of Crime:

> Another reality is that many offenders are motivated by a desire to obtain control over the victim and measure their potential prey for vulnerabilities. Many people with disabilities, because they are perceived as unable to physically defend themselves, or identify the attacker, or call for help, are perfect targets for such offenders. Just as many pedophiles gravitate to youth serving occupations, so do many other predators seek work as caregivers to people with disabilities. Indeed, in one survey, virtually half—48.1 percent—of the perpetrators of sexual abuse against persons with disabilities had gained access to their victims through disability services.

It is difficult to grant credibility to any claims about the precise motivational nature of such crimes since there is so little systematic evidence on the subject. Assuming, however, for the moment that this is an accurate empirical portrayal of such crimes, the type of bias crime persons with disabilities face can be thus characterized as discriminatory, but not animus-motivated.

At the same time, however, violence directed toward people with disabilities can be characterized as motivated by animus. Katz and his colleagues' work,[30] for example, suggest that nondisabled people have a tendency to dislike those who arouse fear or guilt in them (i.e., people with disabilities), and perceive people with disabilities as inferior and responsible for their own fate. They are, in essence, "deserving victims." Similarly, Hahn's work suggests that violence directed toward those with disabilities is an outgrowth of fear best characterized by existential anxiety—the fear of others whose visible traits are perceived as disturbing or unpleasant—which gets expressed as hatred toward people with disabilities. Consistently, Shapiro's book provides ample evidence that persons with disabilities have historically been despised and stigmatized by those without disabilities. This has resulted in the latter denigrating, segregating, and, on occasion, outright attacking the former. As Waxman concluded, "the contention that vulnerability is the primary explanation for disability-related violence is too superficial. Rather, hatred is the primary cause, and vulnerability only provides an opportunity for offenders to express their hatred. Indeed, people who are respected and considered equal are not generally abused." Supporting this view, Longmore and Bouvia describe disability-related violence as a reflection of growing hostility toward those who require and increasingly demand alternative physical and social arrangements to accommodate them.[31]

In the end, these various ways of envisioning the parameters of motivation or bias-intent may prove to be a difference without distinction. Jenness and Grattet's work on hate crime as a "policy domain" suggests that since the invention of the term "hate crime" in the late 1970s, lawmakers and judges have increasingly agreed that the parameters of the discriminatory selection model provide the most legitimate foundation for modern hate crime law. Early in the history of hate crime law, lawmakers experimented with four distinct ways of phrasing the intent standard as they grappled with how to write hate crime law. However, by 1990 two forms of motivational phrasing—the "because of" wording and "intent to harass or intimidate" wording—began to emerge as the most popular. Finally, after 1993, the "because of" phrasing became the dominant form, with roughly half of the adopting states using such language. Thus, the emergent legitimate form of the law does not distinguish between mere bias-intent and hatred. Similarly, appellate court decisions on hate crime cases have, over time, increasingly endorsed the "because of" phrasing in hate crime law. In so doing, courts have maintained that it does not matter what political views or ideologies motivated the act. Rather, all that matters is that a victim was selected "because of" their race, religion, ancestry, etc., quite apart from the degree of malice involved on the part of the perpetrator. This "causation" has caused some to shift from using the term "hate" crime to the term "bias" crime. Presumably, the same logic would apply to violence directed at persons with disabilities. These trends in lawmaking and judicial decision-making suggest that the least stringent form of motivational phrasing, which maps onto the discriminatory selection model, is increasingly dominant.

Having articulated a set of criteria by which "disabilities" could be considered a candidate for inclusion in state and federal hate crime law, it is now appropriate to return to a consideration of what this end result would mean for the "dilemma of difference." Accordingly, in the conclusion that follows, the applicability of "disabilities" to hate crime law is examined in light of its consequences for particularly conceiving of persons with disabilities and generally conceiving of minority groups as both different from and the same as "others."

V. Hate Crime Law, Dilemma of Difference, and Implications

This article describes the general framework and principles underlying an evolving body of hate crime law, indicating how disabilities, as a status provision, might "fit" within its basic parameters. The consistency of disabilities within the hate crime law framework, however, does not directly address the desirability of including or emphasizing it—or any other provision, for that matter—from the standpoint of the dilemma of difference. As suggested at the outset of this article, the dilemma of difference encourages consideration of the practical and political significance of public policies built around the goal of increasing inclusion for particular minority groups. The dilemma is whether those policies should treat a minority group the same as other groups in society or whether the policies should offer them special treatment. As Minow succinctly explained, "the dilemma of difference may be posed as a choice between integration and separation, as a choice between similar treatment and special treatment, or as a choice between neutrality and accommodation."

The dilemma of difference and alternative resolutions to the dilemma of difference are manifest in contemporary policies that surround persons with disabilities in particular, as well as in hate crime law more generally. For example, the former manifestation is most evident in some of the alternatives offered during the Department of Justice's 1998 Symposium on Working with Crime Victims with Disabilities. The policy proposals contained in this position statement are divided into three general areas: physical accessibility, networking and training, and direct services. Changes in each of these areas can be undertaken with the dilemma of difference in mind. For example, increases in accessibility can be accomplished according to so-called "universal design" principles, where the idea is to construct environments and communication tools usable "to the greatest extent possible by the broadest number of users including children, older adults, people with disabilities, people of atypical size or shape, people who are ill or injured, and people inconvenienced by circumstances."[32] Such an approach would allow for the inclusion of people with disabilities without distinguishing them as "special." Likewise, proposals regarding law enforcement training encourage fostering a recognition of and responsiveness to persons with disabilities as potential and actual victims of crime. Here, the content of the educational message is crucial. Officials must be made to move beyond their assumptions about persons with disabilities as pitiable and, instead, emphasize that accommodating and including persons with disabilities is, in fact, a matter of entitlement, not charity. Educational efforts therefore need to simultaneously encourage officials to recognize that crimes against persons with disabilities regularly happen and challenge the initial assumptions those officials might have about persons with disabilities.

The point of implementing these types of changes is to increase recognition and accessibility without engendering subordination and further segregation. Ideally, changes should not emanate from a sense of pity, nor should they reflect the inferiority or dependence of persons with disabilities. Moreover, "special treatment," as it were, should not be a mandated practice, but rather an extra opportunity. Ironically, these examples—the proposals regarding accessibility and law enforcement training reform— achieve a resolution to the dilemma of difference in opposite ways. Universal design principles do not create "special" treatment, but instead work to broaden the sense of "normal" treatment. In contrast, the training programs involve "special" attention to the needs of persons with disabilities, the success of which is dependent upon constantly working to erode officials' assumptions about persons with disabilities as less capable and credible participants in the criminal justice process. Thus, although it reinforces the special character of disabilities, it would remove the stigma of difference and make difference "costless."

Hate crime laws, too, create a novel way of orienting the dilemma of difference, as it relates to "disabilities," as a policy provision and "persons with disabilities" as a target population. As detailed throughout this chapter, hate crime law is, first and foremost, about delineating axes of discrimination that demarcate groups in need of increased attention and responsiveness by the criminal justice system. This delineation is legitimated in light of its differential vulnerabilities to violence. In simple terms, hate crime law is a recent, innovative, and distinct policy option available to, arguably, enhance the status and welfare of persons with disabilities.

Hate crime laws treat persons with disabilities as both "different from" and "the same as" other persons. They do so by simultaneously segregating and integrating persons with disabilities from/into the criminal justice system. As we show below, envisioning crimes against persons with disabilities as a "hate crime" entails affording "special" treatment to those with disabilities. At the same time, it requires treating persons with disabilities the "same" as other minority groups and other individuals victimized by violence because of membership in a socially recognizable group.

With regard to different treatment and segregated practices, including "persons with disabilities" in the formulation of "hate crime" elevates some crimes committed against persons with disabilities to a unique category of criminal conduct. This criminal category—hate crime— evokes unique policing practices,[33] special prosecutorial concerns, and harsher penalties. When applied to persons with disabilities, hate crime law bestows minority status upon fifty-four million people who comprise the disabled population in the United States. Thus, hate crime law has the potential to distinguish persons with disabilities from the rest of the population of potential crime victims.

With regard to same treatment and integrating practices, the institutionalization of disabilities provisions in hate crime law serves to include persons with disabilities into the coalition of status groups already covered under the law, ensuring there is nothing "special" or "different" about persons with disabilities. That is, "persons with disabilities" are extended the "same" treatment afforded to other similarly situated groups, in this case other "target groups" that evidence the presence of a group identity, historical discrimination, and bias-motivated violence directed toward them. In addition, all of the target groups in hate crime law are afforded the same treatment as any other potential crime victim because hate crime laws—like the other anti-discrimination laws that preceded them—are written in a way that elides the historical basis and meaning of hate crime. Hate crime laws elide by translating specific categories of persons—blacks, Jews, gays and lesbians, immigrants, and women, for example—into all-encompassing and seemingly neutral categories (e.g., race, religion, sexual orientation, national origin). In doing so, the laws do not offer any remedies or protections to these groups that are not simultaneously available to all other races, religions, genders, sexual orientations, nationalities, etc. Indeed, members of "majority groups" can and have used hate crime law on their behalf.

It is important to emphasize, however, that the history and content of violence organized around axes of (dis)ability are not equivalent to other forms of discriminatory violence, such as those organized around race or religion. But, anti-gay/lesbian violence is not equivalent to racial or religious-based violence either; nor is violence organized around gender equivalent to violence organized around race, ethnicity, sexuality, etc. Emerging within the context of an American legal tradition that embraces a "sameness" principle, hate crime law does not possess the nuance to treat these different manifestations of intergroup conflict differently. Indeed, sameness in the context of hate crime has meant that laws have been written in a way that equates a hate crime against a black person with one against a white person, thus promoting "within category" sameness. Similarly, hate crimes against persons with disabilities are rendered equivalent to hate crimes against Muslims, thus inscribing "across category" sameness.

At the end of the day, all target groups are treated the same and all sides of demonstrable axes of social inequality and the criminal victimization that informs, maintains, and reflects it are treated the same. Although hate crime law can, at a glance, appear to identify, demarcate, and promote attentiveness to social differences, the way it is written and enforced promotes sameness and overrides differences. Thus, it is possible that hate crime law manages to increase public awareness of criminal victimization of persons with disabilities without defining them as "special."

NOTES

1. See generally Michael J. Lynch & E. Britt Patterson, Race and Criminal Justice passim (1991) (examining the ways race plays a role in the criminal justice system).

2. Linda J. Krieger & Patricia J. Cooney, The Miller-Wohl Controversy: Equal Treatment, Positive Action and the Meaning of Women's Equality, 13 Golden Gate U.L. Rev. 513, 513 (1983).

3. Marlee Kline, Race, Racism, and Feminist Legal Theory, 12 Harv. Women's L.J. 115 (1989); Gary D. LaFree, The Effect of Sexual Stratification by Race on Official Reactions to Rape, 45 Am. Soc. Rev. 842 (1980).

4. Martha Minow, Making All the Difference: Inclusion, Exclusion, and American Law 20–23 (1990).

5. David E. Rovella, Attack on Hate Crimes is Enhanced, Nat'l L.J., Aug. 29, 1994, at A1.

6. James Jacobs & Kimberly Potter, Hate Crimes: Criminal Law and Identity Politics 4 (1998).

7. Valerie Jenness & Ryken Grattet, Making Hate a Crime: From Social Movement to Law Enforcement (2001).

8. Terry A. Maroney, The Struggle Against Hate Crime: Movement at a Crossroads, 73 N.Y.U. L. Rev. 564, 567–68 (1998).

9. These laws appeared as early as the late 1800s in response to perceived escalation of Klan activity. They are distinct from the contemporary hate crime laws insofar as they are considerably older, do not contain a bias "intent standard," do not specify "protected statuses," and most notably, were not introduced under the rubric of "hate crimes legislation." Richard Berk et al., Thinking More Clearly about Hate-Motivated Crimes, in Hate Crimes: Confronting Violence Against Lesbians and Gay Men 126–31 (Gregory Herek & Kevin Berrill eds., 1992); Valerie Jenness & Ryken Grattet, The Criminalization of Hate: A Comparison of Structural and Polity Influences on the Passage of 'Bias-Crime' Legislation in the U.S., 39 Soc. Persp. 129, 129 (1996).

10. Ryken Grattet et al., The Homogenization and Differentiation of Hate Crime Law in the United States: Innovation and Diffusion in the Criminalization of Bigotry, 63 Am. Soc. Rev. 286, 286 (1998); Valerie Jenness, Social Movement Growth, Domain Expansion, and Framing Processes: The Gay/Lesbian Movement and Violence Against Gays and Lesbians as a Social Problem, 47 Soc. Probs. 701, 701 (1995).

11. Bias Crime: American Law Enforcement and Legal Responses passim (Robert J. Kelly ed., 1993); Susan Martin, A Cross-Burning is Not Just an Arson: Police Social Construction of Hate in Baltimore County, 33 Criminology 303 (1995).

12. Peter Fenn & Taylor McNeil, The Response of the Criminal Justice System to Bias Crime: An Exploratory Review 7–8 (1987); Tanya Kateri Hernandez, Bias Crimes: Unconscious Racism in the Prosecution of "Racially-Motivated Violence," 99 Yale L. J. 832 (1990).

13. Sarah Soule & Jennifer Earl, The Differential Protection of Minority Groups: The Inclusion of Sexual Orientation, Gender, and Disability in State Hate Crime Laws, 1976–1995, 9 Res. in Pol. Soc. 3 (2001).

14. Anne Schneider & Helen Ingram, Social Construction of Target Populations: Implications for Politics and Policy, 87 (2) Amer. Pol. Sci. Rev. 334 (1993).

15. John McNeil, U.S. Census Bureau, AMERICANS WITH DISABILITIES, 1994–95, Current Population Reports 1 (1997).

16. Crime Victims with Developmental Disabilities 10–20 (Joan Petersilia et al. eds., 2001).

17. Cheryl Guidry Tyiska, U.S. Dep't of Justice, Working with Victims of Crime with Disabilities passim (1998).

18. Marka G. Hayes, Individuals with Disabilities Using the Internet: A Tool for Information and Communication, 8 Tech. & Disability 153 (1998).

19. Lennard J. Davis, Introduction to The Disability Studies Reader 1–5 (Lennard J. Davis ed., 1997); Barbara Faye Waxman, Hatred: The Unacknowledged Dimensions in Violence Against Disabled People, 9 Sexuality & Disability 185–87 (1991).

20. Jack Levin & Jack McDevitt, Hate Crimes: The Rising Tide of Bigotry and Bloodshed 21–31 (1993).

21. Valerie Jenness & Kendall Broad, Hate Crimes: New Social Movements and the Politics of Violence 42 (1997).

22. Robert A. Goldberg, Grassroots Resistance: Social Movements in the Twentieth Century 141, 194, 223–25 (1991).

23. Valerie Jenness, Managing Difference and Making Legislation: Social Movements and the Racialization, Sexualization, and Gendering of Federal Hate Crime Law in the U.S., 1985–1998, 46 Soc. Probs. 548, 566–67 (1999).

24. Scott Phillips & Ryken Grattet, Judicial Rhetoric, Meaning-making, and the Institutionalization of Hate Crime Law, 34 L. & Soc'y Rev. 584, 584 (2000).

25. Verta Taylor & Nancy Whittier, Collective Identity in Social Movement Communities: Lesbian Feminist Mobilization, in Frontiers in Social Movement Theory 104–29 (Aldon C. Morris & Carol McClurg Mueller eds., 1992).

26. Alberto Melucci, Nomads of the Present: Social Movements and Individual Needs in Contemporary Society 63–67 (1989); Alain Touraine, An Introduction to the Study of Social Movements, 52 Soc. Res. 749 (1985).

27. Louis Harris & Assoc., The ICD Survey of Disabled Americans: Bringing Disabled Americans into the Mainstream 7 (1986).

28. Dick Sobsey, Violence and Abuse in the Lives of People with Disabilities: The End of Silent Acceptance? 13–17 (1994).

29. The Ku Klux Klan: A History of Racism and Violence 16 (Sara Bullard, ed. 1991).

30. Irwin Katz, Stigma: A Social Psychological Analysis, 16–21 (1981); Irwin Katz et al., Ambivalence, Guilt, and the Denigration of a Physically Handicapped Victim, 45(3) J. Personality 419 (1977).

31. Paul Longmore & Elizabeth Bouvia, Assisted Suicide and Social Prejudice Issues, 3 Law & Med. 141 (1987).

32. Center for Universal Design, Principles of Universal Design (1999), at http://www.design.ncsu.edu/cud/.

33. Chuck Wexler & Gary T. Marx, When Law and Order Works: Boston's Innovative Approach to the Problem of Racial Violence, 32 Crime & Delinquency 205, 205 (1986).

QUESTIONS

1. What is the "dilemma of difference"? Why is it a central issue to consider when evaluating different policy approaches to the treatment of people with disabilities?

2. What do you think of proposals to include union members, police officers, children, and the elderly as groups protected under hate crime law?

3. What was the 1994 Violence Against Women Act? What provision of the legislation was struck down as unconstitutional?

4. How are people with disabilities similar to other groups protected under hate crime laws? How are people with disabilities distinct from members of other legally protected groups?

5. Why is disability an overlooked status in research and legal policy making on hate crime?

6. Describe some of the major examples of institutional violence that have been committed against people with disabilities.

7. Considering the arguments for and against including disability as a protected status under hate crime statutes, which do you find most persuasive, and why?

8. How did the Americans With Disabilities Act help pave the way for designation of disability as a status protected under federal hate crime law?

9. Discuss four reasons why hate crimes against people with disabilities are underreported and arguably given insufficient attention by policymakers and the criminal justice system.

10. If we apply the elements of Lawrence's methodology to determine which statuses should be included under hate crime laws, should disability be included?

11. Are hate crimes against people with disabilities more difficult to prosecute under statutes based on the animus model or the discriminatory selection model?

12. The authors contend that hate crime laws promote "sameness" in legal treatment. What are some examples of this? Do you agree?

Part VII

FIGHTING HATE

I n this section we look at different strategies for fighting hate through changing attitudes—media campaigns designed to change negative stereotypes about minorities, victim-offender mediation sessions designed to help both parties, and a campus program that uses a variety of methods to raise community awareness of hate crimes. The approaches to fighting hate described in this section share a common focus on the role that intolerance and prejudice have in hate violence. Thus, fighting hate requires changing the attitudes that serve as precursors to hate crimes and responding to the emotional needs of victims when dealing with the aftermath of hate crimes.

21

Hate Crime and Antiracism Campaigning

Testing the ψ Approach of Portraying Stereotypical Information Processing

Frans Willem Winkel

How can prejudiced stereotypes be changed to reduce racism, bigotry, and hatred? This article describes how mass media campaigns to reduce prejudice can employ a specific psychological approach to change the influence of negative stereotypes on the way people perceive information about other people. The evidence suggests that antiracism campaigns using persuasive strategies are promising but that their effects are conditional.

Hate Crime: Some Trends

In many European countries and the USA hate crime (criminal incidents that are motivated primarily by prejudice) is on the increase (Levin and McDevitt, 1993). In their analysis of hate crime, subtitled 'The rising tide of bigotry and bloodshed,' they note:

> There has been a disturbing increase recently in the use of negative stereotyping. Hatred has become hip, intolerance is in. We are in the midst of a growing culture of hate. A person's group affiliation—the fact that he differs from people in the in-group—is being used more and more to provide a basis for dehumanising and insulting that person. Stereotypes justify hate crimes in the mind of the perpetrator.
>
> —Levin and McDevitt,
> 1993, pp. 33-34

EDITORS' NOTE: From Winkel, F. W. (1997). Hate Crimes and Antiracism Campaigning: Testing the ψ Approach of Portraying Stereotypical Information Processing. *Issues in Criminological and Legal Psychology*, 29, 14-19. Reprinted with permission of the British Psychological Society.

Reports from British metropolitan and regional police forces suggest that the number of racial incidents has been relatively high for a number of years: it increased from 2,844 in 1984, to 7,882 in 1991, and to almost 8,800 in 1993. An upward trend in the number of 'violent incidents with a right-wing motivation' also emerges in Germany. Reports of the Bundes VerfassungsSchutz indicate an increase from a couple of hundred in the 1970s (76 in 1983) to thousands in the 1990s (1990: 306; 1991: 1,483; 1992: 2,585; 1993: 2,232: 1994: 1,345). In France seven racial murders took place in 1995 (versus 1 in 1994). Polls suggest that 76 per cent of people living in communities with no foreigners think there are too many Arabs living in France. Van Donselaar (1995) reports the number of acts of racial violence in the Netherlands to have been well under a hundred before 1991, and to have increased since 1992 (n = 270, 1993: 352, 1994: 1,000).

PSYCHOLOGICAL INTERVENTIONS

An important strategy for influencing these rates is to counter the proliferation of (ethnic) prejudice and to aim to set limits to its social penetration. Cochrane (1995) recently presented an overview of potential psychological interventions. Suggested as fruitful are to: (1) increase the general level of education, (2) enforce laws which make discrimination illegal, (3) legislate for equality, (4) censor the press and other mass media, (5) encourage intergroup contact, (6) reduce environmental frustrations, (7) uniform and unambiguous rejection of all aspects of racism by political and social opinion leaders, and (8) encourage assimilation and intermarriage. Obviously there is an array of psychological measures that may result in reduced prejudice. However, such a goal is not automatically reached: social psychological studies on the 'contact-hypothesis' (Allport, 1954; Amir, 1969; Winkel, 1987) are a case in point. An ignored strategy—which is moreover relatively easy to implement—is the use of mass media campaigns aiming at reducing prejudice in the general public. Here too, success is not guaranteed. Winkel (1996, 1996a) recently reviewed various persuasive communication

strategies that have some empirical backup, *inter alia*: 'exhortation' (Simpson & Yinger, 1972); 'ridiculing the bigot' (Cooper & Jahoda, 1947; Vidmar & Rokeach, 1971; and Wilhoit & De Bock, 1976); 'visualising deprivation of outgroups' (Winkel, 1983; Winkel et al., 1976; and Winkel, 1990); 'eroding' and 'presenting disconfirming evidence' (Gurwitz & Dodge, 1977; Rothbart & Park, 1986; Weber & Crocker, 1983); 'cultural education' (Fiedler et al., 1971; Triandis, 1972; Winkel et al., 1987; Winkel et al., 1988; and Winkel & Vrij, 1990); 'grounded messages' (Vrij & Winkel, 1991; and Vrij et al., 1992), and the ψ approach introduced by Winkel (1996).

Paraphrasing Klapper (1960) and Kurt Lewin, these studies suggest that campaigns may be successful under some conditions, unsuccessful under others, and counterproductive under still other conditions ('law of conditional effects'). A major condition appears to relate to the patterning of the information presented. Brown (1995), for example, notes that more disconfirming evidence is needed to change unfavorable traits relative to favourable ones, and particularly that a dispersed pattern (many less salient counter-exemplars) works somewhat better than a concentrated message-pattern, comprising a few highly salient counter-exemplars. The ψ approach (outlined in the next paragraph) also suggests a specific patterning and structuring of the message.

THE ψ APPROACH

The ψ in the ψ approach means 'portraying stereotypical information-processing.' The idea is to reduce prejudice through subtly elucidating the concept of biased processing, directly confronting the viewers to that process, in order to familiarize them with the way in which prejudicial processing actually works. Ultimately, one aims to prime the notion that biased processing is wrong, and that impulsive judgements may unjustly harm others. Thus, the strategy is pericognitive: presenting disconfirming evidence is expected to work through activating the normative feeling that harming others is undesirable.

An effective ψ message is hypothesised to consist of three steps: (1) implicit priming:

creating an opportunity for stereotype activation, prejudice formation, or for generating undue generalizations; (2) explicit refuting: presenting 'disconfirming evidence' through explicitly refuting the negative stereotype, racial prejudice, or unambiguously countering undue generalizations, and (3) explicit appeal to individualized processing: calling upon the receiver to perceive the target as an individual person. This appeal may be magnified through stigmatizing the receiver if (s)he fails to process individually.

Table 21.1 Intercorrelations of Prejudice-Related Measures

	Dissimilarity	*Curiosity*	*Hostility*
Perceived Dissimilarity	—		
Curiosity	.35**	—	
Hostility	−.28**	−.12	
Fear	−.04	.04	.58**

**Indicates $p < .001$; dissimilar (1) – similar (5)

METHOD

Independent Variable

The independent variable was incorporated in a *set of videos,* resulting from manipulating two spots that were actually used in the Medelanders-Medewerkers campaign, namely 'Tiler,' and 'Pharmacist's Assistant.' While the viewer can hear eastern background music, Tiler in phase 1 portrays images of a man kneeling down making bowing movements, eliciting the suggestion that a muslim is involved in performing ritual acts of prayer (the implicit prime here is: 'they' have weird habits). In phase 2 a white person emerges supplying a pile of tiles. The muslim thus turns out be to be an ordinary tiler. Phase 3 entails a voice-over, saying 'if you look a little bit further, you merely see a tiler.'

Pharmacist's Assistant has a similar structure. This video starts off with images of a Surinamer woman—the viewer hears jazz music in the background—who is busy weighing white powder (suggestion: 'they' are addicts/heroin users). In phase 2 she is moving over to the counter to pass the prescription made to a client, saying 'please take this two times a day.' In phase 3 a voice-over is heard, again saying 'if you look a little bit further, you merely see a pharmacist's assistant.' In the (1) implicit prime or baseline condition subjects were exposed twice to a phase 1 fragment, one relating to 'Tiler' and the other to 'Pharmacist's Assistant.' In condition 2, the ψ condition subjects were exposed to the two full videos. In the enhanced ψ condition (3) subjects moreover heard the

voice-over saying 'if you don't look any further, you are actually like Hitler,' while his image emerges on screen.

DEPENDENT VARIABLES

Prejudice was assessed through two scales: a scale for Perceived (Dis)Similarity from/to Allochthonous Persons (based on Pettigrew and Meertens, 1995) and a scale for affective responses to allochthonous persons (Watson et al., 1988), comprising one scale for positive emotions (Curiosity Scale), and two subscales for negative emotions, namely a fear scale and a hostility scale. Reliabilities were satisfactory: for 'curiosity' (comprising three items: interested, inspired, and enthusiastic) alpha was .72; for 'fear' (n = 5: upset, fearful, afraid, nervous) .78; for 'hostility' (n = 3: hostile, vigilant, irritated) .70, and for perceived dissimilarity (n = 3: in bringing up their children; in religious beliefs and customs, and in sexual norms and behaviour) alpha was .64. All answers were in terms of five-point rating scales.

Pedestrians walking in a huge mall, located at Amsterdam-Buitenveldert served as subjects. They were randomly assigned to experimental conditions. The total sample consisted of 360 persons: 152 males and 200 females (eight missing values). Age varied from 11 to 82 years, with a mean age of 35 (sd = 15 years). As to political preferences the whole spectrum emerged: 112 subjects considered themselves to be left-wing oriented, 74 to be right-wing, and 200 preferred the political middle.

Table 21.2 Testing the ψ Principle: Prejudice-Related Measures on Which Significant Differences Emerged Between Experimental Conditions

	Baseline: Implicit prime	ψ message	Enhanced ψ message
Prejudice related measures			
Perceived dissimilarity	1.67[a]	2.17[b]	2.18[b]
Positive emotions ('Curiosity')	2.11[a]	2.49[b]	2.67[b]
Negative emotions ('Fear')	1.27[a,b]	1.2[a]	1.42[b]

NOTE: Higher score: more emotions and more similarity; different superscripts indicate a significant difference at $p < .05$

RESULTS

To gain insight in the underlying structure of the dependent measures a correlational analysis was performed. Table 21.1 presents an overview of these correlations. The various measures are obviously intercorrelated, but all tend to measure different cognitive and affective components of prejudice. Hostility and fear-responses to foreigners are substantially correlated; perceived similarity to foreigners is associated with enhanced curiostiy in and reduced hostility to allochthonous persons.

Various MANOVA-models were fitted to the data: all two-way interactions with condition were insignificant (condition by sex; political preference; and age: young < 25 years, middle 25–45 years, and older > 45 years of age). At a multivariate level no main effects emerged, apart from a condition (Fm $(8286) = 2.73$; $p < .01$)) and an age effect (Fm $(8274) = 2.37$; $p < .05$). This latter effect is mainly due to univariate differences in hostility (F$(2139) = 3.40$; $p < .05$) and fear responses to allochthonous persons (F$(2139) = 2.65$, $p = .07$). Younger aged subjects tended to report somewhat higher fears and hostilities compared to the other two age groups.

Breaking down the multivariate condition, effect differences specifically emerged regarding perceived similarity (F$(2152) = 6.55$, $p < .01$), curiosity (F$(2150) = 4.27$, $p < .01$), and regarding fear (F$(2154) = 3.47$, $p < .05$). The pertinent means, together with the outcomes of a post-hoc LSD analysis, are summarized in Table 21.2.

Table 21.2 validates our general expectations. Both messages appeared to have an effective communicative structure, resulting in reduced prejudice. Both ψ messages reduced the tendency to perceive allochthonous persons as dissimilar; both appeared to prime positive emotions regarding these persons: feelings of enthusiasm and interest in these groups were enhanced. Moreover, the simple ψ message did not result in enhanced negative emotions: neither as regards fear, nor regarding hostility reactions. However, the enhanced ψ message is partly tended to backfire: fear responses to allochthonous persons were reinforced.

DISCUSSION

The topical emergence of xenophobia, racial tensions, and prejudicial thinking at the agendas of European summit meetings exemplifies the pressing need for developing thorough and concerted European programmes targeting hate-crime control and prevention. Comprehensive programming fails if it merely embraces the various legal measures targeting the behavioral manifestations of prejudice (hate speech, acts of violence and aggression against allochthonous persons); it should also comprise psychological interventions aimed at prejudice reduction in (specific segments of) the general public. Anti-racism campaigns via the mass media form an obvious subcomponent of such programming, which is relatively easy to implement. However, here too, the road to success is a thorny one, given the risk—also embodied in the present findings—that campaigns may sometimes backfire. Yet success is attainable, and in view of the current findings, at least to some extent, under the control of the communicator: the ψ approach empirically emerged as a viable option. The empirical evidence offered here, though suggestive, is extremely slim, and needs thorough elaboration. Further studies into the ψ approach introducing a proper control group, examining individual differences between members of the exposed audience, and further exploring the backfiring dynamics of the enhanced ψ message—are urgently needed. Preferably such studies are part of a series of wider field experimental designs on campaign impact. The review of possible persuasive strategies, touched upon in the introduction, may serve as a basis for developing a more complete victimological research on prejudice reduction.

REFERENCES

Allport, G.W. (1954) *The Nature of Prejudice.* Addison Wesley: Reading, Mass.

Amir, Y. (1969) Contact Hypothesis in Ethnic Relations. *Psychological Bulletin, 71,* 319-342.

Brown, R. (1995) *Prejudice: Its Social Psychology.* Blackwell: Oxford.

Cochrane, R. (1995) Racial Prejudice. *Psychology and Social Issues,* pp. 127-140.

Cooper, E. & Jahoda, M. (1947) The Evasion of Propaganda. *Journal of Psychology, 23,* 15-25.

Fiedler, F.E., Mitchell, R. & Triandis, H.C. (1971) The Culture Assimilator: An Approach to Cross-Cultural Training. *Journal of Applied Psychology, 55,* 95-102.

Gurwitz, S.B. & Dodge, K.A. (1977) Effects of Confirmations and Disconfirmations on Stereotype-based Attributions. *Journal of Personality and Social Psychology, 35,* 495-500.

Klapper, J. (1960) *The Effects of Mass Communications.* The Free Press: Glencoe, Ill.

Levin, J. & McDevitt, J. (1993) *Hate Crimes: The Rising Tide of Bigotry and Bloodshed.* Plenum: New York.

Pettigrew, T.F. & Meertens, R.W. (1995) Subtle and Blatant Prejudice in Western Europe. *European Journal of Social Psychology, 25,* 57-75.

Rothbart, M. & Park, B. (1986) On the Confirmability and Disconfirmability of Trait Concepts. *Journal of Personality and Social Psychology, 50,* 131-142.

Simpson, G.E. & Yinger, J. M. (1972) *Racial and Cultural Minorities: An Analysis of Prejudice and Discrimination.* Harper & Row: New York.

Stichting Program (1994) *Reader Landelijke Themadag Anti-Racisme.* Stichting Program: Rotterdam.

Stomp, O. (1994) *Anti-Racisme. Merchandisen die Hap! Genootschap van Roerige Reclamemakers tegen Racisme.* LBR-Bulletin, 5/6, 9-13.

Tajfel, H. (1981) *Human Groups and Social Categories.* Cambridge: Cambridge University Press.

Triandis, H.C. (1972) *The Analysis of Subjective Culture.* New York: Wiley.

Van Donselaar, J. (1995) *De Staat Paraat. De Bestrijding van Extreem-Rechts in WestEuropa.* Babylon-De Geus: Amsterdam.

Vidmar, N. & Rokeach, M. (1971) Archie Bunker's Bigotry: A Study in Selective Perception and Exposure. *Journal of Communication, 24,* 36-47.

Vrij, A. & Winkel, F.W. (1991) Zet eens een Andere Bril op: De Effecten van een Voorlichtingscampagne over Vooroordelen ten aanzien van Etnische Minderheden bij Autochtone Waarnemers onderzocht. *Migrantenstudies, 7* (2), 44-54.

Vrij, A., Van Schie, E. & Winkel, F.W. (1992) Het Tegengaan van Vooroordelen jegens Etnische Minderheden: een Evaluatie van een Voorlichtingsfilm gebaseerd op SociaalPsychologische Uitgangspunten. *Massacommunicatie, 20* (2), 117-128.

Watson, D., Clark, L.A. & Tellegen, A. (1998) Development and validation of brief measures of positive and negative affect: The PANAS-Scales. *Journal of Personality and Social Psychology, 54,* 1063-1070.

Weber, R. & Crocker, J. (1983) Cognitive Processes in the Revision of Stereotypic Beliefs. *Journal of Personality and Social Psychology, 45,* 961-977.

Wilhoit, C. & DeBock, H. (1976) All in the Family in Holland. *Journal of Comunication, 26,* 75-84.

Winkel, F.W. (1983) Voorlichting en Schade: Het Gevaar van Averechtse CampagneEffecten. *Sociologische Gids, 30* (2), 114-131.

Winkel, F.W. (1984) Changing Misconceptions about Rape through Persuasive Campaigns: A Model. *Victimology, 19,* 957-963.

Winkel, F.W. (1987) (Ed.) *Relaties tussen Groepen: Sociaal-Psychologische Analyses en Interventies* (pp. 71-95). Alphen: Samsom.

Winkel, F.W., Bruunincx, J. & Van Der Kley, H. (1987) Beinvloeding van Etnisch Vooroordeel: De Verwerking van Informatie over Andere Groepen. In F.W. Winkel (Ed.) *Relaties tussen Groepen: Sociaal-Psychologische Analyses en Interventies* (pp. 71-95). Alphen: Samsom.

Winkel, F.W., Koppelaar, L. & Vrij, A. (1988) Creating Suspects in Police-Citizen Encounters: Two Studies on Personal Space and Being Suspect. *Social Behaviour, 3* (4) 307-319.

Winkel, F.W. (1990a) Crime Reporting in Newspapers: An Exploratory Study of the Effects of Ethnic References in Crime News. *Social Behaviour,* 5 (2), 87-101.

Winkel, F.W. (1990) Interaction and Impression-formation in a Crosscultural Dyad: Frequency and Meaning of Culturally Determined Gaze Behaviour in a Police Interview Setting. *Social Behaviour,* 5(4), 335-350.

Winkel, F.W. (1996) Anti-Racism Campaigning: A review of Persuasive Strategies in the context of the Law of Conditional and Restrained Effects. Keynote. Department of Psychology, University of Portsmouth, March, 20.

Winkel, F.W. (1996a) Antiracisme-campagnes: Een overzicht van psychologische overredings-strategieen. *De Psycholoog, 31,* 6, 229-236.

Zaller, J.R. (1992) *The Nature and Origins of Mass Opinion.* Cambridge University Press: Cambridge, MA.

QUESTIONS

1. What were the eight potential psychological interventions discussed at the beginning of the article?

2. Of the eight, which ones do you believe have the greatest potential for success, and why?

3. According to the author, what are the three steps that an effective psychological message should have, and why?

4. What do you think of the Dutch antihate campaign strategies depicted through the illustrations?

5. What are some other ways that you can envision mass media campaigns being used to try to reduce intolerance? Under what conditions are such campaigns most likely to be successful?

6. Under what conditions could psychological strategies actually be counterproductive?

7. What is the "law of conditional effects"?

8. In the experiment described in this article, what were the independent and dependent variables?

9. Describe the different conditions in the experiment and how participants were recruited.

10. In the experiment, why were viewers' implicit prejudices "primed" before presentation of the messages designed to reduce prejudice?

11. What were the results of the experiment?

12. If you were designing a mass media campaign using psychological strategies to reduce prejudice against a particular group or groups in your community, what would your campaign look like?

22

VICTIM-OFFENDER MEDIATION

The Road to Repairing
Hate Crime Injustice

ALYSSA H. SHENK

The criminal justice system does not meet the needs of victims and the community in the aftermath of a crime, and the system's focus on punishment does little to help prevent recidivism. This article explores how using the restorative justice approach in hate crime cases could help victims heal emotionally and ensure that offenders realize the impact of their crimes. In particular, the author examines how victim-offender mediation could provide benefits to victims, offenders, and the community even in cases involving violent hate crimes.

I. INTRODUCTION

For centuries, the adage "Crime Wounds . . . Justice Heals,"[1] has been at the heart of the American criminal justice system. Traditionally, the focus has been on crime as a violation of the law, offering punishment as the appropriate remedy.[2] By limiting reparation to the punishment of the offender, this system has neglected to take into account the needs of the victim, ignoring one of the most important aspects of the justice system.[3]

The American criminal justice system has been appropriately described as being retributive, measuring justice by the amount of punishment inflicted upon the offender.[4] Punishment, although conceivably just, cannot achieve results that will aid in repairing the actual harm done to the victim. Inflicting punishment cannot restore the victims' losses, "answer their questions, relieve their fears, help them make sense of their tragedy or heal their wounds." In the traditional criminal justice system, the victim is rarely given the opportunity to explain what his or her needs are, let alone provide any thoughts on how the case should be resolved. This system has done an excellent job of "keeping crime

EDITORS' NOTE: Originally From Shenk, A. H. (2001). Victim-Offender Mediation: The Road to Repairing Hate Crime Injustice. *Ohio State Journal on Dispute Resolution, 17,* 185-217. Reprinted with permission.

victims, the community, and offenders from deciding how society will respond to crime."

Over the years, there has been a developing trend in the criminal justice system to put the needs of the victims before the interests of the system. The changing mentality of the criminal justice system is symbolic of a move toward restorative justice where the focus is primarily on the needs of victims. This shift in focus includes permitting victims to participate actively in the criminal justice process by giving them a decision-making role while supporting their participation in the process. Restorative justice not only seeks to engage victims in the justice process, but it also turns to the community as well as the offender in order to examine the ways in which an offender may directly repair the harm done to the victim and society. Restorative justice suggests that the criminal justice system can repair the harm done to both victims and the community by utilizing such methods as "negotiation, mediation, victim empowerment, and reparation."

Restorative justice may be applied in many different settings, taking a variety of forms. However, victim-offender mediation has emerged as the most well-known and effective means of employing the theory of restorative justice.[5] Victim-offender mediation emerged in the United States in the late 1970s,[6] and its use continues to flourish.[7] Originally employed in cases involving property crimes or minor assaults, victim-offender mediation programs have become increasingly widespread. In recent years the scope of victim-offender mediation programs has deepened, expanding the process to provide for the mediation of severely violent crimes.

This chapter proposes broadening the scope of victim-offender mediation to include incidents of hate crimes. For centuries hate crimes have been part of life in American society. However, in recent years these crimes have been on the rise with increasing severity. This increase in hate crimes has prompted both federal and state governments to take action. Most efforts to deter hate crimes have been in the form of hate crimes legislation, even though other methods of prevention are being utilized. Although vital to combating incidents of hate crimes, hate crimes legislation without adequate

support does not provide appropriate justice and is not alone sufficient to deter the future commission of hate crimes. Therefore, this chapter proposes the adoption of a paradigm which integrates both hate crimes legislation and a victim-offender mediation process.

This chapter explores the themes of restorative justice and how they impact the resolution of hate crimes in the contemporary American criminal justice system. Part II discusses the restorative justice movement and how it is symbolic of the changing mentality of the criminal justice system. Part III examines the victim-offender mediation process and why it has become the most widely employed form of restorative justice. In addition, this section explores the scope of victim-offender mediation programs and the recent expansion of the process to include crimes of severe violence. Part IV provides an overview of the status of hate crimes in the United States. Part V examines the most prevalent hate crimes being committed in the United States today, recognizing the increased caliber of severity of many of these offenses. Part VI discusses the development of hate crimes legislation in an effort to prevent the further commission of hate crimes. Moreover, this section proposes that an integrated paradigm of hate crimes legislation and victim-offender mediation is necessary to most appropriately address the issue of hate crimes and deter such incidents in the future. Part VII concludes, briefly discussing the movement toward restorative justice and, in particular, the concept of victim-offender mediation and its implications for both hate crimes prevention and the American criminal justice system as a whole.

II. THE RESTORATIVE JUSTICE MOVEMENT

A. The Inadequacies of the Traditional Criminal Justice System

The nature of crime runs deeper than the mere act of breaking the law.[8] Crime is the manifestation of something greater, signifying the destruction of the social fabric of a community, a process by which humans violate both the personal and social relationships of other humans. In simple terms, "crime is the violation of one human being by another." The role of justice is designed to repair the harm done by crime and to rebuild the relationships that were destroyed.

The current criminal justice system and the traditional means of ensuring justice make it difficult for the victim and community to achieve the kind of justice necessary to repair and rebuild.[9] Traditionally, punishment has been utilized as a means of conveying that justice has been done; however, "punishment alone is unlikely to convince the offender to become a contributing member of the community."[10] In addition, punishment is merely a passive act that does nothing to encourage offenders to be accountable for their [crimes]. Therefore, it is important to provide offenders with a chance "to become meaningfully accountable to their victims, and to become responsible for repairing the harm they have caused."

B. Benefits of Restorative Justice Over Traditional Format

The theory of restorative justice has created an outlet to the traditional notions of the criminal justice system by suggesting "a new way of thinking about crime, community, and working together for the future." With this notion of restorative justice comes a vision in which victims play a central role in the way crimes are resolved and the type of reparation received for harm incurred.

Restorative justice has surfaced as a theory directly focused on providing opportunities for those who have been most affected by crime. This "victim-centered response to crime" allows victims, offenders, families and community members "to be directly involved in responding to the harm" resulting from the crime. Restorative justice bestows upon the victim, the community, and the offender an obligation to right the harm that has been done and, in particular, creates a sense of accountability for the offender to accept responsibility and work to repair the harm.

The goals of restorative justice are threefold. First, restorative justice is predicated upon the idea of greater victim involvement. Victims have had little opportunity for their voices to be heard under the traditional criminal justice system. In contrast, restorative justice provides victims with a chance for face-to-face interaction with the person responsible for the crime, so the victim can express directly to the offender the impact of the offense. By engaging in restorative justice programs, victims "regain their personal power by stating their own needs and how their needs can best be met." Second, restorative justice is aimed at promoting a greater sense of community protection. By involving various community members, agencies, and organizations in an effort to "bridge gaps between people and organizations and strengthen community bonds," restorative justice aids communities in furthering their sense of safety and provides them with the ability to engage in active peacemaking. Third, restorative justice focuses on enhancing offender accountability. Restorative justice programs provide a forum in which offenders can learn about the harm that they have inflicted on the victim and ways in which they can make amends to both the victim and the community.

Restorative justice provides something for everyone and instills a great sense of hope that things will get better for the victim, the community, and the offender. Restorative justice affords victims a chance to become a part of the process and to take an active role in achieving justice that will meet their individual needs. As for the offender, restorative justice provides skills and confidence while making real the impact of the crime, all of which aids in future deterrence.

III. VICTIM-OFFENDER MEDIATION: RESTORATIVE JUSTICE IN ACTION

A. The Inner Workings of Victim-Offender Mediation

Restorative justice takes many forms, including victim-offender mediation, family group conferencing, and educational programs for offenders. Among these various programs, victim-offender mediation has emerged as the "most widely developed expression of restorative justice, with more than 25 years of experience and numerous studies in North America and Europe." Over 300 victim-offender mediation and dialogue programs have been established throughout the United States and continue to develop in more than forty-five states.

The first Victim Offender Reconciliation Project (VORP) was established in Kitchener, Ontario, Canada in 1974 as a small experiment conducted by members of the Mennonite church, as well as a local judge and a probation officer. The VORP program made its first appearance in the United States in Elkhart, Indiana in 1978. The VORP model "was designed to address the needs of the parties in a manner which rendered the justice process meaningful to both, enabling them to resolve the conflict in a manner which they considered appropriate, without court imposition."

Since its inception, the use of victim-offender mediation has continued to flourish, as is evidenced by the endorsement that it received from the American Bar Association in 1994. Most often employed in cases involving property crimes or minor assaults, victim-offender mediation programs are frequently found in juvenile courts, law enforcement agencies, probation and corrections departments, and victims' assistance programs.

Generally, there are four phases of the victim-offender mediation process. The first phase is intake, in which the case is referred to victim-offender mediation and is then pre-screened by the mediator. The mediator is responsible for contacting both the victim and offender, and if the mediator finds that both parties are eager to negotiate and "show no overt hostility toward each other," the mediator will accept the case for victim-offender mediation.

The next phase is preparation for mediation. During this phase, the mediator will first arrange individual meetings with each party, in which "the mediator explains the program, answers questions and screens the case for its appropriateness for mediation." In meeting with the victim and offender separately, "if the mediator does not feel she has effectively established trust and rapport with each of the parties, the case is remanded to court." However, if the mediator finds that the case is suitable for mediation and both victim and offender voluntarily agree to participate in the mediation session, the

case is ready for mediation. Preparation for the mediation session may include homework assignments and, in some situations, additional preliminary meetings.

The third phase is the mediation itself. Mediation sessions are designed to "focus upon dialogue rather than upon reaching a restitution agreement, facilitating empathy and understanding between victim and offender." The mediation session generally begins with an explanation of the ground rules and then the victim is given the opportunity to speak first. Once the victim has explained to the offender the effects of the offender's crime, the victim may ask the offender questions, and the offender then has an opportunity to "offer an explanation and/or an apology." In the mediation session, the parties are expected to reach a mutually acceptable agreement, "usually a restitution agreement or work order." If the parties are unable to reach an agreement the case will be remanded back to the court for further proceedings.

The final phase of the victim-offender mediation process is follow-up. After an agreement is reached during mediation, "the offender's performance and cooperation" is monitored to ensure that he or she is acting in compliance with the work or restitution agreement.

This four-part victim-offender mediation process fully embodies all the ideals of the restorative justice concept. Operating under a pure restorative justice theory, this four-stage process provides a secure setting in which victims and offenders can communicate and work together to devise a mutually acceptable plan, obtain answers to questions, and discuss the impact of the offender's behavior.

B. Advantages and Statistically Proven Beneficial Effects of Victim-Offender Mediation

The advantages of engaging in victim-offender mediation are numerous. One of the principal benefits of victim-offender mediation programs "is that they humanize the criminal justice process." When offenders are brought face-to-face with their victims, the harm they have caused becomes very real, making it extremely "difficult for the offenders to rationalize their criminal behavior." Furthermore, by learning that the victim is no longer nameless or faceless, it is hoped that this face-to-face interaction will instill in the offender a sense of compassion for the victim, hence making it more difficult for the offender to replicate his wrongdoings in the future. Another important benefit which victim-offender mediation provides to the offender is emotional and psychological release from the stigma of being labeled a criminal. The overall benefit of victim-offender mediation programs, as indicated by their proponents, is that these programs "will empower the victim while reducing recidivism among offenders." The underlying hope of victim-offender mediation programs is that both victims and offenders will gain a greater understanding of "each other's common humanity and that offenders will be able to take their place in the wider community as valued citizens."

Research conducted on victim-offender mediation indicates an end result in which both victims and offenders are left with a greater sense of satisfaction for both the program and the justice system as a whole. The largest multisite study of VORP programs was conducted in 1994 by Dr. Mark Umbreit. The results of this study provide an excellent overview as to the consensus among victims and offenders about the victim-offender mediation process and the effectiveness of these programs. During a two-year period, 3142 cases were referred to one of four programs. Of those sessions, ninety-five percent resulted in a successful restitution agreement. For victims, there was much greater satisfaction with the mediation process (seventy-nine percent) as opposed to the normal court procedure (fifty-seven percent). Additionally, after engaging in mediation, victims were considerably less apprehensive about being re-victimized. For offenders, the study indicated a much greater sense of accountability among those who engaged in victim-offender mediation, as well as lower recidivism rates.

C. The Scope of Victim-Offender Mediation

Victim-offender mediation programs may not be appropriate for every victim and offender. Therefore, it is imperative that cases are screened on an individual basis to determine whether they are suitable for mediation. Victim-offender mediation programs are most consistently utilized in cases ranging from property crimes to minor assaults, or any other crimes that would not result in receiving prison time.

Recently, the trend in victim-offender mediation has been "toward deepening the process and expanding its scope." Although it has not been commonplace in the past, there is a greater movement toward mediating crimes of severe violence. In cases involving violent crime, victim-offender mediation does not serve as a substitute for punishment. However, it does offer a means of healing and a sense of closure that cannot be achieved by punishment alone. Both "victims and survivors of severely violent crimes, including murders and sexual assaults, are finding that confronting their offenders in safe and controlled settings, with the assistance of the mediator, returns their stolen sense of safety and control in their lives."

In a case of a young man who was robbed and shot in the head by a man who had previously assaulted two other men in the area, the victim's mother engaged in victim-offender mediation. The woman spent ten months preparing for the mediation with an experienced mediator and finally after nine years she was able to come face to face with her son's killer in a high-security prison. The woman felt that the victim-offender mediation process was "a pivotal moment in her long journey of grieving and her search for closure." In this particular case, the woman felt that "she needed to let the man who killed her son know the devastating effect the crime had on her life, and to get answers to many questions." Victim-offender mediation may not be appropriate for all victims of crimes of severe violence, but it has continually proven beneficial in cases such as these in which it has been employed.

IV. Hate Crimes

Those who are bigots do not stop at classes, at races, or again, at gays and lesbians. Those who hate you, hate me. Those who hate, hate everybody. Hate is contagious. . . . No one has the right not to allow you to acquire the dignity, the respect, and the self-respect to which we are all entitled.[11]

For centuries, hate crimes have played a crucial role in shaping world history. In the United States, hate crime is not a new phenomenon. For years, hate crimes have been prevalent in the United States, particularly those inspired by religious and racial biases.

Hate crimes distinguish criminal behavior prompted "by prejudices from criminal conduct motivated by lust, jealousy, greed, politics, and so forth."[12] Unlike other criminal offenses, hate crimes accentuate the underlying attitudes, values, and character of individual offenders. Congress has defined hate crime as that "in which the defendant intentionally selects a victim, or in the case of a property crime, the property that is the object of the crime, because of the actual or perceived race, color, national origin, ethnicity, gender, disability, or sexual orientation of any person."

Among those individuals participating in incidents of hate crime, juveniles and other young people tend to be disproportionately represented. There is a host of factors that may incite these otherwise law-abiding individuals to engage in hate crimes. Some of these crimes are fueled by alcohol and drugs; however, more often then not "the main determinant appears to be personal prejudice, a situation that colors people's judgment, blinding the aggressors to the immorality of what they are doing."[13] Other factors that may lead individuals to commit hate crimes include racial stereotypes, individual incidents with members of a certain minority group, and tentative economic conditions. Regardless of the contributing factors, "once a climate of hate is created, a single incident—such as the videotaped beating of Los Angeles, California, motorist Rodney King—can trigger a wave of hate crimes."

Those criminal acts which are prompted by prejudice, "may carry far more weight" than the average criminal offense because hate crimes reach beyond the victimization of a single target. When a hate crime occurs, it victimizes "every member of the group that the immediate target represents," sending "fear and discomfiture across [an entire] community."

V. PREVAILING HATE CRIMES IN AMERICA

Despite paramount efforts by both "political and community leaders to foster tolerance and understanding, deep-seated racial tensions continue to plague the Nation." Bias-motivated crimes continue to fill the pages of many of the United States' most influential newspapers. In particular, this nation has encountered a tremendous surge in the occurrence of extremely disturbing and even deadly hate crimes.

Hate crimes are committed for a plethora of reasons, including acts against one's race, ethnicity, religion, gender, disability, and sexual orientation. Historically, the brunt of hate crime has fallen upon some classifications more than others. However, since the mid-1980s the issue of hate crimes in the United States has stirred "mounting public scrutiny," primarily resulting from numerous bias motivated incidents involving race, religion, and sexual orientation.

A. Crimes Committed on the Basis of Race

Racial bias is "by far the largest determinant of hate crimes" affecting African Americans, Asian/Pacific Islanders, Native Americans, and Caucasians alike. Although different races have fallen pray to hate crimes, African Americans seem to be the group at greatest risk.

Historically, violence against African Americans has been viewed as the quintessential hate crime because a crime against an African American not only injures individuals, but also serves as a means of intimidating an entire group of people. Since the Nineteenth Century, African Americans have been the victims of cross burnings, church bombings, and murder.

One of the most heinous illustrations of hate crimes committed against blacks in recent years was the dragging death of James Byrd, Jr., forty-nine, of Jasper, Texas in June of 1998. Byrd, a disabled black man, was returning from a family party when three men offered him a ride. The men took Byrd outside of town, chained him by his ankles and tied him to the back of a pickup truck. They then proceeded to drag Byrd along an old logging road until his head and arm ripped apart from his body. Within twenty-four hours of committing this odious crime, the three men, having ties to white supremacy groups, were arrested. Tensions began to rise in the aftermath of this racially charged crime. The New Black Panthers came into town to advise the black residents to arm themselves and the Ku Klux Klan announced that it would begin rallying in the town square. The community as a whole was traumatized, suffering a deep-rooted emotion that would take a great deal of time and effort to mend.

B. Crimes Committed on the Basis of Religion

Attacks upon individuals and institutions on the basis of religion are another highly concentrated source of hate crimes. Religiously motivated hate crimes are generally signified by acts of vandalism and at times even personal attacks. The overwhelming majority of these incidents are targeted at the Jewish religion.

Prejudice against Jews is not a new phenomenon for it has long persisted as a problem in the United States. Jews have continually been excluded "from attending certain schools, entering certain professions, holding certain jobs, or moving into certain neighborhoods." Incidents of hate crimes targeting Jews range from property crimes to physical assault upon individuals. In the instances in which property crimes have been committed, they typically involve acts of vandalism. For example, in 1997 the University of Chicago library discovered anti-Semitic graffiti such as SS lightning bolts and swastikas on several Hebrew and Yiddish books.

Although most incidents against the Jewish religion have involved the desecration "of synagogues and cemeteries and the painting of swastikas on private homes," physical assaults are not atypical. In addition, many Jews as individual members of society have been subjected to anti-Semitic comments. For instance, a fourteen-year-old boy in Gloucester, Massachusetts utilized the Internet to send a series of anti-Semitic death threats to his school teacher. Among the messages received by the teacher, one communication simply stated, "'your

Jewish lungs should be ripped out and your body shot full of holes.'"

In August 1991, the United States experienced one of the most dramatic occurrences of anti-Semitic hate crimes in recent history. The incident transpired in the Crown Heights section of Brooklyn. In a motorcade for Grand Rabbi Menachem Scheerson, a car driven by a Hasidic Jew unintentionally swerved onto the sidewalk, tragically killing a black youth. The death of this young boy was followed by four days of intense rioting in which, "chanting 'kill the Jews,' mobs set fires, destroyed property, and looted stores, and assaulted and harassed citizens."

Several hours after the tragic incident and in the midst of all the rioting, Yankel Rosenbaum, a twenty-nine-year-old rabbinical student, was murdered. Rosenbaum was spotted by a group of African Americans who yelled, "'There's a Jew' and 'Get the Jew.'" Rosenbaum was surrounded by a fifteen-member mob that proceeded to beat and stab him. The act committed against Rosenbaum was "'one of blind, baseless bigotry and putrid violent hate,'" and although the man responsible for stabbing Rosenbaum was acquitted on criminal charges, he was eventually convicted for violating Rosenbaum's civil rights.

C. Crimes Committed on the Basis of Sexual Preference

Although racial and religious prejudice remain prominent sources of hate crimes in this country, incidents involving sexual orientation have become increasingly prevalent in today's society. Hate crimes targeting sexual minorities have become socially tolerable and are perhaps the most rampant "form of hate crime among teenagers and young adults."

Statistically, it is evident that attacks upon sexual minorities are dramatically increasing. What is more alarming, however, is the severity of these attacks. Crimes against gays and lesbians are becoming more and more violent as is evidenced by some of the heinous acts that have occurred in recent years. For instance, in March of 1992 the lesbian and gay organizations' office at Northeastern University in Boston received a telephone call from an anonymous male student who threatened to blow up the office as well as kill all the members of the group. This particular incident is reminiscent of many of the early types of hate crimes committed against sexual minorities.

In the past several years, however, the United States has witnessed crimes against sexual minorities that are shocking the nation due to their extreme insensitivity and caliber of brutality. In October of 1998, the death of Matthew Shepard, a gay college student, in Laramie, Wyoming received national attention. Shepard was lured from a bar by two men who robbed him, brutally beat him with a pistol, and then tied him to a fence where he was left to die. With a smashed skull, Shepard was roped to the fence for close to eighteen hours in near-freezing temperatures before passersby discovered him. By the time he got to a hospital his chances of living were slim, and as a result of severe damage to his brain stem he died five days later.

Comparable to the fatal beating of Matthew Shepard was the February 1999 brutal murder of thirty-nine-year-old Billy Jack Gaither. Two men, angry over an alleged sexual advance made by Gaither, took Gaither to the banks of a creek where they beat him to death with an ax handle and then proceeded to burn his body on top of a set of tires.

VI. Victim-Offender Mediation: The Future Response to Hate Crimes

Hate crimes have long been a tragic part of American history. The increase in incidents of hate crimes in recent years signifies that this nation still has a long way to go in its hate crimes prevention efforts. Crimes committed against individuals on the basis of skin color, religion, and sexual preference remain a powerful presence in today's society. The need to deal with hate crimes is essential in light of the increasing brutality of these bias motivated crimes. There are two overarching paradigms that can be integrated in an effort to deal appropriately with hate crimes and to deter such incidents in the future: hate crimes legislation and the implementation of a victim-offender mediation model.

A. The Development of Hate Crimes Legislation

The first paradigm in place for combating hate crimes is the implementation of some form of hate crimes legislation. The failure to address incidents of hate crimes through legislation will in effect "leave[ ] entire groups of people feeling isolated and vulnerable." Therefore, in an effort to curtail incidents of hate, Congress and the states have been making great strides in developing new legislation. Numerous laws have been enacted that provide enhanced sentencing "for crimes motivated by officially disfavored prejudices," and many states have developed substantive hate crimes laws.

Undoubtedly, the development of hate crimes legislation is vital to combating the recurrence of hate crimes in this country. However, the underlying concern with hate crimes legislation is that it only serves political and symbolic functions. Hate crimes legislation is emblematic in that it permits the public to perceive the legislature as taking a "tough on crime approach" because the legislature is making strong efforts to label these particular offenders and in most cases is providing harsher sentences for those who commit these offenses. In essence, the legislature is doing nothing more than applying the traditional values of the criminal justice system to new legislation— punishment without reparation.

The enactment of legislation alone is not the answer to curtailing hate crimes because it fails to provide the sense of justice originally intended as a basis for establishing hate crimes legislation. Specifically, hate crimes legislation fails to address the needs of the victims. Recognizing these needs is imperative given that many victims of hate crimes are not reporting the incidents despite the increase in hate crimes legislation. There are a myriad of reasons why hate crimes go unreported, one in particular being victims' uncertainty whether perpetrators will be brought to justice.

If hate crimes legislation was designed to help those individuals who fall prey to bias-motivated crime as a result of their race, religion, sexual orientation or other distinguishing feature, then it needs to reassure those individuals that they are being protected and that there is some discernible benefit from prosecuting offenders under a hate crimes statute. Hate crimes legislation is purely retributive in that it only punishes hate-crime offenders after they have committed a bias-motivated crime. In essence, similar to other criminal laws, hate crimes legislation provides little opportunity for offender accountability or personal empowerment for victims. Hate crimes legislation as it now exists is not meeting the needs of victims, offenders, or the community. If hate crimes are going to be dealt with effectively and there is going to be a lasting impact on the offender, it is essential that there be a system put in place that provides not only for punishment of the offender, but for rehabilitation of the offender as well as reparation for the victim.

B. The Implementation of a Victim-Offender Mediation Model

Hate crimes legislation is only one means of dealing with recurring incidents of hate crime. This chapter proposes that there exists a second paradigm for the prevention of hate crimes. By electing to utilize some form of restorative justice, the needs of hate crimes victims will be brought to the forefront, and the underlying goals for establishing hate crime legislation will be more appropriately met. Specifically, by implementing a victim-offender mediation process to complement existing legislation, punishment and rehabilitation will be able to coexist, which in the end will provide a greater benefit to both victim and offender.

Victim-offender mediation is applicable to a wide range of crimes and has proven successful even in cases involving severely violent crimes. Hate crimes may vary in degree from property crimes such as vandalism to more severe crimes such as murder. In recent years, the crimes that have raised national attention have been of the most brutal caliber.

Whether minor or severe, any hate crime causes far more damage to both victim and offender than other types of offenses. Hate crimes, unlike other types of crimes, are driven by characteristics inherent to the personality of the offender. They are not crimes of greed or lust, but rather of personal prejudice, denoting the underlying attitudes and values of individual

offenders. Because the goal of the victim-offender mediation process is to delve beyond the crime itself and explore the underlying thoughts and feelings of both victims and offenders, it seems that this process would reveal the very premise that often leads offenders to commit hate crimes. Such a restorative process would therefore be specially beneficial in handling hate crimes.

There is immeasurable value in utilizing victim-offender mediation in incidents of hate crimes. In particular, there are three principal benefits to be derived by both victims and offenders who engage in the victim-offender mediation process. First, victim-offender mediation humanizes the criminal justice process. Providing for a human element is particularly important in instances of hate crimes because these crimes are premised on harm caused to a particular individual. If a hate crimes offender is punished pursuant to hate crimes legislation, there will likely never be the opportunity to understand how the offender affected a particular individual. However, if victim and offender are afforded the opportunity to meet, it will force the offender to learn of the extent of the damage as well as the reason why his or her actions were so offensive to a particular person or group of people. Moreover, victim-offender mediation provides a forum in which the victim can break down any stereotypes and prejudices held by the offender, which will in turn educate the offender as to the true perception of a certain group of people. This may deter the offender from committing crimes of a similar nature in the future.

Second, victim-offender mediation provides an emotional release for both the victim and offender. This is an important benefit of victim-offender mediation because hate crimes are so highly sensitive and elicit an enormous array of emotions. In general, victims of hate crimes suffer serious psychological effects, more so than do victims of other crimes. Common characteristics among hate crimes survivors include depression, stress, and anger. In addition, hate crimes usually invoke memories of past incidents by members of a particular targeted group. In the case of hate crimes committed against African Americans, whenever such incidents occur there is a tremendous "impact upon the entire society not only for the hurt they cause but for the history they recall, and perpetuate." Similarly, crimes committed against Jews arouse comparable feelings of vulnerability and persecution.

Engaging in victim-offender mediation will also present an excellent opportunity for the offender to release some emotion and relieve the individual from the stigma of being labeled an offender. For example, victim-offender mediation may have been useful in the case of Aaron McKinney, one of the men convicted for killing Matthew Shepard. In that case, McKinney pled to the court that he was sorry for what he had done and was truly ashamed. Participating in victim-offender mediation would have provided McKinney with an opportunity to release some of this emotion as well as express his sentiments to the parents of Matthew Shepard.

Third, victim-offender mediation fills many of the gaps in hate crimes legislation. By placing emphasis on the victim's needs, victim-offender mediation will likely encourage victims to report future incidents of hate crimes because it helps victims to recognize that reporting is part of the healing process and that they have the power to overcome what has happened. In addition, unlike hate crimes legislation, victim-offender mediation assures a reduction in recidivism. By engaging in victim-offender mediation, offenders are less likely to recidivate because once an offender has had an opportunity to meet the victim it becomes more difficult to rationalize committing such crime in the future. For hate crimes offenders in particular, a face-to-face meeting with the victim will hopefully make it harder for them to maintain the same biases they held before the mediation.

It is imperative that victim-offender mediation play an integral role in dealing with and preventing hate crimes. The benefits that it provides to both victim and offender are numerous. The overall implication of expanding the scope of victim-offender mediation to hate crimes is that it will instill a sense of justice that has ceased to exist in the American criminal justice system.

VII. CONCLUSION

The restorative justice movement is slowly changing the face of the American criminal

justice system, teaching us that "the problem of crime can no longer be simplified to the problem of the criminal." Crime is more than breaking the law; it "injures individual victims, communities, offenders, and their families, and it damages relationships." Restorative justice acknowledges that there is much more at stake than the fact that a crime has been committed. The restorative justice vision requires the criminal justice system to delve beyond the surface of crime and to examine closely the harm it causes to real people.

Victim-offender mediation has emerged as the most commonly used form of restorative justice. Although widely used, this country has only begun to "'[push] the envelope'" of victim-offender mediation. In the coming years, there will be continued efforts to expand the application of victim-offender mediation and improve upon the process to allow for maximum healing potential in all crimes that are mediated.

Hate crimes are a paramount example of an area that necessitates a victim-offender mediation process. Hate crimes are much more than a criminal act because they represent deep-rooted biases and are extremely detrimental to both targeted victims and their greater communities. In recent years there have been widespread efforts to curtail hate crimes, as is evidenced by the increase in hate crimes legislation. However, apprehension as to the effectiveness of this legislation has created an overwhelming need to consider other alternatives.

In dealing with incidents of hate crimes, any measures to be taken by the criminal justice system cannot be purely punitive; a restorative approach is also needed. The only way to truly "stop the hate" so that it does not continue to plague future generations of this country is to establish an effective method of prevention. As this chapter proposes, the future of hate crimes prevention lies in a well-integrated system providing for both the application of hate crimes legislation as well as the utilization of a victim-offender mediation process.

NOTES

1. Harry Mika & Howard Zehr, Restorative Justice Signposts, at http://ssw.che.umn.edu/rjp/

resources/documents/cumb99c.pdf (last visited Oct. 8, 2001).

2. Catherine Edwards, Paying for What They've Wrought, INSIGHT ON THE NEWS, July 26, 1999, at 46.

3. Marty Price, Crime and Punishment: Can Mediation Produce Restorative Justice for Victims and Offenders?, at http://www.vorp.com/articles/crime.html (last visited Oct. 8, 2001).

4. See CTR. FOR RESTORATIVE JUSTICE & PEACEMAKING, RESTORATIVE JUSTICE FOR VICTIMS, COMMUNITIES AND OFFENDERS 2 (1996), available at http://ssw.che.umn.edu/rjp/resources/documents/cctr96a.pdf (last visited Oct. 12, 2001)

5. Mark S. Umbreit, What is Restorative Justice, at http://ssw.che.umn.edu/rjp/resources/documents/cumb99c.pdf (Apr. 15, 1999). In the last fifteen years, the number of criminal conflicts which are sent to mediation has grown tremendously. Mark William Bakker, Comment, Repairing the Breach and Reconciling the Discordant: Mediation in the Criminal Justice System, 72 N.C. L. REV. 1479, 1480 (1994).

6. Mark S. Umbreit & Robert B. Coates, Victim-Offender Mediation: A Review of Research in the United States, in MAKING AMENDS 190, 191 (Gwynn Davis ed., 1992).

7. CTR. FOR RESTORATIVE JUSTICE & PEACEMAKING, NAT'L SURVEY OF VICTIM OFFENDER MEDIATION PROGRAMS IN THE U.S. 3 (2000).

8. Mark S. Umbreit & Jean Greenwood, CTR. FOR RESTORATIVE JUSTICE & PEACEMAKING, MULTICULTURAL IMPLICATIONS OF RESTORATIVE JUSTICE: POTENTIAL PITFALLS AND DANGERS 3 (2000).

9. Advocates of restorative justice believe that the traditional notion of retributive justice, which focuses on incarcerative practices as a means of achieving justice, only "add[s] more harm to the world."

10. Marty Price, Can Mediation Produce Justice?, ADR REPORT, Oct. 29, 1997, at 6, available at http://www.vorp.com/articles/justice.html.

11. Charles G. Brown, FIRST GET MAD, THEN GET JUSTICE 161 (1993) (quoting Elie Wiesel, Jewish writer and Holocaust survivor).

12. James B. Jacobs & Kimberly A. Potter, Hate Crimes: A Critical Perspective, 22 CRIME & JUST. 1, 2 (1997).

13. Position Paper, Am. Psychological Ass'n, Hate Crimes Today: An Age-Old Foe in Modern Dress (1998), at http://www.apa.org/pubinfo/hate/homepage.html.

QUESTIONS

1. What is the restorative justice approach, and how does it differ from the regular criminal justice system approach?

2. How can the restorative justice approach help repair the harm done to victims?

3. Describe some examples of hate crimes committed on the basis of race, religion, and sexual preference in recent years.

4. In what ways is hate crime legislation limited in its ability to address the needs of hate crime victims?

5. What are the potential benefits of victim-offender mediation for victims? For offenders? For the community as a whole?

6. What are the four phases of the victim-offender mediation process?

7. What reasons does the author provide for believing that victim-offender mediation will reduce the likelihood of reoffending by hate crime perpetrators?

8. How promising do you think the victim-offender mediation approach is for hate crime cases involving attacks against people (as opposed to attacks on property) in terms of its potential benefits for all parties?

9. What might motivate hate crime offenders to participate in victim-offender mediation?

10. Were you surprised to learn that victim-offender mediation has been used in cases involving murder and other serious violent crimes? If so, why?

11. Does your county have a restorative justice program that includes opportunities for victim-offender mediation? Find out more about actual or proposed restorative justice programs in your community.

12. If you were a crime victim, do you think you would be interested in participating in victim-offender mediation under certain circumstances?

23

STOP THE HATE

Massachusetts Task Force Creates Student Civil Rights Project to Combat Problem

JEREMY MAHONEY

How can students work to inform others of their civil right to be free from hate-motivated harassment and violence? This article describes a project created to respond to intolerance and hate through education and activism. The project employs a wide variety of strategies designed to raise awareness in victims, potential perpetrators, and the broader community.

H
ate crimes create fear, mistrust and hostility among society members.

They occur in communities worldwide and no one is exempt from them. However, society must remain diligent in stopping crimes motivated by racial, religious, national origin, disability, sexual orientation, culture and gender biases. Through the collaborative efforts of educators, law enforcement and communities, issues of hate and bias. . . . motivated violence can be addressed. It is through teaching respect for individual differences that will cease hate and prejudice in society.

The underreporting of hate crimes is a serious problem for both law enforcement and investigators. Witnesses sometimes fear retaliation from perpetrators if they report crimes to police and many victims worry that police will not believe their accounts and will revictimize them. Victims must report these crimes to police, and law enforcement personnel need proper training in identifying bias-motivated crimes. Through expanded training and technical

EDIOTRS' NOTE: From Mahoney, J. (1999). Stop the Hate: Massachusetts Task Force Creates Student Civil Rights Project to Combat Problem. *Corrections Today, 61*(5), 82-86. Reprinted with permission of the American Correctional Association Canhum, MD.

assistance from legal experts, educators and civil rights advocates, police departments will become better equipped to handle incidents of hate-motivated violence as they occur.

Massachusetts recognizes the seriousness of these crimes and is increasing prevention efforts within the school systems. Since many perpetrators of hate crimes are under the age of 20, it is imperative that we identify incidents in schools and colleges. To meet this challenge, the Governor's Task Force on Hate Crimes created the Student Civil Rights Project to provide assistance and support for students, parents, educators and law enforcement by creating school environments that are safe and free of harassment and violence. The Student Civil Rights Project began in 1998 under the leadership of Executive Director Christina Bouras and Student Civil Rights Director David Rudewick. Both individuals provide continual support to schools and law enforcement agencies through training sessions and on-site visits.

INTERNSHIP PROGRAM

The first initiative of the Student Civil Rights Project was the 1998 Summer Internship Program, which brought together a working group of college and high school students from across Massachusetts to explore, identify, review and recommend curriculum and resources that school communities could implement to prevent hatred, prejudice and violence within the school setting. The 10 student interns were from different cultural, religious and ethnic backgrounds and each brought his or her own prejudices, biases and beliefs to the program. They spent a significant amount of time confronting their feelings and attitudes toward people who are different from themselves. Much of the time focused on sharing personal experiences of discrimination or harassment. Each intern was able to recall at least one situation in which he or she had been discriminated against because of individual culture, gender, religion, ethnicity or sexual orientation. It was an enlightening experience for each individual involved.

The 4-week program was held at Northeastern University in Boston. The interns stayed in the campus dormitories. Discussions were held in a conference room and research was conducted in computer labs. The interns received training in civil rights laws and history from legal experts and civil rights organizations. The Anti-Defamation League, Attorney General's Office, Facing History and Ourselves and National Conference for Community Justice were some of the organizations that made presentations during the program. The interns were given the opportunity to venture into the community and research the history of the civil rights marches and the Holocaust. This experience allowed the interns to view the issue of civil rights in different ways.

INTERNET PRESENCE

The centerpiece of the internship program was the creation of a youth-focused Web site— stopthehate.org. The site is an innovative online educational/reporting mechanism designed to provide students, teachers and administrative professionals with tools and resources to combat and reduce bias and hate within the school environment. The site also provides resources and information on victim assistance, diversity awareness and peer mediation. It was created by the interns, who all received training in Web page design and development during the program. Each intern was responsible for conducting research for online materials and resources.

The site aims to appeal specifically to youths and students, so it must be both interactive and educational. It features online journal pages through which youths can share ideas and successes in creating safe environments in their schools. An online bulletin board section hosts an area where youths can leave messages for others about addressing issues of hate, prejudice and violence in their schools and communities. There is an online history section in which youths can read about the Holocaust and the Civil Rights Movement. The section on laws outlines both federal and state laws regarding hate crimes. Youths must become informed and understand that laws exist to protect them from intimidation, harassment and violence. Students need to know the importance of reporting incidents of harassment and violence as they occur. Administrators and law enforcement cannot help create safe environments if students who are either witness to or victims of crimes do not report these incidents.

The most significant aspect of the Web site is the online reporting form with which students can report incidents of hate motivated harassment or violence. The reporting form gives students a way to summon help, particularly if administrators are less than supportive or provide little assistance. The online reports are received by the student civil rights director who then may establish contact with school officials and, if needed, local law enforcement. The greatest challenge students face is having the courage to report incidents of harassment or violence. It is difficult enough for youths to speak out when they are victimized, which is why it is so important that an accessible reporting mechanism is available. The site is linked to the Governor's Task Force on Hate Crimes Web page, which is located on the Executive Office of Public Safety's main site. In addition to an agency overview and listing of activities, the site offers access to publications, resources, hate crime laws and links to other useful sites.

RESOURCE MANUAL

It is essential that resources and support services are available for students, parents, administrators, law enforcement and communities. The Student Civil Rights Project initiated the creation of the Educator's Resource Manual, which contains a comprehensive overview of hate crime laws and prevention steps for schools and communities. In addition, an extensive listing of victim advocacy resources is included. The manuals were distributed to high schools throughout the commonwealth in addition to several middle and elementary schools. Also, the Hate Crimes Resource Manual for Law Enforcement and Victim Assistance Professionals was distributed statewide. It is important that both law enforcement officials and school educators are able to identify incidents when they occur.

RAISING STUDENT AWARENESS

Another initiative of the Student Civil Rights Project was raising awareness in schools about hate crimes, harassment and civil rights issues. This initiative led to the launching of the Poster/Safety Pamphlet Campaign, which targeted schools throughout the commonwealth. The posters, designed to promote awareness and reporting of hate crimes among students, spotlight the Web site and the "stop the hate" message. Additionally, they list resources for victims of anti-gay, lesbian, bisexual and transgender violence and were distributed in localities in which incidents of violence have occurred. The pamphlets contain basic information about harassment, hate crimes and civil rights issues as well as comprehensive and inclusive resources that students can access if they have been victimized. Inclusiveness is key in creating safe environments for all students in Massachusetts schools. The Student Civil Rights Project, in a collaborative effort with the Governor's Commission on Gay and Lesbian Youth, Gay and Lesbian Adolescent Social Services, and the Gay and Lesbian Advocates and Defenders, created and distributed the pamphlets. In addition to providing a general overview of civil rights/hate crimes, they include resources for gay, lesbian, bisexual, transgender or questioning youths.

COMMUNITY OUTREACH

The Student Civil Rights Project conducts extensive outreach to church organizations, youth groups, advocacy groups and civil rights organizations. Much of this outreach is done through collaborative training symposiums for schools, educators and law enforcement. Two regional training sessions were held last fall. The sessions were designed to raise awareness of hate crimes/civil rights issues, while encouraging productive working relationships between school administrators and law enforcement. Presentations were given by the Attorney General's Office, Anti-Defamation League, Provincetown Police Department, Facing History and Ourselves, and other civil rights advocates. The second training session was attended by several high school students and youths from community organizations. It was important that law enforcement and educators hear the students' perspectives on issues of hate, prejudice and violence in the schools. The training sessions are inclusive and cover issues of hate and bias crimes committed because of someone's color, culture, national origin, gender, ethnicity, disability or sexual orientation.

MEDIA ASSISTANCE

The Student Civil Rights Project has used media outlets to encourage discussion about hate, bias, prejudice and violence in Massachusetts schools. Under the direction of the Governor's Task Force on Hate Crimes, the Student Civil Rights Project collaborated with UPN Channel 38 to create a program titled "The Teen Files: The Truth About Hate," which examines bow hate and prejudice affect towns and teens in Massachusetts. This was broadcast along with a 1-hour national segment that explored the beliefs, feelings and attitudes of teens when confronted with issues of hate and prejudice in their own lives and families. A diversity awareness curriculum was compiled and complemented the "Teen Files" segment. The curriculum integrates media literacy with Web technology and offers many opportunities for classroom discussion, reflection and integration of student concepts, ideas and strategies to reduce hate and violence. The result of a collaborative effort by several educational organizations, the curriculum has been used in many classrooms throughout the commonwealth. Future development and improvement of curriculum is one of the many initiatives to be carried out by the Student Civil Rights Project.

A focal point of the Task Force and the Student Civil Rights Project was the release of a public service announcement (PSA) urging witnesses and victims of hate crimes to report incidents via 911, their local police department or on the Web at *www.stopthehate.org* <http://www. stopthehate.org>. This media campaign was crafted to identify the seriousness of hate and bias crimes while stressing the importance of seeking assistance and support. The 30-second PSA was featured in conjunction with the UPN Channel 38, "Teen Files: Healing the Hate"

segment. It has been shown to students and faculty in high schools throughout the commonwealth and also was showcased before the Bureau of Justice Assistance in Washington, D.C., in April. One thousand law enforcement professionals, educators and civil rights advocates throughout the country had the opportunity to learn about the Student Civil Rights Project and the Governor's Task Force on Hate Crimes.

SCHOOL LIAISONS

This past spring, the Student Civil Rights Project requested that all Massachusetts high schools designate a civil rights coordinator. The appointed individual will serve as the contact for the student civil rights director in the event of a hate or bias incident. The coordinator also acts as the liaison between the school and local law enforcement. Many of the schools chose to designate the school principal or a faculty member to hold this position. A training session is being planned for all appointed school-based civil rights coordinators. It is important that the civil rights coordinators have a clear understanding of hate and bias crimes or harassment. They must be properly educated on these issues so that assistance can be provided to students when incidents occur. Many middle and elementary schools have responded through their school superintendents that they are interested in becoming involved with the Student Civil Rights Project. This is positive because students begin to notice differences in their early school years. If youths can become sensitized to issues of diversity, prejudice, hate and violence at an early age, they will be more apt to effectively respond when incidents occur.

THE FUTURE

Throughout the summer months and into the fall, the student civil rights director and the community outreach coordinator will continue to develop the Student Civil Rights Project Web site. This time will give staff the opportunity to conduct additional research for resources and new information on violence prevention resources and services. The community outreach coordinator will continue conducting awareness programs targeting underreporting minority communities.

This fall, the Student Civil Rights Project will be piloting Civil Rights Teams in high schools throughout the commonwealth. Each team will consist of two students from each grade level and a faculty advisor. The teams will help to foster safe environments in their schools and help school administrators address incidents of harassment or violence. In addition to creating safe environments, these teams will develop strategies for encouraging the discussion of issues surrounding prejudice, hate, bigotry and violence. Initially, 10 to 15 schools will be selected to pilot this program, with future plans to incorporate all high schools throughout the commonwealth. A training session for the school-based civil rights teams will take place in October. Presentations will be conducted by civil rights advocates, legal experts and community groups. Each team will receive comprehensive strategies and resources for making their schools safe and violence-free. The task force hopes that these civil rights teams will carry the "stop the hate" message to all students in all Massachusetts schools.

Another initiative of the Student Civil Rights Project includes an online database at stopthehate.org. The database will contain a comprehensive listing of resources for students, educators, law enforcement and communities. The services listed will focus on victim recovery, violence prevention, advocacy organizations and school-based civil rights groups. The database will be updated as new resources are available for online viewing. It will be crucial in getting information out to minority communities where underreporting of hate and bias crimes is prevalent. In building this database, the Student Civil Rights Project has conducted a statewide search of advocacy groups, support services and community-based organizations. The focus of these searches is to spotlight those organizations whose missions are to create communities that are free of violence, hate, bigotry and prejudice. In identifying these groups, a solid network of organizations will be constructed. This network will help provide support for citizens, schools, educators and law enforcement

personnel. Every citizen has an obligation to report incidents of hate, harassment and violence wherever and whenever they occur.

QUESTIONS

1. Why is "teaching respect for individual differences" the way to end prejudice and hate in society, according to the author?

2. Describe the components of the Stop the Hate program. Would you add additional aspects to the program? Why?

3. How does your college or university deal with hate crimes? Specifically, how is the campus community informed about the problem of hate crimes? How are hate crimes reported?

4. Have there been incidents of hate crime at your campus that you are aware of? If so, was the incident or incidents reported to authorities by the victim(s) or witness(es)?

5. Find out the methods your campus uses to compile and report statistics on hate crimes.

6. Go to StoptheHate.org and explore different segments of the Web site. Which aspects of the site do you think are most valuable for the project's goal of increasing tolerance?

7. What would you add or change about the Students and Educators sections of the StoptheHate.org Web site?

8. How can victims (or witnesses) of hate crimes or harassment be encouraged to report?

9. How can victims of harassment or hate crimes report their experiences to campus authorities? Would an online reporting form (such as the one that StoptheHate.org provides) be helpful on your campus?

10. If you were to create a project similar to Stop the Hate on your campus, what would you want students to know about hate violence?

11. What strategies would you use to raise awareness among students, educators, and other members of the campus community?

12. What resources are available in your area for people who want to find out more about working to prevent prejudice, bigotry, and hate crimes?

Part VIII

INTERNATIONAL PERSPECTIVES

This section presents a variety of international perspectives on the social and legal issues involved in defining, preventing, and sanctioning hate crimes. These articles illuminate the American experience with hate crimes by describing the experiences of other countries in ways that provide instructive comparisons. The experiences of the nations described in this section illustrate how societal attitudes are linked to a particular nation's problem with hate crime and how each nation responds to the problem (or fails to respond) in ways that reflect its specific cultural and legal context.

24

RACISM, ETHNICITY, AND HATE CRIME

ROB WHITE

SANTINA PERRONE

This article discusses how a societal culture of racism and intolerance sets the stage for street conflicts involving ethnic minority youth in Australia. Wider societal perceptions of ethnic violence among these youth may fuel majority stereotyping of minority youths as violent, dangerous, and crime prone. Thus violence among minority youth may be perceived as reflective of the nature of ethnic cultures, but this perception overlooks how the marginalization of these youths by the majority culture contributes to discord.

INTRODUCTION

The media construction of 'Otherness' has a major impact upon how young people see themselves, how they see their peers, and how they see themselves in relation to their peers. Media imagery certainly affects mainstream perceptions of the 'ethnic minority'. These images are neither neutral in social content nor with regard to institutional consequence (see, for example, Poynting et al. 2001). The negative portrayal of ethnic minority youth in the media is not, however, simply or solely due to misguided stereotyping and sensationalist reporting. There is a material basis for at least some of the public concerns expressed, albeit in distorted and partial form, through the mass media. This is especially so when it comes to certain types of street violence.

The intention of this chapter is to discuss the nature of street fights involving ethnic minority youth, in order to explore the relationship between violence, racism and the phenomenon of hate crime. Our aim is to demonstrate how one particular paradox of marginalisation may well serve to fuel racist political attacks on

EDITORS' NOTE: From White R., & Perrone, S. (2001). Racism, Ethnicity, and Hate Crime. *Communal/Plural, 9(2),* 161-181. Reprinted with permission of the Centre for Cultural Research (formerly the Research Centre in Intercommunal Studies) from Taylor and Francis.

ethnic minority groups in Australia, and how the actions of young people themselves contribute to this process. To put it simply, street-level violence involving acts of (perceived) hatred against another group (whether offensive or defensive), regardless of the fact that they may ultimately be seen to have been motivated by collective responses to racism and marginalisation, can have the consequence of reinforcing negative perceptions of ethnic minority youth. The street-level behaviour of ethnic minority youth is thus liable to be used against them ideologically and symbolically, as refracted through various prisms of vilification and hate.

The substantive sections of the [chapter] are based upon recent research carried out in Melbourne on so-called ethnic youth gangs (White *et al.* 1999; referred to hereafter as the Melbourne study). In our discussions with them, the young people spoke of two main types of group conflict. On the one hand, there was often reference to 'street fights.' These were seen as violent, occasionally involving weapons, and often linked to racism. Fighting occurred between different ethnic groups, as well as within particular communities. On the other hand, group conflict was also evident in the form of 'school fights.' These included verbal and physical assaults, and again were often associated with racism. In both cases, the young people tended to make assumptions and generalisations about other groups of young people from different ethnic backgrounds, including assumptions about Anglo-Australian young people.

The contribution of this paper is to explore the nature and reasons for these street conflicts. More specifically, it is to place these discussions within the context of resurgent interest in hate crime as a social phenomenon, and the potential consequences of street conflict, especially if perceived to be prejudice based, for wider political debates centring on the place of ethnic minorities in Australian society.

A CLIMATE OF CONFLICT

To appreciate the nature of street conflict between different groups of young people, it is important to emphasise the negative impact of the recent 'race' debate on the Australian social mosaic. In 1996, the populist right-wing candidate Pauline Hanson was elected as an independent member to federal parliament. Later to form her own political party (One Nation), Hanson's political agenda was founded upon racist ideologies (particularly in relation to indigenous people and 'Asians'), while also incorporating a range of nationalist (e.g. support for protectionism) and quasi-statist (e.g. more public assistance to farmers) perspectives. The rise of One Nation, and the implicit acceptance at a federal government level of many of Hanson's ideas and policy prescriptions (especially in areas such as immigration and resettlement policies, as well as indigenous concerns), has reopened public debate on 'race' issues in Australia in a particularly destructive way. They have allowed even the most crude and openly racist sentiments to be voiced without limit, and with considerable legitimacy. This new 'race' openness has been further bolstered by criticisms of so-called 'political correctness' by prominent political leaders, to the extent that to call a racist a racist is now considered taboo in many circles.

Recent work on 'hate crime' in Australia has pointed to the material result of such pronouncements and political movements (Cunneen *et al.* 1997). There has been increased reporting of racial vilification, many new stories of physical violence directed against the person and property of 'outsiders' (whether they be 'Asian,' Aboriginal, gay and lesbian, Jewish, Arab, etc.), and the imposition of official crackdowns on particular communities alleged to be rorting the welfare system or engaging in criminal activity. It is a climate where 'difference' is being highlighted, the 'Other' further entrenched with outsider status, and fear and loathing promoted as part of the mainstream of media and political debate. The seeds of social division, sown through years of economic disparity and institutionalised social discrimination, have re-emerged in the form of great fissures in the multicultural fabric (see White 1998). For many, the reality of life in contemporary Australia is shaped by what can only be described as a climate of hate.

The ramifications of such a climate on the people cohabiting what is one of the most polyethnic countries in the world, have still not been appreciated fully. For example, a number of assumptions are often made about the nature of 'hate crime' and violence directed against minorities. It is assumed, for instance, that the victims of such actions are always associated with minority groups. It is further assumed that the perpetrators are always drawn from the majority, particularly Anglo-Australian, communities. While there is plenty of evidence to support these contentions, especially in regard to the actions of the far right (Cunneen *et al.* 1997), there are complexities and paradoxes in the nature of social conflict that need to be further tested out. This is one aim of the present paper.

Hate crime is generally defined along the following lines:

> A 'hate crime,' synonymous with 'bias crime,' is a prejudice-based criminal offence motivated by the victim's membership within a particular social group. This could include, but may not be limited to, crimes motivated by the victim's real or perceived race, ethnicity, national origin or sexual orientation. (Byers 1999: 47)

There is some dispute over how, or even if, this crime designation can adequately be operationalised in practice. In strict legal terms, two statute-based models of bias crime can be distinguished in the USA (see Lawrence 1999). The 'racial animus' model requires that the defendant has acted out of hatred for the victim's racial group or the victim for being a member of that group. The 'discriminatory selection' model requires that the defendant has selected their victim because of the victim's membership in a particular group. The common thread in these definitions is the 'state of mind' of the bias criminal.

However, in their critique of such statutes, Jacobs and Potter (1998) argue that it is extremely difficult to define a species of crime based upon prejudice or bigotry. The concept is a social construct, one that varies greatly in meaning depending upon whether a broad or a restrictive definition is used. They argue that

hate crime is inherently ambiguous conceptually, and that it is terribly hard to demonstrate empirically—given that, in most cases, it is not possible to determine an offender's motivation. Choices invariably have to be made as to how to define the precise meaning of 'prejudice,' and how to understand the nature of the causal link between the offender's prejudice and their criminal conduct.

There are also varying opinions on how to measure hate crime, and whether or not it is a growing problem. According to Lawrence (1999), for example, the extent of bias crime is essentially dependent upon a combination of objective quantification (e.g. crime reports, violence perpetrated by 'militias'), and changing perceptions (e.g. what was once seen as a 'prank' is now seen as bias-motivated vandalism).

Perception and problem are inextricably related. From this perspective, the spectre of hate crime looms as a very large, and very real, menace to (American) society. Alternatively, the size of the crime problem can be seen to be entirely dependent upon how the definition is manipulated. This is certainly the view of Jacobs and Potter (1988: 28) who argue, for instance, that 'If criminal conduct must be completely or predominantly caused by prejudice in order to be termed hate crime, there will be few hate crimes. If prejudice need only in part to have motivated the crime, hate crime will be plentiful.' They critique the notion that there is a hate crime epidemic. In doing so, they note the lack of reliable, uniform data on hate crime.

The data that have been collected have, nevertheless, been used to develop a profile of the general characteristics of hate crime as such. British and US research, for example, indicates that the majority of hate crimes are committed by young white males, and that minority groups are generally at greater risk of victimisation, both in terms of household and personal offences (United States Bureau of Justice Statistics 1995; Fitzgerald & Hale 1996; Byers 1999). The attack is more likely to be committed by a stranger than a family member or acquaintance, and the perpetrators are half as likely to be under 20 years of age than over (United States Bureau of Justice Assistance 1997). The crime occurs not because of who the victim is, but rather because the victim is what they are (Lawrence 1999). In other words, group membership (or perceptions of such membership) becomes a prime reason for the violence experienced by the victim.

While 'race' appears to be an important predictor of victimisation, the elevated threat is not exclusively attributable to bias motivation; that is, loathing towards the group with which the victim identifies. In other words, there is no evidence to suggest a linear correlation between 'race' and bias-motivated victimisation. This is a significant observation, and is worth bearing in mind when interpreting the findings presented below. Having said this, however, it still needs to be acknowledged that both official and unofficial UK and US data suggest that 'race' is a key motivator of hate crime (Bowling 1993; Ehrlich 1989; United States Bureau of Justice Statistics 1995; Martin 1996).

Consistent with UK portrayals, information derived from the USA reveals a tendency for bias-motivated offences to fall predominantly within a handful of categories, namely: vandalism, assaults and threats (often accompanied by racist language). The effects of such attacks are profound. It has been argued, for instance, that hate crime introduces an additional dimension of harm compared with other types of criminal assault (Kelly 1993; for another view, see Jacobs & Potter 1998). The individualised pain and trauma that characteristically accompanies traditional forms of street crime is further transposed to the collective. Not only is the individual stigmatised on the basis of their social group membership, but, by logical extension, the social group is emotionally harmed. As Kelly (1993; cited in Byers 1999: 47) puts it:

> The designation [of bias crime] is a signal that damage beyond the infliction of physical pain has been done. . . . There is the hurt to victims singled out for the most stigmatised aspects of their identities, and there is a collective emotional harm to entire groups who must live with the knowledge that they are vulnerable to random attack.

The collectivised nature of such crimes has a number of ramifications for group formation among minority youth. In particular, and as demonstrated in our study, the importance of group solidarity and mutual protection become paramount.

Also important to the present paper is the fact that hate crimes tend to be carried out by young males in a group setting. Furthermore, it has been pointed out that 'Young men who have been socialised to be aggressive and to find violent solutions to their problems may end their search for power by physically attacking others who, themselves, lack the power to retaliate' (Levin & McDevitt 1993: 71).

Taking these broad patterns into account, it is useful at this stage to distinguish between different types of hate crime. Differences in the motivation and character of these crimes are summarised in the accompanying typology (adapted from Levin and McDevitt; cited in Byers 1999).

TYPOLOGY OF HATE CRIME

The Thrill Seeker

It is the anticipation of excitement and rush of adrenalin that motivates this class of perpetrator to engage in hate crime. Thrill-seeking hate crimes are customarily—though not exclusively—committed within a youth group context.

The Reactive Offender

The victimisation of a group is motivated by a sense of superiority. The underlying justification for violence lies in the belief that the offender is bestowed with certain 'rights' and 'privileges' not shared by the target group. Violence is therefore viewed as an attempt by the advantaged group to preserve their way of life and defend the rights and privileges which they perceive to be under threat from the 'Others' (e.g. jobs, school places, 'way of life').

The Mission Offender

The motivation for violence is unambiguously racist and/or based upon a political ideology. The violence is premeditated in the sense that it is usually linked to organised hate organisations or groups (e.g. National Action).

In our study of 'ethnic young gangs' we encountered many stories of street fights between diverse groups of young people (White *et al.* 1999). In many cases, racism was perceived to be the motivating trigger factor for the conflicts. What makes this form of violence different from that described in most of the literature on hate crime, however, is that very often the perpetrators, as well as victims, were from minority ethnic backgrounds.

We would suggest that the origins of these conflicts do bear a close relationship to the nature of hate crime, in that they stem from biases and prejudices related to stereotypical views of the 'Other.' Furthermore, the violence generally involves groups of young men acting collectively, attacking other young people primarily on the basis of identification with a particular target group.

The problem with seeing these conflicts as 'hate crimes,' however, is that it tends to transpose the explanation for the violence solely on to the perpetrators, without taking into account the structural location and social status of the parties involved. Such an approach not only may stigmatise ethnic minority youth who engage in street violence of this nature—as being 'racist,' 'violent' and 'dangerous'—but it misses the essential point. That is, that racism permeates the lives of these young people in ways that manifest in both the stereotyping of other groups of young people, and that foster violence as a practical solution to problems of status insofar as it provides an immediacy and tangibility that is difficult to ignore or resist. As it stands, the inter-group violence depicted in our study appears to be more in keeping with the first category identified in the hate crime typology above, than the other categories. Even so, there is much more to the violence than simply that of 'thrill seeking' as such, and moreover, 'us' and 'them' demarcations certainly are central to the conflicts.

CONSTRUCTING THE 'OTHER'

Media images and treatments of ethnic minority young people in Australia are generally very negative. Researchers have commented on how these youth are often presented as being homeless, on drugs, members of gangs, school drop-outs and basically 'bad' and 'dangerous' (Pe-Pua 1996, 1999). The media are seen by young people themselves as a constant source of biased, sensationalist and inaccurate information about their lives and their communities (Maher *et al.* 1999; White *et al.* 1999). It is also frequently the case that particular events are seized upon by the media to reinforce the 'ethnic' character of deviancy and criminality in ways that stigmatise whole communities (Noble *et al.* 1999; Poynting 1999; Poynting *et al.* 2001; Collins *et al.* 2000).

Street Gangs

In the specific case of 'ethnic youth gangs,' the activities and perceptions by and of ethnic minority youth present a special case. The overriding message of most media reports, for example, is that such 'gangs' are entirely negative, dangerous and threatening. Indeed, in recent years the hype and sensationalised treatment of 'youth gangs' have tended increasingly to assume a racialised character (White 1996; see also Lyons 1995; Poynting *et al.* 2001). That is, the media have emphasised the 'racial' background of alleged gang members, and thereby fostered the perception that, for instance, 'young Lebanese' or 'young Vietnamese' equals 'gang member.' The extra 'visibility' of youth ethnic minority people (relative to the Anglo 'norm') feeds the media moral panic over 'youth gangs,' as well as bolstering a racist stereotyping based upon physical appearance (and including such things as language, clothes and skin colour). Whole communities of young people can be affected, regardless of the fact that most young people are not systematic lawbreakers or particularly violent individuals. The result is an inordinate level of public and police suspicion and hostility being directed towards people from certain ethnic minority backgrounds.

With respect to these developments, it is significant that the increased frequency of involvement with the criminal justice system on the part of some ethnic minority young people, particularly in relation to drug offences and the use of violence (see, for example, Cain 1994;

Gallagher & Poletti 1998), has led to heightened media attention of ethnic young people generally. However, the extent of the shifts in criminal justice involvement do not warrant the intensity and universalising tendencies apparent in much media coverage, which tend to provide negative images of ethnic minority people as a whole. The problems associated with police–ethnic minority youth relations have probably contributed to this as well, and form an important part of the 'image-building' in relation to ethnic youth gangs.

Dedicated research and commentaries on gang formation in the Australian context have demonstrated that very often there is great ambiguity amongst both researchers and young people alike regarding the difference between 'gangs' and 'groups' (White *et al.* 1999; Collins *et al.* 2000; Perrone & White 2000). Such work has highlighted the wide variety of group formations amongst young people, and the diversity of activities in which young people engage. It is rare to find groups of teenagers who specifically gather together, over time and in an organised hierarchical network or structure, for the purposes of criminal activity. Rather, crime and anti-social activity tends to be irregular, sporadic and not the central purpose for hanging around together. Group formation itself, however, is frequently associated with types of group identification that periodically manifest in fights with other young people in a community.

Stereotypes, low social status and male aggressiveness were all ingredients in the reasons why young people from diverse ethnic backgrounds engaged in street violence. Often the violence was linked directly to 'racial' or 'ethnic' characteristics.

Street Violence: Group Fights

The study with which we were involved examined the issue of youth gangs by talking directly with young people about the nature of group formation and group activities in their communities and neighbourhoods (White *et al.* 1999). The study was based upon in-depth interviews with 120 young people from six different ethnic and cultural backgrounds across metropolitan Melbourne—including those from Vietnamese, Somalian, Turkish, Pacific Islander and Latin American backgrounds. Young people from Anglo-Australian backgrounds were also interviewed for the purposes of comparison. The young ethnic minority people in each sample were specifically targeted to reflect the dominant ethnic group in their particular region of the city. The sample included a cross-section of young people within the particular ethnic community, some of whom identified as being gang members (although, again, precise definitions were hard to establish even in these cases). Importantly, the interviews were carried out with young people who are often difficult to access or who are rarely consulted about such matters.

A major focus of the research was to investigate the specific problems, challenges and opportunities faced by ethnic minority young people. The ethnic minority young people we interviewed spoke about the difficulties of migration, of leaving familiar homes and cultures, to settle in a new, often quite alien, environment. Differences in language, religion and community values were frequently associated with problems in the resettlement process, and finding a place within Australian social life. Most of the young people lived in low-income households, in low-income areas. Unemployment was a significant problem for both the young people and quite often their parents. Basically the sample comprised young people from working-class neighborhoods who were economically marginalised, and who were socially and culturally on the margins of mainstream Australian society.

The study found that street fighting, and school-based fights, were a fairly common occurrence. The young people were asked about which groups get involved in conflicts with other groups, and why this was so. Table 24.1 presents data on the perceptions of the young people of the different groups that get involved in gang fights. (White *et al.* 1999).

The reasons for the fights between different groups of young people are in one sense already suggested by the findings presented in Table 24.1. That is, there appears to be a strong link between ethnicity and group behaviour involving street and school-based conflicts. Table 24.2 presents another perspective on why fights of this nature happen.

Table 24.1   Young People's Perceptions of the Different Groups That Get Involved in Gang Fights

| Types of groups | Response to each category | | |
	Number (respondents)	*Per cent (respondents)*	*Per cent (response)*
Anglo against other ethnic	45	38.5	30.8
One ethnic against 'different' ethnic	37	31.6	25.3
Ethnic amongst 'similar' ethnic	9	7.7	6.2
Ethnic within ethnic	4	3.4	2.7
No particular/many different combinations	23	19.7	15.8
Another specific combination	3	2.6	2.1
Not based on ethnicity	13	11.1	8.9
Don't know	11	9.4	7.5
Other	1	0.9	0.7
Total	146		100.0

N = 117.
Missing responses = 3 (2.5%).

Table 24.2   Young People's Perceptions of Why Gang Fights Happen

| Types of groups | Response to each category | | |
	Number (respondents)	*Per cent (respondents)*	*Per cent (response)*
Acting/talking smart	26	29.5	22.6
Drugs	7	8.0	6.1
Power struggles/revenge/territory	31	35.2	27.0
Girls	5	5.7	4.3
Don't know	5	5.7	4.3
Other	9	10.2	7.8
Total	115		100.0

N = 88.
Missing responses = 32 (26.7%).

The specific reasons for fighting between different groups are identified as being due to perceptions regarding what are acceptable or unacceptable ways to relate to particular groups and individuals. Racism and treating people with disrespect are crucial elements in the explanation. So too is the sense of ownership and belonging associated with particular local areas and membership of particular youth groups. Social status is thus something that is both contested and defended, and this in turn is generally tied to one's identification with certain people and places.

DIFFERENT EXPERIENCES AND PERCEPTIONS OF STREET CONFLICTS

Dimensions of Racism: Pacific Islander Youth

While overall commonalities were apparent in how the young people perceived the issues, specific differences emerged as well, depending upon the group in question. Each group of young people we talked to thus had different experiences and perceptions regarding group formation, gang membership and gang-related behaviour. A particularly insightful discussion was held with members of the Pacific Islander communities. These respondents were asked about the types of illegal activities young people might engage in, but not for the purposes of money. The leading response was 'fighting/ assaults,' followed by 'drug/alcohol use' and 'car theft/joy riding.'

The main reasons given for engagement in these kinds of activities were fun and excitement, showing off, peer pressure, boredom, problems at home and revenge against other young people. The intensity of feeling associated with fights in particular is indicated in the following quotations:

> PI19: People might feel angry and go out and beat the shit out of somebody, go out and go and you know, like just little things people consider crimes, like going out and getting pissed at the beach, or you know, or smoking drugs, or doing drugs, or—but that's not, is that a crime? Do you think that's a crime?—um stealing cars, just go for a ride. You know, you feel like going for a ride somewhere, so just walk down the street and get someone's car, steal taxis.

> PI20: The teenagers, that's what they get up to [fighting/assaults]. Like the Maoris, especially the Maoris. That's why we've got a really bad name down here. They love beating up the white people, because you know, they can't get to them. Even at school, that's what they do—for fun.

Violence directed against oneself, against property and against others indicates a high level of frustration and alienation. They are also usually linked to what was described as typical youth gang behaviour—in this case, describing groups of young men who acted tough.

The Pacific Islander young people were asked specifically if racism was a reason for belonging to a gang. The issue of racism had a number of different dimensions. In some cases, gang membership was perceived to be a response to *direct threats* to particular groups of young people:

> PI6: Maoris stick together no matter what, because they've all been through a lot of racism in

schools and elsewhere. They get called 'black cunt' and 'sheep fucker.' I've had rocks thrown at me at school and everything because of racism. Most Aussies reckon that Maoris, Samoans and Tongans are all the same; when you try to explain it, they just go 'what?'

> PI7: It could be part of the reason why. Coming to a country like Australia is—I find it a very racist place. Australians are very racist from what I've seen. They've got names for everyone. I didn't know what a 'wog' was before I came here. They put everyone into different categories—you've got your 'wogs' and you've got your 'nips' and you've got your 'skips.' They don't know respect; a lot of kids seem to not know the word respect.

> PI2: They [different gangs] like to fight each other. Australians always fight people from other races.

Another feature of the discussion over racism was the way in which ethnicity came to the fore, not simply as a response to a perceived or actual threat, but as a form of *confirmation of group identity:*

> PI11: You ask me why do I become a certain part of a group or a gang. That group or gang's basically my network of friends and family. If you looked at your life, you've got a network of family and then friends and you're in that circle; basically you see 'em like that—you could class that as a gang. Why do people do it? only because people only associate with certain different people. There are all these other mates on the outside of the circle, they [gang members] spend more time with the people in the immediate circle.

> PI19: They usually have the same focus. If you wanna know why Maoris are in gangs, I'll tell you right now. It's because we are tribal people. We've been like tribal people for like thousands of years right, and we, because we group together because that's what tribal people do, right. And because these children that are born here—like the ones that you've been speaking to—they think you know, they identify with culture from America right, because they think: 'Oh well, I'm black,' you know, 'I wanna be cool.' They don't know who they are; they're lost. They need their identity.

In some cases, however, racism was seen more as *convenient cover for aggressive action* on the part of some group members. In other words, the anti-social or violent behaviour was justified on the basis of racism, but the primary motivation was not seen to reside in racism per se:

> PI4: With some nationalities racism can be a reason. But sometimes I feel that certain Maoris and Samoans or Polynesians, they like to use the word 'racism' as an excuse and they give somebody a thump and like the police say 'why did you do that?' and they say 'well, he called me a black such and such.' I think sometimes people just use that as an excuse and they don't really know what racism is.

> PI20: I don't like the Maoris down here to be honest, even though I'm a Polynesian myself. But they just really, really think that they can boss around the Australians and all that; you know, the white people. And to me, oh, I just get really, really offended, 'cos I know I'm black, but I'm an Australian but, and I hate it when people do that; it really puts you off. But they wanna be, you know, the number one people here in Frankston.

Street fights featured prominently in discussions about the activities of gangs. Aggression between groups was generally seen to be linked to racism or power struggles over territory. Other reasons for the fighting included taking action 'over a woman,' some people being perceived as acting or talking smart, drug-related aggressiveness, or simply some young people just wanting to act tough for the sake of it.

From the point of view of the Pacific Islander youth, when it comes to street fights between groups, rather than simply between individuals or small numbers of young people, there was a strong 'ethnic' dimension. This is reflected in the following quotations:

> PI4: I find that a lot of Australians, not all Australians, but a lot of Australians, are pretty racist towards Oriental people—Vietnamese, Chinese. I've asked a lot of Australians 'why would you want to be racist against the Vietnamese?' and they always say something like

'they're always pulling out machetes' and stuff like that and 'they'll chop you up' and stuff like that. They say 'They should go back to their own country and chop each other up instead of coming over here and chopping us up.' I can't see a normal person who's sober say a racist remark to a Polynesian. I mean if a Polynesian and a Vietnamese were sitting together and there was an Australian guy, I believe that he'd say something racist to the Vietnamese, rather than the Polynesian. Australians think if they say something racist towards a Vietnamese they necessarily won't do nothing, because they're smaller—they come in small sizes. That's why they'll pick on a Vietnamese rather than a Polynesian first.

> PI9: Asians against Australians I'd say. Australians are very racist against the Asian groups.

> PI13: A few years ago it was Maoris and Australians used to fight each other all the time. But not now; not any more. Vietnamese usually fight against the Cambodians and the Australians [now].

> PI15: It's mainly, everyone's onto the Asians. Everyone hates Asians. Doesn't matter which gang, you know, everyone hates them.

> PI17: The Maoris most; [They fight] anybody.

> PI18: It used to be Aussies versus Maoris, but it's not as common any more. There aren't any skinheads around here, there are too many Maoris. There are some Vietnamese, but not enough to make one gang. You need about one hundred to make one gang.

Ethnicity was a major source of social connection for most of the people in the study. There was a familiarity with one another, and a sense of shared experiences. However, the group nature of youth behaviour also manifests itself in the form of fights on the street, and conflicts between groups and individuals within the school setting. In this context, it is understandable that the young people saw gang formation and membership as a rational way to protect oneself.

The process of group formation is linked in several ways to racism. For instance, racist violence directed at certain groups, whether on the street or in the school, by other young people or by state police, can be a trigger for collective responses to the threat. Similarly, gang membership can also, simultaneously, be an important way in which to confirm one's group identity, to determine precisely whom one is and where they fit into the wider world. It also needs to be acknowledged that periodically the notion of racism can be used as a convenient cover for the aggression of the victimised group. In other words, it can be used to justify violence that is substantially motivated by a desire to engage in the violence itself, rather than in responding to racism per se. Angry young men lashing out at the world around them is a quite different phenomenon to concerted community action that attempts to foster an anti-racist social environment.

Racism and Class: Turkish Youth

The young Turkish people in the study were also asked whether or not racism had anything to do with gang formation or gang-related behaviour. Their answers varied. Some argued that racism, or at the least *ethnic identification*, is a major reason for gang membership:

T2: Because 'Turks' stick with 'Turks' and 'Lebos' stick with 'Lebos' and the Asians with the Asians. Because, it's like if you need some help, you can go to one of the gang members and get all of the group to come and help you with your situation.

T4: a lot of for example 'wogs' don't like 'Aussies' or 'Nips', so it's like you've got something against them, but you don't even know why—just because they're different.

T6: I suppose they all can't get along; Turkish can't mix with Australians and I don't know, they just want to see who's tougher.

T14: Mainly Turkish—they're just in their packs out and about.

T14: Racism could start in the playground at school—getting picked on by some other group and then running to the safety of a majority group.

Other young people placed more stress on *immediate local conditions* and other forms of social connection (such as being unemployed, or drug users) as being the main reason for certain types of gang formation:

T9: Living in Broadmeadows and leaving school in year 10, it doesn't leave you much to do really.

T19: Mostly the people that are in the gangs are the druggies of the area; they all like to smoke together.

T10: They're mostly friends, dropouts from the same schools who come together and do things together.

T18: Kids in areas where unemployment levels are much higher than other suburbs; you know, hooligans around the streets.

Still others had the perception that regardless of present social circumstances, the issue of *racism was no longer dominant* in terms of how groups of young people relate to each other, or as the basis for specific group formations:

T18: I wouldn't say racism, because I haven't seen racism for years. Like, Broadmeadows years ago used to be full of racism, like 'What are you doing "wog"' down the street, but not any more.

T8: There used to be [gangs in the area] but not any more. Back in those days there used to be racism. When people like Turkish people, Lebanese or anyone that used to come from overseas, they used to get called like 'wogs' by Australians or the Asians were called 'Nippers' and they'd argue about it and they'll go into a gang to fight 'em and make sure they'd protect one another.

Ignorance and Stereotype:
Latin American Youth

The Latin American youth we spoke with were asked whether or not there were ethnic differences in how different young people used their time. Differences were identified, based upon religious and cultural backgrounds, choice in recreational activity, and time spent with one's family. However, significantly, many of the young people were hard pressed to actually identify of what the specific differences in activity might consist—owing to a lack of knowledge about other groups of young people. This is indicated in the following comments:

LA3: People from Asia do different things than we [Latin Americans] do. I really don't know, but I would think that they do different things. I don't know, I don't really have friends from different backgrounds, so I don't really know.

LA8: I don't know what other people from different backgrounds do, but I believe it's different.

LA9: I think there's a difference in what they do, but I don't know what's different. You know, we never get together with other ethnic groups, so I don't know.

LA11: Not really, maybe a bit. I don't know. If you're . . . like say Italian . . . you're probably lucky. You probably have a lot of spaghetti or lasagne.

LA12: No not really. I just think that like, if you're like with all Spanish people, you do different things. You would like listen to your own kind of like music from where you come from, like Spanish music.

The young people were asked about the difference between a group and a gang. As with the academic literature on gangs, there was some confusion and uncertainty over what demarcated a gang or not. In discussion, however, when asked about what types of gangs were present in their particular neighbourhoods, the young people emphasised 'ethnicity' more than age or criminality. This perception of gangs is particularly interesting given the Latin American young people's general lack of knowledge about other ethnic young people, as discussed above.

The perception that other groups of ethnic minority youth, or Anglo-Australian youth,

constitute 'gangs,' simply by virtue of their ethnic background, is clearly conveyed in the following quotations. In some cases the ignorance regarding the affairs of other young people is manifest in the use of racist descriptions of them:

LA4: Yeah, there are heaps. Well, there's the Vietnamese group, also the drugs—drug dealers. Well, I seen some Africans too; I don't really know if they're gangs or not—the Latinos.

LA5: Aborigines, Australians, Albanians and the 'Wogs.'

LA8: There are many gangs in my local area. Well, most of them are Vietnamese—from an Asian background. There's lots of 'em from Africa—Somalia.

LA11: I've only been here three weeks. I haven't seen any of them. But in my old local area, there were packs. There's the 'Gooks'—that's what everyone else calls 'em. And there's 'Skips in Control'—which they think. There's the 'Wogs' and there's the 'Niggers' and there's the South Americans, which are called 'Latins.'

When specific detail about 'gangs' was sought, many of the young people were unsure about things such as the size of such groups. The names of local 'gangs' either referred to a specific geographical location (e.g. the 3174 gang, based upon the post code for Noble Park) or ethnic background (e.g. the 'Skips in Control' gang). Largely, however, gang membership was perceived to consist of particular kinds of ethnic identification, which was reinforced by the concentration of certain groups of young people in certain suburbs.

The comments on gang fights offer intriguing insights into the nature and dynamics of such activity:

LA3: You can't generalise that one group fights with another. You know, Latin Americans like fighting and they fight against anyone, it doesn't really matter. For example, with the Latin Americans you know, they have two different gangs or groups you know—[one] from one country and [the other] from another country of Latin

America and you know, there's always fighting between countries from Latin America because they have different beliefs, so they fight about practically everything from you know, drinking, to what do you think or how do you speak Spanish—'Do you speak better than me?' But Latin Americans usually prefer to fight between each other, but for example, if they have a fight against another group—the Australians or the Vietnamese or any other race—they unite. For example, the gang from El Salvadorians or the Chilean gangs or whichever gang, they get together and both of them fight against the other gang.

LA4: Well, around here is mainly the Asians against the Asians.

LA8: The Asians get involved in gang fights, especially the Vietnamese in Springvale. You see some of the El Salvadorians getting involved in that, but the Vietnamese are the main ones in Springvale.

LA12: It's usually like Asians versus like Australians.

LA13: I would say at the moment, Australians against Asian people.

LA15: From what I know, it's mostly Lebanese, Turkish, Asians.

LA16: Well around this area, I suppose you hear a lot of trouble between like Turkish and like other countries around that area and Asians against Australians as well.

Fights of this nature were predominantly attributed to 'racism.' As indicated earlier, there appear to be strong ethnic identifications and distinctions amongst the various street-present young people. In addition to tensions between these groups, and within particular communities, there is the additional factor of a volatile social climate engendered by the rise to prominence of the One Nation Party:

LA13: Because of, you know, the racial hatred that there is at the moment in Australia. The Asians are hated by Pauline Hanson and then by every body else. Not every body else, but a lot of

people do support her opinions. And in numbers, you'd be surprised how many people do think, do agree with Pauline in Australia, but they're just silent because they fear that you know, the people, might think badly of them.

Another young person commented that a large part of the problem is ignorance: 'Because they don't like understand their cultures—like the other groups' cultures—and like the story behind their lives' (LA17). The lack of appreciation of other young people's backgrounds, histories and cultures thus is seen to contribute to at least some of the tension between the diverse groups.

STREET CONFLICT, RACISM, AND HATE CRIME

Street violence of various kinds features strongly in the lives of the young people, especially the young men with whom we spoke during the course of the Melbourne study. In and of itself, this is fairly unremarkable given the prevalence of certain types of aggressive physicality within marginalised and working-class communities. Being tough and engaging in acts that put one's bodily integrity at risk are generally associated with working-class male culture (in its many varieties and permutations). Typically, the matters of physique and the physical have been central to working-class forms of aggressive masculinity that celebrate strength, speed, agility and general physical prowess (White 1997/8). Under conditions of economic disadvantage, social stress and group marginalisation, there is even greater recourse to 'the body' as a key site for identity construction and affirmation (see Connell 1995, 2000). Thus, a lack of institutional power and accredited social status appears to leave little alternative to physicality itself as the main form of self-definition, whether this manifests itself as self-destructive behaviour or as violence directed at the other.

We would argue that the material basis for this violence lies in the disadvantages and injuries of social inequality. Social polarisation is the breeding ground for interpersonal violence. The links between economic marginalisation, working-class culture and particular forms of masculinity (reflective of certain hegemonic masculine ideals) have been discussed at length elsewhere (see Segal 1990; Connell 2000). So, too, recent work has provided sophisticated analysis of the ways in which ethnicity, racism and masculinity combine to reinforce particular kinds of behaviour and group formation (Collins *et al.* 2000). In regard to issues surrounding ethnicity specifically, Collins *et al.* (2000: 143) argue that violence and aggression have more to do with questions of status and masculinity than with inter-ethnic conflict. We would broadly agree with this observation. Yet we wish to emphasise, nevertheless, the importance of such conflicts in constructing images of, and social responses to, ethnic minority young men.

The public images of ethnic minority youth are shaped by racialised media portrayals (see, for example, Poynting *et al.* 2001; Collins *et al.* 2000; White *et al.* 1999), and by the manner in which police intervene in their lives (White 1996; Perrone & White 1999; Collins *et al.* 2000). They are also influenced by actual incidents of violence, such as fights and bullying, between groups of young people on the street. Institutionalised racism (in the form of restrictive life chances and the dominance of monocultural norms), economic marginalisation (in the form of unemployment and poverty) and reliance upon particular notions of masculinity (in the form of reliance on physical and symbolic markers of toughness) put these young people into a particularly vulnerable and volatile social situation. This, in turn, is associated with a central paradox in the lives of ethnic minority youth. Specifically, the assertion of identity and collective social power via membership of street groups and engagement in fighting, while forged in the context of rejecting racism and threats from outsiders, simultaneously reinforces the subordinate or 'outsider' position of, and negative directed social reaction directed toward, these selfsame groups of young people.

This paradox of marginalisation can be explored further by once again referring to the literature on hate crime. As discussed previously, hate crime is typically explained in terms of the social circumstances of the perpetrator (e.g. disadvantaged background, reliance on violent solutions to perceived social problems) and situational dynamics relating to the fact that it is associated primarily with young men, acting in groups. In our work, we were struck by how discussions of the motivations and character of hate crime seemed to fit the behaviour and actions of ethnic minority youth. For instance, some Maori young people conveyed the sentiment that they do indeed find excitement and thrills in attacking non-Maori people—it was 'fun' to do, and 'racism' was only a veneer used to justify having a punch-up. For others, fighting was clearly linked to issues of safety and protection, as well as garnering respect from those outside the particular community or group. In this sense, violence was certainly reactive, not so much to preserve perceived advantage (as in some types of hate crime), but to defend oneself against threats. We found no evidence among the young people of violence being based upon a racist or political ideology as such.

Clear lines of group demarcation were constantly drawn throughout the Melbourne research. While membership of any particular group may have been variable (e.g. Laotians and an Anglo-Australian being part of the 'Vietnamese' youth formation), there were broad-brush categorisations used to distinguish 'Australians,' 'Asians,' 'Turkish,' 'Latinos' and so on. People know who the 'wogs' are (with considerable internal variations in terms of precision and categorisation), and who the 'Aussies' are (with very few qualifications or recognition of internal categorical differences). These social distinctions have very real and pertinent effects at a political level. The history of immigration settlement and the particular ways in which 'multiculturalism' has been propagated at an ideological and policy level have undoubtedly contributed to the maintenance of these 'commonsense' divisions (see, for example, Jakubowicz 1989; Jamrozik *et al.* 1995; Vasta & Castles 1996). That is, the institutionalisation of 'difference,' in ways that embed social inequalities across and within groups, is a reflection of broad political and economic processes fostered by the Australian state over time. Our present concern, however, is less with the structural underpinning of social difference than with the impacts that this has at an interpersonal and immediate political level.

The institutional racism and economic marginalisation experienced by the ethnic minority young people in the Melbourne study is linked directly to group formations that function in particular ways to sustain a sense of identity, community, solidarity and protection. The assertion of identity, and the 'valorisation of respect in the face of marginalisation' (Collins *et al.* 2000: 150), manifests itself in the form of group membership and group behaviour that privileges loyalty and being tough (individually and as a member of the identified group) in the face of real and perceived outside threats. It also sometimes takes the form of contempt for 'Aussies' (as the dominant social group) and wariness of other ethnic minority groups that likewise are struggling to garner respect and reputation in a hostile environment.

Street violence that is premised ostensibly upon 'hatred' for other groups, regardless of the material circumstances that provide the social context for such actions, rebounds back upon the group in question in unexpected and unintended ways. Fundamentally, we would argue that in a political environment in which 'race politics' is a predominant feature (witness the recent controversies over asylum seekers, and the anti-immigration electoral platform of the One Nation Party), the spectre of 'ethnic criminality' is effectively bolstered by the actions of ethnic minority youth themselves, as they struggle to negotiate their masculinities, ethnicities and class situations. This is dangerous politically. For to the extent that racism is seen and/or portrayed in strictly attitudinal terms, then the manifest activities of ethnic minority youth can be distorted and sensationalised in ways that portray them as racist, 'un-Australian' and socially divisive. The association of street fights with 'racist' attitudes can be used to assert that the victims of systemic social discrimination are in fact the main perpetrators of hate crimes (defined narrowly as prejudice-based offences).

An inversion of real relations and social processes is thus made possible. This presents the far right with a potential field day politically, while creating major difficulties for governments and authority figures (such as the police) to find remedies to the street conflicts that do not further reinforce the racialisation and criminalisation of such conflicts, and the people involved in them.

It is interesting in this regard to note the feedback from the Anglo-Australian young people interviewed for the Melbourne study. According to many of these respondents, the ethnic basis for group membership was also seen as evidence of 'racism' (in a sense) insofar as young people from similar cultural and ethnic backgrounds were seen to be consciously excluding themselves from the dominant Anglo-Australian society. Racism was thus also construed to mean the close group identification of young people from similar ethnic, national and cultural backgrounds, in ways that affirmed the young person's membership of one section of society (but, in the eyes of the respondents, not another). Ethnic identification was thus conflated with the idea of 'racism.' That is, group formation based upon mutual understanding and shared experiences was seen actively to exclude and include people on the basis of 'race' or 'ethnicity.' From the perspective of the dominant group—the Anglo-Australian young people—this was seen as a problem, even though the processes of exclusion, and emphases on 'difference,' from the dominant group constitute major reasons for this social phenomenon.

CONCLUSION

Superficially, some of the stories of street conflict provided by the young people in our study appear to approximate the usual definitions of hate crime. However, given the social location and status of the young people involved, finer analytical distinctions need to be drawn. For example, we would suggest that the nature of the inter-group conflict, while in some senses 'race-based' or 'ethnicity-based,' is not necessarily 'race-motivated.' That is, the basis of the violence and conflict is not due to intrinsic biases against a particular group, or to discriminatory selection of victims or other young people to fight. Who fights whom is historically, socially and situationally contingent. It depends upon local dynamics, the particularities of immediate neighbourhood and school relationships, and who the newly arrived group is (i.e. the newest 'outsider').

We would argue that making sense of the street conflicts involving different ethnic minority youth requires an appreciation of the material resources available—or, more precisely, not available—to these young people. We would also make the point that the recent concerted undermining of the legitimacy of 'multiculturalism' as a state ideology and policy framework has had, and will continue to have, a major impact on the identification, confidence and opportunities available to ethnic minority youth. In many cases, this will lead to hybrid identity formation, in which young people claim different 'identities' depending upon social circumstance (see Noble *et al.* 1999). However, in cases where physical differences are pronounced relative to the white, Anglo-Australian 'norm,' the impact of the 'race' debate and associated policy revisions will be much greater, and much more difficult to negotiate.

While racism is certainly implicated in the nature of street violence, both via institutional structures that marginalise many ethnic minority young people and through direct face-to-face confrontations, the crucial variable is that of power. Fights between groups of relatively powerless sections of the community is less a matter of 'hate crime' per se than that of social dislocation and marginality. However, this type of violence does tend to reinforce the stereotypes and social divisions upon which racial vilification and hate crime feeds. The perpetrators of violence against one group may thus find themselves branded and ostracised from the mainstream, precisely because they engage in the sorts of activities they do. It may thus confirm the media image—that ethnic minority youth are violent, dangerous and not to be trusted. And it is this image that constitutes a major political resource for the purveyors of race hate in contemporary Australian society.

REFERENCES

Bowling B 1993 'Racial harassment and the process of victimisation: conceptual and methodological implications of the local crime survey', *British Journal of Criminology* 33(2) 231–250.

Byres B 1999 'Hate crimes in the workplace: worker-to-worker victimisation and policy responses', *Security Journal* 12(4) 47–58.

Cain M 1994 *Juveniles in Detention. Special Needs Groups: Young Women, Aboriginal and Indo-Chinese Detainees*, Information and Evaluation Series no. 3 Sydney Department of Juvenile Justice.

Collins J G Noble S Poynting & P Tabar 2000 *Kebabs, Kids, Cops & Crime: Youth, Ethnicity & Crime* Sydney Pluto Press.

Connell R 1995 *Masculinities* Sydney Allen & Unwin.

Connell R 2000 *The Men and the Boys* Sydney Allen & Unwin.

Cunneen C D Fraser & S Tomsen 1997 'Introduction: defining the issues', in C Cunneen D Fraser & S Tomsen (eds) *Faces of Hate: Hate Crime in Australia* Sydney Hawkins Press.

Ehrlich H 1989 'Studying workplace ethnoviolence', *International Journal of Group Tensions* 19(1) 69–80.

Fitzgerald M & C Hale 1996 *Ethnic Minorities: Victimisation and Racial Harassment, Findings from the 1988 and 1922 British Crime Survey*, Home Office Research Study 154 London Home Office.

Gallagher P & P Poletti 1988 *Sentencing Disparity and the Ethnicity of Juvenile Offenders* Sydney Judicial Commission of New South Wales.

Jacobs J & K Potter 1998 *Hate Crimes: Criminal Law and Identity Politics* New York Oxford University Press.

Jakubowicz A 1989 'Social justice and the politics of multiculturalism in Australia', *Social Justice* 16(3) 69–86.

Jamrozik A C Boland & R Urquhart 1995 *Social Change and Cultural Transformation in Australia* Melbourne Cambridge University Press.

Kelly R 1993 *Bias Crime: American Law Enforcement and Legal Responses* Chicago Office of International Criminal Justice.

Lawrence F 1999 *Punishing Hate: Bias Crimes Under American Law* Cambridge MA Harvard University Press.

Levin J & J McDevitt 1993 *Hate Crimes: the Rising Tide of Bigotry and Bloodshed* New York Plenum Press.

Lyons E 1995 'New clients, old problems: Vietnamese young people's experiences with police', in C Guerra & R White (eds) *Ethnic Minority Youth in Australia* Hobart National Clearinghouse for Youth Studies.

Maher L T Nguyen & T Le 1999 'Wall of silence: stories of Cabramatta Street youth', in R White (ed.) *Australian Youth Subcultures: On the Margins and in the Mainstream* Hobart Australian Clearinghouse for Youth Studies.

Martin S 1996 'Investigating hate crimes: case characteristics and law enforcement responses', *Justice Quarterly* 13(4) 455–480.

Noble G S Poynting & P Taber 1999 'Lebanese youth and social identity', in R White (ed.) *Australian Youth Subcultures: On the Margins and in the Mainstream* Hobart Australian Clearinghouse for Youth Studies.

Pe-Pua R 1996 *'We're Just Like Other Kids!': Street-frequenting Youth of Non-English-speaking Background* Melbourne Bureau of Immigration, Melbourne Multicultural and Population Research.

Pe-Pua R 1999 'Youth and ethnicity: images and constructions', in R White (ed.) *Australian Youth Subcultures: On the Margins and in the Mainstream* Hobart, Australian Clearinghouse for Youth Studies.

Perrone S & R White 1999 'The Policing of ethnic minority youth', paper presented at Hate Crime Conference, Sydney, December.

Perrone S & R White 2000 *Young People and Gangs. Trends & Issues in Crime and Criminal Justice* no. 167 Canberra Australian Institute of Criminology.

Poynting S 1999 'When "zero tolerance" looks like racial intolerance: "Lebanese youth gangs", discrimination and resistance', *Current Issues in Criminal Justice* 11(1) 74–78.

Poynting S G Noble & P Tabar 2001 'Middle Eastern appearances: "ethnic gangs", moral panic and media framing', *Australian and New Zealand Journal of Criminology* 34(1) 67-90.

Segal L 1990 *Slow Motion: Changing Masculinities, Changing Men* London Virago.

United States Bureau of Justice Assistance 1997 *A Policymaker's Guide to Hate Crimes* Washington DC United States Department of Justice.

United States Bureau of Justice Statistics 1995 *National Crime Victimisation Survey* (NCVS) Washington DC United States Department of Justice.

Vasta E & S Castles (eds) 1996 *The Teeth are Smiling: the Persistence of Racism in Multicultural Australia* Sydney Allen & Unwin.

White R 1996 'Racism, policing and ethnic youth gangs', *Current Issues in Criminal Justice* 7(3) 302–313.

White R 1997/8 'Violence and masculinity: the construction of criminality', *Arena Magazine* December-January 41–44.

White R 1998 'Globalisation and the politics of race', *Journal of Australian Political Economy* no. 41 37–63.

White R S Perrone C Guerra & R Lampugnani 1999 *Ethnic Youth Gangs in Australia: Do they Exist?* [seven reports—Vietnamese, Latin American, Turkish, Somalian, Pacific Islander, Anglo-Australian, Summary] Melbourne Australian Multicultural Foundation.

QUESTIONS

1. How have political changes such as the rise of the conservative movement contributed to increasing intolerance and bigotry against minorities?

2. How do media images of minorities in Australia contribute to perceptions of ethnic minorities as "the other" and reflect depictions of "ethnic criminality"?

3. How does the culture of racism contribute to conflicts between different minority groups?

4. What were the main reasons for street conflicts, according to the young people interviewed in this research?

5. In what ways were the young minorities studied economically and socially disadvantaged?

6. Why did youths form groups or gangs? What were the purposes of such groups?

7. According to the authors, how are social inequality and racism linked to interpersonal violence among youth?

8. What is the central paradox of marginalization, and how is it illustrated in the lives of the young people in this research?

9. What did you think of the reasons given for intergroup conflicts by the young people interviewed in this research?

10. According to the authors, how might conflicts between ethnic minorities be used by conservatives to reinforce societal perceptions of "ethnic criminality"?

11. Do you see any similarities between the experiences of young people in Australia and the United States in relation to hate crime?

12. Consider the ways in which power is a crucial factor in explaining the origin and impact of youth conflict in Australia.

25

AGGRESSIVE YOUTH CULTURES AND HATE CRIME

Skinheads and Xenophobic Youth in Germany

MEREDITH W. WATTS

The reunification of Germany was followed by a sharp rise in bias crimes. Although the frequency of hate crimes then subsided, it appears that Germany is experiencing a rise in the number of youth who display extreme racist views and sometimes actions. This article examines how youthful perpetrators of hate violence in contemporary Germany are creating an ever-changing youth culture that is difficult to monitor and assess. The German government's efforts to prosecute bigotry in speech and action stand in stark contrast to the American approach, reflecting the different historical and legal cultures of the two nations.

Xenophobic aggression in postunification Germany is not identical with what is called hate crime or hate violence in the United States, nor are the official data kept by the Federal Office for the Protection of the Constitution to monitor bias-inspired crimes directly comparable with U.S. definitions. The law in the Federal Republic of Germany reflects a reaction against the Nazi past and aims to forbid "Nazi" speech and propaganda. The law also provided for the monitoring of acts motivated by right-wing extremism, anti-Semitism, and antiforeigner bias. This produces several special categories of crime that may seem unusual to citizens of the United States, such as (a) disturbing or defaming the dead (the charges invoked to sanction desecration of Jewish grave sites and memorials), (b) "public incitement" and "instigation of racial hatred" (charges used to suppress racist public speech), and (c) distribution of Nazi propaganda or "literature liable to corrupt the young."

EDITORS' NOTE: From Watts, M. W. (2001). Aggressive Youth Cultures and Hate Crime: Skinheads and Xenophobic Youth in Germany. *American Behavioral Scientist, 45*(4), 600-615. © 2001 Sage Publications. Used with permission.

Other aspects of German law forbid the promotion of a Nazi-like political party, denial of the Holocaust, and use of the symbols associated with officially banned groups. The latter provision criminalizes the display of Nazi-era symbols (e.g., the swastika, the "Hitler greeting") but has been steadily expanded to forbid a wide variety of flags, emblems, and other symbols that were employed by groups banned by the Federal Constitutional Court.

What these laws do not do (compared to bias crime legislation in the United States) is define hate crime or hate violence as such, nor do they include any special recognition of gender, disability, or sexual orientation. On the other hand, they go much further than laws in many other contemporary democracies in limiting certain types of biased or racist speech, particularly when it is directed at groups victimized in the Holocaust.

Although the German law obviously reflects a special set of historical and legal circumstances, it results in an exemplary national data effort in certain categories of bias crime. The law requires national reporting of incidents by all police agencies. This ensures data gathering that is more intensive and more complete than is currently the case in most other nations (particularly in comparison with the United States where hate crime reporting is still voluntary and highly variable). As a result, German data provide a better basis than that of most nations for examining trends and developments in certain categories of hate-motivated violence. This feature of the law makes it possible to analyze trends in right-wing and xenophobic[1] violence in Germany, developments that reflect a particular national situation but that also show international characteristics that may help us understand hate violence in other societies as well.

THE COURSE OF
RIGHT-WING VIOLENCE

Perhaps the first question concerns the basic historical development of right-wing violence in Germany. Table 25.1 and Figure 25.1 place the era of "modern" xenophobia in Germany in perspective. In 1989 and 1990, immediately prior to unification, there were fewer than 200 violent

Table 25.1 The Course of Right-Wing Violence in Germany, 1989-1998

Year	Number of Violent Acts[a]
1989	173
1990	178
1991	849
1992	1,485
1993	1,322
1994	784
1995	612
1996	624
1997	790
1998	708

SOURCE: Bundesamt für Verfassungsschutz [Federal Office for Protection of the Constitution] (1997, 1998d). See also Watts (1997, chap. 2).

a. The official term refers to violent acts "which demonstrated or assumed right-wing motivation."

incidents per year. That figure more than quadrupled by 1992 and reached its contemporary peak in the following year. Shock of the German public (expressed dramatically by candlelight processions in sympathy with the victims), consolidation of the criminal justice agencies in the new federal states in the east, and stepped-up enforcement activities by security agencies all played a part in the decline. Since then, there have been oscillations between 600 and 800 violent incidents per year—a decline from the peak but still high compared to the preunification period (for a more extended discussion, see Watts, 1997, chap. 2).

A second question concerns the targets of violence. Unlike federal (and some state) hate crime statutes in the United States, German law does not provide for special reporting of violence based on sexual orientation, gender, or disability. However, it is quite specific about crimes that can be attributed to anti-Semitic, antiforeigner, or right-wing motivation. Since unification (beginning officially in 1990), the targets of attack have remained relatively constant. As Table 25.2 shows, about 60% of the violent incidents have been directed against foreigners. Anti-Semitic attacks, including desecration of graves and memorial sites, have accounted for about 2% of all violent incidents. Foreigners are a significant presence in Germany (with a population of more than

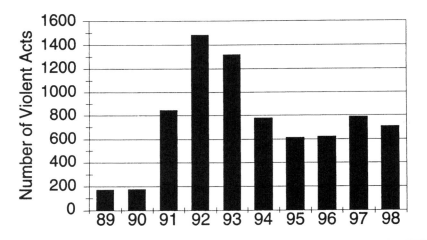

Figure 25.1   Right-Wing Violence

Source: Verfassungsschutzbericht (1997, 1998).

7 million) and account for the vast majority (60%) of attacks against persons. By contrast, the number of Jews in Germany is probably not much more than one hundredth that of foreigners, even allowing for a doubling of the Jewish population over the decade (due primarily to immigration from the former Soviet Union). Thus, whereas only 2% of the total offenses involve Jewish persons or institutions, the per capita rate is high.

Political opponents such as "autonomous" leftist groups and rival youth cultures accounted for another 14% of the total. The last category ("other") contained 24% of the incidents; it refers to offenses where the perpetrators were identifiably right wing but the victims were not foreigners, Jews, or political enemies (examples might be damage to property during a demonstration or assaults against police or bystanders).

Table 25.2   Targets of Right-Wing Violence in Germany, 1995-1998

Type	Number of Offenses[a]	Percentage of Total
Antiforeigner	1,269	60
Anti-Semitic	38	2
Against political opponents	303	14
Other[b]	512	24
Total	2,122	100

SOURCE: Bundesamt für Verfassungsschutz [Federal Office for Protection of the Constitution] (1997, 1998d).

a. The official term refers to violent acts "with demonstrated or assumed right-wing motivation."

b. "Other" includes acts of violence where the perpetrators are identified as "rightists" but where the incident or target does not involve the previous three categories. Examples might be a march in which store windows are broken or a confrontation with citizens or bystanders.

WHO ARE THE PERPETRATORS?

But who are these "rightists"? Increasingly, the perpetrators of hate violence of the past decade have tended overwhelmingly to be young males, usually acting in groups. But how young? And in what kind of groups—skinheads, neo-Nazis, or informal groups of young men looking for excitement?[2] As Table 25.3 shows, modern xenophobia indeed has a youthful face. Data from 1996 show that 30% of the perpetrators were ages 16 to 17 and that more than two thirds of all perpetrators were 20 years of age or younger.

This aggressive activism on the part of teenaged and young adult males represents a historical "modernization" of xenophobic violence. Prior to 1980, those younger than 20 years of age accounted for only 40% of the incidents (see Watts, 1997, p. 269). The earlier form of rightist activism involved somewhat

Table 25.3   Age of Perpetrators (1996)

Age	Percentage	Cumulative Percentage
16-17	30	30
18-20	37	67
21-30	27	94
31-40	3	97
Older than 40	3	100

SOURCE: Bundesamt für Verfassungsschutz [Federal Office for Protection of the Constitution] (1996). (For earlier years, see Watts, 1997, p. 269.)

older perpetrators who were more likely to be associated with neo-Nazi groups (and, presumably, had more developed right-wing ideological positions than today's younger activists). In comparison with this earlier period, today's typical activist is much younger[3] and less likely to be a member of a neo-Nazi organization.

Accompanying this shift toward youthful activism has been a trend away from classic, membership-based organizational forms. The young perpetrators are less likely than their predecessors to be ideologically sophisticated and organizationally connected. This does not mean they are isolated; on the contrary, they are part of a xenophobic culture that includes both the older organizational forms and a heterogeneous (and often highly spontaneous) youth culture. This last point is not an obvious one, but we can make sense of it looking at recent skinhead history and at the data on the organization connections of actual perpetrators. Here, we have two questions: How have developments in the skinhead scene contributed to the subculture of racism? and How much have skinheads contributed to the rise in violence?

TRENDS IN EXTREMISM AND
AGGRESSIVE SUBCULTURES

Historically, only a portion of the skinhead style has been explicitly racist or neo-Nazi. Most histories of the movement point to its British working-class origins and to its multiracialism in membership and music tastes. But, those accounts also point to the split of the skinheads into "left" and "right" factions in the 1980s. Somewhere in between these politicized factions are the apolitical skins (who probably make up the majority). The actual numbers in each group are difficult to identify because the boundaries are fluid, and stylistic variations are not always recognizable to the outsider. To make things more difficult, it is not unusual for German skins to refer to themselves as "more or less left" when they actually mean that they are not right. For young Germans in the east, to be truly left was largely discredited with the fall of the East German regime. This was particularly the case for skinheads, who were likely to see being right as the logical place for rebellion to take place in a socialist society.

The right-wing scene has been notorious for its fluidity and unpredictable actionism, a frustration both for the more orthodox rightists who would like to organize them and for the security agencies who would like to monitor them. However, there is a countervailing tendency that seems to have been accelerating throughout the decade—there are signs that such international groups as the Blood and Honour (British) and the Hammerskins (United States) have added discipline, ideology, and an international network to the right-wing skinhead culture. Not only do both movements have global pretensions, but the latter group refers to itself, ominously, as the Hammerskin Nation.

All this points to a rightist milieu that contains a diverse mix of elements—informal groups of xenophobic youth; "subcultures" with a recognizable, aggressive style (such as skinheads); and ideological groups that are disciplined and organized. Those who identify themselves as rightist skinheads are a dramatic presence among perpetrators (Anti-Defamation League, 1995; Hamm, 1993), but available data suggest that they are only one part of a much broader class of aggressive xenophobes.

In his study of perpetrators in the early 1990s, Willems found that 38% of those arrested for antiforeigner violence in the early 1990s were identified as skinheads (Willems, 1995). Heitmeyer and Müller (1995) found that 46% of their interviewees who were involved in antiforeigner violence thought of themselves as skinheads. Prior to 1990, however, the term *skinhead* hardly surfaced with respect to anti-Semitic or antiforeigner violence—not only was there a smaller amount of violence, but some 90% of the perpetrators in that earlier period were identified with neo-Nazi or other classic right-wing extremist groups (Kalinowsky, 1990). In other words, the 1990s were characterized by a surge in xenophobic violence that was carried by aggressive subcultures that were different from the traditional ideological groups on the right.

In comparison to Germany, information on the role of skinheads in the United States is somewhat less systematic and therefore less conclusive. Levin and McDevitt (1993) estimated that the most ideological perpetrators of hate crimes are probably no more than 1% of the total perpetrators. The authors suggested that skinheads are part of this group of violent perpetrators who attack out of an ideological "mission" to drive out the target group. However, data from Germany and elsewhere suggest that skinheads and other aggressive subcultures may not act primarily from racial or ideological motivations but are motivated by "thrill-seeking" and other opportunistic or criminal motives. Thus, it is difficult to estimate the contributions of skinheads in the perpetration of hate crimes or bias-motivated attacks and just as difficult, at the moment, to compare accurately the various types of perpetrators from one nation to another.

Direct comparison across nations is also made difficult because of the nature of the data (compared to Germany, police reports in the United States are less systematic in establishing the political motivation or membership of the perpetrators). As a result, figures from the United States are not comparable (either in relative accuracy or in estimated magnitude) with those of Germany; however, it is clear that racist skinheads are involved in a number of dramatically violent incidents nationally and internationally (Anti-Defamation League, 1995; Southern Poverty Law Center, 1998).

Thus, to reiterate an obvious point: Only some skinheads are racists, and most racists are not skinheads. Yet, skinheads have played a growing role in xenophobic violence. But, what do we know of the "skinhead" contribution to the broader culture of aggressive xenophobia? To put the numbers in perspective, Willems (1995) found that in addition to the 38% who were identifiable with skinhead culture in some way, about 25% of the perpetrators were associated with right-wing extremist groups. Another

19% were members of informal groups or cliques with no specific ideological identification (most of the remaining perpetrators not accounted for in the above categories had prior records and were classified as "criminal," though this category no doubt overlaps the others). Heitmeyer and Müller (1995) found that roughly 27% of the rightist youth they interviewed were associated with neo-Nazi (rather than skinhead) groups. Taken together, these studies indicate that skinheads make up the largest single category of perpetrators in Germany, with members of neo-Nazi organizations a distant second. By either account, at least one third of the attacks are committed by youth who are not associated with these easily identifiable groups.

Skinheads have represented a major portion of the problem, but they were still only one part of a much broader pattern of violence. According to the German Federal Office for the Protection of the Constitution, the total estimate of "right-wing extremist potential" in Germany grew steadily in the last half of the 1990s. A closer look at the various groups (see Table 25.4) shows that the largest single numerical change has occurred in the estimated strength of right-extremist political parties (these are parties that are "on watch" by the agency but are not classified/banned as "neo-Nazi"). The number of hard-core ideologues represented by the neo-Nazis has remained relatively constant; other growth areas have been among those classified as "violence-prone rightists" and "other groups" (see Figure 25.2). The latter category contains a diverse cluster of Kameradschaften, discussion groups, and informal cliques that seem to have proliferated (but whose numbers are notoriously hard to estimate due to their informal organizational forms).

Also hard to estimate is the exact number of persons in the violence-prone category; yet, it is on this diffuse group that the federal office has focused much of its concern over the decade. This category contains the heart of the perpetrator category—potentially violent young people (mostly males); its numbers are largely a matter of estimate (because there are no "organizations" to infiltrate or membership records to confiscate). It is this category that contains the skinheads, the group with the most identifiable

Table 25.4 Estimated Right-Wing Extremist Potential, 1995-1998

Extremist Group	Year			
	1995	*1996*	*1997*	*1998*
Violence-prone rightists	6,200	6,400	7,600	8,200
Neo-Nazis	1,980	2,420	2,400	2,400
Political parties	35,900	33,500	34,800	39,000
Other groups	2,660	3,700	4,300	4,500
Total	46,740	46,020	49,100	54,100
Total minus multiple memberships	44,610	45,300	48,400	53,600

SOURCE: Bundesamt für Verfassungsschutz [Federal Office for Protection of the Constitution] (1997, 1998d).

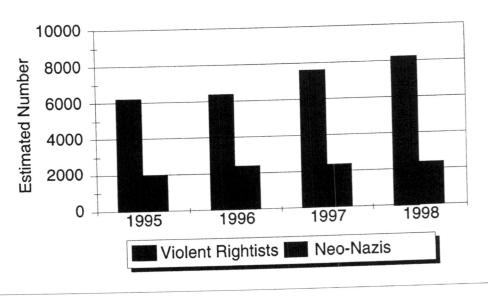

Figure 25.2 Trends in Right-Wing Potential

style and appearance among the violence prone. Obviously, the German government views this category as a growing source of danger. The rise in the number estimated to be violence prone thus reflects an increase in aggressive youth. It is also likely that the increase in their estimated numbers results from a heightened perception on the part of monitoring agencies that the danger from unorganized, aggressive youth is growing. If the numbers are truly on the rise, then it is an increase in the potential—rather than the actual—rate of perpetration. In recent years, the number of violent offenses has declined somewhat (see Table 25.1).

EVOLUTION AND CHANGE IN SKINHEAD CULTURE

The skinhead scene actually consists of many scenes with elements borrowed from other subcultures. For this reason, it is impossible to speak of skinheads as if they all shared an identical culture, ideology, or organizational structure; there are also evolution and change in the scene. Three types of development are worth noting: The first is adaptation of the skinhead style to fit the local political culture. The second is in the increased networking of skinhead groups; this includes organization diffusion above the local level and reflects the internationalization of skinhead style. The third is in the commercialization and commodification of skinhead culture.

In the first development, the international skinhead style (much like other subcultural styles) can be "downloaded" from international media and adapted to fit local conditions. This produces variation not only in the groups themselves but in their local "partners." As local variations include cultural elements that respond to the particular culture and community, the network of potential supporters varies from one place to another. For example, in the United States, racist skinhead groups may be allied locally with neo-Nazi groups, with traditional organizations such as the Ku Klux Klan, or with such groups as Aryan Nations or the World Church of the Creator. In Germany, rightist skinheads may find political partners with neo-Nazi groups or with Kameradschaften and political "discussion groups." White supremacist groups (often imported from the United States) also have some appeal because they offer a racist model that is not associated with the Nazi era (thereby avoiding both the stigma of association with the Nazi period and reducing the likelihood of being banned or prosecuted).

This ideological and associational variation has counterparts in the United States, as in the example of the Nazi Low Riders of Antelope Valley, California. Although the name conjures up images of Los Angeles Latino subculture, this group combined elements of skinhead culture, Nazi ideology, racism, and a business sideline in the methamphetamine trade (Finnegan, 1997). Local variations such as these show that such subcultures are dynamic and difficult to capture in a simple ideological or political definition. Local scenes show a kind of cultural entrepreneurship that combines national and international models with the political culture of the local community.

There also appears to be a growing network of rightist culture on both the local and international levels. Though their impact is difficult to estimate, there is evidence from a number of sources that the right-wing elements of the skinhead scene have become more structured and that they have increased their capacity to cooperate with other groups. Those partner groups often provide the organizational structure, capacity for logistics, and tactical planning

(e.g., for demonstrations) that skinheads have traditionally lacked. Most of all, those groups may provide ideological structure and tutelage.

The hard street-fighting style of many skins has long been used by other rightist groups for its intimidation value. According to former neo-Nazi Ingo Hasselbach (1996), "The skins were our storm troopers—the idiots who cleared the streets for us and intimidated our enemies—and enjoyed a bit of violence anytime" (p. 171). However, there is evidence that by the end of the decade skins had expanded beyond this role of "useful idiots" (Hasselbach's term) and that they had done it beyond national boundaries. In early 1999, skinheads from Croatia, Slovenia, and Germany joined neo-Nazis from Hungary and elsewhere for a demonstration in Budapest. Rightist skins were a common sight at Aryan Nation meetings in the United States, the White Aryan Resistance actively recruited violent skinheads in the early 1990s, and a well-known watchdog organization argues that the skinhead scene is moving "from chaos to conspiracy" (Southern Poverty Law Center, 1998, p. 23). In Germany, connections have developed between the skins and various neo-Nazi groups and, more recently, to rightist political parties; in particular, the National Democratic Party and its youth organization, the Young National Democrats, have actively sought contact and cooperation with right-wing skins (Bundesamt für Verfassungsschutz, 1998a, 1998b, 1998c).

If the actual extent of political networking is a bit difficult to estimate, the evidence for the international commercialization of skinhead culture seems more easily quantifiable. In Germany, data on this trend come from the fact that police and government agencies monitor both "hate speech" and material that is considered "harmful to youth." For example, music and public speech can be targeted for official repression if they are placed by authorities under either of these categories. Thus, in a 1993 operation that would seem unusual to citizens in the United States, German national and provincial agencies prosecuted rightist and "White power" skinhead bands and took legal action against commercial distributors of their music.

In a similar action in 1997, police and security agencies in 10 federal states searched the homes and places of business of 24 individual and corporate distributors of music judged to be

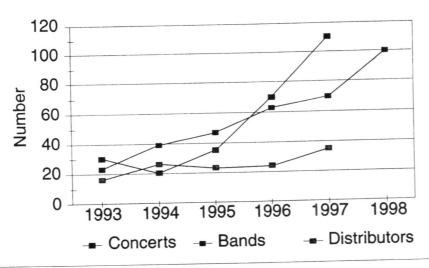

Figure 25.3   Trends in Skinhead Culture

racist. Confiscated in the action were several thousand CDs and various Nazi memorabilia and propaganda material. Also captured were computers, business files, and, in one case, an automatic weapon with ammunition (Landesamt für Verfassungsschutz, 1998).

Despite these periodic waves of concerted suppression and interdiction by authorities, the number of concerts and distributors of skinhead materials (and literature) increased steadily through the late 1990s (see Figure 25.3). The number of bands also increased, showing a 20% surge in 1 year alone (from fewer than 80 in 1997 to roughly 100 in 1998). Repression efforts run up against two major obstacles. The first is the increase in commercialization and commodification, in which skinhead and racist culture is turned into products (e.g., music, clothes) and marketed for economic gain. This produces an economic incentive for the continuation and exploitation of skinhead and racist culture.

The second, interrelated, trend is the internationalization of that commercial culture that allows concerts and distributors to operate effectively from other countries. To escape German sanctions, bands, literature, and concerts are likely to appear in Denmark or Sweden (in fact, it was from Denmark that American neo-Nazi Gary Lauck was extradited to Germany in 1995). Of course, the United States is the prime international center for the distribution of skinhead, White power, and

extremist material. The development of electronic networks such as the World Wide Web has promoted this globalization, increased the commercial availability of rightist materials, and undermined German attempts to suppress skinhead culture. Ideological/commercial Web sites (usually based in the United States but reachable from virtually anywhere) have expanded; Web sites suppressed in Canada, Germany, and elsewhere reappear in the freer cyberspace of the United States where they exist alongside entrepreneurial American extremists.

DISCUSSION

Germans are not alone in the surge of xenophobia and hate crime. There are signs that similar developments are occurring throughout industrial societies undergoing modernization and structural change, stress in employment markets, and a significant influx of people perceived as foreign. Though these structural and social problems all affect Germany, they are common throughout contemporary democracies. So, too, is xenophobic violence and bias crime.

The preceding analysis dealt with rightist potential (and the role of skinheads within it) in one country. The German data are more complete than information available in other nations, but they are not identical with what would be categorized as hate- or bias-crime in the United States. Notably, offenses based on gender and sexual orientation are not included (as indeed they are not in a number of American states). These differences in emphasis make it difficult to compare trends across nations with accuracy. Even so, the data are helpful in pointing out some of the major trends in xenophobic culture in Germany and elsewhere.

Some of our concerns go beyond what the data can clearly tell us. However, we can make some reasonably well-grounded speculations about the role of aggressive youth cultures in contemporary bias crime. I would like to suggest some propositions that seem sensible based in part on the analysis presented here. Each is supported to a greater or lesser extent by current information, but to have more certainty, more comparable data from other nations will be needed. Indeed, we will need far more systematic data for the many jurisdictions of the United States because, unlike Germany, reporting under U.S. hate crime legislation is voluntary and still far from complete.

• First of all, youth cultures are often not just passing fads. The decline of skinhead culture has long been predicted, but it has changed, expanded, and internationalized in the two or more decades since it first appeared. As a style, it has some ephemeral characteristics that will undoubtedly change further and even disappear. But, like rock and roll music (whose death has been predicted for four decades), there is no reason to doubt that this or a similar youth culture will continue to express some form of aggressive xenophobia.

• The early skinhead style originally emerged from British working-class culture as an expression of a strong, working-class masculinity. Segments of it later split into politicized left and right, with the racist segment emerging as an amalgam of aggressive masculinity and explicit xenophobia. This racist tendency was augmented by a sporadic, but growing, connection with ideological elements of the extreme and racist right. What resulted was a three-part poison of aggression, xenophobia, and ideology that has been much more self-sustaining than any of the individual components alone. Where younger persons, particularly males, are confronted with

economic modernization and dislocation for which they are ill prepared, and where scapegoats in the form of various cultural "outsiders" are perceived as threats, this three-part poison will continue to produce aggressive subcultures (of which skinheads are only one contemporary variant).

• The skin/fascho scene has developed elements of a subculture that includes music, fanzines (fan magazines), concerts, and other more or less organized symbolic and cultural events. This helps provide an integration of the scene as well as a sense of identity—of being part of something much larger, more powerful, and even somewhat "dangerous." This provides the basis for a self-sustaining scene—it falls short of being a "movement," but it provides a network through which movement-like connections can develop.

• The skinhead scene has broken out of its parochial/provincial boundaries to establish important links to ideological groups—groups that provide the "intellectual" part of the fascho program, offer a "standing organization," and maintain a durable political opportunity structure. The skins might not be interested in organizing, say, a Rudolf Hess Memorial day (a German neo-Nazi tribute day, substituted for Hitler's birthday, which cannot be celebrated publicly); the neo-Nazis do that. But, the skins can show up, act badly, and lend a show of force and aggressive power. They typically horrify the orthodox rightists, but both groups gain from the odd alliance. Moreover, skinheads have graduated from being what Hasselbach (1996) called "useful idiots"; some have crossed the ideological line and become part of the organizational neo-Nazi right. They maintain links to the skin scene and provide a bridge from the rowdy skinhead style to the more disciplined structures on the right.

• The scene of youthful xenophobic aggression has broken out of its provincialism to establish links to international groups. There are many reports of contacts to a variegated international network, particularly in the United States, United Kingdom, Scandinavia, the Netherlands, and to a lesser degree Spain (relations with the Czechs, Poles, Hungarians, and other central Europeans are somewhat more strained, but they exist). Explicitly racist groups such as Blood and Honour and the Hammerskin Nation provide an international style that is easily downloaded and adapted from the World Wide Web, music, and literature. In Germany, the government estimates that there are more than 200 skinhead or racist Web sites (in the United States, there are far more, of course); many of them are in English to broaden their impact (or because they use North American Internet providers to avoid German censorship).

• Concerts of White power bands are typically discouraged, even prosecuted, in Germany. Bands are raided, CDs confiscated, concerts broken up or forbidden, and leaders prosecuted under German hate speech laws that forbid glorification of Nazis, racist speech, or defamation of victims of the Holocaust. It is even illegal to deny that the Holocaust existed or to slander Jews in public speech. This suppression is undermined by global electronic networks and by support for the scene from abroad.

• The example of skinheads provides some insight into the dynamics of international commercialization—a phenomenon that appears to help stabilize the scene, allow it to expand, and give it a longer life than might have been expected. The same is true, but more so, for right-wing extremist groups and sentiment. This commercial dimension includes cultural artifacts, memorabilia, music, and literature that provide an economic incentive for widening and deepening the scene.

• The structural conditions that produced skinhead groups all over the world are still present. Where they are not solved, skinheads or some other subcultural phenomenon is likely to persist. Status anxiety, identity problems in declining working-class culture, and the compensatory needs of underemployed or threatened young people, particularly males, are continuing problems. These problems, and the youth cultures they produced, extend well beyond the boundaries of the less advantaged. Although the expression of such xenophobia may have significant origins in threatened segments of the housing and labor markets, that xenophobia has been transported politically and culturally to a much broader segment of the population (e.g., middle-class youth, young women, and a variety of nations that have developed "copy-cat" scenes).[4]

• The psychological need for an identity and sense of meaning remains. Not all youth can answer that need with conventional achievement in work, education, and family, but some find it easier or more exciting to use physical and symbolic aggression against out-groups. This form of identity can be extremely unrealistic and dysfunctional (especially when based on a mythopoetic White race, or the like, which either does not exist or, if it does, hardly appoints these youth as its "sword and shield"). This is not a productive identity search, but it will continue to have power where other sources of positive identity are not available.

• Last, although racist skinheads and other aggressive cliques may seem atavistic, they may actually be on the cutting edge of modern xenophobia. Their spontaneous and unpredictable style was traditionally seen as a disadvantage, but a trend in the far right throughout the decade comes to favor this seemingly primitive form of action. Increased repression of extremist groups by various national governments has led to organizational innovations. In the United States, the concept of leaderless resistance sprang up on the far right to promote action that is not controlled by a specific organizational center. The concept was developed among American extremists to replace the standard organizational model that proved vulnerable to government infiltration and prosecution. But, small groups of aggressive youth had long been the source of spontaneous, "unorganized" violence. Skinheads and other aggressive subcultures are part of a fluid milieu that is held together by symbols, idea fragments, cultural events, and electronic media—but often without any classic organizational structure. This relatively unorganized base then provides a place from which the more ideological of them are likely to find their way into parties, movements, and discussion circles. Thus, the language and symbols may often sound like the "same old thing," but underlying the familiar slogans is a significant change—the right has modernized and adapted, and it has taken on a more youthful face than was the case a generation ago.

NOTES

1. The term *xenophobia* can refer to a generalized antipathy toward out-groups in general or toward a specific target group such as foreigners, Jews, homosexuals, and others. In German usage, the term *Fremdenfeindlichkeit* refers to antipathy against foreigners, although *Xenophobie* is increasingly used. I have tried elsewhere to make these distinctions somewhat more carefully. In this discussion, I try (without complete success) to use *xenophobia* when referring to the more inclusive concept. The terms *antiforeigner* and *anti-Semitic* not only denote the more specific antipathies, they also correspond to the primary categories in the official German agency reports.

2. This is not the place for an analysis of the causes and appeals of youthful xenophobia, but some useful starting points are Bergmann (1998); Boehnke, Hagan, and Hefler (1998); Hagan, Merkens, and Boehnke (1995); Oesterreich (1998); Watts (1997, 1999); Watts and Zinnecker (1998); and Willems (1995). For a closer look at the role of young females on the right, see Mushaben (1996).

3. Other discussions of aggressive German youth cultures in the early 1990s can be found in Watts, 1997 (particularly in chaps. 1, 6, 7, and 9). For a more detailed analysis of the shift in public opinion and violence during the 1980s and 1990s, see Watts, 1997 (particularly chap. 2). A detailed chronology of postunification xenophobia is provided by Rainer Erb (cited in Kurthen, Bergmann, & Erb, 1997, pp. 263–285).

4. This conclusion obviously refers to the spread of aggressive youth culture, the primary topic of this discussion. I do not mean it to be a global proposition about the origins of xenophobia or to imply that youth are the source of xenophobia. What I have argued from the German data, though, is that xenophobic youth have been the primary source of rightist violence in the past decade.

REFERENCES

NOTE: Sources are provided in English wherever possible, though in many cases the data reported are available only in German. In those cases, I have provided a translation of the original title and institutional name (when a governmental agency is the data source). Readers interested in the extensive German literature on the subject might start with the bibliographies in Watts (1997) and in Kurthen, Bergmann, and Erb (1997).

Anti-Defamation League. (1995). *The skinhead international: A worldwide survey of neo-Nazi skinheads.* New York: Author.

Bergmann, W. (1998). Violence as social control: Right-wing youth in Germany. In M. W. Watts (Ed.), *Cross-cultural perspectives on youth and violence* (pp. 99–115). New York: JAI.

Boehnke, K., Hagan, J., & Hefler, G. (1998). On the development of xenophobia in Germany: The adolescent years. *Journal of Social Issues, 3,* 585–602.

Bundesamt für Verfassungsschutz [Federal Office for Protection of the Constitution]. (1996). *Verfassungsschutzbericht* [Online]. Retrieved August 15, 1998, from: http://www.bundesregierung. de/02/0201/innen

Bundesamt für Verfassungsschutz [Federal Office for Protection of the Constitution]. (1997). *Verfassungsschutzbericht* [Online]. Retrieved August 15, 1998, from: http://www.bundesregierung.de/02/0201/innen

Bundesamt für Verfassungsschutz [Federal Office for Protection of the Constitution]. (1998a, March). Rechtsextremistische Skinheads. *Entwicklung, Musik-Szene, Fanzines* [Right-wing extremist skinheads: Development, music scenes, fanzines] [Online]. Retrieved November 1, 1998, from: http://www.verfassungsschutz.de

Bundesamt für Verfassungsschutz [Federal Office for Protection of the Constitution]. (1998b, July). *Right-wing extremism in the Federal Republic of Germany: Situation report* [Online]. Retrieved November 1, 1998, from: http//www.verfassungsschutz.de

Bundesamt für Verfassungsschutz [Federal Office for Protection of the Constitution]. (1998c, March). *Right-wing extremist activities in INTERNET* [Online]. Retrieved November 1, 1998, from: http://www.verfassungsschutz.de

Bundesamt für Verfassungsschutz [Federal Office for Protection of the Constitution]. (1998d). *Verfassungsschutzbericht* [Online]. Retrieved August 15, 1998, from: http://www.bundesregierung. de/02/0201/innen

Finnegan, W. (1997, December 1). The unwanted. *The New Yorker,* 61–78.

Hagan, J., Merkens, H., & Boehnke, K. (1995). Delinquency and disdain: Social capital and the control of right-wing extremism among East and West Berlin youth. *American Journal of Sociology, 100,* 1028–1052.

Hamm, M. (1993). *American skinheads: The criminology and control of hate crime.* Westport, CT: Praeger.

Hasselbach, I. (with Reiss, T.). (1996). *Führer-ex: Memoirs of a former neo-Nazi.* New York: Random House. (Portions excerpted in Hasselbach, I. [with Reiss, T.] (1996, January

6). How Nazis are made. The New Yorker, 36–57.

Heitmeyer, W., & Müller, J. (1995). *Fremden-feindliche Gewalt junger Menschen. Biographische Hintergründe, soziale Situations-kontexte und die Bedeutung strafrechtlicher Sanktionen* [Antiforeigner violence of young people: Biographical background, social context and the significance of legal sanctions]. (1995). Bad Godesberg, Germany: Forum.

Kalinowsky, H. H. (1990). *Rechtsextremismus und Strafrechtspflege. Eine Analyse von Strafver-fahren wegen mutmaßlicher rechtsextremististis-cher Aktivitäten und Erscheinungen* [Right-wing extremism and the law: An analysis of legal pro-ceedings of suspected right-extremist activities] (3rd ed.). Bonn, Germany: Bundesministerium der Justiz.

Kurthen, H., Bergmann, W., & Erb, R. (Eds.). (1997). *Antisemitism and xenophobia in Germany after unification.* New York: Oxford University Press.

Landesamt für Verfassungsschutz. (1998). *Landesverfassungsschutzbericht* (Report of the Provincial Office for Protection of the Constitution, Hamburg) [Online]. Retrieved March 29, 1999, from: http://www.hamburg.de/Behoerden/LfV/v-bericht

Levin, J., & McDevitt, J. (1993). *Hate crimes: The rising tide of bigotry and bloodshed.* New York: Plenum.

Mushaben, J. M. (1996). The rise of femi-Nazis? Female participation in right-extremist move-ments in unified Germany. *German Politics, 5,* 240–261.

Oesterreich, D. (1998). Authoritarianism and aggres-sion: German youth and right-wing extremism. In M. W. Watts (Ed.), *Cross-cultural perspec-tives on youth and violence* (pp. 39–51). New York: JAI.

Southern Poverty Law Center. (1998, Fall). Chaos to conspiracy: Racist skinhead violence growing more organized. *Intelligence Report,* pp. 23–24.

Watts, M. W. (1997). *Xenophobia in united Germany: Generations, modernization, and ide-ology.* New York: St. Martin's.

Watts, M. W. (1999). Xenophobia among young Germans in the nineties. In S. Hübner-Funk & M. du Bois-Reymond (Eds.), *Intercultural reconstruction: Trends and challenges* (pp. 117-139). Berlin, Germany: Walter de Gruyter.

Watts, M. W., & Zinnecker, J. (1998). Varieties of violence-proneness among male youth. In M. W. Watts (Ed.), *Cross-cultural perspectives on youth and violence* (pp. 117–145). New York: JAI.

Willems, H. (1995). Development, patterns and causes of violence against foreigners in Germany: Social and biographical characteris-tics of perpetrators and the process of escalation. *Terrorism and Political Violence, 7,* 162–181.

QUESTIONS

1. What are some examples of the differences in the way the German and American legal sys-tems define and respond to bias crimes, espe-cially expressions of bigotry or hate?

2. Since the reunification of Germany in 1990, what categories of people have been the tar-gets of hate crimes?

3. How does the profile of hate crime perpetra-tors in Germany compare with the profile of perpetrators in the United States?

4. How might social changes in Germany, such as reunification, be linked to the rise of xeno-phobia, hate, and right-wing extremism within German youth culture?

5. What role do skinheads play in racist violence in Germany? How does this compare to the role of skinheads in American hate crimes?

6. Why is information on the number and char-acteristics of German youth designated by the government as potentially violence prone dif-ficult to estimate?

7. What do you think of the German govern-ment's legal restrictions on expressions of bigotry? Do you think such restrictions have a significant symbolic and/or practical impact on preventing hate crimes?

8. Describe three types of development that have marked the changes in German skinhead culture.

9. Why is the United States the major international distribution center for extremist material and merchandise?

10. How does the profit motive behind marketing of extremist merchandise provide an incen-tive to maintain and expand extremist cul-tures of hate?

11. How does the internet function as a source of support for the aggressive elements in German youth culture?

12. How are efforts by the German government to suppress hate speech complicated by the expansion of the internet?

26

LEGISLATING AGAINST HATE

*Outlawing Racism and
Antisemitism in Britain*

PAUL IGANSKI

What is the impact of legislation intended to send a message denouncing hate and sanctioning expressions of hate? The right to freedom of expression can come into conflict with the right to be free from being subjected to expressions of intolerance, bigotry, and hate. Therein lies the dilemma for Britain and other societies attempting to craft policies that address hate violence. The author argues that to successfully address the ethical and practical difficulties that are part of this dilemma, British policymakers should examine relevant legislation from other countries to help determine how to navigate the sometimes fine line between condemning and censoring expressions of hate or bigotry.

INTRODUCTION

The new Labour government was elected in 1997 with a manifesto commitment to review legislative provisions against racist violence. It has already put its commitment into action by introducing legislation against racially motivated violence and racist harassment (Home Office, 1997a; House of Lords, 1997). Although they were not stated in the manifesto, a review of provisions against incitement to 'racial'

hatred, and possible legislation against holocaust denial, are also on the policy agenda.

The impetus for legislation has been provided in part by the consistent rise in the number of racist incidents reported to the police in England and Wales across the 1990s, and Home Office commissioned survey evidence revealing a far greater number of racist incidents (Aye Maung and Mirrlees-Black, 1994; Percy, 1998; see also Virdee, 1997). An apparent escalation of racist attacks across a number of European

EDITORS' NOTE: Reprinted by permission of Sage Publications Ltd. From Iganski, P. (1999). Legislating Against Hate: Outlawing Racism and Antisemitism in Britain. *Critical Social Policy, 58*, 129-141.

countries in the late 1980s and early 1990s (Commission of the European Communities, 1993) similarly provided the impetus for policy exhortation for the European Community, most recently by the Kahn Commission (European Parliament, 1995). In many European countries racism in the shape of hostility against visible minority ethnic groups has been far more extensive than antisemitism. Despite the lack of reliable evidence it is also apparent that in many countries the extent of antisemitic incidents appears to have peaked in the mid-1990s. In Britain the Board of Deputies of British Jews reported a year by year rise in recorded antisemitic incidents up until 1994, and a decline since (Institute for Jewish Policy Research, 1997). Nevertheless, many extreme incidents of antisemitism continue to occur in addition to the everyday manifestations of hostility, and the extent of antisemitism remains a concern for many Jews (Hertzberg, 1993).

Abhorrence against violence and other incidents motivated by racism and antisemitism appears to provide a broad consensual support for legislation in Britain, as evidenced most recently by reaction to the murder of Stephen Lawrence (Runnymede Bulletin, 1997: 12). But legislating against racism and antisemitism encounters some fundamental moral dilemmas. Chiefly, it comes into conflict with claims to freedom of expression. Such claims are being used as a political platform by far-right groups in Europe and the United States. As analysis of legislative intervention against racist violence in Britain, and across Europe more generally, is still in its infancy, and as the emerging literature to date has relatively neglected antisemitic manifestations, it is timely to undertake a moral scrutiny of current and potential legislative provisions.

RACIST VIOLENCE

Many manifestations of racist and antisemitic violence, such as physical assaults, verbal threats and damage to property, for instance, are generally prohibited by the criminal law in European countries irrespective of the motivation behind the incidents. However, there have been calls to take account of motivation in the

prosecution of incidents on the grounds that the offences committed are more serious than the same acts carried out without such motivation. In this vein, the House of Commons Home Affairs Committee argued in 1994 that 'an assault motivated by racism is more socially divisive than any other assault, and if allowed to pass unchecked will begin to corrode the fabric of our tolerant society' (House of Commons, 1994a: xxvii–xxviii, para. 77). More recently, Home Office Minister Mike O'Brien, commenting on the government's Crime and Disorder Bill, argued that:

> Society needs to express its particular abhorrence for racial hostility in any form. Today's Britain is a multi-cultural society and those who seek to undermine it strike at the heart of the values of modern Britain. (Home Office, 1997b)

Hence, proponents of legislation commonly argue that it would provide an unambiguous expression of government and public abhorrence of the incidents concerned. The Kahn Commission stopped short of advocating the establishment of a specific offence of racially motivated violence, but it did recommend penalty enhancement in cases of racially motivated crime, as has been permitted in the UK, and as required by Part I of the Criminal Justice Act 1991 (Sections 3(3) and 7(1)).

However, the potential for accounting for racist motivation, either through penalty enhancement provisions, or through a specific offence of racially motivated violence, arguably raises fundamental questions of social justice that should not be obscured by the abhorrence against racist and antisemitic incidents. Chiefly, evidence which might be used to justify penalty enhancement or to secure a conviction under an offence of racially motivated violence—things that the offender said before or after an incident, perhaps membership of an extremist political organization, or even beliefs that they hold—may not be intrinsically unlawful. The prosecution of 'racially-aggravated offences' would therefore at first sight appear to constitute restrictions on freedom of expression, association and thought which had not been a priori proscribed. The justification of using such evidence must be questioned unless the words, activities, beliefs and sentiments which are taken to signify racist motivation are themselves unlawful. There are few circumstances where prohibitions have been applied and in Britain racist speech is proscribed only where it takes the form of an act, as in instances of incitement (discussed later), chanting at a football match (1991 Football Offences Act) and the use of threatening, abusive or insulting words which threaten, provoke, or generate a fear of violence (1996 Public Order Act sections 4 and 5). But using speech as an indicator of racist motivation does not involve regarding speech as an act. Instead, the justification for the imposition of a higher penalty for motivation lies in a principle that the racist offence indicated by the associated speech is a distinct act in itself and not simply the addition of an act of violence and the speech accompanying it. However, the reliability of the indicators used to signify racist motivation raise questions of justice for both the perpetrators and the victims of the acts. For the perpetrator, would alcohol intoxication, provocation, or previous good character, for instance, be used to mitigate the racist element of the act? For the victim, would the absence of abusive speech and other obvious indicators signify that there is no racist motivation involved, or should police and prosecuting authorities routinely question the perpetrators of suspected racial attacks about their attitudes on 'race'? To provide a basis for policy development there is a need to evaluate provisions for penalty enhancement—in countries where they exist, including England and Wales—to determine: the nature of evidence that might be used to indicate racist motivation; any conflicts that such evidence might present in terms of the just treatment of offenders; the means by which evidence might legitimately be obtained; and the weight with which the evidence might be considered by the courts. All of these issues have yet to be explored by policy research.

'HATE SPEECH' AND 'HATE MATERIAL'

Legal instruments and other policy measures against expressions of racism and anti-semitism—in the form of 'hate speech' and 'hate material'[1]—confront a dilemma of striking a balance between the potentially conflicting rights of the right to freedom of expression and the right to freedom of not being subjected to hatred on the basis of 'racial,' ethnic, or religious identity, especially if the hatred is associated with discrimination or violence. Both rights are enshrined in a number of international treaties and declarations.[2]

In Europe, most countries—including former communist countries—have enacted laws against incitement to racial hatred, and although antisemitism is not specifically named in all the laws passed, it would be covered by the provisions of the legislation. There is, though, considerable variation across Europe in the degree to which the laws are applied. In some countries— Denmark, France, Germany, and the Netherlands—they have been actively applied, although the number of prosecutions accounts for a very small proportion of the number of recorded racist incidents (Kohl, 1993). In contrast, little use has been made of the laws in Great Britain and Northern Ireland (Colliver, 1992).

The Kahn Commission advocated that 'a clear prohibition on incitement to racial hatred should be explicitly and unequivocally included in the criminal law,' and additionally that 'the law should provide for the prohibition of demonstrations, publications and other expressions of opinion which incite racial hatred' (European Parliament, 1995: 49). Behind such calls for the curbing of freedom of expression is perhaps the common-sense assumption that hate speech leads to, or provokes, violence and discrimination against the groups concerned. Such a consequence was recently revealed by the prosecution of Mark Atkinson—a leading member of Combat 18 and publisher of the magazine *Stormfront*. Material in the magazine generated hate mail and abusive telephone calls to the mother of heavyweight boxer Frank Bruno and others targeted by the magazine (*The Guardian,* 12 September 1997: 4).

The willingness and rationale behind sacrificing total freedom of expression to protect minority groups was articulated by the House of Commons Home Affairs Committee which stated in its report that:

> Britain enjoys a reputation for promoting a right to free speech. Nevertheless, free speech may in

certain circumstances interfere with other people's rights. For example, it is argued that those who incite racial hatred 'claim the right to free speech, but they misuse that right to preach a doctrine of hate and violence. Surely those who persecute others should themselves be prosecuted by the forces of law and order.' We agree. There must be a limit to the extremes to which the principle of free speech can be taken. (House of Commons, 1994a: xxxii)

Yet only 41 cases in Britain were given the Attorney General's consent for prosecution under the provisions of Part III of the Public Order Act 1986—which deals with incitement to racial hatred—between 1990 and the end of 1997 (http://www.parliament.the.stationary-office.co.uk/cgi-bin/tso_fx). It might be argued that the low number of prosecutions reflects the low incidence of manifestations covered by the Act. It may alternatively reflect the limitations to the provisions of the legislation and its application. Strong arguments have been made in support of this latter claim.[3]

Section 17 of the Public Order Act 1986 specifies that:

[A] person who uses threatening, abusive or insulting words or behaviour, or displays any written material which is threatening, abusive or insulting, is guilty of an offence if (a) he intends thereby to stir up racial hatred, or (b) having regard to all the circumstances racial hatred is likely to be stirred up thereby.

A fundamental limitation of the provisions of the Act, however, lies in the stringent—but yet ambiguous—language used to define exactly what is unlawful. The Act refers to the stirring up of racial 'hatred.' But 'hatred' is a very severe sentiment which may exclude many other reactions which might lead to unlawful behaviour. The Board of Deputies of British Jews has proposed in consequence that 'hatred' should be extended to include 'hostility or contempt.'[4] The Act also refers to the 'stirring up' of racial hatred, which implies an active instigation on the part of the offender, excluding milder impulsion such as encouragement or advocacy. Incitement is also defined to occur through the use of words or material which are 'threatening, abusive and insulting,' and the

strength of feeling conveyed by these words arguably excludes many relatively more moderate and subtle expressions, which could be just as likely to stir up racial hatred (Bindman, 1997). This legislative loophole is acknowledged by the British National Party in its information sheet *Freedom of Speech in Britain—A Brief Legal Primer*, freely accessible on the internet. It argues that the Public Order Act is:

[N]ot quite the weapon it is often thought to be, which is why there is constant pressure, particularly from Zionists, to extend it . . . The fact of the matter is that the more politely one's case is expressed the more damning it is. Abusive language only gains support for the opposition. The act, in substance, banned the use of wild language, not polite and reasoned argument. The legislation can work entirely to our advantage, if only a tiny minority of people would just stop sending out abusive and illegal material anonymously. [http://www.bnp.net/freelaw.html]

It is possible that many expressions—even very moderate expressions of dislike or prejudiced ideas—may either directly provoke or contribute to unlawful acts by striking a chord with particular individuals—who already adhere to such sentiments but needed a provocation to act on them—or, in combination with other expressions have a cumulative effect for some individuals or, in a broader way, by contributing to societal norms which may eventually lead to unlawful behaviour. But to outlaw all these forms of expression would require draconian legislation, which would probably be practically unworkable—even if it were desirable.

The ambiguities inherent to defining incitement might perhaps be removed by limiting provisions to the prohibition of expressions that are intended to—or should have reasonably been anticipated to—*directly* lead to violence or other unlawful behaviour. The onus would be on prosecuting authorities to prove the intent behind the words used, or in the absence of intent, an impact that should have been reasonably anticipated. The actual causal link between the words and subsequent unlawful action would also have to be proved, or in the absence of some action, the potential for action to be provoked would have to be demonstrated by reference to past experience. If the condition of impact is removed from the sentiments expressed, the law would serve to regulate the expression of ideas, beliefs, attitudes and opinions which in themselves would not be unlawful. If they were prohibited, there would be a serious conflict with the rights to freedom of expression enshrined in international treaties and declarations, and in the extreme arguably provide the potential for the repression of political rights and the rights of government critics.

In short, if prohibitions against incitement to racial hatred are to be actively applied, ambiguities in legislative definitions about forms of expression defined as unlawful need to be resolved to provide clear parameters for police and prosecuting authorities. While there has been considerable scholarly analysis of the desirability of legislating against 'hate speech,' there has been little evaluation of the experience of implementing legislation. There is arguably, therefore, a need for policy research to examine how the dilemmas manifest in the ambiguities characterizing the Public Order Act in Britain have been managed in other countries. Hence, in countries where the condition of impact is removed from prohibition of expressions of 'hatred,' an evaluation needs to be made of the justifications used to circumscribe freedom of expression, and to determine how some rights to freedom of expression have been preserved.

HOLOCAUST DENIAL

Holocaust denial might perhaps be regarded as a specific case of 'hate speech.' Denial or distortion of the historical facts of the holocaust is arguably an insidious form of antisemitism, as it commonly surfaces in the guise of supposed scholarly research. The Institute for Historical Review—established in the United States in the late 1970s—and its journal, the *Journal of Historical Review*, have provided the core of the holocaust denial movement (Stern, 1995), although holocaust denial material has emerged from within the majority of European countries. The 'Institute' believes that dissemination of their material is protected under the First

Amendment to the United States Constitution, and by Article 19 of the International Covenant on Civil and Political Rights.[5]

Holocaust denial is particularly offensive as it is often accompanied by claims that Jews have profited from exaggerating the facts of the holocaust, both politically by establishing legitimacy for the state of Israel, and financially by extracting reparations from Germany. Holocaust denial has been promulgated on occasion by prominent political figures, and in one of the most publicized incidents in Europe in recent years Jean-Marie Le Pen, the French Front National leader claimed that: 'The gas chambers are only a detail in the history of the Second World War . . . They occupy only a few lines in the history books' (Institute for Jewish Policy Research, 1996: 125). It is more common, though, for holocaust denial to be promoted in literature disseminated by far-right political groups and in pseudo-academic publications under the guise of historical research.

Holocaust denial is not only directly antisemitic, but it also serves the agenda of neo-nazi and fascist movements by blurring the magnitude of nazi atrocities in World War Two. It is integral to the resurrection of fascism by attempting to remove the stain of the holocaust (Lipstadt, 1994: 23). Stern asks:

> [R]epaint World War II without the Holocaust and what do you get? Perhaps a war between competing systems that each had their demerits—capitalism, fascism, Communism. Perhaps just an ugly phase of history, just as Stalin's USSR was an evil part of history. Without the gas chambers and the Holocaust, Nazi Germany is relativized into just another troubling part of human history. (Stern, 1995: 247)

While the notion of holocaust denial is probably an abomination to the majority of people in contemporary Western Europe, and hence paradoxically limiting any fascist revival which exploits it (Eatwell, 1995), it is possible that it may have a stronger appeal in the coming decades, as through the passage of time there will no longer be any survivors to provide their personal testimony and the collective memory of the holocaust may increasingly fade the further it is removed from direct experience. As

Lipstadt suggests, the objective of the holocaust deniers 'is to plant seeds of doubt that will bear fruit in coming years, when there are no more survivors or eyewitnesses alive to attest to the truth' (Lipstadt, 1994: 24). Against this, though, the memory has been kept alive through the growing attention paid to the holocaust over the past 20 years in many European countries through the mass media, in cinema and documentary films, dramatic performances and other artistic works, and also through the introduction of holocaust studies to some school and University curricula.

Holocaust denial has been outlawed in a number of European countries, most of them Member States of the European Community (Austria, Belgium, France, Germany and Spain). Switzerland is the only non-EC country in Europe to have established such legislation. Each country, apart from Germany, established their legislation in the early 1990s. In addition to the criminal law in Germany, holocaust denial is also subject to the civil law which holds that 'every citizen of Jewish descent is violated in his individual—civil—"personality right" when the holocaust is denied' (Kohl, 1993: 151). In Britain, a Private Members Bill to outlaw holocaust denial was recently, although unsuccessfully, introduced by Mike Gapes MP to Parliament (29 January 1997).

There is little uniformity of provision in the countries where legislation has been established, with variation in the type of offence prohibited, differences in the provisions for bringing prosecutions and provisions for hearings, variation in the penalties that might be imposed, and variation in the relationship between holocaust denial legislation and other legal provisions, such as laws against racial discrimination and incitement to racial hatred.

The Kahn Commission called for the establishment of holocaust denial legislation in all Member States of the European Community, arguing that 'there should be specific offences of Holocaust-denial and the trivialisation of other crimes against humanity' (European Parliament, 1995: 49). The case for outlawing holocaust denial appeals to two broad arguments. First, that it is so intrinsically repugnant that it should be prohibited, and second, that the phenomenon—and hence its influence—is

growing. The moral repugnance of holocaust denial is often not spelt out by commentators, perhaps because it is so obviously self-evident. But repulsion alone arguably cannot justify prohibition, as there are countless other distortions of historical events—many also under the guise of academic scholarship—which are not subject to similar calls for prohibition. It would have to be demonstrated, therefore, that holocaust denial is uniquely offensive. From one perspective such a requirement would be difficult to sustain when confronted by claims to prohibit other distortions of historical events, perhaps for instance that the iniquities of the African slave trade have been exaggerated. Or might a demarcation line be drawn to invalidate claims concerning events that occurred before a particular point in time? How might that time-point be decided? While the holocaust was unique in the modern industrialized world (Stern, 1995: 252), there have been other cataclysmic acts of genocide, for instance, in Cambodia and more recently in Rwanda.

To refuse competing demands to legislate against distorting the historical record of other significant events would present a morally questionable proposition that the historical tragedy of one group is less serious than another. But even if outlawing holocaust denial was devoid of such moral predicaments, there could potentially be a number of practical difficulties with the legislation. There is a potential conflict between censoring holocaust denial and the right of freedom of expression as protected by international treaties. It is also possible that a law could create martyrs out of offenders, especially if they appeal to a defence of their right to freedom of speech and expression. Offenders may be provided with public exposure and publicity that they might not otherwise receive, inflating their significance in the public eye. The definition of holocaust denial would also be problematic as there are many more subtle ways of attempting to distort the historical record than boldly stating that the holocaust was a lie. Very complex legislative provisions would be required to outlaw all of the possibilities, and in effect the legislation would be defining historical truth.

Many calls to outlaw holocaust denial argue that it needs to be curbed as the phenomenon is growing. However, there appears to be no evidence of growth. In addition, while in some countries there appears to be a widespread ignorance characterizing public awareness of the facts of the holocaust, this appears to be due to a lack of information about the holocaust rather than a susceptibility to ideas characteristic of holocaust denial.

In short, it is difficult to justify claims for the establishment of legislation against holocaust denial. However, in view of the arguably uniquely offensive nature of holocaust denial, and the strong claims made to establish specific legislation against it, there is a need for a wide-ranging debate about the merits of establishing legislation that would incorporate the prohibition of holocaust denial in a broader framework of legislation against the trivialization of other crimes against humanity—as the Kahn Commission suggested. This would address some of the moral dilemmas discussed above, although the practical difficulties would remain.

Conclusions

The use—or potential use—of legal instruments against racism and antisemitism confronts dilemmas presented by the often conflicting rights to freedom from acts of violence, threats, hostility, damage and other forms of abusive behaviour, and claims to freedom of expression. It is possible, though, as argued in this article, to legislate against acts of racism and antisemitism without unjustly curtailing the rights of perpetrators of those acts to just treatment themselves. Many practical limitations remain, however, and as there is a dearth of comparative research on the potential, and the effectiveness, of such legal instruments, there is a need for policy learning from the measures that have been established.

Notes

1. 'Hate speech' and 'hate material' include speech, written material, or electronic communication, that is offensive and which may or may not advocate hatred of persons or groups of persons on the basis of their putative 'racial,' national, ethnic, religious, or cultural identity.

2. For instance, Article 4(a) and Article 5 of the International Convention on the Elimination of all Forms of Racial Discrimination, Article 19 and Article 20 of the International Covenant on Civil and Political Rights.

3. In Britain, for instance, see House of Commons, 1994b: Appendix 8, Memorandum by the Board of Deputies of British Jews; Appendix 9, Memorandum by the Anti-Racist Alliance; and by the Commission for Racial Equality, Q. 292, 44.

4. The Board of Deputies of British Jews concluded that 'This may explain in part, the reluctance to prosecute on occasions, or the unwillingness of juries to convict' (House of Commons, 1994b: 100).

5. http://www.kaiwan.com/-ihrgreg/ See also Aryan Nations and BNP homepages for 'revisionist' material.

References

Aye Maung, N., & Mirrlees-Black, C. (1994). *Racially Motivated Crime: A British Crime Survey Analysis*. London: Home Office.

Bindman, G. (1997). 'A Special Case for Holocaust Denial?' *Searchlight* December, 270: 13.

Colliver, S. (Ed.). (1992). *Striking a Balance: Hate Speech, Freedom of Expression and Non-Discrimination*. London: Article 19.

Commission of the European Communities. (1993). *Legal Instruments to Combat Racism and Xenophobia*. Luxembourg: Office for Official Publications of the European Communities.

Eatwell, R. (1995). 'How to Revise History (and Influence People?), Neofascist Style.' In L. Cheles, R. Ferguson and M. Vaughan (Eds.), *The Far Right in Western and Eastern Europe*. London: Longman.

European Parliament. (1995). Committee on Civil Liberties and Internal Affairs, *Consultative Commission on Racism and Xenophobia*. (DOC EN\CM\274\274586.)

Hertzberg, A. (1993). 'Is Anti-Semitism Dying Out?' *New York Review of Books* June 24: 51–2.

Home Office. (1997a). *Racial Violence and Harassment: A Consultation Document*. September 1997. London: Home Office Communications Directorate.

Home Office. (1997b). 'Government to Crack Down on Racist Crime.' Press Release 365/97, [http://www.coi.gov.uk/coi/depts/GHO/coi5881d.ok].

House of Commons. (1994a). *Racial Attacks and Harassment*. Home Affairs Committee, Third Report, Volume I. London: HMSO.

House of Commons. (1994b). *Racial Attacks and Harassment*. Home Affairs Committee, Third Report, Volume II. London: HMSO.

House of Lords. (1997). *Crime and Disorder Bill*. London: HMSO.

Institute for Jewish Policy Research. (1996). *Anti-Semitism World Report 1996*. London: Institute for Jewish Policy Research.

Institute for Jewish Policy Research. (1997). *Anti-Semitism World Report 1997*. London: Institute for Jewish Policy Research.

Kohl, H. (1993). 'Freedom of Speech and Hate Expression: The German Experience.' *New Community* 20(1): 147–54.

Lipstadt, D. (1994). *Denying the Holocaust*. Harmondsworth: Penguin.

Percy, A. (1998). 'Ethnicity and Victimisation: Findings from the 1996 British Crime Survey.' *Home Office Statistical Bulletin* 6/98 London: Home Office.

Runnymede Bulletin. (1997). 'The Inquiry Into the Death of Stephen Lawrence.' *The Runnymede Bulletin* No. 305, July/August: 12.

Stern, K. (1995). 'Denial of the Holocaust: An Anti-Semitic Political Assault.' In J. R. Chanes (Ed.), *Anti-Semitism in America Today*. New York: Birch Lane Press.

Virdee, S. (1997). 'Racial Harassment.' In T. Modood, R. Berthoud, J. Lakey, J. Nazroo, P. Smith, S. Virdee, and S. Beishon (Eds.), *Ethnic Minorities in Britain: Diversity and Disadvantage*. London: Policy Studies Institute.

QUESTIONS

1. What prompted Britain to create legislation against racially motivated violence and anti-Semitism?

2. What are some of the arguments made by proponents of legislation against hate concerning the societal messages such legislation is expected to convey?

3. In what ways does the legislation described in this article raise questions about freedom of expression?

4. How does the Public Order Act raise questions of justice for both victims and perpetrators of hate crimes?

5. An excerpt from the House of Commons Home Affairs Committee report (see page 359, this volume) states that " . . . free speech may in certain circumstances interfere with other people's rights" and cites examples. Do you agree or disagree?

6. How can legislation on hate crimes strike a balance between the right to freedom of expression and the right to freedom from being subjected to hate? Discuss your ideas on this subject.

7. How does the language used in Britain's Public Order Act present difficulties in determining what is unlawful under the act? Discuss examples.

8. Why did the extremist hate group the British National Party inform its members that the Public Order Act could be used to their advantage?

9. What are the problems involved in applying legislation that prohibits expressions that are an "incitement to racial hatred"?

10. Describe the provisions of hate crime legislation in European countries currently. According to this article, are such provisions uniform from country to country?

11. What are the moral and practical difficulties associated with creating and implementing legislation prohibiting Holocaust denial?

12. What are your thoughts on creating legislation prohibiting the "trivialization of crimes against humanity"?

27

THE PERSECUTION OF GYPSIES IN EUROPE

MARGARET BREARLEY

The Roma people, also known as Gypsies, have been subject to persecution for much of history. What is less well known and chillingly documented in this article, however, is that Roma continue to be subject to violence and hate crimes by both governments and private individuals. In Eastern and Central Europe, Roma are frequently stereotyped as undesirables by the media and politicians, and portrayed as responsible for crime and other social ills. Under these conditions, the author warns that Roma could be facing genocide.

The 600-year sojourn of Gypsies in Europe has been hallmarked by repeated acts of hatred against them, as Grattan Puxon (1987) noted: "The history of the Romani people is a story of relentless persecution. From the Middle Ages to the present day, they have been the target of racial discrimination and outright genocide" (p. 1).

Since 1987, the situation of Gypsies throughout Europe has deteriorated sharply.[1] Numbering 7 to 9 million, they are Europe's largest and, after the Jews, arguably the second oldest minority. They are now the most persecuted minority by far. Leading Rom activists argue that Roma are, post-1989, in a similar situation to that of Jews in 1937 (Gheorghe, 1992a; Holl, 1993; cf.

Margalit, 1996); they face mounting oppression in their own countries, yet if they seek to flee as refugees, other nations close the doors to any possible escape.

EARLY HISTORY IN EUROPE[2]

Roma migrated from India some time before A.D. 1000, moving slowly westwards. They settled in the Balkans by the 14th century and reached all major west European cities by the 15th century. The initial response to these dark-skinned and exotic nomads was often antagonistic but sometimes warm, both among local populations and church and secular authorities.

EDITORS' NOTE: From Brearley, M. (2001). The Persecution of Gypsies in Europe. *American Behavioral Scientist, 45*(4), 588-599. © 2001 Sage Publications. Used with permission.

During the 16th century, however, attitudes hardened. The church feared the very popularity of Gypsy fortune-telling and healing and began spreading anti-Gypsy propaganda. Early agrarian capitalism and war forced many non-Gypsies to become homeless beggars; harsh legislation against all vagabonds was passed throughout western Europe and had a major impact on Gypsies. They became outlaws.

In many countries, including England under Henry VIII, it became a capital offence to be a Rom. If caught, a Rom could be tortured, flogged, branded, and banished. If caught a second time, the penalty was death for men and women. In some countries such as the Netherlands, organized Gypsy hunts became fashionable. Male Gypsies could be sent to the royal galleys, chained as oarsmen for decades or even for life. In Hungary, Germany, Spain, and England, Gypsy children as young as 2 or 4 were taken by force and given to non-Gypsies to rear. (This may well be the source of the myth that Gypsies steal non-Gypsy children. Gypsies are passionately devoted parents and often sought to steal away their own children.)

It is noteworthy that this hatred did not stem primarily from local populations, who have traditionally valued Roma for their peripatetic services; technical skills, such as weaving, smelting, basket-making, and expertise with horses; and facility in music and dance. On the contrary, what has been called "sustained genocidal persecution" of Roma stemmed from the highest authorities, from kings and popes. Nobles and magistrates were forbidden to shelter Gypsies on pain of losing their titles and lands. Pope Pius V tried to expel all Gypsies from the domain of the Catholic Church, prompting Spain, Portugal, and France to start shipping Roma to Africa and America as slaves. In large parts of eastern Europe—especially in what is now Romania—Gypsies were enslaved by princes and monasteries from the 14th century onwards; they were freed from the most abject and cruel slavery only in the 1860s, long after slavery had been abolished in the West Indies.

During the 18th century, efforts to exterminate or expel Gypsies were gradually replaced by forcible assimilation and eradication of the Romany language and identity. Measures were still brutal: forcible settlement of nomadic Roma, forcible seizure of children by the state (this continued in Switzerland until 1973), and imprisonment simply for being Gypsy. In Spain, all male Roma were sent to prisons or mercury mines for up to 16 years; many died.

In the 19th century, persecution of Roma diminished, due partly to Enlightenment notions of tolerance and scholarly interest in Romani language, music, and culture and partly to romantic interest in the Gypsy as "noble savage." However, the Aryan racism of Count Gobineau, Richard Wagner, and others, as well as the social Darwinism that grew from this, resulted in Roma being increasingly stigmatized as racially inferior. In 1876, Cesare Lombroso, in *L'uomo delinquente,* characterized Roma as atavistic and criminal (Fraser, 1992, p. 249).

PERSECUTION OF ROMA IN 20TH-CENTURY WESTERN EUROPE

Germany in particular acted on such distorted concepts. In 1899, the Central Office for Fighting the Gypsy Nuisance was opened in Munich, closing only in 1970. Increasing persecution of Roma throughout Germany culminated in what Roma call the Porrajmos, or "Devouring": the Nazi Holocaust. Between 200,000 and half a million Gypsies were murdered by Nazis in extermination camps such as Auschwitz and Treblinka or in their home countries by, among others, Croats, Slovaks, Hungarians, and Romanians (Kenrick, 1994/1995). Many Roma were subjected to inhumane medical experiments or were forcibly sterilized. More than half of all German, Czech, Austrian, Polish, and Latvian Gypsies were killed, whereas nearly all Roma in Belgium, Holland, Croatia, Estonia, and Lithuania were annihilated. Documentation exists showing that one ultimate aim of Nazism was the "complete extermination" of the Roma people (Kenrick, 1989; Kenrick & Puxon, 1995; Polansky, 1998).

Since the Second World War, life has remained hard for Gypsies. In western Europe, nomadism is allowed but has become increasingly difficult because of oppressive laws. Roma generally live in the poorest housing with limited access to health care or education

(CDMG, 1995). Policing can be harsh. National legislation and local bylaws increasingly restrict Gypsy life. Roma in western Europe are widely subject to harassment and racism and, especially in Germany, Spain, and Italy, have been victims of significant hate crimes during the 1990s.

LIVING CONDITIONS OF ROMA IN CONTEMPORARY CENTRAL AND EASTERN EUROPE

In central and eastern Europe, however, conditions are much worse. Indeed, they are so bad that the admission of several former Eastern bloc countries into the European Union (EU) may depend in part on their improving the living conditions of Roma. In most countries, Roma form a substantial proportion of the population: from more than 5% in Hungary to 9% to 10% in Bulgaria, Slovakia, and Romania.[3] Roma are not only one of the largest ethnic minorities but also the most visible one. Their darker complexion renders them instantly recognizable, and they are often referred to contemptuously as "blacks." Moreover, they are always the poorest and most stigmatized minority, at the very bottom of the social spectrum, with consistently the worst housing, the highest rates of homelessness, illiteracy rates as high as 60% in some countries, and with life expectancy up to a third lower than that of non-Gypsies.

Because of their different cultural and linguistic background, Roma children are commonly classified as retarded; in Hungary in the mid-1980s, for example, 36% of all children in "special educational institutions" for "retarded or difficult children" were Gypsies, and 15.2% of all Rom school children were in schools for the handicapped (Crowe, 1995, p. 95). In the Czech Republic, some 20% of Gypsy children are sent to schools for the mentally handicapped ("European Roma rights," 1997; for a full account, see European Roma Rights Centre [ERRC], 1999); some special schools have between 60% and 90% intake of Roma children (Kenrick, 1998, p. 59). Few Roma children attend secondary school; in Romania, 27% of Roma have never attended school, and only 4.5% have attended secondary school. Most leave school by age 9, and only 51.3% of Roma

children under 10 attend school regularly (British Broadcasting Corporation, 1993). Indeed, in many countries, fewer Roma children are in secondary school now than under communism. Their life expectancy rates are far lower than that of the majority populations,[4] whereas their unemployment rates in the postcommunist era are far higher.[5]

PERSECUTION OF ROMA UNDER COMMUNISM AND POSTCOMMUNISM

During the 1990s, Roma have become a near-universal scapegoat for the ills of postcommunist society. Renewed nationalistic ideologies have increased hatred of Roma as a stigmatized ethnic group, indeed as a despised caste of virtual untouchables. Hundreds of Gypsies have been murdered in racially motivated attacks and thousands of their homes destroyed by arson.

One direct cause for this outbreak of anti-Gypsy violence is the growing insecurity and economic hardship of the majority populations. As Professor Netanyahu (1995) stated in his recent book on the origins of the Spanish Inquisition, "The majority's toleration of every minority lessens with the worsening of the majority's condition" (p. 5). Under communism, majority intolerance of Roma had been held in check by strong centralized authority and by the institutions of a police state. The state itself was intolerant of Gypsy identity: The Romani language was effectively banned, Roma were allowed to form no political organizations, and from the 1950s, nomadism was forbidden almost everywhere. Roma were often compelled to take on a non-Roma identity and new names as, for example, Bulgarians or Albanians. Self-employment was forbidden and traditional Roma occupations forcibly stopped. Roma were forcibly settled into housing, often in poor shanty towns or factory-owned flats. In Czechoslovakia, thousands of Gypsy women were forcibly sterilized in the 1970s and 1980s (Pellar, 1995; Tritt, 1992, p. x), and many children were placed in orphanages. But, although these assimilationist policies aimed at erasing Gypsy identity, they at least guaranteed to Roma some security (Ofner, 1990). Gypsies did have a modicum of health care, education, housing, and regular paid work as skilled or unskilled laborers. Above all, Gypsies were protected from open discrimination and violence from the majority population.

This protection has now gone. Following 1989, throughout the former communist states, the non-Gypsy majority's condition has worsened; populations have faced unprecedented financial insecurity, food shortages, and unemployment. Large-scale crime, corruption, and fraud have increased massively. Former members of the nomenclatura and security forces, indigenous mafia gangs, and international crime syndicates are all involved. Existing justice systems are largely powerless to investigate and prosecute major crime. Yet, petty crime by unemployed Roma—and Roma petty crime undoubtedly has increased since 1989 due to increased poverty and high unemployment rates (Pehe, 1993)—is often tackled by mob violence.

HATE CRIMES AGAINST ROMA IN CENTRAL AND EASTERN EUROPE

In 1997 in Bulgaria, where Rom unemployment can reach 95% or even 100% (Project on Ethnic Relations [PER], 1998, p. 12) and many Roma receive no welfare benefits, Romani petty thieves suffered lynch justice that would not have been applied to non-Gypsies. Five men and two girls caught trying to steal five lambs were tied to a tractor and beaten by locals; a Rom was tied to a tree for 7 hours for stealing potatoes and onions (*The Sofia Echo,* 1997). Other Romani petty thieves were publicly caned. In Hungary in 1992, a farmer shot dead two Roma stealing pears (Braham, 1993, pp. 39–40; Crowe, 1995, p. 104). Popular anger against Gypsies can thus serve to deflect widespread popular anger and frustration at less visible—and far more powerful—non-Gypsy criminals.

Hatred of Roma, latent but suppressed under communism, can now be expressed openly. This hatred combines racism, contempt for Roma poverty, resentment for perceived past favoritism toward Roma under communism, and newly found nationalism. A leading Rom activist, Nicolae Gheorghe (1992b), has stated,

"Before the revolution, only the police were violent to Romanies. Now the whole population can be." Individual events can trigger disproportionately massive hate crimes against Roma. "An individual mugging, rape or knife fight involving a single Rom can result in the burning of many or all houses of the whole Roma community" (Snagov Conference Report, p. 16). The following is one of many examples: In Bolentina, Romania, in 1991, after a Rom allegedly raped a village woman, 1,000 villagers drove 137 Roma families from their homes and burned the houses of 26 families to the ground as "retaliation" (*The Times,* 1992). Numerous Roma have died in such arson attacks since 1991.

Mob violence also occurs in response to actions by the authorities: For example, when Roma are forcibly resettled, local villagers or townspeople often violently expel them or set fire to Roma housing. During the 1990s, there have been major pogroms against Rom communities in Poland, Hungary, Slovakia, and Romania (where 30 pogroms occurred between 1990 and 1995, involving lynchings, torching of Rom homes, permanent expulsions, and the deaths of several Roma) ("Lynch Law," 1994). Local instigators of mob violence are rarely prosecuted; instead, assaults on Roma communities are often blamed on the victims themselves, whereas racial motives for such attacks are consistently denied by the authorities.

THE ROLE OF SKINHEADS

The main culprits in hate crimes against Roma are, however, skinheads. Organized groups of skinheads now exist in most former communist states. They are relatively few in number (in the Czech Republic only 5,000), but they enjoy considerable support in the wider population. In Hungary, nearly a quarter of a million young Hungarians fully or partly identify with skinheads (Welfare Ministry statistics, as cited in Kovats, 1994, p. 10). Skinheads are well organized both nationally and internationally and have links to far right political parties. Their ideology is openly neo-Nazi, racist, and violent. In their version of "White supremacy," there is no room for "black" Roma. A widespread skinhead slogan is "Roma to the gas chambers" (European Centre for Research and Action, 1994, p. 19). Although they have murdered Indians, Turks, and other foreigners, the vast majority of their victims have been Gypsies. In the Czech Republic alone, at least nine Roma have been murdered by skinheads since 1991 (Patrin, 1997). Skinheads have killed dozens more in Bulgaria, Serbia, and Slovakia, and many hundreds of Roma have been badly injured in skinhead attacks across central and eastern Europe (ERRC, 1997b).

ROMA VIS-A-VIS CRIMINAL JUSTICE

Few of those responsible are ever brought to justice, partly because many skinheads are still in their teens and partly because of the sympathy they enjoy among the wider population and the police. Indeed, some skinheads are themselves the sons of policemen. When skinheads are occasionally arrested and found guilty, their sentences are always light.

Indeed, one can argue that in many former Eastern bloc countries, the justice system itself and especially the police are guilty of hate crimes toward Roma. There is little tradition in former communist countries of neutral policing; police commonly display the same deep prejudices as those of the wider population. Ample evidence now exists of police contempt for Roma, expressed in racist insults and often violent behavior. In countries such as Romania, for example, there are frequent and violent dawn raids on Roma communities using excessive force to instill fear (ERRC, 1996b, pp. 20-44).

One consistent hallmark of police hatred is that if Roma victims of a crime go to the police, they are then frequently accused themselves of having committed that or another crime. Thus, the innocent Gypsy victim becomes the guilty party, whereas the non-Gypsy culprit conveniently goes unpunished. In some countries, police boost their incomes by regularly demanding bribes and extortionate fines from Roma and by confiscating their property (Helsinki Human Rights Watch Report, 1996a, 1996b, pp. 15–28, 34–37).

There is now substantial evidence from several central and eastern European countries of endemic physical abuse, torture, and indeed killings of Roma both in police custody and in prisons (ERRC, 1996b; Helsinki Human Rights Watch Report 1996a, 1996b).[6] There are commonly no legal mechanisms for Roma to instigate proceedings against police involved in such violence. Roma throughout central and eastern Europe have a well-justified fear of police and security forces. It is almost universally the case that minor crime committed by Roma is punished overzealously, whereas serious crime against Roma receives little or no punishment. It is commonplace for police, prosecutors, and judges to downplay or outright deny the existence of hate crimes toward Roma. This, in turn, encourages the perpetuation of hate crimes because perpetrators know that they are likely to remain immune from prosecution.

POPULAR "ANTI-GYPSYISM"

It is clear from recent public opinion polls that hatred of or contempt for Roma is widespread within the populations of former communist countries. In Croatia, for example, the Roma are the most disliked among all 30 ethnic minority groups, whereas in the Czech Republic, 87% of Czechs polled in November 1996 objected to having Roma neighbors, and about 50% wanted to expel Roma from Czech territory (Institute for Jewish Policy Research and American Jewish Committee, 1997, p. 131). These statistics are typical of most countries in the region. On this basis, one could argue that hate crimes against Roma simply reflect a grassroots phenomenon, an innate antipathy to Roma based on racism and fear of "the other."

The situation is, however, far more complex. Anyone who knows the history of anti-Semitism is well aware that anti-Semitism has generally been inculcated from the top down. From Hellenistic times onwards and especially within Western Christendom, state legislation, ideological writings by intellectuals, propaganda, and inflammatory speeches have all contributed toward the growth of popular anti-Semitism.

So it is with what has been called "Romophobia," hatred of Gypsies. Since 1989, this hatred has been fanned and even taught by some national governments, by many local authorities, by right-wing political parties, and by the media. Any discussion of violent hate crimes against Roma cannot ignore this complicity by those in positions of leadership.

STATE LEGISLATION AND ROMA

A few governments, such as Hungary and Slovakia, have passed legislation to protect Roma as a national minority, and several others, including Bulgaria, have restored many civil and political rights to Roma. But other governments have legislated to exclude as many Roma as possible. The prime example is that of the Czech Republic; it became known in 1992 that the Czech government had prepared a secret report planning to expel all Gypsies in the Czech Republic to Slovakia. Eventually, prior to the split with Slovakia in 1993, Czechoslovakia created such stringent citizenship laws that more than 100,000 Roma living in the Czech Republic who could not fulfill the criteria were left stateless. They were unable to claim any social security or welfare benefits (Brearley, 1996, pp. 19–20). In 1999, several thousand Roma in the Republic were still stateless.

Western governments have followed similar patterns of excluding and then deporting Roma. Between 1991 and 1993, Austria created new asylum and residence laws enabling it to deport large numbers of Roma who had been living legally in Austria for many years, as well as virtually all Roma asylum seekers (ERRC, 1996a). Germany has repatriated tens of thousands of Roma asylum seekers from Romania, Yugoslavia, and elsewhere. Expulsions of Roma at a national level also occur as part of ethnic cleansing; many were deported from Croatia and Bosnia during the recent Balkan wars, during which Roma were forced to clear mine fields and dig frontline trenches (Liegeois & Gheorghe, 1995, p. 18; *Official Bulletin of the International Romani Union,* 1992, p. 11.XII; *The Times,* 1994), and in Kosovo, where tens of thousands of Roma had to flee their homes, they were forced to bury corpses.

Local authorities can send similar messages of contempt for Gypsies through their own expulsions of Roma. Throughout eastern

Europe, large numbers of Roma have been made redundant by state-owned factories and then expelled from urban work-linked flats owned by municipal authorities. Privatization of much of the housing market and the restoration of publicly confiscated land to its former private owners has led to evictions of many Roma families, particularly from rural settlements. Some town mayors have intensified local hostility to Roma, in some cases going so far as to build street walls to divide Gypsies from their neighbors, such as in Madrid, 1994, and Usti nad labem, Czech Republic, 1999; or to evict large numbers of Roma (5,000 from the Selamsiz quarter of Istanbul, 1996).

ROMA AND THE
PUBLIC RHETORIC OF HATE

Moreover, the rhetoric of officials in both local and national government can inflame hatred of Roma. Slovakia is a prime example: In 1993, Prime Minister Vladimir Meciar described Roma as "antisocial, mentally backward, unassimilable and socially unacceptable." He demanded a reduction in family welfare payments to lower the reproduction of these "mentally retarded" people (Fakete & Webber, 1994).

Right-wing political parties, too, are guilty of hate rhetoric. In Italy, where six Roma children have died in hate crimes since 1994 and several others have been seriously wounded, a Northern League member of Parliament described Roma camps outside Florence as "a gathering of thieves and prostitutes, muggers and rapists" and called for Roma to be prevented from entering Florence (Institute of Race Relations European Race Audit, 1995). In Poland, the National Front Party circulated pamphlets demanding that all 90,000 Polish Roma (three times the actual number) be banished and has circulated fly porters with slogans such as "Death to Gypsies" and "Gas the Gypsies" (Braham, 1993, p. 92). Nationalist parties in Romania, Russia, Germany, and elsewhere are responsible for similar anti-Gypsy xenophobia. They, like skinheads and some eastern European governments, would like Roma to emigrate en masse.

THE PORTRAYAL OF ROMA IN THE MEDIA

The media also play a major part in creating hatred of Roma. Although since the early 1990s there have been occasional articles about the economic distress of Roma or romantic aspects of their culture such as music, most reporting on Gypsy affairs is sensationalist, exaggerated, and negative. Language typical of anti-Semitism is often used of Roma. In 1992, for example, two leading German newspapers described Gypsies as "a pure disease" and "a serious plague" (Brearley, 1996, p. 23). Throughout Europe and especially in former communist states, Gypsies are commonly presented in the media in gross stereotypes: as parasites, as genetic criminals, as dangerous. In Bulgaria, for example, there has been "persistent media stigmatising of Roma" since 1989. The media portray Roma as inherently deviant, typifying them as "villains," "incorrigible perpetrators," and "apt to commit crimes." Crime statistics in newspapers are always presented in two columns, "Roma" and "non-Roma," with exaggeratedly high rates shown for Roma crime (Anguelova, 1996; ERRC, 1997a, pp. 18–19; Project on Ethnic Relations, 1996).[7] The same is true for Romania, where in any report on Roma crime, the ethnicity of the alleged perpetrator is always given. This does not happen with crimes committed by any other ethnic group (PER, 1997, pp. 6–8).

There is thus little more neutral journalism than there is neutral policing. The presumption is always on Roma guilt and the innocence of non-Romanies. There is little media interest in positive aspects of Roma life or sympathy with their widespread persecution and no interest in praising Roma values or outstanding public figures (said to include Ava Gardner, Yul Brynner, and Charlie Chaplin). The effect of this undiluted stigmatizing by the media is powerful. Indeed, at a conference in 1996 on the media and Roma in contemporary Europe, organized by the PER, a delegate from the Organisation for Security and Cooperation in Europe (OSCE) argued that according to the OSCE, "anti-Roma violence was the result of racial discrimination in the media, which then became institutionalised in people's minds" (PER, 1996, pp. I, 4).

THE LACK OF NON-ROMA POLITICAL SUPPORT

A further element exacerbating hate crimes is the failure of non-Romany leadership to speak out on behalf of Roma. For example, although there are now within the EU, the OSCE, and nongovernmental organizations many national and international initiatives to assist Roma, trade unions and the churches have remained notably silent in the face of anti-Roma violence. Not until March 1998 did a joint conference of Catholic and Moravian bishops in the Czech Republic make a joint appeal on behalf of Roma in their country. Churches in most other states where Roma are persecuted remain silent.

In this brief article, it is impossible to give a comprehensive account of the current persecution of Roma in Europe. But, even this short summary should suffice to indicate the urgency of their situation. Facing discrimination by national governments and local authorities; denied safe havens as refugees; targeted by a hostile media; and the victim of increasing hatred, violence, and murder from lynch mobs, skinheads, and the police, the Roma of Europe face a bleak future.

To love liberty should mean to stand with and on behalf of Roma. A Romany prayer states, "A land without Gypsies is a land without freedom."[8] A Romany proverb runs, "Cursed is the land from which Gypsies flee" (*O Drom,* 1990). But, Gypsies have no land to which they can flee, and in some of the lands where they have lived for centuries there is arguably a genocidal situation in the making.

NOTES

1. Noted most recently in an Organisation for Security and Cooperation in Europe study on Roma prepared by Max van der Stoel (2000).

2. Compare Fraser (1992), Crowe (1995), and Hancock (1987). For a comprehensive bibliography on Roma, see Tong (1995).

3. Government census figures on Roma populations are often unreliable. For plausible statistics, see Liegeois and Gheorghe (1995, p. 7).

4. E. Kalibova (1995) suggested that Rom life expectancy approximates to that of Czech non-Gypsies in the 1930s, whereas estimates of life

expectancy of Hungarian Roma range between 32 and 55 to 60 years (Braham, 1993, p. 42).

5. In the Czech Republic, unemployment rates are 40% to 50% (Obrmann, 1991); in some regions of Hungary, unemployment rates reach 50%, 80%, or even 100% (Braham, 1993, p. 35; Crowe, 1995, p. 103).

6. In Bulgaria, 14 Gypsies died between 1992 and 1998 while in police custody or as a result of police shootings (*Manchester Guardian,* 2000), and in the first half of 1997 alone, 528 cases of abuse by police officers against Roma were reported (European Roma Rights Centre, 1997a, p. 22).

7. Further examples in *The Sofia Echo,* September 25 through October 1, 1998, pp. 10–11.

8. Cited in *Diveso,* a Gypsy newsletter in Albania.

REFERENCES

Anguelova, K. (1996, March-April). Romophobia in the media. *Focus: Newsletter of the Human Rights Project* [Facts and Fiction], *I,* 1, 13–15.

Braham, M. (1993). *The untouchables: A survey of the Roma people of central and eastern Europe.* Geneva, Switzerland: Office of the United Nations High Commissioner for Refugees.

Brearley, M. (1996, December). *The Roma/Gypsies of Europe: A persecuted people.* London: Institute for Jewish Policy Research.

British Broadcasting Corporation. (1993, April 12). *Summary of world broadcasts (SWB).* London: Author.

Cahn, C. (1996, September). *Divide and deport: Roma and Sinti in Austria.* Budapest, Hungary: European Roma Rights Centre.

CDMG, European Committee on Migration. (1995, May). *The situation of Gypsies (Roma and Sinti) in Europe.* Strasbourg, France: Council of Europe.

Crowe, D. M. (1995). *A history of the Gypsies of eastern Europe and Russia.* London: I. B. Tauris & Co.

European Centre for Research and Action on Racism and Antisemitism. (1994). *Political extremism and the threat to democracy in Europe: A survey and assessment of parties, movements and groups.* London: Institute of Jewish Affairs.

"European Roma Rights Center on Events in Great Britain." (1997, October 22). *Patrin Romani News.*

European Roma Rights Centre. (1997, January). *Time of the skinheads: Denial and exclusion of Roma in Slovakia.* Budapest, Hungary: Author.

European Roma Rights Centre. (1999, June). *A special remedy: Roma and schools for the mentally handicapped in the Czech Republic.* Budapest, Hungary: Author.

Fakete, L., & Webber, F. (1994). *Inside racist Europe.* London: Institute of Race Relations.

Fraser, A. (1992). *The Gypsies.* Oxford, UK: Blackwell.

Gheorghe, N. (1992a, September 30). Gypsies are now the scapegoats as the Jews were before. *The Times.*

Gheorghe, N. (1992b, September 30). Letter to *The Times. The Times.*

Glenny, M. (1994, April 6). "Time runs out in a Balkin powderkeg." *The Times* (Online).

Gughinski, N. (1997a, December). *Profession: Prisoner. Roma in detention in Bulgaria.* Budapest, Hungary: European Roma Rights Centre.

Hancock, I. (1987). *The pariah syndrome: An account of Gypsy slavery and persecution.* Ann Arbor, MI: Karoma.

Helsinki Human Rights Watch Report. (1996a). *Children of Bulgaria: Police violence and arbitrary confinement.* Helsinki, Finland: Author.

Helsinki Human Rights Watch Report. (1996b). *Rights denied: The Roma of Hungary.* Helsinki, Finland: Author.

Holl, K. (1993, June-August). The East European Roma have today the same role as the Ostjuden earlier in this century. *Regards.*

Institute for Jewish Policy Research and American Jewish Committee. (1997). *Antisemitism world report 1997.* London: Author.

Institute of Race Relations. (1995, March). *European Race Bulletin.* London: Author.

Kalibova, E. (1995). La situation demographique de la population tzigane en Tchecoslovaquie [The demographic situation of the Gypsy population in Czechoslovakia]. In C. Auzias (Ed.), *Les familles Roms d'Europe de l'Est* [The Romany families of Eastern Europe]. Paris: Editions Michalon.

Kenrick, D. (1989). Letter to the editor. *Holocaust and Genocide Studies,* 4(2), 251–254.

Kenrick, D. (1994/1995, Winter). The Nazis and the Gypsies: A fresh look. *Jewish Quarterly, 156.*

Kenrick, D. (1998, July). Gypsies: Life on the edge. *Index on Censorship,* 27(4), 55–62.

Kenrick, D., & Puxon, G. (1995). *Gypsies under the Swastika.* Hatfield: University of Hertfordshire Press.

Kovats, M. (1994). *The political development of the Hungarian Roma.* Unpublished master's dissertation, School of Slavonic and East European Studies, London.

LeBore, A. (1992, September 30). Hatred of Gypsies lurks beneath Romania's surface calm. *The Times* (Online).

Liegeois, J.-P., & Gheorghe, N. (1995). *Roma/Gypsies: A European minority* (Minority Rights Group report). London: Minority Rights Group.

"Lynch law: Violence against the Roma in Romania." (1994, November). *Helsinki Human Rights Watch, 6*(17).

Margalit, G. (1996). Antigypsyism in the political culture of the federal republic of Germany: A parallel with antisemitism? In *Analysis of Current Trends in Antisemitism* (No. 9). The Hebrew University of Jerusalem: Vidal Sassoon International Center for the Study of Antisemitism.

Netanyahu, B. (1995). *The origins of the Inquisition in fifteenth century Spain.* New York: Random House.

O Drom. (1990, April), p.35.

Obrmann, J. (1991, December). Minorities not a major issue yet. *RFE/RL Research Report, 11.*

Official bulletin of the International Romani Union. (1992). Berlin: International Romani Union.

Ofner, P. (1990, April). *O Drom,* 34–35.

Pehe, J. (1993, February). Law on Romanies causes uproar in Czech Republic. *RFE/RL Research Report,* p. 19.

Pellar, R. (1995). La fecondite n'est plus en vente [Fertility is no longer on sale]. In C. Auzias (Ed.), *Les familles Roms d'Europe de l'Est* (pp. 66–70). Paris: Editions Michalon.

Polansky, P. (1998). *Black silence: The Lety survivors speak.* Prague, Czechoslovakia: G plus G: Cross-Cultural Communications.

Project on Ethnic Relations. (1996, September). *The media and the Roma in contemporary Europe.* Princeton, NJ: Author.

Project on Ethnic Relations. (1997, June 27–28). *Images and issues: Coverage of the mass media in Romania* [Report of the Project on Ethnic Relations Conference]. Princeton, NJ: Author.

Project on Ethnic Relations. (1998, April). *The Roma in Bulgaria: Collaborative efforts between local authorities and nongovernmental organizations.* Princeton, NJ: Author.

Puxon, G. (1987). *Roma: Europe's Gypsies.* London: Minority Rights Group.

The Sofia Echo. (1997, August 8–14), p. 1.

Steele, J. (2000, April 8). "Gypsies feel the lash of everyone's hatred." *Manchester Guardian,* p. 19.

Szente, V. L. (1996, September). *Sudden rage at dawn: Violence against Roma in Romania.* Budapest, Hungary: European Roma Rights Centre.

The Times. (1992, August 30).

Tong, D. (1995). *Gypsies: A multidisciplinary annotated bibliography.* New York: Garland.

Tritt, R. (1992). *Struggling for ethnic identity: Czechoslovakia's endangered Gypsies.* New York: Helsinki Human Rights Watch Report.

van der Stoel, M. (2000, April 7). *Report on the Situation of Roma and Sinti in the OSCE Area,* Office of the High Commissioner on National Minorities, The Hague: Organisation for Security and Co-operation in Europe.

Watts, L. (1994, July). *Countering anti-Roma violence in Eastern Europe: The Snagov Conference and related efforts.* Project on Ethnic Relations Snagov Conference report (p. 16). Princeton, NJ: Project on Ethnic Relations.

QUESTIONS

1. What are some examples of the persecution and hate crimes that the Roma are experiencing in Europe in historical and modern times?

2. What is the history of Gypsy persecution? How were Roma persecuted during the Holocaust?

3. Describe the living conditions of Roma in contemporary Central and Eastern Europe. What examples stand out most in your mind?

4. How did the situation of Roma under Communism change in the post-Communist era?

5. Describe some of the parallels between the violence currently suffered by Roma and the violence suffered by other groups such as Jews and African Americans during various historical eras. What are the similarities between the experiences of these targeted groups?

6. What is the role of skinheads in violence against Roma?

7. Why is the legal system ineffective in prosecuting and sanctioning crimes against Roma? Discuss several reasons.

8. What are some recent examples of violence committed by government authorities against Roma?

9. Given the article earlier in this section on Germany's approach to bigotry and hate crimes, does it surprise you to learn that Germany has deported Roma asylum seekers by the thousands?

10. Describe some examples of how government and media portrayals of Roma create a "public rhetoric of hate." How does this help create a climate conducive to hate crimes against Roma?

11. Do you think a positive media campaign could be created to counteract negative media portrayals of Roma in European countries today? How might this be accomplished?

12. Why is the author of this article concerned that Roma are currently experiencing a potentially genocidal situation? Discuss the reasons presented in the article.

AUTHOR INDEX

Subject Index

ABOUT THE EDITORS

Phyllis B. Gerstenfeld is Professor and Coordinator of Criminal Justice at California State University, Stanislaus. She received her M.A. and Ph.D. in Psychology from University of Nebraska–Lincoln and her J.D. from University of Nebraska College of Law. She has presented at national conventions and published chapters and papers on hate crimes in a variety of books, encyclopedias, and journals. The author of *Hate Crimes: Causes, Controls, and Controversies* (2004), Gerstenfeld is gaining a national reputation in hate crime research.

Diana R. Grant is Assistant Professor of Criminal Justice Administration at Sonoma State University. She received her Ph.D. in Social Ecology from the University of California, Irvine. Her research interests focus on the social psychology of legal processes and legal decision making.

11139186R0

Made in the USA
Lexington, KY
12 September 2011